Understanding the Entrepreneurial Mind

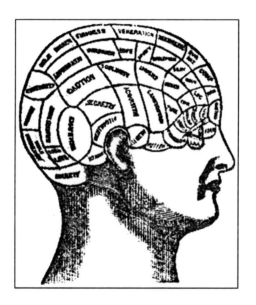

The Phrenological Location of Faculties and Organs of the Brain. (William Windsor, *How to Become Rich: A Treatise on Phrenology, Choice of Professions and Matrimony*, 1898; Accessed through www.gutenberg.org, eBook #21646)

INTERNATIONAL STUDIES IN ENTREPRENEURSHIP

Series Editors:
Zoltan J. Acs
George Mason University
Fairfax, VA USA

David B. Audretsch
Max Planck Institute of Economics
Jena, Germany

and

Indiana University
Bloomington, IN, USA

For further volumes:
http://www.springer.com/series/6149

Alan L. Carsrud · Malin Brännback
Editors

Understanding the Entrepreneurial Mind

Opening the Black Box

 Springer

Editors
Alan L. Carsrud
Ted Rogers School of Management
Ryerson University,
Toronto Ontario,
M5B 2K3 Canada
alan.carsrud@ryerson.ca

Malin Brännback
Department of Business Studies
Åbo Akademi University
Henriksgatan 7
FIN-20500 Turku, Finland
malin.brannback@abo.fi

ISBN 978-1-4419-0442-3   e-ISBN 978-1-4419-0443-0
DOI 10.1007/978-1-4419-0443-0
Springer Dordrecht Heidelberg London New York

Library of Congress Control Number: 2009927133

Printed on acid-free paper

Springer is part of Springer Science+Business Media (www.springer.com)

Acknowledgments

We are deeply indebted to both the Max Planck Institute of Economics in Jena, Germany, and the Ewing Marion Kauffman Foundation of Kansas City, Kansas, for their constant moral and financial support of the process associated with the development of this volume. Without their belief in the value of better understanding the entrepreneur, this book would not have been possible.

We also want to thank our internationally based colleagues, graduate students, friends, and fellow authors in this volume. The intellectual stimulus they have provided to each other during the development of this volume will have a long-term impact on the study of the entrepreneur. A special thanks goes to Diemo Urbig of the Max Planck Institute of Economics in Jena, Germany, for his invaluable assistance in the final editing and checking of the texts. Without his help we would still be held hostage by the details.

Finally, we want to thank our families for allowing us the time, over a nearly 2-year period, for this research and theoretical collaboration. Their tolerance for our frequent trips abroad and early morning phone calls cannot be measured.

Contents

List of Figures

List of Tables

Contributors

Barbara Bird Kogod School of Business, American University, 4400 Massachusetts Avenue, NW, Washington, DC 20016, USA, Phone: +1 (202) 885-1924, bbird@american.edu

Kristie Brandt 9363 Fontainebleau Blvd Apt. H-107 Miami, FL 33172, USA, Phone: +1 (786) 715-2635, kristiebrandt@hotmail.com

Malin Brännback Department of Business Studies, Åbo Akademi University, Henriksgatan 7, FIN-20500 Turku, Finland, malin.brannback@abo.fi

Melissa S. Cardon Lubin School of Business, Pace University, 861 Bedford Road; Pleasantville, NY 10570, USA, Phone: +1 914 773 3716, mcardon@case.edu;

Alan L. Carsrud Loretta Rogers Chair in Entrepreneurship, Professor of Entrepreneurship and Strategy, Ted Rogers School of Management, Ryerson University, Toronto, Ontario, M5B 2K3 CANADA, Phone: 416-979-5000, alan.carsrud@ryerson.ca

Evan Douglas Faculty of Business, University of the Sunshine Coast, Maroochydore DC, Queensland, 4558, Australia, Phone: +61 (0)7 5430 1230, Fax: +61 (0)7 5430 1231, edouglas@usc.edu.au, www.usc.edu.au

Mateja Drnovsek Faculty of Economics, University of Ljubljana, Kardeljeva ploscad 17, 1000 Ljubljana, Slovenia, Phone: + 386 1 589 2 400, drnovsekm@gmail.com

Jennie Elfving Rödsövägen 149, FIN-67400 Karleby, Finland, Phone: + 358 40 5233059, jennie.elfving@gmail.com

Connie Marie Gaglio Director, Ohrenschall Center for Entrepreneurship, San Francisco State University, 835 Market Street Suite 550, San Francisco CA 94103, USA, Phone: +1 (415) 817-4354, cmgaglio@sfsu.edu

Veronica Gustavsson Jönköping International Business School, P.O.B. 1026, SE-551 11 Jönköping, Sweden, Phone: +46 (0)36-101834, Fax: +46 (0)36-101888, veronica.gustavsson@ihh.hj.sem, http://www.ihh.hj.se/doc/1262

Kevin Hindle Chair of Entrepreneurship Research Deakin University, Australia and Visiting Professor of Entrepreneurship, University of Southern Denmark, Phone + 61 3 9244 6100, khindle@swin.edu.au

Daniel F. Jennings Andrew Rader Professor of Industrial Distribution, Texas A&M University, MS 3367, College Station, Texas 77843-3367, USA, Phone: 1 979 845 2972, djennings@tamu.edu

Anne Kirketerp Linstad Universe Research Lab, Alsion 2, DK-6400 Soenderborg, Denmark, Phone: + 45 6550 8122, akl@universeresearchlab.com

Kim Klyver Postdoc, Stanford University & University of Southern Denmark, Department of Entrepreneurship and Relationship Management, Engstien 1, 6000 Kolding, Denmark, Phone: +45 6550 1463, kkl@sam.sdu.dk / kklyver@stanford.edu

Norris Krueger 1632 South Riverstone Lane, #304, Boise ID 83706, USA, Phone: +1 208 440 3747, norris.krueger@gmail.com

René Mauer Chair for Business Studies and Sciences, for Engineers and Scientists, RWTH Aachen, Templergraben 64, D-52064 Aachen, Germany, Phone: + 49/241/80-99362, mauer@win.rwth-aachen.de

Theresa Michl Ludwig-Maximilians-University, Munich School of Management, Ludwigstr. 28, D - 80539 Munich, Germany, Phone: +49 (0)89 2180 3862, Fax: +49 (0)89 2180 3685, michl@lmu.de

Benjamin T. Mitchell Carlson School of Management, University of Minnesota, 321 19th Avenue S, Suite 3-365, Minneapolis, MN 55455, USA, Phone: (612) 625-4463, Fax: (612) 626-1316, mitch516@umn.edu

J. Robert Mitchell Price College of Business, University of Oklahoma, 307 West Brooks, Norman, OK 73019, USA, Phone: (405) 325-5692, jrmitch@ou.edu

Ronald K. Mitchell Texas Tech University, Rawls College of Business, Box 42101, Lubbock, Texas 79409-2101, USA, Phone: (806) 742-1548, Fax: (806) 742-3848, ronald.mitchell@ttu.edu

Erik Monsen Max Planck Institute of Economics, Entrepreneurship, Growth and Public Policy Group, Kahlaische Str. 10, D-07745 Jena, Germany, Phone: +49-3641-686736, monsen@econ.mpg.de

Charles Y. Murnieks US Air Force Academy, Colorado 80840, DSN: 333-1110, USA, Tel: + 1 719-333-3497, charles.murnieks@usafa.edu

Helle Neergaard Department of Management, Aarhus School of Business, Aarhus University, Haslegaardsvej 10, DK-8210 Aarhus V, Denmark, Phone: +45 8948 6607, hen@asb.dk

Arnold Picot Ludwig-Maximilians-University, Munich School of Management, Ludwigstr. 28, D - 80539 Munich, Germany, Phone: +49 (0)89 2180 2252, Fax: +49 (0)89 2180 3685, picot@lmu.de

Leon Schjoedt College of Business, Illinois State University, Campus Box 5580, Normal, IL 61790-5580, USA, Phone: +1 (309) 438-2736, lschjoe@ilstu.edu

Kelly Shaver School of Business and Economics, Beatty 305, College of Charleston, 5 Liberty Street, Charleston, South Carolina, 29401, USA, Phone: +1 (843) 953-2276, Fax: +1 (843) 953-5697, shaverk@cofc.edu

Matthias Spörrle University of Applied Management, Am Bahnhof 2, D - 85435 Erding, Germany, Phone: +49 (0)8122 955 948 0, matthias.spoerrle@myfham.de

Diemo Urbig Max Planck Institute of Economics, Entrepreneurship, Growth and Public Policy Group, Kahlaische Str. 10, D-07745 Jena, Germany, Phone: +49-3641-686771, urbig@econ.mpg.de

Isabell M. Welpe Technical University of Munich, Arcisstr. 21, D - 80333 Munich, Germany, Phone: +49 (0)89 202 38774, Fax: +49 (0)89 202 38775, welpe@wi.tum.de

Susan Winter Office of Cyberinfrastructure, National Science Foundation, 4201 Wilson Blvd., Arlington, VA 22230, USA, Phone: +1 (703)292-8276, swinter@nsf.gov

Introduction

Interest in the functioning of the human mind can certainly be traced to Plato and Aristotle who often dealt with issues of perceptions and motivations. While the Greeks may have contemplated the human condition, the modern study of the human mind can be traced back to Sigmund Freud (1900) and the psychoanalytic movement. He began the exploration of both conscious and unconscious factors that propelled humans to engage in a variety of behaviors. While Freud's focus may have been on repressed sexuality our focus in this volume lies elsewhere. We are concerned herein with the expression of the cognitions, motivations, passions, intentions, perceptions, and emotions associated with entrepreneurial behaviors. We are attempting in this volume to expand on the work of why entrepreneurs think differently from other people (Baron, 1998, 2004).

During the decade of the 1990s the field of entrepreneurship research seemingly abandoned the study of the entrepreneur. This was the result of earlier research not being able to demonstrate some unique entrepreneurial personality, trait, or characteristic (Brockhaus and Horwitz, 1986). It was both a naïve and simplistic search for the "holy grail" of what made entrepreneurs the way they are. However, many of the researchers in this volume have never gave up the belief that a better understanding of the mind of the entrepreneur would give us a better understanding of the processes that lead to the creation of new ventures.

We also hope this book expands on the overviews of the cognitive characteristics of the entrepreneur found in the analyses of data from the Panel Study of Entrepreneurial Dynamics (PSED) work of Gartner et al. (2004). Relevant to this volume are the discussions on cognitions (Shaver, 2004a), career choices (Carter et al., 2004), expectations (goals) (Gatewood, 2004), work and life satisfaction (motivation) (Johnson et al., 2004a), decision style (maps and scripts) (Johnson et al., 2004b), intensity (motivation and passion) (Liao and Welsch, 2004), problem solving (maps and scripts) (Ford and Matthews, 2004), and locus of control and attributions (Shaver, 2004b). This volume differs from that one by being less concerned with results from a specific data set. We focus here on the theoretical foundation for various concepts and conceptual constructs that should be the basis of progressing research.

This book brings together not just commentaries on the cognitive psychology of the entrepreneur but more importantly new approaches to the key research areas that we believe describe the critical processes of the entrepreneur. This book is not designed as merely a review of the literature, nor as the results of collaborative analyses of a specific data set (Gartner et al., 2004), nor as an attempt to describe the entrepreneurial personality. It has been designed to direct future research, teaching, policy making, and practice by challenging one to look at various elements of the "entrepreneurial mind" in terms of how we can go about influencing and fostering those cognitive elements that the entrepreneur uses, consciously and unconsciously, in their daily activities.

What would the field be like now if it had found that entrepreneurs are "born that way"? It certainly could have meant "entrepreneurship cannot be taught." We should be thankful we have yet to find the "genetic traits for being a brain surgeon or an entrepreneur" even though some continue that search via studies of monozygotic twins (Nicolaou et al., 2008). Fortunately and therefore, as academics and teachers, we still have a lot of work to do.

The results of research on entrepreneurial cognitions for the past decade have been quite positive. We now know a lot more about the role of how experience, training, and education can shape motivations, cognitions, and behaviors to help in the creation of entrepreneurs. We have also learned that the cognitive processes of the entrepreneur are far more complex than our initially assumed approaches. Clearly, a better understanding of the mind of the entrepreneur should give us a better understanding of the processes that lead to the creation of new ventures.

In this volume we have gathered a wide range of our colleagues who are championing new explorations of the entrepreneurial mind that move beyond the relative simplistic search for "risk-taking traits" in entrepreneurs or the "entrepreneurial personality." Perhaps, early researchers should have paid attention to Schumpeter's proposition that entrepreneurs do not take risks, but bankers do (1934, p. 137), and risk is in no way part of the entrepreneurial function. We may have moved in a very different direction with respect to the study of risk taking both by the entrepreneur and by bankers in financial markets.

Continuing Search for Research Paradigms

Over 20 years ago researchers considered entrepreneurship a pre-paradigmatic discipline (Carsrud et al., 1986; Vesper, 1987; Carsrud and Johnson, 1989, Stevenson, and Jarillo, 1990) in need of adopting theories from more established disciplines like psychology and sociology, e.g., attribution theory (Shaver and Scott, 1991). Simultaneously, Brockhaus and Horwitz (1986) argued that studies hunting for unique personality characteristics for entrepreneurs had been disappointing and should be discarded. Gartner (1988) concurred when proposing a shift in focus on the firm as the unit of analysis and the external factors impacting their creation.

However, these are examples of researchers naïvely expecting communality in personality types across individual entrepreneurs (in reality a confusion with what a role is) and forgetting that personality characteristics are uniformities within the behavior of the individual (Deutsch and Krauss, 1965). Unfortunately, the field nearly threw the baby out with the bathwater; psychology, and especially individual motivations, had little to add to the study of entrepreneurs. It was to take almost 10 years before *entrepreneurial cognition* was to re-enter the entrepreneurial arena (an extensive review in Mitchell et al., 2007; Busenitz and Barney, 1997; Gaglio and Katz, 2001; Mitchell et al., 2000; Sarasvathy, 2001). The renewed interest in intentions (Krueger and Carsrud, 1993; Krueger et al., 2000), attributions (Shaver et al., 2001), and cognitive elements (Mitchell et al., 2002) propelled a long overdue renaissance for studying the entrepreneurial mind. The reader is referred to Chapters 2–4 on entrepreneurial intentions and Chapter 10 on attributions for a greater discussion of these particular topics.

Despite the call by Shane (2003) for a unifying theory of the field of entrepreneurship, entrepreneurship remains largely in a pre-paradigmatic phase and like most social science-based disciplines lacks a unifying theory. Such an endeavor may in fact be a fruitless pursuit as it is unclear to us how entrepreneurship would specifically benefit from such a unifying theory. To us, diversity is richness, which in turn is the basis for creativity. The opposite would be anorexia, a physiological state incapable of facilitating growth and the creation of new.

Entrepreneurship research is still inhibited by the indiscriminate transfer or, worse yet, the wholesale ignoring of well-tested theories especially from psychology and other behavioral sciences that could advance the study of the entrepreneurial mind and subsequent behaviors. There are clearly alternative perspectives than the firm focused – external and internal – strategy-based strategic positioning (Porter, 1980) or resource-based view of the firm (Penrose, 1959; Wernerfelt, 1984) relevant for entrepreneurship. While these studies are indeed useful, they are on the firm level and tell us nothing about the thinking and motivations of the individual who creates the venture or takes decisions. Such externally oriented theoretical approaches, while valuable in their own right, still act as if the entrepreneur magically appears much like Athena sprung from the head of Zeus full-born and adult. Entrepreneurs create companies and entrepreneurs are people, which places entrepreneurial cognition at the heart of entrepreneurship.

Clearly, the initial search for personality differences between entrepreneurs and non-entrepreneurs was a simplistic, if not naïve, quest. One should have expected successful entrepreneurs to have traits similar to any other successful professional or leader in any career stream (Carsrud et al., 1989; Begley and Boyd, 1987; Carter et al., 2004). The right approach, we suggest, is for appropriately adopting models and theories from psychology and other behavioral science-based disciplines, like marketing, that can be used to better understand entrepreneurial cognitions, motivations, and subsequent behaviors.

The Development Process of This Volume

This book is the result of a rather different editing process than what is customary. Three international book workshops were arranged; the first two in Jena, Germany, under the sponsorship of the Max Planck Institute for Economics. The first was held in December 2007, the second in May 2008. The most recent meeting was held in November 2008 in Miami, Florida, at the Eugenio Pino and Family Global Entrepreneurship Center at Florida International University. This meeting was under the sponsorship of the Kauffman Foundation through its grant to the Pino Center. These meetings were initially focused on entrepreneurial intentions and cognitions, which led to the creation of the *International Research Group on Entrepreneurial Intentions and Cognitions*.

A group of the chapter authors also met at the annual Babson Entrepreneurship Research Conference in Chapel Hill, North Carolina, in June 2008. All of these meetings were aimed not only at coordinating the contributions to this volume but also setting a research agenda to foster further study of the entrepreneurial mind and how those cognitions translate into actual entrepreneurial behaviors.

At each of these workshops discussions centered on the theory base of each concept being proposed for the book. Issues included how chapter topics have been typically researched and theoretical approaches that have been ignored, but could be useful. These discussions sought to tie concepts together in order to improve their operational definitions as well as how they should be researched. The aim was to avoid chapters being isolated silos and instead create integrated chapters. Given that authors are physically located all over the world, this was a bold goal. Despite the distance and thanks to these meetings we think we have come close to our goal. We sincerely hope results will be international research collaborations that will far outlive the commentaries in this particular volume.

The Volume's Structure

This book is divided into a series of clusters, each of which contains several chapters with related topics. For example, three chapters on intentions form one cluster; chapters on motivation, emotions, and passions form another cluster. Each of these clusters is preceded by introduction to that cluster that ties those chapters together and to related clusters. Each chapter in this volume has a designated senior author who was then encouraged to work with a new scholar or scholars.

These author teams were encouraged to challenge those reading their chapters with new models or approaches for looking at the topic at hand. These chapters often put forward propositions that are challenges for future researchers or propose new models for moving various research agenda forward. For example, one cluster ties the other chapters to actual behaviors for the purpose of learning to become an entrepreneur.

Cluster I – Entrepreneurial Perceptions and Intentions

The first cluster consists of chapters related to entrepreneurial perceptions and intentions. The chapter on perceptions offers challenges to current views of how entrepreneurs perceive their world. The chapters on intentions include overviews of the various theories as well as new models of intentions and the concept of informed intentions. The view of entrepreneurial intentions as a linear process is challenged;

for some entrepreneurs intentions drive opportunity recognition and perceptions. We also believe that the reverse can be true.

Cluster II – Cognitive Maps and Entrepreneurial Scripts

The next cluster of chapters takes the discussion to a higher level of abstraction: cognitive maps and entrepreneurial scripts. These chapters represent various theoretical approaches on how entrepreneurs make sense of their world and their ventures. It will be obvious to the reader that different streams of research use different terms to describe the same phenomena. By placing these together we hope one can see the similarities in these concepts and the different ways to study them. Both the chapters take different perspectives on how entrepreneurs construct their reality providing a different methodology with which to study the cognitive structure of the entrepreneurial mind.

Cluster III – Motivations, Emotions, and Entrepreneurial Passion

A book on entrepreneurial cognitions would not be complete without discussions around motivational concepts and motivational states, which can be regarded as the engine, or fuel, for entrepreneurial cognitions and subsequent behaviors. This chapter also ties to some of the new models proposed in the intentions cluster. The motivation chapter in this cluster includes an overview of various motivations that the entrepreneur possesses including work motivation, achievement motivation, and risk avoidance.

The chapter on the role of emotions brings classical research from psychology to bear on emotional states that impact entrepreneurial cognitions and behaviors. We believe this is a neglected research area in entrepreneurship, which would contribute to a deeper understanding of the cognitive triggers of venture creation. Emotions color the thinking and behaviors of entrepreneurs. The final chapter in this cluster is on entrepreneurial passions. The authors explicate how entrepreneurial passion provides a unique contribution to the study of human psychology, which has often not seen passion as a motivator or emotion.

Cluster IV – Attributions, Self-Efficacy, and Locus of Control

This cluster of chapters represents the seemingly subconscious cognitive activities used by entrepreneurs. The chapter on attributions offers important insights that when adequately applied help us understand how entrepreneurs interact with others or how venture capitalists view the entrepreneur. The chapter on self-efficacy ties to one of the key elements in the various models of entrepreneurial intentions, but by itself also ties to elements within various motivational models as found in

another cluster. Finally, the chapter on locus of control goes beyond risk perceptions providing a new model, which is likely to impact research in entrepreneurship
and psychology. An additional discussion on risk can be found in the chapter on
motivation. While self-efficacy and locus of control have been widely researched
the authors in this cluster provide new views of their concepts and methodological
approaches to their study.

Cluster V – Beyond Cognitions to Thinking and Behaving

This final cluster can be considered the transitional chapter from cognitions to
entrepreneurial behaviors. While we have no specific chapter on attitudes, it is
clear that in all of the prior clusters this concept appears and is used. This cluster helps to link attitudes and cognitions to actual behaviors at the micro-level. In
this final cluster we have chapters on thinking, entrepreneurial alertness and opportunity identification, and behaving. These chapters represent more of the application of prior chapters and their ultimate expression in actual behaviors. The chapter on entrepreneurial thinking brings a distinctly different view to the interface
of cognitions and behaviors. The chapter on entrepreneurial alertness provides a
nice summary of from where we have come to where we are now with respect to
entrepreneurial alertness and opportunity identification. Finally, the behavior chapter challenges the reader in terms of research methodology and conceptualization.

References

Baron RA (1998) Cognitive mechanisms in entrepreneurship: Why and when entrepreneurs think
    differently than other people. Journal of Business Venturing 13(4): 275–294.
Baron RA (2004) Social skills. In: Gartner WB, Shaver KG, Carter NM, Reynolds PD (eds) Hand-
    book of Entrepreneurial Dynamics: The Process of Business Creation. Sage, Thousand Oaks,
    CA, pp. 220–234.
Begley TM, Boyd DP (1987) Psychological characteristics associated with performance in
    entrepreneurial firms and smaller businesses. Journal of Business Venturing 2(1): 79–93.
Brockhaus RH Sr, Horwitz PS (1986) The psychology of the entrepreneur. In Sexton DL, Smilor
    RW (eds), The Art and Science of Entrepreneurship. Cambridge, Ballinger, pp. 25–48.
Busenitz LW, Barney JB (1997) Differences between entrepreneurs and managers in large orga-
    nizations: Biases and heuristics in strategic decision-making. Journal of Business Venturing
    12(1): 9–30
Carsrud AL, Johnson RW (1989). Entrepreneurship: A social psychological perspective.
    Entrepreneurship and Regional Development 1(1): 21–32.
Carsrud AL, Olm KW, Eddy GG (1986)Entrepreneurship: Research in quest of a paradigm. In:
    Sexton DL, Smilor RW (eds), The Art and Science of Entrepreneurship. Cambridge, Ballinger,
    pp. 367–378
Carsrud AL, Olm KW, Thomas JB (1989). Predicting entrepreneurial success; effects of multi-
    dimensional achievement motivation, levels of ownership, and cooperative relationships.
    Entrepreneurship and Regional Development 1(3): 237–244
Carter NM, Gartner WB, Shaver KG (2004) Career reasons. In: Gartner WB, Shaver KG, Carter
    NM, Reynolds PD (eds) Handbook of Entrepreneurial Dynamics: The Process of Business
    Creation. Sage, Thousand Oaks, CA, pp. 142–152
Deutsch M, Krauss RM (1965) Theories in Social Psychology. Basic Books, New York

Ford, MW, Matthews CH (2004) Individual problem solving. In: Gartner WB, Shaver KG, Carter NM, Reynolds PD (eds) Handbook of Entrepreneurial Dynamics: The Process of Business Creation. Sage, Thousand Oaks, CA, pp. 196–204.

Freud, S (1900). The Interpretation of Dreams, Standard Editions. London, Hogarth Press 1953

Gaglio CM, Katz JA (2001) The psychological basis of opportunity identification: Entrepreneurial alertness. Small Business Economics 16(2): 95–111

Gartner, WB (1988) "Who is an entrepreneurs?" is the wrong question. American Journal of Small Business 12(4): 11–32

Gartner, WB, Shaver KG, Carter NM, Reynolds PD (2004) Handbook of entrepreneurial dynamics: The process of business creation. Sage, Thousand Oaks, CA

Gatewood EJ (2004) Entrepreneurial Expectations. In: Gartner WB, Shaver KG, Carter NM, Reynolds PD (eds) Handbook of Entrepreneurial Dynamics: The Process of Business Creation. Sage, Thousand Oaks, CA, pp. 153–162

Johnson KL Arthaud-Day ML, Rode JC, Near JP (2004a). Job and Life Satisfaction, In: Gartner WB, Shaver KG, Carter NM, Reynolds PD (eds) Handbook of Entrepreneurial Dynamics: The Process of Business Creation. Sage, Thousand Oaks, CA, pp.163–170

Johnson KL, Danis WM, Dollinger MJ (2004b), Decision-making (innovator/adaptor) style, In: Gartner WB, Shaver KG, Carter NM, Reynolds PD (eds) Handbook of Entrepreneurial Dynamics: The Process of Business Creation. Sage, Thousand Oaks, CA, pp. 171–179

Krueger N, Carsrud A (1993). Entrepreneurial intentions: Applying theory of planned behaviour. Entrepreneurship and Regional Development 5(4): 315–330

Krueger N, Reilly M, Carsrud A (2000) Competing models of entrepreneurial intentions. Journal of Business Venturing 15(5/6): 411–532

Liao J, Welsch H (2004), Entrepreneurial intensity. In: Gartner WB, Shaver KG, Carter NM, Reynolds PD (eds) Handbook of Entrepreneurial Dynamics: The Process of Business Creation. Sage, Thousand Oaks, CA, pp. 186–195

Mitchell RK, Busenitz LW, Bird B, Gaglio CM, McMullen JS (2007) The central question in entrepreneurial cognition research 2007. Entrepreneurship Theory and Practice 31(1): 1–27

Mitchell RK, Busenitz, LW, Lant T, McDougall P, Morse E, Smith J (2002) Toward a theory of entrepreneurial cognition: Rethinking the people side of entrepreneurship research. Entrepreneurship Theory and Practice 27(2): 93–104.

Mitchell RK, Smith B, Seawright KW, Morse EA (2000) Cross-cultural cognitions and the venture creation decision. Academy of Management Journal 43(5): 974–993

Nicolaou N, Shane S, Cherkas L, Spector, TD (2008) The influence of sensation seeking in the heritability of entrepreneurship. Strategic Entrepreneurship Journal 2(1): 7–21

Penrose ET (1959) The Theory of the Growth of the Firm. Basil Blackwell, Oxford.

Porter ME (1980) Competitive Strategy. Free Press, New York

Sarasvathy SD (2001) Causation and effectuation: Toward a theoretical shift from economic inevitability to entrepreneurial contingency. Academy of Management Review 26(2): 243–288

Schumpeter JA (1934) The Theory of Economic Development. Oxford University Press, Oxford

Shane S (2003) A General Theory of Entrepreneurship. Edward Elgar Publishing, Cheltenham

Shaver KG (2004a), Overview: The cognitive characteristics of the entrepreneurs, In: Gartner WB, Shaver KG, Carter NM, Reynolds PD (eds) Handbook of Entrepreneurial Dynamics: The Process of Business Creation. Sage, Thousand Oaks, CA, pp. 131–141

Shaver KG (2004b). Attribution and locus of control, In: Gartner WB, Shaver KG, Carter NM, Reynolds PD (eds) Handbook of Entrepreneurial Synamics: The Process of Business Creation. Sage, Thousand Oaks, CA, pp. 205–213

Shaver K, Scott L (1991) Person, process, choice: The psychology of new venture creation. Entrepreneurship Theory and Practice 16(2): 23–45

Shaver K, Gartner W, Crosby E, Bakalarova K, Gatewood E (2001) Attribution about entrepreneurship: A framework and process for analyzing reasons for starting a business. Entrepreneurship Theory and Practice 26(2): 5–32

Stevenson HH, Jarillo JC (1990) A paradigm of entrepreneurship: Entrepreneurial management. Strategic Management Journal 11(Summer): 17–27

Vesper K (1987) Entrepreneurial academics. Journal of Small Business Management 25(2): 1–7

Wernerfelt B (1984) A resource-based view of the firm. Strategic Management Journal 5:171–180

Part I
Entrepreneurial Perceptions and Intentions

Chapter 1
Perceptions – Looking at the World Through Entrepreneurial Lenses

Evan Douglas

Abstract In this chapter we consider how the perceptions of entrepreneurs might differ from those of non-entrepreneurs and how this might lead individuals to act entrepreneurially when others would not. Perceptions are reality for nascent entrepreneurs who must make business decisions in an uncertain world, based on what they see or what they think they see. We use the analogy of "entrepreneurial lenses" and discuss clear lenses (self-efficacy), rose-colored lenses (cognitive biases), blue lenses (simplistic decision rules), yellow lenses (preference for monetary gains), purple lenses (preference for intrinsic benefits), and telescopic lenses (overestimation of profits and underestimation of risks). We also consider the frames that hold the lenses (framing effects).

1.1 Introduction

It is said that entrepreneurs look at the world through different eyes, see the future better than others do, see opportunities that others do not see, do not see risks that others do see, and so on. But maybe it is not their eyes that make entrepreneurs different but the lenses through which they look. Lenses can change one's view of the world, compensating for deficiencies in our visual acuity or helping us see things in a different way. Lenses bring objects into focus, make objects seem closer or further away, reduce or increase the amount of light admitted to the eyes, change the color of things, and so on. The analogy of looking through lenses can help us understand the thinking and the behavior of entrepreneurs, so in this chapter we examine the lenses that entrepreneurs (metaphorically) look through as they form the intention to behave entrepreneurially and as they exploit entrepreneurial opportunities.

Perceptions are important at various points in the entrepreneurial process. At the beginning of this process, individuals form the intention to become entrepreneurs

E. Douglas (✉)
University of the Sunshine Coast, Maroochydore DC, Queensland, Australia
e-mail: EDouglas@usc.edu.au

A.L. Carsrud, M. Brännback (eds.), *Understanding the Entrepreneurial Mind*, International Studies in Entrepreneurship 24, DOI 10.1007/978-1-4419-0443-0_1, © Springer Science+Business Media, LLC 2009

and enter the "exploration phase" (McMullen and Shepherd, 2006; Choi et al., 2008). The formation of entrepreneurial intentions might precede, or follow, the discovery of the specific entrepreneurial opportunity to be exploited. For some, the formation of the general intention to become an entrepreneur will trigger the search for a desirable entrepreneurial opportunity, while for others the discovery of a specific and desirable entrepreneurial opportunity might trigger the formation of entrepreneurial intentions. Bhave (1994) calls the former case "internally stimulated opportunity recognition" and the latter case "externally stimulated opportunity recognition." In the former case the individual enters the exploration phase wanting to be an entrepreneur and may explore many entrepreneurial opportunities before settling on one to "exploit" (McMullen and Shepherd, 2006) when a sufficiently attractive opportunity presents itself. The alternative case, where the individual discovers the opportunity first and subsequently decides to become an entrepreneur, is exemplified by the scientist who previously had no intention of becoming an entrepreneur, preferring instead to do research and publish papers, but who discovers a new technology and subsequently gains intellectual property protection for that technology. This individual might then be "pushed" (Smilor and Feeser, 1991) by members of his/her social network, and perhaps also by investors, to commercialize the proprietary technology, and consequently forms entrepreneurial intentions and enters the exploration phase of the entrepreneurial process.

In the exploration phase, individuals are "nascent entrepreneurs" meaning that they are actively planning to start their own business (Shaver et al., 2001). In this phase they conduct viability screening on one or more new venture opportunities they perceive. The viability screening process involves gathering information about the resources needed to exploit the specific new venture opportunity, considering whether or not these resources can be assembled to produce and sell the new venture's product or service, and investigating whether there is a sufficient market for that product or service at a price level that will allow profits.

At some point in the exploration phase of the entrepreneurial process, nascent entrepreneurs will form the belief that they have collected enough information and subsequently make the decision to launch the new venture. At this point they enter the "exploitation" phase (Choi et al., 2008) and the nascent entrepreneur becomes an actual entrepreneur and realizes his/her entrepreneurial intentions. In the exploitation phase, the new venture may survive, prosper, and grow, or it may survive as a small-scale business without having any desire for further growth, or it may become bankrupt and not survive. The new venture's subsequent fortunes will depend on the competitive forces that it experiences following its entry into the market, the entrepreneur's (managerial) ability to cope with those competitive forces and the potential vagaries of customer demand, and the entrepreneur's preferences for a growth or a no-growth (perhaps "lifestyle") business (Barringer and Ireland, 2006, 13–14).

The entrepreneurial process takes place in a highly uncertain business environment. When introducing new products, new services, new business processes, and/or new "business models" (Morris et al., 2006) it is not possible to foresee accurately the outcomes of decisions that are made. Vagaries on both the cost and demand sides could deliver financial outcomes that range from fortune to ruin. In order to act decisively in a highly uncertain environment, entrepreneurs must act on what they see, or more correctly, on what they *think* they see, or what they think they *will see* as the scenario rolls out with the passage of time. So, entrepreneurs in a highly uncertain business environment must act upon their perception of reality (Krueger, 1993; Krueger and Brazeal, 1994; Forlani and Mullins, 2000). What entrepreneurs think they see might be an illusion, of course, and their new venture might consequently fail. Alternatively what they think they see, or think they will see, might prove to be an accurate vision of the future. Thus entrepreneurs' perception of their entrepreneurial opportunity is critical to their subsequent exploration and exploitation decisions and to their later success or failure.

The process of entrepreneurship involves the nexus of a specific individual and a specific opportunity (Shane and Venkataraman, 2000), and we note that entrepreneurs not only tend to perceive opportunities differently but also tend to perceive themselves differently. They tend to see themselves as more competent than non-entrepreneurs see themselves. That is, they tend to have higher self-efficacy (Ajzen, 1991; Krueger and Dickson, 1994). Self-efficacy refers to a person's confidence that he/she can accomplish a specific task or related set of tasks. Entrepreneurial self-efficacy relates to the tasks specific to the exploration and exploitation phases of the entrepreneurial process (Chen et al., 1998). This confidence may be based on their possession of superior knowledge about the entrepreneurial opportunity, due to their superior knowledge of market needs and/or the technological potential for serving those needs (Gifford, 2003; Gimeno, et al., 1997; Shane and Venkataraman, 2000). But, in addition, entrepreneurs tend to exhibit *over*confidence in their abilities (Palich and Bagby, 1995). Overconfidence is a common human foible, of course, but entrepreneurs tend to be more overconfident than others (Busenitz and Barney, 1997; Simon, et al., 2000). And, of course, entrepreneurs may be different from non-entrepreneurs in their preferences for monetary outcomes and nonmonetary outcomes (Douglas and Shepherd, 2000).

Accordingly, in this chapter we examine a series of metaphorical lenses through which entrepreneurs perceive reality during the entrepreneurial process. Each of these lenses refers to perceptual differences between entrepreneurs and non-entrepreneurs that cause entrepreneurs to seek less information about potential new business opportunities and thereby causes them to proceed further and with greater speed along the entrepreneurial pathway. These individual differences thus serve to propel the entrepreneurial individual toward an entrepreneurial venture that may succeed or, alternatively, end in failure.

1.2 The Clear-Lens Effect – Differences in Human Capital, Including Knowledge

Do you wear glasses or contact lenses? In any case, you will appreciate that my glasses would most likely be inappropriate for your eyes – they would almost certainly blur your perception of the things around you, because visual acuity differs across human beings. If your eyes have less than perfect natural correction for refraction, you can have a set of lenses made up by an optometrist to a particular prescription that is exactly matched to your eyes so that you will see more clearly. Typically these will be clear lenses that correct your inability to focus on items at different distances.

How does the clear-lens analogy relate to entrepreneurs? The clear lens of the entrepreneurs refers to their ability to see and understand "things entrepreneurial" better than non-entrepreneurs do. That is, the clear lens of the entrepreneurs relates to their prior knowledge and experience of entrepreneurial situations and behaviors. Becker (1964) introduced the term human capital to encompass one's knowledge and abilities, and we focus here on those aspects of human capital that are specific to entrepreneurship. Some people were born to entrepreneurial parents and learned entrepreneurial attitudes, abilities, and behaviors during their childhood. Others learned to be more entrepreneurial at school or university and/or learned from experience in the workplace or at play. In effect, entrepreneurial individuals have honed their own set of clear lenses that allow them to see entrepreneurial opportunities more clearly. The knowledge acquired is specific to entrepreneurship and does not necessarily cause the person to be better at maths or to play a musical instrument well, for example, which may be the forte of others.

Many studies have attempted to relate individual human capital to nascent entrepreneurship, entrepreneurial intentions, entrepreneurial behavior, and entrepreneurial performance (e.g., Aldrich, et al., 1998; Boden and Nucci, 2000; Evans and Leighton, 1989; Shane, 2003, 61–95, for a comprehensive overview). Gifford (1993) distinguished entrepreneurial ability (the ability to recognize a new profit opportunity and to acquire resources to exploit it) from managerial ability (the ability to maintain the profitability of current operations) and argued that possession of these skills in individuals will determine their choice of career as an entrepreneur, intrapreneur, or salaried employee. Gifford (2003) demonstrated that what might seem to be risk aversion or preference might instead be the result of different personal investments in knowledge acquisition. Shepherd et al. (2000) argue that differences in new venture risk perceived by individuals might be due to individual differences between them in terms of their ignorance as producers and managers. In a similar vein, Shane and Venkataraman (2000) argue that entrepreneurs may have domain-specific knowledge that allows them to conclude that a particular new venture is not as risky *for them* as it would be for others. They argue that entrepreneurs who possess proprietary knowledge about new venture opportunities appear (to those who lack the information) to be willing to accept greater risk. Baron (2000) argues that entrepreneurs' lower perceptions of risk relate to their lesser ability to engage in counterfactual thinking. Davidsson and Honig (2003) and Aldrich et al. (1998) argue that individuals have differing capabilities due to their differing "general" human capital (such as age, gender, years of education, and work experience) and "specific" human capital (such as relevant education and industry experience, relatives who are self-employed, and social networks). More recently, Janney and Dess (2006) argue that entrepreneurs may possess specialized knowledge and idiosyncratic resources such that risks perceived by others do not apply to that entrepreneur because he/she has superior human capital.

Greater knowledge and experience in any context affects one's perception of risk in that context. Those with more entrepreneurial knowledge and greater entrepreneurial experience might regard a specific new venture opportunity as relatively low risk, while those with little knowledge and relevant experience might regard the same opportunity as relatively high risk. Entrepreneurial risk can be largely traced to incomplete information (or ignorance) in the minds of consumers, producers, and managers (Shepherd et al. 2000). Shane and Venkataraman (2000) argue that entrepreneurs who possess proprietary knowledge about new venture opportunities appear (to those who lack the information) to be willing to accept greater risk. Janney and Dess (2006) argue that the entrepreneur may possess specialized knowledge and idiosyncratic resources so that risks perceived by others do not apply to this entrepreneur, who has superior human capital resources in that regard. Krueger and Dickson (1994) found that self-efficacy and entrepreneurial risk taking were positively related, indicating that entrepreneurs' confidence in their knowledge and abilities leads them to undertake more risky ventures.

The impact of human capital differences on the perception of risk can be illustrated by two people wanting to jump across a muddy ditch. One is tall and athletic, and the other is shorter and less athletic. The first person was the long-jump champion at high school, while the second was the chess champion. For the first person, jumping across the ditch seems to involve little or no risk, but there is a high probability that the second person will land in the ditch and get muddy and possibly hurt as well. The physical ability and experience of the first person (including task-specific knowledge about how to run up and launch oneself into a long jump) cause that person to have relatively high self-efficacy concerning the task, while the ability, experience, and knowledge of the second person are likely to underlie relatively low self-efficacy for this task and therefore cause a relatively high perception of risk for that person.

Heterogeneity of *social* capital may also mean that the risk perceived by one nascent entrepreneur is less than that perceived by another nascent entrepreneur. Social capital includes the benefits derived from social networks including extended family, community, or organizational groups and individuals (Coleman, 1990; Aldrich et al., 1998). Social capital is expected to enhance the entrepreneur's human capital by enhancing the individual's ability to identify opportunities, gain access to resources, and so on (Birley, 1985; Greene and Brown, 1997). Davidsson and Honig (2003) found that while human capital variables (years of schooling, taking business classes, and work experience) had little or no impact on moving nascent entrepreneurs forward, social capital variables (having parents in business, being encouraged by friends, and having close friends or neighbors who are entrepreneurs) had substantial impact on progressing them from nascent entrepreneurship to launch. Having access to "better" social networks would be expected to provide the nascent entrepreneur with risk-reducing information at little or no cost and thus reduce the perceived risk of the proposed new venture.

Krueger (1993), Krueger and Brazeal (1994), and Krueger and Carsrud (1993) argue that the two main factors underlying the formation of entrepreneurial intentions are the perceived feasibility and the perceived desirability of the entrepreneurial opportunity. McMullen and Shepherd (2006) argue that "knowledge" and "motivation" are the prime drivers of the subsequent decision to exploit the opportunity. In effect, McMullen and Shepherd posit knowledge as a proxy for perceived feasibility and willingness to bear risk as a proxy for perceived desirability in the nascent entrepreneur's decision to exploit the new venture opportunity. Several other authors argue that the nascent entrepreneur's possession of prior and proprietary knowledge and their consequent "alertness" underlies the formation of the intention to become an entrepreneur (Kirzner, 1973, 1979; Busenitz, 1996; Gaglio and Katz, 2001; Gifford, 2003).

The fact that a person has superior human and social capital will become apparent to that individual through interpersonal comparisons and formal or informal contests of various types, such that the person will form an opinion that his/her own capability to undertake and successfully complete specific tasks is superior to others. Accordingly, entrepreneurs tend to exhibit greater self-efficacy for entrepreneurial tasks based on their superior human and social capital that is relevant for the entrepreneurial tasks envisioned. Accordingly, they view the world through "clear lenses" that more clearly show them the outcomes associated with decision making under uncertainty in the context of specific entrepreneurial opportunities. By looking through these clear lenses the entrepreneur is able to form entrepreneurial intentions in the first place, and subsequently takes the decision to exploit and thereby move ahead with the entrepreneurial process, when others would still be seeking information.

1.3 The Rose-Lens Effect – Overconfidence

Humans are notoriously overconfident of their ability to accomplish specific tasks (Simon et al., 2000). Overconfidence in one's abilities has been likened to wearing "rose-colored lenses" (Palich and Bagby, 1995, 443) whereby everything seems "rosy"– i.e., everything is bathed in a soft pink light that makes things look very attractive and/or easier to accomplish. Simon et al. (1999) distinguish between overconfidence, defined as the failure to know the limits of one's knowledge (Russo and Shoemaker, 1998), and illusion of control, this being the overestimation of one's ability to control future events in uncertain situations (Langer, 1975). Boyd and Vozikis (1994) argued that illusion of control will positively impact the entrepreneur's formation of entrepreneurial intention. In this chapter we are essentially rolling these two cognitive biases together and using the term "overconfidence" to mean the overestimation of one's knowledge and abilities in relation to the successful completion of a specific task. Thus the tall athletic person might still fall into the ditch if he miscalculates the width of the ditch or overestimates his jumping ability, or if a headwind begins to blow during his run-up, or if his jumping point collapses as he begins to jump, and so on. The latter two issues are beyond the jumper's knowledge or control, of course, and this parallels the entrepreneur's launch of a new venture in an uncertain business environment.

Overconfidence is a cognitive bias that seems to afflict entrepreneurs more so than other business managers. Cooper et al. (1988) found that entrepreneurs exhibit higher self-efficacy than other managers, and consequently they think that they are better equipped to deal with risks than are non-entrepreneurs. Cooper et al. (1995) argued that higher levels of self-confidence were related to lower levels of information-search activity, and therefore greater risk bearing, due to the entrepreneur's ignorance of the risks being borne. They argued that "the entrepreneur is 'blinded' to the need for more information due to his/her over-confidence" (1995, 110). Palich and Bagby (1995) found that entrepreneurs exhibit overconfidence and tend to downplay the risk they perceive, expecting to triumph over any adverse situations that might arise. They found that entrepreneurs consistently viewed new venture opportunities more positively than others (see also Chen, et al., 1998; Forbes, 2005). Busenitz and Barney (1997) found that while all managers exhibit overconfidence, entrepreneurs exhibit greater overconfidence than do employed managers. Thus, although the actual risk might be perceived accurately, individuals who exaggerate their ability to cope with the perceived risk are more likely to take that risk.

So, in terms of the entrepreneurial process, individuals are more likely to form entrepreneurial intentions if they are overconfident about their ability to successfully accomplish entrepreneurial tasks, other things being equal. Subsequently, and as a nascent entrepreneur, the individual is more likely to want to hurry through the exploration phase (and undertake less information-search activity) due to his/her overconfidence that the venture is a viable business opportunity. Consequently, nascent entrepreneurs will tend to take the exploitation decision sooner than they would if they were not so overconfident, and as they progress in the exploitation phase we should expect their overconfidence to similarly cause lesser levels of information-search activity resulting in "hasty" and probably suboptimal decision making. These rose lenses metaphorically worn by entrepreneurial individuals cause them to perceive the probable outcomes of their decisions more optimistically and to thus induce them to enter and persist in the entrepreneurial process, whereas individuals with a realistic view of their own capabilities would either not enter the process or stall within the process or not take "life-saving" gambles within the process, and thus would not become practicing entrepreneurs, other things being equal.

1.4 The Blue-Lens Effect – The Use of Simplistic Decision Heuristics

The "blue-lens effect" is about sunglasses that cut down the light (and glare) that hits your retinas and thereby allows you to see more clearly the things that you are most interested in (like the road ahead, when driving, for example). Blue lenses cut down the red and green light that is admitted to the photoreceptors in the eyes and thus reduce the amount of fine detail that would be visible when the red, green, and blue lights are combined. (Think of a color (RGB) projector, where the red, green, and blue beams combine to make many other colors and thus convey the finer details to the viewer). The benefit to us of wearing blue lenses is that they cut down eye strain and allow us to concentrate on objects that would have been difficult to see because they are surrounded by too much (multicolored) light. Thus, the decision to wear blue lenses is effectively the decision to sacrifice visibility of the finer details of the overall scene in favor of having better visibility of some items, which seem to be more important at the time.

The analogy for nascent entrepreneurs is that the red and green light sacrificed are like detailed information that the entrepreneur chooses not to have. The entrepreneur is more concerned with charging ahead along a particular road and feels that he/she does not need to have more information about "minor details" that seem unimportant to progress along that road. In the context of the entrepreneurial process, these "unimportant" things might be detailed information about customer preferences, data on the new product's reliability, predictions regarding competitor responses to the entrepreneur's initiatives, and so on.

Fiet (1996) notes that entrepreneurs can undertake information-search activity to reduce the uncertainty and risks of a new venture. Brockhaus (1980) and Brockhaus and Horwitz (1986) found that entrepreneurs in general are no more likely than non-entrepreneurs to be risk averse or risk preferring. Busenitz and Barney (1997) found that entrepreneurs tend to make decisions with less information than other managers. But even if they continue to receive information, individuals are subject to cognitive biases that arise due to the utilization of three main simplified decision rules (or heuristics) (Shaver and Scott, 1991, 33). First, they tend to "anchor" their estimates on past outcomes and tend to not revise their estimates on the basis of new information, and thus they act upon inaccurate assumptions (Tversky and Kahneman, 1974; Busenitz, 1999). Second, they tend to base their decision making upon the most recently acquired or most easily recalled information. This is known as the "availability" heuristic, but of course such data may not be representative of the range of outcomes that should be expected. Third, the "representative heuristic" is the tendency to base decisions on a relatively small number of observations (Tversky and Kahneman, 1974). This apparent belief in the "law of small numbers" (Busenitz, 1999) whereby the decision maker places heavy reliance on a few observations (rather than a representative sample) introduces risk because the limited sample might not be representative of the range of probable outcomes. Thus, relying on a small sample causes the entrepreneur to underestimate risk (Shaver and Scott, 1991; Busenitz, 1999).

Shepherd et al. (2000) argue that the mortality risk of a new venture depends on the novelty of its product, its production technology, and the managerial requirements of the new venture. They explain the liability of newness (Stinchcombe, 1965) in terms of the ignorance (i.e., missing relevant information) in the minds of customers, producers, and managers. This is consistent with the human capital approach – the mortality risk existing in any new venture will depend on which particular entrepreneur or entrepreneurial team is managing the new venture opportunity (as well as the market conditions and technological possibilities). Following the "ignorance" view, Choi et al. (2008) examine the "stopping point" at which entrepreneurs stop *exploring* the new venture opportunity (i.e., truncate information gathering) and start *exploiting* the new business opportunity (i.e., launch the new venture). In effect, the decision to exploit is taken at that point in the viability screening process when the entrepreneur decides that sufficient information has been captured and that the new venture appears to be worth the gamble, and thus the intention to start the new business culminates in a new venture start-up. Thus, Choi et al. (2008) focus attention on the decision to exploit and argue that this decision will be made sooner for the entrepreneur for whom risk tolerance is greater, consumer, producer, and management novelty is lower, knowledge management orientation is explicit rather than tacit, and where potential rivals (followers) can more easily obtain the same information. In concert with the individual-opportunity nexus approach (Shane, 2003) Choi et al. (2008) argue that the decision to exploit occurs in a person–situation context, depending on both the personal characteristics of the entrepreneur and situational characteristics such as novelty and ease of access of followers to important information.

But each one of the lenses discussed in this chapter operates to truncate information-search activity. The blue-lens effect specifically relates to the avoidance of information search due to the decision maker's preference to use simplified decision heuristics. Heuristics are simple "rules of thumb" that can be implemented quickly and inexpensively and which might generally produce an acceptable result. But since they eschew further information search, they may not incorporate relevant information that would improve the decision made and are thus more likely to result in suboptimal decisions being made. That is, heuristics allow quick decisions but these are not likely to be "rational" in the sense of maximizing expected value (Tversky and Kahneman, 1974). Busenitz and Barney (1997) and Busenitz (1999) found that entrepreneurs practice "bounded rationality", using simplified decision heuristics significantly more than do other managers. By using heuristics, entrepreneurs take greater risks than they think they are taking because the heuristic used actually introduces risk to the decision-making process by ignoring relevant information.

1.5 The Yellow-Lens Effect – Differences in Wealth Seeking

The yellow-lens effect is named in recollection of the author's experience while skiing at Whistler Mountain in Canada many years ago. While riding the chair lift up the mountain, my ski goggles fell off my head and disappeared down into a ravine. This was surely unfortunate, since I had just made the confident statement that I could beat my skiing partner to the bottom of the mountain, which provoked him to bet me $10 that I could not. Skiing, and particularly racing down the mountain, would be much more dangerous without goggles – without the yellow lens in those goggles, the glare created by sunlight on the snow makes it difficult to see the moguls that have been carved out by previous skiers and snowboarders. Hitting a mogul unexpectedly may cause you to fall and possibly hurt yourself. Thus, yellow-lens ski goggles are a risk-reducing accessory for skiers and snowboarders. But as the chair lift went higher my friend was having fun saying how he would easily win the race down the mountain, and so I decided to race against him anyway, without my goggles. Yes, it would have been more sensible for me to take the time to get off my skis and go inside the chalet and spend the money to buy a new pair of goggles, but my desire to win the bet was so strong that I stopped thinking rationally and raced down the mountain. I subsequently made my way to the bottom via a series of bone-jolting crashes over unseen moguls and lost the bet of course.

So, the yellow-lens effect for entrepreneurs relates to their urgency to get on with the wealth-making process rather than allocate a little more time and money to the exploration phase such that they gain more risk-reducing information. Both time and money are typically perceived as scarce by the nascent entrepreneur. First, consider the cost of information-search activity. Expenditure on search costs will reduce the net income of the new venture if that search does not result in the capture of additional useful information. Information that is expected to simply confirm the entrepreneur's strongly held belief, for example, that consumers will actually buy the new product or service or that production will proceed smoothly without technical problems, will be perceived as wasted expenditure that simply reduces net income. Because the entrepreneur almost certainly has a preference for more, rather than less, income, such expenditures will be seen as reducing profits from the new venture and thus reducing the entrepreneur's future wealth. Further, we note that the great majority of new ventures are "bootstrap" funded (Winborg and Landstrom, 2000), and thus the opportunity cost of the funds required for search activity is extremely high, competing with prototype development, the cost of manufacturing equipment, marketing expenses, and so forth. When these opportunity costs are added to the direct cost of search activity, it may be perceived as profit maximizing to truncate information-search activity and channel scarce funds into what is thought to be a better use for those funds. But also note that the entrepreneur may think that better-quality information about market demand, technological reliability, and managerial ability will be gained soon after launching the new venture. Thus, proceeding ahead in relative ignorance may be preferred because it consumes less cash prior to launch when cash balances are critical and because it is thought likely to provide better information and thus be a more effective use of the limited funds.

Second, information-search activity requires a significant period of time to set up, to undertake, and to analyze the data derived. The first impact of this is to delay the receipt of initial sales revenues and therefore to reduce the discounted present value of the revenue stream associated with the exploitation of the opportunity. Perhaps, more importantly, the time consumed with continuing to explore rather than to exploit the new venture opportunity may be viewed as an obstacle to winning the race to be "first to market" and subsequently condemns the firm to an inferior profit stream as a follower rather than as a pioneer. The first-mover advantages (Lieberman and Montgomery, 1988) of the pioneer firm are commonly presumed (by nascent entrepreneurs) to provide unassailable competitive advantage, although most pioneers do not survive or even maintain market leadership (Tellis and Golder, 1996). Notwithstanding this reality, we are concerned with the a priori perceptions of nascent entrepreneurs here –the notoriously overconfident entrepreneur expects that pioneering will endow the firm with significant competitive advantages, so any delay due to information-search activity is perceived to negatively affect the net present value of the firm's profits. Whether or not the nascent entrepreneur expects to be the pioneer, he/she may consider that the window of opportunity will soon close and that waiting to gain more reliable demand and cost estimates will mean that the profit opportunity will be lost or diminished. Entering as an early follower can be quite profitable, of course (Tellis and Golder, 1996), but in markets where the early entrants "lock up" strategic resources (Barney, 1991) entering later will be associated with lower profit streams and may even be associated with losses and bankruptcy. Thus the nascent entrepreneur may be expected to adopt a sense of urgency and to avoid time-consuming information-search activity in favor of an earlier decision to exploit and launch into the target market.

To summarize the yellow-lens effect, it is due to the nascent entrepreneur's sense of urgency that the new venture should be launched sooner, rather than later, to gain higher profitability. The more wealth-seeking and materialistic is the nascent entrepreneur, that is, the more he/she values wealth and the goods and services that can be purchased from income, the more the entrepreneur will want to truncate information-search activity and rush ahead to exploit the entrepreneurial opportunity.

1.6 The Purple-Lens Effect – Differences in Intrinsic Motivation

Purple is a beautiful color that evokes visions of the rich robes of royalty, of the gowns of academic processions, and of fortunate people fulfilling their dreams and desires. People say they are having a "purple patch" when everything goes right for them. People use "purple prose" which excessively expresses their passions and emotions. Purple is the color of pleasant emotions, of good feelings, and of psychic satisfaction. Looking through purple lenses would make everything seem purplish, with the purple lenses interacting with the color of objects to become a lighter or darker purple, or some interesting new color – green things seen through purple lenses would look like chocolate brown, for example. Thus wearing purple lenses would change your perception of things and you would see these things in a psychologically more appealing light than otherwise.

The purple-lens effect for entrepreneurs is that they perceive more intensely the emotional benefits associated with an entrepreneurial opportunity, as compared with others who look at the same new venture opportunity. Although we commonly think of profit and growth as the main objectives of entrepreneurs, they pursue entrepreneurship for both monetary and nonmonetary gains. Thus entrepreneurs want to be entrepreneurs partly because of the psychic benefits associated with becoming and being an entrepreneur.

The most commonly cited psychic benefit of being an entrepreneur is "being my own boss" (see, for example, Barringer and Ireland, 2006, 6–7; Shane 2003, 106). All individuals want some degree of independence, manifesting itself in decision-making autonomy, but entrepreneurs seem to self-select on the basis of having a higher preference for decision-making autonomy. Various studies have shown that preference for independence is significantly and positively related to the formation of entrepreneurial intentions (e.g., Douglas and Shepherd, 2002) and significantly distinguishes entrepreneurs from non-entrepreneurs (Shane, 2003, 106–108). Accordingly, entrepreneurs are expected to get more psychic satisfaction out of being their own boss, which is a nonmonetary corollary of becoming an entrepreneur.

Next, entrepreneurs have been shown to have a higher need for achievement (McClelland, 1961) than non-entrepreneurs. Achievement has been defined as follows: "To accomplish something difficult. To master, manipulate, or organize physical objects, human beings, or ideas. To do this as rapidly, and as independently as possible. To overcome obstacles and attain a high standard. To excel one's self. To rival and surpass others. To increase self-regard by the successful exercise of talent" (Murray, 1938, as cited by Shaver and Scott, 1991, 31). Surely this is exactly what entrepreneurs do – entrepreneurship provides people who have a high need for achievement a suitable and accessible way to accomplish something difficult, to overcome obstacles, to excel one's self, and so on.

Digging down a layer, what are the specific achievements that entrepreneurs might really prize? We contend that being recognized as the pioneer in a new market and/or industry may be an achievement of great personal significance to many entrepreneurs. Under the yellow-lens effect we considered the monetary aspects of being the pioneer and gaining first-mover advantages – now, with the purple-lens effect, we are concerned with the psychic benefits of getting to the market quickly and winning the title of pioneer, separate and distinct from any monetary benefits of doing so. Another psychic reward associated with entrepreneurship is recognition for being the intellectual source of great new ideas. Gaining patents has traditionally been a badge of achievement for inventors and many inventors subsequently become entrepreneurs to exploit their inventions. Other innovative ideas, perhaps not patentable, are also widely attributed to entrepreneurs, such as the "invention" of new business models by Michael Dell, by Sam Walton (Walmart), and by Home Depot hardware stores.

Next, being recognized as persons responsible for the rapid growth of their new ventures is personally rewarding for many entrepreneurs. Growth is fraught with risk, since rapid growth associated with new technologies might cause a financial crisis for the new venture if expenses must be paid contemporaneously while revenues are collected with a lag due to credit terms allowed and late payments by customers. Successfully managing the rapid growth of a firm can be expected to generate personal satisfaction for the entrepreneur, which is quite distinct from the satisfaction associated with making profits and/or becoming personally wealthy. Finally, taking a new venture to an initial public offering (IPO) is a huge achievement for entrepreneurs, since relatively few new ventures survive, fewer become highly profitable, and still fewer result in an IPO that allows the founder to realize substantial capital gains. Foreseeing such psychic benefits, and being attuned via their preference structures to gain greater satisfaction from such achievements, the nascent entrepreneur looks at the entrepreneurial process in a much more positive light than does the non-entrepreneur – the nascent entrepreneur sees the exploitation of an entrepreneurial opportunity as a means to achieve these keenly desired emotional benefits.

1.7 Telescopic Lenses – Overestimating Benefits and Underestimating Time and Risk

Telescopes use multiple lenses to magnify what is viewed through these lenses. The situation being observed looks larger than it really is and, moreover, seems to be much closer than it really is. This analogy highlights the way that entrepreneurs tend to overestimate the magnitude of the profits from a new venture opportunity and simultaneously underestimate the proximity of those profits. This is a separate perceptual problem from overconfidence, which addressed a bias individuals have about their ability to cope with specific situations – here we are concerned with the typical entrepreneur's overestimate of the profitability of the new venture and the associated underestimate of the time it will take to set up the new business, gain customers, get paid for sales, get down the learning curve, and so on.

Looking through telescopic lenses certainly gives the entrepreneur the broad picture, and the combination of telescopic and clear lenses may endow the entrepreneur with exceptional "vision" that may be the main reason for the discovery of the new venture opportunity in the first instance. But telescopic lenses compress the finer details of distant things, and these details may become the main impediments to gaining greater profits in a shorter time. As in most new situations, the broad visionary view seems relatively simple and manageable – the "devil is in the details" as people say. Acting upon a telescopic perception of the new venture opportunity will cause the decision to exploit to be taken before it would be if the opportunity was perceived through a single set of clear lenses, since the latter would allow perceptions of problem areas that would require more information search and problem analysis to be undertaken prior to the decision to exploit.

Now, if you were to reverse the telescope and look through the smaller end, objects would seem to be much smaller and to be much further away than they are in reality. But this is what entrepreneurs seem to do when they consider the risks facing the new business venture. They may see them, but they may mistakenly conclude that they are miniscule and far away. For example, entrepreneurs who say "no-one else is doing this, we have first-mover advantage, and therefore we will have sustainable competitive advantage" are likely to be looking through the telescope the "wrong" way. First, there may be others already doing it somewhere, but their cursory scan of the landscape, seen through the wrong end of the telescope, makes existing competitors hard to notice, causes first-mover advantages to appear to dominate smaller but potentially more problematic features of the landscape, and may not reveal as-yet small developments that are likely to grow and render the entrepreneur's first-mover or other competitive advantages easy to copy or obsolete (Barney, 1991).

Note that overconfidence is not the same as overestimation of outcomes or under-estimation of risks (Sitkin and Pablo, 1992). Overconfidence is concerned with self-efficacy that exceeds the individual's capacity to successfully achieve the task at hand. The telescopic-lens effect, on the other hand, concerns the individual's failure to correctly estimate the size and complexity of the entrepreneurial situation. In the rose-lens effect the perceptual error is about one's own capacity, whereas in the telescopic-lens effect the perceptual error concerns the characteristics of the new venture opportunity and the competitive environment.

1.8 Framing the Lenses

While talking about looking through lenses, it would be remiss to ignore the role of the frames that hold the lenses, since they are also critical to how the entrepreneur perceives new venture opportunities. Frames are the structures which surround the lenses and which serve to align the lenses with the eyes such that a person can see through those lenses. Researchers have found that when eliciting information from others, such as in a survey, the way in which a question is "framed", i.e., the context in which the question is considered, has a profound effect on the answer provided. Tversky and Kahneman (1979) introduced "prospect theory" in which the framing of a situation affected the risk behavior of individuals – when the decision maker is presented with a specific decision-making situation that is framed in a pos-itive light, the decision maker would exhibit risk aversion, whereas when framed in a negative light, the decision maker would exhibit risk-seeking behavior. Posi-tive framing of a situation might be as simple as saying "there is a 50% chance of success" whereas negative framing of the same decision problem would be to say "there is a 50% chance of failure". Researchers have found that when the situation is positively framed, the decision maker will tend to act conservatively to protect prior gains, whereas when framed negatively the decision maker will tend to gamble in an attempt to capture some gains from the situation (Tversky and Kahneman, 1974; Busenitz, 1999).

In the context of entrepreneurship, we see entrepreneurs practice "escalation of commitment" by increasing their investment into projects that are not doing very well and, conversely, by holding steady with strategies that have served well in the past, despite new information arising that indicates that the strategy undertaken may not be appropriate for the current circumstances (Tversky and Kahneman, 1974; Shaver and Scott, 1991). Both of these actions may jeopar-dize the entrepreneur's chances of success, of course, yet the entrepreneur's per-ception of the decision problem is effectively constrained by the frame through which he/she is looking at the problem, and the decision-making process is defec-tive in that the entrepreneur's perception is distorted because of the frame through which the decision problem is perceived (see, Sitkin and Pablo, 1992; Sitkin and Weingart, 1995).

1.9 Summary and Conclusion

In this chapter we are concerned with the perceptions of entrepreneurs and how these might differ from the perceptions of non-entrepreneurs. We are interested in entrepreneurial perceptions because these may explain why entrepreneurs step forward to undertake the process of entrepreneurial new venture formation while others hang back and instead choose employment with an established business or other organizations. We illustrated these perceptual differences using the analogy of looking through lenses of different colors. We argue that viewing new venture opportunities through these different lenses causes individuals to be more likely to perceive entrepreneurship as a feasible and desirable career alternative, and thus they are more likely to subsequently form the intention to become an entrepreneur. Thus entrepreneurial individuals become nascent entrepreneurs and enter the exploration phase of the entrepreneurial process whereby they search for risk-reducing information as part of the viability screening process. They also seek information about the availability and accessibility of the resources required to launch the new business venture. At some point, the nascent entrepreneur decides that enough information has been gathered and decides to exploit the new venture opportunity and subsequently transforms from a nascent entrepreneur to an actual (practicing) entrepreneur.

In each phase of the entrepreneurial process, perceptions play a role in driving the individual forward to become a practicing entrepreneur. The clear-lens effect, which is due to greater self-efficacy for entrepreneurial tasks arising from the individual's underlying knowledge and human and social capital advantages that better equip him/her for entrepreneurial actions, allows the entrepreneur to better see the future demand for new products, services, and/or business processes and to better predict the evolution of new technology to serve human preferences and subsequent market needs. Risk analysis is considered from the viewpoint of superior knowledge and human capital, which means that the risk looks smaller through the entrepreneur's eyes, aided as they are by clear lenses. Greater knowledge also means that the entrepreneur will better understand the market and the technology and will make fewer mistakes as a manager in the exploitation phase of the entrepreneurial process.

The rose-lens effect, due to the overconfidence which characterizes entrepreneurial individuals, causes the individual to optimistically inflate the value of entrepreneurial opportunities by overestimating his/her ability to solve problems, to achieve cost and revenue targets, to meet deadlines, to judge the preferences of consumers, and so on. This will tend to hasten progress through the opportunity recognition process and the exploration phase as the nascent entrepreneur underestimates the difficulties and the risks likely to be associated with the new venture. Once into the exploitation phase, the rose-lens effect inhibits the entrepreneur's accurate assessment of market demand, of cost estimates, and so on and thus pushes the entrepreneur forward in the entrepreneurial process when others might have abandoned the process.

The blue-lens effect, due to the excessive use of simplistic heuristics and other cognitive biases that cause decisions to be made without proper data or sufficient analysis, may cause the entrepreneurial individual to make "poor" decisions to proceed ahead in the entrepreneurial process when others would have delayed the decision or abandoned the opportunity. Thus the entrepreneur may select an opportunity for exploration on the basis of simplistic analysis or the exercise of one or more cognitive biases, such as representativeness, availability, and anchoring. In both the exploration and exploitation phases the blue-lens effect causes the entrepreneur to proceed ahead, potentially ignorant of risks being taken, rather than to commit more time for deeper analysis of the decision problem.

The yellow-lens effect, which is due to the entrepreneur's urgency to gain first-mover advantages and the higher profits that first moving is expected to provide, causes the nascent entrepreneur to truncate information search because it costs money and takes time and both of these are perceived to jeopardize the profits to be made from the new venture. Thus the yellow-lens effect causes nascent entrepreneurs to move forward more rapidly in the exploration phase, and to take more risks in the exploitation phase, than would non-entrepreneurial individuals.

The purple-lens effect, which is due to the entrepreneur's greater passion for the process of entrepreneurship and for the achievements and recognitions that are expected to be associated with becoming and being an entrepreneur, causes the entrepreneurial individual to proceed forward in the entrepreneurial process where others would stall, because the entrepreneur tends to place a higher intrinsic value (than others do) on the nonmonetary aspects of becoming and being an entrepreneur.

The telescopic-lens effect describes the bias of perceiving opportunities to be bigger than they really are, to be closer (in time) than they really are and, conversely, to be less risky than they really are. Finally, framing effects were discussed to demonstrate that the way in which an opportunity is presented to the entrepreneur is likely to cause a cognitive bias toward risk aversion (if framed positively) or toward risk seeking (if framed negatively).

Of course, entrepreneurs tend to look through more than one and possibly all of these lenses simultaneously, but we have tried to disentangle the impacts of each of the main factors that collectively operate to induce the individual to proceed more quickly along the path of the entrepreneurial process. Each lens operates to cause the entrepreneur to reduce information-search activity, and thus each lens causes the entrepreneur to accept greater risk, both knowingly and unknowingly, than otherwise, and to increase the incidence of entrepreneurial new business start-ups.

So, are these entrepreneurial lenses a good thing or a bad thing? For individuals they might be either, since they induce the individual to proceed with the entrepreneurial process to an outcome that lies somewhere on a spectrum that ranges from huge success to dismal failure. Indeed, a high proportion of entrepreneurial new ventures do fail (Dunne et al., 1988; Cooper et al., 1988) and most of these failures might be largely due to management ignorance (Shepherd et al., 2000) because most new ventures do not start until there is at least some evidence that the new technology "works" and that there is unmet customer demand. It is up to the entrepreneur (and other members of the top management team) to then launch the new venture and manage the production, marketing, and other business processes. In the management of these business processes clear lenses are a definite advantage, but the other lenses may inhibit effective management processes, perhaps leading to entrepreneurial failure.

For society, these entrepreneurial lenses are overwhelmingly a good thing. If nobody wore these lenses, then nobody would step forward to start new ventures (Busenitz, 1999), and we might still be living in caves. Entrepreneurs take private risks seeking personal gains, to be sure, but successful entrepreneurship is likely to provide societal benefits as well. These external benefits of private entrepreneurship include technical progress, increased productivity, safer living environments, better natural environments, higher standards of living, and so on. Consequently, at a societal level, we encourage the wearing of these entrepreneurial lenses, applauding successful entrepreneurs, and this induces individuals to form entrepreneurial intentions and become involved in the entrepreneurial process. This encouragement for entrepreneurial activity occurs in schools and universities and also in government- and university-supported technology and business incubators.

Thus there is a crucial role for entrepreneurship educators. We need to provide the voice of reason, educating individuals in risk-recognition skills and risk-mitigation strategies to ensure that entrepreneurs have a better awareness of the extent of their ignorance (such that they might "know what they do not know") and how to cope effectively with new venture mortality risk and business risk more generally. Entrepreneurship education will also serve to enhance entrepreneurial alertness (opportunity recognition skills) and viability screening skills. Accordingly, it serves to build human (as well as social) capital and therefore builds entrepreneurial self-efficacy, and thus performs the role of the optometrist in supplying clear lenses to potential entrepreneurs, reducing their managerial ignorance in particular. In addition, entrepreneurial education should be designed to reduce overconfidence and to reduce the use of simplistic decision rules by providing an awareness of the suboptimality of such cognitive biases and heuristics. Finally, entrepreneurial education almost certainly serves to increase the number of entrepreneurial new ventures by promoting the financial and psychic benefits associated with successful entrepreneurship. We hope that by grinding and polishing the individual's clear, yellow, and purple lenses and by discouraging the wearing of rose and blue lenses, entrepreneurial educators will have a significant positive impact on the incidence and success rates of entrepreneurship.

References

Ajzen I (1991) The theory of planned behavior. Organizational Behavior and Human Decision Processes 50: 179–211

Aldrich HE, Renzulli LA, Langton N (1998) Passing on privilege: Resources provided by self-employed parents to their self-employed children. Research and Social Mobility 16: 291–317

Barney JB (1991) Firm resources and sustained competitive advantage. Journal of Management 17: 99–120

Baron RA (2000) Counterfactual thinking and venture formation – The psychology of new venture creation. Journal of Business Venturing 15: 79–91

Barringer BR, Ireland RD (2006) Entrepreneurship: Successfully launching new ventures. Pearson, Upper Saddle River, NY

Becker GS (1964) Human capital: A theoretical and empirical analysis, with special reference to Education. University of Chicago Press, Chicago, IL

Bhave MP (1994) A process model of entrepreneurial venture creation. Journal of Business Venturing 9: 223–242.

Birley S 1985. The role of networks in the entrepreneurial process. Journal of Business Venturing 18: 107–118.

Boden RJ Jr., Nucci AR (2000) On the survival prospects of men's and women's new business ventures. Journal of New Business Venturing 15: 347–362

Boyd NG, Vozikis GS (1994) The impact of self-efficacy on the development of entrepreneurial intentions and actions. Entrepreneurial Theory and Practice 18: 63–77

Brockhaus RH (1980) Risk taking propensity of entrepreneurs. Academy of Management Journal 23: 509–520

Brockhaus RH, Horwitz PS (1986) The psychology of the entrepreneur. In: Sexton DL, Smilor RW (eds), The Art and Science of Entrepreneurship. Ballinger, Cambridge, MA, pp. 25–48

Busenitz LW (1996) Research on entrepreneurial alertness. Journal of Small Business Management 34: 35–44

Busenitz LW (1999) Entrepreneurial risk and strategic decision making. Journal of Applied Behavioral Science 35: 325–340.

Busenitz LW, Barney JB (1997) Differences between entrepreneurs and managers in large organizations: Biases and heuristics in strategic decision making. Journal of Business Venturing 12: 9–30

Chen C, Greene P, Crick A (1998) Does entrepreneurial self-efficacy distinguish entrepreneurs from managers? Journal of Business Venturing 13: 295–316

Choi YR, Levesque M, Shepherd DA (2008) When should entrepreneurs expedite or delay opportunity exploitation? Journal of Business Venturing 23: 333–355

Coleman J (1990) Social capital and the creation of human capital. American Journal of Sociology 94: 94–120

Cooper AC, Folta TB, Woo CY (1995) Entrepreneurial information search. Journal of Business Venturing 10: 107–120

Cooper AC, Woo CY, Dunkelburg WC (1988) Entrepreneurs' perceived chances for success. Journal of Business Venturing 3: 97–108

Davidsson P, Honig B (2003) The role of social and human capital among nascent entrepreneurs. Journal of Business Venturing 18: 301–331

Douglas EJ, Shepherd DA (2000) Entrepreneurship as a utility-maximizing response. Journal of Business Venturing 15: 231–251

Douglas EJ, Shepherd DA (2002) Self-employment as a career choice: Attitudes, entrepreneurial intentions, and utility maximization. Entrepreneurial Theory and Practice 26: 81–90

Dunne T, Roberts M, Samuelson L (1988) Patterns of firm entry and exit in U.S. manufacturing industries. Rand Journal of Economics 19: 495–515

Evans DS, Leighton LS (1989) Some empirical aspects of entrepreneurship. American Economic Review, 79: 519–535

Fiet JO (1996) The informational basis of entrepreneurial discovery. Small Business Economics 8: 419–430

Forbes DP (2005) Are some entrepreneurs more overconfident than others? Journal of Business Venturing 20: 623–640.

Forlani D, Mullins JW (2000) Perceived risks and choices in entrepreneurs' new venture decisions. Journal of Business Venturing 15: 305–322

Gaglio CM, Katz J (2001) The psychological basis of opportunity identification: Entrepreneurial alertness. Journal of Small Business Economics 12: 95–111

Gifford S (1993) Heterogeneous ability, career choice, and firm size. Small Business Economics 5: 249–259

Gifford S (2003) Risk and uncertainty. In: Acs ZJ, Audretsch DB (eds), Handbook of Entrepreneurial Research, Springer, New York, pp. 37–54

Gimeno J, Folta J, Cooper A, Woo C (1997) Survival of the fittest? Entrepreneurial human capital and the persistence of underperforming firms. Administrative Science Quarterly, 42: 750–783

Greene PG, Brown T (1997) Resource needs and the dynamic capitalism typology. Journal of Business Venturing 12: 161–173

Janney JJ, Dess GG (2006) The risk concept for entrepreneurs reconsidered: New challenges to the conventional wisdom. Journal of Business Venturing 21: 385.

Kirzner IM (1973) Competition and Entrepreneurship. University of Chicago Press, Chicago.

Kirzner IM (1979) Perception, Opportunity and Profit: Studies in the Theory of Entrepreneurship. University of Chicago Press, Chicago.

Krueger NF (1993) The impact of prior entrepreneurial exposure on perceptions of new venture feasibility and desirability. Entrepreneurship Theory and Practice 18: 5–21

Krueger NF, Brazeal D (1994) Entrepreneurial potential and potential entrepreneurs. Entrepreneurship Theory and Practice 18: 91–104

Krueger NF, Carsrud AL (1993) Entrepreneurial intentions: Applying the theory of planned behavior. Entrepreneurship and Regional Development 5: 315–330

Krueger NF, Dickson P (1994) How believing in oneself increases risk taking: Perceived self-efficacy and opportunity recognition. Decision Sciences 25: 285–400

Langer EJ (1975) The illusion of control. Journal of Personality and Social Psychology, 32: 311–328

Lieberman MB, Montgomery DB (1988) First mover advantages. Strategic Management Journal 9: 329–346

McClelland DC (1961) The Achieving Society. Van Nostrand, Princeton, NJ

McMullen J, Shepherd DA (2006) Entrepreneurial action and the role of uncertainty in the theory of the entrepreneur. Academy of Management Review 31: 132–152

Morris M, Schindehutte M, Allen J (2006) Is the business model a useful strategic concept? Conceptual, theoretical, and empirical insights. Journal of Small Business Strategy 17: 27–50

Murray HA (1938) Explorations in personality. Oxford, New York.

Palich LE, Bagby DR (1995) Using cognitive theory to explain entrepreneurial risk-taking: Challenging the conventional wisdom. Journal of Business Venturing 10: 426–438

Russo JE, Shoemaker PJH (1998) Decision Traps. Doubleday, New York.

Shane S (2003) A General Theory of entrepreneurship: The individual-opportunity nexus. Edward Elgar, Cheltenham, UK.

Shane S, Venkataraman S (2000) The promise of entrepreneurship as a field of research. Academy of Management Review 26: 217–226

Shaver KG, Carter NM, Gartner WB, Reynolds PD (2001) Who is a nascent entrepreneur? Decision rules for identifying and selecting entrepreneurs in the Panel Study of Entrepreneurial Dynamics (PSED). Paper presented at the Babson College Entrepreneurship Research Conference, Jonkoping.

Shaver KG, Scott LR (1991) Person, process, choice: The psychology of new venture creation. Entrepreneurship Theory and Practice 16: 23–45

Shepherd DA, Douglas EJ, Shanley M (2000) New venture survival: Ignorance, external shocks, and risk reduction strategies. Journal of Business Venturing 15: 393–410

Simon M, Houghton SM, Aquino K (2000) Cognitive biases, risk perception and venture formation: How individuals decide to start companies. Journal of Business Venturing 15: 115–134

Sitkin SB, Pablo AL (1992) Reconceptualizing the determinants of risky behavior. Academy of Management Review 17: 9–38

Sitkin SB, Weingart LR (1995) Determinants of risky decision making behavior: A test of the mediating role of risk perceptions and risk propensity. Academy of Management Journal 36: 1573–1592

Smilor RW, Feeser HR (1991) Chaos and the entrepreneurial process: Patterns and policy implications for technology entrepreneurship. Journal of Business Venturing 6: 165–172

Stinchcombe AL (1965) Social structures and organizations. In: March JG (ed.), Handbook of Organizations. Rand McNally, Chicago, pp. 149–193.

Tellis GJ, Golder PN (1996) First to market, first to fail? Sloan Management Review 37: 65–75

Tversky A, Kahneman D (1974) Judgment under uncertainty: Heuristics and biases. Science 185: 1124–1131

Winborg J, Landstrom H (2000) Financial bootstrapping in small businesses: Examining small business manager's resource acquisition behaviors. Journal of Business Venturing, 16: 235–254

Chapter 2
Toward A Contextual Model of Entrepreneurial Intentions

Jennie Elfving, Malin Brännback, and Alan Carsrud

Abstract In this chapter, the authors challenge the existing linear views of entrepreneurial intentions by proposing a contextual model of entrepreneurial intentions (EIM). This model, initially proposed by Elfving (2008), bridges self-efficacy, motivations, and intentions, in particular it addresses the role that specific goals and motivations play in intentionality. In addition, the chapter addresses the issues of the inconsistent effect of social norms on entrepreneurial intentions. It builds upon the prior work of a broad range of researchers, including those represented in the other chapters in this cluster on entrepreneurial intentions within this volume.

2.1 Introduction

This chapter challenges the existing views of entrepreneurial intentions by proposing a contextual model of entrepreneurial intentions (EIM). It builds upon the prior work of a broad range of researchers, including those represented in the other chapters in this cluster on entrepreneurial intentions within this volume. This chapter also builds on the work of Elfving (2008), which bridges self-efficacy, motivations, and intentions. As is been shown in the chapters in this volume, the ideas adapted from social cognitive theory have widely impacted entrepreneurial research, especially the work in entrepreneurial intentions. While the implementation of perception and cognition has certainly increased our understanding of entrepreneurial behavior and despite the relatively large number of studies done there is really only one model that has been empirically tested to such an extent that it can be viewed as reliable and useful. Although that work is not complete. When studying why people choose to become entrepreneurs and continue being entrepreneurs, it remains one of the most influential models with respect to entrepreneurial cognitions. This model is called the entrepreneurial intention model and was developed by Krueger and his

J. Elfving (✉)
Rödsövägen 149, FIN-67400 Karleby, Finland
e-mail: jennie.elfving@gmail.com

A.L. Carsrud, M. Brännback (eds.), *Understanding the Entrepreneurial Mind*,
International Studies in Entrepreneurship 24, DOI 10.1007/978-1-4419-0443-0_2,
© Springer Science+Business Media, LLC 2009

Fig. 2.1 The classic entrepreneurial intentions model.
Source: adapted from Shapero (1982), Krueger (1993), Krueger and Brazeal (1994), and Krueger et al. (2000)

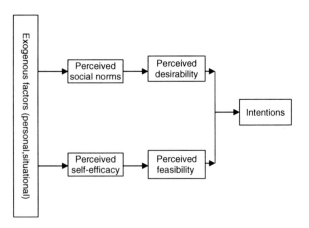

associates (see, for example, Krueger, 1993; Krueger and Brazeal, 1994; Krueger et al., 2000). The model is illustrated in Fig. 2.1.

The model proposed by Krueger and his associates draws heavily on the work of Ajzen and Fishbein and their theory of planned behavior (described in Chapter 7) as well as on the work of Shapero (1982) and his *theory of the entrepreneurial event.* Shapero's work (1975, 1982) focused on factors which make an entrepreneurial event, such as venture creation, happen. His conclusion was that entrepreneurial events are a result of interacting situational and social–cultural factors. Each entrepreneurial event occurs as a result of a dynamic process providing situational momentum that has an impact upon individuals whose perceptions and values are determined by their social and cultural inheritance and their previous experience.

The greatest reason for an entrepreneurial event is a change in the person's life path, e.g., the loss of one's job, a midlife crisis, or an opportunity to take the risk after a financial situation becomes more secure. Changes in one's life path alone, however, are insufficient conditions for an entrepreneurial event to occur. Other influencing factors are, e.g., background, previous experience, and one's perception of feasibility. The division between perceived feasibility and perceived desirability, central in Krueger's model, also originate from Shapero's model (Shapero and Sokol, 1982).

Drawing on these arguments, Krueger (1993) created the entrepreneurial intentions model. The entrepreneurial intentions model assumes that perceived feasibility and perceived desirability predict the intentions to become an entrepreneur. Perceived social norms and perceived self-efficacy are antecedents of perceived desirability and perceived feasibility (Krueger and Brazeal, 1994). Social norms have not always had a significant impact (Krueger et al., 2000). However, one also has to consider that social norms could be expected to vary across cultures, i.e., in some countries, social norms are more supportive of entrepreneurial activity than in others (McGrath and MacMillan, 1992; Davidsson and Wiklund, 1997; Krueger and Kickul, 2006).

According to the model of planned behavior, perceived desirability or personal attitude depends on the perceptions of the consequences of outcomes from performing the target behavior: their likelihood, negative and positive consequences, and both intrinsic and extrinsic rewards (Ajzen and Fishbein, 2005; Kuratko et al., 1997). In short, we are talking about a perceived expectancy framework. Perceptions are dependent on the social context and on what can be regarded as personally desirable. What kind of behavior is considered worthy of a reward and what is not will vary across cultures and societies.

2.2 Social Norms

The social norm measure is a function of the perceived normative beliefs of significant others, such as family, friends, and co-workers, weighted by the individual's motive to comply with each normative belief. Social norms often reflect the influence of an organizational and/or community culture and provide guidelines for what in a culture is regarded as desirable. It is both a very interesting and a very complicated component in the model. Many researchers, however, tend to claim that social norms do not explain additional variances in intentions for would-be entrepreneurs (Krueger et al., 2000). Which certainly may be true within a given culture, but few studies have compared across cultures and societies. Kickul and Krueger (2004) pointed out that if social norms are valid constructs, cultural contexts should be reflected in them, perhaps not as a real measure but at least as a proxy.

One problem when measuring the impact of social norms is that social norms tend to vary both across cultures (McGrath and MacMillan, 1992) and within cultures (Davidsson and Wiklund, 1997). For example, in the United States, starting one's own business is usually considered a measure of achievement and personal success and thus attracts admiration and praise. In Finland, however, the general reaction is often a mix of awe and envy (Carsrud et al., 2007). While bankruptcy is probably never considered something to aim for, it is not the "end of the world" in the United States. In fact, there are those who regard it as an effective learning process (Shapero, 1975).

However, in countries such as Australia, Finland, and Sweden and indeed in most of Europe, those who have gone through bankruptcy will be marked for life (Carsrud et al., 2007; Gustafsson, 2006). In Finland, too much success can also be as much of a sin as failure. This is also true in Latin cultures where extreme success is perceived to mean others have not done well as a result, the concept of "limited good." Consequently, in general, Americans perceive entrepreneurship as much more desirable than Finns or even Canadians. Furthermore, Bryant and Bryant (1998) showed that as social norms in a community change that in turn alters what is more likely to be considered an opportunity. In short, to identify which factors can be labeled as social norms, i.e., to know what to measure may be more difficult than measuring the social norms themselves.

Another challenge when measuring social norms is identifying the correct reference group. The reference group for an entrepreneur or a potential entrepreneur is not necessarily only family and friends, but may actually include colleagues and business partners (Carsrud et al., 2007). Once again this is a context-specific issue. In some countries or cultures, the impact of family may be greater than in others. Recent work by Carsrud et al. (2007) showed it might be useful to distinguish between different kinds of social norms. In this study, they separated general social norms from family social norms and showed that each impacts entrepreneurial intentions differently. The reference group, or role models, can be somebody to look up to, but in some cases, it may equally well be somebody you can be familiar with. If you look at somebody who has started a company and you think "He is no smarter than I am. If he can do it I can do it" that might well function as a triggering event (Shapero, 1975).

2.3 Self-Efficacy

As will be stated in both Chapter 7 and Chapter 11, self-efficacy is one's sense of competence: a belief that we can do something specific (Bandura, 1977, 2001). Self-efficacy is a strong driver of goal-oriented behavior (Baum and Locke, 2004; Bandura, 1977, 2001). Desiring to do something, however, is not enough to lead to intentions. A belief that one can actually do it is also required. For instance, gender and ethnic differences in work preferences and performance can often be traced to differences in self-efficacy. Kourilsky and Walstad (1998) compared perceptions of knowledge with actual knowledge of entrepreneurial skills and showed that although the skill levels of boys and girls were comparable, girls were more likely to feel ill prepared. This might be the result of the gender role of femininity in which self-awareness is stronger, for discussion on this factor, refer to Chapter 7. Support for this was found by Wilson et al. (2004) who demonstrated a direct relationship between self-efficacy and intentions in girls and highlighted the significance of girls' self-efficacy on their entrepreneurial aspirations. As mentioned above, for a more detailed discussion on self-efficacy, the reader is referred to Chapter 11.

2.3.1 Collective Self-Efficacy

Self-efficacy can also be collective, i.e., support from other organizational members of an intention can be needed to support an intention. Perceptions of collective efficacy are likely to be important (Bandura, 1986, 1995). It can be expected that collective self-efficacy enforces social norms and low collective self-efficacy may decrease high personal self-efficacy so as to ultimately inhibit action, i.e., social norms, self-efficacy, and culture are tightly interconnected.

2.3.2 Self-Efficacy as Task-Specific Cognitions

Researchers also point out the importance of "career self-efficacy" as a domain or task-specific construct (Boyd and Vozikis, 1994; Betz and Hackett, 1981; Lent and

Hacket, 1987). Career self-efficacy refers to the perception of self-efficacy in relation to the process of career choice and adjustment. Self-efficacy has been found to predict stated occupational interests and occupational choices among college students (Betz and Hacket, 1981; Lent and Hacket, 1987). Boyd and Vozikis (1994), therefore suggesting that career self-efficacy may be an important variable when studying how entrepreneurial intentions are formed in the early stages of a person's career. However, they also indicated that entrepreneurial intentions were often a result of previous work experience and therefore were not always very strong immediately after graduation, and moreover even if a graduate student did have strong entrepreneurial intentions they might not be acted upon until they had gained enough experience to provide the level of confidence necessary to anticipate venture success (Boyd and Vozikis, 1994; Shane, 2008). Once again the reader is referred to Chapter 11.

2.4 Revising Basic Assumptions About Intentions

Both the theory of planned behavior and the entrepreneurial intentions model are widely used for predicting entrepreneurial intentions and behavior. Using the software "Publish or Perish" (www.harzig.com), 180 references to the entrepreneurial intentions model can be found. This is clear evidence that although some minor changes have been suggested and implemented, the basic structure of the model has remained robust and is commonly accepted. One wonders, however, if that is because the model really is so reliable and well functioning, or whether it is perhaps because no one has made a serious attempt to question the basic assumptions in the model? Brännback et al. (2006a) suggested it might be time to put the model to test and to revise it critically. Considering the wide usage of the model that is indeed a brave suggestion, but it might be needed in order to develop the field of entrepreneurial cognition research.

When reviewing and revising the intentions, model two different questions must be asked. First of all, are there significant errors in the current models that need to be deleted or corrected? Second, are there any significant variables missing from the model? Starting with the first question, recent work by Brännback et al. (2006b), Krueger and Kickul (2006), and Carsrud et al. (2007) unearthed an unusual finding.

While perceived desirability and perceived feasibility were significant antecedents of intentions, as expected, a rudimentary test found that desirability and intent also clearly predicted feasibility, while feasibility and intent also clearly predicted desirability. In fact, the data from their studies seemed to suggest that feasibility may prove – statistically – to be the dependent variable. In their research, when the intent was the dependent variable, $R^2 = .462$ and was driven by desirability (beta $= 0.547$) and feasibility (beta $= 0.217$). When desirability was the dependent variable $R^2 = .464$ and was driven by feasibility (beta $= 0.222$) and intent (beta $= 0.545$). When feasibility was the dependent variable, $R^2 = .284$ and driven by desirability (beta $= 0.297$) and intent (beta $= 0.289$). This would imply that feedback loops exist. Hence, we notice evidence for intention influencing its "predictors."

This finding indicates the intention process may not be linear. Considering that the theory of planned behavior and the entrepreneurial intentions model are linear, we face a serious contradiction (Carsud et al., 2007). However, when looking at previous attitude research (Kelman, 1974; McBroom and Reed, 1992; Allport, 1935), it can be seen that this idea of reciprocal causation is not entirely new. Kelman (1974) claimed that attitudes cause behavior and that behavior causes attitudes (i.e., reciprocal causation exists) and McBroom and Reed (1992) suggested that the two are unrelated or that the two are caused by another third factor. Moreover, Allport (1935) argued that behavior may be predicted by triumvirate of "intention"-like constructs: cognitive, affective, and conative (which very roughly correspond to feasibility, desirability, and the intent to act). Behavior is likely to occur only when all three predictors are in place to some minimal degree. Empirically, this troika tends to be strongly inter-correlated. Given these earlier findings, it is reasonable to assume reciprocal causation within entrepreneurial intentionality as well (Carsrud et al., 2007). Consequently, it is time to explore whether the basic structure of the model really holds.

2.5 A Revised Entrepreneurial Intentions Model

In line with the findings from the work of Carsrud et al. (2007), the study of entrepreneurial intentions can be understood only in a theoretical framework where motivation, goals, and opportunity evaluation are included. The entrepreneurial intentions model (Krueger, 1993; Krueger and Carsrud, 1993; Krueger and Brazeal, 1994; Krueger, 2000) does not include any of these and is therefore a limited framework. However, this model does not explicitly include motivation. This lack of attention to motivation in entrepreneurship research also is pointed out in Chapter 7. Drawing on the elements of the existing models and on the findings from Elfving (2008), a theoretical framework for understanding how entrepreneurial intentions emerge is presented in Fig. 2.2. Elfving (2008) in her qualitative study was not able to determine the variable connections as precisely as in a quantitative study, nor is it possible to say how strong the connections are. This model therefore is to be considered a conceptual framework that still needs to be tested. Nevertheless, this kind of a conceptual framework is necessary in order for research to progress.

The research questions in Elfving (2008) focused on: *What are the characteristics of an entrepreneurial intention? How does an entrepreneurial intention emerge?* The results of that study are summarized in the context-specific entrepreneurial intentions model (context-specific EIM), graphically represented below. From a critical realist point of view, the EIM model illustrates the structure of the entrepreneurial intention formation process. This structure possesses the power to cause entrepreneurial behavior and is therefore helpful when seeking to understand entrepreneurial behavior. However, the role of social norms remains an elusive one as it clearly impacts the model, but it may in fact be an indirect one via motivation, goals, desirability, and self-efficacy. Additional discussion on motivation and goals can be found in Chapter 7.

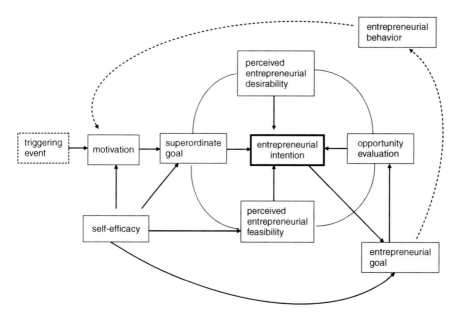

Fig. 2.2 The context-specific entrepreneurial intentions mode

The variables in the model in Fig. 2.2 represent the mechanisms that constitute the structure of an entrepreneurial intention formation process. The structure of
an entrepreneurial intention deeply affects entrepreneurial behavior, but the impact
is mediated through entrepreneurial goals and therefore entrepreneurial goals are
important if one wants to understand entrepreneurial behavior. The existence of different kinds of goals, in this case, superordinate goals and entrepreneurial goals,
also reflects the hierarchy of goals introduced by Bagozzi and Dholakia (1999).
Entrepreneurial goals can be either focal goals or subordinate goals. However, the
transition from entrepreneurial goals to entrepreneurial action is likely to be affected
by non-volitional variables. This model stops at the level of intentions and does
not take a stand on when or how an intention is transferred into action, although
they are implied. Even in the Panel Study of Entrepreneurial Dynamics (PSED) by
Gartner et al. (2004), there remains a group of entrepreneurs who intend to start
something after a prolonged period, even if they have yet to really start a venture.
Even if somebody has a strong intention to do something, something might prevent
the person from pursuing the plan (Gollwitzer and Brandstätter, 1997). This might
include not taking enough actions to make a decision to either quit or start a venture.
The impact of barriers and volitional versus non-volitional behavior occurs after the
intention has emerged and is outside the scope of this chapter.

Entrepreneurial intentions are first and foremost a result of superordinate goals,
perceived entrepreneurial desirability, perceived entrepreneurial feasibility, and
opportunity evaluation. In the context-specific EIM, these variables constitute a circle around the entrepreneurial intention. The variables in the circle reciprocally

impact each other. The results from Elfving (2008) indicated that superordinate goals affect both perception of entrepreneurial desirability and perception of entrepreneurial feasibility. If the main goal is to gain independence, entrepreneurial feasibility and entrepreneurial desirability will be evaluated in relation to how much independence it can provide.

The superordinate goal also impacts opportunity evaluation. The case studies showed motivation and superordinate goals affect what kinds of opportunities the entrepreneurs recognize. Moreover, the results from Elfving (2008) support earlier research findings that desirability and feasibility reciprocally impact each other (Brännback et al., 2006b; Carsrud et al., 2007). It seems that feasibility and desirability are always closely linked: high feasibility increases desirability and vice versa.

Opportunity evaluation is not included in the entrepreneurial intentions model developed by Krueger and his colleagues. (Krueger, 1993; Krueger and Carsrud, 1993; Krueger and Brazeal, 1994; Krueger, 2000). However, Kaish and Gilad (1991), Shane and Venkataraman (2000), Eckhardt and Shane (2003), Gustafsson (2006), and Elfving (2008) support the importance of opportunities and opportunity recognition in the intentional process. The variable opportunity evaluation in the context-specific EIM also includes a tendency to be optimistic and use self-serving biases. The optimism and the self-serving biases result in the entrepreneurs not perceiving themselves as taking risks. This finding is also supported by previous research (Shaver and Scott, 1991; Palich and Bagby, 1995) and consequently is not necessary to include perception of risk as a separate variable.

As Ajzen and Fischbein (2005) point out there is a difference between general attitudes toward a phenomenon and attitudes toward performing a specific behavior: the latter being more likely to result in action. One certainly hopes this is the case in entrepreneurship. The results in Elfving (2008) show perceived entrepreneurial feasibility and perceived entrepreneurial desirability impact *general attitudes toward entrepreneurship*. By also including superordinate goals and opportunity evaluation the behavior is tied to a context and this makes it possible to explore the person's *attitude toward performing a particular entrepreneurial activity*.

If an individual perceives entrepreneurship as feasible and desirable (i.e., in general holds a positive attitude), considers entrepreneurship to be in line with his overall goals in life and additionally sees an opportunity to perform an entrepreneurial act (the two latter constituting a positive attitude toward performing an entrepreneurial activity), then he is likely to form an entrepreneurial intention. The ability to predict attitudes toward a particular entrepreneurial activity, and not only a general attitude toward entrepreneurship, makes the context-specific EIM more precise than the original entrepreneurial intentions model.

Even if self-efficacy and motivation do not impact the formation of an entrepreneurial intention directly, the indirect impact is of such importance that it legitimizes including them in the model. Motivation is discussed in-depth in Chapter 7. Motivation is important because it determines what kind of superordinate goals a person sets in life. The superordinate goals are always set in relation to what is perceived as motivating. Self-efficacy is important because if motivation determines what a person *wants* to do, self-efficacy determines what he thinks he *can* do. Self-efficacy impacts both superordinate goals and entrepreneurial goals. Once again the reader is referred to Chapter 11. However, it is important to remember that self-efficacy is context and content specific (Bandura, 1986, 1989) and both kinds of goals are likely to be impacted by different kinds of self-efficacy. Self-efficacy impacts motivation mainly through commitment, which Bandura (1989) also finds in his research. High self-efficacy improves commitment and thus makes the person more motivated to continue.

Reality consists of many different processes and different structures where one event causes another. The context-specific EIM shows an entrepreneurial intention can result in entrepreneurial goals, which in turn leads to entrepreneurial behavior. Once behavior emerges it may cause changes in motivation. These changes then function as a triggering event, which results in new entrepreneurial intentions. This is seen for example in the case of an individual whose first intention is to start a small business to provide a living for herself. Once she gets started her motivation may change and so will her intentions. She may have formed an intention to explore the possibilities for growth. The triggering mechanisms for these changes can also stem from another source, and in the model, this is illustrated in the variable triggering event. The term is borrowed from Shapero's research (1982).

Finally, the context-specific EIM does not include the variable social norms. That does not mean that social norms are not important or that they do not have an impact but because the results for social norms were mixed further investigation is required before they can be placed in the model with accuracy. It is clear that they belong, especially in various cultures, but exactly how they function is still unclear and requires studying non-American populations.

2.6 Conclusions

We have in this chapter proposed a different model of entrepreneurial intentions, EIM, that ties motivations and goals into the traditional model of intentions. By doing so we are trying to integrate the various cognitive elements of the entrepreneur into a more comprehensive model that will link intentions to behaviors.

References

Ajzen I, Fishbein M (2005) The Influence of Attitudes on Behavior. In: Albarracin D, Johnson B, Zanna M (eds.) The Handbook of Attitudes. Lawrence Erlbaum Associates, Mahwah, pp. 173–221

Allport GW (1935) AttitudesIn: Murchison CM (eds.) Handbook of Social Psychology. Clark University Press, Winchester, MA, pp. 798–844

Bagozzi R, Dholakia U (1999) Goal Setting and Goal Striving in Consumer Behavior. Journal of Marketing, 63: 19–32

Bandura A (1977) Toward a unifying theory of behavioral change. Psychological Review 84: 191–215

Bandura A (1982) Self-efficacy mechanisms in human agency, American Psychologist 37: 122–147

Bandura A (1986) Social Foundations of Thought and Action: A Social Cognitive Theory. Prentice Hall, Englewood Cliffs.

Bandura A (1989) Regulation of Cognitive Process Through Perceived Self-Efficacy. Developmental Psychology 25: 729–735

Bandura A (2001) Social Cognitive Theory: An agentic perspective. Annual Review of Psychology 52: 1–26

Baum J, Locke E (2004) The Relationship of Entrepreneurial Traits, Skill, and Motivation to Subsequent Venture Growth. Journal of Applied Psychology 89: 587–598

Betz N, Hackett G (1981) The relationship of career-related self-efficacy expectations to perceived career options in college woman and men. Journal of Counseling Psychology 28: 399–410

Boyd N, Vozikis G (1994) The Influence of Self-Efficacy on the Development of Entrepreneurial Intentions and Actions. Entrepreneurship Theory and Practice, 18: 63–77

Bryant T, Bryant J (1998) Wetlands and entrepreneurs: Mapping the fuzzy zone between ecosystem preservation and entrepreneurial opportunity. Journal of Organizational Change Management 11: 112–134

Brännback M, Carsrud A, Elfving J, Kickul J, Krueger N (2006a) Why Replicate Entrepreneurial Intentionality Studies? prospects, perils, and academic reality. Paper presented at SMU Edge Conference, Singapore.

Brännback M, Carsrud A, Elfving J, Krueger N (2006b) Sex, Drugs and... Entrepreneurial Passion: An Exploratory Study. Paper presented at Babson conference, Bloomington Indiana.

Carsrud A, Krueger N, Brännback M, Kickul J, Elfving J (2007) The Family Business Pipeline: Where Norms and Modeling Make a Difference. Paper presented at Academy of Management Conference, 2007.

Davidsson P, Wiklund J (1997) Values, beliefs and regional variations in new firm formations rate. Journal of Economic psychology 18: 179–199

Elfving J (2008) Contextualizing Entrepreneurial Intentions, Åbo Akademi Press, Åbo

Eckhardt J, Shane S (2003) Opportunities and entrepreneurship. Journal of Management 29: 333–349

Gartner, WB, Shaver KG, Carter NM, Reynolds PD (2004) Handbook of Entrepreneurial Dynamics: The Process of Business Creation. Sage, Thousand Oaks, CA.

Gollwitzer P, Brandstätter V (1997) Implementation Intentions and effective Goal Pursuit. Journal of Personality and Social Psychology 73: 186–199

Gustafsson V (2006) Entrepreneurial Decision-Making: Individuals, Tasks and Cognition. Edward Elgar, Northampton.

Kaish S, Gilad B (1991) Characteristics of opportunities search of entrepreneurs versus executives: Sources, interests, general alertness. Journal of Business Venturing 6: 45–61

Kelman HC (1974) Attitudes are alive and well and gainfully employed in the sphere of action. American Psychologist 29: 310–324

Kickul J, Krueger NF (2004) A cognitive processing model of entrepreneurial self-efficacy and intentionality. Frontiers of Entrepreneurship Research 2004. Babson College, Wellesley, MA, pp. 607–619

Kourilsky ML, Walstad WB.(1998) Entrepreneurship and female youth: Knowledge, attitudes, gender differences and educational practices. Journal of Business Venturing 13: 77–88

Krueger NF (1993) The Impact of Prior Entrepreneurial Exposure on Perceptions and New Venture Feasibility and Desirability. Entrepreneurship Theory and Practice 18: 5–21

Krueger NF (2000) The cognitive infrastructure of opportunity emergence. Entrepreneurship Theory & Practice 24: 5–23

Krueger NF, Brazeal D (1994) Entrepreneurial potential and potential entrepreneurs. Entrepreneurship Theory and Practice 18: 91–104

Krueger NF, Carsrud AL (1993) Entrepreneurial intentions: Applying theory of planned behaviour. Entrepreneurship and Regional Development 5: 315–330

Krueger NF, Kickul J (2006) So you thought the intentions model was simple?: Navigating the complexities and interactions of cognitive style, culture, gender, social norms, and intensity on the pathways to entrepreneurship. Paper presented at USASBE conference, Tuscon, AZ.

Krueger NF, Reilly M, Carsrud AL (2000) Competing models of entrepreneurial intentions. Journal of Business Venturing 15: 411–532

Kuratko D, Hornsby J, Naffziger D (1997) An Examination of Owner's Goals in Sustaining Entrepreneurship. Journal of Small Business Management 35: 24–33

Lent R, Hackett G (1987) Career Self-Efficacy: Empirical Status and Future Directions. Journal of Vocational Behavior 347–382.

McBroom WH, Reed FW (1992) Toward a Reconceptualization of Attitude-Behavior Consistency. Social Psychology Quarterly 55: 205–216

McGrath R, MacMillan I (1992) More like each other than anyone else?: A cross-cultural study of entrepreneurial perceptions. Journal of Business Venturing 7: 419–429

Palich E, Bagby D (1995) Using cognitive theory to explain entrepreneurial risk-taking: challenging conventional wisdom. Journal of Business Venturing 10: 425–438

Shane S (2008) The Illusions of Entrepreneurship. Yale University Press, New Haven.

Shane S, Venkataraman S (2000) The Promise of Entrepreneurship as a Field of Research. Academy of Management Review 25: 217–226

Shapero A (1975) Who Starts New Businesses? The Displaced, Uncomfortable Entrepreneur. Psychology Today 9: 83–88

Shapero A, Sokol L (1982) Social Dimensions of Entrepreneurship. In: Kent C, Sexton D, Vesper K (eds.), The Encyclopedia of Entrepreneurship, Prentice-Hall, Englewood Cliffs, pp. 72–90.

Shaver K, Scott L (1991) Person, process, choice: the psychology of new venture creation. Entrepreneurship Theory and Practice 16: 23–45

Wilson F, Marlino D, Kickul J (2004) The Embodied Mind, Cognitive Science and Human Experience. MIT Press, London.

Chapter 3
An "Informed" Intent Model: Incorporating Human Capital, Social Capital, and Gender Variables into the Theoretical Model of Entrepreneurial Intentions

Kevin Hindle, Kim Klyver, and Daniel F. Jennings

Abstract This chapter was motivated by a belief, based on a substantial body of research, that prevailing theoretical models of entrepreneurial intensions are under-specified. Currently, such models as represented by the Shapero–Kreuger intentions model (Krueger et al., 2000) are highly focused on cognition in its more limited sense of the thinking process that occurs within an individual's head rather than the broader, contextually embedded process of *social cognition* as conceived by Bandura (1977, 1986) and subsequent scholars. In the chapter, we develop six proportions derived from the literatures of human capital, social capital, and gender as they relate to entrepreneurship. We argue, when it comes to start-up intentions, the entrepreneurial mind is indeed broader than current theoretical models indicate. Accordingly, an enhanced model of informed entrepreneurial intent was developed and discussed.

3.1 Introduction

3.1.1 Background and Overview

In this chapter, we present a model aimed at enhancing the basic entrepreneurial intentions model developed by Krueger and associated researchers (Krueger et al., 2000). We focus on how entrepreneurial intentions are informed by human and social capital and how levels of informed intent differ between genders. The presentation of inquiry begins by presenting the entrepreneurial intentions model as an established theoretical framework. The extant model argues that the concept of self-efficacy is an important influence on people who contemplate and then evaluate both the desirability and the feasibility of a new venture. If the evaluation results in a compelling combination of desirability and feasibility, the person will form the intention to start a new venture.

K. Hindle (✉)
Chair of Entrepreneurship Research Deakin University, Australia and Visiting Professor of Entrepreneurship, University of Southern Denmark
e-mail: khindle@swin.edu.au

A.L. Carsrud, M. Brännback (eds.), *Understanding the Entrepreneurial Mind*, International Studies in Entrepreneurship 24, DOI 10.1007/978-1-4419-0443-0_3, © Springer Science+Business Media, LLC 2009

All models of social attitudes and behavior involve substantial abstraction from the multi-faceted complexity of the real world. We argue, however, that the current model of entrepreneurial intentions is just too abstract because it fails to address aspects of social cognition that evidence indicates simply must be accounted for. At its present level of abstraction, the intentions model is a model of an aspect of what might be called "the entrepreneurial mind." It has given rise to insightful and useful research. However, we will argue that this is in a sense too "narrow minded" a model: it could be improved, making it in a sense a more "broad-minded" model if it were possible to include the influence that *knowledge, information*, and *advice* undoubtedly play when a person formulates his or her intent to start a new venture. We will further argue that it is very important whether the person is a him or a her: gender is as likely to matter in the formation of entrepreneurial intention as it has been shown to matter in many other aspects of the entrepreneurial process. The argument and associated model to be presented in this chapter will use the term "informed intent" as an expression to capture the combined influence of knowledge, information, and advice embedded in the human and social capital a person possesses at the time of forming entrepreneurial intentions. Building on these foundations, a theoretical model was developed including six propositions. Support for the propositions would not only permit but also mandate a redesign of the basic entrepreneurial intentions model.

In summary, the chapter was motivated by a belief, based on a substantial body of research, that prevailing theoretical models of entrepreneurial intensions are under-specified. Currently, such models as represented by the Shapero–Kreuger intentions model (Krueger et al., 2000) are highly focused on cognition in its more limited sense of the thinking process that occurs within an individual's head rather than the broader, contextually embedded process of *social cognition* as conceived by Bandura (1977, 1986) and subsequent scholars.

3.2 Formal Statement of the Research Problem

3.2.1 Entrepreneurial Intentions as a "Mind" Game in the Entrepreneurial Cognition Context

One of the early pioneers of entrepreneurial intentions as a field was Barbera Bird (1988). Norris Krueger, in association with various colleagues, has presented the most prominent and sustained body of work in field. (Krueger, 2003; Krueger, 1993; Krueger and Dickson, 1994; Krueger, 2000; Krueger and Brazeal, 1994; Krueger and Carsrud, 1993; Krueger and Dickson, 1993; Krueger et al., 2000; Shepherd and Krueger, 2002.) His most direct antecedents were Shapero (1982) and Bird (1988). Other empirical workers in the sub-field include the Norwegian scholar, Lars Kolvereid (1996), and British researchers Jenkins and Johnson (1997). Forbes (1999) developed a model that positions entrepreneurial intentions – and its "canon-ical" works (Hindle 2004) – as an integral sub-set of the entrepreneurial cognition literature. Forbes' diagrammatic synthesis is reproduced as Fig. 3.1.

In the Forbes model, a sense-making perspective permits articulation of the salient features of the emerging field of entrepreneurial cognition. The importance

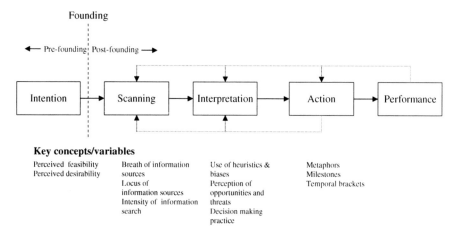

Fig. 3.1 The entrepreneurial cognition continuum

of temporality is represented by a "timeline dichotomy": pre-founding and post-founding. In the pre-founding stage, the emphasis is on organizational *intentions* represented by two key concepts: perceived feasibility and perceived desirability. In the very early days of entrepreneurial intentions research, Barbara Bird (1988) defined the nature of the phenomenon.

> Intentionality is a state of mind directing a person's attention (and therefore experience and action) toward a specific object (goal) or a path in order to achieve something (means) …Research … shows that a person's intentions sustain value or effort despite interruption… Entrepreneurial intentions are aimed at either creating a new venture or creating new values in existing ventures.

In Forbes' synthesis of the post-founding stage, an organizational sense-making framework proceeds from *scanning* (where the conceptual emphasis is upon aspects of information sources), through *interpretation* (where the conceptual emphasis is upon the uses of heuristics and biases, perceptions of opportunities, and threats and decision-making practices) through to *action*. The action phase places conceptual emphasis upon metaphors, milestones, and temporal brackets. The final result is performance. Development of the field of entrepreneurial cognition has grown rapidly. Overview sources include the 2002 special issue of *Entrepreneurship Theory and Practice* edited by Ron Mitchell (see Mitchell et al., 2002); Norris Krueger's overview (2003) in Acs and Audretsch's *Handbook of Entrepreneurship Research* (2003); and Katz and Shepherd's (2003) introduction to JAI Volume 6.

We might think of the emerging field of entrepreneurial cognition as a research "game." It is steeped in psychological antecedents. Axiomatically and logically, the field is very much a "mind game": so is its intentions sub-set: so they should be. J.R. Anderson's *Cognitive Psychology and its Implication* (Anderson, 1990) provides a thorough overview of the "mother" discipline, in language accessible to the non-psychologist. However, we argue in this paper that the extant research and theoretical modeling of entrepreneurial intentions is, currently, *too* much of a mind game. The intentions field, perhaps, has been rather too concerned with the narrower, cerebral, and self-perceptual aspects of the ways in which entrepreneurs think and too little concerned with the wider human and social contexts that influence the thinking. If this imbalance exists, it needs redressing because the very basis of entrepreneurial cognition – its parent field – is supposed to be *social* cognition.

The entrepreneurial cognition field seeks to reassert the importance of the individual, sentient human person as an object worthy of treatment as an empirical unit of analysis in entrepreneurship research. At the heart of this discipline is the core psychological trinity of person, process, and choice (Shaver and Scott, 1991). This heartland recognizes that *social* cognition is the key to understanding entrepreneurial thinking and action at the individual level. The locus of entrepreneurial thinking is not just between peoples' ears; we are bound to consider the complex interaction of mind and environment. The true parent of entrepreneurial cognition as a field is not "cognition" – unadorned – but "social cognition" whose seminal scholar is Albert Bandura. His long list of works find their apogee in his *Social Foundations of Thought and Action: A Social Cognitive Theory* (Bandura, 1986). Furthermore, if we return to the seminal definition of entrepreneurial intentions (Bird, 1988) cited above, she is very specific that intention is a mind game but one that involves experience (which can only be derived in a social context) and is directed toward action (which can only take place in a social context). Granovetter (1985) as argued that too many theories are "under-socialized" and we argue that entrepreneurial intentions models are a case in point.

So, intentionality is indeed "a state of mind," but it is a socially contextualized state of mind and, if existing models of entrepreneurial intentions underplay the social context, it is time the models were improved to include more overt attention to a wider range of human and especially social factors that inform a person's intentions. We need models not just of intent but of informed intent.

3.2.2 Extant Theoretical Framework: Current Status of the Entrepreneurial Intentions Model

The entrepreneurial intention approach emerged in the 1980s drawing heavily on Bandura's (1977) social learning theory. A great deal of previous entrepreneurship literature focused on how psychological traits, demographic, and situational factors distinguished entrepreneurial individuals from non-entrepreneurial individuals. However, the results were disappointing with respect to both explanatory power and predictive validity (Krueger et al., 2000). As a reaction, different entrepreneurial intention models developed. These models offered another way of predicting and understanding entrepreneurship. As previously indicated, Bird (1988) argue that "Entrepreneurs' intentions guide their goal setting, communications, commitment, organization, and other kinds of work" (Bird, 1988: 442). Krueger et al. (2000) indicate that intentions are "... the single best predictor of any planned behavior, including entrepreneurship" (Krueger et al., 2000: 412).

Two entrepreneurial intention models have received predominate attention: the theory of entrepreneurial event (Shapero, 1982) and the theory of planned behavior (Ajzen, 1991). Representing the theory of entrepreneurial event, Shapero (1982) argued that entrepreneurial intentions depend on individuals' perception of the desirability, feasibility, and propensity of the entrepreneurial to act. Individuals' behavior is assumed to continue in same path until something (e.g., job insecurity, job loss, receiving an inheritance, etc.) interrupts the inertia. This interruption makes individuals consider and evaluate other opportunities, including starting a business. The model was developed in order to explain entrepreneurial behavior specifically.

The theory of planned behavior was, in contrast, developed to explain planned behavior in general. Here it is argued that (entrepreneurial) intention depends on individuals' attitudes, subjective norms, and the perceived feasibility (Ajzen, 1991). The planned behavior model has received empirical support (Kolvereid, 1996; Krueger et al., 2000; Shook et al., 2003) and the entrepreneurial event model even stronger support (e.g., Krueger, 1993; Krueger et al., 2000; Shook et al., 2003). Krueger (1993), for instance, found in his study of 126 business students that desirability, feasibility, and propensity to act explained more than half of the variance in the intentions toward entrepreneurship.

So, though models of entrepreneurial intention come in many variations and range in detail and emphasis, the variants have more similarities than differences. An important and influential entrepreneurial intentions model was and remains the one developed and tested by Krueger et al. (2000). Labeled "The Shapero–Kreuger Model," it was presented on page 418 of their study and is reproduced here as Fig. 3.2.

This is, as argued, very much a "mind game" or "between the ears" model of entrepreneurial intent. There are no social capital variables. The only component of the model that may be regarded in some senses as a human capital construct is "self-efficacy" (some scholars regard it as such and some do not). Even if we permit "self-efficacy" to be classified as a component of human capital, it is certainly the most cerebral, subjective, and abstract of all human capital components.

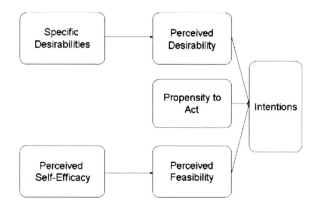

Fig. 3.2 The Shapero–Krueger model of entrepreneurial intent

Education and experience are human capital variables – objective measures of them can be directly obtained. Measures of self-efficacy have to be constructed indirectly. The model developed in this chapter seeks to strengthen the prevailing model by introducing the notion of informed intent. The supposition underlying the attempt to strengthen the model is that the process of developing entrepreneurial intentions is not just contained "between the ears" of an individual – an abstract mechanistic thinking process – it is a process informed by the human capital and social capital that an individual possesses. In this conception, the word "informed" retains two distinct but related meanings. First, "to inform" means "to direct." The combination of human capital and social capital an individual possesses will move a person in certain directions and away from others: toward entrepreneurship or away from it. Second, "to inform" means "to supply with information." A person's human and social capital is literally a source of the information used to form or not to form entrepreneurial intentions and, eventually, to go on to entrepreneurial commitment.

Brännback et al. (2007) have argued that if we are to understand how entrepreneurial intentions evolve, we must embrace theories reflecting the inherent dynamics of human decision making. "While the dominant model of entrepreneurial intentions remains invaluable, capturing the dynamics is necessary to advance our understanding of how intent becomes action." To that end, that offered Bagozzi's Theory of Trying (TT) as a theory-driven model that assumes a dynamic pathway to intent. Their study offers a significant updating of the intentions model because, rather than focusing on intentions toward a static target behavior, Theory of Trying focuses on intentions toward a dynamic goal. The authors of the study reported in this chapter have deliberately used the older and – some might say out dated – intentions model for reasons of clarity of focus. Whether the emergent intentions process is dynamic or static is not our focal issue. We are interested in what informs the process – potentially human and social capital – rather than the nature of the process – dynamic or static.

In summary, our argument is that even the broadest-brush model of entrepreneurial intent should be a model of informed intent.

3.3 Literature Review and Model Development

3.3.1 Overview

In a recent study on the role of human and social capital and technology in nascent ventures, Schenkel et al. (2009) have provided succinct summation of the under-utilized relevance of human and social capital in the modeling that scholars conduct when studying the new venture creation phenomenon.

They argue that research on human and social capital derives from the ideas that actors are both shaped by and contribute to the social construction of their respective economic contexts, citing, inter alia: Aldrich and Zimmer (1986), Burt (1992), Coleman (1988), Davidsson and Honig (2003), and Granovetter (1985).

From a human capital perspective, individuals develop 'corridors' of knowledge (Ronstadt, 1988) from information exposure and practical experience that lead them to being alert to new venture opportunities that they could not see previously (Kirzner, 1979), as well as better prepared to engage in successful exploit efforts (Becker, 1993; Davidsson and Honig, 2003). Similarly, from a social capital perspective individuals presumably develop social relationships throughout time that play a significant role in the enhancement of their alertness to entrepreneurial opportunity (Singh, 2000). Such relationships also allow individuals to engage more effectively efforts to form new ventures because of the socially constructed (Larson and Starr, 1993) and continuously evolving (Aldrich and Zimmer, 1986) nature of these forms of economic organization over time. Schenkel et al. (2009: 1)

Schenkel et al. (2009) agree with Davidsson and Honig (2003) in placing a kind of implied blame on intentions research. They argue that much of the reason that the new venture creation research does not utilize knowledge about social and human capital is *because* "much of the work focuses predominantly on intentions rather than behavior." This is tantamount to saying: "you can't expect intentions-based literature to embrace knowledge about human and social capital." The present authors disagree. We think the intentions literature and its associated theoretical modeling can and should embrace the human and social capital literatures. For good measure, we think that gender is also an issue that can be incorporated within an intentions-based focus.

3.3.2 Human Capital and Entrepreneurial Intentions

Information related to economic opportunity is distributed unevenly across economic marketplace participants (Kirzner 1979). This affects both the opportunities for arbitrage in the existing economy and the opportunity to create new ventures. It has been argued that individuals develop unique knowledge that produces a state of readiness, or "absorptive capacity," allowing some individuals to be more alert to new venture opportunities and create and develop a larger variety of implementation possibilities than those without such knowledge corridors (Kirzner, 1979). Schenkel et al. (2009) point out that implicit within human capital theory is the presumption that the cognitive ability of individuals is increased by the accumulation of knowledge stocks such that it allows some individuals to perceive and act more efficiently and effectively in the marketplace through new venturing activity than others (Kirzner, 1979).

One stream of research – which might be called the "experience" stream – has sought to generate a greater understanding of why and how life context and personal background distinctions may systematically aid the new venture creation process. Another stream stresses "knowledge" as a source of cognitive capability. Human capital theory indicates that both experience and knowledge strengthen the cognitive capability of individuals to recognize opportunities by allowing the "connecting the dots" more effectively among various market forces. For instance, Ucbasaran and Westhead (2002) have shown that experienced entrepreneurs identify more opportunities than novice entrepreneurs. Education is consistently associated with positive economic return when pursuing nascent entrepreneurial activity (Davidsson and Honig, 2003).

It can be generally stated that extant research clearly supports the premise that both knowledge (especially as measurable in the form of education) and experience directly related to new venturing are important both as sources of human capital and informers of judgments concerning the creation of new ventures. We therefore postulate the following.

> Proposition 1 – the education hypothesis: a person of higher education level will be more likely to have the intention to start a new venture than a person of lower educational level.
>
> Proposition 2 – the experience hypothesis: a person with greater experience in starting ventures will be more likely to have the intention to start a new venture than a person with lower experience in starting ventures.

3.3.3 Social Capital and Entrepreneurial Intentions

The literature on entrepreneurial networks and the social capital that results from the connections *between* people (as distinct from human capital which is contained *within* people) developed at the same time as the literature on entrepreneurial intention. Both literatures emerged in the 1980s as a reaction to the deterministic approach taken in many psychological studies of entrepreneurs. However, they developed in parallel and did not intersect. Whereas the literature on entrepreneurial intention changed our understanding of what was occurring *within* the mind of individuals, the entrepreneurial network and social capital literature moved the focus away from the mind of individuals to the social surroundings affecting individuals and their decision making. Owing heavy allegiance to the resource perspective developed by Wernerfelt (1984), entrepreneurial network and social capital literature argues that entrepreneurs obtain non-redundant resources (social capital) from their network that makes them perform better. The social capital resources entrepreneurs obtain from their networks have to be understood broadly and include, among other things, information, advice, social support, and legitimacy.

Sociologists' interest in how people's social networks influence their status attainment (Granovetter, 1973; Bourdieu, 1983) has resulted in three propositions:

- social networks affect the outcome of instrumental actions;
- the nature of resources obtained from social networks is affected by people's original position; and
- the nature of resources obtained from social networks is affected by the strength of ties (Lin, 1999).

Entrepreneurship scholars (e.g., Aldrich and Zimmer, 1986; Greve 1995) have also been interested in social networks and the social capital associated with them. Entrepreneurship research shows that social networks affect opportunity recognition (Singh, 2000), entrepreneurial orientation (Ripolles and Blesa, 2005), and the vocational decision to become an entrepreneur (e.g., Davidsson and Honig, 2003; Morales-Gualdron and Roig, 2005; De Clercq and Arenius, 2006) and growth (Lee and Tsang, 2001). Relatively recently, and most importantly for this study, Hmieleski and Corbett (2006) have argued that social networks influence entrepreneurial intentions.

One of the essential results, which previous entrepreneurship research on social networks and social capital has demonstrated, concerns embeddedness. People embedded in networks containing entrepreneurs tend to be more entrepreneurially oriented. People who have close family members in business (Matthews and Moser, 1995; Sanders and Nee, 1996; Davidsson and Honig, 2003; Menzies et al., 2006) or personally know someone who has started a business (Davidsson and Honig, 2003; Morales-Gualdron and Roig, 2005; Arenius and Kovalainen, 2006; De Clercq and Arenius, 2006; Menzies et al., 2006) seem to have a better chance of becoming entrepreneurs.

Researching in Sweden, Davidsson and Honig (2003) found that people who have parents in business or have close friends or neighbors in business are more likely to become nascent entrepreneurs. De Clercq and Arenius (2006) found positive correlations in both their Belgium and their Finish samples between personally knowing people who have started a business and starting a business oneself. In an analysis of the 2001 GEM database, considering a sample drawn across 29 countries, Morales-Gualdron and Roig (2005) also concluded that personally knowing someone who has started a business has a positive impact on people's decisions to become entrepreneurs. Analyzing a similar sample, but only for the Nordic countries and only for women, Arenius and Kovalainen (2006) found the same relationship. Thus, previous research strongly supports the proposition that personally knowing someone who has started a business is positively correlated with the decision to become an entrepreneur. Accordingly, we formalize the following proposition.

> Proposition 3 – social capital hypothesis: a person with greater social capital will be more likely to have the intention to start a new venture than a person with lower social capital.
> Alternative statement of proposition 3: a person embedded in an entrepreneurial network containing other entrepreneurs will be more likely to have the intention to start a new venture than a person not embedded in a entrepreneurial network containing other entrepreneurs.

3.3.4 Gender Differences

Discussion of the influence of gender on aspects of the new venture creation process is closely entailed with the previously discussed "experience" stream of new venture creation research. Within this stream, three specific characteristics of interest have emerged (1) age, (2) sex (gender), and (3) ethnicity. In this study, we focus on gender.

Despite the high participation by females in entrepreneurial activities around the world (Minniti et al., 2006) and awareness of their role in economic development, there is still too little research in this area (Baker et al., 1997; de Bruin et al., 2006). Nevertheless, a stream of research is emerging. Extant gender research is generally concerned with how female entrepreneurs' *practices* differ from men (e.g., Birley, 1989; Fielden et al., 2003; Klyver and Terjesen, 2007) and the impact on various measures of social and economic performance (e.g., Collins-Dodd et al., 2004; Kim and Ling, 2001; Orser et al., 2006).

It has been suggested that female entrepreneurs are disadvantaged, in part because of a lack of suitable and effective social networks (Fielden et al., 2003; Timberlake, 2005). Research on the social networks of female entrepreneurs is mostly constrained to snapshots at one particular venture stage, such as a new start-up (Menzies et al., 2004) or an existing firm (Cromie and Birley, 1992; Farr-Wharton and Brunetto, 2007), and does not consider the dynamic nature of networks through the entrepreneurship process. Recent reviews call for studies of process differences across individuals' extent of network leverage (Hoang and Antoncic, 2003) and gender (Carter et al., 2001; Godwin et al., 2006). One thing is clear. Though clear patterns of results are not abundant from gender throughout the world, three points do seem well supported. First, a much lower proportion of any country's adult female population participates in entrepreneurship than the proportion of adult males who do so (Brush, 1992). Second, throughout the world women are relatively disadvantaged compared to men with respect to most forms of human capital. Third, in order to succeed at any level of economic endeavor (say employment status in a large corporation) in "a man's world," a woman has to be proportionately better credentialed than a male counterpart. By extension, for the purposes of this model it therefore seems reasonable to argue that a woman may require more human and social capital, in all its forms, than does a man to form the same level of entrepreneurial intentions. Accordingly, we postulate the following propositions.

> Proposition 4A: For the same level of entrepreneurial intention, females will possess higher educational levels than males.
>
> Proposition 4B: For the same level of entrepreneurial intention, females will possess greater startup experience of than males.
>
> Proposition 4B: For the same level of entrepreneurial intention, females will possess greater social capital than males.

3.4 Discussion: An Enhanced Model of Entrepreneurial Intentions

In plain language, the fundamental supposition underpinning this model was that entrepreneurial intensions' researchers could and should broaden our representation of the entrepreneurial mind with respect to our theoretical modeling of the way entrepreneurial intentions are formed. We argued from the literature that a person's entrepreneurial intent is influenced not just by self-efficacy but by other human capital factors and by social capital factors and by gender. All these factors inform the intension to start or not to start a business and we need to model not just intent but *informed* intent. Our informed intention model is illustrated in Fig. 3.3.

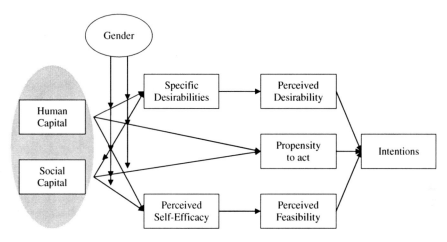

Fig. 3.3 The Informed Intention Mode

Our developed propositions, permit – or mandate – the redrawing of the fundamental Shapero–Krueger entrepreneurial intentions model. In our propositions, we argued that human capital and social capital influenced individuals' likelihood to develop entrepreneurial intentions. However, our argument did not cover the pathway through the Shapero–Kreuger model. This is still to be explored. In Fig. 3.3, we have drawn the most straightforward expected effects, where both human capital and social capital have an influence on, respectively, specific desirability, propensity to act, and perceived self-efficacy. However, as stated, other pathways are possible as well and this is a task for future research to estimate just as it has been the task of previous research to estimate the pathways through the original Shapero–Krueger entrepreneurial intentions model.

In our development of the propositions, we were relatively specific about the content of both human and social capital. We operationalized human capital as education level and experience in starting a venture and social capital as being embedded in an entrepreneurial network containing other entrepreneurs. Regardless of these more or less specific operationalizations, we intend by using the more general concepts of human and social capital to broaden the applicability of the model by explicitly including influences from the knowledge that resides within the individual and the knowledge and influences that flow from the individual's social environment. Thus, the influence of human capital is not limited to education level and experience of starting a venture, and the influence of social capital is not limited to being embedded in an entrepreneurial network containing other entrepreneurs.

Other human capital and social capital variables are highly likely to be relevant and have the potential to influence, respectively, specific desirability, propensity to act, and perceived self-efficacy – or influence through other pathways the original Shapero–Krueger entrepreneurial intentions model.

3.5 Conclusion and Implications

This chapter contains some generic messages important for future research and implications for actual entrepreneurs, educators, and policy makers. Below we will elaborate briefly on these.

Generically, while perhaps the "informed" model of entrepreneurial intensions that we have drawn is not the "right" one in terms of absolute precision, we believe that we are able to argue strongly that *some* kind of informed intent model is now mandatory. On the evidence of the literature review, the notion of informed intent is important. It will no longer be satisfactory to leave social and human capital out of our modeling of entrepreneurial intentions formation and we believe that anything we argue about the importance of experience to the process needs to draw a clear distinction between men and women. The implications for future research are obvious and urgent. The big questions are all about "how." How do human and social capital influence entrepreneurial intentions? Is it via the pathway suggested in the prevailing intentions model or in some other way? Researchers need to formulate designs capable of answering these kinds of questions and thus taking the informed intent model beyond the tentative stage to a clearer picture of path dependency. The authors of this chapter intend to explore this question empirically in future research.

Accepting that intentions are partially formed by human and social capital has essential implications for both actual and, more importantly, potential entrepreneurs. Previously, human capital and social capital were perceived as influential factors for individuals discovering entrepreneurial opportunities and their ability to evaluate and exploit these. However, our enhanced model or entrepreneurial intent suggests that human capital and social capital have an even earlier influence and therefore become even more important to actual entrepreneurs. Not only do they impact individuals' ability to discover, evaluate, and exploit opportunities, but they also impact their intentions to do so. Therefore, ambitions to become an entrepreneur have to be followed by a continuous development and maintenance of both human and social capital.

For educators, the model also has important implications. Educators have previously played an essential role in making those students – with entrepreneurial intentions – capable of discovering, evaluating, and exploiting opportunities. The informed intent model further suggests that they also have a vital role in forming these intentions. A long debate has taken place about how to stimulate entrepreneurial intentions through education.

Although it may be regarded as beyond the scope of this chapter, one specific lesson can be drawn from this model. Educators, apart from providing the general knowledge about many aspects of entrepreneurship, need to stimulate students to develop and maintain their networks. Their social networks are important not only in the process of discovering, evaluating, and exploiting the entrepreneurial opportunity (Shane and Venkatarammen, 2000) but also in the process of shaping the *intention* to do so. So, educators with ambition to stimulate entrepreneurship need to integrate the building of social capital into their teaching. This can be done by intensive interaction with business practitioners and the business environment during a course. Integrating development of business networks into the course is consistent with the fact that human and social capital can be difficult to separate and need to be treated as two interdependent factors (Otteson and Klyver, 2008).

On a higher and more abstract level, the same implications regarding integrating development and maintenance of social networks into education apply to policy makers. From the informed intent model, it seems likely that one crucial way of stimulating not only the capacity but also the intention to become entrepreneurial can be enhanced by an education system that interacts with industry. Thus, interaction between the industry and the education system should be an explicit, formulated policy for every nation wanting to increase the level of entrepreneurial intent among its population. Furthermore, other initiatives that stimulate individuals' development and maintenance of both social and business networks seem to be a way of increasing a population's entrepreneurial intentions.

In a paper entitled, *Watch Out, Isaac! Reciprocal causation in entrepreneurial intent*, Krueger et al. (2007) used a biblical analogy to classify the entrepreneurial intentions model as a kind of "Isaac": a greatly loved "son" of many research "fathers and mothers." They mooted the possibility that they might (for various reasons, including the problem of reciprocal causality) have to do as Abraham was instructed to do in the bible and kill the adored child. In the metaphor of the current book, destroying the entrepreneurial intentions model (killing Isaac) would translate to closing the entrepreneurial mind on the importance of entrepreneurial intentions. The study reported in this chapter has shown that, when it comes to the study of entrepreneurial intentions, we don't have to close the entrepreneurial mind. We just have to broaden it.

References

Acs ZJ, Audretsch DB (2003) Handbook of Entrepreneurship Research: An Interdisciplinary Survey and Introduction. Boston: Kluwer Academic.

Ajzen I (1991) The theory of planned behavior. Organizational Behavior and Human Decision Processes 50: 179–211.

Aldrich, HE and Zimmer, C (1986). Entrepreneurship through social networks. In: Sexton, DL and Smilor, RW (eds.), The art and science of entrepreneurship. New York: Ballinger, pp. 3–23.

Anderson JR (1990) Cognitive Psychology and its Implications (3rd ed.). New York: W.H. Freeman.

Arenius P. Kovalainen A (2006) Similarities and differences across the factors associated with women s self-employment preference in the Nordic countries. International Small Business Journal 24: 31–59.

Baker T, Aldrich HE, Liou N (1997) Invisible entrepreneurs: The neglect of women business owners by Mass Media and Scholarly Journals in the United States. Entrepreneurship and Regional Development 9: 221–238.

Bandura A (1977) Social learning theory. Englewood Cliffs, NJ: Prentice Hall.

Bandura A (1986). Social Foundations of Thought and Action: A Social Cognitive Theory. Englewood Cliffs, NJ: Prentice-Hall.

Becker GS (1993) Human Capital: A Theoretical and Empirical Analysis, with Special Reference to Education. Chicago: University of Chicago Press.

Bird B (1988) Implementing entrepreneurial ideas: The case for intention. Academy of Management Review 13: 442–453.

Birley S (1989) Female entrepreneurs: Are they really different? Journal of Small Business Management 27: 32–37.

Bourdieu P (1983) Forms of capital. In: Richarson J (ed.), Handbook of theory and research for the sociology of education. New York: Greenwood Press, pp. 241–258.

Brännback M, Krueger NF, Carsrud AL Elfving J (2007) "Trying" to be entrepreneurial. MPRA Paper No. 8814, posted 21. May 2008/22:58. Online at http://mpra.ub.uni-muenchen.de/8814. Munich Personal RePEc Archive.

Burt RS (1992) Structural Holes: The Social Structure of Competition. Cambridge, MA: Harvard University Press.

Brush CG (1992) Research on women business owners: Past trends, a new perspective and future directions. Entrepreneurship Theory and Practice 16: 5–30.

Carter S, Anderson S, Shaw E (2001) Women s Business Ownership: Review of Academic, Popular and Internet Literature. Report to the Small Business Service.

Coleman JS (1988) Social capital in the creation of human-capital. American Journal of Sociology 94: 95–120.

Collins-Dodd C, Gordon IM, Smart C (2004) Further evidence on the role of gender in financial performance, Journal of Small Business Management 42: 395–417.

Cozby P (1997) Methods in Behavior Research. London: Mayfield Publishing Co.

Cromie S, Birley S (1992) Networking by female business owners in Northern Ireland. Journal of Business Venturing, 7: 237–251.

Davidsson P, Honig B (2003) The role of social and human capital among nascent entrepreneurs. Journal of Business Venturing 18: 301–331.

de Bruin A, Brush CG, Welter F (2006) Introduction to the special issue: Towards building cumulative knowledge on women s entrepreneurship. Entrepreneurship Theory and Practice 30: 585–593.

De Clercq D, Arenius P (2006) The role of knowledge in business start-up activity. International Small Business Journal 24: 339–358.

Farr-Wharton R, Brunetto Y (2007) Women entrepreneurs, opportunity recognition and government-sponsored networks. Women in Management Review 22: 187–207.

Fielden SL, Davidson MJ, Dawe AJ, Makin PJ (2003) Factors inhibiting the economic growth of female owned small businesses in North West England. Journal of Small Business and Enterprise Development 10: 152–166.

Forbes DP (1999) Cognitive approaches to new venture creation. International Journal of Management Reviews 1: 415.

Godwin L, Stevens C, Brenner L (2006) Forced to play by the rules: Theorizing how mixed-sex founding teams may benefit women entrepreneurs in male dominated contexts. Entrepreneurship Theory and Practice 30: 623–642.

Granovetter MS (1973) The Strength of Weak Ties. American Journal of Sociology 78: 1360–1380.

Granovetter MS (1985) Economic action and social structure: The problem of embeddedness. American Journal of Sociology 91: 481–510.

Greve A (1995) Networks and entrepreneurship – An analysis of social relations, occupational background, and use of contacts during the establishment process. Scandinavian Journal of Management 11: 1–24.

Hindle K (2004) Choosing Qualitative Methods for Entrepreneurial Cognition Research: a Canonical Development Approach. Entrepreneurship Theory and Practice 28: 575–607.

Hmieleski KM, Corbett AC (2006) Proclivity for improvisation as a predictor of entrepreneurial intentions. Journal of Small Business Management 44: 45–63.

Hoang, H. and Antoncic, B. (2003). Network-based research in entrepreneurship – A critical review. Journal of Business Venturing 18: 165–187.

Jenkins M, Johnson G (1997) Entrepreneurial intentions and outcomes: A comparative causal mapping study. Journal of Management Studies 34: 895.

Katz JA, Shepherd D (eds) 2003 Advances in Entrepreneurship, Firm Emergence, and Growth, JAI volume 6. Greenwich, CT: JAI Press.

Kim JLS, Ling CS (2001) Work-family conflict of women entrepreneurs in Singapore. Women in Management Review 16: 204–221.

Kirzner IM (1979) Perception, opportunity and profit. Chicago, IL: University of Chicago Press.

Kirzner IM (1973) Competition and Entrepreneurship, Chicago, IL: University of Chicago Press.

Klyver K, Terjesen S (2007) Entrepreneurial network composition: An analysis across venture development stage and gender. Women in Management Review 22: 682–688.

Kolvereid L (1996) Organizational employment versus self-employment: Reasons for career choice intentions. Entrepreneurship: Theory and Practice 20: 23–31.

Krueger NF (2003) The cognitive psychology of entrepreneurship. In: Acs ZJ, Audretsch DB (eds.), Handbook of Entrepreneurship Research: An Interdisciplinary Survey and Introduction. Boston: Kluwer Academic, pp. 105–140.

Krueger NF (1993) The impact of prior entrepreneurial exposure on perceptions of new venture feasibility. Entrepreneurship: Theory and Practice 18: 5–21.

Krueger NF (2000) The cognitive infrastructure of opportunity emergence. Entrepreneurship: Theory and Practice 24: 5–23.

Krueger NF Brazeal DV (1994) Entrepreneurial potential and potential entrepreneurs. Entrepreneurship Theory and Practice 18: 91–104.

Krueger NF, Carsrud AL (1993) Entrepreneurial intentions: Applying the theory of planned behavior. Entrepreneurship and Regional Development 5: 315–330.

Krueger NF, Dickson PR (1993). Self-efficacy and perceptions of opportunities and threats. Psychological Reports 722(3, pt.2.), 1235–1240.

Krueger NF, Dickson PR (1994) How believing in ourselves increases risk taking: Perceived self-efficacy and opportunity. Decision Sciences 25: 385–400.

Krueger NF, Reilly MD, Carsrud AL (2000) Competing models of entrepreneurial intentions. Journal of Business Venturing 15: 411–432.

Krueger NF, Brannback M, Carsrud A (2007) Watch Out, Isaac! Reciprocal causation in entrepreneurial intent. Paper delivered at *the Australian Graduate School of Entrepreneurship (AGSE) Research Exchange Conference*. Brisbane.

Larson A, Starr JA (1993) A network model of organization formation. Entrepreneurship Theory and Practice 17: 5–15.

Lee DY, Tsang EWK (2001) The effects of entrepreneurial personality, background and network activities on venture growth. Journal of Management Studies 38: 583–602.

Lin N (1999) Social networks and status attainment. Annual Review of Sociology 25: 467–487.

Matthews CH, Moser SB (1995) Family background and gender: Implications for interest in small firm ownership. Entrepreneurship and Regional Development 7: 365–377.

Menzies TV, Doichon M, Gasse Y, Elgie S (2006) A longitudinal study of the characteristic, business creation process and outcome differences of Canadian female vs. male nascent entrepreneurs. International Entrepreneurship and Management Journal 2: 441–453.

Menzies TV, Doichon M, Gasse Y (2004) Examining venture-related myths concerning women entrepreneurs. Journal of Developmental Entrepreneurship 9: 89–107.

Minniti M, Arenius P, Langowitz N (2006) Global Entrepreneurship Monitor: 2005 Report on women and entrepreneurship. Babson College and London Business School.

Mitchell RK, Busenitz L, Lant T, McDougall PP (2002). Toward a theory of entrepreneurial cognition: Rethinking the people side of entrepreneurship research. Entrepreneurship Theory and Practice 27: 93–104.

Morales-Gualdron, ST, Roig S (2005) The new venture decision: An analysis based on the GEM project database. International Entrepreneurship and Management Journal 1: 479–499.

Orser BJ, Riding AL, Manley K (2006) Women entrepreneurs and financial capital. Entrepreneurship Theory and Practice 30: 643–665.

Ottoson H, Klyver K (2008) Entrepreneurial human and social capital – complements or substitutes? Paper presented at NCSB, Tallinn, Estonia.

Ripolles M, Blesa A (2005) Personal networks as fosterers of entrepreneurial orientation in new ventures. International Journal of Entrepreneurship and Innovation 6: 239–248.

Ronstadt R (1988) The corridor principle. Journal of Business Venturing 3: 31–40.

Sanders J, Nee V (1996) Immigrant self-employment: The family as social capital and the value of human capital. American Sociological Review 61: 231–249.

Schenkel MT, Hechavarria DM, Matthews CH (2009) The role of human and social capital and technology in nascent ventures. In Reynolds PD, Curtin RT (eds). New Firm Creation in the United States. Berlin: Springer, pp. 157–185.

Shapero A (1982) Social dimensions of entrepreneurship. In: Kent C, Sexton D, Vesper K (eds.), The Encyclopedia of Entrepreneurship. Englewood Cliffs, NJ: Prentice Hall.

Shane S, Venkataraman S (2000) The promise of entrepreneurship as a field of research. Academy of Management Review 25: 217–226.

Shaver KG, Scott LR (1991) Person, process, choice; The psychology of new venture creation. Entrepreneurship: Theory and Practice 16: 23–45.

Shepherd DA, Krueger NF (2002) An Intentions–Based Model of Entrepreneurial Teams Social Cognition. Entrepreneurship: Theory and Practice 27: 167–185.

Shook CL, Priem RL, McGee JE (2003) Venture creation and the enterprising individual: A review and synthesis. Journal of Management 29: 379–399.

Singh RP (2000) Entrepreneurial Opportunity Recognition Through Social Networks. London: Garland Publishing, Inc.

Timberlake S (2005) Social capital and gender in the workplace. Journal of Management Development 24: 34–44.

Ucbasaran D, Westhead P (2002) Does entrepreneurial experience influence opportunity identification? In: Reynols PD, Autio E, Brush CG, Bygrave WD, Manigart S (eds). Frontiers of Entrepreneurship Research.

Wernerfelt B (1984) A resource-based view of the firm. Strategic Management Journal 5: 171–180.

Chapter 4
Entrepreneurial Intentions are Dead: Long Live Entrepreneurial Intentions

Norris Krueger

Abstract Short of studying actual new venture launches, what could possibly be more potent than understanding the preconditions that enable entrepreneurial activity? Early research focused unsurprisingly on behavior (the "what?" and the "how?" even somewhat the "where?" and the "when?") and since entrepreneurs were obviously special people, on the entrepreneurial person (the "who?"). Intentions are classically defined as the cognitive state temporally and causally prior to action (e.g., Dennett 1989; Krueger 2000). Here that translates to the working definition of the cognitive state temporally and causally prior to the decision to start a business. The field has adopted and adapted formal models of entrepreneurial intentions that are based on strong, widely accepted theory and whose results appear not only empirically robust but of great practical value. But do we have what we think we have? Or have we also opened the door to a much broader range of questions that will advance our theoretical understanding of entrepreneurship and entrepreneurs? We offer here a glimpse of the remarkably wide array of fascinating questions for entrepreneurship scholars.

A Note to Educators and Practitioners

While this chapter is designed to spur more and better research into entrepreneurial intentions, the discussions here have significant value to practice and especially to the classroom. Throughout the chapter you will see direct comments about the practical and pedagogical implications of the issues under discussion. If we cannot serve our scholarly colleagues, our entrepreneurial colleagues, and our educator colleagues, this book misses a great opportunity and we all choose not to do so.

In classrooms and communities, we seek to develop more entrepreneurial students and trainees, we seek to develop better entrepreneurs. Part of that is raising their intentions to start a business; another part is making their intentions more

N. Krueger (✉)
1632 South Riverstone Lane, 304, Boise ID 83706, USA
e-mail: norris.krueger@gmail.com

A.L. Carsrud, M. Brännback (eds.), *Understanding the Entrepreneurial Mind,*
International Studies in Entrepreneurship 24, DOI 10.1007/978-1-4419-0443-0_4,
© Springer Science+Business Media, LLC 2009
51

realistic. To do both requires a deeper, richer understanding of the dynamic process by which entrepreneurial intentions evolve. As you will see, we have recently uncovered intriguing new knowledge about this that can be readily applied (and our scholarly friends will find most intriguing as well.)

4.1 A Critical Overview of Intentions and Entrepreneurial Intentions

4.1.1 Do Intentions Even Exist?

Consider an experiment. The subject is wired up and the experimenter asks the subject to raise either hand. Interestingly, the experimenter can quickly discern which hand the subject will raise before subjects are aware themselves. Next, the experimenter induces the subject to raise either the left or right hand. However, the subject nonetheless perceives the choice as free will, even after being informed of the procedure. A neuroscientist can see our intentions before we perceive we have formulated them? We perceive intent toward a discrete behavior even where it is completely illusory? What does this mean for our models and measures of entrepreneurial intentions that we have carefully developed from proven theory and refined through rigorous empirical analysis? (Libet et al., 1983)

4.1.1.1 A Little History

The rush to describe this amazing phenomenon was like any nascent field of study: It tends to favor description over theory. However, if we are to answer the "Why?" question, we need theory. In remarkably short order, the field of entrepreneurship developed a broad, rich body of observational data that allowed entrepreneurship scholars to begin asking some very intriguing questions of value to scholar and practitioner alike. That success, coupled with the compelling subject matter, allowed the field to increase in breadth. However, the scarcity of well-developed theory was beginning to take its toll. And even where scholars had drawn on theory, they drew upon logical but deeply flawed domains such as personality psychology.

We then saw the entry of serious social psychology and, later, cognitive psychology and developmental psychology. Whatever the gestation processes of new ventures, the sequence of behaviors need not follow any optimal pattern, but the theories offered by social and cognitive (and developmental) psychology immediately provided testable models that seemed quite relevant to entrepreneurship.

For example, the field once upon a time referred to "budding" entrepreneurs, etc., and like much of the early work on the closely related topic of opportunity recognition, the work was atheoretic "dustball empiricism" that rarely moved past *ad hoc* descriptive studies that were all too often unreplicable. Given that a specific class of intentions models (the Fishbein–Ajzen models) were already used heavily in marketing with great practical effectiveness, it seemed painfully simple to test that in entrepreneurship. If you have well-developed theory and robust empirical models, why not test them (Krueger, 1993; Krueger and Carsrud, 1993)?

Since then, formal models of entrepreneurial intentions have been prolific and effective. Perhaps too effective? However, the construct of intentions appears to be deeply fundamental to human decision making and, as such, it should afford us multiple fruitful opportunities to explore the connections between intent and a vast array of other theories and models that relate to decision making under risk and uncertainty. Better still, we have reason to believe that studying entrepreneurs yields findings that speak to a far wider array of human phenomena.

4.1.2 Where Do Intentions "Come From"?

We have long accepted the conventional wisdom that intentions are the consequence of a process that was reasonably well understood by social and cognitive psychology. That is, we typically model intentions of any kind as having a parsimonious, powerful set of predictors that yield significant relationships with remarkable robustness (e.g., Kim and Hunter, 1993).

However, looking closely at entrepreneurial intentions has started to surface some inconsistent pieces of evidence that suggest we may need to re-conceptualize intentions at a more fundamental level. However, the reader will see that this only widens the door to a broad array of interesting and useful questions.

Intentions as Phlogiston? Phlogiston was a theorized element or compound that successfully explained one quirk of oxidation processes. When something oxidized (rusted, burned, etc.) it gained weight. Thus it was proposed that phlogiston was released by oxidization. Since oxidized materials gain weight, phlogiston must have negative weight, as odd as it may seem today.

We poke fun at what is now the obvious absurdity of phlogiston, especially given our current knowledge of oxygen. However, the phlogiston model did accurately explain and predict the consequences of oxidation. The numbers worked. When we learned of oxygen and its role in oxidization, we re-conceptualized the model. Instead of subtracting phlogiston, we add oxygen. Is there any lesson here for social sciences? For intentions? It certainly argues that we need to take a long look at how we conceptualize, model, and measure entrepreneurial intentions. The numbers may work, but is there a better model?

We conceive of intentions as the consequence of obvious antecedents. However, significant correlations or beta weights need not reflect a specific direction of causality. What if the "arrows" between intent and its "antecedents" are bi-directional? What if our intentions models are capturing a static snapshot of a significantly dynamic process? Studying entrepreneurial intentions has begun to raise these very questions (e.g., Brannback et al., 2006; Krueger et al., 2007). A review of the literature suggests that very few successful studies demonstrate that changes in the antecedents of intent actually led to changes in intent. There are zero studies showing that for entrepreneurial intentions. That might even suggest the possibility that even if the causation is reciprocal, what if intent influences its "antecedents" than vice versa?

The logical conclusion is that this review should return to first principles and carefully deconstruct (and re-construct) intentions. We will begin at the beginning and look at a brief history of our models of human intent and of entrepreneurial intentions in general. From there, we will look at how intentions fit into the bigger entrepreneurial picture. We will bring in evidence from other domains that should help us with this quest, especially some striking evidence out of neuroscience. That will suggest a significant number of interesting new questions and of old questions in a new light (such as measuring intentions). From there, we will lay out an ambitious research agenda that explores our new insights into entrepreneurial intentionality and how intentions fit into the bigger picture.

4.1.3 Where Have We Been?

4.1.3.1 Philosophical and Theoretical Grounding

The notion of intentions and intentionality dates back to at least Socrates (who wondered why humans might intend evil or stupid behavior). There has always been some degree of belief that intentionality exists at the core of human agency. Husserl defined *intentionality* as "the fundamental property of consciousness."

Intentional = Planned? Though later philosophers chipped away at that bold assertion, there has long been a sense that human behavior was either stimulus–response (behavior is essentially automatic in reaction to a specific signal or set of signals) or planned, where there are reasonably conscious cognitive processes at work. In fact, one recurring theme across most of the literature on intentions is that all planned behavior is intentional. (Even what appears to be stimulus–response can be the result of habituation or other conditioning. That is, it was planned behavior repeated often enough to become automatic.) Glibly equating planfulness and intent is most convenient for those seeking to model and measure intentions but, as we will see below, potentially misleading.[1]

Channels and Conduits. Another recurring theme across theories and models of behavioral intentions is that intent is a resultant vector, the combination of all the various drivers each with differing direction and magnitude. We add up all the various antecedent forces and the result is intent (again, direction and magnitude).

Moreover, theory, especially empirical study, has tended to find a parsimonious list of critical antecedents for intentions as the reader will see below. All other influences are then channeled through the critical antecedents. For example, exogenous factors such as demographics and psychographics influence the intention to buy a product if and only if the exogenous factor affects one of more critical antecedents.

---

[1] For a nice review, see Dennett (1989); Bratman (1987), who shows intent=choice+commitment to act.

Again, this enhances the parsimony of the model specified but hinges on the assumption that "antecedents" really are.

Static Models. Until recently, most theoretical and empirical models of intentions were static models of a clearly dynamic process. If intentions mirror other human cognitive process, then they are highly likely to be highly dynamic (and those dynamics will tend to be complex.) For example, even if the static model has the correct variables, how will the specification change over time?

Robustness. Despite the above, empirical research finds the various incarnations of the model to be remarkably robust to imperfect sampling frames, flawed measures, and even misspecification of the model (Ajzen, 1987). Meta-analyses (Kim and Hunter, 1993) show that the model explains considerable variance in intent (and intent explains considerable variance in behavior).

There is potentially a significant downside to this robustness, however. For example, the good news may be that we can conceptualize and measure intentions very narrowly and specifically or conceptualize and measure very broadly. However, that is also the bad news in that our "intentions" research may focus on significantly different phenomena.

Here we choose to begin with a definition of intermediate specificity. "Entrepreneurial" intentions refer to the intent to start a business, to launch a new venture. It is important to select a level of specificity where heterogeneous samples will have adequately similar mental models of what the referent means (e.g., Ajzen, 1987). "I intend to start a business" need not match exactly with "I intend to be an entrepreneur" but the bulk of the empirical research to date appears to use this and we will use that as a starting point.

4.1.3.2 Social Psychological Grounding

Building Testable Models. Historically, Martin Fishbein developed the first widely accepted model that simply argued we should be able to consistently identify critical human attitudes or beliefs that would predict future behavior. That critical belief he dubbed "attitude toward the act" and is typically operationalized much as valence is operationalized under expectancy theory. However, he soon noticed that the attitude–behavior link was fully mediated by intentions and that adding intentions dramatically increased explanatory and predictive power.

Fishbein and his protégé, then colleague Icek Ajzen further refined the attitude–intention–behavior model by adding a more contextual influence, that of social norms. That is, other people also have a powerful impact on our decisions. The resulting theory of reasoned action (TRA) includes a measure of "perceived social norms" that elicits the perceived supportiveness of important others weighted by our motivation to comply with their wishes (Ajzen and Fishbein, 1980).

Icek Ajzen then took yet another step and identified a third critical antecedent that corresponded to instrumentality in the expectancy framework, perceived behavioral control. This third iteration was called the theory of planned behavior (TPB). PBC simply measures the perception that the target behavior is within the decision maker's control. Typically, it is proxied with a measure of perceived competence at the task such as perceived self-efficacy. Ajzen (2002) later formalized this by arguing that PBC was a combination of locus of control (this is controllable) and self-efficacy (I am capable of doing this). In Chapter 12 of this book the reader will see a significant assessment and expansion of Ajzen's claim addressing the complexities of control beliefs. Moreover, Chapter 11 argues that a deeper understanding of self-efficacy and its drivers should prove particularly useful in better understanding of both intention and action subsequently. In any event, TPB remains the single most used model of human intentions to this day (Ajzen, 1987, 2002) (Table 4.1).

Table 4.1 Evolution of intentions models

Model/ Variable	Desirability	Social norms	Feasibility	Other
Fishbein	Attitude	n/a	n/a	
TRA	Attitude	Social norms	n/a	
TPB	Attitude	Social norms	Perceived behavioral control	
Shapero-Krueger	Perceived desirability	(Included at left)	Perceived feasibility	Propensity to act

Measurement Issues and Opportunities. The social (and cognitive) psychological approach not only led to theory-driven testable models but it also affords the opportunity to use well-tested constructs and measures. However, it also raises the need for clarity and consistency in our definitions and operationalizations. For example, if we are constantly using variables that reflect our perceptions of situations and conditions (even self-reflection) it is imperative that we fully understand the key perceptual processes that influence entrepreneurial decision making. Chapter 1 will provide the reader with much greater depth than we could do here.

Another issue that scholars often fail to fully explicate is the notion of "control," a term that sometimes we use rather glibly. However, Chapter 12 offers clear directions on that point.

4.1.3.3 A Brief History of Entrepreneurial Intentionality

Meanwhile, scholars interested in entrepreneurial behavior were obviously quite concerned with the decision that lead up to an individual starting a new venture. "Budding entrepreneur" was commonly used, though an altogether fuzzy, ill-defined term.

One of the earliest scholars to use the term, albeit indirectly, was Shapero (1982) who developed what he called the model of the "entrepreneurial event" that is conceptually similar to Ajzen's theory of planned behavior. Shapero equated intent to the identification of a credible, personally viable opportunity. For a perceived opportunity to be credible it had to be perceived by the decision maker as desirable (TPB's attitude and social norm) and feasible (essentially self-efficacy). He also added another antecedent, propensity to act, which captured the potential for a credible opportunity to become intent and, thus, action.

Unlike Ajzen and Fishbein's models, however, Shapero recognized that there were forces that moderated the intent–behavior linkage. Complex goal-focused behaviors may require some sort of precipitating factor, whether the perceived presence of a facilitating factor or the removal of a perceived critical barrier. Interestingly, the Ajzen framework assumes that the target behavior is within one's volitional control (no barriers or facilitators can intervene). Independent of Shapero, Bagozzi quickly noted this problematic facet of TPB.

Relevance to this Book: The reader would be well served to step back and review Chapter 14 on opportunity recognition. For more detailed discussion of moving intent into action, please review Chapter 3 on informed intent and especially Chapter 15 on entrepreneurial behaviors.

Meanwhile, as social psychology rose to prominence in entrepreneurship research, so too did the notion of intentionality. In two landmark papers, Barbara Bird argued persuasively that intentionality seemed central to entrepreneurial behavior (1988, 1989). Indeed, entrepreneurs were clear exemplars of intentionality. At the same time, Jerome Katz and Bill Gartner (1988) identified intentionality as one of the four critical facets of an emerging new venture.

However, Shapero's model had gone untested empirically, nor had the theory of planned behavior, until Krueger (1993) tested the Shapero model empirically and found very strong confirmation of the model. In turn, this suggested it might be useful for entrepreneurship scholars to turn to this literature. Krueger and Carsrud (1993) made the case that entrepreneurship really needed to take a long look at the theory of planned behavior. Simultaneously, Krueger and Brazeal (1994; Krueger, 2000) further explored the applicability of the Shapero model to multiple settings (i.e., both organizational and individual entrepreneurship) by adding insights from Ajzen's work to Shapero's original conception. Ultimately, Krueger et al. (2000) performed a competing hypotheses test that compared Shapero's model and TPB, finding that both models held. However, a *post hoc* examination suggested that adding social norms explicitly to the Shapero model increased explanatory power (see Fig. 4.1).

Other leading scholars were quick to adopt formal models of entrepreneurial intentions as well. Lars Kolvereid picked up the torch for the theory of planned behavior and quickly became the best-known user of TPB in entrepreneurship (e.g., 1996). Per Davidsson added the useful angle of exploring entrepreneurial intentions toward growth (Davidsson, 1991). Today, intentions models are seemingly *de rigueur*, with an easy variable to measure and considerable empirical robustness. However, this explosion of studies using a formal model such as the Shapero–Krueger model or TPB or simply using entrepreneurial intentions as a stand-alone variable has raised some intriguing questions.

The first question is obviously how we are defining "entrepreneurship." Drawing from the careers literature (e.g., Lent et al., 1994 review) the target can be conceptualized and measured narrowly or broadly but it is critical for scholars to clear about their definitions. As noted earlier, here we have chosen the broader, more inclusive

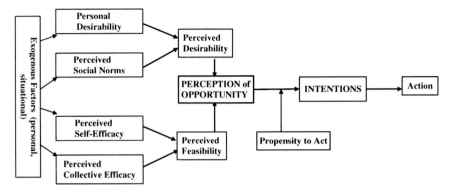

Fig. 4.1 Intentions model (adapted from Shapero,1982; Krueger & Brazeal, 1994; Krueger, 2000)

definition of starting a venture while retaining the notion that intent is a cognitive state causally prior to action. However, this raises the issue that terms can easily be perceived very differently by different stakeholders in the process (see Chapter 1). Consider also the evidence in Chapter 5 that entrepreneurs, managers, students, etc., have often strikingly different maps of the entrepreneurial process. Might that have important consequences for specifying the model? (Below we will mention how cognitive style seems to affect how to specify the model.)

Another issue is whether we are looking at intentions toward entrepreneurship independent of competing alternatives. Shapero's (1982) notion of displacement and its role in the entrepreneurial event assumes a bounded rationality perspective where some displacing event (whether push or pull) would drive a reappraisal of career options. We already know from the broader study of human intentions (e.g., Dennett, 1989) that we can hold competing, even conflicting intentions. How do we effectively model that?

Moreover, as entrepreneurs take each step forward, their intent may easily change. Sarasvathy's (2001) work shows that entrepreneurial decision making is often far from linear. Under effectuational thinking the pathway to the goal is likely to change as the entrepreneur works to find feasible and desirable paths toward a goal (which itself may well be a moving target). If entrepreneurs are effectuating we are likely to see intentions evolve in similarly nonlinear fashion. We certainly may wish to think about intentions as a stepwise process and consider modeling intentions toward each step.

Consider too the notion of bricolage (Baker and Nelson, 2005). If entrepreneurs move forward with limited resources and must improvise with what they perceive as available, then what does that mean for how we model intent? For example, if the implementation of a step depends on choosing between a superior, but less controllable option and an inferior option that is seen as very controllable, it might be logical for the entrepreneur to select the seemingly inferior option.

While the model tends to hold overall, a glittering R-squared might be masking some deeper issues. Those issues already signal a need to take a long second look at how we model intentions (not just entrepreneurial intentions) and perhaps an equally long second look at the construct of intentions itself. As we peer more deeply into how we might use formal models of intentions on entrepreneurial phenomena, there are multiple opportunities to develop intellectually interesting and practically useful new insights.

4.1.4 Where Are We Now?

4.1.4.1 Chinks in the Armor? The Rise of Disconfirming Evidence

Recall that these models are predicated on the logic of a formative model, that is, there are antecedents that combine to form the target variable. One early study by Liska (1984) suggested that the "antecedents" may instead comprise a reflective model. More interestingly, Bagozzi and colleagues noticed that if we relax Ajzen's assumption that behavior is fully volitional, that requires that we think in terms of "trying." The seminal piece, "Trying to Consume" (Bagozzi and Warshaw, 1990) forced several changes in modeling intentions effectively, especially if we are seeking to predict and not just explain.

Volition. Heckhausen (2007) frames it nicely that we too often conflate motivation (why we pursue an action) and volition (how we choose to pursue it), drawing on work as far back as Ach (1910) who demonstrated the central role of willpower as separate from motivation but mutually influencing.

The most important consideration here is that if the behavior is only partially volitional, as with goal attainment, it is inherently dynamic and must be modeled as such. A static snapshot could prove hopelessly inadequate. Second, human cognition is itself inherently complex, given the unavoidable embeddedness of even simple economic decisions in social and cultural contexts. Thus, intentions models must capture the important aspects of that. For example, we probably need to consider alternative behaviors/goals. Our intentions toward a specific career choice may not be terribly informative without looking at our intentions toward an alternative career. A third key aspect that we now need to examine is that human cognition tends to have both a rational component and an emotional component. Even the simplest "pure" economic decision has been shown to have an emotional dimension. For a classic example, witness how decision makers suddenly shift toward risk acceptance under Kahneman and Tversky's (1979) loss frame.

4.1.4.2 Reciprocal Causation?

The most interesting hints about the existing models come from looking at specifying the intentions model in reverse (Krueger et al., 2007). Interestingly, early results show that the impact of intentions on the "antecedents" is stronger than the impact of antecedents on intent. Could it be that the correlations are so strong because this is a dynamic process where intent influences attitudes which influence intent, etc.? Note that the data appear to argue that the anchoring construct is intent (which in turn argues that at least our initial attitudes may be anchored on some initial intent). Note that Allport's (1935) model treated what we call "intent" as but one of three critical antecedents of human action (cognitive, affective, and conative[intent]) that interacted in complex dynamic fashion.

Reciprocal causation goes a long way toward explaining anomalies such as the paucity of research that shows changes in attitudes leading to subsequent changes in intentions. What if we have that backward? Another anomaly this might address is that many intentions studies have found weak, even non-existent support for the influence of social norms on intent. Conceptually, social norms should be a potent predictor. However, what if social norms only influence initial intentions but attenuate as the intentions process evolves?

So, how might we begin to take advantage of these insights? (Note to the reader: Testing dynamic models can be dauntingly complex to implement properly, but we urge scholars to deploy dynamic models more often. Testing for reciprocal causation may be enlightening in many entrepreneurial phenomena.) Most important, if intentions at least partly drive subsequent attitudes, what drives initial intent? That is, what are the deeper beliefs that partially anchor intent?

4.1.4.3 Anchoring

If we propose that the dynamic process by which intentions evolve is anchored on some initial intent, we are still faced with the issue of understanding the origins of that initial intent. In a recent paper, Shaver (2007) called on scholars to closely examine the reasons that we attach to our intentions. That is, to what do intenders (and non-intenders?) attribute as the cause or source of their intentions? (Here I would suggest that readers interested in the key attributional processes of entrepreneurs read Chapter 10.)

Often these anchoring beliefs are very deeply held, often well outside of our mindful consideration. Kahneman and Tversky (e.g., 1979) long ago noted that human decision making often invoked an "anchor and adjust" heuristic where in novel situations we anchor our beliefs on initial information, then adjust for later information. Self-efficacy beliefs have proven to follow that dynamic (Bandura, 2001; Chapter 11).

4.2 The Future of Entrepreneurial Intentions

4.2.1 The Next Generation?

4.2.1.1 The Theory of Trying

However, as Fig. 4.2 suggests, Bagozzi's theory of trying might be conceptually closest to how human actually make decisions, but the model becomes rather unwieldy in comparison to the theory of planned behavior. If a scholar finds similar levels of statistical significance in both models, the far more parsimonious TPB is

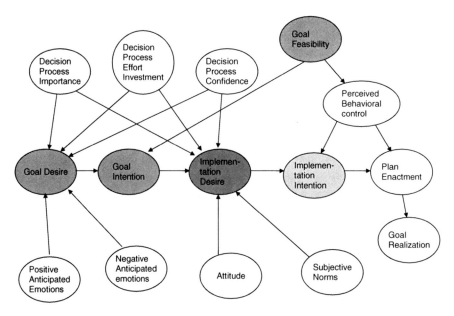

Fig. 4.2 Toward a theory of trying

an easy choice. And, despite being a static snapshot of a complex, messy dynamic process, it still offers considerable explanatory power. Nonetheless, the cutting edge remains the model depicted below (e.g., Bagozzi et al., 2003; Dholakia and Bagozzi, 2002; Brannback et al., 2007).

4.2.1.2 Implementation Intentions

Gollwitzer and Brandstatter (1997) focused on a phenomenon that we also see in Bagozzi's model, that of implementation intentions, following Ach's (1910; Heckhausen, 2007) work showing motivation and volition were usefully separable and allows us an immediate way to include a dynamic element. We may focus on a person's intentions toward a goal, but once that goal is formulated there is no guarantee that the goal will be implemented. We formulate important goals all the time but really with no intent to actually implement. (Consider all the people who have an extremely strong goal intent toward smoking cessation but just a routinely fail to develop strong implementation intentions.)

The theory of trying and its variants should prove rich, fertile territory for entrepreneurship scholars (Brannback et al., 2007). At minimum, it would certainly be important for scholars to simply notice the distinction between goal intent and implementation intent: Is someone's "entrepreneurial intention" a goal intent (they intend to begin the process) or an implementation intent (they intend to actually get the venture launched)?

4.2.2 The New Cutting Edges

For scholars interested in identifying even newer ground for intentions research, there are some intriguing directions to consider. We will focus on an overview of the fascinating (and useful) insights being generated by neuroscientists, and then discuss deep anchoring beliefs and implications for entrepreneurial learning and pedagogy.

4.2.2.1 Neuroentrepreneurship?

Consider the kind of experiment that opened this chapter. This work by Benjamin Libet dates all the way to 1983 (Libet et al., 1983) but, perhaps oddly, only now are intentions researchers fully grasping its significance. This pre-cognitive awareness is hardly an isolated phenomenon deriving from the explosively growing body of research in neuroscience[2].

To accompany neuroeconomics and neuromarketing, we now even have the research topic of neuroentrepreneurship (Stanton et al., 2008). The neuroscience perspective enables us (or forces us depending on one's receptivity) to examine the neural and biological substrates of human decision making. As noted earlier, in the early days of entrepreneurship research we focused on surface phenomena, what we say and do. Herbert Simon famously called this the *semantic* layer of human cognition. Below the semantic layer was the *symbolic* level which holds beliefs, attitudes, and assumptions. However, below that is the *neurological* layer which represents the biological substrate of cognition. (Note that all cognitive activity is neural at its heart; neuroscientists seek to explore the biological underpinnings that lie beneath conscious processing.) By delving rigorously to this level we can ask some new questions and do a better job asking (and answering) existing questions of great interest.

Consider too that entrepreneurs are increasingly the focus of neuroscientists in research at Cambridge and Vanderbilt. However, these studies need involvement by entrepreneurship scholars. Focusing purely on risk taking or managing hot cognitions makes a contribution but think of the opportunities to do even more[3].

The Cambridge study (Lawrence et al., 2008) assumed that entrepreneurs need to manage emotion-laden decision making ("hot" cognition) and concluded that the neurological evidence argued that this is highly learnable. However, that skill applies to far more than entrepreneurs; entrepreneurship scholars could help narrow their focus (see Chapter 8).

The Vanderbilt study (Zald, 2008) assumed that entrepreneurs are inherently risk takers and found that those high on sensation-seeking propensity have more

---

[2]In North America, there are at most 2,000 entrepreneurship scholars and educators, but well over 25,000 neuroscientists. The pace of research in this area will continue to explode and entrepreneurship scholars would be well served to identify ways to collaborate (e.g., Krueger and Day, 2009)

[3]See also the nascent efforts in neuroentrepreneurship under the aegis of the Experimental Entrepreneurship ("X-Ent") group at the Max Planck Institute of Economics in Jena, Germany

receptors for dopamine (greater rewards for stimulating activity). Given that the entrepreneurship field has largely debunked risk taking as a predictor, how might we guide future research? What if this neurological propensity anchors individuals to prefer risky activity and if they also have a deep belief such that their mental prototype of "entrepreneur" includes "risk taker"?

Neuroscience is not just clever theory with glitzy multi-color brain images. It has practical implications too. Consider the experiment where subjects are asked to watch a video and count the number of times that a basketball is passed. In mid-video, a person in a gorilla suit walks through the screen and well over 50% of the observers fail to notice (Simons and Chabris, 1995). What does that say to educators and practitioners? We are wired to be relatively blind to change; if our attention is focused in one direction, it can be very difficult to notice something else. The marketplace is filled with "gorillas" and the entrepreneur who notices the "gorilla" reaps a competitive advantage. Or does she? If you are looking closely for the gorilla you may fail to notice the basketball passes. Where we choose to focus our intentions may be critical. We need to study this but we also need to make sure students and practitioners are aware of phenomenon such as this.

For another example, the area of the brain that processes spatial relationships tends to grow significantly larger in long-time London cab drivers (Maguire et al., 2006). Where might we see such hypertrophy in, say, serial entrepreneurs?

"My brain made me do it!" Experiments in the spirit of Libet make a persuasive case that many times, our brain generates intentions not only before we are aware of them but occasionally despite our conscious attempts to change them. Think back to Socrates' question of why anyone would intend evil or stupid behavior. If intentions are merely the resultant vector of various unobserved neural or hormonal activities, the brain can make choices contrary to what we would develop "logically." So where might we start looking to explore what might really be driving intentions? We return again to deep beliefs.

4.2.2.2 Deep Beliefs

Most human decision making occurs anyway via automatic processing. Oversimplifying a bit, we possess a large set of if–then rules to guide our behavior. Many decisions simply derive from a relatively limited set of decision rules based on an equally limited set of very deep anchoring assumptions. Only relatively few human decisions are processing mindfully and even there we might find these deep assumptions still in play. Consider the "three-year-old" technique of surfacing deep assumptions. We ask "Why do you do this?" and with each answer, you respond as a 3-year-old might with another "Why?" It may take seven or eight rounds of "Why?" before you identify the anchoring assumption, not a task we would undertake routinely.

As such it becomes very important to understand as best we can what deep assumptions lie beneath our intentions (Krueger, 2007). Moreover, these assumptions also represent the critical architecture of how we structure our knowledge (including our cognitive scripts, schemas, and maps). This certainly seems to be the next frontier in entrepreneurial intentions research, if not entrepreneurial cognition in general, and we urge the reader to give significant thought to these issues.

Role Identity. Consider, for example, role identity and related constructs like 3d role demands. Our mental prototypes of "opportunity" and "entrepreneur" differ widely and are almost certainly anchored by powerful deep assumptions. These beliefs need not be functional for even experienced entrepreneurs but it is likely that novice entrepreneurs will hold beliefs that are incorrect or simply limited (Krueger, 2007). Despite the effort required to surface these deep beliefs, it may be the only way to truly understand these mental prototypes that are so important (e.g., Baron, 2004, 2006).

Sapir–Whorf: Deep Cultural Beliefs? Here is an example of a broad, complex research question that demonstrates the range of solid issues raised by studying entrepreneurial intentions. Can you intend to be an entrepreneur, if there is no word for "entrepreneur"? An interesting, if philosophical question that might prove extremely fascinating and of great potential utility in public policy is the one raised by the Sapir–Whorf hypothesis from anthropology. At its simplest, it asserts that if there is no word for an activity in a culture, it is very hard for members of that culture to conceptualize that activity to any significant degree. That is, it reflects a deep belief or the absence of one needed for genuine entrepreneurial activity. While we can readily envision that entrepreneurs (as we know them) have existed since the dawn of human commerce, no ancient language has a word that remotely captures our modern meaning. The modern word "entrepreneur" is itself only a few hundred years old. It might be very telling to see a linguistic analysis that compares the words used to describe entrepreneurs with economic development.

Deep Beliefs and Relevance to this Book. Most of the other chapters in this book are either critically dependent on deep beliefs or help mold them. Chapter 6 on scripts Chapter 5 on cognitive maps are two obvious places to begin thinking about deep beliefs, how they arise, and how they affect entrepreneurial decision making. These chapters in particular offer focused, detailed insights that tell us how deep beliefs can play out and how scripts and maps in turn influence how our deep beliefs can evolve.

Consider also that self-efficacy beliefs can affect mental prototypes and role identity through critical life experiences and self-efficacy can, in turn, influence how other beliefs change (Bandura, 2001; Neergaard and Krueger, 2005 and especially Chapter 11).

It would seem more than plausible that entrepreneurial passion reflects truly deep anchoring beliefs (Melissa Cardon, Mateja Drnovsek, Chuck Murnieks) as would entrepreneurial emotions (Isabell Welpe). The "lenses" that filter our perceptions are likely influenced greatly by deep beliefs (Evan Douglas) as would our patterns of causal attribution (Kelly Shaver), control beliefs (Erik Monsen and Diemo Urbig), other decision making processes (Veronica Gustavsson), and our processes of enacting opportunities (Connie Marie Gaglio).

However, do we not wish for prospective and current entrepreneurs to have a mindset that supports successful entrepreneurial thinking? That requires an understanding of what that mindset might comprise, whether we refer to the expert mindset discussed in Chapter 6 or we refer to "informed" intent as discussed by Hindle and Klyver.

What are the deep beliefs that consistently characterize a truly informed intent (Chapter 3)? What are the deep beliefs that underlay the cognitive scripts of expert entrepreneurs (Chapter 6)?

4.2.2.3 Deep Beliefs and Relevance for Teaching and Practice

However, all this is of equal, if not greater importance to educators and practitioners when we restate the issue in terms of how do we learn those assumptions? How do our deep knowledge structures arise and how do they influence (and are influenced by) entrepreneurial learning (Krueger, 2009)? And consider again all the growing evidence from neuroscience that this deep "wiring" (whether innate or learned) is germane to how entrepreneurs think and act. For an entrepreneur to become fully mindful of the string human propensity toward change blindness should prove to be of significant practical value. Let us next turn to this very question.

4.2.2.4 Implications for Entrepreneurial Learning and Pedagogy

What we are learning has enormous potential implications for entrepreneurial education (and in some ways we see best practice in pedagogy that fits the dynamic model of intent even better than the static case). Consider Fig. 4.3 carefully. The process of learning (and ideally the process of educating) does much more than add knowledge content to the learners. The old behaviorist model of students as relatively passive vessels to be filled with information has largely given way to the constructivist model which assumes that the real objective of education is to help learners to evolve how they structure that knowledge. In short, train minds not memories.

However, it is equally important to recognize that while this process may increase their attitudes and intentions toward entrepreneurship, we must also increase them in productive directions. To inspire an ill-informed student to launch a venture borders on the negligent. Isn't what we want to do is move learners from a mindset more like that of a novice entrepreneur toward a mindset more like that of an expert entrepreneur? We proposed the term "informed intent" for a symposium of the ICSB and as you will see from their chapter, Kevin Hindle and Kim Klyver have advanced the concept considerably. But that construct hinges on that expert mindset which is reflected in cognitive scripts (Chapter 6) and maps (Chapter 5) and those chapters will address these issues in much greater depth.

Nonetheless, it is important for the reader to know we have ample to reason to believe that (a) the expert mindset exists and (b) we can use what we know about the expert mindset to guide our teaching (e.g., Mitchell, 2005; Krueger, 2009) to move learners toward a truly informed intent. The constructivist model teaches us that learners' intentions and related attitudes will change but only insofar as they reflect changes in deep anchoring beliefs (Krueger, 2009). To change how we structure

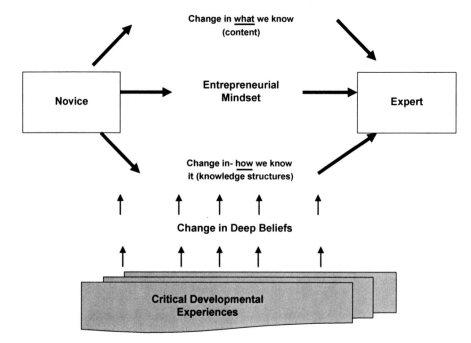

Fig. 4.3 Changing deep beliefs: critical developmental experiences

what we know, especially in the direction of a more informed, expert intent, the learner goes through multiple critical developmental experiences that change their deep beliefs. (Learners will thus need guidance from those who share or understand deeply the expert entrepreneurial mindset.)

Why is this important and why is this important to our discussions here about entrepreneurial intentions? It is important to emphasize the need for a more expert, informed intent. But it also speaks to the possible reality that even under reciprocal causation, intentions may drive attitudes more than the reverse. That is, the process may begin with some initial intent. To the degree that we can help anchor learners with this informed intent at the outset, learners benefit.

4.3 Key Future Research Directions

This chapter promised the researcher a broad, rich view of the many research opportunities offered by entrepreneurial intentions. We have thus far identified several critical areas of research: Deep beliefs, identifying critical development experiences, and formally testing Bagozzi's theory of trying (with special attention to implementation intentions) but it may not yet be clear how these fit together.

To that end, we offer three different ways that we might profitably take a deeper look at entrepreneurial intentions:

(1) Explicitly test for reciprocal causation
(2) Explicitly test for contingencies
(3) Explicitly test the impact of deep beliefs on "phase changes" as intentions evolve
(4) Explicitly testing a "stepwise" model of how intentions evolve

4.3.1 Reciprocal Influence Model

Intent and Action – Dynamic Not Static Another important area that we have already begun to address is moving from static models toward different dynamic perspectives. We have already argued that we need to test models that do not assume unidirectional causality. It is highly likely that we will find reciprocal causality to be the norm, just as we find in other dynamic cognitive processes (e.g., Allport, 1935). While this argues immediately for monitoring intentions and their assumed antecedents longitudinally, the discussion above argues the utility of three particular aspects. The first is that if intent is initially anchored on some deep assumptions, we need to identify those. (We discuss that below.) The second is that we need to explore the cognitive consequences such as post-decision attributions. Third, the theory of trying and the work on implementation intentions argue that we need to do a much better job of understanding perceived barriers to (and facilitators of) entrepreneurial action.

Entrepreneurial Rationalization? However, what if we confirm that intentions influence attitudes significantly more than the reverse, even with significant reciprocal causation? Recall that Shaver (2007; also his Chapter 10 here) argued that we need to include the attributional perspective, that we should identify the reasons that entrepreneurs have for their intentions. Note that beneath those surface attributions are likely deep anchoring assumptions that we need to find.

Barriers and Triggers. Another nonlinearity that the theory of planned behavior cannot directly help us with is the partial volitional control that characterizes many entrepreneurial behaviors. Shapero (1982) argued that central to the entrepreneurial event were those factors that either facilitated entrepreneurial action or offered a perceived barrier. Adding barriers to the model adds to the messiness, but isn't it interesting that outside of Bagozzi – and entrepreneurship researchers – it is rare to see intentions research that deals overtly with barriers or facilitators (Krueger, 2003)? If you realize that rigorous analysis of entrepreneurial barriers is painfully rare, the reader should be able to see fertile ground for extensive study that will add genuine value to our understanding of entrepreneurship. Consider, for example, the interaction between deep beliefs and barriers. Different motivations and different volitions might manifest itself in the barriers and ways to avoid them that entrepreneurs perceive.[4] But it also would provide genuine value to educators: Consider the diagnostic value of an instrument that rigorously assessed perceived entrepreneurial barriers.

---

[4]This "walls and holes" model surfaced in discussions at Max Planck in 2008 by volume authors Diemo Urbig, Erik Monsen, Alan Carsrud, Malin Brannback, and this author.

4.3.2 Contingencies

Another "messiness" that has arisen of late with the intentions model is that the paths by which intentions evolve may vary systematically. For example, Krueger and Kickul (2006) found that the cognitive style index had a sizable impact on the intentions model. In fact, the model was specified differently for those scoring with an intuitive cognitive style than for analytic style. For an example from leadership studies, Anderson et al. (2006) found gender-specific construct perceptions in leadership. That is, the same scale might measure consistently different things for different people. Or do variables such as gender or cognitive style actually change the decision calculus?

But what other contingencies might yield similar results? Two strong possibilities can be found in this book. How might passion change the model(Chapter 9)? For example, Keynes argues that "animal spirits" were the real motive force behind enterprising activity (Brannback et al., 2006). In this book, Chapter 12 suggests that differences in control beliefs might drive differences in how we model intention. Intentions when one believes that powerful others dominate your key outcomes might well differ from intentions when one has a very strong internal control belief. Also, studying entrepreneurs would permit us to see if intentions evolve differently under pure risk than under pure uncertainty.

Three other seemingly obvious contingencies remain untested. What about differences in the intentions model between necessity entrepreneurs and opportunity entrepreneurs? Should we not see meaningful differences between high and low entrepreneurial intensity? Differences in regulatory focus (promotion versus prevention) are already considered to generate different cognitive scripts (e.g., McMullan and Shepherd, 2002; Baron, 2004).

4.3.3 Deep Beliefs and Phase Change Model

Cognitive developmental psychology has long noted that human psychosocial development occurs in reasonably distinct stages connected by transition periods that are inherently experiential (Erikson, 1980). In children, it is the "terrible twos" that demarcates infancy and early childhood. We see very different knowledge structures in these different stages; we also see consistent (and diagnostically useful) phenomena that characterize transition. This affords us a good sense of someone's psychosocial development and how to help them navigate transitions. What if entrepreneurial intentions evolve similarly, exhibiting phase changes?

Phase Changes. If we plot intentions against a key attitude such as self-efficacy, we tend to see evidence that the optimal fit is not linear. It may be that noise and measurement error are amplified unpredictably, but one can also make the case that we are actually seeing one or two inflection points in the data that reflect a phase change in the evolution of entrepreneurial thinking.

That is, as entrepreneurial intentions evolve, they go through different stages. Just as entrepreneurial ventures move from ideation to nascency to launch, might not intentions follow a similar pattern, moving from one cognitive regime to another? (Consider Drnovsek's troika of inventor, founder, and developer.) If so, we should see interesting cognitive differences between the regimes.

How do knowledge structures differ across the phases? What are the critical developmental experiences associated with each phase *and* with each transition? (Fig. 4.3) Such evidence would also be of invaluable diagnostic assistance to educators and to practitioners.

An Illuminating Controversy? One of my favorite controversies recently is the sizable fraction of subjects in the PSED database who are nascent and have been for years. They have not launched; they have not quit; they are still trying. Are they simply noise or do they represent something very interesting?[5] Beyond the obvious idea of applying the theory of trying to them, isn't there a construct question here? In a world where so many people want to start a business and so many people want to believe that they are, maybe all our research has missed a very important point. Intent without the right action is not intent, it is dreaming. (Do I intend to start a business? Yes! Do I expect to start soon? Not necessarily.)

However, a nascent entrepreneur is committed (or believes she is) to a course of action. What do we gain if we identify nascency as the genuine "intending"? The careers literature distinguishes a stage prior to intent, "interest" (e.g., Lent et al., 1994). Might this also suggest a three-stage phase change model: Interest, Intent, Launch? Even if this is too limiting, this thought suggests that we may want to think long and hard about where "intent" really begins?

Deep Beliefs. However, if deep anchoring beliefs influence entrepreneurial intentions but influence differently as intentions evolve, then we might well identify different specifications for the model. Consider differences in motivation and volition (Ach, 1910), Heckhausen (2007) in this simple thought experiment suggested by Elfving, et al., 2008). One music entrepreneur believes "I am an entrepreneur. Therefore I start a business." The other believes "I am passionate about music. Being an entrepreneur enables that." One has passion for entrepreneurship, the other for music, yet both start a music business. It might be relatively straightforward to identify what lies beneath those surface beliefs. Kets de Vries (1996) argued from a psychoanalytic perspective that all humans have critical core beliefs that trigger significant action.

In any event, we would again propose that if this approach is valid, then we should see very different cognitive regimes for each phase: different scripts, schemas and maps, and different deep anchoring beliefs. Returning to our previous discussion on education and learning, we should also be able to identify the critical development experiences that correspond to different phases and especially to the transitions.

---

[5]This issue was raised by the book editors and gratefully acknowledged.

4.3.4 Stepwise Model

Finally, consider one additional frontier for entrepreneurship research. How many studies merely ask about starting a "business"? Instead we need to drill down into the facets of the intended business (e.g., Krueger et al., 2009). That is, consider the related notions of effectuation (Sarasvathy, 2001) and bricolage (Baker and Nelson, 2005).

While entrepreneurs may have a strong, well-developed intent toward launching a venture, their path may change dramatically. Even if the overall intent and attitudes need not change significantly, their intent toward the "next step" may change radically. As such, we would argue that it might be quite rewarding to monitor entrepreneurial intentions at both the overall level and for each step of their trajectory.

In Sum. . .

I began with the metaphor of the old phlogiston theory. Our existing model of entrepreneurial intentions is no phlogiston; Its underlying theory base remains strong as ever. But like oxidation, we may well find a model whose theory is even stronger and whose ability to explain, predict and to be useful to educators and practitioners is significantly better.

Studies of pre-entrepreneurial behaviors demonstrate a dizzying array of successful (and unsuccessful) patterns and sequences of activities. There simply is no single optimal path – based on behaviors. Intentions remain critical to our understanding. However, looking at entrepreneurial intentions suggests that we need to re-think how entrepreneurs arrive at their intent. That re-think will contribute to how we teach/train and how we counsel entrepreneurs.

Consider the PSED "perma-nascents" who reflect a process where applying cognitive science offers us some new clues. Who knows what *else* we will find? I am honored to lead off this book but every chapter in this book will be useful and provocative in this journey.

References

Ach N (1910) Über den Willen. Leipzig: Verlag von Quelle & Meyer.
Ajzen I (1987) Attitudes, traits and actions: Dispositional prediction of behavior in social psychology. Advances in Experimental Social Psychology 20(1): 1–63.
Ajzen I, Fishbein M (1980) Understanding Attitudes and Predicting Social Behavior. Englewood Cliffs, NJ: Prentice-Hall.
Ajzen I (2002) Perceived behavioral control, self-efficacy, locus of control and the theory of planned behaviour. Journal of Applied Social Psychology 32(4): 665–683.
Allport GW (1935) Attitudes. In: Murchison C.M. (ed.), Handbook of Social Psychology. Winchester: Clark University Press.
Anderson N, Lievens F, van Dam K, Born M (2006) A construct-driven investigation of gender differences in a leadership-role assessment center. Journal of Applied Psychology 91: 555–566.

Bagozzi R, Warshaw P (1990) Trying to consume. Journal of Consumer Research 17(2): 127–140.

Bagozzi R, Dholakia U, Basuron S (2003) How effectful decisions get enacted: The motivating role of decision processes, desires and anticipated emotions. Journal of Behavioral Decision Making 16(4): 273–295.

Baker T, Nelson R (2005) Creating something from nothing: Resource construction through entrepreneurial bricolage. Administrative Science Quarterly 50(3): 329–366.

Bandura A (2001) Social cognitive theory: An agentic perspective. Annual Review of Psychology 52: 1–26.

Baron RA (2004) The cognitive perspective: A valuable tool for answering entrepreneurship's basic "why" questions. Journal of Business Venturing 19(2): 221–239.

Baron R (2006) Opportunity recognition as pattern recognition: How entrepreneurs 'connect the dots' to identify new business opportunities. Academy of Management Perspectives 20(1): 104–119.

Bird B (1988) Implementing entrepreneurial ideas: The case for intentions. Academy of Management Review 13(3): 442–454.

Bird B (1989) Entrepreneurial Behavior. Glenview, IL: Scott Foresman and Company.

Brannback M, Carsrud AL, Krueger N, Elfving J (2006) Sex, drugs and entrepreneurial passion: An exploratory study. Babson Entrepreneurship Research Conference, Bloomington, IN.

Brannback M, Carsrud AL, Krueger N, Elfving J (2007) "Trying" to be an entrepreneur. Babson Research Conference, Madrid.

Bratman M, (1987) Intention, Plans, and Practical Reason. Harvard University Press: Cambridge MA.

Carsrud AL, Brannback M, Krueger N, Kickul J (2007) Family Business Pipelines. Philadelphia, PA: Academy of Management.

Davidsson P (1991) Continued entrepreneurship. Journal of Business Venturing 6(6): 405–429.

Dennett DC (1989) The Intentional Stance. Cambridge, MA: MIT Press.

Dholakia U, Bagozzi R (2002) Mustering motivation to enact decisions: How decision process characteristics influence goal realizations. Journal of Behavioral Decision Making 15: 167–188.

Elfving J, Brannback M, Carsrud AL, Krueger N (2008) Passionate entrepreneurial cognition: Illustrations from multiple Finnish cases. Working paper under review.

Erikson E (1980) Identity and the Life Cycle. New York: Norton.

Gollwitzer P, Brandstätter V (1997) Implementation intentions and effective goal pursuit. Journal of Personality and Social Psychology 73: 186–199.

Heckhausen J (2007) The motivation-volition divide. Research in Human Development 4(3–4): 163–180.

Kahneman D, Tversky A (1979). Prospect theory: An analysis of decision under risk. Econometrica 47(2): 263–292.

Katz J, Gartner W (1988) Properties of emerging organizations. Academy of Management Review 13(3): 429–441.

Kets de Vries M (1996) The anatomy of the entrepreneur: Clinical observations. Human Relations 49(7): 853–883.

Kim M, Hunter J (1993) Relationships among attitudes, intention and behaviour. Communications Research 20(3): 331–364.

Kolvereid L (1996) Prediction of employment status choice intentions. Entrepreneurship Theory and Practice 21(1): 47–57.

Krueger N (1993) The impact of prior entrepreneurial exposure on perceptions of new venture feasibility and desirability. Entrepreneurship Theory and Practice 18(1): 521–530.

Krueger N (2000) The cognitive infrastructure of opportunity emergence. Entrepreneurship Theory and Practice 24(3): 5–23.

Krueger N (2003) Entrepreneurial resilience: Real and perceived barriers to implementing entrepreneurial intentions. Paper at Babson Conference. Jönköping, Sweden.

Krueger N (2007) What lies beneath? The experiential essence of entrepreneurial thinking. Entrepreneurship Theory and Practice 31(1): 123–138.

Krueger N (2009) The microfoundations of entrepreneurial learning and education. In: Gatewood E, West GP (eds.) The Handbook of Cross Campus Entrepreneurship. Cheltenham, UK: Elgar.

Krueger N, Brannback M, Carsrud AL (2007) Watch Out, Isaac! Reciprocal causation in entrepreneurial intent. Australian Graduate Scholar Exchange conference, Brisbane.

Krueger N, Brazeal D (1994) Entrepreneurial potential and potential entrepreneurs. Entrepreneurship Theory and Practice 18(1): 5–21.

Krueger N, Carsrud AL (1993) Entrepreneurial intentions: Applying the theory of planned behaviour. Entrepreneurship and Regional Development 5: 315–330.

Krueger N, Day M (2009) What can entrepreneurship learn from neuroscience? Presentation at USASBE Conference, Anaheim.

Krueger N, Kickul J (2006) So you thought the intentions model was simple? Navigating the complexities and interactions of cognitive style, culture, gender, social norms, and intensity on the pathways to entrepreneurship. USASBE conference, Tucson, AZ.

Krueger N, Kickul J, Gundry L, Wilson F, Verma R (2009) Discrete choices, trade-offs and advantages: Modeling social venture opportunities and intentions. In: Robinson J, Mair J, Hockerts K (eds.) International Perspectives on Social Entrepreneurship. UK: Palgrave.

Krueger N, Reilly M, Carsrud AL (2000) Competing models of entrepreneurial intentions. Journal of Business Venturing 15: 411–532.

Krueger N, Schulte W, Stamp J (2008) Beyond intent: Antecedents of resilience and precipitating events for social entrepreneurial intentions and action. USASBE Conference, San Antonio, TX.

Krueger N, Welpe I (2007) Experimental Entrepreneurship: A Research Prospectus. Working paper. (also: papers.ssrn.com/abstract_id=1146745)

Krueger N, Welpe I (2008) The influence of cognitive appraisal and anticipated outcome emotions on the perception, evaluation and exploitation of social entrepreneurial opportunities. Babson Entrepreneurship Research Conference, Chapel Hill, NC.

Lawrence A, Clark L, Labuzetta JN, Sahakian B, Vyakarnum S (2008) The innovative brain. Nature 456: 168–169.

Lent R, Brown S, Hackett G (1994) Toward a unifying theory of career and academic interests, choice and performance. Journal of Vocational Behavior 45: 79–122.

Libet B, Gleason C, Wright E, Pearl D (1983) Time of conscious intention to act in relation to onset of cerebral activity: Unconscious initiation of a freely voluntary act. Brain 106: 623–642.

Liska A (1984) A critical examination of the causal structure of the Fishbein/Ajzen attitude-behavior model. Social Psychology Quarterly 47(1): 61–74.

Maguire E, Woollett K, Spiers H (2006) London taxi drivers and bus drivers: A structural MRI and neuropsychological analysis. Hippocampus 16(17): 1191–1201.

McMullen J, Shepherd D (2002) Regulatory focus and entrepreneurial intention: Action bias in the recognition and evaluation of opportunities. Paper presented at Babson conference.

Mitchell RK (2005) Tuning up the global value creation engine: Road to excellence in international entrepreneurship education. In: Katz J, Shepherd D (eds.) Advances in Entrepreneurship, Firm Emergence and Growth 8, JAI Press, pp. 185–248.

Neergaard H, Krueger N (2005) Still playing the game? RENT XIX conference, Naples, Italy.

Sarasvathy S (2001) Causation and effectuation: Toward a theoretical shift from economic inevitability to entrepreneurial contingency. Academy of Management Review 26(2): 243–263.

Shapero A (1982) Social dimensions of entrepreneurship. In: Kent C, Sexton D, Vesper K (eds.) The Encyclopedia of Entrepreneurship. Englewood Cliffs, NJ: Prentice Hall, pp. 72–90.

Shaver K (2007) Reasons for Intent. Presentation at the International Council for Small Business (ICSB) Conference, Turku, Finland.

Simons D, Chabris C (1995) Gorillas in our midst: Sustained inattentional blindness for dynamic events. British Journal of Developmental Psychology 13: 113–142.

Stanton A, Day M, Krueger N, Welpe I, Acs Z, Audretsch D (2008) The Questions (Not So) Rational Entrepreneurs Ask: Decision-making through the Lens of Neuroeconomics, Professional Development Workshop, Academy of Management Conference, Anaheim CA.

Zald D (2008) Midbrain dopamine receptor availability is inversely associated with novelty-seeking traits in humans. Journal of Neuroscience 28(53): 14372–14378.

Part II
Cognitive Maps and Entrepreneurial Scripts

Chapter 5
Cognitive Maps in Entrepreneurship: Researching Sense Making and Action

Malin Brännback and Alan Carsrud

Abstract In this chapter, we show that cognitive maps are a viable way of both examining the cognitive structures of entrepreneurs and understanding the differences between entrepreneurs and managers in their cognitive structures. We demonstrate that these maps differ in their use and differ based on prior experience and perceptions. We tie this research stream in organizational behavior and strategic management to a potential research approach in the study of the cognitions of entrepreneurs. We also demonstrated how maps are tied to goals and to actions and thus to entrepreneurial motivations and perceptions. We also conclude that this stream of research into the cognitive maps of entrepreneurs has yet to be fully explored. Certainly maps can yield significant new insights into how entrepreneurs view their world and translate that either into successful or into unsuccessful new ventures. Finally, we demonstrate that entrepreneurial researchers likewise have such cognitive maps that influence, sometimes without awareness, their own views of the world.

5.1 Introduction

Isn't it quite fascinating that we with a few lines and symbols on a paper can "see" oceans and land, perceive borders between countries and distances between cities, re-live memories from vacations and start longing for friends in distant places. The map gives a world. This world determines how we interpret the world in front of us. At the same time we know at heart that the world does not at all look like this. We know it with certainty. Yet we use this map to orientate ourselves in the global room. It seems as if we cannot do anything else. But, the fact remains: *This is not the world!* The world is not flat. (Kristensson Uggla, 2002, 18)[1]

M. Brännback (✉)
Department of Business Studies, Åbo Akademi University, Henriksgatan 7,
FIN-20500 Åbo, Finland
e-mail: malin.brannback@abo.fi

[1] This quote is one of the author's translation from the book Slaget om verkligheten (Kristensson Uggla, 2002; the title would translate as *The battle about reality*), which is currently available only in Swedish.

A.L. Carsrud, M. Brännback (eds.), *Understanding the Entrepreneurial Mind*,
International Studies in Entrepreneurship 24, DOI 10.1007/978-1-4419-0443-0_5,
© Springer Science+Business Media, LLC 2009

In his book Kristensson Uggla (2002) discusses our relationship to maps by asking us to take a really good look at the map shown in Fig. 5.1. He assumes most of us probably recognize it. "Most of us know it from our childhood. This is how we have been taught the way the world 'looks like' and when we have it in front of us we think we have a perspective of the world – the entire world. It is safe and stable...most of us can easily find Bangkok, Munich or Santiago de Chile." Kristensson Uggla then asks us to conduct an experiment, "...turn the map upside down and something suddenly occurs: It is no longer easy to find places! Try fast to find Bolivia, Bangladesh or Belgium." He asks if we found it difficult and concludes that we most probably did. "You can also try to turn it 90° to the left or the right and you are probably equally lost. Why? Because, we are used to the world 'looking like' it does when it is turned the right way up" (Kristensson Uggla, 2002, 17–18).[2]

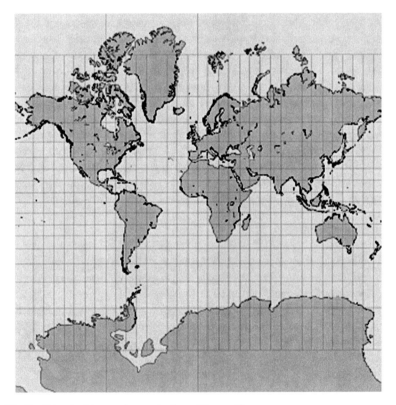

Fig. 5.1 Traditional – Mercator's – projection of the world
(source: http://www.progonos.com/furuti/MapProj/Normal/ProjNav/projNav.html accessed February 11, 2009)

---

[2]The translations are made by one of the authors.

Take a look at Fig. 5.2 – The TO-map – a world map from the sixteenth century. It depicts a world where Europe, Africa, and Asia are separated by the Danube (*Tanis*), the Nile, and the Mediterranean. This map was not used for navigating in the physical geography but for navigating in the spiritual geography. It is a map of the meaning of life, a religious map. How do we know that? Kristensson Uggla explains, the horizon is turned toward the east (*Oriens*), a "wrong" direction according to the modern world (which has for centuries been oriented towards the west (*Occidens*). The TO-world was oriented toward the east because at the time it was thought that Paradise was in the east, but above all, that Christ would return from the east.

The world map shown in Fig. 5.1 as "the real" picture subsequently replaced the TO-map. Kristensson Uggla continues to ask (p. 27): How has this map (Fig. 5.1) organized our thinking of the world? Europe is in the middle, sided by America and Asia and above Africa, reflecting a kind of geopolitical power relationship. Moreover, a two-dimensional projection of a three-dimensional globe portrays the proportions to the advantage of Europe. In this Mercator's projection, the United Kingdom is the same size as India and does not reveal the actual fact that Asia and America are about four times larger than Europe, Africa is three times larger than Europe, and that Australia also is larger than Europe.

While a map is a representation of territory or a journey from one place to another and it also has the ability to represent the environment with varying degrees of detail. It is also a model or image capable of focusing minds, helping to understand and make sense, for taking particular courses of action (Cummings and Wilson, 2003). The focus of this chapter is on the territories of minds, sense making, and action.

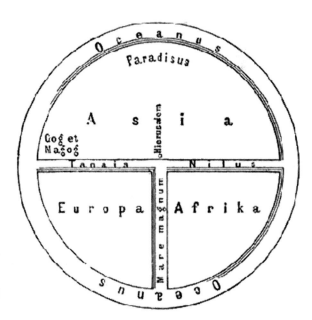

Fig. 5.2 The TO-map, sometimes also known as the Beatine map (http://en. wikipedia.org/ wiki/T_and_O_map accessed February 11, 2009)

While the geographical functionality of maps is important it is beyond the scope of this chapter. We focus here on the cognitive maps that entrepreneurs use to guide their creation of a new venture.

Maps of minds, sense making, and action are known as cognitive maps. Cognitive maps, which are some times called schemas or scripts, are concepts from the field of cognitive psychology that have been studied and used in organization theory and strategic management for several decades (see, for example, Bougon et al., 1977; Bougon, 1992; Fiol and Huff, 1992; Hodgkinson et al., 1999). Today managerial and organizational cognition is a well-establish research area (for a detailed review see Walsh, 1995). However, cognitive maps are not only representation of individual perceptions. Cognitive maps, or cognitive mapping, are powerful research techniques to study exactly how people "see" things and how these sights differ and impact subsequent action. This chapter explores how cognitive maps, as perceived by the entrepreneurs and others, can be used in research on the entrepreneur and the entrepreneurial process. In Chapter 6, there is a detailed discussion on entrepreneurial scripts.

5.2 Cognitive Maps – Territory of Mind

Cognitive maps, within managerial and organizational cognition, have been described as sense-making tools that can be used to map out territories (cognitive or physical) and are the basis for action (Weick, 1990). Maps emphasize spatial relatedness and are replacements for space. Maps communicate a sense of place, a sense of *here* in relation to *there*. Literally and figuratively maps put people into their places, e.g., the market (potential, served, actual, target), the competitive environment, the United States, the European Union, China, etc., or the industry (semi-conductors, biotechnology, or fast food). Maps establish a landscape or a domain (Huff and Jenkins, 2002). Fiol and Huff (1992, 267) define cognitive maps as "...*graphic representation that locate people in relation to their information environments. Maps provide a frame of reference for what is known and believed. They highlight some information and fail to include other information, either because it is deemed less important, or because it is not known. They exhibit the reasoning behind purposeful actions.*"

In management research, it is often claimed that the theoretical foundation for cognitive maps is a psychological one: Personal Construct Theory, developed by Kelly (1955) (Eden, 1988; Eden and Ackermann, 1998). Cognitive maps are seen as personal construct systems. In developing the Personal Construct Theory, Kelly assumes the individual to be inherently curious about the surrounding reality. Kelly argues that a person is gradually making sense of his or her reality. Reality is seen as dynamic and that (p. 15) "...*all our interpretations of the universe are subject to revision or replacement.*" Kelly argues that experience is vital for sense making in that it functions as a constantly correcting compass of facts. Experience is seen as the extent of what we know although its validity can be disputed. The compass enables the creation of patterns that map on to the already known, in other words it takes a map to create a map. Maps are tools for finding *explanations*, for making sense by sometimes creating powerful narrative-like stories.

While experience is important, it does not guarantee the validity of personal constructs. That is, the constructs need not be accurate. Karl Weick (1990, 7) argues: "If cognitive maps are imperfect renderings of territory, and if people have had extensive experience with other territories in their lives, then present maps...create a composite virtual map that capitalizes on what the person already knows." Experience prefigures our perceptions and at the same time underscores the subjective nature of cognitive maps. That is, we tend to see what we expect to see (Louis and Sutton, 1991). Past experience builds on a top-down or a "theory-driven" conceptualization (Walsh, 1995) of new information where experience affects an individual's ability to encode and draw conclusions from the new. Put slightly differently: what is out of mind is out of sight or to quote the quote in Chapter 6 by Mitchell, Mitchell, and Mitchell – "Never Mind!" This in turn brings on the notion of explicitness and tacitness. The latter is especially challenging as we may not always be capable of explaining what we see (Polanyi, 1967; Nonaka, 1990). Yet, if the difference between the expected and the actual is large, experience becomes the compass of comprehension – of sense making. Cognitive maps therefore are forms of heuristics. Therefore, it becomes vital to distinguish between relevant past experience, through selection, omission, and organization.

With respect to venture creation, when almost everything is new the challenge becomes to select among open-ended possibilities. Moreover, past experience may only be partially relevant. For example, past experience in the same industry may indeed be helpful. But if the past experience is anchored in the operations of a large, multi-national firm, it may not give much appropriate guidance for anyone about to create a small firm. This is because the individual's cognitive map lacks any experience in how to create a venture, or how to function in a small firm reality. Likewise, experience in one sector of high technology does not allow for generalizations across different sectors or industries within high technology (Brännback and Carsrud, 2008).

If we re-write the basic thesis of Personal Construct Theory into an entrepreneurial context we would arrive at the following: "we presume the business world really exists and the entrepreneur is gradually coming to understand it. We assume that the entrepreneur's thought really exist, though the correspondence between what the entrepreneur thinks exists and what actually does exist is constantly changing." Accordingly, we may argue that an entrepreneur needs to make sense of his/her reality to predict and to control – to find and to solve problems.

The concept of territory is a cognitive abstraction and symbolization of events and things, which through the use of *language* are expressed or represented for creating a mental map (Weick, 1990). However, the way we create a map differs between individuals. That is, we end up having different cognitive maps. Hence although all entrepreneurs are not alike and all managers are not alike, thus managers and entrepreneurs will have different cognitive maps. Mapping occurs through selection, omission, and organization things and events into some seemingly coherent pattern.

While maps and territories are seen as distinct, this distinction is anything but clear in strategic thinking – and entrepreneurial thinking. Weick (1990) argues that the ability to distinguish between map and territory is a left-brain activity, while strategic thinking is considered a right-brain activity. Mintzberg (1976) argues that planning takes place in the left brain and the actual managing or implementation takes place in the right brain. With respect to strategic plans, Mintzberg speculates that this may be one of the reasons why so many plans failed. This line of reasoning could well explain why so many business plans fail – not just to get funded, but much more, fail to get effectively implemented. Maps are the territory and yet most of managerial activity is socially constructed, i.e., the map creates the territory. Thereby maps prefigure self-confirming perceptions and actions. Maps as such are passive, while managerial and entrepreneurial life rests on the notion of constant activity and motion.

Weick (1990) argues that maps on a sufficiently high level of abstraction loose their ability to provide a vehicle for identifying differences. Things and events start to look alike. Consequently, when firms engage in, for example, benchmarking in order to map or place the firm in the competitive landscape, this exercise becomes fruitless or inaccurate if conducted on a too high level of abstraction. That said, Weick (1990) continues to observe that managerial maps need not be too accurate to convey spatial relatedness. Certainly this may be the case with the entrepreneur operating in an uncertain environment while trying to create a yet new venture. Perhaps this would explain why some people prefer to purchase a franchise where the cognitive map is more explicit, detailed, and perhaps more accurate.

The symbolization of events brings forth another important characteristic of cognitive maps – the ability to deal with *time* and therefore represent the dynamic nature of events. As noted in Chapter 7, there are time dimensions which need to be taken into account. Events occur with respect to some specific timeframe, whether they are single events or repeated events, whether they are past, present, or future events. While time is important in business, it is also problematic as temporality introduces instability into the map. This in turn calls for a constant refinement of the map – and the territory. Weick (1990) argues that those individuals more capable of selecting, omitting, and organizing are more flexible and therefore more capable of creating more accurate maps. The issue of time ties back to experience.

Experience and time are problematic for other reasons as well. Implicitly, experience and time place events in some kind of order, where one event is assumed to lead to another – a causal relationship, which is too often assumed to be linear. This in turn often leads us to project the past onto the future, as if the future already took place. In other words, the best predictor of future behavior is past behavior. This kind of causal and predictive logic is how we like to represent events and things in organizations, e.g., decision-making processes. It is like the map of the world in the beginning of this chapter. Yet we know that a linear and causal modeling of decisions is not an accurate representation of how decisions are made. We do this as it allows for "as accurate calculations as possible" (Ackoff, 1970, 1977, 1978) of events and their predicted future and because this is our conception of rational behavior.

The assumption of rationality does not conveniently allow for the inclusion of such fuzzy entities like intuition, gut feelings, experience, fate, luck, or tradition (March, 1976). But, even more so these models do not reflect or accommodate for change per se and with respect to goals. They do not deal with the fact that goal development and choice are independent processes conceptually and behaviorally (March, 1976; Saraswathy, 2001). More on goals and goal motivation can be found in Chapter 7. As human beings, we seek to minimize the cost of failure as opposed to determine the level of affordable loss. Entrepreneurs, operating with restricted amounts of resources, face the reality of calculating the latter – the affordable loss – and to apply inverse causality, i.e., effectuation (Saraswathy, 2001, 2003, 2008). We return to the discussion of causation versus effectuation in the section below discussing uses of cognitive maps.

To deepen our understanding of cognitive maps in the context of entrepreneurship, we will take a detour into the areas of organization theory and strategic management. These are where cognitive maps, or cognitive mapping, have been used for decades as means for representing managerial and collective thoughts. Thus maps provide sense making of organizational and strategic behaviors, i.e., actions (Huff, 1990).

5.3 Cognitive Maps in Management and Entrepreneurship

Research on managerial and organizational cognition gained wider interest with the emergence of the concept of strategic groups (Porter, 1980; Dess and Davis, 1984; Hodgkinson, 1997). The review by Walsh (1995) shows an impressive amount of 70 different concepts. A large proportion of the concepts reflect a top-down theory-driven information-processing construct. This rationale seeks to identify (i) knowledge structures that represent some information environment in relation to some important consequences, (ii) the origins of the knowledge structures, and (iii) how they evolved, so that guidance to change efforts can be made. Research exists on all four ontological levels of analysis: individual, group, organizational, and industry. Nevertheless, a large proportion of this research has focused on large organizations and groups of non-owner managers.

Earlier research on cognitive maps focused on identifying and mapping causal relationships in strategic decisions (Axelrod, 1976), in particular with reference to strategy concepts like cause maps (Bougon et al., 1977) and causal maps (Fahey and Naranyanan, 1989). These terms are often used as synonyms to cognitive maps. As the conceptual names suggest these maps are used for mapping causal relationships following the state-of-the-art rationale for decision-making and problem-solving processes. Early research also studied the impact of heuristics and biases on strategic decision under high uncertainty (Hodgkinson et al., 1999). Later studies revealed that cognitive maps were useful for surfacing perceptions of strategic alternatives (Bowman and Johnson, 1992; Calori et al., 1994; Reger and Palmer, 1996; Hodgkinson et al., 1999), studying competitive comparison (Porac and Thomas, 1990; Daniels et al., 1994; Hodgkinson, 1997), structuring complex or messy problems (Eden et al., 1983; Eden and Huxham, 1995; Fiol and Huff, 1992).

Cognitive maps in the context of entrepreneurship have not been extensively studied although early research on managerial and organizational cognition held the understanding of an individual's screens as important (Cyert and March, 1963; March and Simon, 1958; Walsh, 1995). A computer search, with keywords *entrepreneurship* and *cognitive maps,* on Business Source Premier and Blackwell Synergy[3] results in three (!) articles from 1988, 1999, and 2000. The first does not cover entrepreneurship at all (Schwenck, 1988), the second is on corporate entrepreneurship (Russell, 1999) but is in one of the top entrepreneurship journals, and the third (Hines, 2000) compares two qualitative methods for studying entrepreneurial decision making but is not an entrepreneurship journal. Hence, entrepreneurship and cognitive maps, or cognitive mapping, appear to be rather unchartered waters. One might rightfully wonder why. One reason may be that entrepreneurial cognition as a specific area of research is rather recent (Busenitz and Barney 1997; Mitchell et al., 2002, 2007; Krueger, 2007), but somehow that seems like a bad excuse rather than a valid explanation as cognitive maps in organization theory and strategy certainly are not new.

Therefore, to open up cognitive maps in entrepreneurship, we rely on the ideas and findings from organization theory and strategy to elucidate what cognitive maps are, what they have been used for, and how they can be used to improve our understanding of entrepreneurs and the entrepreneurial. Implicitly, and quite explicitly, we suggest that cognitive maps and cognitive mapping could – and should – be used in entrepreneurship much in the same way as they have been in organization theory and strategy. Much simplified one can argue that the cognitive map for the entrepreneur is that of the individual, or singular of the collective or plural organizational strategy. We are not concerned with large organizations versus small firms. The focus here is on cognitive mapping as a method for capturing a "personal construct system" of the entrepreneur (Kelly, 1955; Eden, 1988; Eden and Ackermann, 1998) rather than the representations of collective thought as often portrayed in organizational theory and strategy. A personal construct system represents the beliefs, values, and embedded expertise and knowledge structures.

---

[3]These were chosen as they cover the top entrepreneurship journals

5.4 On Those Who Decide and Think Versus Those Who Appear Not to

Analyzing how the research field of entrepreneurship talks about the entrepreneur and entrepreneurial work contrasted with that of managers and managerial work provides a simple illustration of cognitive maps in entrepreneurship. Such a map would be a *researcher's cognitive map*. That is, a personal construct system of the researcher, of what entrepreneurship is to them. In the research literature, the entrepreneur is characterized as the *innovator*, the *creator* of the new (Schumpeter, 1934), the *locator* of new ideas and *implementer* of ideas, the *exerciser* of leadership (Baumol, 1968), the actor in the process-conscious market theory who exhibiting deliberate behaviors (Kirzner, 1973, 1979), and the *possessor* of idiosyncratic knowledge enabling opportunity recognition (Shane and Venkatarman, 2000; Gaglio and Katz, 2001; Shane, 2003; Eckhart and Shane, 2003). While all of these descriptions of the entrepreneur may indeed be true, the entrepreneur is rarely described explicitly as a *decision maker* or a *thinker*, whereas managers are explicitly described by researchers as decision makers and thinkers.

Generally, whether an activity is recognized as entrepreneurial or not tends to be justified by the nature of the action a person (the entrepreneur) undertakes (Landström, 2005).[4] In other words, the focus is on *action* and *activities* undertaken – in most cases – by a person who is assumed to have carefully and consciously thought about those actions *prior* to the action. As researchers, we like to see entrepreneurship as rational behavior, as a phenomena occurring as a result of rational thought and decision-making process following a linear causal logic. A business plan can be seen as documentation of such a thought process. Thus a business plan is physical representation of a cognitive map, an attempt to make tacit knowledge explicit.

In the literature on managerial and organizational cognition, managers are described as strategic decision makers who make decisions about highly complex issues requiring careful thinking. Decision making involves cognition and CEOs (in large organizations) have therefore been considered *cognizers* (Calori et al., 1994). Strategic decisions are said to depend on the cognitive orientation of managers, and strategies are abstractions of managerial thought (Weick, 1979; Daft and Weick, 1984; Prahalad and Bettis, 1986; Mintzberg, 1987). Porac and Thomas (1990) argued that decision makers act on a cognitive map of the environment and therefore any strategic response to changes in the competitive environment is based on mental models of competitive strategies. Changes in the competitive environment will, in turn, reciprocally affect mental models (Porac et al., 1989, Hodgkinson, 1997). A related concept introduced by Prahalad and Bett (1986) – dominant

---

[4]In The Early History of Entrepreneurial Theory Hoselitz (1951) points out that the earliest use and meaning of entrepreneur was formed during the Middle Ages, i.e., long before Cantillon or Say, and was celui qui entreprend quelque chose – a person who gets things done.

logic – describes the kind of mental maps developed through experience in one business context that some times are not applicable in another (Prahalad and Bettis, 1986, Bettis and Prahalad, 1995).

However, it is not only the words used by researchers to describe the activities by entrepreneurs versus managers that are different. As earlier pointed out, it is often a question of more than one manager engaging in some activity. The challenge is to arrive at a collective decision or forming a collective thought that becomes the basis for collective action. In recognizing that there are multiple perceptions, opinions, and actors involved, it has been understood that these may be in conflict with each other. Managerial and organizational cognition has also studied the homogeneity versus heterogeneity of managerial and organizational thought (Daniels et al., 1994). The number of individuals involved has been considered large and the issues are many and complex. These have to be negotiated into a common understanding. Thus cognitive maps have proven instrumental for visualization and clarification in such situations.

Implicitly entrepreneurship seems to have been perceived differently by researchers, that is, much less complex and involving one or only a limited number of individuals. Keeping track of thoughts, perceptions, or opinions in a less complex context has not required a tool for graphical representation. There seems to be a naive distinction between managers and entrepreneurs; the former is a decision maker or a group of decision makers (in large firms) (Learned et al., 1965) and the latter is an innovator or creator, often alone (in small firms). The latter is not explicitly considered a decision maker. Yet, one can only wonder if cognitive maps are any more different between managers and entrepreneurs than between any two individuals?

In reviewing studies on managerial and organizational cognition, it is possible to identify two views; a traditional one which takes the collective top-down approach, and one, which argues that managerial and organizational cognition is diverse and determined by individual cognition (Daniels et al., 1994) – a bottom-up approach. Entrepreneurship is a bottom-up process, or could even be the top *and* the bottom. Even if it has been long argued that entrepreneurs are different from managers, it is rarely pointed out that this difference could be due to *thought* although it is argued that entrepreneurs appear to perceive their environment, opportunities, risk, etc., differently than those who are not entrepreneurs – some of whom apparently are managers. This has certainly been the case with respect to the concept of risk as discussed in Chapter 7 and Part IV.

That is, it is implied that there may be differences in the cognitive structures or knowledge structures for entrepreneurs versus managers. Knowledge structure also refers to thinking and an ability to articulate (language) the thought enabling the construction of a model or a *map* of thought – a cognitive map. A map, as we recall, is a graphical representation that provides a frame of reference (Weick, 1990; Fiol and Huff, 1992).

Researchers in entrepreneurial cognition explicitly argue that entrepreneurs appear to *think* differently or appear to structure the reality they live in differently from others (Busenitz and Barney 1997; Mitchell et al., 2002, 2007; Carsrud, et al., 2009). The specific interest into entrepreneurial cognition boils down to a single question that previous researchers had not been able to answer adequately: why some people and not others are able to recognize opportunities (Mitchell et al., 2002)? Mitchell et al. (2002) argue that the ability to recognize opportunities is due to different cognitions among entrepreneurs, i.e., entrepreneurial cognition, probably much in the same way as managerial strategizing tends to differ depending on differences in managerial cognition (Daniels et al., 1994). Entrepreneurial cognition is defined as (p. 97): "...*the knowledge structures that people use to make assessments, judgments or decisions involving opportunity evaluation and venture creation and growth.*" The definition implies that there are knowledge entities that can be organized in a meaningful way that will lead to some form of action: assessments, judgments, decisions, evaluations, and creation, i.e., cognitive maps.

5.5 Cognitive Maps as Research Tools

As earlier stated cognitive maps have been used to structure messy organizational and strategic problems in order to focus attention, trigger memory, reveal gaps, highlight key factors, and supply missing information for individuals or groups of individuals. Such maps can be placed on a continuum depending on the purpose of the map.

The purpose will determine the amount of the required interpretive input. Maps requiring less interpretation represent methods that manifest context. Such maps will rarely identify cognitive structures, but when further analyzed will provide us with maps involving extensive interpretation with increasingly complicated models of cognition. In management – and entrepreneurship – this becomes increasingly important, as most firms regardless of size are context specific. The context can be industry, market, country, and nature of the firm (public traded versus family firm). It is not unimportant to understand the context of the firm. In fact it is important to remember that entrepreneurial firms often exist in multiple contexts.

Huff (1990) suggests five different uses for cognitive maps: (i) maps that assess attention, association, and importance of concepts; (ii) maps that show dimensions of categories and cognitive taxonomies; (iii) maps that show influence, causality, and system dynamics; (iv) maps that show the structure of argument and conclusion; and (v) maps that specify schemas, frames, and perceptual codes.

5.5.1 Maps Assessing Attention, Association, and Importance of Concepts

These maps seek to identify frequent use of related concepts and how these are associated with related concepts to unravel particular themes. The basic assumption is that perception is influenced by language and many languages have more than one word for describing various phenomena. Consequently, within entrepreneurship research such maps could well be used for studying differences in perception of the term *entrepreneur* between researchers and entrepreneurs, or between other stakeholders like venture capitalists or policy makers. Cognitive maps would be instrumental to study what different people associate with concepts like entrepreneurship and entrepreneurial work.

Let us examine the words used to describe entrepreneurship. The word entrepreneur, or entrepreneurship, when translated to different languages may acquire multiple meanings. In Swedish, two different words can be used: entreprenör and företagare. The former is a direct translation of the English word, whereas the latter translates back into English as "one who does." In Finnish, the word is yrittäjä, which translates back to English as "one who tries" (and a firm is yritys, which literarily translates as "a trial"!). But, in addition to the direct linguistic translations, these words often embed a much wider and richer tacit meaning, which when used trigger different associations and perceptions of an individual as well as the associated activities (Johannisson, 2005). It is not uncommon that entrepreneurs do not recognize themselves in the academic descriptions of entrepreneurs. Similarly, many that the academic research community would describe as entrepreneurs would not call themselves entrepreneurs, e.g., artists, or creators of non-profit social service organizations.

One method of looking at cognitive maps is content analysis. Krippendorff (2004), for example, describes content analysis as a form of cognitive map, especially when used for studying words and the use of words. But, from the above we can see that this is not entirely unproblematic. It is not clear if frequency of words indicates saliency. Likewise do changes in the words used indicate change in attention or understanding. Finally, it is not clear if a valid comparison of word use can be made as variations frequently occur across individuals, organizational, or national cultures (Huff, 1990). Therefore, it is suggested that word counts should be used with additional methods of analysis when using this approach to study cognitive maps of entrepreneurs.

5.5.2 Maps of Categories, Cognitive Taxonomies, and Cognitive Frameworks

Frequently within research we categorize for pedagogic reasons in order to facilitate sense making and learning for students. Categories and specific links between concepts create an organized memory, which supports additional thought processes. Sometimes the categories are artifacts and not necessarily true representations of reality. A good example is provided from the field of strategy and categorization of schools of thought in strategy. Mintzberg et al. (1998) argues for ten schools of thought that are quite different from the list of ten by Karlöf (1987) and much broader than the six schools of thought suggested by Gilbert et al. (1988) or the simple two-category description offered by Kristamuljana (1994). Moreover, these are academic classifications and it is not likely to find a company operating according to one particular school of thought. Hence, the practical relevance – other than educational – can be disputed. Most managers would likely not use those terms to conceptualize what they do strategically unless trained to do so.

Similar maps have also been drawn in attempts to make sense of entrepreneurship (Grégoire et al., 2006) and more recently social entrepreneurship (Hill et al., 2008). While most category maps are organized as hierarchies, concepts can also be organized in a network manner. These are called semantic networks and it has been argued that they provide a more relevant representation than the hierarchical maps (Huff, 1990). For example, Hill et al. (2008) use semantic networks in mapping out social entrepreneurship.

Maps of categorization can be used in the visualization a firm's competitive environment (Figs. 5.3 and 5.4). This can be done on firm level but also on industry level. Our example below is from the field of biotechnology, where the scientific and technological advances in the 1970s came to change the prevailing paradigm for drug development in the pharmaceutical industry. Moreover, this scientific breakthrough had implications for multiple other industries and fundamentally created a new one, or did it? It all began in November 1973 when Stanley Cohen and Herbert Boyen published an article. The article reported on the scientific breakthrough of recombinant DNA and this is commonly regarded as the genesis of modern biotechnology. Over a period of 10 years, a new paradigm of drug development emerged – biology-based drug development. At first, traditional pharma companies saw little reasons to worry. After all, the firms that seemed to enter the market where small companies employing a few university scientists involved in small-scale protein production for R&D. These could in no way be threatening to large pharma companies more than 100 years old.

This view was seriously jolted through the commercial breakthrough, which took place on October 14, 1980, when Genentech went public and listed their stock on the US stock exchange. Genentech had been founded a few years earlier and employed some 20 persons had gone from small-scale protein production for R&D purpose to

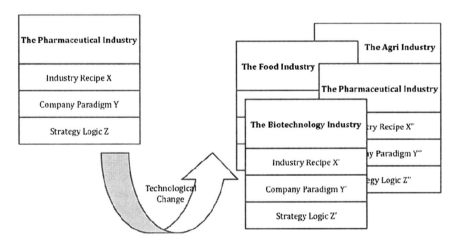

Fig. 5.3 The effect of technological change on the pharmaceutical industry

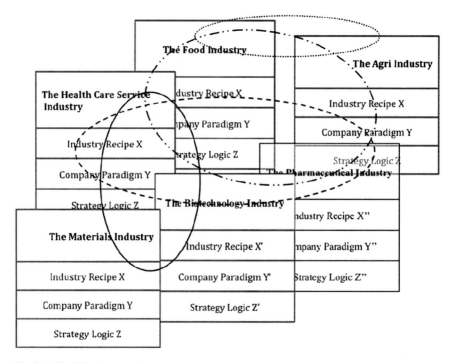

Fig. 5.4 The life science sector

large-scale production for commercial purposes. What happened that day in October nobody had been able to anticipate? Genentech was going to sell one million shares for $35 a piece (Brännback and Carsrud, 2008). What was going on?

In Fig. 5.3, we have first depicted the pharmaceutical industry to the left and a major technological change. Until this change, there was a prevailing industry recipe, company paradigm, and strategy logic. On a macro-level, we have industry recipe which certain common beliefs and assumptions – dominating opinions, which are held as consistent and realistic and which give the actors about the "rules of the game" Grinyer and Spender (1979). A sub-set of an industry recipe is the *company paradigm* (Spender, 1989; Johnson and Scholes, 1988), which is a representation of managerial perceptions and views of how to succeed in their business environment. These two levels then feed into the strategy logic of the firm, which are concepts on the individual level. This represents the thinking of key person(s) in the firm. To the right in Fig. 5.3, we have four "industries," which were more or less directly affected by the scientific breakthrough. The agricultural industry had with the lead of Monsanto in the 1970s started to explore the use of biotechnology (Pence, 2002). This in turn would lead to the introduction of genetically modified crops, which in turn would impact the food industry (Charles, 2001). It was also claimed that biotechnology would also impact the materials as well as computing and military industries (Oliver, 1999). Ultimately the health-care industry would also be strongly affected.

In Fig. 5.4, we have depicted the increasing complexities, which today is commonly referred to as the life science sector. The circles imply that the industry, or the served markets, were no longer the neat "boxes" but were converging and could in principle exist anywhere. Thus, competitive analysis would have to be carried out by think-outside-the-box rationale. Competitors could come from entirely other industries. Another example is that data available in 2000 indicating the number of profitable biotechnology firms in the world. The range was from 22 to 75, which must be a sign of different yardsticks of measurement (Brännback et al., 2001).

Clearly the figures above serve as rich cognitive maps for researchers to express the complexity of their findings. If researchers use such maps, it is not so difficult to conceive that entrepreneurs and those in start-up teams have similar such maps to express their cognitive views of their firm and its relations with others in an industry.

5.5.3 Maps of Causal Relationships and Arguments

It is not surprising that maps showing causal relationships are the most frequently used in management literature. These are traditional models of managerial decision making and problem solving based on causal rationality (Bougon et al., 1977; Huff, 1990). Causal relationships represent one of the very human ways of comprehending and explaining events. Causal inference allows for interpretation. Causal explanations provide powerful means by which to conduct post hoc analyses of attributions. Biases in attribution and the influence of attribution on the propensity to act are important aspect of this line of research. It is also possible to use causal maps to study changes in belief about the industry environment.

Although the maps in Figs. 5.3 and 5.4 depict categorization it can also be argued that they are representations of changes in the perceptions of the industry environment. Graphic representations of causal relationships among concepts require the identification of nodes and directions of the causal relationship. Of particular interest are then such nodes, which can take opposite values or directions (Fig. 5.6).

In Fig. 5.5, two versions of a causal map have been depicted. In both cases, the argument starts with nuclear power and how it will impact general welfare. In the upper version, a positive causal relationship is represented and in the lower string a negative causal relationship is established. These maps were constructed based on arguments in the public press for and against building a new nuclear power plant in Finland. This discussion was rampant in the early 1990s (Brännback and Malaska, 1995). Those in favor and those against a new nuclear power plant had quite different views on what would create an increased general welfare for society.

A larger representation of the causal relationship between the arguments in the discussion is shown in Fig. 5.6. Arguments are often built based on a causal logic and therefore the distinction between *cause-maps* and *argument maps* are sometimes unclear. Argument maps are often used – as in the case of nuclear power – to represent arguments for and against an action. However, arguments are often inconclusive and the challenge is to find arguments strong enough to be considered valid as a basis for decision. Clearly, the decision is likely to be subjective.

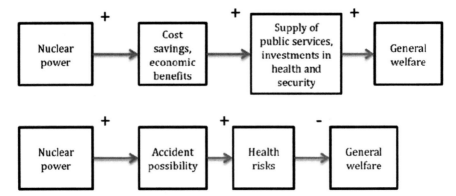

Fig. 5.5 Two cause maps (Brännback, 1996)

While the goal of causal maps is to clarify it is easy to see that they can become quite messy. Moreover, causal maps and argument maps show all arguments on the same level of certainty. It is also difficult to assess the role of time, i.e., these maps are not temporal but monotonic (Huff, 1990). Nevertheless causal maps are powerful tools as decision aids supporting the choice of alternatives. Decision trees are examples of causal and argument maps. One could certainly research both the cause maps and the argument maps of entrepreneurs as they use these in creating their venture or in convincing a venture capitalist to invest in that firm. The former would be a cause map, while the latter might be an argument map.

5.5.4 Entrepreneurial Maps of Causal Relationships

The above shown illustrations are examples of cognitive maps on a high level of abstraction. We will yet provide another illustration of how cognitive maps can differ from each other. This example concerns a quasi-experiment analyzing how perception of a very real entrepreneurial reality may differ considerably (Carsrud et al., 2009). Prior knowledge and experience seem to partially explain the differences in the generated collective cognitive maps.

Three groups of people with very different experience backgrounds participated: a group of business students with no or very little practical experience, but with presumably a recent relevant theoretical education; a group technology entrepreneurs with practical experience in a related industry; and a group of managers in a large firm with practical experience and extensive understanding of the product and market used in the experiment.

The task was for the participants to select five critical success factors from a list of 21 that would be important for pursuing a specific growth strategy for a high-technology and a low-technology product. The strategies were the following: no growth, 20% annual market share growth over a period of 5 years regardless of profitability, and 20% annual profit growth over a period of 5 years. The two

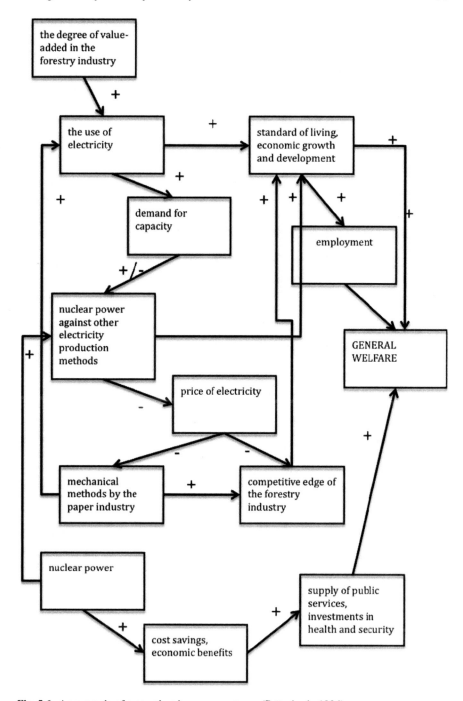

Fig. 5.6 An example of a causal and an argument map (Brännback, 1996)

products were the following: organic pasta (500 g) sold at a 20% price premium and functional food pasta (500 g) sold at a 20% price premium. Organic pasta was characterized as a low-technology product and the other as and high technology. For both, the element of technology, either its absence or its presence is used in the claim of the product's superiority. Functional food[5] is a sub-category of the life science sector. The technology entrepreneurs had experience in a related industry – another life science sector – biomaterials. While biomaterials and functional food are clearly different products, there are similarities in the fundamental science of these two sectors (e.g., biology, biochemistry, chemistry, and medicine). It was, therefore, assumed that these entrepreneurs would possess a technology-based experience that would enable them to understand the products and the markets in order to assess growth strategies. The manager group consisted of experienced middle managers employed in the same food-processing company. The company is a large food processing company, which has in recent years brought innovative products, functional foods, to the market. Recently, the company had launched a functional food pasta on the market. Thus, it was assumed that the task in the experiment was reflected in a real-life situation for this group. The only experience that the students might possess was that of consuming these products – at least ordinary pasta if the functional food version.

Each respondent was assigned *one* product and *one* strategy for which to select five critical success factors and rank them in order of importance with respect to their assigned task scenario. Finally the respondents were asked to make these considerations in two growth phases: start-up and take-off. This is important as the theory pertains that critical success factors will change depending on what stage a firm is in. Thus, the quasi-experimental design reflected the kinds of decision-making situations an entrepreneur would frequently face.

Results revealed clear differences in cognitive maps between the three groups, on all dimensions: the products, the strategies, and the different growth phases. The managers and the technology entrepreneurs were apparently better in envisioning the growth strategies as if they had already been accomplished. However, for students they remained open-ended possibilities with no linkage to hands-on experience. For the students, it seemed as if they created some order, *any order*, out there. However, the task was aimed at creating a specific order relating to a growth strategy. In fact, students had problems in distinguishing between "no growth" and "annual profit growth" strategies and they could not at all distinguish between market share growth and annual profit growth strategies. They showed clear problems with conceptualizing the factors generating revenues and what generated profits. This is interesting as they were students within a school of business administration.

---

[5]Functional food contains an ingredient, a micro-nutriment, or a natural chemical product for which we have scientific results showing either significant and beneficial interactions with the bodily functions or a reduced risk of developing certain diseases. Functional food must remain foods and must demonstrate their effects in amount that can normally be expected to be consumed in the diet: they are not pills or capsules, but part of a normal food pattern

While in a seminar for Group 2 this issue was subject to a lengthy discussion, where it was pointed out that although the managers had been able to distinguish between the strategies this rationale does not reflect the reality of the managers' reasoning. We were told that when launching a product, annual profit growth is not the target – although admitting it ought to be so. The actual target is market share growth (regardless of profit target). Profits are monitored by senior executives and owners, not primarily by operating managers! This certainly shows the impact of specific goals on the maps of managers.

A fourth group of data was collected on business school professors. Their patterns of cognitive elements showed little correspondence to the other three groups. This may be the result of having lumped together marketing, accounting, management, and international business professors together. In addition, a large number failed to compete adequately the questionnaire. Therefore, for publication purposes this group was not reported in Carsrud et al. (2009).

5.6 Conclusions

In this chapter, we have attempted to show that cognitive maps are a viable way of both examining the cognitive structures of entrepreneurs and understanding the differences between entrepreneurs and managers in their cognitive structures. We have also attempted to show that these maps will differ in their use and will differ based on prior experience and perceptions. We have tied a research stream in organizational behavior and strategic management to a potential research approach in the study of the cognitions of entrepreneurs. We have demonstrated how maps are tied to goals and to actions and thus to entrepreneurial motivations and perceptions.

It is clear that this stream of research into the cognitive maps of entrepreneurs has yet to be fully explored. Certainly maps, and entrepreneurial scripts, could yield significant new insights into how entrepreneurs view their world and translate that either into successful or into unsuccessful new ventures.

Finally, we have tried to demonstrate that entrepreneurial researchers likewise have such cognitive maps that influence, sometimes without awareness, their own views of the world. An interesting research question yet to be explored would be the difference in cognitive maps of entrepreneurship researchers who have actually started a venture versus those researchers whose sole experience is via research journals and theoretical discussions. We have attempted to study the cognitive maps of business faculty. In this unpublished research they clearly are not like managers, entrepreneurs, or students. We have yet to describe or explain their rather unusual maps.

References

Ackoff RL (1970) The Concept of Corporate Planning. Wiley & Sons, New York.
Ackoff RL (1977) Optimization + Objectivity = Opt out. European Journal of Operational Research 1: 1–7

Ackoff RL (1978) The art of problem solving. Wiley&sons, New York

Axelrod R (1976) Structures of Decisions. Princeton University press, Princeton NJ

Baumol WJ (1968) Entrepreneurship in economic theory. The American Economic Review 58: 64–71

Bettis RA, Prahalad CK (1995) The dominant logic: Retrospective and extension. Strategic Management Journal 16: 5–14

Bougon M, Weick K, Binkhorst D (1977) Cognition in organizations: an analysis of the Utrecht Jazz Orchestra. Administrative Science Quarterly 22: 606–639

Bougon MG (1992) Congregate cognitive maps: A unified dynamic theory of organization and strategy. Journal of Management Studies 29: 369–389

Bowman C, Johnson G (1992) Surfacing competitive strategies. European Management Journal 10: 210–219

Brännback M (1996) Strategic Decisions and Decision Support Systems. Åbo Akademi Press, Åbo

Brännback M, Carsrud A (2008) Do they see what we see? A critical Nordic tale about perceptions of entrepreneurial opportunities, goals and growth. Journal of Enterprising Culture 16: 55–89

Brännback M, Malaska P (1995) Cognitive mapping approach analyzing societal decision-making. World Futures 44: 231–245

Brännback M, Hyvönen P, Raunio H, Renko M, Sutinen R (2001) Finnish Pharma Cluster – Vision 2010, Target Programme initiated by the Finnish Pharma Cluster, TEKES Technology Review 112/2001

Busenitz LW, Barney JB (1997) Differences between entrepreneurs and managers in large organizations: Biases and heuristics in strategic decision-making. Journal of Business Venturing 12: 9–30

Calori R, Johnson G, Sarnin P (1994) CEOs cognitive maps and the scope of the organization. Strategic Management Journal 15: 437–457

Carsrud A, Brännback M, Nordberg L, Renko M (2009) Cognitive maps and perceptions of entrepreneurial growth: A quasi-experimental study in differences between technology entrepreneurs, corporate managers, and students. Journal of Enterprising Culture 17: 1–24

Charles D (2001) Lords of the Harvest, Biotech, Big Money, and the Future of Food. Perseus Publishing, Cambridge Mass.

Cummings S, Wilson D (2003) Images of Strategy. Blackwell Publishing, Oxford UK

Cyert RM, March JG (1963) A Behavioral Theory of the Firm. Prentice Hall, Engewood Cliffs NJ

Daft RL, Weick KE (1984) Toward a model of organizations as interpretation systems. Academy of Management Review 9: 284–295

Daniels K, Johnson G, de Chernatony L (1994) Differences in managerial cognitions of competition. British Journal of Management 5: S21–S29

Dess GG, Davis PS (1984) Porter's (1980) generic strategies as determinants of strategic group membership and organizational performance. Academy of Management Journal 27: 467–488

Eckhardt JT, Shane S (2003) Opportunities and entrepreneurship. Journal of Management 29: 333–349

Eden C (1988) Cognitive mapping. European Journal of Operational Research 36: 1–13

Eden C, Jones S, Sims D (1983) Messing About in Problems. Pergamon Press, Oxford

Eden C, Huxham, C (1995) Action research for study of organizations. In: Clegg S, Hardt C, Nord W (eds.), Handbook of Organization Studies. Sage, Beverly Hills

Eden C, Ackermann F (1998) Making Strategy: The Journey of Strategic Management. Sage, London

Fahey L, Narayanan VK (1989) Linking changes in revealed causal maps and environmental change: An empirical study. Journal of Management Studies 26: 361–378

Fiol CM, Huff AS (1992) Maps for managers: where are we? Where do we go from here? Journal of Management Studies 29: 267–285

Gaglio CM, Katz JA (2001) The psychological basis of opportunity identification: entrepreneurial alertness. Small Business Economics 16: 95–111

Gilbert, D. R., Hartman, E., Mauriel, J. J., Freeman, R. E. (1988) A Logic of Strategy. Ballinger Publishing Company, Cambridge, MA

Grégoire DA, Noël MX, Déry R, Béchard J-P (2006) Is there conceptual convergence in entrepreneurship research? A co-citation analysis of frontiers of entrepreneurship research, 1981–2004. Entrepreneurship Theory and Practice 30: 333–373

Grinyer PH, Spender J-C (1979) Recipes, crises, and adoption in mature industries. International Studies of Management and Organization 9: 113–133

Hill TL, Kothari T, Shea M (2008) The Emergence of Social Entrepreneurship as a Research Domain: Implications for Entrepreneurship Theory. Paper presented at Babson Entrepreneurship Research Conference Chapel Hill NC 3–6.6 2008

Hines T (2000) An evaluation of two qualitative methods (focus group interviews and cognitive maps) for conducting research into entrepreneurial decision making. Qualitative Market Research: An International Journal 3: 7–16

Hodgkinson GP (1997) The cognitive analysis of competitive structures: A review and critique. Human Relations 50: 627–654

Hodgkinson GP, Bown NJ, Maule AJ, Glaister KW, Pearman AD (1999) Breaking the frame: An analysis of strategic cognition and decision making under uncertainty. Strategic Management Journal 20: 977–985

Huff As (1990) Mapping Strategic Thought. Wiley & Sons, Chichester UK

Huff AS, Jenkins M (2002) Mapping Strategic Knowledge. Wiley & Sons, Chichester, UK

Johannisson B (2005) Entreprenörskapets väsen (in Swedish, The essence of entrepreneurship), Studentlitteratur, Lund

Johnson G, Scholes K (1988) Exploring Corporate Strategy. Prentice Hall, London

Karlöf B (1987) Business Strategy in Practice. John Wiley, Chichester, UK

Kelly GA (1955) The Psychology of Personal Constructs. W.W. Norton & Company Inc., New York

Kirzner IM (1979) Perception, Opportunity and Profit. University of Chicago Press, Chicago, IL.

Kirzner IM (1973) Competition and Entrepreneurship. University of Chicago Press, Chicago, IL.

Krippendorff K (2004) Content Analysis: An Introduction to its Methodology. Sage, Thousand Oaks CA.

Kristamuljana S (1994) Flexible strategies: Two schools of thought, Paper presented at the EIASM Workshop on Schools of Thought in Strategic Management 12–13.12 Rotterdam.

Kristensson UB (2002) Slaget om verkligheten, filosofi, omvärldsanalys, tolkning (in Swedish, The Battle about reality), Brutus Östlings Bokförlag Symposium, Stockholm.

Krueger NF (2007) What lies beneath? The experiential essence of entrepreneurial thinking. Entrepreneurship Theory and Practice 31: 123–138

Landström H (2005) Pioneers in Entrepreneurship and Small Business Research. Springer, Berlin

Learned EP, Christensen CR, Andrews KR, Guth WD (1965) Business Policy: Texts and cases. Homewood Il, Irwin

Louis MR, Sutton RI (1991) Switching cognitive gears: From habits of mind to active thinking. Human Relations, 44:55–76

March JG (1976) The technology of foolishness. In: March JG, Olsen JP (eds.) Ambiguity and Choice in Organizations. Universitetsforlaget, Bergen, Norway, pp. 69–81

March JG, Simon HA (1958) Organization. Wiley & Sons, New York

Mintzberg H (1976) Planning on the left side and managing on the right side. Harvard Business Review 54: 49–58

Mintzberg H (1987) The strategy concept I: Five Ps for strategy. California Management Review 30: 11–24

Mintzberg H, Ahlstrand B, Lampel J (1998) Strategy Safari. Prentice Hall, London

Mitchell RK, Smith JB, Morse EA, Seawright K, Peredo AM, McKenzie B (2002) Are entrepreneurial cognitions universal? Assessing entrepreneurial cognitions across cultures. Entrepreneurship Theory and Practice 26: 9–32

Mitchell RK, Busenitz L, Bird B, Gaglio CM, McMullen J, Morse E, Smith B (2007) The central question in entrepreneurial cognition research 2007. Entrepreneurship Theory and Practice 31: 1–27.

Nonaka I (1990) The knowledge creating company. Harvard Business Review 68: 96–104

Oliver RW (1999) The Coming Biotech Age, The Business of Bio-Materials. McGraw-Hill, New York

Pence GE (2002) Designer Food. Rowman & Littlefield Publishers Inc., Lanham.

Polanyi M (1967) The Tacit Dimension. Routledge & Kegan Paul Ltd., London

Porac JF, Thomas H (1990) Taxonomic mental models in competitor definition. Academy of Management Review 15: 224–240

Porter ME (1980) Competitive Strategy. The Free Press, New York

Prahalad CK, Bettis R (1986) The dominant logic: A new linkage between diversity and performance. Strategic Management Journal 7: 485–501

Reger RK, Palmer TB (1996) Managerial categorization of competitors: Using old maps to navigate new environments. Organization Science 7: 22–39

Russell RD (1999) Developing a process model of intrapreneurial systems: A cognitive mapping approach. Entrepreneurship Theory and Practice 23: 65–84

Saraswathy SD (2001) Causation and effectuation: Toward a theoretical shift from economic inevitability to entrepreneurial contingency. Academy of Management Review 26: 243–263

Saraswathy SD (2003) Entrepreneurship as the science of the artificial. Journal of Economic Psychology 24: 203–220

Saraswathy SD (2008) Effectuation: Elements of Entrepreneurial Expertise. Edward Elgar, New York

Schumpeter J (1934) The Theory of Economic Development. Harvard University Press, Boston

Schwenck CR (1988) The cognitive perspective on strategic decision making. Journal of Management Studies 25: 41–55

Shane S (2003) A General Theory of Entrepreneurship. Edward Elgar, Cheltenham

Shane S, Venkataraman S (2000) The promise of entrepreneurship as a field of research. Academy of Management Review 25: 217–226

Spender J-C (1989) Industry Recipe – An Enquiry into the Nature and Sources of Managerial Judgement. Basil Blackwell, New York

Walsh JP (1995) Managerial and organizational cognition: Notes from a trip down memory lane. Organization Science 6: 280–321

Weick KE (1979) The Social Psychology of Organizing (2nd ed.). Addison-Wesley, Reading, MA.

Weick KE (1990) Cartographic myths in organizations. In: Huff AS (ed) Mapping Strategic Thought. Wiley & Sons, Chichester UK, pp. 1–10

Chapter 6
Entrepreneurial Scripts and Entrepreneurial Expertise: The Information Processing Perspective

Ronald K. Mitchell, Benjamin T. Mitchell, and J. Robert Mitchell

Abstract Entrepreneurial scripts that represent entrepreneurial expertise enable researchers to begin to map the entrepreneurial mind. This chapter provides a complete demonstration of the steps needed by researchers to uncover the structure and content of the expert script knowledge structures that entrepreneurs utilize and to relate the use of these scripts to substantive organizational and entrepreneurial consequences.

6.1 Introduction

What is Mind?
No matter.
What is matter?
Never mind.[1]

Q: Is this passage believable?

A: In the case of entrepreneurship, the relationship between mind and matter is never more evident than in the new combination/creative destruction process (Shumpeter, 1934) invoked by entrepreneurs. But remarkably, until the role of the entrepreneurial mind was explicitly considered in individual entrepreneur-focused research, the connection between mind and matter – entrepreneur and new venture performance – remained elusive.

About 15 years ago (1994), a new narrative began in the search for the "E" in new venture formation entrepreneurship, with the suggestion that entrepreneurship be studied as a form of expertise (Mitchell, 1994; Dew et al., 2009). Previously, until Herron (1990) demonstrated that entrepreneurial skill and skill propensity

---

R.K. Mitchell (✉)
Rawls College of Business, Texas Tech University, Lubbock, Texas 79409-2101, USA
e-mail: ronald.mitchell@ttu.edu

[1] The above passage is a reordering and repunctuation of a quotation by Albert Baez (1967) used by Tom Stonier in the Prologue to his book *Information and the internal structure of the universe*, 1990: Springer-Verlag: London.

A.L. Carsrud, M. Brännback (eds.), *Understanding the Entrepreneurial Mind*,
International Studies in Entrepreneurship 24, DOI 10.1007/978-1-4419-0443-0_6,
© Springer Science+Business Media, LLC 2009

are related to venture performance, the persistent attempts of researchers to link the entrepreneur himself/herself to performance (Cooper et al., 1986; Kunkel, 1991; MacMillan and Day, 1987; McDougall, 1987; Sandberg, 1986) met with little success. At that time, it was industry structure and venture strategy that weighed most heavily in this calculus (e.g., Sandberg, 1986). Now, in this newly forming narrative, the focus is turning to the expert scripts of entrepreneurs to distinguish entrepreneurial experts from novices (e.g., Mitchell and Chesteen, 1995; Gustafsson, 2004), entrepreneurs across cultures (e.g., Mitchell and Seawright, 1995; Mitchell et al., 2000, 2002), and common entrepreneurial cognitions across levels of analysis (Smith et al., 2009). In fact, Dew et al. (2009: 4) suggest that what makes the scientific study of entrepreneurial expertise interesting is the commonality underlying cognitive processes that support expertise across domains (e.g., Glaser, 1984) while each individual domain – such as entrepreneurship – exhibits a rather narrow set of entrepreneurial cognition principles that are typically very specific and are therefore highly useful in developing expertise through teaching entrepreneurship-specific problem-solving and decision-making techniques (e.g., Mitchell, 2003, 2005). The common thread is human information processing.

One of the important ideas that the information processing perspective has contributed to the study of the problem-solving and decision-making techniques used in management is the concept of a script: a knowledge structure or schema (Lord and Maher, 1991a; Walsh, 1995), which refers to organized knowledge about an information environment that gives meaning to concepts or stimuli (Fiske and Taylor, 1984). Research interest in the mental templates that guide top-down information processing (Abelson and Black, 1986) has been generated in part because of the possibility that the exceptional schema-based performance of experts (Ericsson et al., 1993; Glaser, 1984) – that has been demonstrated in a variety of fields such as chess (Chase and Simon, 1973b), computer programming (McKeithen et al., 1981), law enforcement (Lurigio and Carroll, 1985), and physics (Chi et al., 1982) – might be harnessed and effectively operationalized within the field of management. However, until recently, research results in the study of managerial and organizational cognition have been fragmented (Walsh, 1995) and have been limited to particular substantive (content) areas (Lord and Maher, 1991a). Further, no general approach has yet been suggested that provides an example of how to systematically examine management-domain specialties such as entrepreneurship, to articulate their knowledge structure, and then to utilize such structures in their further study.

In a recapitulation of the information processing perspective in management research, Walsh (1995) urges scholars in the field to (1) uncover the content and structure of particular knowledge structures that managers might use and (2) " ... relate the use of this knowledge structure to consequences of substantive organizational importance ... " (Walsh, 1995, 282). In this chapter, consistent with this call and using the past 15 years as a guide, we illustrate the knowledge structures of individuals who specialize in new venture formation – the "E" in new venture formation entrepreneurship.

This chapter addresses both aspects of Walsh's (1995) call to first illuminate and then to operationalize knowledge structure research in a substantive area. To accomplish this we must tell the information processing story: to explain how the concepts have developed and lay out the key definitions, as we do in the first section. In the second section of the chapter we take on Task #1: to describe and demonstrate the steps needed to uncover (illuminate) entrepreneurial expert scripts (the structure and content of the knowledge structure used by individual entrepreneurs). Then, in the third section of the chapter, we take on Task #2: and relate the use of this knowledge structure to substantive consequences by describing a prototypical approach for identifying the script-based components of new venture formation expertise and for distinguishing entrepreneurial expertise in individuals (e.g., experts from novices) that has now become somewhat well established in the literature and suggest a template for future research. We conclude in the fourth section, by looking toward the future of entrepreneurial scripts-based research as set within the context of researching the entrepreneurial mind.

6.2 Concepts and Definitions

Information processing theory attempts to explain how information is acquired, stored, and retrieved from the memory of individuals (Neisser, 1967). In its short history, the study of human information processing has developed through three somewhat overlapping phases, each one leading ever closer to enabling the study of the entrepreneurial mind. Table 6.1 presents a chronology of key research that has led to the current capability of researchers to use information processing theory (Table 6.1, Section 1), expert information processing theory (Table 6.1, Section 2), and the notion of expert scripts (Table 6.1, Section 3) as one important means by which the entrepreneurial mind can be investigated.

As illustrated in Section 1 of Table 6.1, information processing theory has its roots in the idea that information is a function of human action and that human action can differ vis-à-vis the processes that result in information – that is, information processing. Of particular importance in this phase of research is the (fitting) recognition that there are systematic elements to the processes/processing of information. This results in the development of models that can explain these differences. Lord and Maher (1990) highlight four of these general models each of which provide implicit frameworks for research: rational, limited capacity, expert, and cybernetic. While they note that no single framework is superior, each approach possesses a unique capacity to explain elements of information processing for specific situations and purposes. Of particular interest to management scholars is the expert model because of its potential for explaining dramatic individual-based performance differences between the group with expertise and the group without.

According to expert information processing theory, experts store and retrieve information from long-term memory differently than do novices. Experts utilize

Table 6.1 Information processing, expert information processing, and expert scripts – a selected chronology

Year	Author(s)	Excerpt	Application to this chapter narrative
		Section 1: INFORMATION PROCESSING THEORY	
1937	von Hayek. FA	…before we can explain why people commit mistakes, we must first explain why they should ever be right (1937, 34); Two concepts of data (that explain this) are really fundamentally different and ought to be kept carefully apart … (1) that the subjective data possessed by individuals are mutually compatible; and (2) whether the individual subjective sets of data correspond to the objective data (1937, 39–40)	Knowledge depends on explanations that render data into information
1956	Miller, GA	(Consists of) …experiments in absolute judgment: …experiments on the capacity of people to transmit information … (and) would not have been done without the appearance of information theory (1956, 81)	Such an exercise of human judgment requires a theory of information
1972	Newell, A; Simon, HA	…states the theory [information processing theory] in comprehensive form (1972, 14)	The notion that humans "process" information provides a theoretical foundation for future work
1977	Shiffrin, RM; Schneider, W	A general framework for human information processing is proposed; the framework emphasizes the roles of automatic and controlled processing (1977, 127)	Types of processing are then explored, e.g., automatic and controlled
1979	Lachman R; Lachman, J; Butterfield, EC	An analogy to computers explains the operation of the information-processing system as a whole. In this analogy, information processing is guided by preexisting routines which are similar to computer programs. These routines are stored in long-term memory, but their execution involves short-term memory or attentional capacity (from Lord and Mayer, 1990)	Processing considerations lead to the rise of the computer metaphor to describe human information processing
1986	Bourne, LE; Dominowski, RL; Loftus, EF; Healy, AF	Cognitive psychologists face the enormous task of explaining phenomena…in systematic, scientific terms. The approach that seems to show the most promise of providing an explanation is based on the notion that human beings are systems for processing information (1986, 11–12)	The computer metaphor further develops; and humans are conceptualized as information processing systems

Table 6.1 (continued)

Year	Author(s)	Excerpt	Application to this chapter narrative
1990	Lord, RG; Maher, KJ	A general taxonomic system of alternative information-processing models (rational, limited capacity, expert, and cybernetic) found in the management and psychological literatures is developed (1990, 9)	Several types of information processing models develop and are summarized for relevance to the management literature
1995	Walsh, JP	A host of research challenges are identified to help develop a better understanding of knowledge structure representation, development, and use in organizations (1995, 280)	Information processing in organizations presents research challenges
1997	Hinsz, VB; Tindale, RS; Vollrath, DA	A selective review of research highlights the emerging view of groups as information processors .... A combination of contributions framework provides an additional conceptualization of information processing in groups (1997, 43)	A natural extension of individual information processing to organizations suggests a group level of analysis
1998	Schwarz, N	Since the late 1970s, theorizing in psychological social psychology has been dominated by the computer metaphor of information processing models, which fostered an emphasis on "cold" cognition and the conceptualization of individuals as isolated information processors.... The emerging picture is compatible with social psychology's latest metaphor, humans as motivated tacticians who pragmatically adapt their reasoning strategies to the requirements at hand (1998, 239)	As the study of humans within organization develops, the field migrates away from the computer metaphor of information processing toward a notion of humans as motivated tacticians with pragmatically adaptive reasoning
		Section 2: EXPERT INFORMATION PROCESSING THEORY	
1946 (1965)	De Groot, AD	Investigated the cognitive requirements and the thought processes involved in moving a chess piece. .. (and suggested) that visual memory and visual perception are important attributors and that problem-solving ability is of paramount importance	An initial linkage is suggested between expert task performance (e.g., in chess) and visual memory and visual perception
1973	Simon, HA; Chase, WG	.. proposed the first general theory of expertise, and it was based on the human–information processing theory (Newell and Simon, 1972), which assumes that normal, healthy human adults do not differ in terms of basic short-term memory capacity and other fundamental characteristics of elementary cognitive processes (from Ericsson, 2005, 234)	The idea develops that experts are different cognitively: specifically in terms of information processing

Table 6.1 (continued)

Year	Author(s)	Excerpt	Application to this chapter narrative
1973	Chase, WG; Simon, HA	Chase and Simon (1973a, b) extended de Groot's (1946) original findings and demonstrated a new paradigm for studying the complex memory representations of experts (from Ericsson, 2005, 235)	A new way to study the complex memory of experts is proposed
1973	Chase, WG; Simon, HA	This paper develops a technique for isolating and studying the perceptual structures that chess players perceive (1973a, 55)	Puts forward techniques that might be useful for studying expert perceptions
1981	Chase, WG; Ericsson, KA	. . skilled memory is the rapid and efficient utilization of memory in some knowledge domain to perform a task at an expert level . . . (herein) we present our analysis of the cognitive processes underlying this memory feat, and we want to use this specific example to develop what we think are the important theoretical principles that we have discovered about skilled memory (1981, 141)	Introduces the idea that skilled memory might explain expert performance
1982	Chase, WG; Ericsson, KA	A theory of skilled memory is proposed in which the size of working memory expands as skill increases (1982, 1)	Elaborates the idea of skilled memory as an expansion of expert working memory
1983	Fiske, ST; Kinder, DR; Larter, WM	. . for experts , but not for novices , knowledge-based inferences were mediated by their clustering of recall . . . . Expert/novice differences in the use of shared knowledge content encourages more focus on individual differences in strategies for the use of prior knowledge in social cognition (1983, 381)	Proposes the idea (that is later dominant in the literature) that expertise involves both a knowledge base and problem-solving processes
1992	Day, DV; Lord, RG	. . to understand more fully the role of managerial cognition in organizations. As such, we (found that) . . . experts rely on well-developed, context-dependent Entrepreneurial cognitions in the early stages of their decision making. It is argued that such Entrepreneurial cognitions allow organizational experts to make sense of strategic issues . . . (1992, 35)	Begins to suggest the application of expert entrepreneurial cognitions to organizations
1993	Ericsson, KA; Krampe, RT; Tesch-Romer, C	. . explains expert performance as the end result of individuals' prolonged efforts to improve performance . . . . Individual differences, even among elite performers, are closely related to assessed amounts of deliberate practice. Many characteristics once believed to reflect innate talent are actually the result of intense practice extended for a minimum of 10 years (1993, 363)	Introduces the notion of deliberate practice as a key explanation for individual differences in expert performance

Table 6.1 (continued)

Year	Author(s)	Excerpt	Application to this chapter narrative
1994	Ericsson, KA; Charness, N	Counter to the common belief that expert performance reflects innate abilities and capacities, recent research in different domains of expertise has shown that expert performance is predominantly mediated by acquired complex skills and physiological adaptations (1994, 725)	Counters the "innate abilities" argument that has previously predominated in explanations for expert performance
1994	Mitchell, RK	Differences in new venture formation expertise are explained (where) entrepreneurship theory and expert information processing theory are combined (to result) in the following: (1) the composition of new venture formation expertise is delineated on the basis of empirical findings, (2) The classification of individual venturers into more finely discriminated categories between expert and novice is made more practical, and (3) the process of creating additional expertise in new venture formation novices is documented, better understood, and improved (1994, 5)	Suggests that expert scripts might explain new venture formation (entrepreneurship)
1995	Ericsson, KA; Kintsch, W	In the proposed theoretical framework cognitive processes are viewed as a sequence of stable states representing end products of processing. In skilled activities, acquired memory skills allow these end products to be stored in long term memory and kept directly accessible by means of retrieval cues in short-term memory, as proposed by skilled memory theory. These theoretical claims are supported by a review of evidence on memory in text comprehension and expert performance in such domains as mental calculation, medical diagnosis, and chess (1995, 211)	Begins to explain how expertise works (e.g., underlying processes, etc.)
1996	Mitchell, RK	Under the principles of information processing theory, expert scripts explain the remarkable performance differences between otherwise "mystical" experts, and novices. Where script content is traced from entrepreneurial oral histories to shared interpretations, insider knowledge is demystified, and practical, understandable insights about how insider-entrepreneurs think are obtained. In this way management history serves the cause of management science (1996, 51)	Provides qualitative evidence and theory to support expert information processing explanations for entrepreneurship

Table 6.1 (continued)

Year	Author(s)	Excerpt	Application to this chapter narrative
1998	Gobet, F; Simon, HA	… this paper re-examines experimentally the finding of Chase and Simon (1973a) that the differences in ability of chess players at different skill levels to copy and to recall positions are attributable to the experts' storage of thousands of chunks . … (Results) are highly correlated with those of Chase and Simon. We conclude that the two-second inter-chunk interval used to define chunk boundaries is robust, and that chunks have psychological reality (1998, 225)	Links the concept of chunking to expert script explanations
1998	Sarasvathy, DK; Simon, HA; Lave, L	We compared entrepreneurs with bankers in their perception and management of a variety of risks. Problems included financial risk, risk to human life and health, and risk of a natural disaster. Cluster analysis and content analysis of think-aloud protocols revealed surprising details. Entrepreneurs accept risk as given and focus on controlling the outcomes at any given level of risk; they also frame their problem spaces with personal values and assume greater personal responsibility for the outcomes. Bankers focus on target outcomes – attempting to control risk within structured problem spaces and avoiding situations where they risk higher levels of personal responsibility (1998, 207)	Suggests an expertise-based explanation for traditionally trait-based explanations for entrepreneurship (e.g., risk taking)
1999	Kintsch, W; Patel, VL; Ericsson, KA	A distinction is made between short-term working memory, which is capacity limited, and long-term working memory, which is available to experts in their domain of expertise (1999, 186)	Links work and long-term memory to domain expertise
2003	Ericsson, KA	Discussed here are the implications for broad attainability of highly skilled memory performance in professional and everyday activities (2003, 233)	Refines memory-based explanations for expertise in the professions
2003	Mitchell, RK	Performance comes from cognitions created through deliberate practice (Ericsson et al., 1993), which depends upon individuals' endowments (Ericsson and Charness, 1994; Gardner, 1983; Gardner, 1993) (2003, 195)	Suggests deliberate practice to be a key factor in individual-based explanations for entrepreneurship

Table 6.1 (continued)

Year	Author(s)	Excerpt	Application to this chapter narrative
2004	Ericsson, KA; Delaney, PF; Weaver, G; Mahadevan, R	Our paper describes a general experimental approach for studying the structure of exceptional memory (2004, 191)	Delves deeply into the mechanisms used in exceptional memory feats, specifically in the information encoding process
2005	Ericsson, KA	… a new trend (is emerging) towards capturing the expert performance with representative tasks in the laboratory and focus on how this superior performance is acquired through training and extended deliberate practice (2005, 233)	Suggests how the study of expert performance can benefit from laboratory studies of deliberate practice
2005	Mitchell, RK	The … implication of the findings in Mitchell and Chesteen (1995) is to establish links among deliberate practice, script enhancement, and transaction cognition theory. The link between deliberate practice and script/ expertise enhancement is established through confirmation of the relationship between certain deliberate practice activities – in this case direct contact with individuals who are more expert, which students analyzed metacognitively (by being required to "think about their thinking") – and changes in the subjects' cognitive scripts . … There exist both empirical evidence and evidence from educational practice, which suggest that (the deliberate practice model) may in fact, be generalizable to the education of global entrepreneurs (2005, 190, 206)	Refines the educational implications for the deliberate-practice-based education of entrepreneurs in a general (global) setting
2009	Dew, N; Read, S; Sarasvathy, SD; Wiltbank, R	In support of theory, this study demonstrates that entrepreneurial experts frame decisions using an "effectual" logic (identify more potential markets, focus more on building the venture as a whole, pay less attention to predictive information, worry more about making do with resources on hand to invest only what they could afford to lose, and emphasize stitching together networks of partnerships); while novice use a "predictive frame" and tend to "go by the textbook" (2008, 1)	Begins the further exploration of how expert information processing translates to the actual processes whereby entrepreneurs select and enact decisions

Table 6.1 (continued)

Year	Author(s)	Excerpt	Application to this chapter narrative
		Section 3: SCRIPTS/ KNOWLEDGE STRUCTURES	
1976	Abelson, RP	Script processing in attitude formation and decision making	Relates scripts and decision making
1977	Schank, RC; Abelson, RP	Sometimes having recourse to knowledge of a standard sequence of events, the reasons for which we have already determined to our satisfaction, is useful in the understanding process. When a waitress comes to our table with food in a restaurant it is not necessary to figure out what caused her to arrive. It is sufficient to have knowledge of the causal sequence of events in restaurants to allow us to behave appropriately. This knowledge leaves more cognitive capacity available for use in more interesting tasks. It also allows a certain amount of ellipsis in textual accounts of situations that have a commonly recognized sequence of events. These standard sequences of events have been termed scripts (Schank and Abelson, 1977, as cited in Abbott and Black, 1986, 130)	Develops further the idea that understood task sequence helps to explain expertise due to added cognitive capacity
1982	Glaser, R	… experts store and retrieve information from long-term memory differently than novices do (1982, 292)	Begins to explore expert–novice distinctions in terms of information retrieval
1984	Glaser, R	The interaction between the development of problem-solving and learning skills and the acquisition of structures of domain-specific knowledge is discussed. Suggestions are made for developing thinking abilities in the context of the acquisition of knowledge and skill (1984, 93)	Provides a foundation for both distinguishing experts and novices, and also for explaining the learning processes leading to expertise
1986	Leddo, J; Abelson, RP	… the hierarchical, goal–subgoal organization of scripts permits individuals to make attributions that depend upon how events proceed sequentially … the opportunity to distinguish novices from experts occurs at two key points in expertise-specific situations, when the performance of an expert script (an attempt to utilize expertise) might fail … these points occur either: (1) at the time of script "entry," or (2) as individuals engage in "doing" the things that serve the main goal of a script … script "entry" depends upon " … having the objects in question" … "doing" depends upon two subrequirements: ability and willingness (1986, 121)	Suggests a general sequential structure useful to the study of professional expertise that leads to the higher-level constructs that appear in new venture formation expertise: arrangements, willingness, and ability

Table 6.1 (continued)

Year	Author(s)	Excerpt	Application to this chapter narrative
1987	Lord, RG; Kernan, MC	This paper focuses on the role cognitive scripts, a unique type of knowledge schema, play in generating purposive behaviors in organizations (1987, 265)	Links scripts to organization
1987	Read, SJ	A model of causal reasoning based on Schank and Abelson's (1977) analysis of knowledge structures is presented. The first part of this article outlines the necessary characteristics of such a model . . .. The second part of this article analyzes how the knowledge structures outlined by Schank and Abelson (1977) – scripts, plans, goals, and themes – can be used to construct such causal scenarios, and it presents a process model for the construction of such scenarios (1987, 288)	Suggests the nature of the causal scenarios that provide a basis for the measurement and analysis of expert scripts
1987	Olson, JR; Rueter, HH	. . . methods developed by cognitive science to reveal human knowledge structures . . . are (in) two classes of investigative methods, direct and indirect (1987, 152)	Provides a foundation for the script-cue measurement method
1988	Glaser, R	Experts efficiently translate problem information in a situation into problem solutions (1988, 269)	Suggests how cueing might enable the classification of experts from novices
1995	Mitchell, RK; Chesteen, SA	In this paper we link entrepreneurial expertise with the notion of an expert "script" as a means for enhancing entrepreneurial expertise. The focus of this paper is an instructional pedagogy that improves students' entrepreneurial expertise through the application of the recommendations of expert information theorists regarding script acquisition. Expert information theory suggests contact with expert scripts as a primary means for acquiring expertise. Concepts from the simulation and gaming literature are employed to design the pedagogy which features such contact as its primary emphasis (1995, 288)	Applies current expert information processing theory to suggest a way to enhance new venture formation expertise and to measure the results using script cues
1999	Glass, RS; Oz, E	This study uses verbal protocol analysis to identify and compare the information cues used by experts and novices (while) performing software diagnosis tasks (1999, 40)	Describes how protocol analysis can also be used to assess expert information cueing

Table 6.1 (continued)

Year	Author(s)	Excerpt	Application to this chapter narrative
2000	Woloschuk, W; Harasym, P; Mandin, H; Jones, A	This study sought to determine the extent to which faculty and students were implementing and utilizing scheme-based problem solving ... the benefits of schemes for problem solving was also evident (2000, 437)	Further develops the problem-solving element of deliberate practice
2000	Mitchell, RK; Smith, JB; Seawright, KK; Morse, EA	Arrangements, willingness, and ability scripts are found to be associated with the venture creation decision, while some two-way interaction effects involving arrangements scripts were also significant. Cultural values of individualism and power-distance are found to be associated with willingness and ability cognitive scripts, and to also to be associated with the venture creation decision through interaction with arrangements scripts. These results support and extend theory, and provide preliminary evidence of consistency in cognitive scripts across cultures (2000, 974)	Applies expert information processing theory and script-cue recognition methods to test a model of cross-cultural entrepreneurship
2001	Day, EA; Arthur, W; Gettman, D	The purpose of this study was to examine the viability of knowledge structures as an operationalization of learning in the context of a task that required a high degree of skill (2001, 1022)	Applies scripts/ knowledge structures to the learning in a high-skill task domain
2002	Mitchell, RK; Smith, JB; Morse, EA; Seawright, KW; Peredo, AM; McKenzie, B	In this study we examine three research questions concerned with entrepreneurial cognition and culture: (1) Do entrepreneurs have cognitions distinct from those of other business people? (2) To what extent are entrepreneurial cognitions universal? (3) To what extent do entrepreneurial cognitions differ by national culture? ... using data collected in a field setting that included 990 respondents in eleven countries. We find ... that individuals who possess "professional entrepreneurial cognitions" do indeed have cognitions that are distinct from business non-entrepreneurs ... further confirmation of a universal culture of entrepreneurship ... and in answer to question three, we find (a) observed differences on eight of the ten proposed cognition constructs, and (b) that the pattern of country representation within an empirically-developed set of entrepreneurial archetypes does indeed differ among countries. Our results suggest increasing credibility for the cognitive explanation of entrepreneurship in the cross-cultural setting (2002, 9)	Applies scripts/ knowledge structures to differentiating entrepreneurs from nonentrepreneurs and to establishing the extent to which entrepreneurial cognition is more universal across cultures. On the basis of scripts, a set of entrepreneurial cognitive archetypes is developed

Table 6.1 (continued)

Year	Author(s)	Excerpt	Application to this chapter narrative
2003	Davis, MA; Curtis, MB; Tschetter, JD	. . . a key factor in differentiating expert and novice performance is the way individuals organize their knowledge . . . measures of structural knowledge quality predicted individual differences in performance self-efficacy (2003, 322)	Further explores expert knowledge organization
2004	Zohar, D; Luria, G	. . . script orientation . . . predicted climate level, whereas script simplicity and cross-situational variability predicted climate strength (2004, 322)	Applies script-based observation to explain other organizational features: e.g., climate
2005	Jones, DK; Read, SJ	Experts relied more on events; used a more historical analysis consisting of past states, events, goals, and actions; and, most important, relied heavily on causal reasoning to create a coherent, understandable causal scenario or narrative. In addition, experts' overall explanation networks were significantly more connected (but less centralized) than those of the other groups (2005, 45)	Suggests how expertise – as a social phenomenon (e.g., networks) – might operate in general
2006	Bradley, JH; Paul, R; Seeman, E	. . . experience alone is not an indicator of expertise. Other factors, such as the cognitive ability to correctly structure those experiences, must also be present (2006, 77)	Reaffirms that expertise and experience are not synonymous
2007	Corbett, AC; Hmieleski, KM	In this article, we examine the interplay and divergence between the role schema of individuals in corporations and the event schemas necessary to launch a new venture. By examining these schemas together, we show how the corporate context can create tension between corporate entrepreneurs' role schemas and the event schemas necessary for entrepreneurship (2007, 103)	Further dimensionalizes the expert/ novice analysis repertoire by differentiating between corporate and independent entrepreneurship
2007	Corbett, AC; Neck, HM; DeTienne, DR	. . . we advance the literature on entrepreneurial human capital by linking cognitive scripts used by corporate entrepreneurs in project termination decisions to corresponding levels of learning (2007, 829)	Applies entrepreneurial scripts in the corporate entrepreneurship setting

Table 6.1 (continued)

Year	Author(s)	Excerpt	Application to this chapter narrative
2009	Dew, N; Read, S; Sarasvathy, SD; Wiltbank, R	In support of theory, this study demonstrates that entrepreneurial experts frame decisions using an "effectual" logic (identify more potential markets, focus more on building the venture as a whole, pay less attention to predictive information, worry more about making do with resources on hand to invest only what they could afford to lose, and emphasize stitching together networks of partnerships); while novice use a "predictive frame" and tend to "go by the textbook" (2008, 1)	Again, further dimensionalizes the nature of entrepreneurial expertise by demonstrating differences in the underlying logics (e.g., framing) between experts and novices
2008	Kabanoff, B; Brown, S	We explore the content and structure of top managers' strategic knowledge structures by measuring differences in the level of attention they give in annual reports to strategic issues and themes that Miles and Snow used to describe their main strategic types (2008, 149)	Addresses the need to further uncover the content of various expert scripts (e.g., Walsh, 1995)
2008	Seawright, KW; Mitchell, RK; Smith, JB	This research examines cognitive similarities and differences among Russian and U.S. entrepreneurs and nonentrepreneurs. Manova and multiple discriminant analysis results found similarities between U.S. and Russian experts and U.S. and Russian novices with respect to Arrangements, Willingness, and Ability scripts, but differences in these scripts were found between experts and novices, particularly in Russia (2008, 1)	Applies entrepreneurial script explanations to analyze the unexpectedly low entrepreneurship levels in a newly forming market economy
2008	Sarasvathy, S	Suggests how entrepreneurs use logic and insight used to convert problems into opportunities. Effectuation empirics are observations of 27 entrepreneurs which revealed how each individual converted "as if" circumstances into "even if" ones. Cognition of these entrepreneurs compared to MBA students showed stark differences between the ways the two groups approached problem solving. MBA's largely used "causal logic" – starting with a specific goal or desired effect and working towards that end. In contrast, the entrepreneurs used "effectual logic," beginning with themselves and being creative with the resources they had to work with	Provides fine-grained analysis and characterization of entrepreneurial thinking processes as distinct from those of novices

Table 6.1 (continued)

Year	Author(s)	Excerpt	Application to this chapter narrative
2008	Mitchell, RK; Mitchell, JR; Smith, JB	In this article, we: (1) elaborate on the critical dimensions that represent a multi-construct view of the new transaction commitment mindset and describe ways that these dimensions can be measured; (2) examine the extent to which the recognition of new venture failure impacts the new transaction commitment mindset; and (3) explore the implications of the interaction between failure recognition and the new transaction commitment mindset for an entrepreneur's decision to continue or abandon opportunity creation efforts (2008, 1)	Begins the more fine-grained exploration of entrepreneurial mindsets by assessing the impact of recognizing failure on the opportunity creation process
2009	Smith, JB; Mitchell, JR; Mitchell, RK	… this paper: (1) clarifies the nature of the relationship between entrepreneurial expert scripts and constructs that might represent an entrepreneurial mindset at the individual level of analysis, (2) identifies analogous relationships at the economy level of analysis where the structure found at the individual level informs an economy-level problem, (3) presents a NAFTA-based illustration analysis to demonstrate the extent to which cognitive findings at the individual level can be used to explain economy-level phenomena, and (4) extrapolates from our analysis some of the ways in which script-based comparisons across country or culture can inform the more general task of making information processing-based comparisons among entrepreneurs across other contexts	Elaborates the usefulness of scripts to enable explanations of how individual-level phenomena (e.g., entrepreneurial scripts) impact economy-level outcomes (e.g., NAFTA trade-issue resolution). Suggests an approach to burgeoning interest in cross-level entrepreneurial cognition research

highly developed knowledge systems based in long-term memory to establish and maintain exceptional capabilities in specialty areas (Lord and Maher, 1990). These knowledge systems are organized around context-relevant scripts (Read, 1987). The main assertion of the expert information processing model is that experts outperform novices within their area of expertise because they can recognize immediately that which novices require great effort to discover – compliance of expertise-specific circumstances with an expert script. The cornerstone literature upon which expert information processing theory concepts are based are presented in Section 2 of Table 6.1. A critical contribution of expert information processing research that is evident in this section is its usefulness in elucidating the latent structure of superior performance. By so doing, it provides a pathway for improving performance. This explanation stands in opposition to previous research that deterministically viewed superior performance as being based in innate abilities and traits. In this way, expert information processing research is fundamental to entrepreneurship research. Interestingly, it is one element of expert information processing theory that has become highly useful in the investigation of the entrepreneurial mind: the notion of expert scripts.

The term " expert script" refers to highly developed, sequentially ordered knowledge in a specific field (Glaser, 1984; Leddo and Abelson, 1986; Lord and Maher, 1990; Read, 1987). Scripts are defined as commonly recognized sequences of events that permit rapid comprehension of expertise-specific information by experts (Schank and Abelson, 1977), as cited in Abbott and Black, 1986. An expert script is most often acquired through extensive real-world experience, and it dramatically improves the information processing capability of an individual (Glaser, 1984), although not without the danger of promoting thinking errors such as stereotypic thinking, the inhibition of creative problem solving, and the discouragement of disconfirmation of the script in the face of discrepant information (Walsh, 1995). Expert information processing theory generally treats the terms knowledge structure and expert script as synonymous.

The cornerstone literature upon which expert script concepts are based are presented in Section 3 of Table 6.1. The research that is highlighted in this section of the table is important to entrepreneurship because it articulates the action-based steps of experts in their decision making. This is important to the field of entrepreneurship given the central role of individual action in socioeconomic activity (Commons, 1931). Additionally, research on expert scripts/knowledge structures also provides an important link between information processing-specific research and the broader literature on entrepreneurial cognition (cf. Mitchell et al., 2007).

Based upon the foregoing conceptual chronology, we are then, in Table 6.2, able to summarize the key terms and definitions that form the foundation of this essay.

We therefore turn our attention to the next section, which describes an approach that can be used to uncover structure and content in entrepreneurial expert scripts.

Table 6.2   Key terms and definitions

Term	Definition
Ability	Possessing the rudimentary techniques and skills necessary to a specialized domain (Leddo and Abelson, 1986: 121)
Cue	Pieces of information in expertise-specific problem statements that enable experts to infer further knowledge about the situation
Cue recognition	The ability to recognize a context-relevant cue from other (distracter) information in the environment
Distracter statement	A plausible, even appealing alternative to a script cue to those who are unfamiliar with the content domain (i.e., novices)
Doing	See *script doing*
Entry	See *script entry*
Expert	An individual who shows expertise in a given domain; someone with a large knowledge based in a particular content domain (Lord and Maher, 1990)
Expert information processing theory	One of the general models of information processing theory where individuals "rely on already developed knowledge structures to supplement simplified means of processing information" (Lord and Maher, 1990: 13)
Expert script	Highly developed, sequentially ordered knowledge in a specific field (Glaser, 1984; Leddo and Abelson, 1986; Lord and Maher, 1990; Read, 1987), acquired through extensive real-world experience; synonymous with *knowledge structure*
Expertise	The ability of an individual to, with excellent performance, perform a task in a particular domain
Feasibility	Having the resources available to accomplish a task
Human information processing	The view that human beings are systems for processing information (Bourne et al., 1986)
Information processing	See *information processing theory*
Information processing perspective	See *information processing theory*
Information processing theory	A theory that views an individual as a processor of information (Newell and Simon, 1972, 5) and attempts to then explain how this information is acquired, stored, and retrieved from memory (Neisser, 1967)
Knowledge categories	Broad mental categories that, when differentiated and linked, permit experts to make sense of new knowledge (Bower and Hilgard, 1981)
Knowledge structure	Organized knowledge about an information environment that gives meaning to concepts or stimuli (Fiske and Taylor, 1984)
Norm	Standard practices that guide experts to perform correctly in their area of specialty (Leddo and Abelson, 1986: 107)
Novice	An individual who does not show expertise in a given domain. Often a beginner who does not have experience in that domain

Table 6.2 (continued)

Term	Definition
Preliminary knowledge scaffold	Temporary models that "help organize new knowledge and offer a basis for problem solving that leads to the formation of more complete and expert schemata" (Glaser, 1984, 101)
Principle of coherence	Requires the use of sufficient knowledge to produce the most intelligible interpretation (Read, 1987)
Principle of concretion	Constrains interpretation to the use of the most concrete knowledge possible (Read, 1987)
Principle of least commitment	Suggests that people make no more than the minimum assumptions necessary to produce a coherent interpretation (Read, 1987)
Principle of exhaustion	Requires that an interpretation account for all the data (Read, 1987)
Principle of parsimony	Instructs people to produce an interpretation that maximizes the connections among inputs (Read, 1987)
Schema	See *knowledge structure*
Schematize	To organize knowledge in chunks or packages so that, given a bit of appropriate situational context, an individual has available many likely inferences on what might happen next in a given situation (Abelson and Black, 1986)
Script	Commonly recognized sequences of events that permit rapid comprehension of expertise-specific information by experts (Schank and Abelson, 1977); mental representations of the causality-connected actions, props, and participants that are involved in common activities (Galambos et al., 1986: p. 19)
Script cue	See *cue*
Script-cue recognition	See *cue recognition*
Script doing	Accomplishing the main action and achieving the purpose of the script. Depends on both *ability* and *willingness*
Script entry	Concerns the availability of the objects necessary for the enactment of the script. Depends on *feasibility*
Sequence	The order that a series of events/actions is in regarding a script
Structure guidelines	Criteria that help to describe the structure of relevant scripts. The guidelines include following specific metarules of story comprehension, construction steps, and rules of causal syntax
Willingness	The propensity to act

6.3 The Structure and Content of Entrepreneurial Scripts

In this section of the chapter we (1) define the structure of expert scripts, (2) identify generalized techniques which consistently furnish the essential content of such scripts, and (3) demonstrate these techniques in the case of entrepreneurs.

6.3.1 Structure

The structure of expert scripts is described in the expert information processing theory literature by several key studies (Abelson and Black, 1986; Chi et al., 1988; Glaser, 1984; Leddo and Abelson, 1986; Read, 1987) which provide the definitions needed to clarify the nature of script structure. The definitional aspects of script structure presented in the subsections that follow move from the more general to the more specific.

6.3.1.1 Sequences and Norms

The most general element of expert script structure is based upon unique differences in the knowledge organization of experts versus novices. Glaser suggests that the knowledge of novices is topical versus contextual; i.e., it is organized around the literal objects explicitly apparent in a problem statement. Hence, limitations in the thinking of novices are due to their inability to infer further knowledge from the literal cues in expertise-specific problem statements. Conversely, experts' knowledge is organized around principles and abstractions that (1) are not apparent in problem statements, (2) subsume literal objects, and (3) derive instead from a knowledge about the application of particular subject matter, leading experts to generate relevant inferences within the context of the knowledge structure or script that they have acquired (Glaser, 1984). Thus expert scripts specify context, because (1) they have a "sequential structure" and (2) they incorporate the " norms" that guide the actions of experts in their area of specialty (Leddo and Abelson, 1986: 107). Accordingly, the first, general specification of the structure of an expert script is that it should include both sequences and norms.

6.3.1.2 Categories

Experts make sense of new situations by drawing upon previously stored knowledge (Cohen and Levinthal, 1990). Bower and Hilgard suggest that this knowledge is stored in broad categories which, when differentiated and linked, permit individuals to make sense of new knowledge (Bower and Hilgard, 1981). In the case of new venture formation, these knowledge categories might include individual attributes (IA) (Carbonnell, 1979; Chi et al., 1988), individual experiences (IE) (Abelson and Black, 1986; Glaser, 1984), individual resources (IR) (Chi et al., 1988), organizational characteristics (OC) which make the knowledge structure context-specific (Lord and Maher, 1990), and prior training (PT) (Cohen and Levinthal, 1990). By pointing to areas that are important to description at the individual level of analysis, which affect outcomes at the group (expertise) and organizational (organizational formation) level (e.g., individually possessed expertise that potentially affects expertise in new venture formation) (Krackhardt, 1990; Rousseau, 1985; Walsh, 1995), these five possible knowledge categories also assist the researcher with a mid-range "preliminary knowledge scaffold" (Glaser, 1984) that supports the later identification of substantive content.

6.3.1.3 Structure Guidelines

Expert information processing theory also contains quite specific criteria that help
to describe the structure of viable scripts. The identification of specific structure
criteria is important, since the criteria utilized within any script definition framework form a "template" of sorts that can then be applied to proposed depictions
of scripts to test for compliance with expert information processing theory. Read
provides such a model. The model applies five principles or " metarules" of story
comprehension[2] (Read, 1987, 294) identified in expert information processing theory (Granger, 1980; Kay, 1982; Marr, 1977; Wilensky, 1983) that affect an individual's understanding of social interaction. The model itself consists of a six-step
construction process[3] (Read, 1987). Based upon the work of Schank and Abelson
(1977), Read's model employs six rules of causal syntax[4] that govern how various elements in a script can be causally linked. Although not explicitly recognized
by Read, Glaser adds that scripts should be constructed such that they provide literal cues in the problem statement that trigger inference on the part of the subject,
since the ". . . inability to infer further knowledge from the literal cues in the problem statement" is argued to be the reason for the ". . . problem solving difficulty of
novices" (Glaser, 1984, 99). We consider Glaser's observation regarding the differential nature of cue recognition between experts and novices to be a primary tool
for uncovering the structure and content of particular knowledge structures (scripts).
The metarules, construction steps, and rules of causal syntax, along with the nature
of the information used in script-cue development, combine to form specific script
structure criteria that may be used to judge the conformance of scripts to expert
information processing theory.

6.3.1.4 Structure Definition

Scripts thus consist of sequences, which identify precedence relationships in a goal–
subgoal framework (Read, 1987) to which adhere the norms that define the expert
expectations of each step in that sequence. Further, scripts subsume knowledge categories (five are suggested in the case of new venture formation as noted previously).
Finally, scripts are structured according to at least one of three sets of structure
guidelines against which they can be evaluated for compliance, provided that they
are also in compliance with the inferential cueing criterion specified by Glaser.

---

[2]Metarules include the principles of coherence, concretion, least commitment, exhaustion, and
parsimony.

[3]Construction steps include (1) making categorizations about people and situations, (2) connecting
subsequently observed actions with the initial scenario, (3) evaluating congruence between actions
and the underlying plan, (4) identifying the plan's goal, (5) evaluating whether the goal is part of a
larger plan or whether it is an end in itself, (6) identifying the goal's source.

[4]Rules of causal syntax include the following: (1) actions and events can result in state changes,
(2) states can enable actions and events, (3) states can disable actions, (4) states can initiate mental
states, (5) acts can initiate mental states, and (6) mental states can be reasons for actions.

6.3.2 Content

There appear to be two primary alternatives that might be used in the articulation of script content. The first alternative is comprehensive enumeration, that is, to attempt to "take a census" of all the content that relates to a particular domain. The second alternative is some type of sampling upon which inference respecting the "content whole" might be made. Comprehensive enumeration poses significant operational difficulty due to the idiosyncratic and dynamic nature of knowledge in the multitude of expert domains that exist. In fact, the impracticality of comprehensive enumeration may be one of the reasons that the identification of script content has been somewhat daunting to researchers, especially in the management domain. We speculate that one possible reason for the seeming impasse in the identification of script content is because of the assumption that few if any acceptable alternatives to comprehensive enumeration exist. This assumption likely has its roots in expert information processing theory, which has developed largely to support research in artificial intelligence (AI) and expert systems. In this research stream, comprehensive enumeration has been a virtual necessity, due to the requirements of the computer processing medium used to operationalize and test AI and expert systems.

However, there appears to be no such constraint within the management domain. With its roots in the social sciences, and by extension, in the use of inferential statistics as the tool for operationalization and testing, management science has deemed methods which rely upon the sampling of populations for inferential purposes to be acceptable. It is but a minor extension of this logic to suggest that, at least as a beginning point for management research into the content of expert scripts, a sampling of script content might be a practical alternative to comprehensive enumeration. Sampling has the advantage of serviceability, but presently lacks guidelines for operationalization. This chapter develops and operationalizes the sampling alternative, based on the concepts of script-cue recognition.

6.3.2.1 Cue Recognition

A fundamental assertion of expert information processing theory is that experts interpret cues in problem statements differently than do novices (Glaser, 1984). Interestingly, the reason for the dissimilarity of interpretation is traceable to differences in the way that individuals organize knowledge. Expert knowledge is "schematized," i.e., organized in chunks or packages so that, given a bit of appropriate situational context, an individual has many likely inferences available on what might happen next in a given situation (Abelson and Black, 1986). The notion of " knowledge chunks" prompts the speculation that if little bits of situational context (representations from expert scripts) were to be provided to individual experts and novices as cues, their ability to recognize the context as applicable to them individually might confirm the structure and content of an expert script, while also revealing individual levels of expertise. Further, the cue recognition approach suggests that sampling versus full enumeration of script content should be sufficient to discriminate experts from novices.

6.3.3 New Venture Formation Content Identification

A possible approach to uncovering the structure and content of scripts, then, is for the researcher to identify a representative body of literature (in this case a representative body of new venture formation literature) and to construct script cues on the basis of that literature. Then, utilizing the guidelines within expert information processing theory which specify the criteria for script structure, these cues are examined for consistency with expert information processing theory. In this section, the script structure guidelines and content identification techniques previously described are utilized to produce "script cues." The literature review and analysis method utilized consists of six steps as follows:

1. identify examples of new venture formation-specific knowledge;
2. classify these into those that primarily deal with the *sequence* of expert actions and those that deal with the *norms* that guide those actions;
3. focus on the five suggested knowledge categories of new venture formation: (1) individual attributes (IA), (2) individual experiences (IE), (3) individual resources (IR), (4) organization characteristics (OC), and (5) prior training (PT);
4. further subdivide the focus areas into knowledge that is related to *content* (to the substantive area) and knowledge that is related to *structure* (to the operation of scripts);
5. develop script recognition cues; and
6. compare these cues to the script construction criteria of expert information processing theory to ensure compliance of the cues with theory.

The foregoing steps outline a relatively general adaptation process that can be utilized by researchers in many domains to extract "script cues" from a given literature that are consistent with expert information processing theory. In the following section, the application of this method in the new venture formation context is demonstrated.

6.3.4 Script Structure and Content

A fairly large sampling of literature that describes the individual attributes, experiences, resources, and prior training possessed by entrepreneurs, and the characteristics of successful new ventures themselves, is available. Regarding the extent of the literature review, the application of the "sampling" approach suggested earlier necessitates the exercise of some latitude in judgment on the part of the researcher. Given the objectives of this chapter, it was deemed appropriate to utilize approximately 3 years of a specialized journal plus related texts in entrepreneurship. Accordingly, the literature review was undertaken by reviewing issues of *The Journal of Business Venturing*, the bibliographies of several prominent entrepreneurship texts, relevant expert information processing theory articles, the cognition-related work in entrepreneurship, and the reading lists for various doctoral seminars in strategy and entrepreneurship. From among several hundred titles reviewed, 28 citations that, based upon the judgment of the researchers, conform to the previously defined structure and content criteria were selected to demonstrate the sampling of knowledge from which new venture formation scripts derive. Sample citations are included both in the References section of this chapter and in Table 6.3, which illustrates the results of the sampling process. Table 6.3 citations for each knowledge category are organized under the headings " Sequence" and " Norms" and are subdivided under these two headings into references dealing with "Content" (new venture formation) and those dealing with "Structure" (expert information processing theory), as suggested in the previously developed framework.

With structure and content examples from relevant literatures selected, it becomes possible to derive script cues. The set of script recognition cues from which the items utilized in this chapter are drawn are shown in Table 6.4.

The next step in the analysis is to evaluate the structural and content veracity of script cues for compliance with expert information processing theory criteria. For the sake of simplicity and to demonstrate the "usability" of the suggested framework, a set of decision rules that follow from expert information processing theory has been adopted for convenience in this chapter and is proposed at least as a beginning point for extensions of this approach. These decision rules, along with the abbreviations used in the analysis, are as follows:

1. A script recognition cue should comply with either a "metarule," a script construction "step," or a causal "syntax" rule (Read, 1987).
2. A script recognition cue should derive from one of the knowledge categories, e.g., individual attributes (IA), experiences (IE), resources (IR) or prior training (PT), and/or organizational characteristics (OC).
3. The script recognition cue should describe either new venture formation sequences (SQ), norms (N), or both (SQ/N).
4. The script recognition cue should contain either content (C) or structural (S) elements.
5. A citation (Cite) from the entrepreneurship or expert theory literature should support, respectively, structure or content.

Table 6.5 provides examples of the results of the analysis. For each major set of theory criteria (metarules, script construction steps, and syntax rules), each of the knowledge categories is analyzed and construction implication exemplars are suggested. This analysis offers evidence that the script recognition cues derived in this chapter comply with expert information processing theory.

Table 6.3 Script content by knowledge area: new venture formation (content) and expert information processing theory (structure) literatures

Area	Sequence	Norms
IA	Content	Content
	More risk averse individuals become workers, while less risk averse individuals become entrepreneurs (Kihlstrom and Laffont, 1979); the search for an opportunity- resource match is a key feature of the entrepreneurial opportunity structure (Glade, 1967); project completion tied to Meyers–Briggs profile type (Ginn and Sexton, 1990); entrepreneurs have high tolerance for the ambiguity characteristics of new, unfolding situations (Schere, 1982)	Entrepreneurs have the qualities of assertiveness and initiative (McClelland, 1968); are moderate risk-takers who can tolerate ambiguity (Sexton and Bowman-Upton, 1985); are creators of new enterprise/combinations (Low and MacMillan, 1988; Schumpeter, 1934); use lock-in type strategic commitment to attain sustained competitive advantage (Ghemawat, 1991); have significant differences in attributes as identified by the Meyers–Briggs instrument (Ginn and Sexton, 1990)
	Structure	Structure
	Experts acquire a greater knowledge base in a specific domain (Glaser, 1984)	Expert action presupposes willingness even though mistakes might be made (Krueger, 1993)
IE	Content	Content
	Entrepreneurs engage in a deliberate process of network building (MacMillan, 1983); knowledge lies waiting to be discovered – entrepreneurs simply recognize changes which have already happened and exploit them (Loasby, 1983); previous venture experience is significant to venture performance (Stuart and Abetti, 1990); failure episodes cited as related to level of experience (Vesper, 1980)	Observed entrepreneurial attributes are the product of experience (Low and MacMillan, 1988); entrepreneurs' low need for support and conformity and high need for dominance and autonomy affects the nature of their experiences (Sexton and Bowman-Upton, 1985); entrepreneurs usually start firms related to their previous work (Cooper and Dunkelberg, 1987)
	Structure	Structure
	Experts possess a more elaborate schema which comes from more extensive experience (Chi et al., 1982); have better and less biased recall of relevant information (Fiske et al., 1983; McKeithen et al., 1981)	Becoming an expert takes extensive past experience (Lord and Maher, 1990); experts have better and less biased recall of relevant information (Fiske et al., 1983; McKeithen et al., 1981)
IR	Content	Content
	Sustained competitive advantage is a result of having and engaging strategic resources (Barney, 1991); the number of previous venture involvements is by far the most significant individual resource in early performance (Stuart and Abetti, 1990)	Entrepreneurs who raised their own venture funds had higher proportionate success (Vesper, 1980)

Table 6.3 (continued)

Area	Sequence	Norms
	Structure	Structure
	Script entry depends upon having the objects required (Leddo and Abelson, 1986); novices do not have the resources (Perkins, 1985)	Proper script entry depends upon having the objects required (Leddo and Abelson, 1986)
OC	Content	Content
	The venture incubation process is fostered by contact with other entrepreneurs (Smilor and Gill, 1986); the process of internalizing commercial information implies increasing control of assets in a firm, i.e., entrepreneurship (Casson, 1982); establishing barriers to entry linked to strategic position (Porter, 1985); the steps of entrepreneurial decision making occur within a specific organizational setting (Glade, 1967); new ventures develop in stages (Churchill and Lewis, 1983)	Organizations where isolating mechanisms are high and appropriability is low have good entrepreneurial strategy (Rumelt, 1987); the entrepreneurial locus of control holds promise for distinguishing successful from unsuccessful ventures (Brockhaus, 1982); experienced venture capitalists have one or two major areas of emphasis which predominate in their thinking, e.g., management, unique opportunity, appropriate return (Hisrich and Jankowicz, 1990)
	Structure	Structure
	Experts' mental structures play an integral part in comprehending familiar events in a setting (Read, 1987); experts efficiently translate problem information in a situation into problem solutions (Glaser, 1988)	Experts efficiently translate problem information in a situation into problem solutions (Glaser, 1988)
PT	Content	Content
	Entrepreneurs expose themselves to information differently (Kaish and Gilad, 1991); understanding how value is built is a precondition for sustained competitive advantage (Ghemawat, 1991; Porter, 1985)	Entrepreneurship is a distinctly new discipline which should be studied (McMullan and Long, 1990); entrepreneurs tend to be better educated (Cooper and Dunkelberg 1987); more successful entrepreneurs had or acquired key skills (Vesper, 1980)
	Structure	Structure
	Experts acquire a greater knowledge base in a specific domain (Glaser, 1984); experts explain failure in terms of script knowledge (Leddo and Abelson, 1986)	An expert's schema is organized around key principles (Lord and Maher, 1990); story understanding affects attributions (Read, 1987)

Table 6.4 Script recognition cues based on expert information processing theory and new venture formation literatures

	Script cue
1.	I am rarely surprised by developments in a new business.
2.	Are you more attracted to people who are ready to take action?
3.	I have more highly developed contacts in the new venture area specifically.
4.	If asked to give my time to a new business I would decide based on how this venture fits into my past experience.
5.	There are times when after I finish a job I wish that I had done it better or worked harder at it.
6.	My knowledge about new businesses is fairly elaborate, due to the many variations I have observed.
7.	When investing in a new venture, I think it is worse to wait too long, and miss a great opportunity.
8.	I own assets such as proprietary technology, patents, or an operating business.
9.	When confronted with a new venture problem I can recall quite vividly the details of similar situations I know about.
10.	I have occasionally divulged a confidence when I should not have.
11.	When someone describes a problem with a new business I recognize key features of the problem quickly and can suggest alternatives from examples I can cite.
12.	It is worse to waste your time thinking over an opportunity than to plunge in without knowing all the risks.
13.	I have personally earned 150% compounded return per year on at least three ventures over 3 years, in cash.
14.	My new venture is/will be protected from competition by patent, secret technology, or knowledge.
15.	I have sometimes said mean, spiteful, or hateful things to people close to me.
16.	It is more important to know about creating new ventures.
17.	I want to get a piece of the big money.
18.	I presently control acquisition or expansion funds in an ongoing business or have my own funds available for venturing.
19.	New ventures, small business, and entrepreneurship are distinctly different disciplines.
20.	In the last 3 years the size of the pool of people and assets I control has grown.
21.	I have occasionally felt envious enough of the possessions of other people to think about stealing.
22.	I like to read periodicals which deal specifically with new ventures and start-up businesses.
23.	Imagine you have just funded a new venture: Would you be worried about not investing enough?
24.	I have started at least three successful new ventures.
25.	I value high payoffs; intelligent craftsmanship; being one-up; well-organized projects; dependability.
26.	During the last 3 years, it is the general consensus that my performance as an entrepreneur has increased.
27.	I am more aware of many new venture situations, some of which succeeded and others which failed, and why.
28.	If you had additional money to put to work, would you put it into a venture where you have a "say," even if there is no track record?
29.	New venture success follows a particular script.
30.	If I try to assess the condition of a new business a few questions lead to the relevant information.

Table 6.4 (continued)

	Script cue
31.	I do not mind being committed to meet a regular payroll if it means that I can have a chance at greater financial success.
32.	I am looking for a place to invest my resources.
33.	I am action oriented.
34.	I have failed in at least one new venture.
35.	My new venture is/will be protected from competition by franchise or other territory restrictions.
36.	I could raise money for a venture if I did not have enough.
37.	Do you want things open to the possibilities?
38.	I have enormous drive, but sometimes need others' help to complete projects.
39.	I understand how to buy low and sell high.
40.	The new venture stories I recall illustrate principles necessary for success.
41.	I am more comfortable in new situations.
42.	I feel more confident that I know a lot about creating new ventures.
43.	I like getting buyers and sellers together.
44.	When I see a business opportunity I decide to invest based upon how closely it fits my "success scenario."
45.	I can often see opportunities for my plans to fit with those of other people.
46.	If I have a lot of free time available, it is more desirable to find a new venture to put your time and expertise into than to engage in recreation.
47.	I am very good at a specialty that is in high demand.
48.	I often see ways in which a new combination of people, materials, or products can be of value.

Table 6.5 Script recognition cue compliance evaluation

Script cue	Script structure criterion (Read, 1987)	Area	SQ/N	C/S	Cite
6. My knowledge about new businesses is fairly elaborate, due to the many variations I have observed.	Step: Explicit embedding	IE	SQ	S	Chi et al. (1982): Experts possess a more elaborate schema
11. When someone describes a problem with a new business I recognize key features of the problem quickly and can suggest alternatives from examples I can cite.	Syntax: Mental states reason for action	OC	SQ/N	S	Glaser (1988): Experts efficiently translate problem information into problem solutions
22. I like to read periodicals which deal specifically with new ventures and start-up businesses.	Metarule: Concretion	PT	SQ/N	S	Glaser (1984): Experts acquire a greater knowledge base in a specific domain

Table 6.5 (continued)

Script cue	(Read, 1987)	Area	SQ/N	C/S	Cite
7. When investing in a new venture, I think it is worse to wait too long and miss a great opportunity.	Syntax: Acts enable mental states	IA	N	S	Leddo and Abelson (1986): Doing presupposes willingness even though mistakes might be made
2. Are you more attracted to people who are ready to take action?	Syntax: Mental states can be reasons for actions	IE	N	C	McClelland (1968): Initiative and assertiveness are characteristic of entrepreneurs
46. If you have a lot of free time available, is it more desirable to find a new venture to put your time and expertise into?	Metarule: Principle of least commitment	IR	N	C	Glade (1967): Opportunity search by entrepreneurs versus nonventure use of resources
	Script structure criterion				
3. I have more highly developed contacts in the new venture area specifically.	Steps: Connection to subsequent action	IE	SQ	C	MacMillan (1983): Entrepreneurs use a deliberate process of network building
8. I own proprietary technology, patents, an operating business.	Steps: Evaluation of congruence	OC	SQ/N	S	Leddo and Abelson (1986): Script entry depends on having the objects required
47. I am very good at a specialty that is in high demand.	Syntax: States can disable action	PT	SQ/N	C	Vesper (1980): More successful entrepreneurs had or acquired key skills
35. My new venture is/will be protected from competition by patent, secret technology, or knowledge.	Syntax: States can disable action	OC	SQ/N	C	Rumelt (1987): Isolating mechanisms imply good new business strategy
9. When confronted with a new venture problem I can recall quite vividly the details of similar situations I know about.	Steps: Connection of subsequently observed actions	IE	SQ/N	S	McKeithen et al. (1981): Experts have better recall of relevant information and it is less biased
19. New ventures, small business, and entrepreneurship are distinctly different disciplines.	Metarule: Concretion	PT	N	C	McMullan and Long (1990): Entrepreneurship is a distinct discipline

Area: The knowledge categories include individual attributes (*IA*), experiences (*IE*), resources (*IR*) or prior training (*PT*), and/or organizational characteristics (*OC*)

SQ/N: *SQ* sequence; *N* norms

C/S: *C* content; *S* structure

6.3.5 Summary

We have demonstrated an approach for "excerpting" representative and structurally consistent script content from a literature. It accomplishes the first objective of this chapter, which is to uncover the structure and content of particular knowledge structures that managers might use (Walsh, 1995: 282), in this case, new venture formation expert scripts – the terms scripts and knowledge structures often being used interchangeably. The result is a set of script cues that comply with the standards of expert information processing theory. The development of these script cues then makes it possible to address the second objective of this chapter, which is to relate the use of the identified knowledge structure (in our case entrepreneurial scripts) to consequences of substantive organizational importance.

6.4 Discriminating Experts and Novices

In this next part of the chapter we therefore explain in general terms how researchers can specify and test script-cue recognition-based models of the entrepreneurial mind. This objective may be accomplished in two steps: (1) components of the knowledge structure are derived and (2) the resulting component/constructs are used to classify sample cases by discriminating between new venture formation experts and novices.

6.4.1 Components

In interpreting the results of three studies that seek experts' explanation for script failure, Leddo and Abelson (1986) identify an opportunity to explore the components of expertise. Their findings suggest three possible components of expertise that might be observed empirically in making distinctions between experts and novices. Essentially, Leddo and Abelson propose that the opportunity to distinguish novices from experts occurs at two key points in expertise-specific situations, when the performance of an expert script (an attempt to utilize expertise) might fail. These points occur either (1) at the time of script "entry" or (2) as individuals engage in "doing" the things that serve the main goal of a script (e.g., take steps to form a new organization).

Script "entry" depends on "...having the objects in question" (Leddo and Abelson, 1986, 121). For example, an expert helicopter pilot requires a helicopter, an expert seismic geologist a seismograph, an expert trauma physician a well-equipped emergency room. Script "doing" means accomplishing the main action and achieving the purpose of the script. "Doing" depends on two subrequirements: ability and willingness. Ability is defined as possessing the rudimentary techniques and skills necessary to a specialized domain (e.g., closing the deal may depend on one's persuasive skill) (Leddo and Abelson, 1986, 121). Willingness, in turn, is defined as the propensity to act.

In the case of entrepreneurs, the "Entry" and "Doing" action thresholds of expert information processing theory parallel the theoretical (Shapero, 1982) and empirical (Krueger, 1993) action thresholds that explain individual intentions to form a new venture. Thus "Entry" (the beginning processes of organizational formation) depends on feasibility – specifically on arrangements resources from that environment such as capital, opportunity, and contacts, and "Doing" depends on a combination of ability and willingness. Since expert information processing theory suggests that expertise results from an individual's use of an expert script, it can be argued that new venture formation expertise ought to be related to individual scripts containing the "Entry"-based component "feasibility" and the "Doing" components "ability" and "willingness." It follows that discrimination among new venture formation experts and between experts and novices should be possible using these constructs. Thus, one common theme in the expertise-based entrepreneurial information processing literature is the following general proposition:

> Proposition: New venture formation expertise should consist of three components of expertise represented by the constructs: (1) arrangements, (2) willingness, and (3) opportunity-ability.

This proposition suggests a latent structure as a foundation to guide the identification and definition of a measurement model. This model is based on the script-cue recognition items derived using the previously described approach suggested by expert information processing theory (arrangements, willingness, and opportunity-ability). Once the entrepreneurial script components of this model are defined, researchers are then set up to discriminate, or classify, individuals' entrepreneurial expertise between expert and novice by testing the likely hypothesis, as further developed in the following paragraphs.

6.4.2 Classification

In addition to uncovering the components of managerial knowledge structures, we also – in this portion of the chapter – attempt to relate the use of knowledge structures to consequences of substantive organizational importance, specifically the formation of new ventures. We suggest that because of the well-known role of entrepreneurial outcomes, e.g., new organizations create jobs, foster innovation, and help keep an economy competitive in an era of increasing globalization, our better understanding of the nature of the influence of individuals' entrepreneurial mind on new business formation will have sustained importance to the scholarly community, because of its importance to the business community, and to society as a whole. In particular, the capability for researchers to reliably distinguish between expert and novice entrepreneurial minds opens new pathways for scholars to help people to calibrate their preparation to venture (e.g., Kruger and Dunning, 1999) and to better interpret venturing events (e.g., to become aware of the conditions under which failure is only a bump in the road, and when it is "game over," e.g., Mitchell et al., 2008)

This distinguishing capability is an applied specialty, where expert information processing theory, which suggests how to discriminate experts from novices, explains how experts use specialized scripts to outperform novices in domain-specific tasks such as entrepreneurship. Novices are expected to recognize cues in script problem statements differentially from experts (Glaser, 1984). To the extent that the occurrence of successful new venture formation by individuals is associated with expertise, discrimination between experts and novices using script-cue-based indicators of expert information processing entrepreneurs is possible. The following general hypothesis is representative of expectations in the discrimination task:

> Hypothesis: Differences exist among the mean vectors of entrepreneurial script-cue recognitions across expert and novice groups.

The research methodology that has developed to enable classification of individuals into expert and novice entrepreneur groups is script-cue recognition based and uses the three theoretical components of expertise suggested by expert information processing theory: arrangements, willingness, and opportunity-ability (e.g., Mitchell, 1994; Mitchell et al., 2000). In the next section of the chapter we present the "highlight films" of this methodology. Our purpose is to assist future generations of researchers who would like to use scripts-based research to further explore the entrepreneurial mind and to get a high-level view of the methods available and thus become familiar with the general issues and approaches that such future researchers should be cognizant of in their own work.

6.4.3 A Methods Template

In our research, we have established an empirical methodology that can apply the results of the literature review and analysis methodology described in the prior section of this chapter. We summarize it, using the standard methods section format: data gathering, measurement, analysis present in brief overview to provide an illustration as a point of departure for future research.

6.4.3.1 Data Gathering

Data in this type of research consist of observations of the script-cue recognitions of individuals. Data are collected through the use of a questionnaire that incorporates specific script-cue recognition items in an a priori relationship to the proposed theoretical components. In the past we have used various strategies for obtaining respondents: usually by working with an SBDC or Chamber of Commerce or through local assistants in a variety of countries and settings. In response to the present difficulty of accessing sampling frames for probability samples in social science research (Pedhazur and Schmelkin, 1991), and in international entrepreneurship research in particular (McDougall and Oviatt, 1997, 303), a purposeful sampling approach is justified (Mitchell et al., 2000). Acceptable samples range in approximate size from 200 to 1,000 respondents depending upon the nature of the study.

6.4.3.2 Measurement

Each item in the questionnaire consists of a "two-alternative" multiple choice-type question. One alternative is the script cue as developed previously. The other, we suggest, should be a distracter statement, a plausible, even appealing alternative to those who are unfamiliar with new venture creation. Distracter statements that appeal to individuals' notions of social desirability (Crowne and Marlowe, 1964) or that conform to commonly accepted entrepreneurial myths add additional distinguishing power to script-cue recognitions as an empirical reference point, since the likelihood that novices will select a script cue is markedly diminished by the availability of an appealing but wrong choice that only an expert could avoid. Each script-cue recognition is coded "1," each nonrecognition "0," and these are added together to create interval-scaled variables (Nunnally, 1978).

6.4.3.3 Data Analysis

For empirically identifying the components of the scripts in the entrepreneurial mind, each script recognition cue should be logically linked to the construct that it represents (e.g., arrangements, willingness, and opportunity-ability). To examine the data structure and discriminant validity, an exploratory factor analysis is conducted on the set of variables linked to these constructs to ascertain the empirically derived components. If successful, items that load on factors consistent with the expectations of theory are used to form scales. Each resulting scale constitutes an indicator. To examine convergent validity, a reliability analysis using Cronbach's alpha is conducted.[5]

To verify that the constructs fit the latent structure expected, confirmatory factor analysis is used. Confirmatory factor analysis can be constrained in accordance with theory (Jöreskog, 1971). In this case the model is constrained to the three-factor expert information processing theory components of new venture formation expertise that are expected. Given the substantive specifications, statistical tests are used to determine whether or not the sample data are consistent with the theoretical constructs. Such tests as a P2 measure of the goodness of fit (Jöreskog and Sorbom, 1989), the overall goodness of fit index, the adjusted goodness of fit index, and the root mean square residual give indications of the fit of the confirmatory model with the sample data.

---

[5]Over the history of measurement there has been a wide-ranging discussion concerning formative and reflective indicators. Howell et al. (2007) suggests that the current thinking would support the use of Cronbach's alpha in this case to be appropriate.

Classification of individuals into expert and novice entrepreneur groups[6] is also script-cue recognition based and uses the three theoretical components of expertise suggested by expert information processing theory: arrangements, willingness, and opportunity-ability. A multiple scale/two group multiple discriminant analysis is conducted to test the expert–novice discrimination hypothesis. The multiple discriminant analysis shows the level of association between a criterion variable with multiple categories (new venture formation expert and novice) and multiple predictor variables (expert information processing theory components of new venture formation expertise) as represented in the following functional relationship: Group Membership = f (Arrangements, Willingness, and Opportunity-ability). Interpretation of the findings is accomplished by evaluating the significance of the statistics related to the discriminant function, assessing the classification effectiveness of the discriminant model (jackknife analysis), and examining the discriminant loadings where applicable.

6.4.3.4 Summary

Over the past decade, we have been able to use the foregoing approach to answer Walsh's (1995) call: (1) uncover the content and structure of particular knowledge structures that managers might use and (2) "...relate the use of this knowledge structure to consequences of substantive organizational importance..." (Walsh, 1995, 282). What might then be in store for future research using entrepreneurial scripts to illuminate the recesses of the entrepreneurial mind?

6.5 Toward Further Study of Entrepreneurial Scripts

Consistent with the call by Walsh for research that moves "... beyond individual minds in our considerations of supra-individual knowledge structures" (Walsh, 1995, 311), this chapter highlights research wherein information processing in entrepreneurship is viewed as the result of human action wherein differences exist between the scripts of novices and the scripts of experts. At the very least, the foregoing analysis of expert cognitions in the specialized field of new venture formation shows that it is possible for management scholars to uncover the structure and content of a particular group knowledge structure – that of new venture formation experts – and relate the use of this knowledge structure to consequences of substantive organizational importance: discriminating new venture formation experts from novices using expert script cues. Unlike much of the previous work in the area, this portion of the chapter highlights the pioneering of the theoretical representation of

---

[6]We have defined entrepreneurial experts as individuals who have (1) formed three or more businesses, at least one of which is a profitable ongoing entity; (2) formed a (nonlifestyle) business that has been in existence for at least 2 years; (3) experience in a combination of (1) and (2) that indicates a high-level organizational formation knowledge; or (4) career experience indicating high levels of familiarity with organizational formation.

knowledge structure attributes at the group (expert versus novice) level of analysis. It demonstrates practical steps that researchers can take to excerpt relevant script cues from a management literature. Then, like the large body of earlier work in the study of cognition in organizations (e.g., Wagner, 1987), the empirical portion of the chapter utilizes the representation that is derived in a questionnaire-based interaction between respondent and researcher to record and observe cognition-based behavior (in this case script-cue recognition), thus adding to the empirical work of Bougon et al. (1977) and Krackhardt (1987, 1990) a study that tests knowledge structure attributes at the group level of analysis.

There is a very real sense among information processing scholars such as Lord and Maher (1990, 1991b) that the consideration of alternative information processing models (such as thinking of people as expert information processors who utilize script-based knowledge structures) might suggest alternative methodologies for our examination of the practice of management. Aside from making progress in developing our general capabilities for describing and applying knowledge structures, this expert information processing theory-based alternative to understanding new venture formation may also bring other benefits. Specifically, the expert information processing theory-based lens has several implications for theory and practice in the new venture formation domain.

First, the application of expert information processing theory in this chapter shows the process whereby an understanding is developed (a) that new venture formation expertise has three components consistent with Leddo and Abelson (1986) and with cognition-based models of entrepreneurial intention (Krueger, 1993; Shapero, 1982) (Section 2 – Part I) and (b) that we can develop script-cue recognition items that serve as indicators of these component-constructs (Section 2 – Part II).

Second, there appear to be specific implications of the classification results. This chapter demonstrates how research can enable discrimination between new venture formation experts and novices using the script-cue-based indicators of expert information processing theory. As a research community, our having made (and continuing to make) this distinction is important, because it has provided theoretical and empirical assistance in resolving dilemmas surrounding the domain of entrepreneurship, particularly in its role in research on entrepreneurial cognition. The results reported in this chapter take a firm step in this direction. On the basis of the classification results, entrepreneurs no longer must be thought of stereotypically, and identified one-dimensionally as "born risk-takers" (Coulton and Udell, 1976), as having a high need for achievement (McClelland, 1965), as the product of an "enterprising childhood" (Litvak and Maule, 1971), or as masters of strategy and industry structure (Sandberg, 1986). Building on the notion of entrepreneurial skill advanced by Herron (1990), this chapter suggests that on the basis of script-cue recognitions, experts in new venture formation will consistently recognize cues from new venture formation scripts (Glaser, 1984; Read, 1987) better than will novices. The effectiveness ratios that we have found and reported over the years support this notion, showing that the discriminant function derived in the study contributes to improved discrimination between experts and novices.

Third is a look to the future. One of the most useful features of exploratory research is its potential for future research. Each step taken in this research has produced opportunities to extend the research. For example, the first part of the chapter introduces script structure criteria to the study of management cognitions, proposes a "sampling" versus "full enumeration" as a means for utilizing the content of expert scripts in research, and suggests explicit steps for the extraction and generation of script cues from a pool of scholarly literature. Are the script structure criteria fully tractable? Does sampling have too high a cost in the potential elimination of script richness? Is replication possible using the explicit steps suggested? Indeed, in answering one question, the first part of this research raises multiple follow-on issues.

Further, in the chapter we have been able to identify several weaknesses in the script-cue recognition items used to measure expert information processing theory constructs. Future research should examine the items from the present questionnaire to ascertain which ought to be used as exemplars for the construction of new script cues. Also, given what is now known about the common constructs of new venture formation expertise, it appears possible to select script cues that may more clearly be identified by respondents as relating to particular conceptual domains, thus "tightening up" the correlation between item and construct, and enhancing the overall internal consistency of the scales. A means whereby this instrument could capture the *strength* of script-cue recognitions would also be helpful.

Last, the chapter provides a starting point for other researchers who seek to utilize expert information processing theory to distinguish experts from novices vis-à-vis other relevant questions for entrepreneurship. For example, although this study was conducted using data obtained from respondents who function in the US economy, this is not to suppose that new venture formation expertise is limited to the United States alone. Indeed, cross-cultural application of the instrument used in this research has provided indications of new venture formation expertise as applied in other economic settings (e.g., Mitchell et al., 2000, 2002; Smith et al., 2009). Also, an underlying assumption of this research is that script cues extracted from the entrepreneurship literature apply on a cross-gender basis. This should be tested, and further research that uses the women in entrepreneurship literature as the basis for script-cue generation should be considered.

6.6 Conclusion

We demonstrate in this chapter that the suggestion that successful new venture formation is associated with individual knowledge-based scripts is a nontrivial suggestion. Further, we highlight how the process underlying this assertion fits into the larger research progression of work on information and information processing. As the previous 15 years have demonstrated, the link between expertise and new venture formation is very useful in helping entrepreneurship researchers illuminate the underlying dynamics of new venture formation so that the productive–destructive aspects of starting businesses can be better managed. As has long been the case, the results of new venture formation are dichotomous. Newly formed organizations tend to be either highly rewarding successes or painful failures (Timmons, 1990). Unrivaled formation rates also coincide with unequaled failure rates (Cooper et al., 1988; Shapero and Giglierano, 1982). The success– failure dichotomy continues to challenge the researchers who study new venture formation to illuminate the underlying dynamics so that the productive–destructive aspects of the process can be better managed.

In this chapter we offer a deeper understanding of the influence of expert entrepreneurs as a group on new venture formation, highlighting the role of their expert scripts. Such an understanding is of critical importance at this point in time, especially given the impact of new venture formation on new jobs, innovation, and the global competitiveness of an economy. Accordingly, the scholarly community, the business community, and society as a whole stand to benefit greatly if "entrepreneurship as expertise" continues to live up to its potential as an integrating and explanatory notion. It is indeed heartening to be able to report that the structure and content of expert knowledge structures can be systematically identified and then utilized for making distinctions that are of organizational significance in a specific domain. We hope that these findings offer encouragement to others who might wish to replicate these findings in other areas of management specialty. Although the steps taken in this research are but a beginning, possibilities for additional insight portend. That "script," however, is yet to be written.

References

Abbott V, Black JB (1986) Goal-related inferences in comprehension. In: Galambos JA, Abelson RP, Black JB (eds), Knowledge Structures. Lawrence Erlbaum Associates, Inc., Hillsdale, NJ, pp. 123–142

Abelson RP (1976) Script processing in attitude formation and decision making. In: Carroll JS, Payne JW (eds), Cognition and Social Behavior. Erlbaum, Hillsdale, NJ, pp. 33–45

Abelson RP, Black JB (1986) Introduction. In: Galambos JA, Abelson RP, Black JB (eds), Knowledge Structures. Lawrence Erlbaum Associates, Inc., Hillsdale, NJ, pp. 1–18

Barney J (1991) Firm resources and sustained competitive advantage. Journal of Management 17: 99–120

Baez AV (1967) The New College Physics: A Spiral Approach. W. H. Freeman and Company, New York

Bougon M, Weick K, Binkhorst D (1977) Cognition in organizations: An analysis of the Utrecht jazz orchestra. Administrative Science Quarterly 22: 606–639

Bourne LE, Dominowski RL, Loftus EF, Healy AF (1986) Cognitive Processes (2nd ed). Prentice-Hall, Englewood Cliffs, NJ

Bower GH, Hilgard ER (1981) Theories of Learning. Prentice-Hall, Englewood Cliffs, NJ

Bradley JH, Paul R, Seeman E (2006) Analyzing the structure of expert knowledge. Information and Management 43: 77–91

Brockhaus RHS (1982) The psychology of the entrepreneur. In: Kent CA, Sexton DL, Vesper KH (eds.), Encyclopedia of Entrepreneurship. Prentice-Hall, Englewood Cliffs, NJ, pp. 39–56

Carbonnell JG (1979) Subjective understanding: Computer models of belief systems. Yale University, New Haven, CT

Casson M (1982) The market for information. In: Casson MC (ed), The Entrepreneur: An Economic Theory. Martin Robertson, Oxford, pp. 201–217

Chase WG, Ericsson KA (1981) Skilled memory. In: Anderson JR (ed.), Cognitive Skills and Their Acquisition. Erlbaum, Hillsdale, NJ, 141–189

Chase WG, Ericsson KA (1982) Skill and working memory. The Psychology of Learning and Motivation, 16: 1–58

Chase WG, Simon HA (1973a) Perceptions in chess. Cognitive Psychology 4: 55–81

Chase WG, Simon HA (1973b) The mind's eye in chess. In: Chase WG (ed), Visual Information Processing. Academic Press, New York, pp. 215–281

Chi MTH, Glaser R, Farr MJ (1988) The Nature of Expertise. Lawrence Erlbaum Associates, Inc., Hillsdale, NJ

Chi MTH, Glaser R, Rees E (1982) Expertise in problem solving. In: Sternberg RJ (ed.), Advances in the Psychology of Human Intelligence. Lawrence Erlbaum Associates, Inc., Hillsdale, NJ, pp. 7–75

Churchill NC, Lewis VL (1983) The five stages of small business growth. Harvard Business Review 83(3): 30–50

Cohen WM, Levinthal DA (1990) Absorptive capacity: A new perspective on learning and innovation. Administrative Science Quarterly 35: 128–152

Commons JR (1931) Institutional economics. American Economic Review 21: 648–657

Cooper AC, Dunkelberg WC (1987) Entrepreneurial research: Old questions, new answers, and methodological issues. American Journal of Small Business 11: 1–20

Cooper AC, Dunkelberg WC, Woo CY (1988) Survival and failure: A longitudinal study. In: Kirchhoff BA et al. (eds.), Frontiers of Entrepreneurship Research. Babson Center for Entrepreneurial Studies, Wellesley, MA

Cooper AC, Willard GE, Woo CY (1986) Strategies of high-performing new and small firms: A reexamination of the niche concept. Journal of Business Venturing 1: 247–260

Corbett AC, Hmieleski KM (2007) The conflicting cognitions of corporate entrepreneurs. Entrepreneurship Theory and Practice 31: 103–121

Corbett AC, Neck HM, DeTienne DR (2007) How corporate entrepreneurs learn from fledgling innovation initiatives: Cognition and the development of a termination script. Entrepreneurship Theory and Practice 31: 829–852

Coulton R, Udell GG (1976) The national science foundation's innovation center – An experiment in training potential entrepreneurs and innovators. Journal of Small Business Management (April): 1–20

Crowne DP, Marlowe D (1964) The Approval Motive. John Wiley, New York

Davis MA. Curtis MB, Tschetter JD (2003) Evaluating cognitive training outcomes: Validity and utility of structural knowledge assessment. Journal of Business and Psychology 18: 191–206

Day DV, Lord RG (1992) Expertise and problem categorization: The role of expert processing in organizational sense-making. Journal of Management Studies 29: 35–47

Day EA, Arthur W, Gettman D (2001) Knowledge structures and the acquisition of a complex skill. Journal of Applied Psychology 86: 1022–1033

Dew N, Read S, Sarasvathy SD, Wiltbank R forthcoming (2009) Effectual versus predictive logics in entrepreneurial decision-making: Differences between experts and novices. Journal of Business Venturing

Ericsson KA (2003) Exceptional memorizers: Made, not born. Trends in Cognitive Psychology 7: 233–235

Ericsson KA (2005) Recent advances in expertise research: A commentary on the contributions to the special issue. Applied Cognitive Psychology 19: 233–241

Ericsson KA, Charness N (1994) Expert performance. American Psychologist 49: 725–747

Ericsson KA, Delaney PF, Weaver G, Mahadevan R (2004) Uncovering the structure of a memorist's superior "basic" memory capacity. Cognitive Psychology 49: 191–237

Ericsson KA, Kintsch W (1995) Long-term working memory. Psychological Review 102: 211–245
Ericsson KA, Krampe RT, Tesch-Romer C (1993) The role of deliberate practice in the acquisition of expert performance. Psychological Review 100: 363–406
Fiske ST, Kinder DR, Lartner WM (1983) The novice and the expert: Knowledge-based strategies in political cognition. Journal of Experimental Social Psychology 19: 381–400
Fiske ST, Taylor SE (1984) Social Cognition. Addison-Wesley, Reading, MA
Galambos JA, Abelson RP, Black JB (1986) Scripts. In: Galambos JA, Abelson RP, Black JB (eds), Knowledge Structures. Lawrence Erlbaum Associates, Inc., Hillsdale, NJ, pp. 19–20
Gardner H (1983) Frames of Mind. Basic Books, New York
Ghemawat P (1991) Commitment: The Dynamics of Strategy. The Free Press, New York
Ginn CW, Sexton DL (1990) A comparison of the personality type dimensions of the 1987 Inc. 500 company founders/CEOs with those of slower-growth firms. Journal of Business Venturing 5: 313–326
Glade WP (1967) Approaches to a theory entrepreneurial formation. Explorations in Entrepreneurial History 4: 245–259
Glaser R (1982). Instructional psychology: Past, present, and future. American Psychologist, 37, 292–305
Glaser R (1984) Education and thinking. American Psychologist, 39: 93–104
Glaser R (1988) Expertise and learning: How do we think about instructional processes now that we have discovered knowledge structures? In: Klahr D, Kotovsky K (eds.), Complex Information Processing: The Impact of Herbert Simon. Lawrence Erlbaum Associates, Inc., Hillsdale, NJ, pp. 269–282
Glass RS, Oz E (1999) Information cues in decision making: An empirical investigation. Journal of Computer Information Systems 39: 40–47
Gobet F, Simon HA (1998) Expert chess memory: Revisiting the chunking hypothesis. Memory 6: 225–255
Granger R (1980) When expectations fail: Toward a self-correcting inference system. Paper presented at Annual Meeting of the National Conference on Artificial Intelligence, Stanford, CA.
Groot de AD (1965) Thought and Choice in Chess. Noord-Hollandsche Uitgeversmaatschappij, Amsterdam.
Gustavsson V (2004) Entrepreneurial Decision-Making: Individuals, Tasks and Cognitions. Jönköping International Business School, Jönköping, Sweden
Hayek v FA (1937) Economics and knowledge. In: Hayek FA v (ed), Individualism and Economic Order. Routledge and Kegal Paul, London, pp. 33–54
Herron L (1990) The Effects of Characteristics of the Entrepreneur on New Venture Performance. University of South Carolina Press, Columbia, SC
Hinsz VB, Tindale RS, Vollrath DA (1997) The emerging conceptualization of groups as information processors. Psychological Bulletin 121: 43–64
Hisrich RD, Jankowicz AD (1990) Intuition in venture capital decisions: An exploratory study using a new technique. Journal of Business Venturing 5: 49–62
Howell RD, Breivik E, Wilcox JB (2007) Reconsidering formative measurement. Psychological Methods 12: 205–218
Jones DK, Read SJ (2005) Expert-novice differences in the understanding and explanation of complex political conflicts. Discourse Processes 39: 45–80
Jöreskog KG (1971) Simultaneous factor analysis in several populations. Psychometrika 36: 409–426
Jöreskog KG, Sorbom D (1989) LISREL 7: A Guide to Program and Application. SPSS, Inc., Chicago, IL
Kabanoff B, Brown S (2008) Knowledge structures of prospectors, analyzers, and defenders: Content, structure, stability, and performance. Strategic Management Journal 29: 149–171
Kaish S, Gilad B (1991) Characteristics of opportunities search of entrepreneurs versus executives: Sources, interests, general alertness. Journal of Business Venturing 6: 45–62
Kay P (1982) Three Properties of the Ideal Reader. Unpublished Manuscript, University of California, Berkeley, CA

Kihlstrom RE, Laffont J-J (1979) A general equilibrium entrepreneurial theory of firm formation based on risk aversion. Journal of Political Economy 87: 719–748

Kintsch W, Patel VL, Ericsson KA (1999) The role of long-term working memory in text comprehension. Psychologica 42: 186–198

Krackhardt D (1987) Cognitive social structures. Social Networks, 9: 109–134

Krackhardt D (1990) Assessing the political landscape: Structure, cognition, and power in organizations. Administrative Science Quarterly 35: 342–369

Krueger NF (1993) The impact of prior entrepreneurial exposure on perceptions of new venture feasibility and desirability. Entrepreneurship Theory and Practice 18: 5–21

Kruger J, Dunning D (1999) Unskilled and unaware of it: How difficulties in recognizing one's own incompetence lead to inflated self-assessments. Journal of Personality and Social Psychology 77: 1121–1134

Kunkel SW (1991) The impact of strategy and industry structure on new venture performance. The University of Georgia Press, Athens, GA

Lachman R, Lachman J, Butterfield EC (1979) Cognitive Psychology and Information Processing: An Introduction. Lawrence Erlbaum Associates, Inc., Hillsdale, NJ

Leddo J, Abelson RP (1986) The nature of explanations. In: Galambos JA, Abelson RP, Black JB (eds), Knowledge Structures. Lawrence Erlbaum Associates, Inc., Hillsdale, NJ, pp. 103–122

Litvak IA, Maule CJ (1971) Canadian entrepreneurship: A study of small newly established firms. Ottawa: Department of Industry, Trade and Commerce

Loasby B (1983) Knowledge, learning and enterprise. In: Wiseman J (ed.), Beyond Positive Economics. St. Martin's Press, New York, pp. 104–121

Lord RG, Kernan MC (1987) Scripts as determinants of purposeful behavior in organizations. Academy of Management Review 12: 265–277

Lord RG, Maher KJ (1990) Alternative information-processing models and their implications for theory, research, and practice. Academy of Management Review 15: 9–28

Lord RG, Maher KJ (1991a) Cognitive theory in industrial and organizational psychology. In: Dunette MD, Hough LM (eds), Handbook of Industrial and Organizational Psychology. Consulting Psychologist Press, Palo Alto, CA, pp. 1–62

Lord RG, Maher KJ (1991b) Leadership and Information Processing: Linking Perceptions and Performance. Unwin-Hyman, Boston

Low MB, MacMillan IC (1988) Entrepreneurship: Past research and future challenges. Journal of Management 14: 139–161

Lurigio AJ, Carroll JS (1985) Probation officers' schemata of offenders: Content, development, and impact on treatment decisions. Journal of Personality and Social Psychology 48: 1112–1126

MacMillan IC (1983) The politics of new venture management. Harvard Business Review, 83(6): 8–16

MacMillan IC, Day D (1987) Corporate ventures into industrial markets: Dynamics of aggressive entry. Journal of Business Venturing 2: 29–39

Marr D (1977) Artificial intelligence: A personal view. Artificial Intelligence 9: 37–48

McClelland DC (1965) Need achievement and entrepreneurship: A longitudinal study. Journal of Personality and Social Psychology 1: 389–392.

McClelland DC (1968) Characteristics of successful entrepreneurs. Paper presented at Proceedings of the Third Creativity, Innovation, and Entrepreneurship Symposium, Framingham, MA

McDougall P (1987) An Analysis of New Venture Business Level Strategy, Entry Barriers, and New Venture Origin as Factors Explaining New Venture Performance. Unpublished doctoral dissertation. University of South Carolina, Columbia, SC.

McDougall PP, Oviatt BM (1997) International entrepreneurship literature in the 1990s and directions for future research. In Sexton DL & Smilor RW (eds.), Entrepreneurship 2000. Upstart Publishing, Chicago, IL, pp. 291–320

McKeithen KB, Reitman JS, Reuter HH, Hirtle SC (1981) Knowledge organization and skill differences in computer programmers. Cognitive Psychology 13: 307–325

McMullan WE, Long WA (1990) Developing New Ventures: The Entrepreneurial Option. Harcourt Brace Jovanovich, San Diego, CA

Miller GA (1956) The magical number seven, plus or minus two: Some limits on our capacity for processing information. Psychological Review 63: 81–97.

Mitchell RK (1994) The Composition, Classification, and Creation of New Venture Formation Expertise. University of Utah, Salt Lake City, UT

Mitchell RK (1996) Oral history and expert scripts: Demystifying the entrepreneurial experience. Journal of Management History 2: 50–67

Mitchell RK (2003) A transaction cognition theory of global entrepreneurship. In: Katz JA, Shepherd D (eds), Cognitive Approaches to Entrepreneurship Research. In JAI Press: Advances in Entrepreneurship, Firm Emergence and Growth, 6: 183–231

Mitchell RK (2005) Tuning up the global value creation engine: The road to excellence in international entrepreneurship education. In: Katz JA, Shepherd D (eds), Cognitive Approaches to Entrepreneurship Research. In JAI Press: Advances in Entrepreneurship, Firm Emergence and Growth, 8: 185–248

Mitchell RK, Busenitz L, Bird B, Gaglio CM, McMullen J, Morse E, Smith B (2007) The central question in entrepreneurial cognition research 2007. Entrepreneurship Theory and Practice 31: 1–27

Mitchell RK, Chesteen SA (1995) Enhancing entrepreneurial expertise: Experiential pedagogy and the entrepreneurial expert script. Simulation and Gaming 26: 288–306

Mitchell RK, Mitchell JR, Smith JB (2008) Inside opportunity formation: Enterprise failure, cognition, and the creation of opportunities. Strategic Entrepreneurship Journal 2: 225–242

Mitchell RK, Seawright KW (1995) The implications of multiple cultures and entrepreneurial expertise for international public policy. In: Bygrave WD et al. (eds), Frontiers of Entrepreneurship Research. Babson College, Babson Park, MA, pp. 143–157

Mitchell RK, Smith JB, Morse EA, Seawright K, Peredo AM, McKenzie B (2002) Are entrepreneurial cognitions universal? Assessing entrepreneurial cognitions across cultures. Entrepreneurship Theory and Practice 26: 9–32

Mitchell RK, Smith JB, Seawright KW, Morse EA (2000) Cross-cultural cognitions and the venture creation decision. Academy of Management Journal 43: 974–993.

Neisser U (1967) Cognitive psychology. Appleton-Century-Crafts, New York

Newell A, Simon HA (1972) Human Problem Solving. Prentice Hall, Englewood Cliffs, NJ

Nunnally JC (1978) Psychometric Theory (2nd ed). McGraw-Hill, New York

Olson JR, Rueter HH (1987) Extracting expertise from experts: Methods for knowledge acquisition. Expert Systems 4: 152–168

Pedhazur EJ, Schmelkin LP (1991) Measurement, Design, and Analysis: An Integrated Approach. Lawrence Erlbaum Associates, Inc., Hillsdale, NJ

Perkins DN (1985) General cognitive skills: Why not? In: Chipman SF, Segal JW, Glaser R (eds.), Thinking and Learning Skills. Lawrence Erlbaum Associates, Inc., Hillsdale, NJ. pp. 339–363

Porter ME (1985) Competitive Advantage: Creating and Sustaining Superior Performance. Free Press, New York.

Read SJ (1987) Constructing causal scenarios: A knowledge structure approach to causal reasoning. Journal of Personality and Social Psychology, 52: 288–302

Rousseau DM (1985) Issues of level in organizational research: Multi-level and cross-level perspectives. In: Research in Organizational Behavior. JAI Press, Greenwich, CT, pp. 1–37

Rumelt RP (1987) Theory, strategy, and entrepreneurship. In: Teece DJ (ed.), The Competitive Challenge: Strategies for Industrial Innovation and Renewal. Cambridge, MA, Ballinger, pp. 137–158

Sandberg WR (1986) New Venture Performance: The Role of Strategy and Industry Structure. D.C. Health and Co, Lexington, MA

Sarasvathy SD, Simon HA, Lave L (1998) Perceiving and managing business risks: Differences between entrepreneurs and bankers. Journal of Economic Behavior and Organization, 33: 207–225

Sarasvathy SD (2008) Effectuation: Elements of Entrepreneurial Expertise. Edward Elgar, Northampton MA

Schank RC, Abelson RP (1977) Scripts, Plans, goals and Understanding. Lawrence Erlbaum Associates, Inc., Hillsdale, NJ

Schere J (1982) Tolerance of ambiguity as a discriminating variable between entrepreneurs and managers. Proceedings, Academy of Management 404–408

Schumpeter J (1934) The Theory of Economic Development. Harvard University Press, Boston, MA

Schwarz N (1998) Warmer and more social: Recent developments in cognitive social psychology. Annual Review of Sociology, 24: 239–264

Seawright KW, Mitchell RK, Smith JB (2008) Comparative entrepreneurial cognitions and lagging Russian new venture formation: A tale of two countries. Journal of Small Business Management 46(4): 512–535

Sexton DL, Bowman-Upton N (1985) The entrepreneur: A capable executive and more. Journal of Business Venturing 1: 129–140

Shapero A (1982) Social dimensions of entrepreneurship. In: Kent C, Sexton D, Vesper K (eds.), The Encyclopedia of Entrepreneurship. Prentice Hall, Englewood Cliffs, NJ, pp. 72–90

Shapero AN, Giglierano J (1982) Exits and entries: A study in yellow pages journalism. In: Vesper KH e. a. (Ed.), Frontiers in Entrepreneurship Research. Babson Center for Entrepreneurial Studies, Wellesley, MA, pp. 113–141

Shiffrin RM, Schneider W (1977) Controlled and automatic human information processing: II. Perceptual learning, automatic attending, and a general theory. Psychological Review 84: 127–190

Simon HA, Chase WG (1973) Skill in chess. American Scientist 61: 394–403

Smilor RW, Gill MDJ (1986) The New Business Incubator. Lexington Books, Lexington, MA

Smith JB, Mitchell JR, Mitchell RK (2009) Transaction commitment and entrepreneurial cognition: Cross level theory development and implications. Entrepreneurship Theory and Practice, 33–34

Stonier T (1990) Information and the Internal Structure of the Universe: An Exploration into Information Physics. Springer-Verlag, London

Stuart RW, Abetti PA (1990) Impact of entrepreneurial and management experience on early performance. Journal of Business Venturing 5: 151–162

Timmons JA (1990) New Venture Creation: Entrepreneurship in the 1990's. Irwin, Homewood, IL

Vesper KH (1980) New Venture Strategies. Prentice-Hall, Englewood Cliffs

Wagner RK (1987) Tacit knowledge in everyday intelligent behavior. Journal of Personality and Social Psychology 52: 1236–1247

Walsh JP (1995) Managerial and organizational cognition: Notes from a trip down memory lane. Organization Science 6: 280–321

Wilensky R (1983) Planning and Understanding: A Computational Approach to Human Reasoning. Addison-Wesley, Reading, MA

Woloschuk W, Harasym P, Mandin H, Jones A (2000) Use of scheme-based problem solving: An evaluation of the implementation and utilization of schemes in a clinical presentation curriculum. Medical Education 34: 437–442

Zohar D, Luria G (2004) Climate as a social-cognitive construction of supervisory safety practices: Scripts as proxy of behavior patterns. Journal of Applied Psychology 89: 322–333

Part III
Motivations, Emotions, and Entrepreneurial Passion

Chapter 7
Motivations: The Entrepreneurial Mind and Behavior

Alan Carsrud, Malin Brännback, Jennie Elfving, and Kristie Brandt

Abstract In this chapter various theories and approaches to motivational research are reviewed and applied to the study of the entrepreneur. These are discussed with respect to both necessity and opportunistic entrepreneurship. Various models that integrate internal and external motivation are explored and the concept of risk is examined as a form of motivation. The role of goals and goal setting is also discussed in the motivational framework and is tied to intrinsic and extrinsic motivations. In addition, work and life satisfaction are reviewed as they impact entrepreneurial motivation with specific attention paid to career motivation. Finally, achievement motivation is discussed, not only in terms of a unidimensional model, but also in terms of a multi-dimensional model to predict the performance of firms using the motivation characteristics of the entrepreneur.

7.1 Assumptions and a Brief History

In this chapter we address the complex roles that "motivations" play in entrepreneurial cognitions, intentions, and behaviors and suggest various models and theories that might be useful in the study of entrepreneurial motivations. We do not assume that somehow entrepreneurs are "unique" in their type of motivations from non-entrepreneurs, as did many earlier entrepreneurship researchers. We do, however, believe that entrepreneurial motivations impact entrepreneurial activity and the success of their ventures as demonstrated by Carsrud et al. (1989) and Elfving (2008). We also believe that the individual entrepreneur's motivations can directly impact the performance of their firm, even beyond the start-up phase. That impact, however, will be complex and moderated by a number of factors, including those found in a resource-based view of the firm. We assume that how motivations are

A. Carsrud (✉)
Loretta Rogers Chair in Entrepreneurship, Ted Rogers School of Management,
Ryerson University, Toronto, ON, M5B 2K3 Canada
e-mail: alan.carsrud@ryerson.ca

A.L. Carsrud, M. Brännback (eds.), *Understanding the Entrepreneurial Mind*,
International Studies in Entrepreneurship 24, DOI 10.1007/978-1-4419-0443-0_7,
© Springer Science+Business Media, LLC 2009

expressed and the foci of those motivations differ for entrepreneurs in various situations and at different stages of their venture's development.

While we believe emotions are a form of motivation and are clearly related, we refer the reader to the chapter in this book directly addressing emotions and their role in entrepreneurial cognitions and behaviors. In addition, while traditional researchers in emotion would not consider "passion" an emotion, the concept of "entrepreneurial passion" is obvious and often referred to by anyone who has interacted with entrepreneurs. Thus, there is a chapter in this book on passion as well.

The study of motivation can be traced to the early works of Freud (1900, 1915) in which his use of the term "instincts" operates a great deal like "drives" or "motivations" (Deutsch and Krauss, 1965). For Freud (1915), "instincts" were persistent pressures to change an internal state by external activities, often via "unconscious mental activity" (Deutsch and Krauss, 1965). To Freud, instincts (or motivations) influenced behavior on both conscious and unconscious levels.

Given that one's most fundamental drivers are biologically based, it follows that obtaining what is necessary for survival is a strong human motivation. That basic motivation is inherent in all humans and makes achieving success and avoiding failure a necessity. Since the beginning of time we, as the collective human race, are motivated to survive. In its most basic form, motivation, as defined by Maslow (1946), is the human drive to satisfy the body's need for survival, with its highest form reflected in achievement motivation (Ach). Achievement motivation is a research stream initially fostered by Atkinson (1957, 1964). A unidimensional approach was taken by McClelland and Winter (1969), and a multi-dimensional approach was also taken by Spence and Helmreich (1978) and Carsrud et al. (1989). For example, Atkinson (1957, 1964) builds his model of achievement motivation on his prior theory, levels of aspirations (clearly something entrepreneurs often do and yet which few entrepreneurship researchers have directly studied). Could aspiration level explain why some people choose to build high growth firms and others choose life-style firms? His theory addresses the tendency of individuals to both achieve success (creating a successful venture) and avoid failure (starvation). We will continue to discuss achievement motivation later in this chapter.

7.2 Motivations to Survive Versus Motivations to Grow

Survival-oriented motivation can be seen in the "necessity entrepreneur" identified in the Global Entrepreneurship Monitor (GEM) studies (Reynolds et al. 2002). This type of entrepreneur is more concerned with avoiding the failure of starvation than other types of entrepreneurs. We have evolved a long way from the days of cavemen (and cavewomen) and in our modern world, we obtain what we need for survival by working to obtain the monetary means required to purchase what we need and want, thus the evolution of motivation. Most people do this by working as an employee for a corporation or other types of organization. They have a particular role to play within that setting and specific tasks they must fulfill in order to be rewarded a predetermined amount of money (hence work or task motivation)

(Pinder, 1984, 1998). Whether or not the individual likes the job that he or she must perform or the company in which he or she works can sometimes take a back-seat to the more pressing issue of making money in order to support one's self and family.

However, not everyone fits into the role of an employee working for another person within an organization. Some decide to blaze their own trail through the business world as entrepreneurs, hence the "opportunistic entrepreneur" of the GEM studies (Reynolds et al., 2002) who is focused on the achievement of success through exploiting an opportunity for some form of gain. Here the intention of the entrepreneur and the pursuit of the recognized opportunity are critical. Obviously, the question of what motivates the pursuit of an opportunity should be of interest to researchers, entrepreneurs creating ventures, and policy makers wishing to foster entrepreneurial behaviors. Researchers have spent a great deal of time looking at opportunity recognition, but not the motivation behind the search. For more on opportunity, the reader is referred to the chapters in Part V.

Clearly, commercially oriented entrepreneurs are working to earn money, power, prestige, and/or status. But these might not be the only "rewards" or "motivations" they are striving for, as anyone working with either social or biotechnology entrepreneurs will attest to. The search for a disease cure may be a far more powerful motivator than making money, especially if it is the entrepreneur's child that has the disease. Entrepreneurs have the same motivations as anyone for fulfilling their needs and wants in the world; however, they use those motivations in a different manner – they create ventures rather than just work in them.

In this chapter, we examine the role of various types and theories of motivation in conjunction with cognition, intentions, and behaviors of entrepreneurs. We continue to highlight the fact that entrepreneurs do not necessarily possess motivations that are distinct from others, but rather it is how they use those motivations that help determine the ultimate success or failure of their ventures. This chapter assumes that there is a complex interactive model of entrepreneurial cognitions and behaviors that is consistent with the nature of the other chapters in this book, particularly the chapters on locus of control, intentions, emotions, and passion.

We still have much to learn about the entrepreneur, especially with respect to the role of motivation in the entrepreneur. The sociologist Homans (1961) proposed the motivational principles of hedonism and the theory of the "economic man," which still have relevance to the study of mankind, especially the entrepreneur. The utilitarian emphasis on the role of "reward," "drive reduction," "pleasure," "reinforcement," or "satisfiers," as proposed by psychological theories of motivation in learning (Deutsch and Krauss, 1965), can still inform the entrepreneurial researcher and guide their research endeavors. McClelland (1985) summed up the role of motives, values, and skills as those factors that determine what people do in their lives. We believe that entrepreneurship researchers have yet to adequately tie those three factors together although social values clearly impact the development of social ventures and not-for-profit organizations.

7.3 Drive Theories and Incentive Theories

Traditionally, motivation has been studied in order to answer three kinds of questions: (i) What activates a person? (ii) What makes him, or her, choose one venture over another? and (iii) Why do different people respond differently to the same stimuli? These questions give rise to three important aspects of motivation: *activation, selection-direction,* and *preparedness of response* (Perwin, 2003). Existing motivational theories can be divided roughly into *drive theories* and *incentive theories.* Drive theories suggest that there is an internal stimulus, e.g., hunger or fear, driving the person and that the individual seeks a way to reduce the resulting tension. The need for tension reduction thus represents the motivation (Freud, 1924; Murray, 1938; Festinger, 1957). On the other hand, incentive theories emphasize the motivational pull of incentives, i.e., there is an end point in the form of some kind of goal, which pulls the person toward it, such as achievement motivation in the entrepreneur (Carsrud et al., 1989). In other words, in drive theories the push factors dominate, while in incentive theories the pull factors dominate. The cognitive approach to personality psychology has traditionally emphasized the pull factors and the incentive nature of motives (Perwin, 2003).

7.4 Diversity and Complexity of Motivational Theories

Fisher (1930) noted that there are fundamentally two schools of motivational theories, one based in economics and the other rooted in psychology. These have been in conflict with each other for decades. Recently, Steel and König (2006) and Wilson (1998) called for the use of *consilience,* which they describe as the linking of facts and fact-based theory across disciplines to create a common framework between the two schools. We also see this lack of *consilience* in entrepreneurship research with respect to its view of the entrepreneur. This might account for the lack of progress in our understanding of the entrepreneurial mind and how it ties to the venture creation process. If the multi-disciplinary nature of entrepreneurship research is to return to looking at motivation as an explanatory factor in entrepreneurial behavior, it must also bridge the wide variety of theories of motivation and tie them to environmentally oriented theories like RBV (Penrose, 1959). Likewise, any motivational and resource-based models adopted by entrepreneurship researchers must also have some temporal components as there is an inherent time dimension in opportunity recognition and firm creation.

Entrepreneurship could become indebted to the recent work of Steel and König (2006) on motivation. They have brought together various theories of motivation as applied in economics, management, and psychology (with a time dimension) into what they call temporal motivational theory (TMT). In addition, Locke and Latham (2002, 2004) have married task motivation and goal setting in their recent commentaries. What is interesting is that these two approaches to motivation have yet to be adopted by entrepreneurship researchers. This is despite the fact that entrepreneurs are both time constrained, as in Steel and König's (2006) model, and goal focused, as in the Locke and Latham (2002, 2004) approach. Perhaps it is time for the research community to take a new look at this reality.

Another advantage of both of these theoretical approaches is that they can also be used to look at group motivation and in turn be used to study entrepreneurial teams. We take the view that there is cognitive control of motivation as well as motivational impact on cognitions, building on the work of Freud (1900, 1915), Zimbardo (1969), and others. This concept of reciprocal effects is important in understanding entrepreneurial motivations and has also been shown to be true for entrepreneurial intentions (Brännback et al., 2007).

7.5 Motivation, Cognitive Dissonance, and Risk

The complexity of motivations is exhibited in cognitive dissonance and risk avoidance, both of which are strong motivators for humans. Research on cognitive dissonance and the need to avoid failure (Cohen and Zimbardo, 1969) can be used to explain why entrepreneurs will often do anything to avoid failure in their venture, such as persisting when any non-entrepreneurs would have quit. It is important to remember that cognitive dissonance has much to offer the study of entrepreneurs as well as the behavior of venture capitalists and angel investors.

For example, people high in success motivation, who voluntarily commit themselves to a task promising failure (this would be true of most opportunistic entrepreneurs aiming at high growth firms), will show greater cognitive dissonance the greater the probability of failure (Cohen and Zimbardo, 1969). To reduce dissonance, the entrepreneur would be expected to either lower their success motivation *or* their motivation to avoid failure. It is possible that entrepreneurs use very different processes of dissonance reduction than say, managers. It is interesting that this kind of research has not been done to see which dissonance reducer the entrepreneur would enact. Furthering this point, Atkinson (1957) has shown that these two motivations are separate and have different implications for behavior.

However, when risk was previously studied by entrepreneurship researchers, this distinction seems to have been forgotten. Risk was looked at as a risk-taking propensity, or a personality trait, and not seen as two parts of a motivational paradigm that included dissonance. Even the recent commentaries on risk-taking behavior (Lumpkin and Erdogan, 2004) (Segal et al., 2005) have not used this approach. Atkinson (1957) also saw the need for success as a basic motivational process to feel competent and self-determining in relation to one's environment. This will later be discussed in more detail in conjunction with multi-dimensional achievement motivation.

Building on Atkinson (1957) and Deci (1975), further discussion on the relationship between success and risk can include the motivation of success (M_s). This motivation is constant in an individual and has an incentive value (I_s), with the achievement of a difficult goal (such as starting a new firm) having more incentive value than a less difficult goal. The incentive value is equal to one minus the probability of success $(I_s + 1 - P_s)$. Thus, the tendency to approach starting a firm (T_s) would be seen as

$$T_s = M_s \times P_s \times I_s.$$

Therefore, a person with a strong tendency to start a venture which is moderately risky will be the most pronounced in entrepreneurs with a high motive for success.

Another motivation, fear of failure (F), is also present. That is, the fear of failure is a motive to avoid such failure. There are also expectancies about failure and an incentive value for failure as well. The motive to avoid failure (F) is relatively stable (Deci, 1975) and the emotions of shame and embarrassment accompanying failure as an entrepreneur are greater the easier the task: the greater the shame, the greater the incentives to avoid failure. Thus we have $I_f = -(1 - P_f)$. The tendency to avoid failure (T_{af}) becomes

$$(T_{af}) = (F \times P_f \times I_f).$$

Combining these formulas, we can say that the tendency to approach or avoid an entrepreneurial venture (E) is equal to the tendency of approach success plus the tendency to avoid failure (the latter being a negative number) (Deci, 1975). Thus

$$E = (M_s \times P_s \times I_s) + (F \times P_f \times I_f).$$

This kind of modeling could be useful in helping us understand how individuals go about choosing one venture over another or, conversely, in making the decision to stop undertaking a venture.

7.6 Memories as Motivators

Memories of past risks and failures are also related to the issue of risk. Through his review of the motivation to succeed and the role of failure memories, Schlachet (1969) could provide us with a useful model about the impact of serial entrepreneurship on the motivation to start, or not start, subsequent ventures. The motivation of serial entrepreneurs remains unexplored, especially with respect to the impact of memories of risk and prior successes and failures. This may explain why serial entrepreneurs perceive risk differently from less-experienced individuals.

7.7 Intrinsic and Extrinsic Motivations in Entrepreneurs

Although motivation can exist in many forms, it ultimately comes from two places: from inside one's self and from one's outside environment. Motivation could come internally from the emotional high one feels when launching a firm or externally from the admiration of society or money received from the venture. That is, motivation can be *intrinsic* and *extrinsic*. Intrinsic motivation refers to a personal interest in the task, e.g., achievement motivation (Carsrud et al., 1989), and extrinsic motivation refers to an external reward that follows certain behavior (Perwin, 2003; Nuttin, 1984). Therefore, intrinsic motivations include a large proportion of self-development and self-actualization. Note, however, intrinsic and extrinsic motivations are not mutually exclusive; one can be motivated by both to perform an act (Nuttin, 1984; Elfving, 2008).

Ryan and Deci (2000) view motivation as the core of biological, cognitive, and social regulation. They further state that it involves the energy, direction, and persistence of activation and intention. To help better understand the role of both intrinsic and extrinsic motivations, Ryan and Deci (2000) take into account self-determination theory (SDT). SDT spotlights the importance of one's inner-evolved resources for personality development and behavioral self-regulation. Through this theory, Ryan and Deci (2000) empirically identified three inherent psychological needs that are necessary for self-motivation and personality integration. These are the need for competence, relatedness, and autonomy. If these needs are satisfied within an individual concerning a particular act, they will be more inclined to persist at completing the task with intrinsic motivation. Conversely, if these needs are not fully met, they will be more likely to be extrinsically motivated by external factors (Ryan and Deci, 2000). Of course, extrinsic and intrinsic motivations can occur together, but Ryan and Deci point to SDT in helping to determine the primary motivator. Applied to entrepreneurs, the extent to which their venture fulfills the needs defined by SDT will contribute to their intrinsic and extrinsic motivation levels.

Entrepreneurial motivation is tied to both internal and external factors (Elfving, 2008). Internally, entrepreneurs may be motivated to succeed and accomplish a goal, while externally they may be motivated to be their own boss and obtain wealth. One's need for success is another way of looking at need for achievement (Ach) where one tries to match some standard of excellence, for example, an icon of entrepreneurship such as Bill Gates of Microsoft. More likely, entrepreneurial motivations may be learned or influenced by role models of successful entrepreneurs in one's own family. Directly related to one's intrinsic motivation is one's locus of control. For a more detail discussion on locus of control of motivation, which has a long tradition of research, the reader is referred to the chapter in this book on the topic. Likewise, achievement motivation (Ach) is a special form of intrinsic motivation (Deci, 1975; Elfving, 2008) and is discussed in detail later in this chapter.

Perhaps no psychologist has had greater impact on the study of intrinsic and extrinsic motivations than Edward Deci (1975) and more recently with the work of Quigley and Tymon (2006) and Elfving (2008). While most entrepreneurial research assumes the entrepreneur is motivated by external rewards such as money, power, status (an economic view of human motivation), we are left with the reality that some people engage in entrepreneurial activities as ends in themselves. This classic definition of intrinsic motivation (Deci, 1975) could certainly play a role in why social entrepreneurs start social ventures even when there is no apparent reward for doing so other than some internally generated satisfaction. The idea that an individual engages in entrepreneurial behaviors because of the need for stimulation (a form of intrinsic motivation) is not revolutionary, but the fact that serial entrepreneurs do this habitually may provide some interesting insights into such behavior. That is, once an entrepreneur has had the stimulation of starting a firm, they frequently return to that behavior because of intrinsic motivation and the internal and external rewards they received doing that behavior in the past. They might persist in trying for internal reasons even if they have never been rewarded externally through a successful venture. They reduce the cognitive dissonance of perceived possible failure by believing they can be successful this time.

7.8 Obsession, Passion, and Entrepreneurial Motivations

Likewise, entrepreneurs have often been described as being fully absorbed in their ventures and even overcommitted to the point of obsession. Koch (1956) pointed out that those engaged in tasks by intrinsic motivation were more highly organized and energized. This might explain why the panel studies (Reynolds et al., 2002) on entrepreneurs found that even those who did not successfully start a business said that they would try again with a new venture. To have ceased starting a venture and yet want to try again is an indication of intrinsic motivation, which needs to be better understood in addition to the role of that motivation in relation to entrepreneurial intentions. This is a part of what we might call "entrepreneurial passion." For a longer discussion on passion, the reader is referred to the chapter on that topic within this book. Finally, external motivations or rewards would include relatively intangible things such as status, power, social acceptance, with the more tangible eternal rewards being money, stock options, and other forms of compensation.

7.9 Final and Instrumental Motivation

Moreover, it is sometimes appropriate to separate between *final* and *instrumental* motivation (Nuttin, 1984; Elfving, 2008). When one is doing something to reach a certain goal, one has a final motivation. However, when one is doing something that indirectly leads to the final goal, one has an instrumental motivation. For example, one might have a final goal of losing weight and therefore one attends a cooking class in order to learn how to make healthier food. Attending the cooking class is an instrument to reach the actual goal and thus, the cooking class acts as an instrumental motivation.

As noted, when looking at different kinds of motivations we can understand a person's behavior only when we put it into a context. We have to look at how he perceives his initial position, i.e., his construction of the behavioral world, and what goals he sets. We can understand his motivation and behavior only in that context. In other words, the behavior or the motivation has to be put in relation to something else, which Nuttin (1984) argues in his relational model of motivation. He suggests that we should study motivation in the context of the individual–environment relationship. How a person behaves and what is perceived as motivating depends on the person's cognition of the environment and his interaction within it. Motives, goals, and plans do not arise from empty nothingness; they are shaped by their interaction with the environment (Huuskonen, 1989).

According to Nuttin (1984), motivation is rooted in a state of need. We can feel a need to have more independence or a need to be loved and this need motivates us to act. Through a cognitive process, the state of need is gradually processed into a more focused orientation, i.e., we make a plan and set goals. Thus, we have taken the step from phase 1 to phase 2 in the behavioral process. These needs cause some tension, but it is worth noting that in this case we are not talking about the type of purely negative tension which occurs in drive theories. According to Nuttin (1984), people want to have a certain amount of tension in their lives. Consequently, in this case, tension should be viewed mainly as a positive challenge as in the case of the entrepreneur building a new venture. Nuttin (1984) points out that once we have reached one goal, i.e., released the tension, we tend to set a new goal immediately, i.e., deliberately create a new tension.

7.10 Life, Work, Career Satisfaction as Motivators

Another way to look at intrinsic and extrinsic motivations is to look at satisfaction in one's life and work; these are very motivating forces for most individuals. Dissatisfaction at one's current job can propel an employee to attempt to become an entrepreneur. One does not have to lose a job to become an entrepreneur, as in necessity entrepreneurship. One can quit a job and become an opportunistic one. If the outcomes of one's work climate are not meeting their needs or are causing excessive amounts of stress and unhappiness, motivation to change those circumstances can flourish. Hence, this serves to motivate or drive opportunity recognition and propels the venture creation process. Of course, corporate downsizing, economic conditions, or other forces outside of one's control can force motivation through the necessity to continue supporting one's self (Elfving, 2008), but it is also true that people leave safe and secure employment to become entrepreneurs. This is often because they perceive some other combination of internal and external rewards outside of working for someone else to be more valuable and motivating.

The role of the need for success, power, status, and affiliation (Wainer and Rubin, 1967) by entrepreneurs has yet to be fully explored. If entrepreneurship is not viewed positively in a society, it is hard to imagine that entrepreneurs are motivated by power or status in these conditions (Brännback et al., 2007). Could such variables differentiate between entrepreneurs focused on growth-oriented ventures and lifestyle entrepreneurs? Entrepreneurs who set out with a particular vision of their future success can be motivated through the goal of potential future rewards, even though the present work might not be as satisfying or externally rewarding. They may perceive opportunities in very different ways because of their underlying motivations. A longer discussion on perception can be found in another chapter in this book.

7.10.1 Career Motivations

Also related to work satisfaction are the motivational factors related to career motivation. Internal and external forms of motivation are clearly evident in work motivation. Work motivation, as described by Pinder (1984, 1998), is the combination of internal and external factors that initiate work-related behaviors, and determine its form, direction, intensity, and duration (Ambrose and Kulik, 1999). For entrepreneurs, it is important that they have a high level of work motivation. While work motivation has been applied to employees and managers, it seems to be lacking in the study of the entrepreneur. The classic work of Hackman and Oldham (1976) on work design has never been applied to how entrepreneurs design their work (or firm), yet it is clear that entrepreneurs are motivated by the kinds of firms they build. It is interesting that entrepreneurship researchers have seemingly avoided the extensive literature on work motivation (Pinder, 1984, 1998) which can link to the literature on intentions, goals, goal setting, leadership, and even job enrichment. Recent researchers Gächter and Falk (2000) and Quigley and Tymon (2006) have continued this research stream.

7.11 Goal and Goal Setting

Goals and goal setting are clearly parts of any entrepreneurial activity and often serve as motivators for behavior. It is a critical part of any planned behavior as we will note later in this chapter. Setting and working toward goals is a driving motivational force for entrepreneurs. Improving one's life and the lives of their family members can also be a very motivating goal. In addition, many entrepreneurs self-report that they are motivated to be their own boss and work for themselves instead of being just another face within an organization.

Motivation in relation to goals, however, is not a static state: entrepreneur's motives change throughout their life as their goals change. Something started for one reason may continue for another (Nurmi and Salmela-Aro, 2005). The importance and impact of goals has gained a lot of attention in motivational research (see, for example, Locke and Latham, 2002; Bagozzi and Warshaw, 1990; 1992; Bay and Daniel, 2003). In fact, being capable of changing goals and motives is a way for people to adjust to changing situations. As Nuttin (1984) points out, motivation is shaped in the individual–environment context. If environmental factors change, entrepreneurs need to be able to alter their motives in order to cope with and make sense of the new situation (Salmela-Aro et al., 2005).

7.12 Achievement Motivation

One motivational construct that received considerable attention early in the process of understanding the entrepreneur is achievement motivation (Ach) (McClelland et al., 1953; McClelland, 1961, 1965; Brockhaus, 1980, 1982; Gasse, 1982; Carland et al., 1984; Carsrud et al., 1989), with all studies cited here finding varying results. Interestingly, it was Carland et al. (1984) who said that the small business owner sees their business as an extension of their personality, while the entrepreneur is characterized by innovative business behavior. However, McClelland and Winter (1969) did find that achievement motivation was the differentiating factor between small business entrepreneurs and other business leaders. Recently, there has been renewed interest in this motivational concept (Collins et al., 2004; Langen-Fox and Roth, 1995; Tuuanaen, 1997; Steward and Roth, 2007; Lumpkin and Erdogan, 2004; Hart et al., 2007).

One thing that drives that innovative business behavior of the entrepreneur is certainly a motivational characteristic of any successful individual: achievement motivation (Ach). Carsrud et al., (1989) used a multi-dimensional measure of Ach and clearly demonstrated the significant impact of a multi-dimensional measure of Ach on the productivity of a group of retail building supply firms that were started by their owners and ranged from small firms (four employees and revenues of $550,000) to medium size firms (156 employees and revenues of $18,000,000). While one could argue these were small business owners and not really innovative growth-oriented entrepreneurs, the fact remains that they all started their firms and their levels of achievement motivation did significantly impact the subsequent success of those firms. It is not that motivations differ between entrepreneurs and non-entrepreneurs, but instead that motivations can impact the resulting performance of the firm, most likely via the intentions and goals of the entrepreneurs.

McClelland (1961, 1965) used a projective technique, thematic apperception test or TAT, and found achievement motivation in men but not in women. Today's entrepreneurship researcher would be hard-pressed to administer the TAT, but if McClelland's findings were true, then there is the issue of why male entrepreneurs have such motivation and female ones do not when we know from common experience that this is not the case. Much of the research problems in the initial measurement of Ach centered on assuming it as a unidimensional concept initially studied via projective clinical techniques. Komives (1972) saw Ach as a lifestyle value quite similar to the conceptualization and measurement process of Mehrabian (1968). It is also important to note that how a concept is operationally measured affects its usefulness in the study of a given phenomenon.

One such approach to a multi-dimensional measure of Ach is the *Work and Family Orientation Inventory* (WOFO) (Helmreich and Spence, 1978). It contains three sub-scales that may have particular resonance with the study of entrepreneurship that go beyond the "lifestyle" concerns of the more unidimensional scales of Mehrabian (1968) and Komives (1972). The WOFO sub-scales refer to "mastery needs," "work orientation" (Protestant work ethic), and "interpersonal competitiveness." These dimensions of Ach are assessed through questions such as "I like to work hard" (work orientation), "I prefer to work in situations that require a high level of skill" (mastery needs), and "I feel that winning is important in both work and games" (interpersonal competitiveness). It should be clear from the above questions that these scales are tapping into some underlying motivational characteristics of the entrepreneur. Consider the typical observations about entrepreneurs: they work hard, they have to master any number of different skills and tasks, and they have to be able to work with others in their team. It should also be obvious that the motivational concept of "mastery" has a great deal in common with the concept of self-efficacy (Krueger et al., 2000; Bandura and Locke, 2003; Zhao et al., 2005;Wong et al., 2006). For more on self-efficacy, one is referred to the cluster of chapters on intentions and the chapter on self-efficacy in this book.

A series of studies (Spence and Helmreich, 1978; Helmreich and Spence, 1978; Helmreich et al., 1978; Helmreich et al., 1980; Helmreich, 1982; Carsrud et al., 1982; and Helmreich et al., 1986; Carsrud et al., 1989) demonstrated that the quality and quantity of academic and vocational performance can be significantly predicted by varying combinations of multi-dimensional factors of Ach as measured by the WOFO. These studies indicate that the best performance is typically exhibited by those individuals scoring *high* in mastery needs and work orientation, but *low* in interpersonal competitiveness. This combination of factors could also be used to describe self-efficacy. These vocational situations, including entrepreneurial ventures (Carsrud et al., 1989), are ones in which having to interact and motivate others is a necessity. Interpersonal competitiveness, which may be popularly considered a trait of entrepreneurs and Type A personalities, is in fact not a trait of those that are successful (Carsrud et al., 1989).

Finally, if it is correct that McClelland and Winter (1969) found Ach to be a differentiating factor between small business owners and entrepreneurs, such a result could be the outcome of the differences in the interactions of "mastery," "work orientation," and "mastery needs," rather than the presence or absence of overall Ach. This might also explain the observed Ach differences between men and women found by McClelland using the TAT.

7.13 Personality Factors and Motivation

Given that we all have basic, primal motivation, let us consider the influence of specific personality types on how that motivation is cultivated.

7.13.1 Type A and Type B Personalities

In psychological research, personality types can be classified into two subgroups: Type A and Type B. People with Type A personalities tend to be extremely driven, focused, high-strung, and goal-orientated. Type A's are characterized as excessive and competitive, with a strong sense of urgency. Additionally, they are seen as possessing a sustained drive for success, a willingness to compete, and habitual actions associated with mental and physical functions (Liao and Welsch, 2004). Price (1982) suggested that this is a learned set of behaviors and is more likely in competitive and open economies where success is a function of individual effort and progress is seen in tangible forms.

Individuals with Type B personalities are more laid back and easygoing. Little research has examined whether individuals with certain types of personalities end up forming different types of firms. For example, do Type A's develop technology firms while Type B's build lifestyle ventures? Likewise, there is research to show differences in optimism versus pessimism in entrepreneurs (Manove, 2000), which might be beneficial in predicting bankruptcy or failures. An additional area of personality traits that remains to be explored is gender-related traits, which have been shown to have "motivational qualities."

7.13.2 Masculinity and Femininity

Another way of looking at personalities is to look at differences between groups of entrepreneurs. While there are going to be motivational differences between men and women, many of these may be associated not with gender per se, but with sex-role orientations that reflect more masculine and feminine behaviors: hence, masculinity and femininity (Spence and Helmreich, 1978). These traits show predominance of one gender over the other, but both genders can demonstrate these characteristics.

For example, a positive masculine trait with motivational characteristics is instrumentality – the desire to make things work and understand their operation. A negative masculine trait that has motivational impact is hostility – the desire to dominate through physical action in order to bring harm to another. While both men and women can possess these traits, men tend to show them to a greater degree than women. Certainly instrumentality is a trait one would expect to see in technology-based entrepreneurs, which might explain why even today males outnumber women in engineering professions and subsequently in new technology-based firms.

Positive feminine traits such as expressivity – the desire to be sensitive to others and their feelings and to be sensitive to one's own feelings have positive implications for marketing. Being able to listen to what customers need, want, and fear may be far easier for women than it is for men. However, a negative side of femininity, which has motivational implications, is verbal aggression. This tenacity to be aggressive verbally toward others can have significant impact on both organizational performance as well as staff morale within new ventures. Again, while both men and women can possess these traits, women tend to show them to a greater degree than men.

7.14 Motivations, Attitudes, and Behaviors

We know that in order to understand people's behavior, we have to understand their cognitive processes and their perceptions of the particular behavior or act. Accordingly, people make decisions to undergo a certain act, such as becoming an entrepreneur. While cognitive processes involves beliefs, desires, intentions, and motives, Perwin (2003) argues that special attention needs to be paid to the motives themselves or any underlying motivations. In an entrepreneurial context, it is assumed that people form intentions to perform an entrepreneurial act when they possess positive attitudes toward that very act, i.e., entrepreneurship. Why do these attitudes emerge and how do they subsequently affect behavior?

7.14.1 The Impact of Motivation on Behavior

According to Nuttin (1984), there are three phases in every behavioral process. These are (i) the construction of a behavioral world, (ii) processing of the person's needs into goals and plans, and (iii) carrying out the behavioral operations needed in order to reach the goal or fulfill the plan. The first phase has to do with the situation in which the individual finds himself.[1] Before he can do anything, he starts by processing the informational data into a meaningful picture. In the second phase, he decides what he wants to do, i.e., which goal to reach, and in the third phase he executes his plans. From the point of view of understanding human behavior, we have to understand how people perceive a certain situation and what goals they set.

Nuttin also argues that motives are what take people from one phase to another. Nuttin (1984, 14) defines motivation as "the dynamic and directional (i.e., selective and preferential) aspect of behavior. It is motivation that, in the final analysis, is responsible for the fact that a particular behavior moves toward on category of objects rather than another." Here motives and motivation are used synonymously.

7.15 Goal-Directed Behavior, Motivation, and Intentions

Goals can be seen as mental representations, or schemes, of what the future could be like, enabling people not to give up (Perwin, 2003). As previously mentioned, goals are central units in Bandura's social cognitive theory. According to Bandura, self-efficacy partly determines what people intend to achieve and what kind of goal they set for themselves (Bandura, 1989). Goals activate people and in that way often serve as the important link between intention and action (Perwin, 2003; Nuttin, 1984). This indicates that goals play a role in predicting human behavior. In fact, the importance of goals when studying human behavior has been considered so important that it has led to its own field of research: the *theory of goal setting* (see, for example, Locke and Latham, 2002; Latham and Locke, 1991; Locke et al. 1988; Baum et al., 2001; Baume and Locke, 2004; Shane et al., 2003).

Locke and Latham (2002) propose that goals impact both performance and behavior through four different mechanisms. First of all, goals have a directive function. They help us to turn our attention and efforts toward activities relevant to the goal and ignore activities which are irrelevant. Second, goals serve as energizers. The higher the goals, the greater efforts we make to achieve them, as stated in Bandura's (1989) theory of self-efficacy. Third, goals affect persistence. The higher the goal, the longer we are willing to work for it. Finally, goals can lead to arousal,

---

[1] Throughout this chapter the authors have chosen to use the pronoun he when referring to an individual, but this has been only for ease or reading and in no way implies that women cannot be entrepreneurs

discovery, and emergence of strategies. The relationship between goals and performance is stronger the more committed people are. How committed individuals are
depends on the importance of the outcome (how important is it to succeed) and
how likely their success is in their own estimation (self-efficacy). The existence of
feedback is another important factor in goal theory. People need to be able to check
where they stand in relation to their goal so that they can determine whether they
need to make adjustments in their behavior in order to attain the goal (Locke and
Latham, 2002; Lent et al., 1994). Social cognitive theory implies there is a reciprocal
relation between self-efficacy, outcome expectations, and goal systems (Bandura,
1986).

Behavior goals are neither entirely ignored nor explicitly included in the work
of Ajzen and Fishbein (1977). Essentially, all behaviors can be labeled as goals in
the theory of planned behavior. Goals can be defined as every positive outcome that
one seeks to gain through reasoned behavior (e.g., Ajzen and Fishbein, 1977). For
example, if an entrepreneur goes to venture capitalists in order to raise funds, the
act of going to the venture capitalist constitutes a planned behavior and gaining
money for the venture is the goal. However, Bagozzi and Warshaw (1990, 1992)
have opposed this definition of goals and claim the theory of planned behavior is
designed to explain only performances which are solely dependent on an intention,
i.e., volitional behavior where no impediments prevent the implementation of the
intention. Thus, in effect, ignoring the fact that impediments may have an effect on
whether the performance will be successful or not. For example, one may have the
intention to buy a business, but the intention may not be acted upon because of a lack
of financing or a lack of suitable firms for sale. An intention does not always lead
directly to an action (Bagozzi and Warshaw, 1990). As noted earlier, Ajzen (1985)
did add behavioral control into the model in order to include the influence of external
factors, but this addition did not satisfy Bagozzi and Warshaw, who subsequently
developed their own model called the *theory of trying* (Bagozzi and Warshaw, 1990).
This model is illustrated in Fig. 7.1.

While Ajzen and Fishbein's theories treat action as a single performance,
Bagozzi (1992) preferred to view action as an attempt, or a sequence of attempts,
through which to achieve a final performance. Bagozzi made a critical remark with
respect to the nature of entrepreneurial venture creation: *Sometimes there is a significant time-lag between when the decision is made and an opportunity to act on it*
(Bagozzi et al., 2003; Shane, 2008). This was emphasized by using the words "goal
striving" or "trying."

Bagozzi and Warshaw (1990) distinguish between *intermediate goals* and *end-
state goals*. For example, one might buy a house (intermediate goal) in order to
achieve a higher standard of living (end-state goal). Applying the theory of planned
behavior might be useful when deciding which house to buy, but the theory of
planned behavior fails to predict whether the end-state goal is achieved or not.

In the theory of trying, an attitude toward a reasoned action is replaced by an
attitude toward trying and an intention is restricted to an *intention to try*. Moreover,
Bagozzi and Warshaw (1990) added the impact of past behavior and some additional
background factors. In the theory of planned behavior, intentions and performance

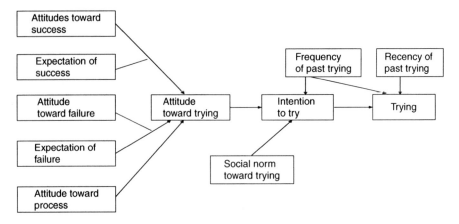

Fig. 7.1 Theory of trying
(Source: Bagozzi and Warshaw, 1990, 131)

are influenced by past behavior only through background factors (Ajzen and Madden, 1986; Ajzen and Fishbein, 2005). However, Bagozzi and Warshaw (1990) argued that past behavior could make a substantial contribution to understanding future behavior and could also possibly influence behavior directly without impacting the formation of intention. Frequently occurring behavior is often mindless and therefore its performance is determined by cognitive schemes.

In the theory of trying, the impact of past behavior is divided into the *frequency of past behavior* and how *recently that past behavior occurred*, representing the role of memories in affecting future intentions. The frequency of past behavior is assumed to impact the *intention to try* as well as the *trying directly*. It is also believed to impact the intention to try even when intentions are not yet fully formed on a cognitive level. Consider, for example, asking an entrepreneur if he is going to attend a trade fair within the next year. Perhaps he has not yet planned which trade fair to attend, but if he knows that he usually attends two trade fairs each year, he is most likely to answer that he will probably attend one within the next year even though he does not yet have a clear plan which trade fair to attend. The frequency of past trying affects trying directly as in habitual behavior. Moreover, how recent the past trying occurred is also believed to have an impact because of the increased likelihood of recalling and reporting more recent behavior rather than behavior which happened in the more distant past. Recent behavior is therefore assumed to be overweighed in the formation of an intention. For example, if one has just succeeded in starting a company, one is likely to believe one can do it again. Likewise, if one has just failed in something, one is probably not very keen to try again immediately (Bagozzi and Warshaw, 1990).

The determinants of attitudes toward trying in the theory of trying are adapted from Lewin's early work on goals (Lewin et al., 1944). Lewin suggests attitudes toward trying were the result of an individual weighing success against failure. In the theory of trying, self-efficacy is present through the subject's subjective assessments of the probability of success (Bay and Daniel, 2003).

In the original test of the theory of trying, attitudes were not significantly predicted by the attitudes toward failure and the expectations of failure. Later work proved the usefulness of the model, but concurrently draws attention to the fact that the significance of the attitude variables fluctuates (see, for example, Bagozzi and Kimmel, 1995; Bagozzi et al., 1992; DeHart and Birkimer, 1997). Both Bagozzi and Dholakia (1999) and Bay and Daniel (2003) picked up on this shortcoming and introduced *the concept of the hierarchy of goals*, which should be used in addition to the theory of trying. Bay and Daniel (2003, 669) state

> *Individuals develop "programs" intended to implement their principles and life goals. Within these programs, goals are arranged in a hierarchical order depending on how close they are to the overall goal of the program. Lower-level goals are intended to set the stage for the achievement of higher level-goals.*

As seen in Fig. 7.2, Bagozzi and Dholakia (1999) suggest that goals can be divided into three levels: focal goals, lower level subordinate goals, and higher level superordinate goals. The focal goal is located in the center of the hierarchy and answers the question "What is it that I strive for?" Lower level subordinate goals answer the question "How can I achieve what I strive for?" and higher level superordinate goals answer to the question "Why do I want to achieve what I strive for?"

Most empirical tests of the theory of trying are carried out on a fairly low level of goals, such as losing weight or mastering a new piece of software. Bay and Daniel (2003) wanted to show that if the goal is of a higher level, it may have a different impact on behavior. It is clear that this theory has much to offer the study of entrepreneurship, which is consistent with Locke and Latham's remark on the importance of the goal and the commitment of the actor (Locke and Latham, 2002). It is fair to assume, for example, that one relates differently to purchasing an ice

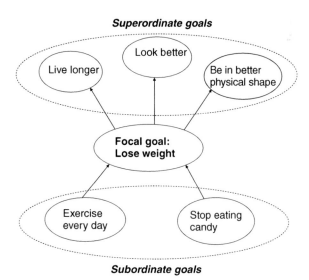

Fig. 7.2 Hierarchy of goals (Source: adapted from Bagozzi and Dholkia, 1999, 24)

cream cone than to finding one's life partner. To test their assumption, Bay and Daniel (2003) choose to study the decision of high school students to complete their education. In that study, both the attitude toward success and the attitude toward failure were significant predictors of the attitude toward trying. As noted earlier, the attitude toward failure had rarely been found significant in earlier tests of the theory of trying. The results supported the assumption that goal-directed behavior can be placed on a continuum and that goals affect behavior differently depending on their position in the hierarchy.

The idea of a hierarchy of goals is also found in the work of Lawson (1997a, b). Similar to Bagozzi and Dholakia (1999), he proposes that goals can be organized at three different levels: system, principle, and program. The system level is the highest level and reflects the idealized self but does not lead to direct action. The principle level reflects a harmonious life and although it too does not lead to direct action, an understanding is formed at this level of what action could be taken. Finally, the program level results in action. At the two highest levels intentions are still ill-formed. Only at the lowest level (the program level) are well-formed intentions incorporated (Lawson, 1997a, b).

The work of Gollwitzer and Brandstätter (1997) contributes to the discussion by illustrating the link between intentions, motivation, and goals and by presenting the ideas of *implementation intentions* and *goal pursuit*. As seen in Fig. 7.3, they describe people's goal pursuits as a continuum including four action phases. The first phase, the *predecisional phase*, is an awakening of desires and wishes. In the second phase, the *preactional phase*, goal-directed behavior is initiated. In the third phase, the *actional phase*, the goal-directed actions are brought to a successful ending. Finally, in the fourth phase, the *postactional phase*, the outcome is evaluated by comparing what has been achieved to what was originally desired.

The four action phases are connected through crucial transition points. Gollwitzer and Brandstätter (1997) label the first transition point *goal intention*. A goal intention, for example, can be "I intend to become an entrepreneur." However, as was previously stated, an intention is not enough to lead to an action as there might be several impediments along the way. There may also be different ways of achieving the goal that one may have to choose between in order to avoid the risk of failing to seize a specific opportunity. An *implementation intention* can then function as a mediator and take the goal pursuit one step further. It serves to translate the goal state from a higher level of abstractness to a lower level and to link

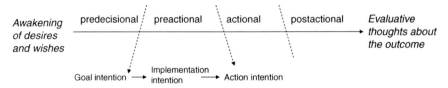

Fig. 7.3 Goal intentions and implementation intentions
(Source: adapted from Gollwitzer and Brandstätter, 1997)

a certain goal-directed behavior to a situational context. An implementation intention could be, for example, "I intend to start my own company when I have finished my studies." An implementation intention results in a commitment to perform a specified goal-directed behavior once a critical situation has occurred. Furthermore, people who have formed an implementation intention should possess the cognitive structures needed to recognize opportunities when they emerge. Thus, Gollwitzer and Brandstätter (1997) conclude that a goal is more likely to be achieved if an implementation intention exists. Gollwitzer and Brandstätter (1997) also succinctly mention the connections to Ajzen's theory of planned behavior and imply that the theory of planned behavior is a good framework when applying their theoretical ideas. Evidently noticing this suggestion for improvement, Ajzen (2001) emphasizes that translating intentions into action is a complex process which needs more research.

More recently, Bagozzi et al. (2003) have added the implementation intention into their original model (Bagozzi and Warshaw, 1992). The resulting model, called a model for effortful decision making and enactment, is designed to explain the mechanisms through which decision making influences goal striving and enactment (see Fig. 7.4).

The model suggests that behavioral decisions are made on two levels. First at the level of goals (or goal intention), and second at the level of the action needed to attain the goal (implementation intention). The mediating role of motivational constructs (goal and implementation desires), emotional constructs (positive and negative anticipated emotions), and attitude constructs (attitudes, social norms,

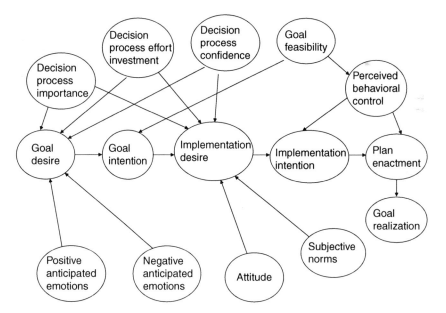

Fig. 7.4 Model for effortful decision making and enactment
(Source: Bagozzi et al., 2003, 276)

feasibility, confidence, and perceived behavioral control) are also taken into account in the model. Desires are believed to be sufficient antecedents of intentions. Anticipated emotions include the assessment of the prospect of both success and failure. How one feels about succeeding and failing will, according to Bagozzi et al. (2003), affect which goals are set. The role of attitude constructs responds to the arguments presented in the theory of planned behavior.

Since goals impact our decisions and decisions are made frequently in our lives, our chosen goals will influence many aspects of our lives, including career choices. The importance of goals when choosing a career has been studied through social cognitive career theory (Lent and Brown, 2006; Lent et al., 1994). The model developed by Lent and Brown and their associates includes variables related to the core person (e.g., self-efficacy, outcome expectation, interest, goals) as well as variables related to the contextual setting (e.g., support, barriers, background). The model is illustrated in Fig. 7.5.

This model implies that people develop a career interest in fields they view themselves to be efficacious in, and in which they anticipate a positive outcome. Personal interests further affects which goal one sets and which actions one chooses to undertake. Outcome expectations and self-efficacy expectations can also directly impact goal and action choices (Lent et al., 1994). *It is noteworthy that there are no obvious dependent variables in the model. Lent and Brown (2006) argued that social cognitive variables can be viewed as dependent or independent, depending on whether one intends to study what shapes the variables, or the outcome that the variables foster.*

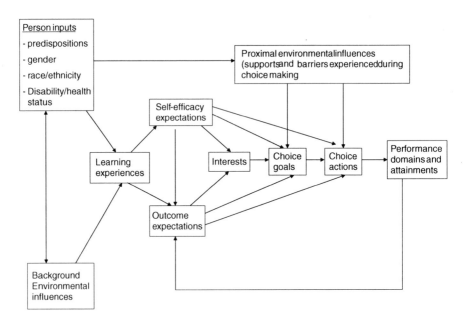

Fig. 7.5 Social cognitive career theory
(Source: Lent et al., 1994, 93)

7.16 Tying Motivation to Cognitions and Goals

If we take the discussion on intrinsic and extrinsic motivations and merge it into the discussion on goals and cognitions, we can create a description of the characteristics that different types of entrepreneurs have (Elfving, 2008). In this chapter, we have attempted to cover a broad range of concepts that have strong motivational properties that could impact entrepreneurial cognitions and behaviors. We have also tried to show how various motivations are tied to entrepreneurial intentions and attitudes, as seen in Fig. 7.6. We have also suggested several potentially fruitful areas of research using motivational concepts that could reveal a lot about what drives entrepreneurs. In turn, this could potentially help us better design programs and policies to support such motivations and subsequent behaviors.

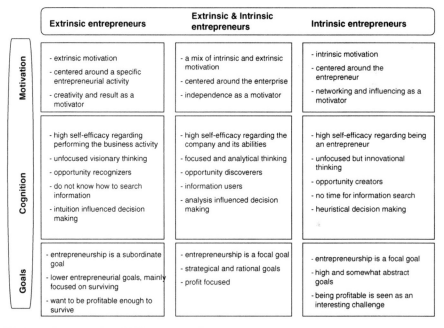

Fig. 7.6 Characteristics of different types of entrepreneurs (Source: Elfing, 2008, 144)

References

Ambrose ML, Kulik CT (1999) Old friends, new faces: Motivation research in the 1990s. Journal of Management 25: 231–292.

Ajzen I (1985) From intentions to actions: A theory of planned behavior. In: Kuhl J, Beckmann J (eds.), Action Control: From Cognition to Behavior. New York: Springer-Verlag, pp. 11–39.

Ajzen I (2001) Nature and operation of attitudes. Annual Review of Psychology 52: 27–58.

Ajzen I, Fishbein M (1977) Attitude-behavior relations: A theoretical analysis and review of empirical research. Psychological Bulletin 84: 888–918.

Ajzen I, Fishbein M (2005) The influence of attitudes on behavior. In: Albarracin D, Johnson B, Zanna M (eds.) The Handbook of Attitudes. Mahwah: Lawrence Erlbaum Associates, pp. 173–221.

Ajzen I, Madden TJ (1986) Prediction of goal-directed behavior: Attitudes, intentions, and perceived behavioral control. Journal of Experimental Social Psychology, 22: 453–474.

Atkinson JW (1957) Motivational determinants of risk-taking behavior. Psychological Review 64: 359–372.

Atkinson JW (1964) An Introduction to Motivation. New York: Van Nostrand.

Bagozzi R (1992) The self-regulation of attitudes, intentions, and behavior. Social Psychology Quarterly 55: 178–204.

Bagozzi R, Davis F, Warshaw P (1992) Development and test of a theory of technological learning and usage. Human Relations 45: 659–686.

Bagozzi R, Dholakia U (1999) Goal setting and goal striving in consumer behavior. Journal of Marketing, 63: 19–32.

Bagozzi R, Dholakia U, Basuroy S (2003) How effortful decisions get enacted: The motivating role of decision processes, desires, and anticipated emotions. Journal of Behavioral Decision Making 16: 273–295.

Bagozzi R, Kimmel P (1995) A comparison of leading theories for the prediction of goal-directed behaviours. British Journal of Social Psychology 34: 437–461.

Bagozzi R, Warshaw P (1990) Trying to consume. Journal of Consumer Research, 17: 127–140.

Bagozzi R, Warshaw P (1992) An examination of the etiology of the attitude-behavior relation for goal-directed behaviors. Multivariate Behavioral Research 27: 601–634.

Bandura A (1986) Social Foundations of Thought and Action: A Social Cognitive Theory. Englewood Cliffs: Prentice Hall.

Bandura A (1989) Regulation of cognitive process through perceived self-efficacy. Developmental Psychology 25: 729–735.

Bandura A, Locke EA (2003). Negative self-efficacy and goal effects revisited. Journal of Applied Psychology 88: 87–99.

Baum J, Locke EA (2004) The relationship of entrepreneurial traits, skill, and motivation to subsequent venture growth. Journal of Applied Psychology 89: 587–598.

Baum J, Locke EA, Smith K (2001) A multidimensional model of venture growth. Academy of Management Journal 44: 292–303.

Bay D, Daniel H (2003) The theory of trying and goal-directed behavior: The Effect and moving up the hierarchy of goals. Psychology and Marketing 20: 669–684.

Brännback M, Carsrud A, Kickul J, Krueger N, Elfving J. (2007) Trying to be An Entrepreneur? A Goal-specific Challenge to The Intentions Model, Babson Conference Entrepreneurship Research, Madrid, Spain. 7-9.6. 2007.

Brockhaus RH (1980) Risk taking propensity of entrepreneurs. The Academy of Management Journal 23: 509–520.

Brockhaus RH (1982). The psychology of the entrepreneur. In: Kent CA, Sexton DA, Vesper, KH (eds) Encyclopedia of Entrepreneurship. Englewood, NJ: Prentice-Hall, pp. 39–55.

Carland JW, Hoy F, Boulton WR, Carland JAC (1984) Differentiating entrepreneurs from small business owners: A conceptualization. Academy of Management Review 9: 351–359.

Carsrud AL, Dodd BG, Helmreich RL, Spence JT (August, 1982) Predicting performance: Effects of scholastic aptitude, achievement motivation, past performance, and attributions. Paper presented at the convention of the American Psychological Association, Washington, DC.

Carsrud AL, Olm KW, Thomas JB (1989) Predicting entrepreneurial success; effects of multidimensional achievement motivation, levels of ownership, and cooperative relationships. Entrepreneurship and Regional Development, 1: 237–244.

Cohen AR, Zimbardo PG (1969) Dissonance and the need to avoid failure. In: Zimbardo PG (ed). The Cognitive Control of Motivation: The Consequences of Choice and Dissonance. Glenview, IL: Scott Foresman and Company.

Collins C, Hanges P, Locke EA (2004) The relationship of achievement motivation to entrepreneurial behavior: A meta-analysis. Human Performance 17: 95–117.

Deci EL (1975) Intrinsic Motivation. New York: Plenum Press.

DeHart D, Birkimer J (1997) Trying to practice safer sex: Development of the sexual risks scale. The Journal of Sex Research 34: 11–28.

Deutsch M, Krauss RM (1965) Theories in Social Psychology. New York: Basic Books.

Elfving J (2008) Contextualizing Entrepreneurial Intentions: A Multiple Case Study on Entrepreneurial Cognitions and Perceptions. Turku, Finland: Åbo Akademi förlag.

Festinger L (1957) A Theory of Cognitive Dissonance. Evanston, IL: Row, Peterson.

Fisher I (1930) The Theory of Interest. New York: MacMillan.

Freud S (1900) The Interpretation of Dreams. Standard Editions, London: Hogarth Press 1953.

Freud S (1915) Instincts and their vicissitudes. In: Freud S (ed) Collected Papers. Vol 4, New York: Basic Books, pp. 60–83.

Freud S (1924) A General Introduction to Psychoanalysis. New York: Permabooks.

Gächter S, Falk A (2000) Work motivation, institutions, and performance. In: Zwick R, Rapoport A (eds.), Advances in Experimental Business Research. Kluwer Academic Publishers, 2002.

Gasse Y (1982) Elaborations on the psychology of the entrepreneur. In: Kent CA, Sexton DA, Vesper KH (eds) Encyclopedia of Entrepreneurship. Englewood Cliffs, NJ: Prentice-Hall, pp. 57–66.

Gollwitzer P, Brandstätter V (1997) Implementation intentions and effective goal pursuit. Journal of Personality and Social Psychology 73: 186–199.

Hackman JR, Oldham GR (1976) Motivation through the design of work: Test of a theory. Organizational Behavior and Human Performance 16: 250–279.

Hart JW, Stasson MF, Mahoney JM (2007) The big five and achievement motivation: Exploring the relationship between personality and a two-factor model of motivation. Individual Differences Research 5: 267–274.

Helmreich RL (1982) Pilot Selection and Training. Paper presented at the meeting of the American Psychological Association, Washington, DC.

Helmreich RL, Beane WE, Lucker GW, Spence JT (1978) Achievement motivation and scientific attainment. Personality and Social Psychology Bulletin 4: 22–226.

Helmreich RL, Sawin LL, Carsrud AL (1986) The honeymoon effect in job performance: Temporal increases in the predictive power of achievement motivation. Journal of Applied Psychology 71: 185–188.

Helmreich RL, Spence JT (1978) The work and family orientation questionnaire: An objective instrument to assess components of achievement motivation and attitudes towards family and career. JSAS Catalog of Selected Documents in Psychology, 8, 35, (Ms. No. 1677).

Helmreich RL, Spence JT, Beane WE, Lucker GW, Matthews KA (1980) Making it in Academic Psychology: Demographic and Personality Correlates of Attainment. Journal of Personality and Social Psychology 39: 896–908.

Homans GE (1961) Social Behavior: Its Elementary Forms. Harcourt: Brace&World.

Huuskonen V (1989) Yrittäjäksi ryhtyminen motivoitumis- ja päätöksentekoprosessina. Turku: Publications of the Turku School of Economics.

Koch S (1956) Behavior as "intrinsically" regulated: Work notes toward a pre-theory of phenomena called "motivational". Nebraska symposium on motivation 4: 42–87.

Komives JL (1972) A preliminary study of the personal values of high technology entrepreneurs. In: Cooper AC, Komives JL (eds.) Technical Entrepreneurship: A Symposium. Milwaukee, WI: Center for Venture Management, pp. 231–242.

Krueger N, Reilly M, Carsrud AL (2000). Competing models of entrepreneurial intentions. Journal of Business Venturing 15: 411–532.

Langen-Fox JL, Roth S (1995) Achievement motivation and female entrepreneurs. Journal of Occupational and Organizational Psychology 68: 209–218.

Latham GP, Locke EA (1991) Self-regulation through goal-setting. Organizational Behavior and Human Decision Processes 50: 212–247.

Lawson R (1997a) Consumer decision making within a goal-driven framework. Psychology and Marketing 14: 427–449.

Lawson T (1997b) Economics and Reality. London: Routledge.

Lent R, Brown S (2006) On conceptualizing and assessing social cognitive constructs in career research: A measurement guide. Journal of Career Assessment 14: 12–35.

Lent R, Brown S, Hacket G (1994) Toward a unifying theory of career and academic interests, choice, and performance. Journal of Vocational Behavior 45: 79–122.

Lewin K, Dembo L, Sears P (1944) Level of aspiration. In: Hunt M (eds) Personality and the Behavior Disorders. New York: Ronald, pp. 333–378.

Liao J, Welsch H (2004) Entrepreneurial intensity. In: Gartner WB, Shaver KG, Carter NM, Reynolds PD (eds.) Handbook of Entrepreneurial Dynamics: The Process of Business Creation. Thousand Oaks, CA: Sage, pp. 186–195.

Locke EA, Latham GP (2002) Building a practically useful theory of goal setting and task motivation. American Psychologist 57: 705–717.

Locke EA, Latham GP (2004) What should we do about motivation theory? Six recommendations for the twenty-first century. Academy of Management Review 29: 388.

Locke EA, Latham GP, Erez M (1988) The determinants of goal commitment. Academy of Management Review 13: 23–39.

Lumpkin GT, Erdogan B (2004) If Not Entrepreneurship, Can Psychological Characteristics Predict Entrepreneurial Orientation? – A Pilot Study. ICFAI Journal of Entrepreneurship Development 1: 21–33.

Manove M (2000) Entrepreneurs, Optimism and the Competitive Edge. Boston: Boston University and CEMFI.

Maslow AH (1946) A theory of human motivation. Psychological Review 50: 370–396.

Mehrabian A (1968) Male and female scales of the tendency to achieve. Educational and Psychological Measurement 28: 493–502.

McClelland DC (1961) The Achieving Society. Princeton: D. Van Nostrand Company.

McClelland DC (1965) Achievement motivation can be developed. Harvard Business Review (November-December).

McClelland DC (1985) How motives, skills, and values determine what people do. American Psychologist 40: 812–825.

McClelland DC, Atkinson JW, Clark RA, Lowell EL (1953) The Achievement Motive. New York: Appleton-Century-Crofts.

McClelland DC, Winter DG (1969) Motivating Economic Achievement. New York: Free Press.

Murray HA (1938) Explorations in personality. New York: Oxford University Press.

Nurmi J-E, Salmela-Aro K (2005) Motivaatio elämänkaaren siirtymissä. In: Nurmi J-E, Salmela-Aro K (eds.) Mikä meitä liikuttaa: modernin motivaatiopsykologian perusteet. Jyväskylä: PS-Kustannus, pp. 54–66.

Nuttin J (1984) Motivation, Planning, and Action. Leuven: Leuven University Press and Lawrence Erlbaum Associates.

Penrose E (1959) The Theory of the Firm. Oxford: Basil Blackwell.

Perwin L (2003) The Science of Personality. Oxford: Oxford University Press.

Pinder CC (1984) Work Motivation: Theory, Issues, and Applications. Glenview, IL: Scott, Foresman.

Pinder CC (1998) Work motivation in organizational behavior. Upper Saddle River, NJ: Prentice Hall.

Price VA (1982) Type A Behavior Pattern: A Model for Research and Practice. New York: Academic Press.

Quigley NR, Tymon Jr. WG (2006). Toward an integrated model of intrinsic motivation and career self-management. Career Development International 11: 522–543.

Reynolds PD, Bygrave WD, Autio E, Cox L, Hay M (2002) Global Entrepreneurship Monitor: 2002, Executive Report. Kansas City, MO: Kauffman Center for Entrepreneurial Leadership.

Ryan RM, Deci EL (2000) Self-determination theory and the facilitation of intrinsic motivation, social development, and well-being. American Psychologist 55: 68–78.

Salmela-Aro K, Saisto T, Halmesmäki E, Nurmi, J-E (2005). Motivaation merkitys siirryttäessä vanhemmuuteen. In: Nurmi J-E, Salmela-Aro K (eds.) Mikä meitä liikuttaa, 2nd ed. Jyväskylä: PS kustannus, pp. 84–104.

Schlachet PJ (1969) The motivation to succeed and the memory for failure. In: Zimbardo PG (eds.) The Cognitive Control of Motivation: The Consequences of Choice and Dissonance. Glenview, IL: Scott Foresman and Company.

Segal G, Bogia D, Schoenfeld J (2005) The motivation to become an entrepreneur. International Journal of Entrepreneurial Behaviour and Research 11: 42–57.

Shane S (2008) The Illusions of Entrepreneurship. New Haven: Yale University Press.

Shane S, Locke EA, Collins C (2003). Entrepreneurial motivation. Human Resource Management Review 13: 257–279.

Spence JT, Helmreich RL (1978) Masculinity and Femininity: Their Psychological Dimensions, Correlates, and Antecedents. Austin: The University of Texas Press.

Steel P, König CJ (2006) Integrating theories of motivation. Academy of Management Review 31(4): 880–913.

Steward, WJ Jr., Roth PL (2007) A meta-analysis of achievement motivation differences between entrepreneurs and managers. Journal of Small Business Management 45: 401–421.

Tuuanaen M (1997) Finnish and US entrepreneurs' need for achievement: A cross-cultural analysis. In: Ann J, Carland J (eds.) The Proceedings of the Academy of Entrepreneurship. Cullowhee, NC: Academy of Entrepreneurship, Inc., pp. 8–20.

Wainer A, Rubin IM (1967) Motivation of R&D Entrepreneurs; Determinants of Company Success. Alfred P. Sloan School of Management: Massachusetts Institute of Technology.

Wilson EO (1998) Consilience: The Unity of Knowledge. New York: Alfred A. Knopf.

Wong P-K, Lee L, Leung A (2006) Entrepreneurship by circumstances and abilities: The mediating role of job satisfaction and moderating role of self-efficacy. MPRA Paper No. 596.

Zhao H, Seibert SE, Hills GE (2005) The mediating role of self-efficacy in the development of entrepreneurial intentions. Journal of Applied Psychology 90: 1265–1272.

Zimbardo PG (1969) The Cognitive Control Of Motivation: The Consequences Of Choice And Dissonance. Glenview, IL: Scott Foresman and Company.

Chapter 8
The Role of Emotions and Cognitions in Entrepreneurial Decision-Making

Theresa Michl, Isabell M. Welpe, Matthias Spörrle, and Arnold Picot

8.1 Theoretical Foundations

This chapter examines the role of emotions and cognitions in entrepreneurial decision-making and how they interact in this process. First, definitions of the terms emotions and cognitions are outlined. Second, entrepreneurial decision-making processes and the role of emotions and cognitions within these processes are presented. Afterward, we briefly describe three representatives of cognitive appraisal theories of emotion with the focus on entrepreneurship. Finally, we present a model of how to study emotions and cognitions in entrepreneurial decision-making and point out implications for future research, for practice, and for teaching.

8.1.1 Emotions

The term "emotion" can be traced back to the Latin words *e(x)* (out/out of) and *motio* (movement/action/excitement), thus indicating that some (inner) movement or excitement is being transported out of an individual inner state to the public.

Emotions in business contexts have been ignored for a long time. However, studies in psychology, humanities, and social sciences assign an important role to emotions in human behavior. Because neuroscience can now specify the physiological correlates of emotional activities and is able to explicitly connect them with decision-making (e.g., Cohen 2005, Phelps 2006), emotions are increasingly integrated into research on decision-making processes and behavior in business contexts (cf. Côté 2005, Côté and Morgan 2002, Fisher and Ashkanasy 2000). The field of neuroeconomics investigates research on emotions in decision-making by linking neuroscience and economics and opens the "black box" of decision-making (e.g., Camerer et al. 2004, Lieberman 2007, Shiv et al. 2005).

T. Michl (✉)
Munich School of Management, Ludwig-Maximilians-University, Ludwigstr. 28, D – 80539, Munich, Germany,
e-mail: michl@lmu.de

A.L. Carsrud, M. Brännback (eds.), *Understanding the Entrepreneurial Mind*, International Studies in Entrepreneurship 24, DOI 10.1007/978-1-4419-0443-0_8, © Springer Science+Business Media, LLC 2009

Since William James (1884)[1] answers to the question of "what is an emotion" has been vehemently discussed, but although there is a large body of literature, it fails to provide one undisputed definition. Scherer (2005) calls the counting of definitions of emotion "hopeless". The large amount of different conceptualizations of emotion can be explained by differing underlying theoretical frameworks and thus accentuating or devaluating different aspects of an emotion. Componential theories of emotion describe emotions' main components and propose that emotions have the following attributes in common (e.g., Meyer et al. 2001, cf. Försterling and Spörrle 2005):

- Emotions are current psychological states of an individual and have a certain quality (positive emotion, e.g., happiness, or negative emotion, e.g., sadness), intensity (e.g., strong fear or weak fear), and duration (e.g., short-term fear or long-term fear).
- Emotions focus on certain targets and usually an individual can name the object why he/she is, for example, happy or sad.
- Emotions are typically (consciously) experienced by the individual (experience aspect).
- Emotions reveal psychological changes, e.g., flushing, increased heartbeat frequency (psychological aspect), which are connected with certain behavior tendencies, e.g., running away with fear, showing your teeth because of anger (behavioral aspect).

Discrete emotion theories (e.g., Scherer 2005, Ekman 1972, 1992) suggest a number of basic emotions such as joy, love, anger, fear, sadness, disgust, and surprise. Scherer (2005), for example, proposes anger, fear, joy, and sadness as typical basic emotions that are frequently experienced. Following the Geneva Emotion Wheel (GEW, see references) in Fig. 8.1, pride, elation, happiness, satisfaction, relief, hope, interest, surprise, anxiety, sadness, boredom, shame/guilt, disgust, contempt, hostility, and anger can be added to these emotions (cf. Scherer 2005). The 16 emotions in the GEW – the upper limit of amount of basic emotions is often considered as 14 (Scherer 2005) – are divided into four emotions per quadrant. The intensity of the emotions is represented by the size of the circle, with small circles representing weak emotional intensity, e.g., weak fear, and large circles representing strong emotional intensity, e.g., strong fear. Additionally, there are negative or positive emotions and high controllable or low controllable causes for emotions. If an outcome is (not) congruent with the goals of an individual and the cause for that outcome was controlled by that individual, the individual will show (anxiety) pride about this outcome. If an outcome is (not) congruent with the goals of an individual and the cause for that outcome was not

---

[1] Scherer (2005) criticizes that William James (1884) asked the wrong question with "what is an emotion," but should have rather asked "what is a feeling."

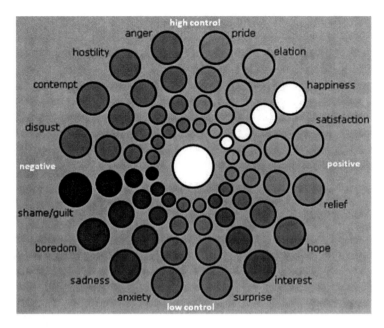

Fig. 8.1 Prototype version of the Geneva Emotion Wheel

controlled by that individual, the individual will show (sadness) surprise about that outcome. For example, when entrepreneurs (do not) receive profit from an investment decision, they will feel (angry) proud, if they appraise this decision (i.e., the cause for the outcome) as controlled by themselves. On the other hand, when entrepreneurs (do not) receive profit from an investment decision, because the profit depends on an unexpected economic boost (crisis), they will feel (sad) surprised.

8.1.2 The Difference Between Emotion, Affect, Mood, and Feeling

As mentioned above, emotions are directed on a certain object and they are timely limited. Mood and affect describe a milder experience, do not necessarily have a clear reason (i.e., stimulus) and are longer lasting. Feelings are the conscious subjective experience of emotion and mood (Barsade and Gibson 2007, Meyer et al. 2001). Baron (2008) defines affect as individuals' current moods and feelings.

In the following we use emotion as a general term, because as far as it concerns the current status of entrepreneurial research emotions, affects, moods, and feelings to some extent produce comparable effects in decision-making (e.g., Baron 2008, Lyubomirsky et al. 2005).

8.2 Cognitions

The term "cognition" derives from the Latin word *cognoscere* (to recognize/to discover).

Cognitions in general are all processes by which sensory input is transformed, reduced, elaborated, stored, recovered, and used (Neisser 1967). Thus, entrepreneurial cognition can be seen as the cognitive process through which entrepreneurs acquire, store, transform, and use information (e.g., Busenitz and Arthurs 2007, Mitchell et al. 2004, Sternberg 2004). Additionally, Mitchell et al. (2002) propose a definition of entrepreneurial cognitions:

> Entrepreneurial cognitions are the knowledge structures that people use to make assessments, judgments, or decisions involving opportunity evaluation, venture creation, and growth. (Mitchell et al. 2002, p. 97)

Some of the problematic aspects of entrepreneurial cognitions, such as counterfactual thinking and affect-infusion (cf. Forgas 1995), self-serving bias, planning fallacy, and self-justification (Baron 1998), overconfidence and representativeness error (Busenitz and Barney 1997), illusion of control, and misguided belief in the law of small numbers (Simon et al. 2000), however, occur in entrepreneurial environments characterized by high uncertainty or novelty, information overload, strong emotions, time pressure, and fatigue (cf. Mitchell et al. 2002, Picot et al. 2005, Picot et al. 2008). On the other hand, positive aspects of entrepreneurial cognitions are, for example, making an entrepreneurial decision based on cognitive mechanisms such as expert scripts (Mitchell et al. 2000 and Chapters 5 and 6).

Because the creation of a new business venture is, fundamentally, a social activity, some researchers (cf. Mitchell et al. 2002, Shaver and Scott 1991) are concentrating on the process of social cognition which beyond others also includes aspects of attention, memory, categorization, and inference. Originally, there are two aspects of social cognition (Fiske and Taylor 1984), one being the person in the situation, and the other one being cognition and motivation (see also Chapter 7). A recent definition of social cognition is provided by Baron et al. (2009) as the ways in which individuals interpret, analyze, remember, and use information about the social world.

8.3 Emotions and Cognitions in Entrepreneurial Decision-Making

In this section, we demonstrate the influence of emotions and cognitions on entrepreneurial decision-making and how emotions and cognitions interact in this process. Although we first outline the influence of emotions and cognitions on entrepreneurial decision-making separately, researchers and practitioners have already agreed that emotions and cognitions cannot be studied without each other. Only for reasons of clarity do we focus on the influence of emotions on entrepreneurial decision-making and then on the influence of cognitions on entrepreneurial decision-making before we show their interacting effects on entrepreneurial decision-making. Previous studies on the connection between emotions and cognitions (e.g., Forgas 2000) indicated that they are connected in a bidirectional link, i.e., emotions affect cognitions and cognitions in turn influence emotions (Baron 2008).

8.3.1 The Role of Emotions in Entrepreneurial Decision-Making

Emotions in the entrepreneurial process have not been examined by many scholars so far (e.g., Cardon et al. 2005, Goss 2005, 2007, Shepherd 2004), but in entrepreneurship literature they are often connected to information processing and decision-making (e.g., Baron 2000a, Goss 2007, Schindehutte et al. 2006). Because entrepreneurs have specific tasks in highly unpredictable, uncertain, and rapidly changing environments (Picot et al. 2005), they cannot follow certain well-learned scripts. Instead, they often have to trust their "gut feeling" which under such circumstances are especially strong (Baron 2008). Emotions, however, influence the decision-making process and judgments, even when they are unrelated to each other and stem from sources completely independent of the context (Baron 2008). But considering the fact that individuals are able to control or suppress their positive and negative emotions, some studies (e.g., Shiv et al. 2005, Spencer 2005) proved that those individuals, who make decisions (seemingly) independent of their emotions, are more successful and make more efficient decisions. Besides, Baron (1998, 2000b, 2008) postulates that entrepreneurs will experience very intense emotions in their decisions, as they generally show a high commitment to their ventures.

The following two sections outline possible effects of positive and negative emotions on entrepreneurial decision-making processes. It must be mentioned here that neither negative nor positive emotions have a uniformly beneficial or detrimental effect on entrepreneurial decision-making.

8.3.2 The Effect of Positive Emotions on Entrepreneurial Decision-Making

There are numerous studies which provide evidence for the beneficial effects of individuals with positive emotions and even though it has been postulated that emotion-related conditions such as passion, enthusiasm, and affection provide important impulses in the entrepreneurial process (Baum and Locke, 2004, Cardon et al. 2005, Smilor 1997, see also Chapter 9), positive emotions have hardly been considered. Many studies have proven that positive emotions lead to more efficient decision-making (e.g., Estrada et al. 1997, Isen 2000), higher involvement with tasks (e.g., Lyubomirsky et al. 2005), and approach behavior (e.g., Baron 2000a, Krause, 2004 and Chapter 15). Additionally, positive emotions might explain why some entrepreneurs are able to tolerate intense levels of stress (Baron 2008) and could therefore be more successful than other entrepreneurs not holding this external pressure.

Some studies (e.g., Ardichvili et al. 2003, Baron 2004, Baron 2008, Forgas 2000) also demonstrated negative effects of positive emotions and showed that positive emotions such as joviality and happiness might lead entrepreneurs to not fully evaluate all possible outcome alternatives and consequently result in hasty and premature decisions. This could happen when entrepreneurs stop the information search for a decision too early (cf. Bless 2001, Picot et al. 2008), because they are already so enthusiastic about their present idea and believe that they cannot find a better one (e.g., Fiet et al. 2004). It was also shown that positive emotions often increase individuals' willingness to take risks because they feel more optimistic and capable of dealing with potential problems (e.g., Weiss 2002) and expect positive outcomes (e.g., Busenitz and Barney 1997) which increase the tendency to make risky decisions. In addition, there is evidence (e.g., Cacioppo et al. 1993) that entrepreneurs' emotions are contagious, resulting, if the emotions are positive, in being more persuasive for investors, employees, and customers. Positive emotions in this instance could serve for a better success of the new venture. However, it cannot be assumed that positive emotions in general are more helpful for the success of a new venture than are negative emotions.

8.3.3 The Effect of Negative Emotions on Entrepreneurial Decision-Making

Negative emotions such as anxiety and shame do not have an exactly opposing effect compared to positive emotions, but they are rather heterogeneous. Negative emotions have been found to result in avoidance behavior (e.g., Krause 2004, Lazarus et al. 1980), even though some studies also uncovered that negative emotions can have a positive influence on decision-making through higher concentration and more detailed processing (Schwarz et al. 1991). But negative emotions could make entrepreneurs also more risk averse so that they only make decisions when the option is evaluated as totally safe in order to minimize risks and negative outcomes. Higgins (2005) and Brockner et al. (2004) call this a "prevention focus," preventing entrepreneurs from engaging in entrepreneurial action although it could be beneficial. Negative emotions might also be contagious and lead to little support from the social network, e.g., investors, customers, employees (Baron 2008). Little or no support from the social network because of negative emotions might also negatively influence the success of a new venture because extensive social networks are seen as a critical success factor (e.g., Birley 1985, de Koning 1999, Low and McMillan 1988, Ozgen and Baron 2007). Shepherd (2003, 2004) examined negative emotions connected with business failure and could show that potential entrepreneurs are more discouraged by fear of failure than that they are driven by the prospects of great success.

8.3.4 The Role of Cognitions in Entrepreneurial Decision-Making

All inner processes associated with entrepreneurial activity are at least partly cognitive processes. Therefore, one might argue that entrepreneurial activity is influenced by cognitive biases, and cognitive biases were indeed found to strongly influence entrepreneurial decision-making (e.g., Baron 2004, Busenitz and Barney 1997, Shaver and Scott 1991). Baron (2004) even proposes that especially entrepreneurs are more susceptible to such biases than other persons.

In general, individuals have a strong tendency to weigh negative information more heavily than positive information (negativity bias, e.g., Mitchell et al. 2002, Picot et al. 2008). Additionally, individuals tend to notice information that is connected to information they already know (e.g., von Hippel 1994). This strongly influences decisions in a wide range of contexts, especially in the decision-making context of entrepreneurship. The so-called optimistic bias describes an individual's tendency to expect positive outcomes and events (e.g., Busenitz and Barney 1997, Simon et al. 2000) and also influences evaluation and exploitation processes. A derivative of the optimistic bias is the planning fallacy which involves individuals' tendencies to assume that they can achieve more than they actually can during a specific period of time, or that they can complete tasks sooner than is actually practicable (e.g., Bühler et al. 1994). If that is not the case and the tasks take longer than planned to complete, it may lead to the dissatisfaction of investors, customers, and other stakeholders. Finally, the confirmation bias influences individuals' decision-making processes. The confirmation bias refers to the tendency to seek, notice, and remember information that confirms current preferences or beliefs and to overlook and ignore information that is not consistent with current preferences or beliefs (e.g., Nickerson 1998, Picot et al. 2008). This might seriously interfere with the perception and evaluation process of information that could be necessary for the success of the new business. The affect infusion model (Forgas 1995) assumes that the strength of emotion affects individuals' judgments, but interestingly, that does not happen consistently.

Baron and Ensley (2006, Baron 2008) compared one cognitive framework that underlies opportunity recognition, namely pattern recognition, of novice and experienced entrepreneurs. Previous literature calls this prototype theory (e.g., Whittlesea 1997) and Hahn and Chater (1997) developed a basis for it with different theories of pattern recognition. It is not surprising that individuals differ in their cognitive frameworks since these are shaped through unique life experiences. In essence, prototypes serve as templates for individuals and seek to notice links between diverse events or trends and to perceive recognizable and meaningful patterns in these linkages (Baron and Ensley 2006). They (Baron and Ensley 2006) argue that entrepreneurial opportunities have similar characteristics that can be recognized by individuals. Therefore, cognitive frameworks employed by entrepreneurs do indeed develop with increasing experience as theories of pattern recognition suggest (e.g., Whittlesea 1997). Experienced entrepreneurs acquire these well-developed cognitive frameworks through processes of learning – processes that occur as they gain experience in the intricacies of starting a new business.

However, it should certainly not be assumed that the development of increasingly strong and developed prototypes is beneficial in all respects or all instances (cf. Garud and Rappa 1994), e.g., for the success of a new venture.

8.3.5 The Interaction Between Emotions and Cognitions in Entrepreneurial Decision-Making Processes

According to Scherer (2005) some researchers still see emotions and cognitions as two independent but interacting phenomena. However, there is more and more common sense that emotions and cognitions cannot be studied separated from each other, but that only an integrative view will lead to an understanding of their effects on entrepreneurial decision-making. Cognitive science research has proven a strong and complex link between emotions and cognitions (Baron 2008, Tice et al. 2000) and the expanding entrepreneurship literature (e.g., Koellinger et al. 2007, Lee et al. 2005, Shepherd 2004, Sternberg et al. 2007) provides also clear evidence that emotions have a systematic influence on entrepreneurial decision-making. In the last two centuries, three integrative fields of research aroused: the study of the influence of emotions on the memory, on cognitive information processing and attention, and on decision-making (Baron 2008).

The mood-dependent memory is therefore a study subject for the interaction of emotions and cognitions as it perceives, stores, and recalls certain information only in certain moods (Baron 2008, Blaney 1986, Bower 1981, Eich et al. 1994). Individuals primarily remember things they learned in a certain mood when they are in a similar affective state again. For example, entrepreneurs remember sad things when they are in a similar sad situation, and they remember happy things when they are in a similar happy situation. Additionally, if entrepreneurs in negative (positive) moods remember more negative (positive) situations, the current negative (positive) emotional state will be enhanced and entrepreneurs will feel even worse (better). This influences entrepreneurs' decision-making as they only recall selected mood-dependent information on which the decision is based.

As mentioned above, strong positive emotions will result in cognitive strategies for coping and tolerating high levels of stress (Baron 2008, Carver and Scheier 2001). While individuals under weak stress are more concentrated and motivated in their tasks, individuals under strong stress might not be able to "think" anymore – a so-called "black out"– and are unable to explain the simplest relationships. In addition to the influence of the emotions' intensity on cognitions, there are also indications that the quality of emotions determines how information is processed and stored (Baron 2008).

Emotions also have been found to influence individuals' perceptions of the external world (e.g., Baron 2008, Forgas 1995, 2000), e.g., objects, experiences, people, whereas individuals displaying positive emotions tend to perceive the external world as positive and individuals displaying negative emotions tend to perceive the opposite (Baron 2008). For example, happy entrepreneurs tend to see their situation as positive (what it is not necessarily), whereas sad entrepreneurs tend to see their situation negative. In line with that, entrepreneurs with positive emotions tend to perceive a broader range of stimuli than entrepreneurs with negative emotions (e.g., Isen 2002, Schiffman 2005). Thus, positive emotions enhance individuals' entrepreneurial alertness (e.g., Baron 2008). Positive emotions were also found to enhance creativity (creative cognition) (cf. Isen 1999), an important aspect of entrepreneurial cognitions, as happy individuals show a higher cognitive flexibility, i.e., a wider range of ideas and associations (e.g., Baron 2008, Ward 2004). However, individuals in positive emotions and a higher cognitive flexibility were also found to be easier to distract (e.g., Dreisbach and Goschke 2004). Besides, negative emotions under some circumstances were also found to increase creativity, although not as strong as positive emotions (e.g., Baron 2008).

When individuals experience strong positive or negative emotions their capacity to think systematically and to evaluate information carefully is significantly influenced (Baron and Ensley 2006, Ruder and Bless 2003), e.g., strong emotions increase the tendency to engage in heuristics ("short-cuts") rather than systematic thinking (e.g., Baron 2008, cf. Tversky and Kahneman 1974).[2] Thus, strong emotions reduce cognitive activity and might lead to serious judgment and decision errors (Baron 2008). Some findings indicated that individuals in positive emotions are more likely to engage in heuristics than individuals in negative moods because they do not want to threaten their positive state through the effort of systematic thinking (e.g., Mackie and Worth 1989, Park and Banaji 2000). Others show that individuals with positive emotions engage more in systematic thinking when clear situational cues require the effort of cognitive activity (e.g., Lyubomirsky et al. 2005). When engaging in heuristic thought, decisions are typically made faster as individuals make this decision based on past decisions. For example, if an entrepreneur made the decision that he or she does not like a certain investor, he or she might make the same decision after one year again. The second decision is a "short-cut" as it refers to a decision already made in the past without further considering emotions. Thus, if we think that we make the most rational decisions, because we take our time to collect and evaluate information, emotions are most likely to influence our decisions in that process (cf. Baron 2008).

Additionally, individuals in a positive mood are more likely to judge a statement as true compared to individuals in a negative mood (Garcia-Marques et al. 2004). Besides, there is a decision-making strategy called "satisficing" (e.g., Baron 2008), which occurs when entrepreneurs choose the first best alternative. This strategy is particularly applied when entrepreneurs experience positive emotions and it results

---

[2] In the early 1970s, Tversky and Kahneman described a research orientation which has dominated the judgement and decision-making literature ever since. They argued that individuals make use of cognitive heuristics, i.e., simple rules of thumb to make "quick-and-easy" decisions, which reduce the complexity of a decision under uncertainty. Heuristics in general, however, are quite useful, but sometimes they also lead to serious and systematic errors, i.e., cognitive biases. Tversky and Kahneman defined three cognitive heuristics for risk judgments, namely representativeness, availability, and anchoring-and-adjustment.

in fast and quite efficient decisions. There is a strategy mostly applied in negative emotions called "maximizing" (e.g., Baron 2008) with which entrepreneurs evaluate exhaustively any possible alternative.

In the following section, we present three cognitive appraisal theories of emotion. These theories are best suitable for future research on entrepreneurial decision-making as they allow looking at cognitions and emotions at the same time.

8.4 Cognitive Appraisal Theories of Emotion

In this section three cognitive appraisal theories of emotion (or appraisal theories) are presented, namely Richard Lazarus' cognitive appraisal theory of emotion, Albert Ellis' theoretical foundations of his rational emotive behavior therapy (REBT), and Bernard Weiner's attribution theory of emotion.

In general, appraisal theories assume that the emotions elicited by an event depend on how the event is appraised by a person along a number of appraisal dimensions (cf. Siemer and Reisenzein 2007). These emotions influence individuals' behaviors and, as a consequence, cognitions. Cognitive theories of emotion to some extent differ in the number and the defining content of the assumed appraisal dimensions (Scherer 1999).

8.4.1 Richard Lazarus' Cognitive Appraisal Theory of Emotion

Richard S. Lazarus, a pioneer in the study of cognition and its relation to emotion, differentiates between two kinds of cognition: (a) knowledge (i.e., a person's understanding of his/her environment) and (b) appraisals (i.e., the evaluation of knowledge and of what is necessary for a person to convert his/her knowledge of the world into something of personal significance) (Lazarus 1991). Thus, knowledge is a precondition for the appraisal of a given stimulus or situation. Appraisals, in turn, are again divided into two types: primary and secondary appraisal (Lazarus 1991). Primary appraisal is an evaluation of knowledge about a certain situation or stimulus in respect to relevance for and incongruence with person's goals and motivations, whereas secondary appraisal predominantly relates to the individual's perceived ability to cope with the situation or a potential failure in this situation.

Appraisal processes are hypothesized to generate emotions: Only when the knowledge about a specific stimulus is evaluated in a way indicating that this stimulus is relevant for the individual's goals (primary appraisal) emotions will occur. Secondary appraisal will influence the individual's perception of the stimulus as a threat. For instance, a person might experience the emotion of challenge if a stimulus is appraised as being relevant of an individual's goals (motivational relevance) but incongruent with them (motivational incongruence) and if the individual perceives his or her own coping potential to be sufficient to handle the stimulus (secondary appraisal). Given the same constellation of motivational relevance and incongruence, but an evaluation of one's own coping potential as being insufficient, the resulting emotion would be fear.

Primary appraisal is a necessary prerequisite of every emotion (this assumption of Lazarus has been explicitly or implicitly integrated in practically all existing cognitive theories of emotion), whereas secondary appraisal is not: For instance, the emotion of happiness is hypothesized to merely result from an appraisal of a stimulus as being motivationally relevant and congruent.

As a result of this process, the appraisal and its attendant emotion influence the quality of the person–environment encounter and the way the person might behave in the particular situation. The altered person–environment encounter is then reappraised, the reappraisal leading to yet another change in the emotion quality and intensity of the encounter (Lazarus 1991), creating, in effect, a sort of continuous loop. Transferring this to the field of entrepreneurship, if an entrepreneur interprets a specific opportunity as being in high contrast with his or her goals (e.g., a situation, in which there is a high risk of losing all private savings which is in high incongruence with the entrepreneur's goal of being financially independent) this appraisal will result in emotional states of fear. As a consequence, the encounter will be avoided and cognitively devaluated.

The theory of Lazarus has been applied to different areas of the field of the study of organizations. In the context of innovation, Krause (2004) shows that if managers have a high primary appraisal of innovation (i.e., they see innovation as an important factor in the process of changing the situation), they demonstrate more innovation-related behaviors. Next to that, Casson (1982), Endres and Woods (2006), and Shane (2003) claim that entrepreneurs act differently from other types of individuals because they perceive situations differently, thus indicating that cognitive processes of entrepreneurs to some extent might also be different in terms of primary and secondary appraisal.

8.4.2 Albert Ellis' Rational Emotive Behavior Therapy

Albert Ellis focuses on irrational beliefs, maladaptive emotions, and resulting dysfunctional behaviors. In 1955, he developed the rational emotive behavior therapy (REBT) on the basis of a large clinical practice, which is the reason why he mainly considers negative emotions. In his model (e.g., Ellis 1977, 1991, Ellis and Dryden 1997), people experience undesirable activating events about which they can have rational and/or irrational beliefs which then lead to emotional, behavioral, and cognitive consequences. Rational beliefs about an event express individuals' preferences, whereas irrational beliefs about an event are characterized through illogically high insistence and demandingness (Ellis and Dryden 1997). Rational beliefs are, e.g., "I'd prefer to succeed and be lovable, but I never have to do so," or "I'd very much like others to treat me fairly and considerately, but there is no reason why they must do so,"or "I greatly desire my life conditions to be comfortable and pleasant, but I never need them to be that way" (Ellis 1991, p. 144). Irrational beliefs are, e.g., "I absolutely must have my important goals unblocked and fulfilled," or "I can't bear it," or "I'm a worthless person," or "I'll always fail to get what I want and only get what I don't want now and in the future" (Ellis 1991, p. 144). More specifically, irrational beliefs can be classified into four different types: demandingness, awfulizing, global evaluation of self-worth/self-downing, and low frustration tolerance (cf. David et al. 2002). Consequently, rational beliefs are hypothesized to result in functional consequences (i.e., individuals are better able to deal with difficult situations), whereas irrational beliefs should result in dysfunctional consequences (i.e., individuals are less able to deal with difficult situations; David et al. 2002).

Ellis refers to irrational beliefs as "hot cognitions" and to rational beliefs as "warm cognitions." Events which are non-evaluative and therefore hardly result in emotional reactions are referred to as "cold cognitions" (Ellis 1991). Ellis and Dryden (1997) propose a causal relationship between appraisal dimensions, i.e., rational and irrational beliefs, and emotional reactions, i.e., adaptive and maladaptive emotions (cf. Spörrle and Försterling 2007, 2008): Rational beliefs ("warm cognitions") cause adaptive emotions (e.g., fear, sadness), whereas irrational beliefs ("hot cognitions") cause maladaptive emotions (e.g., anxiety, depression). Transferring this to the field of entrepreneurship, an entrepreneur confronted with a potential opportunity is hypothesized to experience the (maladaptive) emotion of anxiety if he or she perceives the self-worth to be inevitably associated with the success in this situation; in case of failure he or she will experience depression. On the other hand, if the success is only associated with high motivational relevance (i.e., importance) the entrepreneur will only experience (mild levels of) fear; in case of failure he or she will experience sadness.

Thus, Ellis' REBT suggests that rational cognitions lead to adaptive emotions and result in functional behavior, whereas irrational cognitions lead to maladaptive emotions and dysfunctional behavior. Empirical approaches to apply REBT theory to organizational contexts (e.g., Spörrle and Welpe 2006, Spörrle et al. 2006, 2008) do not come as surprise since Ellis himself (Ellis, 1972) has suggested to do so. Despite this applicability within economic contexts, there is no research examining REBT theory with respect to entrepreneurial activity. Entrepreneurs who think rationally will show adequate negative, adaptive emotions such as fear, which will result in functional, i.e., effective decisions and behaviors, whereas entrepreneurs who think irrationally will show negative maladaptive emotions such as anxiety resulting in poor decisions and ineffective behavior.

8.4.3 Bernard Weiner's Theory of Emotion

Bernard Weiner's theory of emotion is another important representative of appraisal theories and his theory has been widely applied in many fields of psychology (cf. Reisenzein et al. 2003), work and organizational behavior, e.g., help giving in organizational settings (Drach-Zahavy and Somech 2006, Lepine and van Dyne 2001), or performance evaluation of employees and personnel decisions (e.g., Struthers et al. 1998). In Weiner's theory the emotion-eliciting appraisals are causal attributions (Scherer 1999). His theory (Weiner 1980) focuses on emotions such as anger, shame, pride, or joy and shows how they can be explained by ratings on causal dimensions such as locus, stability, and controllability. Locus refers to whether the cause is perceived to be internal, e.g., ability and effort, or external, e.g., task characteristics and chance. Stability determines whether the internal or external causes are temporary or permanent. Ability (internal cause) and task characteristics (external cause) can be seen as stable and permanent causes. Effort (internal cause) and chance (external cause) are variable and temporary causes. In addition, events can be rated as controllable, e.g., effort, or uncontrollable, e.g., ability, task characteristics and chance, depending on the extent of personal influence (Reisenzein et al. 2003). These attributions cause emotions which in turn influence behavior (Weiner 1980, 1985). In this process of emotion formation Weiner (1985) proposes a sequence of cognitions becoming increasingly complex. First, the event is generally evaluated as positive or negative. At this stage, outcome-dependent emotions such as happiness or sadness arise. The second step is the causal ascription of the event and its results are attribution-dependent emotions. For example, if entrepreneurs perceive the cause of the outcome to be internal and controllable, they experience pride for a positive and guilt for a negative outcome. When the event is attributed to an external cause emotions such as anger or pity are felt. Anger is associated with the perception of a high level of controllability, whereas pity is associated with a high level of uncontrollability (Weiner 1985). Positive and negative emotions in turn give the impulse and the direction for behavior (Weiner 1980). Thus, Weiner (1980) proposes that emotions mediate the relationship between cognitions and behavior or behavioral tendencies.

8.5 A Model to Study Emotions and Cognitions in the Entrepreneurial Decision-Making Process

In this section, we propose a model based on the well-known stimulus–organism–response model (S–O–R) to study emotions and cognitions in the entrepreneurial decision-making process and the resulting behaviors or behavior tendencies. After behaviorists (e.g., Pavlov, Watson) introduced the stimulus–response model and considered the organism as a "black box," Woodworth (1921) added the organism to the strict stimulus–response model of the behaviorists. He proposed that the stimulus influences the organism and leads to a certain behavior, however, the stimulus does not have to end automatically in a response.[3] Although most modern psychologists subscribe to different versions of the S–O–R model, they recognize that only

---

[3]This concept was later transferred into a formula by Kurt Lewin (1890–1947), who established that behavior is a function of both person and environment or $B = f(P, E)$.

Stimulus   Organism   Response

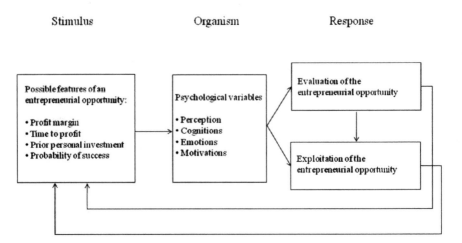

Fig. 8.2 S–O–R model to study entrepreneurial decision-making

the stimulus and the response can be observed directly. All variables of the organism, namely perceptional, cognitive, emotional, and motivational variables must be inferred from their indicators (e.g., physiological measures) or the relationship that is observed between classes of stimuli and classes of responses (Shaver and Scott 1991). It was Shaver and Scott (1991) who first introduced the S–O–R model to the field of entrepreneurship research. As well as in Shaver and Scott's (1991) model, the stimulus in this model (Fig. 8.2) is an entrepreneurial opportunity described by some possible parameters such as profit margin, time to profit, prior personal investment, probability of success, and risk propensity. The organism consists of psychological variables such as perception, cognitions, emotions, and motivations, which might lead to a response that could in the first loop of entrepreneurial decision-making be described as the evaluation and exploitation of the entrepreneurial opportunity in this model. After the decision to exploit an entrepreneurial opportunity, the entrepreneurial opportunity will change into a new stimulus with other features which will again be processed in the organism and might lead to further evaluations of entrepreneurial decision options, entrepreneurial decision outcomes, and entrepreneurial behavior.

The entrepreneurship literature proposes various characteristics which influence the decision to exploit an entrepreneurial opportunity. In this paragraph, we want to stimulate some possible features of entrepreneurial opportunities which are the stimulus of all entrepreneurial decisions. Shaver and Scott (1991), following Cromie (1988), give several reasons which influence the decision to become an entrepreneur such as desire for autonomy, interest in personal achievement, dissatisfaction with current job, desire to make money, and unhappiness in current career. When evaluating a certain business idea, entrepreneurs as well as managers lay their focus on the break-even point, potential market size, potential profit, available government funds, and the ratio of investment size to total assets (Busenitz and Barney 1997). Other researchers discovered that lower probabilities and levels of potential financial loss as well as lower levels of perceived risk are crucial for the decision to exploit an entrepreneurial opportunity (e.g. McNamara and Bromiley 1997, Palich and Bagby 1995, Simon et al. 2000). Additionally, Shane and Venkataraman (2000) detected that an entrepreneurial opportunity with large expected demand, high industry profit margins, young technological life cycle, medium density of competition in a particular opportunity space, low capital cost and medium population level learning from other entrants increases the likelihood of exploiting an entrepreneurial situation. For most individuals, exploitation is more likely when the value of the opportunity preponderates the costs to generate that value, financial capital is high, strong social ties to resource providers is available, useful information/knowledge about entrepreneurship resulting from prior experience is given, the transferability of this information/knowledge is possible, and prior entrepreneurial experience exists (Shane and Venkataraman 2000). However, it must be mentioned that features that increase the probability of entrepreneurial opportunity exploitation do not necessarily increase the probability of success. According to Forlani and Mullins (2000) and Shane and Venkataraman (2000), profit margin, level of personal investment, time to profit margin, and probability of success are assumed to be the most important for the entrepreneurial evaluation and exploitation process which is why we propose them as possible situational features in the S–O–R model.

8.6 Implications

Against the background of this chapter and the derived S–O–R model for the entrepreneurial decision-making process, several implications can be made. In this section, we give recommendations how the role of emotions and cognitions in entrepreneurial decision-making can be further investigated, how emotions and cognitions should be integrated in entrepreneurship practice, and how entrepreneurship teaching can approach emotions and cognitions in the decision-making process of (potential) entrepreneurs.

8.6.1 Recommendations for Future Research

Considering that the field of emotions and cognitions is not only under researched in the domain of entrepreneurship but also in psychology and economics, basic emotion research needs to be done in order to create a fundamental understanding of how emotions influence decision-making and how they interact with cognitions in decision-making processes. Our proposed S–O–R model could serve as a theoretical framework for this intention as it allows to directly looking at the psychological variables, especially emotions and cognitions, of the organism by integrating cognitive appraisal theories of emotions in future research. As far as we are aware, cognitive appraisal theories of emotions have not been investigated in the context of entrepreneurship so far, although they enable one to look at emotions and cognitions at the same time. The GEW presented above can be used as an instrument to investigate the dimensional layout of the emotion qualities on pure appraisal dimensions (arrangement of emotion terms in two-dimensional space) and the intensity of the associated subjective feeling (distance from origin) (Scherer 2005). Especially negative emotions such as fear and anxiety (e.g., Koellinger et al. 2007, Lee et al. 2005, Shepherd 2004, Sternberg et al. 2007) deserve a closer look as previous research (e.g., Vaish et al. 2008) indicated that the approach component of positive affect is less important for entrepreneurial decisions and actions than the avoiding component of negative affect ("negativity bias"). However, a challenge in the research of emotions and their effects on cognitions is that emotions are often multi-dimensional, e.g., anger combined with sorrow or pleasure combined with fear (Baron 2008). Also emotion-related constructs such as passion, optimism, and enthusiasm (e.g., Baron 2008, Baum and Locke 2004, Cardon et al. 2005) should be added to future research in this field. Additionally, entrepreneurial cognitions such as creativity play a crucial role in entrepreneurial decision-making (Baron 2008, Hamidi et al. 2008, Hills et al. 1997, Kay 1986) and should therefore also be integrated in future research.

Another interesting research topic here is (potential) entrepreneurs' environment and their social life as emotions and cognitions are shaped through these. Entrepreneurs' environment is characterized through certain surrounding conditions such as the regulatory, economic, and social conditions which should not be neglected in future research of emotions and cognitions (e.g., Ardichvili et al. 2003, McMullen and Shepherd 2006). Network theories (e.g., Low and McMillan 1988) propose that entrepreneurs who have extended networks identify significantly more opportunities than solo entrepreneurs (e.g., Ozgen and Baron 2007, Singh et al. 1999). Additionally, the quality of entrepreneurs' networks affects characteristics such as entrepreneurial alertness and creativity (Hills et al. 1997). Granovetter (1973), for example, argues that weak ties are stronger "bridges" to information sources than strong ties, because most people have more weak than strong ties. De Koning (1999) classifies entrepreneurs' social networks into inner circle, "action set", partnerships, and a network of weak ties. Then again, Birley (1985) differentiates informal (family, friends, business) and formal (banks, accountants, lawyers) networks. She found that entrepreneurs rely heavily on the informal network, but seldom tap into the formal network. Especially children of entrepreneurial parents have information that is unavailable to children whose parents did not start or purchase a firm (Shaver and Scott 1991) and therefore entrepreneurs tend to come from families where the parents already own/owned a business (Cooper and Dunkelberg 1987). As a result, the extent and the quality of social networks increase the amount and the quality of information (cf. Picot et al. 2008). Regarding the social networks of entrepreneurs it can be concluded that entrepreneurs evolve opportunities by pursuing three cognitive activities (information gathering, thinking through talking, and resource assessing) through active interaction with an extensive network of people.

Also socio-demographic factors and their connection to emotions and cognitions should be investigated in future entrepreneurship research. For example, the exploration of gender, age, or education with regard to the influence of emotions and cognitions on entrepreneurial decision-making could bring promising results.

Some researchers (e.g., Dess et al. 2003, Hitt et al. 2001, McGrath and MacMillan 2000) argue that entrepreneurship research should be integrated with strategic management and innovation management research as they have entrepreneurial opportunities as a base for decisions. Moreover, these decisions cannot follow given theoretical frameworks as they, just as entrepreneurial decisions, have to be made under rapidly changing and uncertain conditions.

Finally, there are numerous possibilities derived from classical psychological methods of experiments, interrogation, and observation as well as methods from neuroscience (cf. Cacioppo and Gardner 1999) to study to the role of emotions and cognitions in the entrepreneurial decision-making process. The most important thing to keep in mind, however, is that emotions and cognitions cannot be studied without each other, but always need to be investigated together.

8.6.2 Recommendations for Practice

From the study of emotions and cognitions in entrepreneurial decision-making several recommendations for practice can be given. (Potential) entrepreneurs should be aware that they have a "subjective" view of objectivity when it comes to entrepreneurial decisions. (Potential) entrepreneurs might also be interested to know that their emotions systematically influence the decisions they make. As we outlined how the interaction of emotions and cognitions influence entrepreneurial decision-making, (potential) entrepreneurs might also want to know which emotions and cognitions lead to which behavior. For example, judgments are highly dependent on affective states and the probability of negative events is considered higher by depressive individuals than by happy individuals. Negative thinking from entrepreneurs in a negative mood could lead to decisions which are more likely to be poor for their venture than from positive thinking entrepreneurs. Additionally, there are findings (e.g., Saavedra and Early 1991) that individuals in a positive affective state feel a higher self-efficacy than individuals in a negative affective state. In addition, entrepreneurs should be aware of the emotions of their employees, investors, customers, etc., and try to handle them efficiently. For example, if entrepreneurs are able to pass their positive emotions to their customers, they will be more willing to try new products (Kahn and Isen 1993) because their risk propensity in low involvement decisions is higher in positive emotions. However, high involvement decisions are avoided in positive emotions as individuals do not want to spoil it with a bad decision (Arkes et al. 1988). Hence, entrepreneurs could learn how to become aware of their affective states in cognitive and emotional awareness trainings.

As previous research (e.g., Vaish et al. 2008) showed that the approach component of positive affect is less important for entrepreneurial decisions and actions than the avoiding component of negative affect ("negativity bias"), entrepreneurship trainings and coachings should rather focus on the reduction of negative emotions and the coping of failure than on the enhancement of positive emotions. However, happy entrepreneurs are more successful than sad entrepreneurs because happy people focus more on increasing their knowledge structure, learning new skills, or on social contact with others. Thus, happy entrepreneurs generally get more involved with their environment which in turn leads to more success in many instances regarding their new venture (e.g., Baron 2008, Fredrickson 2001).

Following cognitive appraisal theories of emotions, emotional reactions can be changed by changing their underlying appraisals and attitudes. If an entrepreneur is very angry about a controllable goal with incongruent outcome, the entrepreneur might be well advised to ascribe the incongruent outcome to an uncontrollable cause in order to attenuate a strongly negative emotional reaction.

8.6.3 Recommendations for Teaching

Kuratko (2005) writes that the number of colleges and universities in the United States that offer courses related to entrepreneurship has grown from a handful in the 1970s to over 1,600 schools in 2005 offering about 2,200 entrepreneurship courses. These numbers show that entrepreneurship teaching increased in the last 30 years, however, this does not say that these courses teach the "right" things. As most researchers could agree, entrepreneurial attitudes are an important prerequisite to enhance entrepreneurship propensity (e.g., Gasse 1985, Gorman et al. 1997). Teaching these attitudes as one part of entrepreneurial education could be divided into different stages of learning: in elementary school, high school, college, and university. Additionally, Gorman et al. (1997) emphasize the importance to distinguish among entrepreneurship, enterprise, and small business management education and to differentiate each of these from traditional approaches to management education.

Interpretations and appraisals play an important role for entrepreneurial decisions and behavior and are shaped by individual social and environmental background. This could be a connecting factor for teaching in the field of entrepreneurship and interpretations and appraisals could also be a link for the motivation of entrepreneurial decision-making and action. Entrepreneurship teaching could stimulate interpretations and appraisals of entrepreneurial decision-making and action. As, for example, creativity was found to be an important cognition for entrepreneurial action (e.g., Baron 2008, Hamidi et al. 2008, Hills et al. 1997, Kay 1986), Hamidi et al. (2008) argue that creative exercises could lead to a higher likelihood to engage in entrepreneurial action.

Entrepreneurship, innovation, and strategic management courses could and should teach, besides mere information and knowledge, emotion and cognition management, especially, dealing with negative affective states. These course variables could also be taught to analysts and project managers as those could be advised on the importance of the subjective appraisals and actual affect in decision-making and judgments.

Darwin (1872) already found emotional expressions to be independent of cultures and that emotions are part of our genetic fundamentals. Thus, emotions themselves might not be easily taught directly, but recognizing emotions, understanding the causes of emotions, anticipating the impacts of emotions, controlling emotions, and hiding or suppressing emotions should be the central subject of entrepreneurship teachers, because (potential) entrepreneurs recognizing their emotions and knowing about possible impacts of their emotions on their cognitions (and subsequent behaviors) are more likely to make better entrepreneurial decisions for their enterprises.

References

Ardichvili A, Cardozo R, Ray S (2003) A theory of entrepreneurial opportunity identification and development. Journal of Business Venturing 18:105–123

Arkes HR, Herren LT, Isen AM (1988) The role of potential loss in the influence of affect on risk-taking behavior. Organizational Behavior and Human Decision Processes 42:181–193

Baron RA (1998) Cognitive mechanisms in entrepreneurship: why and when entrepreneurs think differently than other people. Journal of Business Venturing 13:275–294

Baron RA (2000a) Counterfactual thinking and venture formation: the potential effects of thinking about "what might have been". Journal of Business Venturing 15:79–91

Baron RA (2000b) Psychological perspectives on entrepreneurship: cognitive and social factors in entrepreneurs' success. Current Directions in Psychological Science 9:15–18

Baron RA (2004) The cognitive perspective: a valuable tool for answering entrepreneurship's basic "why" questions. Journal of Business Venturing 19:221–239

Baron RA (2008) The role of affect in the entrepreneurial process. Academy of Management Review 33:328–340

Baron RA, Byrne D, Branscombe NR (2009) Social psychology. Allyn & Bacon, Boston

Baron RA, Ensley MD (2006) Opportunity recognition as the detection of meaningful patterns: evidence from comparisons of novice and experienced entrepreneurs. Management Science 52:1331–1344

Barsade SG, Gibson DE (2007) Why does affect matter in organizations? Academy of Management Perspectives 21:36–59

Baum JR, Locke EA (2004) The relationship of entrepreneurial traits, skill, and motivation to subsequent venture growth. Journal of Applied Psychology 89:587–598

Birley S (1985) The role of networks in the entrepreneurial process. Journal of Business Venturing 1:107–117

Blaney P (1986) Affect and memory: a review. Psychological Bulletin 99:229–246

Bless H (2001) The relation between mood and the use of general knowledge structures. In: Martin LL, Clore GL (eds) Mood and social cognition: contrasting theories. Lawrence Erlbaum Associates, Mahwah

Bower GH (1981) Mood and memory. American Psychologist 36:129–148

Brockner J, Higgins ET, Low MB (2004) Regulatory focus theory and the entrepreneurial process. Journal of Business Venturing 19:203–221

Busenitz LW, Arthurs JD (2007) Cognition and capabilities in entrepreneurial ventures. In: Baum JR, Frese M, Baron R (eds) The psychology of entrepreneurship. Lawrence Erlbaum Associates, Mahwah

Busenitz LW, Barney JB (1997) Differences between entrepreneurs and managers in large organizations: biases and heuristics in strategic decision-making. Journal of Business Venturing 12:9–30

Bühler R, Griffin D, Ross M (1994) Exploring the "planning fallacy": why people underestimate their task completion times. Journal of Personality and Social Psychology 67:366–381

Cacioppo JT, Gardner WL (1999) Emotion. Annual Review of Psychology 50:191–214

Cacioppo JT, Klein DJ, Berntson GG, Hatfield E (1993) The psychophysiology of emotions. In: Lewis M, Haviland JM (eds) Handbook of emotions. Guilford Press, New York

Camerer C, Loewenstein G, Prelec D (2004) Neuroeconomics: why economics needs the brain. Scandinavian Journal of Economics 106:555–579

Cardon MS, Zietsma C, Saparito P, Matherne BP, Davis C (2005) A tale of passion: new insights into entrepreneurship from a parenthood metaphor. Journal of Business Venturing 20:23–45

Carver CS, Scheier MF (2001): Optimism, pessimism, and self regulation. In: Chang EC (ed.) Optimism and pessimism. APA, Washington

Casson M (1982) The entrepreneur. Barnes and Noble Books, Totowa

Cohen JD (2005) The vulcanization of the human brain: a neural perspective on interactions between cognition and emotion. Journal of Economic Perspectives 19:3–24

Cooper AC, Dunkelberg WC (1987) Entrepreneurial research: old questions, new answers and methodological issues. American Journal of Small Business 11:11–23

Cromie S (1988) Motivations of aspiring male and female entrepreneurs. Journal of Occupational Behaviour 8:251–261

Côté S (2005) A social interaction model of the effects of emotion regulation on work strain. Academy of Management Review 30:509–530

Côté S, Morgan LM (2002) A longitudinal analysis of the association between emotion regulation, job satisfaction, and intentions to quit. Journal of Organizational Behavior 23:947–962

Darwin C (1872) On the Origin of Species. John Murray, London

David D, Schnur J, Belloiu A (2002) Another search for the "hot" cognitions: appraisal, irrational beliefs, attributions, and their relation to emotion. Journal of Rational-Emotive & Cognitive-Behavior Therapy 20:93–131

De Koning A (1999) Conceptualizing opportunity recognition as a socio-cognitive process. Centre for Advanced Studies in Leadership, Stockholm

Dess GG, Ireland RD, Shaker ZA, Floyd SW, Janney JJ, Lane PJ (2003) Emerging issues in corporate entrepreneurship. Journal of Management 29:351–378

Drach-Zahavy A, Somech A (2006) Professionalism and helping: harmonious or discordant concepts? An attribution theory perspective. Journal of Applied Psychology 36:1892–1923

Dreisbach G, Goschke T (2004) How positive affect modulates cognitive control: reduced perseveration at the cost of increased distractibility. Journal of Experimental Psychology: Learning, Memory and Cognition 30:343–353

Eich E, Macaulay D, Ryan L (1994) Mood dependent memory for events of the personal past. Journal of Experimental Psychology 123:201–215

Ekman P (1972) Universals and cultural differences in facial expressions of emotion. In: Cole J (ed) Nebraska symposium on motivation. University of Nebraska Press, Lincoln

Ekman P (1992) An argument for basic emotions. Cognition & Emotion 6:169–200

Ellis A (1972) Executive leadership. Institute for Rational-Emotive Therapy (Albert Ellis Institute), New York

Ellis A (1977) The basis clinical theory of rational-emotive therapy. In: Ellis A, Grieger R (eds) Handbook of Rational-Emotive Therapy. Springer, New York

Ellis A (1991) The revised ABC's of rational-emotive therapy (RET). Journal of Rational-Emotive & Cognitive-Behavior Therapy 9:139–172

Ellis A, Dryden W (1997) The practice of rational emotive therapy (RET). Springer, New York

Endres M, Woods C (2006) Modern theories of entrepreneurial behavior: a comparison and appraisal. Small Business Economics 26:189–202

Estrada CA, Isen AM, Young MJ (1997) Positive affect facilitates integration of information and decreases anchoring in reasoning among physicians. Organizational Behavior and Human Decision Processes 72:117–135

Fiet JO, Clouse GH, van Norton WI Jr (2004) Systematic search by repeat entrepreneurs. In: Butler J (ed) Research in entrepreneurship and management. Information Age Publishing, Greenwich

Fisher CD, Ashkanasy NM (2000) Special issue on emotions in work life. Journal of Organizational Behavior 21:123–129

Fiske S, Taylor S (1984) Social cognition. Addison-Wesley, Reading

Forgas JP (1995) Mood and judgment: the affect infusion model (AIM). Psychological Bulletin 117:39–66

Forgas, JP (2000) Feeling and thinking: affective influences on social cognition. Cambridge University Press, New York

Forlani D, Mullins JW (2000) Perceived risks and choices in entrepreneurs' new venture decisions. Journal of Business Venturing 15:305–322

Fredrickson BL (2001) The role of positive emotions in positive psychology: the broaden-and-build theory of positive emotions. American Psychologist 56:218–226

Försterling F, Spörrle M (2005) Emotion. In: Frey D, von Rosenstiel L, Hoyos CG (eds) Wirtschaftspsychologie [Economic Psychology]. Beltz PVU, Weinheim

Garcia-Marques T, Mackie DM, Claypool HM, Garcia-Marques L (2004) Positivity can cue familiarity. Personality and Social Psychology Bulletin 30:585–593

Garud R, Rappa M (1994) A socio-cognitive model of technology evolution. Organization Science 5:344–362

Gasse Y (1985) A strategy for the promotion and identification of potential entrepreneurs at the secondary school level. Paper Presented at the Frontiers of Entrepreneurship Research. Babson College, Wellesley

Geneva Emotion Wheel (GEW) available under Research Tools at http://www.unige.ch/fapse/emotion.Accessed 10 January 2009

Gorman G, Hanlon D, King W (1997) Some research perspectives on entrepreneurial education, enterprise education and education for small business management: a ten year review. International Small Business Journal 15:56–77

Goss D (2005) Entrepreneurship and 'the social': towards a deference-emotion theory. Human Relations 58:617–636

Goss D (2007) Enterprise ritual: a theory of entrepreneurial emotion and exchange. British Journal of Management 19:120–137, OnlineEarly Articles

Granovetter M (1973) The strength of weak ties. American Journal of Sociology 78:1360–1380

Hahn U, Chater N (1997) Concepts and similarity. In: Lamberts K, Shanks D (eds) Knowledge, concepts, and categories. Psychology Press, Hove

Hamidi, DY, Wennberg K, Berglund H (2008) Creativity in entrepreneurship education. Working Paper Series in Business Administration

Higgins ET (2005) Value from regulatory fit. Current Directions in Psychological Science 14: 209–213

Hills GE, Lumpkin GT, Singh RP (1997) Opportunity recognition: perceptions and behaviors of entrepreneurs. Frontiers of Entrepreneurship Research 1:203–218

Hippel von PT (2004) Biases in SPSS 12.0 missing value analysis. The American Statistician 58:160–164

Hitt MA, Ireland RD, Camp MS, Sexton DL (2001) Strategic entrepreneurship: entrepreneurial strategies for creating wealth. Strategic Management Journal 22:479–491

Isen AM (1999) Positive affect. In: Dalgleish T, Power MJ (eds) Handbook of cognition and emotions. John Wiley & Sons, Chichester

Isen AM (2000) Positive affect and decision making. In: Lewis M, Haviland Jones JM (eds) Handbook of emotions. Guilford Press, New York

Isen AM (2002) Missing in action in the AIM: positive affect's facilitation of cognitive flexibility, innovation, and problem solving. Psychological Inquiry 13: 57–65

James W (1884) What is an emotion? Mind 9:185–205

Kahn B, Isen AM (1993) The influence of positive affect on variety-seeking among safe, enjoyable products. Journal of Consumer Research 20:257–270

Kay CJ (1986) The identification of catalysts preceding decision-making as described by innovators and entrepreneurs. University of San Francisco, San Francisco

Koellinger P, Minniti M, Schade C (2007) "I Think I Can, I Think I Can": Overconfidence and Entrepreneurial Behavior. Journal of Economic Psychology 28:502–527.

Krause DE (2004) Kognitiv-emotionale Prozesse als Auslöser von Innovationen. Empirische Überprüfung der Lazarus-Theorie im Innovationskontext [cognitive-emotional processes as trigger for innovations. Empirical examination of Lazarus' theory in the context of innovation]. Zeitschrift für Personalpsychologie 3:63–78

Kuratko DF (2005) The emergence of entrepreneurship education: development, trends, and challenges. Entrepreneurship Theory and Practice 29:577–598

Lazarus RS (1991) Cognition and motivation in emotion. American Psychologist 46:352–367

Lazarus RS, Kanner AD, Folkman S (1980) Emotions: A cognitive-phenomenological analysis. In: Plutchik R, Kellerman H (eds) Emotion. Theory, Research, and Experience. Academic Press, New York

Lee L, Wong PK, Foo MD (2005) Antecedents of entrepreneurial propensity: findings from Singapore, Hong Kong and Taiwan. http://mpra.ub.uni-muenchen.de/2615/1/MPRA_paper_2615.pdf. Accessed 10 of January 2009

Lepine JA, van Dyne L (2001) Peer responses to low performers: an attributional model of helping in the context of groups. Academy of Management Review 26:67–84

Lieberman MD (2007) Social cognitive neuroscience: a review of core processes. Annual Review of Psychology 58:259–289

Low MB, McMillan IC (1988) Entrepreneurship: past research and future challenges. Journal of Management 14:139–161

Lyubomirsky S, Kennon SM, Schkade D (2005) Pursuing happiness: the architecture of sustainable change. Review of General Psychology 9:111–131

Mackie DM, Worth LT (1989) Differential recall of subcategory information about in-group and out-group members. Personality and Social Psychology Bulletin 15:401–413

McGrath RG, MacMillan IC (2000) The entrepreneurial mindset. Harvard Business School Press, Boston

McMullen JS, Shepherd DA (2006) Entrepreneurial action and the role of uncertainty in the theory of the entrepreneur. Academy of Management Review 31:132–152

McNamara G, Bromiley P (1997) Decision making in an organizational setting: cognitive and organizational influences on risk assessment in commercial lending. Academy of Management Journal 40:1063–1088

Meyer WU, Reisenzein R, Schützwohl A (2001) Einführung in die Emotionspsychologie [Introduction to Emotion Psychology]. Huber, Bern

Mitchell RK, Busenitz L, Lant T, McDougall PP, Morse EA, Smith JB (2002) Toward a theory of entrepreneurial cognition: rethinking the people side of entrepreneurship research. Entrepreneurial Theory and Practice 4:93–104

Mitchell RK, Busenitz LW, Lant T, McDougall PP, Morse EA, Smith JB (2004) The distinctive and inclusive domain of entrepreneurial cognition research. Entrepreneurship Theory and Practice 28:505–518

Mitchell RK, Smith B, Seawright KW, Morse EA (2000) Cross-cultural cognitions and the venture creation decision. Academy of Management Journal 43:974–993

Neisser U (1967) Cognitive psychology. Prentice Hall, Englewood Cliffs

Nickerson C (1998) Corporate culture and the use of written English within British subsidiaries in the Netherlands. English for Specific Purposes 17:281–294

Ozgen E, Baron RA (2007) Social sources of information in opportunity recognition: effects of mentors, industry networks, and professional forums. Journal of Business Venturing 22:174–192

Palich LE, Bagby DR (1995) Using cognitive theory to explain entrepreneurial risk-taking: challenging conventional wisdom. Journal of Business Venturing 10:425–438

Park J, Banaji MR (2000) Mood and heuristics: the influence of happy and sad states on sensitivity and bias in stereotyping. Journal of Personality and Social Psychology 78:1005–1023

Phelps EA (2006) Emotion and cognition: insights from studies of the human amygdale. Annual Review of Psychology 24:27–53

Picot A, Dietl H, Franck E (2005) Organisation – Eine ökonomische Perspektive [Organisation – An Economic Perspective]. Schäffer-Poeschel, Stuttgart

Picot A, Reichwald R, Wigand RT (2008) Information, Organization and Management. Springer, Berlin

Reisenzein R, Meyer W-U, Schützwohl A (2003) Einführung in die Emotionspsychologie III. Kognitive Emotionstheorien [Introduction to emotion psychology III. Cognitive emotion theories]. Huber, Bern

Ruder M, Bless H (2003) Mood and the reliance on the ease of retrieval heuristic. Journal of Personality and Social Psychology 85:20–32

Saavedra R, Early PC (1991) Choice of task and goal under specific conditions of general and specific affective inducement. Motivation and Emotion 15:45–65

Scherer KR (1999) Appraisal theory. In: Dalgleish T, Power MJ (eds) Handbook of cognition and emotion. John Wiley & Sons, Chichester

Scherer KR (2005) What are emotions? And how can they be measured? Social Science Information 44:695–729

Schiffman HR (2005) Sensation and perception: an integrated approach. John Wiley & Sons, New York

Schindehutte M, Morris M, Allen J (2006) Beyond achievement: entrepreneurship as extreme experience. Small Business Economics 27:349–368

Schwarz N, Bless H, Bohner G (1991) Response scales as frames of reference: the impact of frequency range on diagnostic judgments. Applied Cognitive Psychology 5:37–49

Shane S (2003) A general theory of entrepreneurship. The individual-opportunity nexus. Edward Elgar, Cheltenham

Shane S, Venkataraman S (2000) The promise of entrepreneurship as a field of research. Academy of Management Review 25:217–226

Shaver KG, Scott LR (1991) Person, process, choice: the psychology of new venture creation. Entrepreneurship and Regional Development 16:23–45

Shepherd DA (2003) Learning from business failure: propositions of grief recovery for the self-employed. Academy of Management Review 28:318–328

Shepherd DA (2004) Educating entrepreneurship students about emotion and learning from failure. Academy of Management Learning and Education 3:274–287

Shiv B, Loewenstein G, Bechara A (2005) The dark side of emotions in decision-making: when individuals with decreased emotional reactions make more advantageous decisions. Cognitive Brain Research 23:85–92

Siemer M, Reisenzein R (2007) The process of emotion inference. Emotion 7:1–20

Simon M, Houghton SM, Aquino K (2000) Cognitive biases, risk perception, and venture formation: how individual decide to start companies. Journal of Business Venturing 15:113–134

Singh R, Hills GE, Hybels RC, Lumpkin GT (1999) Opportunity recognition through social network characteristics of entrepreneurs. Frontiers in entrepreneurship research. Babson College, Wellesley

Smilor RW (1997) Entrepreneurship: reflections on a subversive activity. Journal of Business Venturing 12:341–346

Spencer J (2005) stock trading favors the fearless, study suggests. Wall Street Journal August 22:C1/C6

Spörrle M, Försterling F (2007) Which thoughts can kill a boxer? Naïve theories about cognitive and emotional antecedents of suicide. Psychology and Psychotherapy: Theory, Research and Practice 80:497–512

Spörrle M, Försterling F (2008) Zum Zusammenhang von Kognition, Emotion und Verhalten: Empirische Überprüfungen der Einschätzungstheorie von Albert Ellis [Concerning the relationship between cognitions, emotions and behavior: empirical examinations of Albert Ellis' appraisal theory]. Verhaltenstherapie und Verhaltensmedizin 29:122–137

Spörrle M, Welpe IM (2006) How to feel rationally: linking Rational Emotive Behavior Therapy with components of emotional intelligence. In: Ashkanasy NM, Zerbe WJ, Härtel CEJ (eds) Research on emotion in organizations: Individual and organizational perspectives on emotion management and display. Elsevier, Oxford

Spörrle M, Welpe IM, Försterling F (2006) Cognitions as determinants of (mal) adaptive emotions and emotionally intelligent behavior in an organizational context. Psicothema 18:165–171

Spörrle M, Welpe IM, Ringenberg I, Försterling F (2008) Irrationale Kognitionen als Korrelate emotionaler Kompetenzen aus dem Kontext emotionaler Intelligenz und individueller Zufriedenheit am Arbeitsplatz [Irrational cognitions as correlates of emotional competences from the context of emotional intelligence and individual workplace satisfaction]. Zeitschrift für Personalpsychologie 7:113–128

Sternberg RJ (2004) Successful intelligence as a basis for entrepreneurship. Journal of Business Venturing 19:189–202

Sternberg R, Brixy U, Hundt C (2007) Global Entrepreneurship Monitor (GEM) – Länderbericht Deutschland 2006. [GEM – country report Germany 2006] Leibniz University Hannover, Institut für Arbeitsmarkt- und Berufsforschung, Hannover/Nürnberg

Struthers CW, Weiner B, Allred K (1998) Effects of causal attributions on personnel decisions: A social motivation perspective. Basic and Applied Social Psychology 20:155–166

Tice DM, Bratslavaky E, Baumeister RF (2000) Emotional distress regulation takes precedence over impulse control: if you feel bad, do it! Journal of Personality and Social Psychology 80: 53–67

Tversky A, Kahneman D (1974) Judgement under uncertainty: Heuristics and biases. Science 185:1124–1130

Vaish A, Grossmann T, Woodward A (2008) Not all emotions are created equal: The negativity bias in early social-emotional development. Psychological Bulletin 134:383–403

Ward TB (2004) Cognition, creativity, and entrepreneurship. Journal of Business Venturing 19:173–188

Weiner B (1980) A cognitive (attribution)-emotion-action model of motivated behavior: An analysis of judgments of help-giving. Journal of Personality and Social Psychology 39:186–200

Weiner B (1985) An attributional theory of achievement motivation and emotion. Psychological Review 92:548–573

Weiss HM (2002) Deconstructing job satisfaction: separating evaluations, beliefs and affective experiences. Human Resource Management Review 12:173–194

Whittlesea BWA (1997) The representation of general and particular knowledge. In: Lamberts K, Shanks D (eds) Knowledge, concepts, and categories. MIT Press, Cambridge

Woodworth RS (1921) Psychology: A Study of Mental Life. H. Holt, New York

Chapter 9
Collective Passion in Entrepreneurial Teams

Mateja Drnovsek, Melissa S. Cardon, and Charles Y. Murnieks

9.1 Introduction

Affective processes of individuals and teams at work are increasingly becoming acknowledged as important drivers of business decision-making processes and organizational behaviors. In particular, there has been an increasing interest in the notion of passion and its role in entrepreneurship. Business practitioners reckon that to stand even a chance of winning in a cutthroat environment dominated by larger, richer competitors, an entrepreneur needs to have "passion[1]" – the "fire of desire" that enables an entrepreneur to surmount even the most difficult obstacles. As reflected in the words of Jack Welch[2]: "If there's one characteristic all winners share, it's that they care more than anyone else. No detail is too small to sweat or too large to dream. It doesn't mean loud or flamboyant. It's something that comes from deep within." He is referring to the notion of passion. Martha Stewart says it even more clearly: "Without passion, work is just work. Passion is the first and most essential ingredient for planning and beginning a business."

Academics are also beginning to focus on how affective processes play an important role in facilitating entrepreneurial success. In general, affect is noted to have a profound influence on cognitive processes, motivation, and individual well-being in entrepreneurship. For example, Baron (2007, 2008) examines how both positive and negative affect biases cognitions, helps or hurts in social network development and resource acquisition, and enhances or reduces stress tolerance. Foo et al. (2008) look at how feelings as a particular affective process influence the effort entrepreneurs exhibit toward current or future venture-related tasks. Shepherd (2003) argues that even negative emotions are important to the entrepreneurial process and, in the case of grief, can inhibit learning from entrepreneurial failures.

M. Drnovsek (✉)
Faculty of Economics University of Ljubljana, Kardeljeva ploscad 17, 1000 Ljubljana, Slovenia,
e-mail:drnovsekm@gmail.com

[1] http://archives.emergic.org/archives/2001/10/17/index.html
[2] http://www.straightfromthegut.com/meet/meet_qa.html

A.L. Carsrud, M. Brännback (eds.), *Understanding the Entrepreneurial Mind*,
International Studies in Entrepreneurship 24, DOI 10.1007/978-1-4419-0443-0_9,
© Springer Science+Business Media, LLC 2009

More recently, Shepherd (2009) consider how anticipatory grief (experienced prior to actual business liquidation) may actually reduce the emotional cost of venture failure and enable entrepreneurs to recover more quickly because they have a chance to let go of the business slowly rather than more abruptly. Overall, such work suggests that affective processes are a critical aspect of entrepreneurship, and key questions such as what affect does during the entrepreneurial process are beginning to be answered.

Affect is an umbrella term encompassing a broad range of feelings that individuals experience, including momentary states elicited by short-term affective experiences (i.e., emotions) and affect-oriented traits, which are more stable tendencies to feel and act in certain ways (Watson and Clark 1984). Emotions connote affective experiences that are reactive to external events, while feelings refer to emotion experiences that are more reflective. While the entrepreneurial process is filled with innumerable emotions and feelings (Baron 2008), one of the key affective elements therein is passion (Smilor 1997). Although scholars have conceptualized it in various ways, we draw from Cardon et al. (2009) and define entrepreneurial passion as *consciously accessible, intense positive feelings experienced by engagement in entrepreneurial activities associated with roles that are meaningful and salient to the self-identity of the entrepreneur.* We reserve a deeper discussion of this definition for the next section, but here emphasize two key aspects that distinguish passion from other types of affect experienced by entrepreneurs: (1) the feelings characteristic of passion are positive and intense and (2) they are focused upon activities or role identities that are meaningful to the self-identity of the entrepreneur. Recent theoretical developments (Cardon et al. 2009; Murnieks and Mosakowski 2006) have suggested that passion, working through its constituent components of intense emotions tied to salient identities, has significant impacts on goal-related cognitions, behaviors, and key outcomes for entrepreneurs who experience it.

As conceptualized herein, entrepreneurial passion is a specific type of affective state – a feeling that is different from other entrepreneurial emotions based on the dimensions of intensity, duration, and links to self-identity (Cardon et al. 2008). Passion involves consciously experienced changes in core affect that are attributed to relevant stimuli that are processed using reflection and categorization and stored as key connectors in networks of linkages associated with the focal object (Damasio 2003; Schwarz and Clore 2007) while emotions are typically episodic and last for a relatively short time span. Therefore, in contrast to emotions, entrepreneurs may continue to feel passion even after the stimuli has disappeared or dissipated. Finally, entrepreneurial passion and emotions also differ on whether the affective experience involves linkages to one's self-identity. Any external objects or activities can trigger changes in the emotions experienced by entrepreneurs (even simple things like getting stuck in traffic on the way to work) while entrepreneurial passion is evoked through engagement in activities associated with one or more meaningful roles that are salient to the entrepreneur's self-identity. Thus passion is central to an entrepreneur's sense of self and is a dominant affective state compared to emotions. Because passion has primary characteristics of feelings it can last a long period of time independently of external stimuli. Therefore passion is distinct from state-like emotions and moods, such as happiness, joy, or frustration (for further discussion of the differences, see Cardon et al. 2008).

Even acknowledging passion as a central element of the entrepreneurial process, one of the key questions left unanswered is what entrepreneurial passion does when the entrepreneur experiencing it is part of a founding team, rather than operating as a solo entrepreneur. Many new ventures are founded by teams rather than individuals (Chowdhury 2005; Lechler 2001), and such firms are often more successful than those founded by lone entrepreneurs (Birley and Stockley 2000; Kamm et al. 1990). While the actual statistics vary by industry, Kamm et al. (1990) indicate that the percentage of ventures founded by teams (versus individuals) ranges as high as 70%. Typically, entrepreneurial teams are formed in order for individuals to take advantage of complementarities in skill sets, network connections, or goals among the team.

The aim of this chapter is to integrate work on the emergence and dynamics of entrepreneurial passion of individuals and work on the composition and dynamics that occur within entrepreneurial teams. We define the term "collective passion" *as the combined entrepreneurial passion experienced by members of a team of entrepreneurs, including potential differences in the level and focus of each member's individual passion.* When looking at collective passion we are particularly interested in whether all team members need to be passionate or whether the passion of one or two people is enough to yield the productive benefits of passion for the organization. Acknowledging different role identities that entrepreneurs subscribe to while pursuing venture opportunities, we examine how the experience of passion that results from different role identities (Cardon et al. 2009) may be especially functional for collective passion among entrepreneurial teams.

We begin with a systematic review of the role of passion in entrepreneurship using literature that has taken a solo entrepreneur approach to provide a foundation for building our arguments at the team level. In so doing we utilize a recently proposed conceptual model of passion that seeks to understand the affect–cognition–behavior linkages that lead to effective outcomes in entrepreneurship. Observing that most of the existing work on entrepreneurial passion is intraindividual, our research departs to focus on how passion may operate across individuals to influence behavior. The interindividual's perspective of passion has a particular practical relevance since many entrepreneurial ventures are started by teams of entrepreneurs rather than by individuals (Kamm et al. 1990). Given the variety of entrepreneurial role identities that could be present within a team, we suggest that performance of a particular team may be driven by the team's affective diversity, particularly as it relates to the experienced entrepreneurial passion among team members. We provide some initial suggestions as to how an entrepreneur can best manage their passion within different types of entrepreneurial teams. We conclude the chapter with discussion of the implications of a team-based approach to entrepreneurial passion, both for scholars and business practitioners, and suggest some directions for future research.

9.2 Entrepreneurial Passion: Individual's and Shared

We draw from the work of Cardon and colleagues (in press) to define entrepreneurial passion as consciously accessible, intense positive feelings experienced by engagement in entrepreneurial activities associated with roles that are meaningful and salient to the self-identity of the entrepreneur. This conceptualization includes two important elements that compel further scrutiny: (1) entrepreneurial passion involves intense positive feelings and (2) it results from engagement in activities tied to important entrepreneurial role identities.[3] First, the observation that passion involves intense positive feelings is reflected in many writings where entrepreneurial passion is described with words such as enthusiasm, zeal, and intense longing (e.g., Baum and Locke 2004; Bird 1989; Brännback et al. 2006; Cardon et al. 2005). Using the circumplex model of affect (Russell 2003; Seo et al. 2004), passion corresponds to feelings that are highly intense and positive, similar to excitement, elation, and joy, but distinct from states that are negative and intense (e.g., upset, stressed) and states that are not at all intense (e.g., fatigued, calm), or positive but not intense (e.g., contented).

Second, passion feelings involve experienced changes in affect that are attributed to salient entrepreneurial identities. Feelings arise as entrepreneurs successfully, or unsuccessfully, act to validate their entrepreneurial identities (Burke 1991; Stryker 2004; Murnieks and Mosakowski 2006). According to social psychology, identities represent internalized expectations of characteristics and behaviors attached to societal roles (Cast 2004). Roles are defined as positions in society, such as teacher, doctor, or entrepreneur, and are defined by certain characteristics, actions, and expectations. Once these roles are internalized into one's self-concept, they become identities and help a person define himself/herself accordingly (Burke 1991). Identity theory acknowledges that any individual can have several identities, which are therefore organized hierarchically such that an identity situated higher in the hierarchy is more salient and more central to self-meaning than those placed lower (Stryker 1989; Stryker and Burke 2000). In general, individuals are more strongly motivated to enact or validate identities ranked higher in salience (Stryker and Serpe 1982) as these serve to confirm one's sense of self (Burke 1991). Stryker (2004) points out that highly salient identities, such as the entrepreneurial one for entrepreneurs, are likely to be associated with particularly intense emotions, such

---

[3]In this chapter we use role identity as a proxy for a set of entrepreneurship-specific activities. Based on a taxonomy of entrepreneurial activities developed by Gartner et al. (1999), three role identities can be envisioned: (1) an inventor identity where the entrepreneur's passion is for activities involved in identifying, inventing, and exploring new opportunities; (2) a founder identity, where the entrepreneur's passion is for activities involved in establishing a venture for commercializing and exploiting opportunities; and (3) a developer identity, where the entrepreneur's passion is for activities related to nurturing, growing, and expanding the venture once it has been created. All three of these role identities are prevalent and important for entrepreneurship and we do not suggest a specific hierarchy.

as passion, because of the relative importance of these identities to the individual involved.

Cardon et al. (2009) extend identity theory in entrepreneurship by arguing for the existence of multi-faceted entrepreneurial self-concepts. More specifically, they contend that rather than a singular, monolithic entrepreneurial identity existing at the core of the entrepreneurial self-concept, perhaps many different types of entrepreneurial identities are prominent. They offer three distinct identities as possibilities: (1) an *inventor* identity where the entrepreneur's passion is for activities involved in identifying, inventing, and exploring new opportunities, (2) a *founder* identity, where the entrepreneur's passion is for activities involved in establishing a venture for commercializing and exploiting opportunities, and (3) a *developer* identity, where the entrepreneur's passion is for activities related to nurturing, growing, and expanding the venture once it has been created. All three of these role identities are prevalent and important drivers of entrepreneurial behavior. Although some entrepreneurs may be equally passionate about all three of these identities, others may weigh one identity as significantly more meaningful to them than the others.

While the particular identity (inventor, founder, or developer) evoking passion may vary across entrepreneurs, little debate exists concerning the numerous functional cognitive and behavioral impacts likely to result. First, in most instances, entrepreneurial passion is thought to be a powerful motivational resource that drives entrepreneurs' thoughts, actions, and pursuit of activities. For example, several scholars note that passion involves a strong motivation to work hard (Baum et al. 2001), as well as a dedication or desire to make a difference (Bierly et al. 2000). Similarly, passion leads to tenacity, a willingness to work long hours and make personal sacrifices (Cooper et al. 1988; Odiorne 1991), high levels of initiative and goal commitment (Cardon et al. 2009), and persistence toward goals despite obstacles (Utsch and Rauch 2000).

Second, passion, by definition, is composed of intense positive feelings. A large body of research indicates that positive feelings, such as the ones inherent in passion, may have several benefits for individuals operating in entrepreneurial contexts. For example, Baron (2007, 2008) contends that positive affect facilitates idea generation and opportunity recognition by encouraging creativity and cognitive flexibility. Experimental studies have shown that individuals experiencing positive affect (i.e., passion) are more adaptive to environmental stimuli and are thus able to create more unusual associations, recognize patterns and relatedness among emerging stimuli more readily, and are more likely to pursue creative problem-solving strategies (Isen 2000; Isen and Labroo 2003). In addition, positive feelings facilitate perceptual processing of stimuli, direct perceptual attentive systems, and enhance task involvement (Pham 2004). Furthermore, a host of scholars have shown that positive affect can promote more efficient decision making (Estrada et al. 1997; Isen and Means 1993), which is beneficial for entrepreneurs working in highly dynamic environments (Baron 2008). Positive affect has also been linked to improved health (Lyubomirsky et al. 2005) and the ability to tolerate increased levels of stress, both of which are viewed as advantageous for entrepreneurs (Baron 2008). To the extent that the passion experienced by entrepreneurs is composed of positive feelings similar to the ones studied by researchers above, the benefits should transfer to entrepreneurs as well.

Even though passion possesses many positive aspects for entrepreneurs, passion may also have a "dark side." For example, if intense entrepreneurial emotions such as passion are unchecked, they can lead to discrediting negative information (Branzei and Zietsma 2003) and interfere with learning from failure (Shepherd 2003). Too much passion may lead to obsession, which has been shown to have numerous deleterious effects for individuals (Vallerand et al. 2003). Obsessive passions have been linked to anxiety and depression (Rousseau and Vallerand 2003), as well as increased physical injuries stemming out of rigid adherence to an activity despite the negative impacts on one's health (Rip et al. 2006). Another detrimental consequence of obsessive passion includes zealous behavior that crowds out other activities and people for the entrepreneur. For example, both Séguin-Lévesque et al. (2003) and Vallerand et al. (2003) found that obsessive passions for certain activities were positively related to relationship conflicts with spouses or significant others. Vallerand (2008) speculates that these problems occur because the obsessive passion controls the individual and precludes his/her ability to disengage from the focal activity so they may invest the time needed to maintain other important interpersonal relationships. An all-consuming passion for entrepreneurial activities, or for certain entrepreneurial role identities, may have similar harmful effects on the myriad of interpersonal relationships entrepreneurs must maintain both for the health of their businesses and in their personal lives.

Even though entrepreneurial passion typically involves the experience of positive affect (Cardon et al. 2009), obsessive passions have been shown to generate negative affect as well (Rousseau and Vallerand 2003). Negative emotions such as shame arise when an individual is not able to, or is prevented from, engaging in activities related to his/her passion (Vallerand et al. 2003). To the extent that obsessive passions involve the experience of negative affect, there are additional problems that might arise for entrepreneurs. For example, Baron (2008, 2007) contends that negative affect can inhibit entrepreneurs' abilities to respond to dynamic environments, make them abnormally averse to even moderate levels of risk inherent in the venturing environment, and prompt them to reject promising opportunities. The various dysfunctions of passion have received scant attention from entrepreneurial scholars so far and although it is beyond the scope of this chapter, such a stream deserves greater theoretical and empirical analysis.

Given that a growing amount of attention has been paid to affect and passion at the individual level in entrepreneurship, an important question that arises is how entrepreneurial passion works among entrepreneurial teams. In such teams, an entrepreneur not only needs to manage his/her own passion but also must work with the potential configuration of collective passion among team members. We begin addressing this question by first reviewing extant literature on entrepreneurial teams.

9.3 Entrepreneurial Teams

An entrepreneurial team is a group of people, rather than an individual entrepreneur, involved in the creation and management of a new firm (Cooper and Bruno 1977; Connor and Rueter 2006). Many new ventures are founded by teams rather than individuals (Chowdhury 2005; Lechler 2001), and such firms are often more successful than those founded by lone entrepreneurs (Birley and Stockley 2000; Kamm et al. 1990). Commonly cited reasons for such success are the team's diversity in experience, diversity in ways of thinking, and the larger set of social networks that result from multiple founders. Team entrepreneurship can further enhance performance because both physical and emotional labor can be divided and members can specialize in particular tasks or parts of the firms' development (e.g., Timmons 1999). When the knowledge and skills of entrepreneurial team members complement one another (Westhead et al. 2005), teams are strengthened due to their expanded knowledge base, potential for higher cohesion, and ability to cover for one another (Pasanen and Laukkanen 2006).

Over the last few years, the research on entrepreneurial teams has developed in three primary research streams. The first focuses on the personal connections between team members, such as whether the firm is a family firm with blood-related team members (Haveman and Khaire 2004), or started by a married couple or co-preneurs (e.g., Connor and Rueter 2006), and how such personal connections change the process of founding or managing the business. A second research stream explores demographic aspects of entrepreneurial team composition, such as gender, age, functional background, industry experience, or education of team members, and the extent to which these are homogenous or heterogeneous within the entrepreneurial team (e.g., Chowdhury 2005; Amason et al. 2006). In a third stream the shared or collective cognitions of teams are explored, such as how decisions are made in teams or how teams handle conflict. Effective decision making is particularly important in entrepreneurial environments, which are often highly unpredictable and filled with rapid change, which makes the process chaotic, complex, and compressed in time (Aldrich and Martinez 2001; Baron 2008). In such environments entrepreneurs cannot reach decisions by following learned scripts (cognitive behaviors) and prescribed behaviors, but instead, have to work together to collectively chart a new course, which necessitates navigating through the complex dynamics of the entrepreneurial team.

Some of the complex dynamics of entrepreneurial teams involve their affective processes, yet surprisingly little attention has been paid to the affective dynamics in entrepreneurial teams. The broader literature on teams in organizations suggests that the affective processes resident within teams impact their performance (e.g., Kelly and Barsade 2001) and that positive affect operating between group members can significantly improve team processes (Barsade et al. 2000; Walter and Bruch 2008). Importantly, affective processes contribute to both the overall performance of an organization and the specific processes that lead to performance, such as effective decision making, creativity, and leadership (see Barsade and Gibson 2007 for a review). The teams' literature addresses affective processes in many ways, one of which is to examine the affective diversity or the degree of difference in affective traits that exist between group members (See Barsade and Gibson 2007 for a review). This is the approach followed in this study.[4]

Affective diversity has been shown in prior management research to influence group outcomes, such as group cohesion, social loafing (Duffy and Shaw 2000), and performance of an organization (Barsade et al. 2000). Relatedly, positive affect within a group (conceptualized as the mean level of positive affect in the team) has been shown to reduce cognitive conflict while improving co-operation and task performance (George 1995). However, in addition to the mean level of the positive affect in the team, positive affective diversity can also make a critical difference to overall team functioning and outcomes. Affective diversity is a result of the cumulative affective fit or misfit among group members (Barsade et al. 2000). This fit or misfit is important for effective group functioning because people prefer to work and affiliate with others who tend to be similar on a variety of attributes (Berscheid 1985), such as demographic and personal characteristics, adherence to a specific value system, or emotional processes. Positive affect in particular has been shown as reinforcing in its own right (Lott and Lott 1974) because of the similarity – attraction (Byrne 1971) that happens when it is experienced. In this vein, positive affect, such as entrepreneurial passion experienced by team members, provides information about the affective similarity in the team, and such similarity further reinforces positive emotions and attraction among team members (Barsade et al. 2000). Although the social psychology literature offers robust and reliable findings on affective similarity attraction processes within groups, prior research in entrepreneurship has not yet unveiled how affective processes (for example different passions) that are evoked based on different entrepreneurial identities operate within entrepreneurial teams and how this contributes to the team's performance.

In analyzing affective similarity based on entrepreneurial passion that is present among team members, we propose three different team compositions: (a) balanced passion teams, where entrepreneurial passion for each of the three key role identities (inventor, founder, developer) is felt by at least one team member and each team member has entrepreneurial passion for at least one of the entrepreneurial roles; (b) focused passion teams, where passion for only one entrepreneurial role identity is represented on the team, which means that all team members have entrepreneurial

---

[4]Even though "affective diversity" has traditionally been applied to individual differences in affective traits or personalities between people (Barsade et al. 2000), we contend that this theoretical lens is still appropriate to use when examining the collective passion of entrepreneurial teams. The primary difference between emotion states (like passion) and emotion traits (the traditional focus of affective diversity) is that the former has a clearly identifiable target while the latter emerges from a personality predisposition and, as such, does not need to have a clear target (Barsade et al. 2000). Despite this difference in sources, the effects of both state and trait affect, once produced, may be similar (Baron 2008; Lyubomirsky et al. 2005). Using a lens, such as affective diversity, that acknowledges the social nature of affect (e.g., Parkinson, 1996) allows us to examine the interpersonal effects of passion.

passion for the same role identity, and (c) mixed passion teams, where some team members experience entrepreneurial passion, regardless of which roles evoke such passion, while others do not experience passion for any of the entrepreneurial roles. These different constellations of collective entrepreneurial passion evoke two primary questions: (1) What are the unique team dynamics within teams with each type of collective passion? (2) What are the specific things that the lead entrepreneur should do in managing the collective passion of the team in order to optimize team and organizational performance?

9.4 Entrepreneurial Passion and Team-Level Processes

Prior organizational research has identified several key outcomes of affective diversity, including individual-level attitudes and self-perception of team members (such as an individual's satisfaction with group functioning) as well as group-level social processes such as team rapport (O'Reilly et al. 1993; see Barsade et al. 2000 for a review). We focus on three specific team dynamics that are likely related to the type of collective passion experienced by entrepreneurial teams: team cohesion, cognitive conflict, and affective conflict. All three have been shown to significantly affect group and organizational performance (Barsade et al. 2000; Jehn 1995), and thus are important for optimal entrepreneurial team functioning and performance. Table 9.1 shows a summary of the arguments that follow.

Table 9.1 Entrepreneurial team affective dynamics

Type of collective passion within team	Team social cohesion	Cognitive conflict	Affective conflict
Balanced team (entrepreneurial passion for each of the three key role identities (inventor, founder, developer) is felt by at least one team member and each team member has entrepreneurial passion for at least one of the entrepreneurial roles)	Moderate	Moderate	Moderate
Focused team (passion for only one entrepreneurial role identity is represented on the team, which means that all team members have entrepreneurial passion for the same role identity)	High	High	Low
Mixed team (some team members experience entrepreneurial passion, regardless of which roles evoke such passion, while others do not experience passion for any of the entrepreneurial roles)	Low	Moderate	High

9.4.1 Team Cohesion

Team cohesion is a force that ties group members closer together. Even though it has two dimensions, emotional and task-related cohesion, a commonly used definition sees it broadly as feelings of belongingness or attraction to the group (Eisenberg 2007). Team cohesion reflects synergistic interactions between team members, including use of positive communication (Barrick et al. 1998). Team cohesion can greatly enhance team performance, since it leads to higher satisfaction and team morale, as well as greater communication and efficiency in completing tasks (O'Reilly et al. 1993). The main factors that influence group cohesiveness are members' similarity, group size, entry difficulty, group success, and external competition and threats (Beal et al. 2003). Often, these factors work through enhancing the identification of the individual with the group one belongs to as well as beliefs of how the group can fulfill one's personal needs. In the case of entrepreneurial founding teams and passion, we focus on members' similarity because it holds most relevance for cohesion. The more group members are similar to each other on various characteristics the easier it is to achieve cohesiveness. We note that group size and external competition can also impact cohesiveness (it is easier to agree on different goals and co-ordinate work in smaller groups; external threats can increase awareness of member similarity and need to band together to address the shared threat (Eisenberg 2007), but we leave further discussion of these phenomenon in entrepreneurial teams to future research. In what follows we elaborate how collective passion influences team cohesion processes.

Affectively homogenous groups in general are more cohesive because of their greater level of familiarity, attraction, and trust based on their shared affectivity (Barsade, et al. 2000). Because of this, teams with different types of collective passion may exhibit different levels of team cohesion. In particular, we expect that focused teams (where team members are all passionate about the same role) will be the highest in team cohesion. This occurs because members of such teams are likely to feel most similar to one another; they all experience passion feelings rather than apathy toward organizational activities; and they all experience passion for the *same* set of activities, whether that be related to inventing, founding, or developing the organization. There is some evidence that entrepreneurs prefer to associate with other entrepreneurs interested in the same part of the process as themselves. For example, professional associations in entrepreneurship typically follow identity lines, such as associations of inventors (United Inventors Association, for example) or associations of founders (Young Entrepreneur's Association). Even popular lists of accomplished entrepreneurs such as the Inc. 500 (a list of the 500 fastest growing small organizations in the United States each year) group entrepreneurs together who share a similar passion for growth of their ventures (the developer role identity).

Research in both the entrepreneurship and management literatures analyzing organizational value congruence between team members (agreement about task, goal and mission targets, and priorities) supports the idea that entrepreneurs with passion for the same role identity will experience high team cohesion. For example, Ensley and Pearson (2005) found that as value congruence increased among venture teams, so did team cohesion. In a study of 387 management executives, Boxx et al. (1991) came upon the same conclusion. Thus we expect team cohesion to be highest among focused passion teams.

We expect team social cohesion to be lowest among mixed collective passion teams. In such teams, some members are passionate for entrepreneurial roles, while others experience no passion for venture-related activities, which is a powerful dissimilarity. These teams possess the highest degrees of organizational value divergence, which will lead to lower team cohesion (Boxx et al. 1991; Ensley and Pearson 2005). Moreover, the dissimilarity in values among these teams is particularly relevant because the team members experiencing passion are likely to hold the venture and its activities as central elements of their self-identities, while the team members who do not experience passion are much less likely to define themselves in terms of the venture. This represents a significant mismatch in affective similarity, which would suggest low social cohesion.

Team cohesion is likely to be moderate among balanced teams, where each team member experiences passion for some aspect of the venture's activities (and are therefore similar in that regard), although the focus of such passion is by definition on different role identities (and therefore leads to affectivity dissimilarity among team members). We contend that balanced teams experience moderate cohesion because they possess moderate organizational value congruence and moderate affective similarity. These teams possess more value congruence and affective similarity than mixed passion teams (and therefore have more team cohesion than mixed passion teams) but less value congruence and affective similarity than focused passion teams (and subsequently have less team cohesion than focused passion teams).

9.4.2 Team Conflict

Models of the effects of team diversity on team performance are careful to point out that the former rarely impacts the latter directly. Rather, the effects of diversity from elements like collective passion on team performance are likely mediated by team conflict (Pelled 1996; Pelled et al. 1999). A clash of interests, values, actions, or directions often sparks a conflict, which further calls for a process of adjustment. Typically, team conflict has been divided into relationship (affective), task (cognitive), and process conflict (see Jordan et al. 2006 for a review). Task conflict focuses on conflict over work content or tasks (e.g., how the task should be performed; Jehn 1995), which is typically resolved using rational arguments and discussion, and thus is often labeled cognitive conflict. Process conflict refers to disagreements over the team's approach to the task, methods used, and its group processes (Jehn 1995), and can be subsumed under the label cognitive conflict. Affective conflict (i.e., relationship conflict) refers to emotional disagreement between individuals (interpersonal incompatibility; Jehn 1995) that can generate strong negative emotions, such as anger or hostility. Prior research has shown that the emergence of relationship conflict and its effects consistently turns up differently from cognitive conflict, given that the first is primarily emotion based while the latter lacks emotions (Pelled et al. 1999). Of note, some researchers argue that all team conflict is inherently emotional because it involves perceptions of threats to individuals or team goals (Jordan and Troth 2004). Jehn and Bendersky (2003: 200) suggest that "both relationship and [cognitive] conflicts may be characterized by strong or weak emotional components." Despite these differences, there does appear to be consensus that two major kinds of conflict are cognitive and relationship conflict, thus we address both.

In general, cognitive conflict is viewed as productive for team performance, while relationship conflict is destructive (Amason 1996). Cognitive conflict helps with team decision making because it allows group members to approach challenges from different perspectives ultimately resulting in better decisions (Amason and Schweiger 1994). Such conflict also helps performance because it allows group members to criticize and challenge ideas within the group, rather than fall prey to group think (Janis 1982). The benefits of cognitive heterogeneity in teams are especially critical in unstable or uncertain environments, which are the dominant context for entrepreneurial teams (Ensley et al. 2000). In contrast, relationship conflict can be very destructive to team processes and performance. In groups that experience relationship conflict, there is often greater anxiety, psychological strain, lack of receptiveness to other members' ideas, and lack of listening to and assessing new information impartially (Pelled 1996; Barsade et al. 2000). Disagreements over ideas are often taken as personal attacks and are destructive and isolating, which reduces group effectiveness (Amason 1996). Essentially, with relationship conflict, the team spends energy addressing the conflict rather than the task at hand (Barsade et al. 2000), while with cognitive conflict team energy is spent addressing the task, which promotes team effectiveness and performance. Unfortunately, past research indicates that cognitive and relationship conflicts are often related (Pelled et al. 1999; Simons and Peterson 2000), with cognitive conflict leading to relationship conflict. Therefore, the trick is to try and promote the former without having it trigger or morph into the latter (Ensley et al. 2000).

Diverse teams in general are less predictable in terms of attitudes and behaviors than homogenous teams, and this unpredictability can lead to both affective and cognitive conflict. Demographic heterogeneity (O'Reilly et al. 1993), personality differences (Barsade et al. 2000), and differences in values (Jehn et al. 1999) can all lead to greater conflict within a team. That said, different types of team diversity have been linked to different types of conflict. Studies have shown that functional diversity (diversity in educational or work experiences related to the job) is related to cognitive conflict (Jehn et al. 1999; Pelled et al. 1999) while organizational value diversity is linked to relationship conflict (Lankau et al. 2007). We consider the ramifications of this research for different types of entrepreneurial teams next.

With respect to cognitive conflict, in this chapter, we make the assumption that all the venture teams possess somewhat diverse functional backgrounds (while this may not be true in all cases, we assume that most ventures are not founded by entrepreneurs with identical work and educational backgrounds). Thus, we take it as a starting point that the different teams, with their varying compositions of passion, will experience at least a moderate degree of cognitive conflict owing to their functional diversity. We must mention though that functional diversity is not the only factor determining the amount of cognitive conflict that arises during team inter-actions. Team cohesion also factors into the conflict equation because, as Ensley et al. (2002) contend, individuals within an entrepreneurial team must trust one another and tolerate dissent in a constructive manner if the disagreements char-acteristic of cognitive conflict will be allowed to emerge. Otherwise, individuals will be unwilling or afraid to voice contrary opinions for fear of repercussion. This point is reinforced by Barsade et al. (2000) who contend that groups with high lev-els of positive affective similarity have been also shown to exhibit higher levels of cooperativeness than affectively heterogeneous groups because of greater feelings of familiarity, attraction, and trust that are engendered from affective similarity – attraction processes that work to reinforce a group's cooperation and cohesion. In a study of 70 new ventures, Ensley et al. (2002) empirically demonstrate that teams with higher cohesion experience greater cognitive conflict.

Based on these findings, we suggest that focused passion teams will demonstrate the greatest cognitive conflict because they possess the highest cohesion. As such, they will possess the highest levels of trust and be most willing to disagree with one another. Because they have high team cohesion, they will be comfortable with one another and comfortable airing ideas that are in contrast to one another. Thus the functional advantages of cognitive conflict are most likely to emerge in teams high in cohesion, here focused passion teams. Balanced and mixed passion teams will also demonstrate some degree of cognitive conflict, but less so than focused passion teams because of their lower cohesion, and thus lower interpersonal trust.

In terms of relationship conflict, teams with focused collective passion should exhibit the lowest relationship conflict, because their affective similarity, and thus their team cohesion, is the highest. In a focused team, members all experience high levels of passion feelings and they are all focused on the same entrepreneurial role identity. This suggests a high level of affective similarity and thus a high level of cohesion. High affective similarity and cohesion are likely to reduce the incidence of social categorization among team members. Categorization involves classifying individuals into distinct social groups, and to the extent that one classifies individ-uals into groups different from oneself, cohesion may fall and relationship conflict may arise (Pelled 1996). Focused passion teams are least likely to categorize one another as different because of the similarity in their feelings of passion. They are most likely to recognize that they all possess deep emotional attachments to the ven-ture resulting from the identical focus of their passion to the same entrepreneurial role identity (inventor, founder, or developer). Moreover, these teams are least likely to let cognitive conflict transform into relationship conflict because they do not take dissenting opinions personally since the higher levels of trust and cohesion present in focused passion teams keep cognitive conflict targeted on task-related issues rather than on interpersonal attacks. Our contention is supported by Ensley et al. (2002) who show that entrepreneurial teams with higher cohesion exhibit lower relationship conflict, as well as by Simons and Peterson (2000) who empirically demonstrate that greater intragroup trust reduces the incidence of cognitive conflict triggering relationship conflict.

Following the logic offered above, teams with mixed collective passion will exhibit the highest relationship conflict, because their affective similarity, and thus their cohesion, will be lowest. These teams are the most likely to experience social categorization (Pelled 1996) as individual members view themselves as distinct and different from one another due to stark differences in the existence of (whether or not they feel passion) and focus of (if they feel it, for which identity) their passion feelings. As such, the cognitive conflicts that occur in these teams are most likely to morph into relationship conflict because there is a lack of trust, understanding, and a sense of shared belonging among team members. Disagreements about tasks or processes are more likely to be misinterpreted as personal attacks since it is evident that not all the individuals share the same level or type of passion for the venture and related activities.

Finally, balanced collective passion teams will have moderate levels of relationship conflict, driven primarily by their moderate levels of cohesion. Cohesion in these teams is moderate because the members all experience passion (similarity) but it is focused on different things (dissimilarity). These teams benefit from more cohesion than mixed passion teams, and thus have higher trust, and as a result, lower relationship conflict. Even though their passions are aimed in differing directions, members of balanced passion teams still recognize that everyone has a passion for some aspect of the venture (compared to mixed passion teams where certain members do not feel any passion for the venture at all). Possessing at least some degree of passion for the venture, even if it is directed at different entrepreneurial identities, should help to elevate intragroup trust and mitigate the transformation of cognitive conflict into relationship conflict. Unfortunately, these teams do not possess the high levels of trust and cohesion present in focused passion teams, so they are likely to experience more relationship conflict than focused passion teams.

9.5 The Entrepreneurial Mind Must Manage Collective Passion

Although the focus of this research is on collective passion and team-related processes, within any entrepreneurial team there is usually one individual who is the leader of the team, either formally or informally (Shane et al. 2003). In all three types of teams, in order for the team and organization to work optimally, the lead entrepreneur must be able to recognize which type of collective passion is shared among the team and manage the team dynamics specific to that type of passion. We next discuss management challenges specific to each particular team composition.

In a focused team, team cohesion and cognitive conflict are high, while relationship conflict is low. Greater team cohesion, affective similarity, and value congruence lead to more trust within the team, and therefore differences in opinion can be aired constructively with little harm to interpersonal relationships. Team leaders are most likely to use delegation and participative leadership in a team with greater cohesion (Barsade et al. 2000). Because of the high levels of team cohesion and productive cognitive conflict, the team leader might be driven into thinking that the team processes are all working well, so there are no potential tensions. However, because all team members feel passion for the same role identity, there is a possibility to ignore challenges or tasks in the environment related to the other two roles. A focused passion team is less likely to want to engage in activities associated with entrepreneurial identities outside their passion realm. For example, an entrepreneurial team passionate about the inventing role may be less interested in founding the business or commercializing the inventions they have discovered, making the team less flexible to business demands that they do so. This may result in the team missing the market opportunity for their products or services, which is dysfunctional for team performance.

One recommendation for this team leader might be that he/she use the resources that are freed up from having to manage interpersonal problems among the team (i.e., the team does not have much relationship conflict, so the leader has more time to focus on other things) and focus on an effort to predict what skills and resources will be needed that the team does not currently possess. These resources can either be brought into the firm, such as by hiring employees or contractors with those key skills, or the responsibility for them can be shared equally among team members. Some effort should be expended in this type of team on ensuring a fair distribution of tasks among team members, particularly those unrelated to the focal role identity, so that each member of the team has the responsibility for some non-identity meaningful activities. Otherwise, an unfair distribution could lead to eventual affective conflict for team members taking on responsibility for activities that are less enjoyable to them. However, such a rotation could be harmful from a competence standpoint. In sum, a focused passion team is optimal in terms of team cohesion, cognitive conflict, and relationship conflict, but may be at greatest risk of lacking some of the competencies needed to attain maximum venture performance.

In a balanced team, team cohesion, cognitive conflict, and relationship conflict are all moderate. In balanced passion teams, the situation is the shadow of the focused passion team. The team is optimally balanced for handling changes in the environment (everyone has a desire to do something different in the business) but this can lead to lower cohesion and thus more problems with interpersonal interaction. If no one shares one person's passion (the opposite of focused passion teams) that person can begin to feel isolated (see our arguments about social categorization above). Isolation can reduce trust and raise affective conflict. The team leader has to work actively to break the cognitive conflict to affective conflict link by engaging in team-building activities. These team members are all highly emotionally invested in the venture, but in different aspects (owing to different identities) and that could be a powder keg of relationship conflict. The team leader must work to prevent small disagreements from growing into larger disputes. Energy spent on team building and development of team cohesion could be extremely beneficial in a balanced passion team, because this would lead to more open sharing of cognitive conflicts, which would result in optimal decision making for the team, since all aspects of the venture's business are represented in the team (passion is experienced for all three role identities). Team leaders in a balanced passion team must also provide greater clarity about goals, values, and tasks for the team in order to develop shared understanding (Vyakarnam and Handelberg 2005), which can help the team function more optimally.

In a mixed passion team, team cohesion is low, while cognitive conflict is moderate and relationship conflict is high. This is the most challenging type of team for the lead entrepreneur to manage. Low social cohesion and high relationship conflict make it likely that there will be a lot of interpersonal conflicts and that those conflicts will often be perceived as personal attacks. There is likely to be a lack of communication and a lack of focus on tasks. Moderate cognitive conflict means there will be diversity in thinking, but not at an optimal level, primarily because the low team cohesion will spur distrust between members and make them hesitant to voice their divergent ideas. The lead entrepreneur in this type of team has to set up appropriate systems to manage the interpersonal tensions and stressors and to make sure to provide an environment for decision making that is safe for all members. Techniques like rotating the devil's advocate role, non-judgmental brainstorming sessions, or the use of organizational development facilitators for key decisions may be helpful. It is critical in this type of team that team members understand the overall organizational and team goals and also understand each other's contributions to the team (Mohrman et al. 1995). This is so that team members can be on the same "wavelength" about business cycles and strategies to be successful (Watson et al. 1995). Scholars note that in addition to shared understanding of goals (Vyakarnam and Handelberg 2005), team members should also communicate about venture team structure (Bird 1989) and their individual and shared values in order to increase team success. There is also a chance that a mixed passion team will have key areas where no team member feels passionate, leading to the challenges noted for focused passion teams where some types of critical venture activities may tend to be ignored. In contrast to focused passion teams (where everyone has a passion directed at the same role identity within the same venture) and balanced passion teams (where everyone has a passion directed at different role identities, but still within the same venture), mixed passion teams suffer from perceptions among team members that their colleagues may not have any passion at all for any aspect of the venture. These differences between individuals can reduce commitment of team members to one another and to the venture (Bishop and Scott 1996). Lead entrepreneurs must take measures to ensure that all members of the team (passionate and non-passionate) understand the commitment of the entire team to the venture's overall success. Thus leaders of mixed passion teams have a dual challenge of managing the interpersonal tensions within the team and managing potential skill gaps among team members.

9.6 Discussion and Implications

In this chapter, we extend the recent work on affective processes of entrepreneurs (e.g., Baron 2007; 2008) by integrating work concerning the individual entrepreneurial passion of solo entrepreneurs with work on the composition and dynamics that occur within entrepreneurial teams to propose a new conceptualization of *collective passion* and its effects. Building upon recent developments of entrepreneurial passion by Cardon and colleagues (in press) we elevate the concept of passion to the group level and conceptualize collective passion as the combined entrepreneurial passion experienced by members of a team of entrepreneurs, including potential differences in the level and focus of each member's individual passion. We believe that exploration of collective passion is important for two reasons: (1) entrepreneurial passion has been argued to be a powerful motivational resource that leads to attainment of entrepreneurial goals despite formidable obstacles and (2) there is an evident gap in extant research surrounding how entrepreneurial passion works within teams, especially where a lead entrepreneur not only needs to manage his/her own passion but must also work with the various potential configurations of passion among team members. We outline several contributions of our work for future theoretical and empirical research and implications for business practice below.

Our main conceptual contribution to the entrepreneurship literature stems from raising the discussion of entrepreneurial passion from the individual to the group level. This has implications for future research on entrepreneurial passion as well as on entrepreneurial teams. First, we introduce the concept of collective passion based on the experience of different role identities within the entrepreneurial team. Specifically, we show how diversity of entrepreneurial passions may influence emergence of a collective passion within the team and how this affects team-related processes as well as the venture's performance. We ground our analysis on the proposal of three different team compositions based on individually experienced entrepreneurial passions: balanced passion teams, focused passion teams, and mixed passion teams. By introducing collective passion as an important characteristic of entrepreneurial teams we contribute to the literature on entrepreneurial teams beyond current discussions of personal connections between team members, demographic aspects of entrepreneurial team composition, collective cognitions, and how such characteristics change the process of founding and managing the entrepreneurial team. We show that affective processes within teams may influence overall venture performance directly and indirectly through team dynamics and processes. More specifically, we explore the effects of collective passion on two important within-team dynamics: team cohesion and team conflict. We argue that in a focused team, team cohesion and cognitive conflict will be high and relationship conflict will be low because all team members feel passion for the same role identity. In a balanced entrepreneurial passion team, team cohesion, cognitive conflict, and relationship conflict will all be moderate. Finally, it seems that a mixed passion team is likely to face low team cohesion, moderate cognitive conflict, and high relationship conflict. This implies a variety of leadership challenges that entrepreneurial minds are likely to face within founding teams.

Another contribution of this chapter lies in our examination of different sources for passion among entrepreneurial team members. The majority of the research in management and entrepreneurship analyzing affect does so with little consideration for the eliciting stimulus. Scholars tend to assume that as long as emotions created by varying stimuli are the same, the effects will be identical (Baron 2008). For example, a commonly used procedure for inducing emotions in laboratory studies (e.g., Lerner and Keltner 2001) involves asking subjects to write about a situation that makes them feel the target emotion (sad, angry, happy, etc.). In such an induction, there is no control over the actual eliciting stimuli (i.e., subjects are free to select any stimulus they want); the focus is solely upon creating the desired emotion. While this practice is common in laboratory research, most theories of emotion, especially those involving cognitive appraisals or reappraisals (e.g., Cacioppo et al. 1999; Feldman Barrett et al. 2007; Lambie and Marcel 2002), assert that conscious consideration of the stimulus is of paramount importance. Though it is possible for different stimuli to elicit identical emotions (as is presumed in experimental research) even small differences in the stimuli may contribute to varied emotional experiences. We consider such differences in this study by examining different sources (i.e., the various entrepreneurial identities) for entrepreneurial passion. Further, we examine how different targets for entrepreneurial passion may catalyze different reactions among the other members of the entrepreneurial team. This approach relies on the interpersonal focus in affective diversity theory that emphasizes how emotions are social entities (Parkinson 1996) and, as such, those emotions felt and expressed by one individual can affect other members of a team. It is important to remember that not all entrepreneurial passions are created equally, that they do not all have identical effects, and that lead entrepreneurs must be able to recognize these differences if they are to effectively manage their ventures.

9.6.1 Implications for Practitioners

In this chapter, we highlight the importance of managing affective resources, both within oneself and among the top management team of the new venture. Managing the various constellations of entrepreneurial passion mentioned in this chapter must be preceded by the ability to recognize affective diversity. An important element of an individual's entrepreneurial development is to nurture one's competencies to perceive, understand, and regulate emotions. In this respect, development of an entrepreneurial mindset should explicitly include development of one's specific affective abilities. Entrepreneurs who possess the ability to accurately detect variances in passion among their colleagues have an advantage in being able to manage those differences. Thus, it appears that the construct of emotional intelligence is relevant here. Emotional intelligence involves the ability of an individual to accurately sense and reason about emotions and to use one's knowledge about those emotions to enhance thought and action (Mayer et al. 2008; Salovey and Mayer 1990). Entrepreneurs who possess greater emotional intelligence appear better equipped to manage the various different types of collective passion we discuss. In addition to being aware of variances in an entrepreneurial team's collective passion composition, several relationship management strategies may be worthwhile to consider.

Finally, when thinking of appropriate strategies to manage collective passion within teams, one needs to realize that team dynamics can easily change. Therefore, it is important that the lead entrepreneur avoids tunnel vision during his/her monitoring of ongoing team processes. Prior research shows that affective processes are not only personality dependent, but other factors such as technology, industry, and physical space have been shown to critically influence dynamics of affective processes within a group. Prior research of emotions in small groups (Kelly and Barsade 2001) has shown that in order to fully understand the dynamic and reciprocal nature of group affect one needs to consider the feedback loop from group emotion to affective antecedents of group emotion. In other words, relationship management strategies that are employed by the lead entrepreneur in order to secure entrepreneurial team performance goals have influences on the lead entrepreneur himself/herself and his/her recurring affective processes. Such feedback loops need to be considered in future work on affective processes within entrepreneurial teams.

We realize that it is difficult and probably impractical to train entrepreneurs to feel the specific types of entrepreneurial passion needed in order to achieve total balance within a team. Thus, not every entrepreneurial venture is likely to enjoy the cohesion and conflict advantages emerging from focused passion or balanced passion teams that are discussed above. Perhaps not every venture should be forced to conform to a focused or balanced passion team though, because we must be cautious as to how much we try to "manage" another person's passions. Remember that our own passions derive much of their drive and power from a sense of authenticity and feeling that resonates with who we truly are (our self-identity), not who someone else wants us to be. Thus, to some extent, it is either unrealistic or unwise for a lead entrepreneur to try to alter his/her colleagues' passions directly. Tinkering too much with someone else's passion could diminish the uniquely individual quality that harmonizes that passion with the entrepreneur's role identity, thus depleting one's motivational fire. Our intent in this chapter is not aimed at managing passions, but rather in helping lead entrepreneurs to realize the structure of the collective passion they may be confronted with in their entrepreneurial team. By acknowledging the diversity of passion and affective similarity that a particular entrepreneurial team is facing, an emotionally intelligent lead entrepreneur will take care to sample the affective impulses of the team and use this information to craft behaviors and responses in emotionally charged situations (Rafaeli and Sutton 1990). In order to enhance one's affective regulation skills, several specific tools have been suggested, such as affective computing (Shepherd 2004), and reflection-based activities, such as journaling (Brown 2003), as well as others. This provides new opportunities for lead entrepreneurs to enhance the effectiveness of their entrepreneurial teams.

9.6.2 Future Research Avenues

We believe that the idea of collective passion within entrepreneurial founding teams poses exciting new questions in researching the emergence and dynamics of entrepreneurial teams. The concept provides a starting point to explore questions such as Why do some entrepreneurial teams succeed in achieving individual as well as team-level venture-related goals, whereas other teams break apart when challenges or unexpected successes are confronted? It would be fascinating to explore whether specific teams fail because of too much affective similarity in collective passion (so that there is a lack of competence and necessary skills) or too much affective dissimilarity among passions (so that there is too much cognitive and/or relationship conflict). Further, using a longitudinal research lens one could explore how success or failure in one venture, with one type of collective passion composition, facilitates or debilitates subsequent team building and venturing by the individuals involved.

In this research we have undertaken a relatively static view of entrepreneurial team dynamics. Yet, entrepreneurship teams are not static and members come and go (Ucbasaran et al. 2003) as the venture grows and the specific challenges experienced shift. A more robust view of the affective diversity of an entrepreneurial team would ideally use a longitudinal research design. Indeed, empirical testing of the proposed concepts and exploration of team composition may add additional information about which types of collective passion teams are prevalent in practice. Since our arguments are conceptual at this juncture, empirical examination is needed to see whether entrepreneurs put teams together pragmatically by accounting for different skill sets or are rather driven by affective similarity in passions among possible colleagues. To what extent do entrepreneurs consider the felt passion of potential team members prior to them joining the team and to what extent do the constellations of collective team passions impact firm cohesion, conflict, and ultimately performance or the departure of team members after the venture has been founded? Dynamic, longitudinal field research is needed to address such issues.

In this chapter we have included two team dynamics variables: team cohesion and team conflict. Future conceptual and empirical research could extend the list of team performance-related variables to include other factors such as team coordination, goal setting, learning, feedback monitoring, and backup behavior (LePine et al. 2008). Further, does collective passion directly influence venture performance or are these effects always mediated by team dynamic factors such as those considered above?

Finally, in order to pursue empirical testing of the proposed concept, original scale development work is needed to capture the phenomenon of collective passion. Currently there are no measures of individual entrepreneurial passion, much less of collective team passion. In addition, the concept of affective diversity appears in literature on teams as a trait-like concept, while we are suggesting it may be an interpersonal variable instead. As such, scale validation, and possibly new scale development, needs to be done concerning both collective passion and affective diversity as it is used in this chapter. Initial testing of measures and research designs would require field studies. The MIT Media Lab study of social networks has demonstrated some success in capturing real-time data about entrepreneur's daily experience of emotions and subsequent adaptive behaviors (Eagle 2005) and could be a useful starting point for further research.

9.7 Conclusion

Research on affect and passion in entrepreneurship has seen a recent surge and theoretical and empirical work is developing at a fast pace (e.g., Baron 2008; Cardon et al. 2009). As we continue to push the boundaries with studies of affect and passion among individual entrepreneurs, we must be mindful of the context in which we hope to apply our research. New ventures cannot arise without the efforts of individual entrepreneurs (McMullen and Shepherd 2006), but most new ventures are the product of teams of entrepreneurs, not individual ones (Kamm et al. 1990). As such, it behooves us to extend our theorizing on individual constructs like affect and passion to the team level. We have taken a first step in this chapter toward pushing thinking about the interactions of affect and passion in teams. However, much more needs to be done in terms of analyzing how passion permeates and pervades team cognitions and actions, and ultimately influences venture outcomes. We hope that we have stimulated discourse among scholars concerning the importance of these factors in our field.

References

Aldrich HA, Martinez MA (2001) Many are called, but few are chosen: An evolutionary perspective for the study of entrepreneurship. Entrepreneurship Theory and Practice 25: 41–56

Amason AC, Schweiger DM (1994) Resolving the paradox of conflict, strategic decision making and organizational performance. International Journal of Conflict Management 5: 239–253

Amason AC (1996) Distinguishing the effects of functional and dysfunctional conflict on strategic decision making: Resolving a paradox for top management teams. Academy of Management Journal 39: 123–148

Amason AC, Shrader RC, Tompson GH (2006) Newness and novelty: Relating top management team composition to new venture performance. Journal of Business Venturing 21: 125–148

Baron RA (2007) Behavioral and cognitive factors in entrepreneurship: Entrepreneurs as the active element in new venture creation. Strategic Entrepreneurship Journal 1: 167–182

Baron RA (2008) The role of affect in the entrepreneurial process. Academy of Management Review 33:328–340

Barrett LF, Mesquita B, Ochsner KN, Gross JJ (2007) The experience of emotion. Annual Review of Psychology 58: 373–403

Barrick M, Stewart G, Neubert MJ, Mount M (1998) Relating member ability and personality to work-team processes and team effectiveness. Journal of Applied Psychology 83: 377–319

Barsade SG, Gibson DE (2007) Why does affect matter in organizations? Academy of Management Perspectives 21: 36–59

Barsade SG, Ward AJ, Turner JDF, Sonnenfeld JA (2000) To your heart's content: A model of affective diversity in top management teams. Administrative Science Quarterly 45: 802–836

Baum JR, Locke EA (2004) The relationship of entrepreneurial traits, skill, and motivation to new venture growth. Journal of Applied Psychology 89: 587–599

Baum JR, Locke EA, Smith KG (2001) A multidimensional model of venture growth. Academy of Management Journal 44: 292–303

Beal DJ, Cohen R, Burke MJ, McLendon CL (2003) Cohesion and performance in groups: A meta-analytic clarification of construct relation. Journal of Applied Psychology 88: 989–1004

Berscheid E (1985) Interpersonal attraction. In: Lindzey G, Aronson E (eds) Handbook of Social Psychology. Random House, New York, pp. 413–484

Bierly PE, Kessler EH, Christensen EW (2000) Organizational learning, knowledge, and wisdom. Journal of Organizational Change Management 13: 595–618

Bird BJ (1989) Entrepreneurial Behavior. Scott Foresman and Co, Glenview, IL

Birley S, Stockley S, 2000 Entrepreneurial teams and venture growth. In: Sexton DL, Landstrom H (eds) The Blackwell Handbook of Entrepreneurship. Blackwell Publishers, Malden, MA. pages

Bishop JW, Scott KD (1996) Multiple foci of commitment in a team environment. Academy of Management Proceedings, pp. 269–273.

Boxx WR, Odom RY, Dunn MG (1991) Organizational values and value congruency and their impact on satisfaction, commitment and cohesion: An empirical examination within the public sector. Public Personnel Management 20: 195–205

Branzei O, Zietsma C (2003) Entrepreneurial love: The enabling functions of positive illusions in venturing. Paper Presented at the Babson-Kauffman Entrepreneurial Research Conference. Babson College, Wellesley, MA.

Brown RB (2003) Emotions and behavior: Exercises in emotional intelligence. Journal of Management Education 27: 122–134

Brännback M, Carsrud A, Elfving J, Krueger NF (2006) Sex, [drugs], and entrepreneurial passion?: An exploratory study. Paper Presented at the Babson-Kauffman Entrepreneurial Research Conference. Bloomington, IN.

Burke PJ (1991) Identity processes and social stress. American Sociological Review 56: 836–849

Byrne D (1971) The Attraction Paradigm. Academic Press, New York.

Cacioppo JT, Gardner WL, Berntson GG (1999) The affect system has parallel and integrative processing components: Form follows function. Journal of Personality and Social Psychology 76: 839–855

Cardon MS, Wincent J, Singh J, Drnovsek M (2005) Entrepreneurial passion: The nature of emotions in entrepreneurship. In: Weaver KM (ed), Proceedings of the Sixty-fifth Annual Meeting of the Academy of Management CD, ISSN 1543–8643.

Cardon MS, Wincent J, Singh J, Drnovsek M (2008) The different faces of entrepreneurial affect: why entrepreneurial emotion and passion are distinct. Paper Presented at 2008 Academy of Management Conference, Anaheim, CA.

Cardon MS, Wincent J, Singh J, Drnovsek M (2009) The nature and experience of entrepreneurial passion. Academy of Management Review.

Cast AD (2004) Well-being and the transition to parenthood: An identity theory approach. Sociological Perspectives, 47(1): 55–78.

Chowdhury S (2005) Demographic diversity for building an effective entrepreneurial team: Is it important? Journal of Business Venturing 20: 727–746

Connor JJ, Rueter MA (2006) Parent-child relationships as systems of support or risk for adolescent suicidality. Journal of Family Psychology 20: 143

Cooper AC, Dunkelberg WC, Woo CY (1988) Entrepreneurs' perceived chances for success. Journal of Business Venturing 3: 97–109

Cooper AC, Bruno AV (1977) Success among high-technology firms. Business Horizons 20: 16–28

Damasio AR (2003) Fundamental feelings. Nature 413(6858): 781

Duffy MK, Shaw JD (2000) The Salieri syndrome. Small Group Research 31: 3–23

Eagle NN (2005) Machine Perception and Learning of Complex Social Systems. Unpublished PhD dissertation, Massachusetts Institute of Technology, Cambridge, MA.

Eisenberg J (2007) Group Cohesiveness, In: Baumeister RF, Vohs KD (eds), Encyclopedia of Social Psychology, Sage, Thousand Oaks, CA, pp. 386–388

Ensley MD, Pearson AW (2005) An exploratory comparison of the behavioral dynamics of top management teams in family and nonfamily new ventures: Cohesion, conflict, potency and consensus. Entrepreneurship: Theory and Practice 29: 267–284

Ensley MD, Pearson AW, Amason AC (2000) Understanding the dynamics of new venture top management teams: Cohesion, conflict and new venture performance. Journal of Business Venturing 17: 365–386

Estrada CA, Isen AM, Young MJ (1997) Positive affect facilitates integration of information and decreases anchoring in reasoning among physicians. Organizational Behavior and Human Decision Processes 72: 117–135

Foo M, Uy MA, Baron RA (2008) How do feelings influence effort? An empirical study on entrepreneurs' affect and venture effort. Paper Presented at 2008 Academy of Management Conference, Anaheim, CA.

Gartner WB, Starr JA, Bhat S (1999) Predicting new venture survival: An analysis of "Anatomy of a Startup" cases from Inc. magazine. Journal of Business Venturing 14: 215–232

George JM (1995) Leader positive mood and group performance: The case of customer service. Journal of Applied Social Psychology 25: 778–794

Haveman HA, Khaire MV (2004) Survival beyond succession? The contingent impact of founder succession on organizational failure. Journal of Business Venturing 19: 437–463

Isen AM (2000). Positive affect and decision making. In: Lewis M, Haviland-Jones J (eds) Handbook of Emotions. Guilford Press, New York, pp. 417–435

Isen AM, Labroo AA (2003) Some ways in which positive affect facilitates decision making and judgment. In: Schneider SL, Shanteau JR (eds) Emerging Perspectives on Decision Research. Cambridge press, New York, pp. 365–393

Isen AM, Means B (1993) The influence of positive affect on decision-making strategy. Social Cognition 2: 18–31

Janis IL (1982) Groupthink: Psychological Studies of Policy Decisions and Fiascoes. Houghton-Mifflin, Boston

Jehn KA (1995) A multi-method examination of the benefits and determinants of intragroup conflict. Administrative Science Quarterly 40: 256–282.

Jehn KA, Bendersky C (2003) Intragroup conflict in organizations: A contingency perspective on the conflict-outcome relationship. In: Staw B, Kramer R (eds), Research in Organizational Behavior. Elsevier, New York, pp. 189–244

Jehn KA, Northcraft GB, Neale MA (1999) Why differences make a difference: A field study of diversity, conflict, and performance in workgroups. Administrative Science Quarterly 44: 741–763

Jordan PJ, Lawrence SA, Troth AC (2006) The impact of negative mood on team performance. Journal of Management and Organization 12: 131–145

Jordan PJ, Troth AC (2004) Managing emotions during team problem solving: Emotional intelligence and conflict resolution. Human Performance 17: 195–218

Kamm JB, Shuman JC, Seeger JA, Nurick AJ (1990) Entrepreneurial teams in new venture creation: A research agenda. Entrepreneurship: Theory and Practice 14: 7–17

Kelly JR, Barsade SG (2001) Mood and emotions in small groups and work teams. Organizational Behavior and Human Decision Processes 86(1): 99–130

Lambie JA, Marcel AJ (2002) Consciousness and the varieties of emotion experience: A theoretical framework. Psychological Review 1092: 219–259

Lankau MJ, Ward A, Amason A, Ng T, Sonnenfeld JA, Agle BR (2007) Examining the impact of organizational value dissimilarity in top management teams. Journal of Managerial Issues 1: 11–34

Lechler T (2001) Social interaction: A determinant of entrepreneurial team venture success. Small Business Economics 16: 263–278

LePine JA, Piccolo RF, Jackson CL, Mathieu JE, Saul JR (2008) A meta-analysis of teamwork processes: Tests of a multidimensional model and relationships with team effectiveness criteria. Personnel Psychology 61: 273–307

Lerner JS, Keltner D (2001) Fear, anger, and risk. Journal of Personality & Social Psychology 81: 146–159

Lott AJ, Lott BE (1974) The role of reward in the formation of positive interpersonal attitudes. In: Huston TL (ed) Foundation of Interpersonal Attraction. Academic Press, New York, pp. 171–192

Lyubomirsky S, King L, Deiner E (2005) The benefits of frequent positive affect: Does happiness lead to success? Psychological Bulletin 131: 803–855

Mayer J, Roberts R, Barsade SG (2008) Human abilities: Emotional intelligence. Annual Review of Psychology 59: 507–536

McMullen JS, Shepherd DA (2006) Entrepreneurial action and the role of uncertainty in the theory of the entrepreneur. Academy of Management Review 31: 132–152

Mohrman SA, Cohen SG, Mohrman A Jr. (1995) Designing Team Based Organizations: New Forms for Knowledge Work. Jossey Bass, San Francisco CA

Murnieks C, Mosakowski E (2006) Entrepreneurial passion: An identity theory perspective. Paper Presented at the 2006 Academy of Management Conference. Atlanta, GA.

O'Reilly CA, Snyder R, Boothe J (1993) Effects of executive team demography on organizational change. In: Huber G, Glick W (eds) Organizational Change and Redesign. Oxford University Press, New York, pp. 147–175

Odiorne J (1991) Competence versus passion. Training and Development 45: 61–65

Parkinson B (1996) Emotions are social. British Journal of Psychology 87: 663–683

Pasanen M, Laukkanen T (2006) Team-managed growing SMEs: A distinct species? Management Research News 29: 684–700

Pelled LH (1996) Demographic diversity, conflict, and work group outcomes: An intervening process theory. Organization Science 7: 615–631

Pelled LH, Eisenhardt KM, Xin KR (1999) Exploring the black box: An analysis of work group diversity, conflict and performance. Administrative Science Quarterly 44: 1–28

Pham MT (2004) The logic of feeling. Journal of Consumer Psychology 14: 360–369

Rafaeli A, Sutton RI (1990) Busy stores and demanding customers: How do they affect the display of positive emotion? Academy of Management Journal 33: 623–637

Rip B, Fortin S, Vallerand RJ (2006) The relationship between passion and injury in dance students. Journal of Dance Medicine & Science 10: 14–20

Rousseau FL, Vallerand RJ (2003) The role of passion in the subjective well-being of the elderly. Revue Quebecoise de Psychologie 24: 197–211

Russell JA (2003) Core affect and the psychological construction of emotion. Psychological Review 110: 145–172

Salovey P, Mayer JD (1990) Emotional intelligence. Imagination, Cognition, and Personality 9: 185–211

Schwarz N, Clore GL (2007) Feelings and phenomenal experiences. In: Higgins ET, Kruglanski A (eds) Social Psychology: Handbook of Basic Principles. Guildord Press, New York, pp. 385–407

Séguin-Lévesque C, Laliberté M-L, Pelletier LG, Blanchard C, Vallerand RJ (2003) Harmonious and obsessive passion for the internet: Their associations with couple's relationships. Journal of Applied Social Psychology 33: 197–221

Seo M, Barrett LF, Bartunek JM (2004) The role of affective experience in work motivation. Academy of Management Review 29: 423–440

Shane S, Locke EA, Collins CJ (2003) Entrepreneurial motivation. Human Resource Management Review 13: 257–279

Shepherd DA (2003) Learning from business failure: Propositions of grief recovery for the self-employed. Academy of Management Review 28: 318–329

Shepherd DA (2004). Educating entrepreneurship students about emotion and learning from failure. Academy of Management Learning and Education 3: 274–287

Shepherd DA (2009). Grief recovery from the loss of a family business: A multi- and meso-level theory. Journal of Business Venturing 24: 81–97

Simons TL, Peterson RS (2000) Task conflict and relationship conflict in top management teams: The pivotal role of intragroup trust. Journal of Applied Psychology 85: 102–111

Smilor RW (1997) Entrepreneurship: Reflections on a subversive activity. Journal of Business Venturing 12: 341–346

Stryker S, Burke PJ (2000) The past, present, and future of an identity theory. Social Psychology Quarterly 63: 284–297

Stryker S, Serpe RT (1982) Commitment, identity salience and role behavior: Theory and research example. In: Ickes W, Knowles ES (eds) Personality, Roles and Social Behavior. Springer Verlag, New York, pp. 199–218.

Stryker S (1989) Further developments in identity theory: Singularity versus multiplicity of self. In Berger J, Zelditch M, Anderson B (eds) Sociological Theories in Progress. Sage, London

Stryker S (2004) Integrating emotion into identity theory. In: Turner JH (ed) Theory and Research on Human Emotions, Elsevier Ltd, New York, pp. 1–23

Timmons JA (1999) New Venture Creation: Entrepreneurship for the 21st Century. McGraw Hill, Irwin

Ucbasaran D, Lockett A, Wright M, Westhead P (2003) Entrepreneurial founder teams factors associated with team member entry and exit. Entrepreneurship, Theory and Practice 28: 107–127

Utsch A, Rauch A (2000) Innovativeness and initiative as mediators between achievement orientation and venture performance. European Journal of Work & Organizational Psychology 91: 45–63

Vallerand RJ (2008) On the psychology of passion: In search of what makes people's lives most worth living. Canadian Psychology 49:1–13

Vallerand RJ, Blanchard CM, Mageau GA, Koestner R, Ratelle CF, Leonard M (2003) Les passions de l'ame: On obsessive and harmonious passion. Journal of Personality and Social Psychology 85: 756–767

Walter F, Bruch H (2008) The positive group affect spiral: A dynamic model of the emergence of positive affective similarity in work groups. Journal of Organizational Behavior 29: 239–261

Watson D, Clark LA (1984) Negative Affectivity: The disposition to experience negative emotional states. Psychological Bulletin 96: 465–490

Watson WE, Ponthieu LD, Critelli JW (1995) Team interpersonal process effectiveness in venture partnerships and its connection to perceived success. Journal of Business Venturing, 10(5): 393–411

Westhead P, Ucbasaran D, Wright M (2005) Experience and cognition: Do novice, serial and portfolio entrepreneurs differ? International Small Business Journal 23: 72–98

Vyakarnam S, Handelberg J (2005) Four themes of the impact of management teams on organizational performance: Implications for future research of entrepreneurial teams. International Small Business Journal 23: 236–256

Part IV
Attributions, Self-Efficacy, and Locus of Control

Chapter 10
Why? Attributions About and by Entrepreneurs

Kelly G. Shaver

Abstract To help explain events and behavior, people search for causes. In some cases the identified causes are found within persons, in other cases they are found in the environment, in still other cases they are found in the interaction between person and environment. When provided with multiple opportunities for observation, people typically follow a principle of covariation. With only one chance for observation, people rely on causal schemata. Although attributional inferences are often correct, there are two primary classes of attributional error. First, there is a natural difference in perspective between actors and observers. Actors are "looking outward," concentrating on factors in the environment, but observers are concentrating only on the actor. This perspective difference leads observers to over-attribute events to persons, paying too little attention to situational factors, a cognitive mistake known as the fundamental attribution error. Second, there are errors created by the observer's motivation. Three examples are the self-serving bias, the need to believe in a just world, and defensive attribution. These errors and objective attribution processes are described and illustrated by examples from entrepreneurship.

10.1 Introduction

Attributions are the explanations people offer for the occurrence of events and behavior. The attributions made depend in part on the individual's vantage point and in part on that person's own motivations. This chapter begins with a general description of attribution processes, next considers how vantage point can influence attributional judgments, then turns to some of the errors and biases that originate from internal motivation, and finally provides examples of the way the attribution approach has been used in the study of the entrepreneurial mind.

K.G. Shaver (✉)
School of Business and Economics, College of Charleston, Beatty 305, 5 Liberty Street, Charleston, SC, 29401, USA
e-mail: shaverk@cofc.edu

A.L. Carsrud, M. Brännback (eds.), *Understanding the Entrepreneurial Mind*, International Studies in Entrepreneurship 24, DOI 10.1007/978-1-4419-0443-0_10, © Springer Science+Business Media, LLC 2009

10.1.1 Origins of the Attribution Approach

Why did that happen? Few endeavors are more human than the search for the meaning of events in one's physical and social world. Adequate understanding helps us to account for what has occurred in the past and to predict the future much more reliably. By contrast, inadequate understanding of the causes of events can be the basis for divorces, international conflicts, and the philosophical argument between evolutionary science and creationism. In the present context, the target of causal analysis is neither international nor philosophical, but rather is the more limited domain of business success or failure. Even there the goal is not to identify all the true causes of venture survival or demise, but to show how causal accounts offered by the people involved may serve as important contributing factors.

The particular value of an attribution-based approach is in its ability to describe entrepreneurial performance in ways not reached by other psychological theories. As a prime example, consider the case of "habitual" entrepreneurs, people who start one entrepreneurial business after another. Many of these habitual entrepreneurs have enjoyed an unbroken string of successes, but many others have also had their share of failures. The psychological literature is chock full of motivational principles that explain why people continue to do something at which they are successful. But principles behind repetition of successes – such as that old standby, the principle of reinforcement (Skinner, 1953) – are at a loss to account for starting over after failure, failure, and more failure. On the other hand, an entrepreneur's beliefs about why failures have occurred can be the basis for persistence.

As a body of scientific inquiry, attribution is a description of how people answer the "why" question. Attribution theory (and its associated research) is the formal study of the sorts of explanations people give for the causes of events and behavior (their own and that of others). This area of inquiry is now more than a half-century old, as the beginnings are usually traced to the pioneering work of Fritz Heider (1958). In his book Heider offered a detailed explanation of the processes that individuals use to account for the causes of both events and behavior. For brevity, we shall concentrate on attributional explanations of human behavior, mentioning the causes of events only in passing where relevant. Notice that Heider's objective was not to describe why behavior occurs, but rather to describe why people think actions occur.

In the literature this has been characterized as a "naive" – as distinguished from a "scientific" – explanation. The difference is more easily apparent today than it was in Heider's time. At some level, the scientific explanations of human behavior are soon likely to involve functional magnetic resonance imaging (fMRI) that provides an image of the specific brain cells that are activated during one sort of thought or another. Whether such scientific explanations begin to hold sway or not, naive psychologists (read "ordinary people") are likely to retain the terms provided by everyday language. To use some of Heider's words, if we observe a person accomplishing a task, we say that the person "can" do the task, perhaps because his or her "ability" exceeds the "task difficulty" or perhaps because of "opportunity" or "luck." We also believe that the person who accomplished the task was "trying" to do so in the

sense of having an intention to succeed and exerting "effort" in the direction specified by that intention. Though we recognize that accidents happen, we are reluctant
to believe that jobs are completed by accident, but rather that some level of willing
participation by the actor was essential. Even in a future era of widespread fMRI,
phrases such as "wanted to" and "tried to" are unlikely to disappear from everyday
discourse.

Heider's contribution was to identify how the various causal factors might be
related to one another. Specifically, he argued that behavior was the consequence of
an interplay between personal force and environmental force, the now familiar

$$B = f(P, E).$$

Four specific aspects of personal force have received the most attention, whereas
two aspects of environmental force have been seen as central. On the personal side,
ability is the skill or power that constitutes the individual's capabilities; trying is the
motivational component, usually subdivided into intention and exertion. In the literature, these elements of personal force are also described as dispositional properties
of the person, enduring characteristics that observers hope to infer from behavior.
On the environmental side there is task difficulty (usually an impediment, though
tasks can also be easy) and there is also luck (which can of course be either positive toward the outcome or negative). These are dispositional properties within the
environment.

The creation of a new business venture is a process extending through time. It
requires both resources and effort, all directed at a particular objective, with the process being brought back "on track," should it stray along the way. It is inconceivable
that all of this could be accomplished by accident, so we are certain that personal
causality, directed by intention, was centrally involved. So although the particular intentions behind entrepreneurial behavior (discussed in Chapters 2 through 4)
are important, the question of whether there is any intention at all is usually not
at issue.

Under these circumstances, it makes more sense to speak only of the "effort"
component of trying. Thus, following Weiner et al. (1972), only ability, effort,
task difficulty, and luck are usually considered in the attributional analysis of
entrepreneurial action. The first two are dispositional properties of the person, the
second two are dispositional properties of the external world. Within each of these
categories, one element of force is stable (ability, task difficulty), whereas one element of force is variable (effort, luck). We shall return to some implications of this
fourfold characterization in Section 10.4.2.

10.1.2 More About the Situation

Within a few years of the publication of Heider's pioneering analysis of the "naive
psychologist," two prominent experimental social psychologists offered detailed
(and testable) expansions of Heider's principles. In the first of these, Jones and

Davis (1965) argued that beyond difficulty and luck there were two additional environmental forces affecting behavior. One of these is the set of prior actions the person has taken. The other is the set of behavioral alternatives that exist at the time the person chooses one action over another. Taking the person's past history and present alternative choices into account, Jones and Davis argue that we learn the most about the internal dispositions of the individual when he or she does something that is unexpected or, in their terms, out of role. An entrepreneur who makes a presentation to angel investors and asks for support is simply doing what is expected in (even demanded by) the situation. Performances like this tell us little about the entrepreneur's internal confidence in the venture. But one who says "government grants are paying for research and development, so we're simply letting you know now that we'll be back" is doing something unexpected. That he or she would choose to do so suggests a much higher level of internal confidence. Thus the latter performance is more likely to whet an investor's appetite. And not merely because of the added credibility that government support provides the venture, but also because of what the claim says about the entrepreneur's own confidence in the enterprise. For present purposes, the primary contribution made by Jones and Davis's work is to lead us to take a more finely grained view of the environment.

10.1.3 A Model of Causal Judgment

The second expansion of Heider's basic ideas was the work of Kelley (1967, 1972, 1973). Among Kelley's ideas, two are of particular relevance here. The first is a principle of covariation that with deceptive simplicity argues that events and behavior will be attributed to factors that vary when the events or behavior go from absent to present. In an analogy to the statistical analysis of variance, Kelley's theory asks that we consider both main effects and interaction effects along three separate dimensions. The three are entities, time/modality, and persons. Experience suggests that these are more clearly described by illustration than by definition (but if definitions are needed, along with a comparison of Kelley's theory to that of Jones and Davis and that of Heider, please see Shaver, 1975).

   Put yourself in the role of a private venture investor (more of an angel than a professional venture capitalist). Over the course of several months a series of possible deals will come your way. Some will be restaurant concepts, others will be Web-based businesses, still others will be biotechnology. These various classes of potential investments are the entities. Because you belong to an organized angel investor group, some of the proposals will be made in front of the entire group. Some of these proposals will be informal, others will have that perfected "road show" quality. You may also come across possible investments at cocktail receptions (or those of us who teach students to make good "elevator pitches" are wasting our time). Or deals may come out of the blue, brought to you by fellow investors who would like to broaden participation. The ways in which opportunities present themselves are, in the theory's terms, the variations in time and modality: not all deals show up at the same time and the level of formality in presentation varies from one to the next.

Finally, because you are a member of an investment group, there are other persons available to you for purposes of comparing impressions and notes.

Now for the main and interaction effects. Suppose you want to jump at every biotech start-up you discover, no matter how you heard of it, no matter how formal the presentation was, and no matter what other potential investors thought about the project. That is a main effect for the entity: Your desire to invest depends solely on the venture's being in a defined class of possible enterprises. Alternatively, suppose that regardless of the nature of the business being proposed or the way in which the pitch is delivered, you choose to invest only when accompanied by others whose judgment you trust. Then the cause of your investment decision is a main effect for the persons dimension, not involving either entities or time/modality. Skipping to the most complex interaction effect (in this three-dimensional attribution world), suppose you elect to write a check only if (a) the company is a Web-based business that has (b) made a highly convincing formal presentation in front of the angel group (c) several others of whom have also agreed to invest. In this instance each of the dimensions plays a part – in conjunction with the others – in the investment choice.

Why does this sort of attributional analysis matter? Well, change your perspective to that of the entrepreneur seeking funding. To attract this particular investor, do you need (a) the right kind of business, (b) the right sort of presentation, (c) the right audience, or (d) some combination of the above? Recognizing that there are only 24 hours in every day, you will want to make your "pitch time" as effective as possible, and that requires that you know something about the causes of a listener's investment decisions.

The second of Kelley's ideas about the nature of causal judgment that has implications for entrepreneurship is the notion of causal schemata, best described by the way in which it differs from the principle of covariation. Inherent in the principle of covariation is the idea that attributional judgments require multiple comparisons, often made over time. One entity is compared to another, one mode of presentation is compared to another, one person's view of the world is compared to that of another person. One reason that the statistical analysis of variance is appropriate as a model for covariation is that the various comparisons are not unlike what a scientist might do to investigate the causes of an event. But, continuing Heider's approach, people are naive scientists, ones who follow a limited version of the scientific method. More importantly, people – unlike scientists – are perfectly comfortable making definitive attributions without all the necessary evidence. Kelley argues that they do this by reference to causal schemata, mental models that fill in for missing data.

One such model is the schema for multiple necessary causes: at the simplest level, two necessary causes. Consider what is needed to make ice. Obviously, one requirement for ice is water, the other requirement for ice is an ambient temperature below freezing. Bitter cold without water produces no ice; water without freezing temperature remains water, even though it might get quite cold to the touch. Applications of the idea of multiple necessary causes to the entrepreneurial domain, however, are not always so simple. Indeed, they may be a matter of definition rather than a matter of universal agreement.

For example, think about what it means for an entrepreneur to be "in business." Many naive psychologists (and more than a few business researchers) would say that an entrepreneur who has sold a product or service and has collected money would be "in business." By this definition, selling something and collecting cash are the two necessary causes of being in business. There are, however, other definitions. Consider the Panel Studies of Entrepreneurial Dynamics (PSED, both I and II), described in books by Gartner et al. (2004) and Reynolds and Curtin (2009). In both data sets a nascent entrepreneur is defined as a person who (a) is currently in the process of organizing a business venture, (b) expects to own part of that venture, but whose venture (c) has not generated sufficient income to pay a salary for the founder for longer than 3 months. Thus, within this research paradigm, it is not having sales that converts a person from a nascent entrepreneur into a "firm," but rather having sales that are large enough for a long enough time. There are sound theoretical and empirical reasons for this particular definition, but it is still different from the definition offered by the naive psychologist.

In addition to the cognitive schema for multiple necessary causes, there are the more interesting schemata for multiple sufficient causes. These are cognitive representations of the fact that many physical and social events (or for that matter, behaviors) might be brought about in any of several different ways. An obvious example from entrepreneurship would be the failure of a newly formed company. A new business can fail if it is inattentive to its market, if the demands from its suppliers are too high, if there are already too many competitors in the local industry, if substitutes for its products or services can be obtained easily, if it burns too quickly through its cash reserves, or if it happens to be sabotaged from within. Readers will note that many of these accounts sound very much like Porter's (1980) "five forces." For present purposes it is sufficient to note that any, some, or all the problems might produce the death of the new firm.

The attributional problem is different depending on whether the presumed causes of an event are necessary or sufficient. When asked to explain the occurrence behavior or events that have only multiple necessary causes, an observer can easily "reason backward" to conclude that all the necessary causes must have been present. On the other hand, when asked to explain behavior or events that have multiple sufficient causes, the observer's task is substantially more complicated. Now the task is to decide which of the multiple sufficient causes, alone or in combination, might have produced the event. Here Kelley argues that the judgments follow one of two schematic principles – discounting or augmentation. If there are multiple sufficient facilitative causes of an event or action, the discounting principle states that each will be reduced by some function of the number of possible multiple sufficient causes. If, however, some of the multiple factors are impediments to the occurrence of the event or action, and it occurs in the face of these impediments, then according to the augmentation principle, more weight will be given to the facilitative causes that are present. An entrepreneur who succeeds "against all odds" will be perceived to be even more capable than if success had come easily. Note that this perception of the entrepreneur as more capable may be correct, but it may not be.

10.2 Alternative Views of the World

As much as the various attribution theories ask us to pay attention to the situations that surround behavior, attributions are still mental constructions made by people, about people. Indeed, people are seen as the prototypical causes of events, and certainly of their own behavior. We shall consider this in more detail in a moment, but first, a bit of metatheoretical diversion. Having earlier referred to the principle of reinforcement, readers familiar with the rest of Skinnerian behaviorism (1953) will wonder whether it is philosophically correct to argue that people are the prototypical causes of events. In the behaviorist view of the world, there is no "action" in the usual (agentic) sense of the word. Rather, there is only "behavior," itself conditioned entirely by the individual's past history and current reinforcement setting. In other words, people only "respond," they do not "do." This disagreement between the behavioristic view and the view taken by attribution theory cannot be resolved by reference to data or even by an attempt to build an integrating theory that permits both views. Rather, the disagreement is on a metatheoretical level – the level of the philosophical assumptions on which theory is built. I have previously conducted an extended discussion of these issues (Chapters 2 and 4 in Shaver, 1985) and cannot repeat that discussion here. Suffice to say that the philosophical foundation of the attribution approach is libertarianism (not the political sort). The libertarian resolution of the dilemma of determinism relies on the writings of Reid (1863) and, later, Campbell (1957). The essence of the position has been captured by Feinberg (1981) who noted that "human actions, unlike other events in nature, are subject to a special kind of explanation: the actor's own *reasons* for acting" (p. 329, emphasis in original). It is worth noting that legal systems in most of the world are based on assumptions that people have choices, make choices, and so should endure the consequences of bad choices (though none of these assumptions is congenial to the deterministic view of the world). As does the legal system, individual perceivers act as if they believe that people can make choices. Indeed, people are often even less forgiving than is the legal system. People's proclivity to see others as the origins of their actions leads to two related errors in the attribution process.

Both errors arise from the fact that, as Heider (1958) noted, "behavior engulfs the field." The first implication of this principle is that the world view of an actor is different from the world view of an observer. If you are attempting to organize a new business venture, you will concentrate on the obstacles facing you – the need to identify a market, the necessity of conquering the competition, the problem of generating enough cash to stay afloat. In short, as the actor in the setting, you will concentrate on everything that is going on around you and your business. You will see yourself, and describe yourself, as merely responding to the situational demands that are "out there." The rest of us (observers), however, will pay less attention to what is going on around your business than we will to you and what you are doing. We will see you testing the market, erecting barriers to competition, and managing your income and expenses.

This difference in perspective leads to what is known as the "fundamental attribution error" (Ross, 1977). This error is the pervasive tendency for observers to

(a) overestimate the contributions of the person and (b) underestimate the constraints or contributions inherent in the external environment. More than a statement about the nature of causality, the fundamental attribution error is also a statement that perceivers make about the enduring dispositional properties of the actor. In a way most congenial to the libertarian philosophical view noted above, we will not only see you as doing things, we will see you as doing what you want to do. This is precisely where the question "what is being done?" turns into the attributional question "why did you do that?" In the present context it should be pointed out that a version of this error could contribute to an investor's over-reliance on a management team and under-reliance on the nature of the product or service being proposed. Specifically, an entrepreneur's passion for a particular venture may be misinterpreted as an internal level of drive that could be applied successfully to some other venture. Because of Kelley's covariation principle, this assumption of internally based skills and tenacity is likely to be even stronger if the target person is a habitual entrepreneur with several successes to his or her credit. Yes, past behavior is very helpful in predicting future success, but it may not be quite as helpful as we think it might be.

10.3 Biases and Motivations

The fundamental attribution error is brought about by two facts: that we see human beings as agents and that not all human beings share identical perspectives on the actions taken or consequences produced. In short, this error is a product of the situations in which people find themselves, no matter who those people might be. There are, however, other complications in the attribution process that are the product of the internal motives of both actors and perceivers. These include self-serving biases, overconfidence biases, defensive attributions, and the need to believe in a just world. The first two are normally found among actors, the second two are normally found among observers.

Beginning with biases deriving from the motivations of actors, perhaps the most common is the "self-serving bias" (Bradley, 1978). Deciding that a particular event is to be attributed to internal factors, or as Heider would describe it, personal force, has obvious implications for self-esteem. We like to think of ourselves as capable, perhaps a bit more capable than we really are. The result is if something positive gets produced, we rarely take less credit than we deserve (normally, we take a bit more credit). On the other hand, if something bad happens, we prefer to talk about why it was not our fault. In short, we attribute successes internally, failures externally.

There is a long string of studies in the social psychological literature that supports this general conclusion, even when the "success" and "failure" are artificially created in the experimental laboratory. It is important to emphasize how many separate demonstrations of self-serving biases there have been, because in the entrepreneurial world, one often finds exactly the reverse: entrepreneurs seem to have no trouble saying things like "Well, it didn't work, but at least I can learn from my mistakes."

In short, entrepreneurs appear to be acting counter to a very well established pattern. Nor do entrepreneurs (at least the very successful ones) take all the credit for themselves. Rather, they include everyone involved in the project among those to receive accolades.

What might be the difference between the self-attributions of entrepreneurs and the self-attributions in so many other instances? One possibility that suggests itself is the nature of the domain in which the success or failure has occurred. The successes that are followed by self-aggrandizement are often personal performances of one sort or another, not performances of a business, the success of which clearly depends on factors outside the firm as well as on factors within the founder. As for denials of fault for failure, most of the research that shows such denials deals with moral failures, which are generally disapproved by society, rather than with business failures, which in the United States at least are often considered "the cost of doing business."

Turning to motivated attributional biases within the perceiver, several have the strategic objective of protecting ourselves from harm. This very human tendency is reflected in the notion of a "need to believe in a just world" and in the idea of "defensive attribution". Although the need to believe in a just world was originally developed to explain an observer's tendency to hold accountable a truly innocent victim (Lerner and Simmons, 1966), it also applies in the context of new venture creation. The basic idea is that in a "just" world people would not suffer for no reason. Often it is their own behavior that got them into trouble, and to the degree that this is obvious, the just world need would not come into play. Do stupid things, pay the price. No more explanation needed. The trouble begins when there is no stupid or dangerous behavior performed, but the target person still suffers. This situation suggests that we, too, might suffer through no fault of ours. The self-protective motive then takes over, and because bad behavior is effectively ruled out, we come to believe that the victim suffered because of being a "bad person." If we see an entrepreneur fail at a venture that has plenty of financial and people resources, an excellent product appreciated by its customers, and no particularly effective competition, we wonder what could have happened. A small portion of our attributional mind says to itself, "was this a form of karma, retribution for some hidden character flaw?"

The need to believe in a just world is an attributional luxury available only to those who never expect to be in the entrepreneur's shoes. For people who share the entrepreneur's ambitions, interests, and work patterns – such as other entrepreneurs – a harsh statement about the victim's character has the unfortunate potential to harm the self. Pointing one finger at someone else leaves three fingers pointing back at you. This possibility leads to a still more convoluted attempt at self-protection called defensive attribution. Although originally developed in the context of the attribution of responsibility for accidental occurrences (Shaver, 1970), defensive attribution can also be seen in an entrepreneurial context.

An observer who never expects to be in the entrepreneur's position (an investor, or a service provider, for example) is free to insist that the entrepreneur either made serious errors or was, in the just world sense, deserving of the negative outcome.

On the other hand, a perceiver who is doing the same things (another entrepreneur, perhaps even in the same or a similar business) is wary of claiming that the victim made critical mistakes. Moreover, to the extent that the perceiver considers herself or himself personally similar to the target entrepreneur, the natural conclusion is "Good grief, I might have done exactly the same thing!" From this perspective, the failure will be bad enough in itself, no reason to add condemnation (by self or others) to the mix. Because of their differing perspectives, actors and perceivers are likely to give discrepant explanations for success and failure. In addition to their differing perspectives, however, actors have internal motives (self-serving biases, defensive attribution) that are different from those of observers (needs to believe in a just world). Given their differences in perspective and motivation, it is almost a wonder that actors and observers ever agree on the causes of behavior or events.

10.4 Attributions in Venture Organization

To this point, basics of the attribution approach have been outlined and examples have been used to illustrate ways in which attribution processes could be involved in entrepreneurial behavior and performance. With this as background, we now turn to ways in which attribution has found its way into the research literature.

10.4.1 Measuring Attributions

As intuitively convincing as particular examples might be, there is an essential difference between reasoning by example and reasoning by reference to data. Only the latter provides scientific insight into the functioning of the entrepreneurial mind. Some attributional principles are easy to demonstrate in a scientifically acceptable way. For example, the fundamental attribution error is so easily reproducible that it has become a classroom illustration in social psychology courses. In such cases, half of a class of students is told "After completing the general education requirements and considering options for a college major, a good friend of yours has decided to major in accounting." Then the respondent is asked to indicate a belief that this choice reveals (a) something about the person, (b) something about the major itself, or (c) neither. The other half of the class is given exactly the same information and response scale, with the sole exception that in the description of the major choice the words "a good friend of yours has" are replaced by "you have." With great regularity, the friend's choice produces a predominant response of (a), something about the person, but that alternative is almost never the predominant response for one's own choice (b, something about the major, is preferred).

It is one thing to use a simple experimental design to test for differences in the attributions made by actors and observers. It is something quite different to take the everyday descriptions offered by entrepreneurs and show that they can be characterized in clear attributional terms. Difficult, yes; impossible, no (Shaver et al., 2001). As noted above, the four primary contributors to the performance of intentional actions are ability, effort, task difficulty, and luck. Ability and effort are dispositional properties of the person, with ability considered "stable" and effort considered "variable." In this context, stability does not mean permanence, as a person's ability can, and often does, grow over time. But such growth takes a long time rather than changing from moment to moment. Effort, on the other hand, can be turned on and off like a switch. Within the realm of environmental force, task difficulty is the stable element, whereas luck is the variable one. The four elements are usually considered as being represented by two conceptual dimensions – locus of causality (internal/external) and stability (stable/variable). The challenge is to use these dimensions to describe the explanations entrepreneurs provide for their desire to start a business.

In the PSED I, nascent entrepreneurs who had been identified through a random-digit-dialing screening procedure were interviewed by members of the University of Wisconsin Survey Research Laboratory. One of the very first interview questions asked was "Why do you want to start this business?" Respondents gave open-ended answers that the interviewers tried to capture verbatim. There were understandable variations in the personal shorthand systems interviewers used to try to accomplish this objective, and no doubt there were pieces of information that were lost. There was, however, no evidence of any systematic bias.

The attributional coding began with parsing of the entire response into separate thoughts using linguistic disjunctives like commas, periods, and words like "and" or "or." Nearly 85% of the respondents gave answers that included three or fewer elements. Elements containing personal pronouns, references to the self or to a personality characteristic were coded as internal to the person; elements with references to external factors such as the economy, competition, or demand were coded as external to the person. For the stability variable, answers were coded as stable if they described enduring properties of the person or environment that were unlikely to change in the short term. They were coded as variable if they had a decidedly probabilistic nature, could be changed from moment to moment based on whim, or depended to any substantial degree on the actions of other people. This brief description cannot do justice to the complexity of the coding process (which employed a coding manual in excess of 30 pages that included particular examples and the rationale for whatever code would be applied to that example). The procedure, however, produces inter-rater reliabilities above 0.90. Readers interested in further details are referred to the paper itself, which also includes an appendix containing two "training sets" of 50 items each that can be used to teach how the system should be used to produce reliable distinctions among internal and external, and stable and variable, causes.

10.4.2 Why Attributions Matter

Given that it is possible to measure internal versus external attributions with acceptable reliability, the next question is whether the attributional model is a valid description of entrepreneurial behavior. At least two studies suggest that the answer is affirmative.

The first of these two was a study of entrepreneurs who took advantage of the consulting opportunities made available by a large urban Small Business Development Center (Gatewood et al., 1995). As part of their initial client meeting with the SBDC staff, female and male entrepreneurs completed a scale assessing their beliefs about personal efficacy and were asked why they wanted to start their proposed business. Responses to the "why" were coded by an early version of the procedure outlined above, one that separated the answers according to the two dimensions of locus of causality and stability. A year later the respondents were contacted again, and nearly 60% of them replied to a mail questionnaire. This mail questionnaire listed 29 separate activities involved in starting a business and asked how many hours the respondent had spent on each one. The 29 activities were grouped into five categories: gathering market information, estimating potential profits, finishing the groundwork for the company, structuring the company, and setting up business operations. Finally, all respondents were asked whether they had delivered their product or service to customers and collected the payment for it. (Obviously, this definition of "being in business" is simpler than the one used in the PSED research.)

Two findings from the study are particularly interesting. First, among the activities there was a significant bias in favor of action: respondents who reported being in business had, during the preceding year, devoted nearly 18 times the hours to setting up business operations than the respondents who did not meet the criterion for being in business. Second, thinking also helps, although it needs to be the right sort of thinking. Specifically, general beliefs about personal efficacy did not differ between respondents who had gone into business and those who had not. The attributions, however, showed important results that differed between men and women. Among people who had gone into business, females had (a year earlier) expressed reasons for wanting to be in business that had been coded as internal and stable. Among people who had gone into business, males had (also a year earlier) expressed reasons for wanting to do so that were coded primarily as external and stable. The coding had been done without knowledge of the sex of the respondent, so differences between explanations offered by men and women are an indication that the nature of the attributions matters.

A second illustration that attributions matter comes from a study of the problems and opportunities identified by small businesses on a survey done by a major metropolitan newspaper (Gartner and Shaver, 2004). Newspaper surveys have obvious limitations in terms of such things as restrictions on the number of questions that can be asked, inability to collect much in the way of demographic information, and representativeness of the responses. On the other hand, they frequently do produce large numbers of data points. This particular research examined the responses of nearly 1,700 business owner/managers to two questions: "What is the biggest opportunity facing your business?" and "What is the biggest problem facing your business?"

Answers were coded into the familiar dimensions of locus of causality and stability. Each respondent's first-mentioned opportunity was coded into one of the four cells produced by the cross-classification of internal/external by stable/variable. The same coding was done for each respondent's first-mentioned problem. Next, each respondent was placed into one of 16 cells based on (a) which of the four categories contained his or her first-mentioned opportunity and (b) which one contained his or her first-mentioned problem. Where problems were concerned, by far the most frequent causal combination was external-variable. Where opportunities were concerned, the most frequent category was external-stable. Not surprisingly, the cell where these two codings intersect – external-stable for opportunities and external-variable for problems – was the most frequently occurring combination. Notice that this pattern is different from the one that would be expected to be self-serving (internal for failure, external for success). The difference may be that the self-serving pattern is usually offered to explain events in the past, where nothing can be done about the situation. Here, however, opportunities are in the future, so entrepreneurs would like to believe that they are "out there" and will remain so. By contrast, the problems (that are also "out there") are variable. This pattern looks like an "enterprise-serving bias": "Opportunities will be there when my business needs them, problems will either go away on their own or can be remedied." Compared to respondents who had any of the other 15 possible attributional patterns, respondents in the enterprise-serving cell expected higher growth for the future. Whether such growth will be achieved is another matter, but it is important that the enterprise-serving bias was related to anticipated future growth. Overall, the research briefly summarized here adds to our confidence that entrepreneurial attributions (a) can be measured reliably and (b) have implications for both individual and firm performance.

References

Bradley GW (1978) Self-serving biases in the attribution process: A reexamination of the fact or fiction question. Journal of Personality and Social Psychology 36: 56–71.

Campbell CA (1957) On Selfhood and Godhood. Allen & Unwin, London.

Feinberg J (ed.) (1981) Reason and Responsibility (5th ed). Wadsworth, Belmont, CA.

Gartner WB, Shaver KG (2004) Opportunities as attributions: The enterprise-serving bias. In: Butler J (ed.) Opportunity Identification and Entrepreneurial Behavior. Information Age Publishing, San Francisco, CA, pp. 29–46.

Gartner WB, Shaver KG, Carter NM, Reynolds PD (2004) Handbook of Entrepreneurial Dynamics: The Process of Business Creation. Sage Publications, Thousand Oaks, CA.

Gatewood EJ, Shaver KG, Gartner WB (1995) A longitudinal study of cognitive factors influencing start-up behaviors and success at venture creation. Journal of Business Venturing 10: 371–391

Heider F (1958) The Psychology of Interpersonal Relations. Wiley, New York.

Jones EE, Davis KE (1965) From acts to dispositions: The attribution process in person perception. In: Berkowitz L (ed), Advances in Experimental Social Psychology. Academic Press, New York. pp. 219–266

Kelley HH (1967) Attribution processes in social psychology. In: Levine D (ed), Nebraska Symposium on Motivation. University of Nebraska Press, Lincoln, NE. pp. 192–238

Kelley HH (1972) Causal schemata and the attribution process. In: Jones EE, Kanouse DE, Kelley HH, Nisbett RE, Valins S, Weiner B (eds), Attribution: Perceiving the Causes of Behavior. General Learning Press, Morristown, NJ. pp. 151–174

Kelley HH (1973) The processes of causal attribution. American Psychologist 28: 107–128

Lerner MJ, Simmons CH (1966) Observers' reaction to the "innocent victim": Compassion or rejection? Journal of Personality and Social Psychology 4: 203–210

Porter ME (1980) Competitive Strategy: Techniques for Analyzing Industries and Competitors. The Free Press, New York.

Reid T (1863) Of the liberty of moral agents. In: Hamilton W (ed), The Works of Thomas Reid (6th ed). Maclachlan & Stewart, Edinburgh, pp. 599–636

Reynolds PD, Curtin RT (eds.) (2009) New Firm Creation in the United States: Initial Explorations with the PSED II Data Set. Springer Verlag, New York

Ross LD (1977) The intuitive psychologist and his shortcomings. In: Berkowitz L. (ed.), Advances in Experimental Social Psychology. Academic Press, New York, pp. 173–220

Shaver KG (1970) Defensive attribution: Effects of severity and relevance on the responsibility assigned for an accident. Journal of Personality and Social Psychology 14: 101–113

Shaver KG (1975) An Introduction to Attribution Processes. Winthrop, Cambridge, MA.

Shaver KG (1985). The Attribution of Blame: Causality, Responsibility, and Blameworthiness. Springer-Verlag, New York.

Shaver KG, Gartner WB, Crosby E, Bakalarova K, Gatewood EJ (2001) Attributions about entrepreneurship: A framework and process for analyzing reasons for starting a business. Entrepreneurship Theory and Practice 26: 5–32.

Skinner BF (1953) Science and Human Behavior. Macmillan, New York

Weiner B, Frieze IH, Kukla A, Reed L, Rest S, Rosenbaum RM (1972) Perceiving the causes of success and failure. In: Jones EE, Kanouse DE, Kelley HH, Nisbett RE, Valins S, Weiner B (eds), Attribution: Perceiving the Causes of Behavior. General Learning Press, Morristown, NJ, pp. 95–120

Chapter 11
Self-Efficacy: Conditioning the Entrepreneurial Mindset

René Mauer, Helle Neergaard, and Anne Kirketerp Linstad

11.1 Introduction

Since Bandura's original work (Bandura 1977a), the self-efficacy concept has become an important variable within social psychology research. However, it has also been invoked in numerous other areas of research: organization theory, human resource theory, cognition and behavioral theory, as well as identity theory, in connection with topics such as health, stress, leadership, commitment, ethnicity, religion, gender, culture, social class, because it emphasizes values that we perceive as important in the Western world such as achievement and performance (Gecas 1989).

The literature addressing the self-efficacy concept is thus enormous and continuously growing. Hence, a complete review of the psychology literature on self-efficacy is outside the scope of this chapter. However, the prolific interest in the concept indicates its potential. Nevertheless, although much of the work underpins the importance of predicting and improving performance and enhancing specific behavior in the various fields, much still remains unclear about the antecedents of self-efficacy and the processes that produce and reinforce self-efficacy. Further, research has predominantly been concerned with measuring levels of self-efficacy ex ante and ex post some participation in an experimental setting (see, e.g., Zimmerman et al., 1992 for an exemplar). In other words, research that addresses the underlying determinants of self-efficacy has been much less widespread (Gist and Mitchell 1992).

The aim of this chapter is twofold: First, it seeks to broaden our understanding of the self-efficacy concept. Second, it develops suggestions for new avenues of research into the self-efficacy concept. It sets out to achieve these objectives through an exploration of the origins of the concept, moving on to its impact in the field of entrepreneurship. After a short summary of the chronological development, the chapter will focus on three main issues around entrepreneurial self-efficacy: its measurement, its impact as an influencing factor, and its antecedents, which

R. Mauer (✉)

Chair for Business Studies and Sciences, for Engineers and Scientists, RWTH Aachen,
Templergraben 64, D-52064, Germany
e-mail: mauer@win.rwth-aachen.de

A.L. Carsrud, M. Brännback (eds.), *Understanding the Entrepreneurial Mind*,
International Studies in Entrepreneurship 24, DOI 10.1007/978-1-4419-0443-0_11,
© Springer Science+Business Media, LLC 2009

will finally lead to suggestions for understanding the pedagogy needed to promote entrepreneurial self-efficacy in the different social arenas of life.

11.2 The Psychological Origin of Self-Efficacy

Alfred Bandura's social cognitive theory of self-efficacy refers to individual's assessment of their competences and ability to overcome adverse conditions and obstacles and the belief that future actions will be successful (Bandura 1977a, 1986, 1997). According to Bandura (1986), self-efficacy concerns the extent to which an individual believes in his or her capabilities to mobilize the motivation, cognitive resources, and causes of action needed to meet given situational demands. These beliefs influence "what challenges to undertake, how much effort to expend the endeavor (and) how long to persevere in the face of difficulties" (op. cit., p. 29). Thus, an individual's self-efficacy reflects the impact of past experiences on his or her assessment of capacity for performance attainment.

Bandura operates with two types of assessments or expectations: efficacy and outcome expectations (Bandura 1977b). The former refers to a belief about an individual's own competence that she/he can successfully perform a certain action and has been addressed extensively by research over the years, both out- and inside entrepreneurship. The latter refers to an estimate about the social system's responsiveness to that action. This distinction is important because if an individual perceives the social (or political) system as being unresponsive or unappreciative of entrepreneurial action then there is no need for behaving entrepreneurially, even if that individual feels that she/he has the competence and ability to achieve the desired objective. Thus, the environment's positive responsiveness is penultimate to action. Research into this part of the equation is rare, if it exists at all.

However, whether the assessment of both self-efficacy and outcome expectations is positive or negative is predominantly dependent on the preference for or resistance to a particular behavior that each individual has built up (Stern 1985). If something is perceived as a dangerous or risky behavior then an individual is likely to abstain from carrying out this behavior. A preference for or resistance to a particular behavior is built up through somatic markers (Damasio 1994, Bechara and Damasio 2005).

11.2.1 Somatic Markers and Self-Efficacy

The theory of somatic markers is concerned with associating emotions with events (Damasio 1994). Likewise, somatic markers will build up in an individual and the predominance of either the positive or the negative experiences associated with a particular behavior will dominate the individual's choice of reaction. Hence, the first time a person meets a certain feedback she/he will use this to refer back the next time a similar or same feedback is experienced. Thus, if a girl climbs a tree and falls down hurting herself then her mother has two options: either to create a positive somatic marker for "failing fast" – oh, that hurt but that is what may happen when you climb a tree – get back on the horse and practice. Or she can run to the rescue and say "never ever do that again, it is so dangerous to climb trees." The former creates a positive somatic marker, the latter a negative one for experimenting. If the mother does this every time the little girl tries something that might hurt her or she might fail to do, then she may gradually build a resistance to attempt risky behavior. Basically, the process can be likened to a washbasin with a plug and a dripping tap. On its own a drip is just a drip. But if drips are collected the basin fills up. Further, a drip can be either warm or cold. Whether the water is ultimately warm or cold depends on the predominance of one or the other (not taking into account evaporation and a general cooling of warm water!). And that is what happens: drips of somatic markers are stored in the subconscious, deep within the inner system of our brains. Thus, abstaining from a certain action is not necessarily a conscious act, but rather a subconscious one. Somatic markers become reinforced throughout our lives and our choices in life will reflect our individual "stores" of somatic markers (Damasio 1994).

Damasio is, however, not sufficiently precise in describing how this process takes place and how it becomes internalized. Stern (1985), on the other hand, delivers an explanation in his theory of "representations of interactions generalized" (RIGs). RIG is a developmental psychological term about how people build notions of others. It starts the minute the baby is born and continues all through our lives. The basic premise of this theory is that in order to navigate in the world, all the impressions of events and individual reactions that we meet in our lives are interpreted, internalized, and eventually generalized. Every time we meet something or someone, then this meeting builds on what previous experiences we have had with this something or someone, simply because we cannot continue to build new impressions. It is a way to create a continuous and "normal" picture of others, against which we perceive new impressions of them. The reason we can experience something as "different" is because we have a memory (our RIG) of what it usually is like. These RIGs can produce either positive or negative memories, or as Damasio calls them guiding stars or black holes (Damaiso 1994). Whether they function as one or the other means that individuals, without thinking about it, will avoid negative somatic markers before they even become a possibility. It entails that the emotions and feelings that are connected to certain results and those results that produce positive emotions and feelings in us will be preferred over those that produce negative emotions and feelings. Thus, they may be seen as personality shaping as well as behavior ruling. It also entails that being conscious about your RIGs is an underlying mechanism of potential change.

Thus, unknowingly, the parents of the little girl may be conditioning her mind against undertaking any risky behavior and this may in time translate into a disposition not to become an entrepreneur because this is often portrayed as a risky behavior. This means that in order to break such a pattern, it is necessary to find methods of "unconditioning the mind" – of displacing the cold water with warm and further at a greater speed than that with which it was originally built up. Research consistently shows that women score lower on self-efficacy than men (Hackett and

Betz 1981; Carter et al. 1997; Fletcher 1999; Neergaard and Eythórsdóttir 2008). This indicates that girls are conditioned in a different way and that women make choices based on different experiences to men. This is not to say that it is not possible to overcome RIGs, but it is necessary to find methods of "unconditioning" – of breaking the patterns. Hence, taking a critical case perspective, if ways of enhancing women's self-efficacy can be identified, then we will also have found a way of increasing the level of men's (Neergaard 2007). However, because these patterns of behavior are based on a subconscious conditioning, they *are* very difficult to change. Further, the deeper the RIGs are built in our culture, the more difficult it is to change them. Thus, the Jante Law can best be described as a universal, national RIG, see Box 11.1.

Box 11.1 Janteloven (The Jante Law) (based on Sandemose 1933)

Du skal ikke tro, du er noget~~~(You shall not think that you are special)
Du skal ikke tro, du er lige så klog som os~~~(*You shall not think that you are of the same standing as us*)
Du skal ikke tro, du er klogere end os~~~(*You shall not think that you are smarter than us*)
Du skal ikke indbilde dig, du er bedre end os~~~(*You shall not fancy yourself as being better than us*)
Du skal ikke tro, du ved mere end os~~~(*You shall not think that you know more than us*)
Du skal ikke tro, at du er mere end os~~~(*You shall not think that you are more important than us*)
Du skal ikke tro, at du duer til noget~~~(*You shall not think that you are good at anything*)
Du skal ikke le af os~~~(*You shall not laugh at us*)
Du skal ikke tro, at nogen bryder sig om dig~~~(*You shall not think that anyone cares about you*)
Du skal ikke tro, at du kan lære os noget~~~(*You shall not think that you can teach us anything*)

The impact of the Jante Law on Danish/Scandinavian culture is pervasive and Danes are, in general, very skeptical of success (Smith and Neergaard 2008). The Jante Law also partly explains the power of the social democratic values espousing equality, which are simultaneously an advantage and a problem. They represent an advantage, because they helped create the Nordic welfare model, which redistributes wealth from the rich to the poor, so that the difference between the two groups is reduced. They constitute a problem, because the incentive to better oneself – and therefore be smarter, special, or better in some way – is reduced. Thus, having a self-efficacious feeling may be affected by such universal beliefs.

Since patterns of behavior are built up over long periods of time, they cannot be broken just in one go. It is necessary to create a trustful teaching environment that provides continuous experiences of success. Thus, just one successful experience may not be sufficient to change an internalized experience. Further, it is necessary to identify differentiated challenges that are right for the individual and make sure that each individual has positive experiences – as a single negative experience will just bring home the original aversion against carrying out a certain act. Therefore, teaching needs to include ways of impressing on potential entrepreneurs that it may be the expectation and perception of how difficult it might be that is the worst part. It can be likened to jumping from the 10-m diving board – it is walking out toward the edge that is the worst part.

A high level of self-efficacy is achieved through repeated performance accomplishments and the overcoming of obstacles through effort and perseverance (Wood and Bandura 1989) and produces the belief in one's capabilities to mobilize the motivation, cognitive resources, and courses of action needed to exercise control over events in one's life (Wood and Bandura 1989). So how can we teach self-efficacy? Bandura's (1997) self-efficacy framework operates with four sources of self-efficacy or ways in which we are subconsciously conditioned toward achievement: mastery experiences, vicarious experience (also known as modeling), social/verbal persuasion, and judgment about physiological and affective state. As will be shown, each of these operates in the individual–environment nexus. Wood and Bandura (1989) further distinguish between possessing skills and the ability to use them well and consistently under difficult or adverse circumstances. The question is then how and in which circumstances an individual learns to cultivate these skills and the ability to use them well. That is, complete mastery of a skill is no guarantee that the skill will be used, especially under stress or in the face of high stakes; no self-efficacy, no behavior. In order to identify how it is possible to support positive representations, replace or transform possible negative ones, to produce self-efficacious behavior, we can use Bandura's framework.

11.2.1.1 Mastery Experiences

Bandura describes how the gradual generation of an ability may result in a mastery experience. The experience has to be sufficiently difficult to achieve and contain a potential danger of failure. If this action succeeds then it will count as a mastery experience. Thus, a task, which is to easy achieve, will not provide a change in perception. In other words, we are concerned with tasks that will bring about a more competitive, risk taking, self-reliant, or ambitious attitude such as participating in competitive sports activities, hence generating self-efficacious attitude.

11.2.1.2 Vicarious Experience/Modeling

According to Bandura (1977b, 1986), vicarious experience means that we learn through imitating or repeating the behavior of others. Bandura suggests that most modeling is based on behavioral observation. It occurs when a certain social behavior, e.g., entrepreneurship, is informally observed and then adopted by an individual. Hence, the learning occurs by example rather than by direct experience (Bandura 1977b). In other words, role models are individuals on whom you can mirror your own behavior and use as a guide for your own action and are usually persons whom the individual admires and whose opinions are trustworthy. The good role model delivers the first stepping-stone or guide for action so it is perceived as less dangerous to navigate through uncertain and potentially challenging waters. Scherer et al. (1989) found that the presence of a high-performing parent entrepreneur had a positive impact on an individual's choice of an entrepreneurial career. However, role models do not necessarily have to be actual entrepreneurs or parents although they can be, but a role model always has to be relevant and believable for the situation in which the individual finds himself or herself in. Thus, women may mirror themselves in different role models than men.

11.2.1.3 Social/Verbal Persuasion

Bandura describes the influence that our environment has on our beliefs of what is acceptable or non-acceptable behavior through the discourse or peer pressure. For instance, the reason for the low participation of women in entrepreneurship in many countries may be due to the fact that entrepreneurship is often associated with long working hours, and particularly young women of childbearing age may deselect entrepreneurship because the environment does not allow for this double role. This goes hand in hand with ideas about social identity because it typically involves peers – family, other women's acceptance – or other groups who can be defined as culture bearers.

11.2.1.4 Judgment About Physiological State

In order to heighten beliefs in coping efficacy with corresponding improvements in performance it is important to eliminate emotional reactions to subjective threats through mastery experiences (Bandura 1989). He describes the importance of being conscious of physical and emotional reactions in different situations and how you perceive and interpret these reactions because this impinges on your ability. If you are unable to register and interpret your own bodily reactions and emotions when you have reached your limit, then you will ultimately fail in what you are doing and therefore you will have an unsuccessful experience. This is why we see a high extent of very clever and highly motivated entrepreneurs who "burn out." The relation between bodily reactions, emotions, and feelings of success is thus very close. There is some taboo surrounding the verbalization of emotions in teaching environments, which may make it very difficult to change this situation.

Therefore, in order to facilitate entrepreneurial behavior we need to promote certain behavioral patterns. The way to do this may potentially include a facilitating, coaching approach to making individuals think reflexively about their own RIGs or exposing them to exercises that slowly push their limits for certain behavior. For example, in teaching entrepreneurs who may fear rejection from the first customer, a teacher could ask "Are there situations in which you feel comfortable in contacting new persons?" And "Are there then potential ways in which you extrapolate from this situation to situations where you feel uncomfortable?" Such future-oriented and solution-driven questions do not break the therapeutic space but more subtly facilitate an emotionally safe solution that will condition the mind toward a more positive interpretation of oneself. Figure 11.1 shows the interrelationship between the four sources of self-efficacy and the process of transforming behavioral patterns. The idea is that for each of the sources it is possible to design a curriculum and appropriate teaching methods. This will naturally be different depending on the age and the stage of education, which will be shown in a later section.

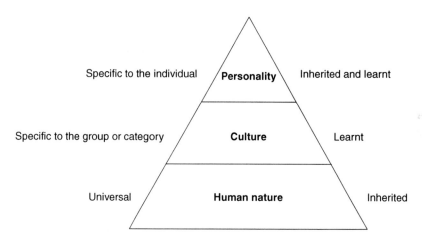

Fig. 11.1 The three levels of mental programming/conditioning (Hofstede 1991: 6)

11.2.2 Measuring Self-Efficacy in Psychology

There are various approaches to measuring self-efficacy. Generally they fall into three different groups (Gecas 1989): task-specific measures (Bandura's own approach), domain-specific measures (e.g., health, political, entrepreneurial), and general measures. What can be learnt from the existing studies in, e.g., the health literature is that self-efficacy is a significant factor in overcoming various disorders, addictions, and phobias. Indeed, recovery from different types of illness seems to be more rapid in individuals with high levels of self-efficacy (Schwalbe and Gecas 1988).

However, according to Gecas (1989) the measurement of self-efficacy in the psychology literature is still rather primitive. Even the general measures have predominantly been concerned with measuring levels of self-efficacy ex ante and ex post some participation in an experimental setting (see, e.g., Zimmerman et al., 1992 for an exemplar). A positive attitude or state of mind seems to work, but how it works is still a mystery (Gecas 1989). In other words, research that addresses the underlying determinants of self-efficacy is lacking in this body of research and this is important if attempts to improve levels of self-efficacy in individuals are to succeed (Gist and Mitchell 1992). Therefore, we need to identify the triggering factors of the type of behavior we want to improve, e.g., entrepreneurial behavior. However, how entrepreneurship research has addressed the measurement of self-efficacy will be discussed later.

11.3 ESE: Entrepreneurial Self-Efficacy

Two ambitions have driven the transfer of psychological constructs in general and more specifically that of self-efficacy into the entrepreneurship literature. First, there is our general ambition as entrepreneurship scholars to produce more entrepreneurs, as we strongly believe in their positive economic influence, a fulfilling lifestyle, and an attractive life option. Second, the field has failed for a long time to find personality traits in entrepreneurs that could differentiate them from other groups (see, e.g., Gartner 1988). The field has now turned to drill into the entrepreneur's head, searching for distinct entrepreneurial characteristics both specific enough to be descriptive of core entrepreneurial concepts and at the same time broad enough to embrace all varieties of entrepreneurs.

11.3.1 The History of Entrepreneurial Self-Efficacy Research

In order to delineate the growing impact of self-efficacy in entrepreneurship research, we propose to look back to 1989. Bandura (1977a) published his seminal work on self-efficacy in the context of human agency, and Gist (1987) introduced self-efficacy to the management literature with a discussion of implications for organizational behavior and human resource management. Then, Scherer et al. (1989) published a study on the role model performance effects on the development of entrepreneurial career preferences. These are among the pioneers in drawing on concepts from the field of psychology (namely Social Learning Theory), introducing them to the field of entrepreneurship, thereby starting a valuable interdisciplinary discussion. Their results revealed that the existence of a parent role model, cf. Bandura's "modeling" concept, increases a variety of antecedents to the child's entrepreneurial career choice: entrepreneurial career expectancy (what is later labeled as intention, see, e.g., Bird 1988) and entrepreneurial preparedness including – what Scherer et al. (1989) call – education and training aspirations as well as entrepreneurial task self-efficacy (op. cit., p. 66).

For the next decade, entrepreneurship researchers developed the concept of entrepreneurial self-efficacy. It moved slowly from the psychological corner of career choice research – where it had also been overlooked as a viable career option (Boyd and Vozikis 1994, p. 74) – via intentions research into the center of the entrepreneurship field. While studies after 1998 mostly used the term entrepreneurial self-efficacy, there is a rather broad variety of terms used up to this point. Boyd and Vozikis (1994) are exemplary of a noteworthy development step: building upon the work of Scherer et al. (1989), thus tying their research to the career-related self-efficacy discussion. However, they finally end up labeling their own scale "entrepreneurial self-efficacy" – or ESE. The concept was then popularized in the entrepreneurship discussion by Krueger and Brazeal (1994), who defined it as an attribute of personal competence and control, which helps convert perceived failures into learning experiences. For them, there is no question about the importance of the concept: "No self-efficacy, no behavior" (op. cit., p. 94). Yet, Krueger and Brazeal used the terms "perceived venture feasibility" and "perceived venture self-efficacy" and built a scale by adapting a set of obstacles for corporate ventures from MacMillan et al. (1986).

The term entrepreneurial self-efficacy finally emerged as the combination of self-efficacy as a task-specific psychological concept and entrepreneurship as a bundle of tasks that are supposed to represent the entrepreneurial career choice. The concept gains a foothold when it started to manifest itself in the titles of top tier journal articles. Chen et al. (1998) were among the first to mention entrepreneurial self-efficacy in the title of a research paper, thereby moving the concept into the focus of the field. Their study tied directly in with the dissatisfaction of the field in searching for general entrepreneurial traits, trying to identify distinctively entrepreneurial characteristics. Chen et al. (1998) were able to show that entrepreneurial self-efficacy offered the potential to differentiate entrepreneurs from non-entrepreneurs. Thus, they carried out the task-specific adaptation of self-efficacy to the entrepreneurial domain, opening up a fruitful discussion on the relevant entrepreneurial facets that needed to be included in valid measurement scales for entrepreneurial self-efficacy. They also contributed to the debate in the literature by differentiating the concept from other psychological concepts as locus of control which had shown "only limited success in differentiating entrepreneurs from higher achievers and internalizers in other spheres of life" (op. cit., p. 312) and the importance of the contribution is cemented by the inclusion in Shane and Venkataraman's (2000) seminal article on entrepreneurship as a field of research. Shane and Venkataraman (op. cit., pp. 222–224) mentioned cognitive properties as an important field of study in context with the discovery of opportunities, pointing explicitly to the value of incorporating entrepreneurial self-efficacy in entrepreneurship research.

Since 1998, the number of articles on entrepreneurial self-efficacy has been constantly growing. Roughly until 2004, research mainly focused on either creating scales for entrepreneurial self-efficacy or testing existing scales in varying contexts (Kourilsky and Walstad 1998; DeNoble et al. 1999; Anna and Chandler 2000; Drnovsek and Glas 2002; Lucas and Cooper 2004; Forbes 2005; Hao et al. 2005). Originally stemming from career research, many of these studies examined the impact of entrepreneurial self-efficacy on entrepreneurial intentions. Especially in the context of training programs, entrepreneurial self-efficacy was employed to check the program's effectiveness (e.g., Peterman and Kennedy 2003; Lucas and Cooper 2004). A basic discussion point was the fact that self-efficacy emerged as an important mechanism to overcome perceptions of risk. Hence, the mechanism fitted well into the venturing process (e.g., Boyd and Vozikis 1994; Krueger and Brazeal 1994; Krueger et al. 2000), which also led to studies trying to explain gender differences in entrepreneurial activity (e.g., Kourilsky and Walstad 1998; Anna and Chandler 2000).

Since 2004, research has begun to take on a more nuanced approach, surrendering assumptions of direct relationships, discussing moderating and mediating effects, and inquiring more intensely about antecedents of entrepreneurial self-efficacy (e.g., Hao et al. 2005; Hmieleski and Baron 2008; Forbes 2005; Wilson et al. 2007; Hmieleski and Corbett 2008). For the years 2007 and 2008 alone, a total of 14 studies building on the existing body of entrepreneurial self-efficacy research were published. This is certainly an indicator of the growing interest in and impact of ESE and signifies the need for further research. Therefore, the next section will address those three issues that may be pertinent to the future development of the discussion on entrepreneurial self-efficacy.

11.3.2 Measurement of ESE

When comparing scales of entrepreneurial self-efficacy, the scales used by Scherer et al. (1989), Chandler and Jansen (1992) as well as Krueger and Brazeal (1994) offer interesting starting points. Building upon a scale by Betz and Hackett (1981), Scherer et al. (1989, p. 59) asked participants whether they believe in their capabilities of performing tasks such as accounting, production, marketing, human resources, and general organizational tasks. Obviously, these tasks belong to the field of management as a whole and are hardly idiosyncratic for the field of entrepreneurship research. The reason for this is that the discussion started in the field of career research where task-specific adaptations of the construct were carried out through definition of typical task sets for the particular career path (see also Lucas and Cooper 2004 for a more recent study within the career choice stream). Therefore, the entrepreneurial career path seems at first sufficiently described by general management functions, at least if compared to scales for entirely different career paths like teachers or parents. In a comparable approach and almost simultaneously, Chandler and Jansen (1992) developed an entrepreneurial competences scale, combining entrepreneurial, managerial, and technical-functional roles in order to cover the full spectrum of entrepreneurial activity. Anna and Chandler (2000) followed up on this scale, inquiring for self-efficacy on competences like opportunity recognition, formal planning, economic management, and human/conceptual competence. Further, Krueger and Brazeal (1994) propose their perceived venture self-efficacy scale with 27 items on obstacles for ventures. This scale has been taken up again in recent studies in the *Journal of Developmental Entrepreneurship* (Sequeira et al. 2007; Mueller and Dato-On 2008).

Although the psychology literature also uses a general self-efficacy scale, entrepreneurship researchers have mostly adopted a task-specific understanding. Studies still using the general self-efficacy scales have been carried out by, e.g., Markman et al. (2002) and Markman and Baron (2003). In 1998, Chen et al. consolidated the existing research and built a scale combining the works of Scherer et al. (1989), Boyd and Vozikis (1994), and Krueger and Brazeal (1994), stressing the understanding of entrepreneurial self-efficacy as a key prerequisite for entrepreneurs and a key impact factor for entrepreneurial intentions. In order to create their scale, they further drew upon the literature on entrepreneurial roles (Long 1983; Kazanjian 1988; Miner 1990). Chen et al. (1998) argued that enlisting a full list of entrepreneurial activities would be highly impractical and alternatively chose exemplary activities, which they believed characterize this special "career choice" of entrepreneurship. In conclusion, they define entrepreneurial self-efficacy as the belief of an individual to be capable (efficacious) to successfully perform a set of typical entrepreneurial activities. Chen et al. (1998) finally produced a list of 26 items to represent the domain of entrepreneurship. Five factors turned out to underlie the item structure: marketing, innovation, management, risk taking, and financial control. Results showed the scale's capacity to successfully differentiate founders from non-founders. In comparison to Scherer et al. (1989), it even revealed a development from rather managerial functions to a more entrepreneurial conceptualization. However, among the five factors, Chen et al. only found two to be uniquely entrepreneurial, namely innovation and risk taking. They concluded that the three managerial competences are necessary for entrepreneurs in a more general sense but do not differentiate them from other managers.

However, DeNoble et al. (1999) criticized the scales by Chandler and Jansen, as well as Chen et al., for not being sufficiently entrepreneurship specific. DeNoble et al. (1999) proceeded in a similar way to build a different scale. Eight entrepreneurs generated 100 statements, which were condensed to 35 skills and behaviors, which were further reduced by exploratory and confirmatory factor analysis to six dimensions: developing new product or market opportunities, building an innovative environment, initiating investor relationships, defining a core purpose, coping with unexpected challenges, and developing critical human resources. Results showed that this set of skills and behaviors influences entrepreneurial intentions (DeNoble et al. 1999). More recently, this scale has been identified as an alternative to the scale by Chen et al. for its robustness in predicting entrepreneurial performance (Hmieleski and Baron 2008; Hmieleski and Corbett 2008). Despite its questionable fit with the entrepreneurial domain, Chen et al.'s scale has become a cornerstone for entrepreneurial self-efficacy measurement in the literature and has since been used in a variety of studies (e.g., Drnovsek and Glas 2002; Forbes 2005; Hao et al. 2005; Steffens et al. 2006; Urban 2006; Wilson et al. 2007). Hao et al. (2005) and Sardeshmukh and Corbett (2008) further advanced the scale and moved it even closer to the core of entrepreneurial activity: identifying new business opportunities, creating new products, thinking creatively, and commercializing an idea or new development.

11.3.3 Impact of ESE and Moderating Effects

As previously mentioned, the entrepreneurial self-efficacy literature has its infancy in career research. Accordingly, many of the early studies tried to explain differences in career choice. However, Krueger and Brazeal (1994) relate their measure of perceived venture self-efficacy to models of entrepreneurial intent. As entrepreneurial self-efficacy, the concept became popularized as an antecedent to entrepreneurial activity. Chen et al. (1998) found "a significant and consistent positive effect of entrepreneurial self-efficacy on the likelihood of being an entrepreneur" (op. cit., p. 310). While this relationship has been reproduced by other studies (DeNoble et al. 1999; Krueger et al. 2000), research on the direct impact on performance has produced less congruent results. Anna et al. (1999) and Forbes (2005) both reported a positive impact of entrepreneurial self-efficacy on subjective performance measures. However, Chandler and Jansen (1997) found no such performance impact for entrepreneurial self-efficacy in their attempt to predict causal relationships between entrepreneurial competences (entrepreneurial, managerial, and technical self-efficacies) and emerging venture performance. Managerial efficacy turned out to be a significant predictor of subsequent performance, while the entrepreneurial and technical dimensions did not predict performance. Neither could Chen et al. (1998) provide a link. They offered a set of possible explanations for the unexpected results. First, self-efficacy in general is used to predict performance at the individual level. They believed the relationship with venture performance to be more complex. Second, they noted that self-efficacy has been a good predictor for performance that followed closely in time and not so much for more distant performance effects. Third, "although higher self-efficacy definitely motivates entrepreneurial entry, it may not always positively affect performance" (op. cit., p. 313). This links directly to the results of more recent studies, e.g., Hmieleski and Baron (2008) cite references from the psychology and management literature that have found positive relationship between self-efficacy and growth (e.g., Baum et al. 2001; Baum and Locke 2004). However, it is necessary to note that these studies have used adapted self-efficacy scales in which they do not ask for entrepreneurial functions but for the *ability* to grow a business. The authors conclude their own literature review stating that entrepreneurs high in self-efficacy seem to be "higher performing in that the firms they lead tend to grow more quickly and be more profitable than those led by entrepreneurs who are comparably lower in entrepreneurial self-efficacy" (Hmieleski and Baron 2008, p. 60). However, their own results question a direct impact and show moderating effects on the performance impact of entrepreneurial self-efficacy.

In terms of moderating effects, Chen et al. (1998) include the environment in their theoretical discussion as one part of a triangle of reciprocal causation of (i) cognition, (ii) behavior, and (iii) environment, which all seem to influence the relationship between self-efficacy and performance. In conclusion, they advocate a consideration of the environment, shaping it so that it is supportive to entrepreneurs. They claim that individuals feel to be more self-efficacious when they can assess their own entrepreneurial capacity within a supportive environment (op. cit., p. 314). Other studies have also suggested further moderating effects: Sequeira et al. (2007) found that the structure of the entrepreneur's personal network moderates the relationship between self-efficacy and entrepreneurial intentions as well as action. Hmieleski and Baron (2008) are able to predict entrepreneurial performance but find the relationship to be moderated by dispositional optimism and environmental dynamism. Hence, entrepreneurial self-efficacy and high levels of optimism can coalesce to inadequate levels of over-confidence with negative effects in a dynamic environment. Therefore, entrepreneurship education programs should be required to teach tools of self-regulation (Hmieleski and Baron 2008). In another recent study, Hmieleski and Corbett (2008) examine the relationship of improvisational behavior on new venture performance and entrepreneurs' job satisfaction. In this study, they find entrepreneurial self-efficacy to moderate the relationships. While the improvisation–performance relationship is positively moderated, the improvisation–satisfaction relationship is negatively moderated, which opens up further avenues of research on interaction effects (Hmieleski and Corbett 2008).

Finally, some studies have analyzed mediating roles of self-efficacy: Luthans and Ibrayeva (2006) find a direct and mediating effect of self-efficacy on performance in the context of transition economies. Hao et al. (2005) were among the first to look back into the chain of causalities to the antecedents of entrepreneurial self-efficacy, discussing the mediating role of self-efficacy on intentions. The latter shows that entrepreneurial self-efficacy mediates the impact of perceptions of formal learning, entrepreneurial experience, and risk propensity on entrepreneurial intentions.

11.3.4 Antecedents of ESE

A discussion on antecedents to entrepreneurial self-efficacy brings us back to the field of psychology with its emphasis on mastery experience, modeling/vicarious experience, social persuasion, and physiological factors as antecedents to entrepreneurial self-efficacy. By now, a variety of studies have started to look more intensely into these antecedent concepts to entrepreneurial self-efficacy (Scherer et al. 1989; Forbes 2005; Hao et al. 2005; Barbosa et al. 2007; Carr and Sequeira 2007; Wilson et al. 2007; Mueller and Dato-On 2008; Sardeshmukh and Corbett 2008). Scherer et al. (1989) emphasized the necessity of a *parent role model* and its impact on entrepreneurial self-efficacy. They saw a need to develop theory in terms of the underlying mechanisms, in their case how an entrepreneurial role model influences career preferences (op. cit., p. 67). Hao et al. (2005) found that *training programs, previous experience, and risk propensity* – three of the most frequently identified individual-level antecedents of entrepreneurship – drive entrepreneurial self-efficacy and subsequent intentions to become an entrepreneur. They advised to "incorporate as many diverse types of learning experiences related to the promotion of greater entrepreneurial self-efficacy as is practical" (op. cit., p. 1270). Forbes (2005) discussed the impact of *strategic decision making* on entrepreneurial self-efficacy, showing that the type of decision making in a venture influences self-efficacy beliefs. He also hypothesized that there has not been a lot of antecedent research due to the fact that effect relationships of entrepreneurial self-efficacy are more straightforward (op. cit., p. 616). Carr and Sequeira (2007) discussed the importance of the *family influence* on entrepreneurial self-efficacy. Wilson et al. (2007) found a strong influence of *entrepreneurship education* on entrepreneurial self-efficacy. The results from their gender study with female participants of different age groups suggest that it is important to provide entrepreneurial training at an early age (Wilson et al. 2007). Krueger and Brazeal (1994, p. 94) summarized the importance of antecedent research as follows: "We learn self-efficacy from actual mastery of the behavior and from believable models of the behavior. It is enhanced by believable information about the behavior and emotional support for performing the behavior (Bandura 1986). These antecedents prove important to promoting the perceived feasibility of new ventures."

Thus, what is not found in the literature is a stringent breakdown of the antecedent discussion in connection with "diagnosis and treatment" of entrepreneurial self-efficacy. Given the current state of research, we propose to focus on two aspects in future research:

1. What can we do in the process of early-age formation to foster entrepreneurial self-efficacy?
2. How is it possible to influence children, adolescents, or young adults with low levels of entrepreneurial self-efficacy to develop the respective cognitive resources?

Chen et al. (1998) provided a variety of suggestions. For example, they proposed entrepreneurship programs to focus not only on entrepreneurial skills but also on entrepreneurial self-efficacy. They put experience first, be it in meeting role models or in working on their own projects or together with other entrepreneurs. They saw treatment in practical training to enhance innovation and risk taking, their two significant dimensions of entrepreneurial self-efficacy. Accordingly, all other antecedents of self-efficacy may be analyzed in terms of applicable tools for entrepreneurship education and training and how this can tie in with the design of a favorable learning environment.

Thus, while research on entrepreneurial self-efficacy has produced valuable knowledge on the measurement of the concept as well as it effects, there seems to be a pertinent need for research on its antecedents and even on the underlying factors or mechanisms that influence the antecedents. Entrepreneurial self-efficacy, the type of subconscious "social persuasion" that arises through individual's interaction with the environment (Bandura 1977b), which embeds itself deep within us without our conscious knowing, needs to be brought out in the open if we are to address it in practice.

11.4 Entrepreneurial Self-Efficacy Contextualized

So far we have seen that self-efficacy is a rather complex psychological concept that dropped into entrepreneurship via career choice research. The question by Krueger and Brazeal, "*What specific factors lead to the perception of self-efficacy for potential entrepreneurs in a community?*" goes right to the crux of the matter (Krueger and Brazeal 1994, p. 99). They continue, "Unanswered is the question of how to encourage entrepreneurship in a discouraged population. Can we use the model to identify tactics to overcome learned helplessness?" and remind us "Entrepreneurs are made, not born." (Krueger and Brazeal 1994, pp. 101, 102). Few have attempted to answer these questions empirically and the origin and underlying components of self-efficacy still need to be investigated.

Therefore, we may need to center the discussion on which particular mechanisms produce these characteristic attitudes and beliefs and possibly internalized to the extent that they can be perceived and appear as "inherent." Many successful entrepreneurs have little further education and even less entrepreneurship education. Instead, they have a kind of drive that sets them apart and although many have no leadership training at all, they tend to lead their companies with vision and spirit and success. So if entrepreneurial behavior is not taught, from whence does it arise? Although traits may not be inherent at first, they may become internalized as a result of a socializing or educational experience and in time become what we perceive as "inherent" personality traits. According to social psychologists, such acquisition takes place through various forms of experiential learning at some point in life and often in what is popularly called the formative years. Indeed, according to Carland et al. (1988) based on Myers and Myers (1980), personality is something that is largely set during the formative years, that is, attitudes and beliefs are learned. The crucial question is where in the social arenas of their lives do entrepreneurs learn the building blocks of entrepreneurial thinking? One way of exploring this question is by looking to anthropology. Hofstede (1991) suggested that human nature is universal and inherited and cannot be changed. However, what is generally referred to as culture and personality can be programmed or conditioned into the minds of individuals, cf. Fig. 11.1.

Most entrepreneurship scholars agree that the notion of a fixed "entrepreneurial personality" is unlikely at best, but equally that entrepreneurs do think differently (Shaver and Scott 1991). At the same time, both scholars and practitioners appear to assume that much of these differences must arise from various processes of socialization that might explain, even predict, the base rate characteristics of aspiring entrepreneurs (Starr and Fondas 1992). Indeed, Mitchell et al. (2002) demonstrated that cultural differences explain some of the variance in venture-creation decisions among countries. Thus, they seem to agree with Hofstede (1991) who further suggested that cultural programming may take place at different levels in the environment and that a culture consists of both values and practices. National values are more universal – hence, if a nation does not espouse entrepreneurial values generally then this will affect how families bring up their children, see Fig. 11.2. In other words, The Jante Law can be perceived as a national value that inhibits entrepreneurial behavior causing reactions such as the "Tall Poppy Syndrome." Naturally, the family also has an influence on the values transmitted to its children, but if these are very different from the universal ones, then it becomes much more difficult for the child to act in ways that are expected by the social environment. It will thus be much easier for a child brought up in a culture permeated with entrepreneurial values to choose a career as an entrepreneur. Entrepreneurship research has also suggested that growing up in a family business can do much to mold one's entrepreneurial thinking (Krueger 1993). These experiences provide the

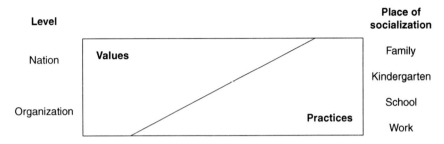

Fig. 11.2 Places of cultural programming (Hofstede 1991: 182)

children with very early understandings of what they can do in life, how they can influence their own lives, what options are open to them, and how the environment is going to react. This section will continue to provide exemplars of how infants, young children, adolescents, and young adults may be conditioned toward a self-efficacious behavior and an entrepreneurial career in the different "social arenas" of their lives.

Bandura (1997) discusses two different ways in which children are conditioned toward self-efficacious behavior, a positive and a negative. The former is produced through support, encouragement, and positive modeling. For example, children who are given challenging or "risky" tasks at an early age, encouraged to undertake these tasks, and praised for the results will experience higher levels of self-efficacy as exemplified earlier in this chapter. The latter results from experience with learning to overcome adverse conditions or experiences. Bandura's (1977a, b; 1986; 1994; 1997) examples are generally concerned with much more adverse conditions such as parental drug abuse, but for the purposes of this chapter, examples that relate to the generation of entrepreneurial behavior will be sought out. Table 11.1 provides an overview of examples of potential influential factors on self-efficacy at the various stages of children's development. Chell (2008) similarly operates with a concept called concept cognitive-affective units. These are among others concerned with expectancies and beliefs that arise from experience of the social world influence of how an individual behaves depending on what she/he believes might happen in a particular situation (op. cit., p. 149). Furthermore, individuals choose desirable courses of action whose potential outcomes will hold particular values for them and avoid the undesirable. Again, these patterns of action and reaction are conditioned into individuals over time as they encounter new challenges to be overcome. Chell (2008) proposes that this generates an "if … then situation-behavior profile" and that an individual's reaction to a challenge is therefore not random (op. cit., p. 150). Table 11.1 attempts to exemplify what type of mechanisms may influence an individual's "if–then" reaction pattern. Some of the influential mechanisms naturally transcend the whole period from infancy to adulthood. However, the content of the mechanism may change.

Clearly, the family is the most important socialization environment (Gecas 1989). The conditioning of the mind commences already in infancy when parents provide

Table 11.1 Bandura's framework contextualized

	Mastery experience	Vicarious experience/modeling	Social/verbal persuasion (discourse)	Judgements about physiological state
Infancy and early childhood (home, kindergarten and preschool)	• Choice of toys and activities	Reference groups: Parents	• Fairy tales • Children's TV • Kindergarten teachers	• Physical exercises and activities
Adolescence (school, high school)	• Participation in sports at a high level	Reference groups: Parents, peers	• Media • Teachers: • Ways of teaching and rewarding appropriate behaviour	• Physical exercises and activities: participating in sports
Young adulthood (university)	• Participation in sports at a high level • Teachers	Reference groups: Family, peers, successful entrepreneurs (real life cases)	• Teachers • Media • Peers • Coaches and mentors	• Participation in sports at a high level • Preparing and attending exams

support, encouragement, and instill expectations in their children so that children come to perceive themselves as competent. Thus, parents who provide a stimulating, challenging, and responsive environment and give their children the freedom to engage in it produce more efficacious children. Children may also learn to develop coping strategies by modeling their parents (Bandura 1997).

11.4.1 Infancy and Early Childhood

Although parents will influence all the stages of development, this is probably the stage at which parents may have the most influence, because they make the most choices on behalf of their children. Thus, even in infancy and early childhood, parents may unwittingly condition their children in ways that do or do not support entrepreneurial behavior at a later age. For example, old-fashioned nursery stories and fairy tales are often inundated with negative messages surrounding the ability to rise above one's station in life. The majority of Hans Christian Anderson's fairy tales present negative outcomes for those individuals who had the audacity to wish for a better future. The most loved fairy tale, and one which signifies the essence of Danish culture, is that of the little mermaid, who gave up her ability to speak to become human. She ends up as froth on the waves in the wake of the Prince's wedding because she could not convince him to love her. The little Match-girl, a truly entrepreneurial child, selling matchsticks on the streets (that nobody will buy), dies in the cold of winter wishing for a better future. Further, many fairy tales portray the woman (princess) as a person who should just sit back, inactive, and wait for the young, handsome prince to rescue her. Neither produces associations that provide for much entrepreneurial thought. Entrepreneurial is the Prince who thinks up various ways of coming to her rescue or finding ways to overcome the obstacles on his way. Thus, choosing the right literature is the first step not only in infancy but also later on and books that stress young children's ability to influence their own everyday life may provide them with a different interpretation of their opportunities.

Children's hour on TV may be another example of a major influencing factor. Today, many parents use the TV as a babysitter, rather than involving the children in whatever activities they are undertaking themselves unlike in former times when children learnt how to master various activities from their parents. Further, the learning that the child takes away from watching TV depends on what program is chosen. Crucial to this discussion is thus how the content of TV programs may condition children to perceive themselves and their interaction with the environment. According to Danesi (2002), TV influences the way individuals derive meaning for their daily life routines. Open, friendly, and welcoming programs that stress friendship and sharing such as is portrayed by Teletubbies (UK), Teddy and Chicken (DK) or aggressive and hostile, survival of the fittest/smartest as portrayed by many of the cartoons on, e.g., Cartoon Network, will eventually if watched sufficiently frequently have a certain impact, positive or negative.

Parents may further inadvertently influence their children's level of entrepreneurial self-efficacy through their choice of toys. Indeed, construction toys provide children of both sexes opportunities for the development of an inquisitive mind. Toys may also function as role models – e.g., recently Peter Pan's Tinkle Bell doll and its associated products have provided girls with a new type of role model, who is opinionated, resourceful, and skilled.

Female role models dominate kindergartens and primary schools in most of the Western world and mostly the environments surrounding these locations are devoid of potentially dangerous element such as tall trees for building tree houses and climbing. Thus, activities are likely to be influenced by the dominant gender and include fewer choices that may involve risky behavior. Children are rarely allowed to make their own toys or reinterpret natural elements as something else, simply because the opportunity to do so is removed. Most playgrounds are fitted with pre-molded fixtures, which represent no danger to children. Therefore, the thrill of doing something that might be a little bit risky has to be found elsewhere.

Today, parental fear of potential harm coming to their children, which is often exacerbated by the media, also hampers children's freedom to experience and experiment with life as well as their urge and ability to decide for themselves. Children are driven to and picked up from school. Given the freedom to walk or bike, they learn to take care of themselves and make their own decisions, which is a good basis for future self-reliance. Over-controlling parents may easily have an effect on their children that counteracts entrepreneurial behavior.

11.4.2 Adolescence

For adolescents values and standards of conduct that are consistent with those of the home have usually been adopted – and the choice of friends tends to reflect a similar value system and behavioral norm and these peers are more likely to uphold their behavioral standards rather than to breed family conflicts (Bandura 1997, p. 177), but even adolescents who have been subjected to fractured families, poverty, or abuse (substance and physical) can result in one of two outcomes. These children may become as delinquent as their environment or they can learn to navigate successfully in these troubled waters and overcome the problems resulting in a high level of self-efficacy, and breaking the mold of social heritage. Thus, adolescents may be able to expand and strengthen their sense of efficacy by learning how to deal successfully with potentially troublesome situations in which they are unpracticed. Success in managing problem situations instills a strong belief in one's capabilities that provides staying power in the face of other, unrelated difficulties – e.g., a child who is mobbed in school, called names, or excluded from peer group activities may develop coping strategies that are centered on being "better" than those who undertake the mobbing or exclusion and not needing anyone else to succeed.

The approach to teaching seems to have an impact right from primary grade. Teachers who use a responsive classroom approach and provide rich classroom experiences have a greater chance of successfully influencing self-efficacy (Rimm-Kaufman and Sawyer 2004). Thus, the American model of awarding good and desirable behavior by handing out gold stars or other types of rewards assist youngsters in building self-efficacy. It is a subtle way of social persuasion to achieve the behavior wanted.

After-school activities such as participating in competitive sports may also help build self-efficacious behavior. Potentially, there are a number of such activities that may cultivate self-efficacy in one way or another by supporting the ability to overcome constraints, learn the ropes of the game, and endure and cope with difficulties. For example, competitive sports cultivate the aptitude to constantly better yourself, to endure hardship, and make judgments about how much pressure you can cope with. It helps improve perceptions and interpretations of environmental uncertainty and provide coping strategies in the entrepreneurial competitive arena, which is a crucial element in self-efficacy (Neergaard and Krueger 2005). Hence, children who participate in competitive sports are socialized into an entrepreneurial mindset – they feel more competitively competent. They may feel spurred on by apparent obstacles rather than feel discouraged by them. Neergaard and Krueger (2005) found that entrepreneurs who were athletic high-achievers in adolescence and as young adults used their knowledge from their previous sports activities such as focus and persistence to develop appropriate business practices.

11.4.3 Young Adulthood

The media influences the self-schemata of efficacy dependent on physical appearance (strength or beauty) and produces sensitivity to social evaluation (Bandura op.

cit., p. 178). Young adults watching programs such as "Top Model" will evaluate themselves against the apparent criteria set up by the program: skinny and beautiful. Hence, it is likely that documentary programs, which showcase entrepreneurs, will have a potential to "teach appropriate lessons" about entrepreneurship (Neergaard and Smith 2004) because young adults utilize media representations to evaluate their own lives and emulate various components of its content, such as lifestyle (Danesi 2002). Thus, if young adults see that society values individuals who are able to start a company and make a solid profit which gives access to a certain lifestyle, then they may attempt to copy that behavior. Thus, competitive programs such as "The Apprentice" may have similar impact on young would-be entrepreneurs as "Top Model" has on young girls. They want to be the chosen one, the one who has what it takes, and in order to obtain that they have to decode what underlying mechanisms may produce the "right" behavior. A study undertaken by Thompson and Dass (2000) suggests that experiential learning through simulations rather than lectures and cases increases student self-efficacy and strategic planning/thinking ability. The Apprentice is a real-life experiment: a simulation and may thus be copied successfully in class, if teachers understand how to avoid giving the students negative experiences rather than positive ones. Thus, it would be undermining the objective to provide derogatory comments, such as those typically given by the judging panels of the above-mentioned programs.

Another method that might be useful for teaching young entrepreneurship is coaching, as Malone (2001) found that coaching enhances self-efficacy. Such a measure may be used in classes where students are supposed to start their own company. They can be assigned a teacher who acts as a coach cum supervisor with whom to discuss their progress and the challenges they meet. This method assists them in finding their own solutions and thus finding ways to overcoming problems that they can use the next time they encounter a similar type of problem. In other words, they learn to master the skill of entrepreneuring.

This account of potential sources or mechanisms of self-efficacy is by no means claimed to be exhaustive. Some of the mechanisms highlighted above are general in nature, others specific. General mechanisms are those that take place in another context than entrepreneurship, but the learning gained can be extrapolated to an entrepreneurial setting, such as athletic experiences. These may not necessarily produce specific behavior in specific situations, but in conjunction with more specific mechanisms may be sufficient to tip the scales. Specific mechanisms are those particularly entrepreneurial, such as having parents or family who are entrepreneurs. It is probably easier to identify and measure the impact of specific mechanisms than that of the general mechanisms. Further, some of mechanisms transcend the various spheres of life: parents who are entrepreneurs do not stop influencing a child as it grows up; however, the child's interpretation of an entrepreneurial life may develop and change depending on how its mind is conditioned along the way. Figure 11.3 further provides an overview of some of the behavioral patterns that may be possible to reproduce in the classroom in order to (re)condition the student mind toward entrepreneurial action.

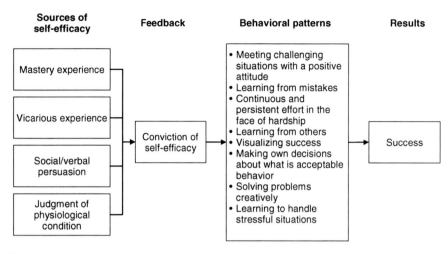

Fig. 11.3 A general model for successful training of self-efficacy (based on Bandura 1997)

11.5 Future Perspectives and Concluding Remarks

Psychologists such as Bandura have long argued that there is an interaction between contextual factors and self-efficacy. Self-efficacy can thus only be produced if the contextual constraints allow this expression. Nevertheless, there has been a void in research and theory development on the relevant context conditions in entrepreneurship research. This chapter has hopefully helped kick off this discussion. Clearly, what is presented constitute only a few ideas. Better theoretical conceptualizations of the contextual/environmental variables that interact to produce self-efficacy are needed. Further, such research might help us establish why differences in entrepreneurial start-ups exist across nations. If underlying national cultural conditions have an impact, a change process may take a long time before it has an impact. In the matter of Denmark with its egalitarian ethos, which permeated school policies in the 1970s and 1980s, it might be difficult to replace traditional teaching methods with teaching methods that acknowledge that children are different, have different skills and interests, and should be taught accordingly.

Additionally, it might be helpful to gather evidence about successful entrepreneurship teaching methods in order to explore if and how these can be related to Bandura's self-efficacy framework, and which methods are most successful in reconditioning children and youngsters toward a more entrepreneurial mindset. Studies can be undertaken in two ways: either retrospective or longitudinal studies. Retrospective studies can trace the exposure of existing entrepreneurs to each of the four factors in Bandura's framework, as attempted by Neergaard and Krueger (2005) who explored the entrepreneurial skills generated through participation in competitive sports activities. Longitudinal studies could experiment with groups of young children and follow their development over time. Such an experiment is currently being undertaken by Danfoss Universe Research Lab in Denmark.

Finally, it should probably be noted that it is not possible to instill immediate changes in individuals. Even if students become aware of their RIGs, it will take continuous, positive conditioning to alter old emotions and patterns of behavior. A conditioning or reconditioning of the mind takes time so if we want future generations to be more entrepreneurial, now may be is the time to start figuring out how to influence their paths.

References

Anna AL, Chandler GN (2000) Women Business Owners in Traditional and Non-Traditional Industries. Journal of Business Venturing 15: 280–303

Anna AL, Chandler GN, Jansen E, Mero NP (1999) Women Business Owners in Traditional and Non-Traditional Industries. Journal of Business Venturing 15: 279–303

Bandura A (1977a) Social Learning Theory. Prentice Hall, Englewood Cliffs. NJ

Bandura A (1977b) Self-efficacy: Toward a Unifying Theory of Behavioral Change. Psychological Review 84: 191–215

Bandura A (1986) Social Foundations of Thought and Action. Prentice Hall, Englewood Cliffs, NJ

Bandura A (1989) Self-regulation of Motivation and Action through Internal Standards and Goal Systems. In: Pervin LA (ed) Goal Concepts in Personality and Social Psychology. Hillsdale, Erlbaum, NJ

Bandura A (1994) Self-efficacy. In Ramachaudran VS (Ed.), Encyclopedia of Human Behavior. Academic Press, New York, pp. 71–81

Bandura A (1997) Self-efficacy The Exercise of Control. W.H. Freeman and Company, New York

Barbosa SD, Gerhardt MW, Kickul JR (2007) The Role of Cognitive Style and Risk Preference on Entrepreneurial Self-efficacy and Entrepreneurial Intentions. Journal of Leadership & Organizational Studies (Baker College) 13: 86–104

Baum JR, Locke EA (2004). The Relationship of Entrepreneurial Traits, Skill, and Motivation to Subsequent Venture Growth. Journal of Applied Psychology 89: 587–598

Baum JR, Locke EA, Smith KG (2001) A Multidimensional Model of Venture Growth. Academy of Management Journal 44: 292–303

Bechara A, Damasio AR (2005) The Somatic Marker Hypothesis: A Neural Theory of Economic Decision. Games and Economic Behavior 52: 336–372

Betz NE, Hackett G (1981) The Relationship of Career-Related Self-efficacy Expectations to Perceived Career Options in College Women and Men. Journal of Counseling Psychology 28: 399–410

Bird B (1988) Implementing Entrepreneurial Ideas: The Case for Intention. Academy of Management Review 13: 442–453

Boyd NG, Vozikis GS (1994) The Influence of Self-Efficacy on the Development of Entrepreneurial Intentions and Actions. Entrepreneurship: Theory & Practice 18: 63–77

Carland JW, Hoy F, Carland JAC (1988) "Who is an Entrepreneur?" Is a Question Worth Asking. American Journal of Small Business 12: 33–39

Carr JC, Sequeira JM (2007) Prior Family Business Exposure as Intergenerational Influence and Entrepreneurial Intent: A Theory of Planned Behavior Approach. Journal of Business Research 60: 1090–1098

Carter NM, Williams M, Reynolds PD (1997) Discontinuance Among New Firms in Retail: The Influence of initial Resources, Strategy and Gender. Journal of Business Venturing 12: 125–145

Chandler GN, Jansen E (1992) The Founder's Self-Assessed Competence and Venture Performance. Journal of Business Venturing 7: 223–237

Chandler GN, Jansen E (1997) Founder Self-efficacy and Venture Performance: A Longitudinal Study. Academy of Management Proceedings. Academy of Management, San Diego, California

Chell E (2008) The Entrepreneurial Personality: A Social Construction. Routledge, London, UK

Chen CC, Greene PG, Crick A (1998) Does Entrepreneurial Self-efficacy Distinguish Entrepreneurs from Managers? Journal of Business Venturing 13: 295–316

Damasio A (1994) Descartes' Error: Emotion, Reason, and the Human Brain. GP Putnam's Sons, New York

Danesi M (2002) Understanding media semiotics. Arnold, New York.

DeNoble AF, Jung D, Ehrlich S (1999) Entrepreneurial Self-efficacy: the Development of a Measure and its Relationship to Entrepreneurial Action. Frontiers of Entrepreneurship Research. Babson College, Wellesley, MA

Drnovsek M, Glas M (2002) The Entrepreneurial Self-efficacy of Nascent Entrepreneurs: The Case of Two Economies in Transition. Journal of Enterprising Culture 10: 107–131

Fletcher C (1999) The Implications of Research on Gender Differences in Self-assessment and 360 Degree Appraisal. Human Resource Management Journal 9: 39–46

Forbes DP (2005) The Effects of Strategic Decision Making on Entrepreneurial Self-efficacy. Entrepreneurship: Theory & Practice 29: 599–626

Gartner WB (1988) Who Is an Entrepreneur? Is the Wrong Question. American Journal of Small Business 12: 11–32.

Gecas V (1989) The Social Psychology of Self-efficacy. Annual Review of Sociology 15: 291–316

Gist ME (1987) Self-efficacy: Implications for Organizational Behavior and Human Resource Management. Academy of Management Review 12: 472–485

Gist ME, Mitchell TR (1992) Self-efficacy: A Theoretical Analysis of its Determinants and Malleability. Academy of Management Review 17: 183–211

Hackett G, Betz NE (1981) A Self-efficacy Approach to the Career Development of Women. Journal of Vocational Behavior 18: 326–339

Hao Z, Seibert SE, Hills G (2005) The Mediating Role of Self-efficacy in the Development of Entrepreneurial Intentions. Journal of Applied Psychology 90: 1265–1272

Hmieleski KM, Baron RA (2008) When does Entrepreneurial Self-efficacy Enhance Versus Reduce Firm Performance? Strategic Entrepreneurship Journal 2: 57–72.

Hmieleski KM, Corbett AC (2008) The Contrasting Interaction Effects of Improvisational Behavior with Entrepreneurial Self-efficacy on New Venture Performance and Entrepreneur Work Satisfaction. Journal of Business Venturing 23: 482–496

Hofstede G (1991) Cultures and Organizations: Software of the Mind. McGrawHill, London, UK

Kazanjian RK (1988) Relation of Dominant Problems to Stages Growth in Technology-Based New Ventures. Academy of Management Journal 31: 257–279

Kourilsky ML, Walstad WB (1998) Entrepreneurship and Female Youth: Knowledge, Attitudes, Gender Differences, and Educational Practices. Journal of Business Venturing 13: 77–89

Krueger NF (1993) The Impact of Prior Entrepreneurial Experience on Perceived New Venture Feasibility and Desirability. Entrepreneurship Theory & Practice 18: 5–21

Krueger NF, Brazeal DV (1994). Entrepreneurial Potential and Potential Entrepreneurs. Entrepreneurship: Theory & Practice 18: 91–104

Krueger NF, Reilly MD, Carsrud AL (2000) Competing Models of Entrepreneurial Intentions. Journal of Business Venturing 15: 411–433

Long W (1983) The Meaning of Entrepreneurship. American Journal of Small Business 8: 47–56

Lucas WA, Cooper SY (2004) Enhancing Self-efficacy to enable Entrepreneurship: The Case of CMI's Connections. MIT Working Paper, Cambridge, MA

Luthans F, Ibrayeva ES (2006) Entrepreneurial self-efficacy in Central Asian Transition Economies: Quantitative and Qualitative Analyses. Journal of International Business Studies 37: 92–110

MacMillan IC, Block Z, Narasimha PN (1986) Corporate Venturing: Alternatives, Obstacles Encountered, and Experience Effects. Journal of Business Venturing 1: 177–192

Malone JW (2001) Shining a new Light on Organizational Change: Improving Self-efficacy through Coaching. Organization Development Journal 19: 27–36

Markman GD, Balkin DB, Baron RA (2002) Inventors and New Venture Formation: The Effects of General Self-efficacy and Regretful Thinking. Entrepreneurship: Theory & Practice 27: 149–165

Markman GD, Baron RA (2003) Person-Entrepreneurship Fit: Why Some People are More Successful as Entrepreneurs than Others. Human Resource Management Review 13: 281–301

Miner JB (1990). Entrepreneurs, High Growth Entrepreneurs, and Managers: Contrasting and Overlapping Motival Patterns. Journal of Business Venturing 5: 221–235

Mitchell RK, Smith JB, Morse EA, Seawright KW, Peredo AM, Mckenzie B (2002) Are Entrepreneurial Cognitions Universal? Assessing Entrepreneurial Cognitions across Cultures. Entrepreneurship: Theory and Practice 26: 9–33

Mueller SL, Dato-On MC (2008) Gender-Role Orientation as a Determinant of Entrepreneurial Self-efficacy. Journal of Developmental Entrepreneurship 13: 3–20

Myers IB, Myers PB (1980). Gifts Differing. Consulting Psychological Press, Palo Alto, CA

Neergaard HN (2007) Sampling in Entrepreneurial Settings. In: Neergaard HN, Ulhøi JP (eds.), Handbook of Qualitative Research Methods in Entrepreneurship. Edward Elgar, Cheltenham, UK

Neergaard HN, Eythórsdóttir I (2008) The Icelandic Female Entrepreneur: Self-efficacy and Growth Intentions. 31st ICSB Conference, Belfast

Neergaard H, Krueger N (2005) Still Playing the Game? RENT (Research on Entrepreneurship and Small Business), 15th November 2005

Neergaard HN, Smith R (2004) Images of Women's Entrepreneurship: Do Pictures Speak Louder than Words? Conference paper, RENT XVIII, Copenhagen

Peterman NE, Kennedy J (2003) Enterprise Education: Influencing Students' Perceptions of Entrepreneurship. Entrepreneurship: Theory & Practice 28: 129–144

Rimm-Kaufman SE, Sawyer BE (2004) Primary-Grade Teachers' Self-efficacy Beliefs, Attitudes toward Teaching, and Discipline and Teaching Practice Priorities in Relation to the Responsive Classroom Approach. Elementary School Journal 104: 321–341

Sandemose A (1933) En flyktning krysser sitt spor. Vinters Forlag, Oslo

Sardeshmukh SR, Corbett AC (2008) Strategic Renewal in Family Firms: Role of Successor's Work Experience and Entrepreneurial Self-efficacy. Academy of Management Proceedings 1, Anaheim, CA

Scherer RF, Adams JF, Wiebe FA (1989) Role Model Performance Effects on Development of Entrepreneurial Career Preference. Entrepreneurship: Theory & Practice 13: 53–71

Schwalbe ML, Gecas V (1988) Social Psychological Consequences of Job-Related Disabilities. In: Mortimer JT, Borman KM (eds) Work Experience and Psychological Development Through the Life Span. Westview, Boulder, CO

Sequeira J, Mueller SL, McGee JE (2007) The Influence of Social Ties and Self-efficacy in Forming Entrepreneurial Intentions and Motivating Nascent Behavior. Journal of Developmental Entrepreneurship 12: 275–293

Shane S, Venkataraman S (2000). The Promise of Entrepreneurship as a Field of Research. Academy of Management Review 25: 217–226

Shaver KG, Scott LR (1991) Person, Process, Choice: The Psychology of New Venture Creation. Entrepreneurship Theory & Practice 16: 23–45

Smith R, Neergaard H (2008) Rescripting the Danish-American Dream: An Exploration of the Embeddedness of Enterprise Cultures and Discourses. Journal of Asia Entrepreneurship and Sustainability 4: 60–85

Starr JE, Fondas N (1992). A model of entrepreneurial socialization and organization formation. Entrepreneurship, Theory and Practice 17: 67–76

Steffens PR, Fitzsimmons JR, Douglas EJ (2006) A Choice Modeling Approach to predict Entrepreneurial Intentions from Attitudes and Perceived Abilities. In: Proceedings Babson College Entrepreneurial Research Conference, Bloomington, Indiana. Available at SSRN: http://ssrn.com/abstract=1263730.

Stern D (1985) The Interpersonal World of the Infant: A View from Psychoanalysis and Developmental Psychology. Basic Books, New York

Thompson GH, Dass P (2000) Improving Students' Self-efficacy in Strategic Management: The Relative Impact of Cases and Stimulations. Simulations and Gaming 31: 22–41

Urban B (2006) Entrepreneurship in the Rainbow Nation: Effect of Cultural Values and ESE on Intentions. Journal of Developmental Entrepreneurship 11(3): 171–186

Wilson F, Kickul JR, Martino D (2007) Gender, Entrepreneurial Self-efficacy, and Entrepreneurial Career Intentions: Implications for Entrepreneurship Education. Entrepreneurship: Theory & Practice 31: 387–406

Wood RE, Bandura A (1989) Impact of Conceptions of Ability on Self-regulatory Mechanisms and Complex Decision Making. Journal of Personality and Social Psychology 56: 407–415

Zimmerman BJ, Bandura A, Martinez-Pons M (1992) Self-Motivation for Academic Attainment: The Role of Self-efficacy Beliefs and Personal Goal Setting. American Educational Research Journal 29: 663–676

Chapter 12
Perceptions of Efficacy, Control, and Risk: A Theory of Mixed Control

Erik Monsen and Diemo Urbig

12.1 Introduction

Entrepreneurship involves the establishment of new organizations and the development of new economic activities. Its consequences have not been experienced before and thus are rife with risk and uncertainty. Those who engage in such activities have consequently been considered as being willing to take on more risk and uncertainty than others. Empirical work, however, has demonstrated that entrepreneurs are not willing to take more risks than non-entrepreneurs (Busenitz and Barney 1997; Miner and Raju 2004; Palich and Bagby 1995; Wu and Knott 2006). Therefore, a corresponding *difference in general risk propensity hypothesis* is not supported by research findings. Alternatively, a *difference in risk perception hypothesis* has been suggested. In other words, even if entrepreneurs and non-entrepreneurs have similar risk preferences, entrepreneurs may perceive less risk by overestimating their chances for success (Baron 1998). Differences in risk perception, or how an individual perceives patterns of odds and probabilities, have been of particular interest to economists dealing with economic decisions under risk and uncertainty (Bernardo and Welch 2001; Felton et al. 2003; Puri and Robinson 2007; Weber and Milliman 1997; Wu and Knott 2006) as well as management scholars examining entrepreneurial decision making and entrepreneurs' positively biased perceptions of their venture's risk (Baron 1998, 2004; Busenitz and Barney 1997; Forlani and Mullins 2000; Keh et al. 2002; Norton and Moore 2006; Simon et al. 2000).

E. Monsen (✉)
Max Planck Institute of Economics, Entrepreneurship, Growth and Public Policy Group,
Kahlaische Str. 10, D-07745 Jena, Germany
e-mail: monsen@econ.mpg.de

A.L. Carsrud, M. Brännback (eds.), *Understanding the Entrepreneurial Mind*,
International Studies in Entrepreneurship 24, DOI 10.1007/978-1-4419-0443-0_12,
© Springer Science+Business Media, LLC 2009

12.1.1 Risk Perceptions, Self-Efficacy, and Internal Locus of Control

The perception of risk and, thus, expectancies about the outcomes of an entrepreneurial activity depend on various other expectancies, including the probabilistic estimates of outcomes and the controllability of outcome attainment (Sitkin and Pablo 1992; Sitkin and Weingart 1995). In particular, Miller (2007) describes how the outcomes of types of entrepreneurial processes (e.g., opportunity recognition, opportunity discovery, and opportunity creation) are dependent on contingencies that can be unpredictable, unknowable, and uncontrollable. Bandura (1997) suggests a simpler model based on social cognitive theory, in which outcome expectancies depend on two major elements that underlie Miller's three dimensions: *self-efficacy*, the belief of whether or not one is able to put required actions into practice, and *locus of control*, the belief of whether or not one's outcomes depend mainly on one's own actions or on factors not under one's control.

Empirical studies in the area of entrepreneurship provide initial justification for the inclusion of both self-efficacy and locus of control in our model of risk perception. Regarding self-efficacy, Krueger and Dickson (1994) report that business executives who show greater self-efficacy will perceive opportunities and threats differently and will take more risks. Likewise, Simon et al. (2000) demonstrate for students and Keh et al. (2002) demonstrate for entrepreneurs that the evaluation of a business opportunity depends on control beliefs. While self-efficacy (Gatewood et al. 1995; Gatewood et al. 2002; Krueger and Dickson 1994) and locus of control (Keh et al. 2002; Simon et al. 2000) have been investigated separately in entrepreneurship research, their joint effects have not. Further, other sources of efficacy and control have likewise received little or no attention.

12.1.2 From a Single to a Multidimensional Model

In their Nobel Prize winning paper, Tversky and Kahneman (1992) list five major empirical phenomena that descriptive theories of decision making should deal with: framing effects, nonlinear preferences, source dependence, risk seeking, and loss aversion. It is interesting to note that of the five phenomena only source dependence has not been incorporated into more recent decision-making theories (compare, for example, Steel and König 2006). Source dependency describes the fact that the evaluation of risk and uncertainty might depend on the source, which could be a throw of the dice or a task that one has to solve based on their own competence. In fact, different combinations of sources of risk could explain why different people perceive the total risk differently. For example, entrepreneurship researchers including Busenitz and Barney (1997) and Janney and Dess (2006) have proposed that one reason why entrepreneurs and managers of large firms perceive risk differently is "that entrepreneurs face a different composition of risks than their non-entrepreneurial counterparts" (Janney and Dess 2006: 387).

This empirical need to develop a more comprehensive model of risk perception that takes into account source dependency is demonstrated by research into the additional impact of efficacy beliefs regarding factors external to the individual (Gist and Mitchell 1992; Wu and Knott 2006), as well as efficacy beliefs regarding specific external factors including collective efficacy (DeTienne et al. 2008; Shepherd and Krueger 2002) and belief in good luck (Day and Maltby 2005). For example, in their study of market entry decisions for the US banking industry, Wu and Knott (2006) are one of the first pair of researchers to demonstrate in the same study that both one's own abilities and one's expectancies regarding external factors (in their case, market volatility) affect risk taking differently.

Similar to efficacy, external sources of control beliefs should also be addressed in a more comprehensive model of compound-risk perception. The examples for efficacy beliefs mentioned in the paragraph above (i.e., internal versus external and collective versus luck) parallel Levenson's (1974, 1981) work on social activists, which proposes that external locus of control should distinguish between powerful others and chance. Further, Bandura's (1997) work on self-efficacy was strongly influenced by earlier work on control beliefs by Rotter (1966). Rotter (1966) discusses the role of beliefs about whether or not the reasons for success and failure are located within a person or outside a person, i.e., an internal or external locus of control. However, based on the analysis of sociopolitical activists (an interesting form of social entrepreneur), Levenson (1974, 1981) and Levenson and Miller (1976) argue that one needs to distinguish external drivers of outcomes with respect to chance and powerful others. This is a critical distinction as powerful others can be influenced by social action but chance cannot. Therefore, coping with dependency on powerful others differs from coping with bad luck.

12.1.3 The Theory of Mixed Control

In this chapter, we follow Krueger's (2003) call for more theory-based research on entrepreneurial cognition and contribute by developing a model of compound-risk perception. Based on the aggregated insights of the existing theories related to multiple sources of efficacy and locus of control, we introduce the *theory of mixed control*, a theory developed by Urbig and Monsen (2009) that incorporates both efficacy beliefs and control beliefs to explain outcome expectancies and thus perceptions of risk. While both constructs have been anticipated in research on entrepreneurship, recent results reported in psychological research on the interaction of both constructs have not received attention by entrepreneurship research. Furthermore, self-efficacy has been frequently investigated in the entrepreneurial context, but beliefs regarding the efficacy of external factors of success are only beginning to receive attention from researchers.

The interaction of efficacy and control beliefs as well as a corresponding integration of beliefs regarding one's own efficacy and the efficacy of external factors is at the core of the theory of mixed control. This theory considers outcome expectancies as being composed of expectancies regarding three distinct sources of risk (self, others, and chance). Beliefs about the efficacy of these elements are weighted by the degree to which these elements are perceived to control the outcome. This reflects one important empirical observation that deviates from traditional decision theories: Entrepreneurship is a complex activity involving multiple sources of risk. While the second part of this chapter deals with this multidimensionality, the third part briefly discusses a second important empirical observation: Expectancies are not only learned, but can be endogenous and thus depend on future actions of the entrepreneur. The chapter concludes with a discussion of contributions of the theory of mixed control for more robust decision research.

12.1.4 Distinctions and Definitions

For this chapter three distinctions are vital: unconditional versus conditional expectancies, preference versus perception, and single- versus multidimensional conceptualizations of sources of risk.

Expectancies regarding an event describe beliefs of the likelihood of the occurrence of an event. Unconditional expectancies are related to a single event or a set of independent events (e.g., P[A] and P[O]). *Efficacy beliefs*, the expectancy that a particular antecedent or source A will be helpful or useful (e.g., $e_A \approx$ P[A]), positive outcome expectancy, the expectancy that a particular positive outcome O will occur (e.g., $\pi \approx$ P[O]), and perceived risk, the expectancy that a particular positive outcome will not occur (i.e., $\rho = 1 - \pi$) are considered unconditional expectancies. For example, in the entrepreneurship literature, risk has been defined as the probability or likelihood of a downside loss or upside gain from the pursuit of an opportunity (compare Janney and Dess 2006). In contrast, when defining locus of control, Rotter (1966) refers to the conditional expectancy that an event (e.g., outcome O) happens given that another event (e.g., behavioral antecedent A) occurs. An event is considered to "control" another event if the occurrence of the first event affects the likelihood of the second event. We, therefore, refer to the expectancy that both events are linked by a causal relation (e.g., $c_A \approx$ P[O|A]) as *control beliefs*. This is reflected later in this chapter in our theory of mixed control and model of compound-risk perception, in which "unconditional" *perceived risk* ρ is one minus positive outcome expectancy π, which is the sum of the products of multiple source-dependent "unconditional" efficacy beliefs and "conditional" control beliefs:

$$\rho = 1 - \pi = 1 - \sum_x c_x e_x \qquad (12.1)$$

The second distinction to be made is between preference and perception. Whereas perceived risk reflects the expectancy or probability of an outcome, risk preference reflects the shape of the utility function for a series of related risky choices (Weber and Milliman 1997). Kahneman and Tversky (1979) emphasize this point by distinguishing overweighing reflecting a preference from overestimating reflecting a biased perception. Perceptions of risk and the sources of risk may not only affect the evaluation of businesses opportunities. Entrepreneurs may also have specific preferences regarding both the level of risk they are willing to assume and the sources of that risk (Janney and Dess 2006; Miller 2007; Monsen et al. in press), which can moderate the impact of risk perceptions on decision making (Pablo et al. 1996). These can lead to counterintuitive results, which the core perception-only model in this chapter does not address. For example, given that many entrepreneurs have a taste for variety (Astebro and Thompson 2007), they may choose to take a risk in an area which they are low on efficacy, but do so with the confidence that they will quickly learn what they need to know. Furthermore, given that many entrepreneurs have a need for autonomy and control (Cromie 1987; Kuratko et al. 1997; Monsen et al. 2007), entrepreneurs may give more weight to control than non-entrepreneurs in evaluating opportunities. Before we address the role of risk preferences on decision making, however, we need to better understand and have a better core model of how those risks are perceived, independent of preferences. Therefore, in this chapter, we focus on risk perception and only consider the effects of control and efficacy beliefs on outcome expectancies.

The third distinction is between single- and multidimensional conceptualizations of sources of risk. Traditional research on self-efficacy and internal locus of control can be considered single-dimensional, in that it focuses on the individual self. However, entrepreneurial productivity (Parker 2006) and persistence (DeTienne et al. 2008) are affected by both entrepreneurial ability and market forces, thus, more dimensions should be considered. For example, Gist and Mitchell (1992) propose that self-efficacy is determined by both internal and external factors. Of particular interest for this chapter, Gist and Mitchell propose that external factors can be attributed to factors "under the control of others" (1992: 196) and "luck-oriented factors" (1992: 197). Regarding dependence on others, recent research on entrepreneurship has identified collective efficacy as an important construct for explaining entrepreneurial intentions (Shepherd and Krueger 2002) and persistence (DeTienne et al. 2008). Furthermore, in a three-dimensional conceptualization of locus of control developed for research into social activists, Levenson (1974, 1981) introduces not only powerful others but also chance as an additional driver of outcomes (see also Bonnett and Furnham 1991; Furnham 1986). Closing the theoretical circle, Bandura (2001) outlines in a recent review article on social cognitive theory multiple sources of agency, including personal, proxy, collective, and fortune. All in all, this suggests that an individual's perception of risk is driven not only by personal efficacy and control beliefs but also by their beliefs of whether other people or chance rules the world and how these may help or hinder one's success.

12.1.5 Roadmap for Chapter

Given the multidisciplinary nature of entrepreneurship research and its connection with disciplines as distinct as psychological and economic research, our discussion will be along three lines. First, we briefly review the current theoretical and empirical literature on efficacy, control, and risk perception and develop in a step-by-step manner our theory of mixed control. Next, to make our theory more precise and testable, we develop in parallel a mathematical formulation of our compound-risk perception function. Finally, to concretely illustrate what our theory means in day-to-day practice, we conclude each section of the theory and mathematical development with a hypothetical story of a day in the life of "Joe the Entrepreneur," as he wrestles with the question of whether to become an entrepreneur or not.

12.2 Static Theory of Mixed Control

The theory of mixed control considers risk perception as a process and perceived risk, i.e., outcome expectancies, as the dependent variable. The theory describes how people's overall perceived risk regarding desired or undesired outcomes is influenced by other more specific expectancies regarding the efficacy and control of three generic sources: self, others, and chance. Grounded in a review of the current theoretical and empirical literature on efficacy, control, and risk perception, we develop our theory of mixed control in a step-by-step manner. Beginning with established research on the independent effects of self-efficacy and internal locus of control on risk perception, we then apply recent ideas and research on the interaction of self-efficacy and control beliefs to extend our model. Next, we go beyond the single dimension of the self and first add a general external source of efficacy, followed by a division between others and chance as independent external sources of efficacy and control. At the close of the section, we discuss how our compound-risk perception function can be used to augment current existing decision-making theories.

In parallel, in order to make our theory more precise and testable, we develop a corresponding mathematical formulation of our compound-risk perception function and theory of mixed control, which parallels the formalization by Urbig and Monsen (2009). Mathematical modeling is not uncommon in the field of entrepreneurship (Minniti and Bygrave 2001; Parker 2006) and provides a useful second language to precisely express the meaning of the text-based theory and to test its consistency and coherence (Lévesque 2004). To begin, we consider the function $f(\cdot)$ that maps a set of independent variables onto positive outcome expectancy π and perceived risk $\rho = 1 - \pi$. If, for instance, positive outcome expectancy π depends positively on self-efficacy e_s we will write that the function $\pi = f(e_s)$ is characterized by $\delta f(e_s)/\delta e_s > 0$. While π represents the perceived expectancy of a specific outcome, the function f could be considered as the perceived production of risks associated with a specific outcome. We will exemplify the general mathematical model with a specific function $\pi = f(e_s)$, e.g., $\pi = e_s$.

Finally, to more concretely illustrate and explain what our theory and math mean in day-to-day practice, we conclude each section of the theoretical and mathematical development with a hypothetical story of a week in the life of "Joe the

Entrepreneur." As the week progresses from Monday to Friday, and our theory and model become more complex, Joe's life will become correspondingly more complex and as such closer to the reality of day-to-day real-world entrepreneurship.

12.2.1 Independent Effects of Self-Efficacy and Control Beliefs

To begin, typical models for including control beliefs and self-efficacy into entrepreneurship decision making (Keh et al. 2002; Simon et al. 2000) and intentions (Wilson et al. 2007; Zhao et al. 2005) models consider only self-efficacy, only control (Gatewood et al. 2002; Krueger and Dickson 1994), or an independent combination in the form of the theory of planned behavior (Krueger et al. 2000). For example, in a recent revision of the theory of planned behavior, Ajzen (2002) defines the construct of perceived behavioral control as reflecting beliefs about self-efficacy and beliefs about controllability. This raises the question of whether self-efficacy or locus of control matters more in risk taking. Using three carefully designed economic experiments, Goodie and Young (2007) found that while both control and efficacy affect risk-taking behavior, perceptions of control played the more dominant role in risk-taking decisions. Therefore, we initially consider self-efficacy e_s and control beliefs c_s as independent drivers of risk perception $\rho = 1 - \pi$ and outcome expectancy π in our mathematical model as

$$\pi = f(e_s,c_s) \text{ with}$$
$$(1)\ \delta f(e_s,c_s)/\delta e_s > 0 \text{ and } \delta f(e_s,c_s)/\delta c_s > 0 \qquad (12.2)$$
$$\text{Example: } \pi = c_s + e_s$$

On Monday, "Joe the Entrepreneur" is not yet an entrepreneur, but has woken up with a new and innovative business idea that he is seriously considering. He believes that he has the necessary skills and self-discipline, but is that enough? Before he decides to quit his job and become an entrepreneur, he decides to wait another day, to sleep on it, and to see how he feels the next morning.

12.2.2 Interaction of Self-Efficacy and Control Beliefs

Since self-efficacy and control beliefs appear to have very similar effects and are often correlated, some consider self-efficacy and locus of control to be reflective of the same univariate core construct (Judge et al. 2003) or the same multivariate construct (Spreitzer 1995; Thomas and Velthouse 1990). However, researchers in the areas of job stress as well as general decision making have demonstrated that self-efficacy and locus of control are distinct constructs and can have not only additive but also interactive effects. In research on job stress, Schaubroeck and Merritt (1997) not only found an interaction effect between perceptions of control and self-efficacy but also found that this interaction moderates the relationship of job demands and job stress, measured by blood pressure. Given that being an entrepreneur is stressful, ambiguous, and uncertain (Monsen and Boss 2009; Schindehutte et al. 2006), we expect to see a similar interaction effect between beliefs of self-efficacy and control and the evaluation of risky opportunities (for example, Mullins and Forlani 2005; Norton and Moore 2006).

Sharpening this line of thought, we claim that the effect of self-efficacy on outcome expectancies and perceived risk is moderated by control beliefs (Bandura 1997; Krueger 2003). Bandura (1997) argues that the judgment about the likelihood of an outcome is based on two types of expectancies: self-efficacy beliefs describe the belief that one's effort will produce a required performance, while control beliefs describe the strength of the belief that the performance will cause a specific outcome. In Bandura's (1997) words, "Controllability affects the extent to which efficacy beliefs shape outcome expectancies" (Bandura 1997: 23).

Bandura's (1997) idea that control beliefs affect the extent to which self-efficacy influences outcome expectancies can be generalized to the idea that control beliefs moderate the extent to which efficacy beliefs influence judgments of outcome probabilities and corresponding risk perceptions. The idea is that if outcomes cannot be controlled, i.e., external factors control the outcome, then beliefs about the efficacy of external factors drive a person's risk perception. While management researchers have been talking conceptually about this moderating effect for some time (compare Gist 1987; Gist and Mitchell 1992), none to our knowledge have empirically tested this interaction hypothesis in the context of risk perception and entrepreneurial decision making.

Krueger (2003: 114) similarly emphasizes that the "more internal the attribution of causality (e.g., skill or effort)" and the more "controllable" the situation, the stronger the impact of self-efficacy on initiating and persisting in entrepreneurial activity. In other words, a multiplicative model suggests that if one perceives zero self-efficacy (or zero internal locus of control), the outcome expectancy will be zero and the individual will perceive maximum risk, irrespective of the perceived internal locus of control (or self-efficacy).

Our mathematical model thus needs to be extended as follows. The general formalization now utilizes an additional level of derivatives and it requires that these derivatives with respect to one variable are zero if the other variable is zero. An example of this is a simple multiplicative combination of self-efficacy and control beliefs. This model closely reflects the description provided by Bandura (1997).

$$\pi = f(e_s, c_s) \text{ with}$$
$$(1)\ \delta f(e_s,c_s)/\delta e_s \geq 0,\ \delta f(e_s,c_s)/\delta c_s \geq 0,\ \text{and}\ \delta\delta f(e_s,c_s)/\delta c_s\delta e_s \geq 0$$
$$(2)\ \delta f(e_s,0)/\delta e_s = 0,\ \delta f(0,c_s)/\delta c_s = 0$$
$$\text{Example: } \pi = c_s e_s$$

(12.3)

On Tuesday, "Joe the Entrepreneur" wakes up and once again considers his innovative new business idea. While others might be as skilled if not more so than he, Joe feels increasingly more confident that his self-discipline will be a deciding factor in his eventual success.

12.2.3 Adding External Sources of Efficacy and Control

Bandura's (1997) work on self-efficacy was strongly influenced by earlier work on control beliefs by Rotter (1966). Rotter (1966) discusses the role of beliefs about whether or not the reasons for success and failure are located inside a person or outside a person, i.e., an internal or external locus of control. Rotter (1966) conceptualized locus of control as unidimensional, such that a low internal locus of control is equivalent to a high external locus of control:

$$c_e = 1 - c_s \leftrightarrow c_s + c_e = 1 \qquad (12.4)$$

There is, however, a missing element: While self-efficacy beliefs matter if one has internal control, beliefs about the efficacy of external factors that would matter if one has an external locus of control are not included. While Gist and Mitchell (1992) were one of the first to propose the need to consider both internal and external sources of efficacy, Judge et al. (1997) are to our knowledge among the first to operationally define these external factors; which they call "external core evaluations". However, Judge et al. (1998) concluded that controlling for core self-evaluations, which includes self-efficacy and internal locus of control, external core evaluations do not have a unique effect on job attitudes. In contrast, testing the effects of external efficacy beliefs on dispositional optimism, Urbig and Monsen (2009) have found significant effects. These authors also report that external control beliefs moderate the influence of external efficacy beliefs.

The basic idea is that in such situations where external factors control one's outcomes, beliefs about external factors instead of beliefs about internal factors should determine one's outcome expectancies and perceived risk. This empirical need to develop a more comprehensive model of risk perception that takes into account external sources is likewise demonstrated by research into the additional impact of efficacy beliefs regarding factors external to the individual (Wu and Knott 2006). For example, in their study of market entry decisions for the US banking industry, Wu and Knott (2006) are one of the first pair of researchers to demonstrate in the same study that both one's own abilities and one's expectancies regarding external factors (in their case, market volatility) affect risk taking.

For the mathematical formulation of our theory we thus have to add beliefs about the efficacy and control of external factors. We furthermore include that an increase in control beliefs regarding one factor, i.e., self or external, moderates the influence of the corresponding efficacy belief.

$$\pi = f(e_s,c_s,e_o,c_e) \text{ with}$$
(1) $c_s + c_e = 1$
(2) $\delta f(e_s,c_s,e_e,c_e)/\delta e_x \geq 0$, and $\delta\delta f(e_s,c_s,e_e,c_e)/\delta c_x \delta e_x \geq 0$ (12.5)
(3) $\delta f(e_s,c_s,e_e,c_e)/\delta e_x = 0$ if $c_x = 0$
Example: $\pi = c_s e_s + c_e e_e$ with $c_s + c_e = 1$

This formula, where the outcome expectancy is a sum of efficacy beliefs which are weighted by the degree of control they have, can be transformed into the following form:

$$\text{Example: } \pi = (e_s + e_e)/2 + (c_s - c_e)(e_s - e_e)/2 \tag{12.6}$$

This formula demonstrates that the effect of changes in efficacy beliefs depends on the difference of the beliefs in the control of internal (self) and external factors and clearly separates two elements. The first term, i.e., the average of self-efficacy and external efficacy beliefs, reflects the positive direct effect of efficacy beliefs on outcome expectancies. The second term describes that the effect of efficacy beliefs on outcome expectancies and perceived risk is moderated by the difference in control beliefs.

On Wednesday, "Joe the Entrepreneur" starts to write his business plan and realizes that current regulations will make implementing his business idea much more difficult than he originally expected. Further, he does not believe that the government will make an exception for him. Thus, despite his initial self-confidence in his own skill to carry through with his idea, he is beginning to have second thoughts.

12.2.4 Distinguishing Between Others and Chance as External Sources of Efficacy and Control

At this stage, where outcome expectancies are positively influenced by efficacy beliefs regarding internal as well as external factors and where these effects are moderated by corresponding control beliefs, we have finished the development of the basic version of the theory of mixed control. There is, however, one extension that is useful and necessary to remain consistent with existing literature, i.e., external factors need to be differentiated with respect to other people and chance. For example, Gist and Mitchell (1992: 193) discuss external factors such as "group interdependence" (others) and "distractions such as noise" (chance). Bandura (2001) similarly talks about multiple sources of agency, including personal, proxy, collective, and fortune. To distinguish between the efficacy (or expected helpfulness) of other people and the efficacy (or expected helpfulness) of good luck, we introduce the more precise terms: *other efficacy* and *chance efficacy* plus *other control* and *chance control*.

Not only has literature already suggested distinguishing efficacy beliefs with respect to other people and chance, but there is also an older stream of literature suggesting differentiating external control with respect to others and chance. More specifically, based on the analysis of sociopolitical activists (an interesting form of social entrepreneur), Levenson (1974, 1981) and Levenson and Miller (1976) argue that one needs to distinguish external drivers of outcomes with respect to powerful others (social environment) and chance (natural environment). This idea of distinguishing between powerful others and chance is later applied to the economic

(Furnham 1986) and entrepreneurship education context (Bonnett and Furnham 1991). At the heart of this critical distinction is the idea that powerful others can be influenced by social action but chance cannot. Therefore, coping with dependency on powerful others differs substantially from coping with bad luck. For example, the accumulation and leveraging of social capital is one strategy to address the former and the application of a real options approach is one strategy to address the latter (Janney and Dess 2006).

Regarding other efficacy and other control, recent research on entrepreneurship has identified collective efficacy as an important construct for explaining entrepreneurial intentions (Shepherd and Krueger 2002) and persistence (DeTienne et al. 2008). Collective efficacy refers to beliefs about whether or not a group of people is able to implement required actions to succeed, and thus incorporates self-efficacy and efficacy beliefs regarding other people. In addition to collective efficacy as a source of agency, Bandura (1997, 2001) additionally talks about proxy control. Proxy control refers to the internalization of external control through social networking. Proxy control is therefore a socially mediated control, where a person convinces another person with influence to exert this influence to the benefit of the person out of direct control. In this chapter, we introduce the concept of other efficacy and control, which separates the self from the collective and respectfully refers to the likelihood that others will help the individual and degree of control others can exert regarding attainment of the desired outcome. For extra clarity, it should be noted that Bandura (1997, 2001) (see also, Fernández-Ballesteros et al. 2002), as well as DeTienne et al. (2008) and Shepherd and Krueger (2002), define collective efficacy as a group's shared belief in its capabilities to organize and execute required actions to produce a given level of attainment. In contrast, other efficacy considers an individual's own beliefs and perceptions about the efficacy of others to help the individual (compare Schaubroeck et al. 2000).

Moving forward, external efficacy and control beliefs do not only comprise beliefs about other people but also beliefs about nature, fortune, and chance. If not other people's help, it might still be fate or luck that makes things happen. While literature on collective efficacy refers to the first, entrepreneurship literature and general psychology research have rarely and inconsistently investigated beliefs in good luck (Day and Maltby 2005; see also the discussion in Urbig and Monsen 2009), despite the important role good luck, fortune, and random chance always play both in entrepreneurship (Minniti and Bygrave 2001) and in life (Bandura 1982, 1998, 2001).

At the first glance the term chance efficacy might sound strange or even like a contradiction in terms. It has, however, been used to describe beliefs of jazz artists in the popular press who practiced an artistic technique called aleatory or aleatoricism:

> Aleatory enjoyed its best run in the 1960s, when the influence of John Cage's philosophy, if not his actual music, tickled the imagination of avant-gardists the world over. However, so few composers managed to exploit chance with much success, even in timid ways, that interest in such experiments gradually dried up. Today, Mr. Lutoslawski is one of few remaining believers in the *efficacy of chance* in music, possibly because as a Pole he feels attracted to the idea of freedom in any guise. (Henahan 1988: 36)

Jazz has been used as a metaphor for improvisation and creativity in the management (Crossan et al. 2005) and in the entrepreneurship literatures (Hmieleski and Corbett 2008). Jazz is a particularly relevant metaphor for our theory of mixed control, as jazz combines individual (self) and group (other) skills and abilities with the chance of the moment:

> in jazz improvisation: group members bring a rich repertoire of musical skill and memory and seek to enhance it through the collective experience of composing and playing in the moment (Hatch 1998, 1999) (Crossan et al. 2005: 140).

Therefore, based on a rich repertoire of research on sources of external efficacy and control beliefs, we conclude that it is appropriate to distinguish at least three dimensions of control: self, others, and chance. Our formal model is thus enhanced as follows:

$$\pi = f(e_s, c_s, e_o, c_o, e_c, c_c) \text{ with}$$
$$(1) \ c_s + c_o + c_c = 1$$
$$(2) \ \delta f(e_s, c_s, e_o, c_o, e_c, c_c)/\delta e_x \geq 0, \text{ and } \delta\delta f(e_s, c_s, e_o, c_o, e_c, c_c)/\delta c_x \delta e_x \geq 0$$
$$(3) \ \delta f(e_s, c_s, e_o, c_o, e_c, c_c)/\delta e_x = 0 \text{ if } c_x = 0$$
$$\text{Example: } \pi = c_s e_s + c_o e_o + c_c e_c \text{ with } c_a + c_o + c_c = 1$$

$$(12.7)$$

Similar to the transformation from Equation (12.5) into (12.6), where only the internal and external dimensions were considered, we can perform the same transformation for the three-dimensional version.

Example: $\pi = (e_s + e_e)/2 + (c_s - c_e)(e_s - e_e)/2 + (c_o - c_c)(e_o - e_c)/2$
with $e_e = (e_o + e_c)/2$ and $c_e = (c_o + c_c)$

$$(12.8)$$

Comparing the two- with the three-dimensional example of the outcome expectancy function, only the third term is new. We thus have a formal representation where the different models, starting from self-only models, to internal-versus-external models, to three-dimensional models, are nested into each other. One can thus use the three-dimensional model and explicitly test whether or not splitting of the external factors is statistically significant in a particular context or not.

On Thursday, "Joe the Entrepreneur" decides to role the dice and to pursue his new business idea. Despite the fact that government regulations and officials may stand in his way, Joe feels that in this chaotic and fast changing world, luck plays a major role in who makes it big. Fortunately, luck has never let Joe down in the past, and he believes that luck will be on his side in the future.

12.2.5 An Alternative Full-Multiplicative or Production Function Model

Up to this point, we have simply added together the terms representing the three sources of risk perception (i.e., self, other, chance). One potential limitation of this functional form is that a zero-level expectancy regarding one source does not result in corresponding zero-level expectancy for the overall outcome. In other words, expectations associated with different sources are independent of one another, an assumption that could lead to positively biased predictions of outcome expectancies and correspondingly negatively biased predictions of perceived risk. An alternative, multiplicative variation of our TMC theory assumes that source-specific risks are not independent. This implies that a zero-level expectancy regarding one source results in corresponding zero-level expectancy for the overall outcome, independent of the other sources. A Cobb–Douglas-style function, a form commonly used in the economics literature to represent economic production and growth (Cobb and Douglas 1928), can represent this variation of the model:

$$\pi = f\left(c_s, c_o, c_c, e_s, e_o, e_c\right) = e_s^{c_s} e_o^{c_o} e_c^{c_c} \tag{12.9}$$

On Friday, "Joe the Entrepreneur" once again reconsiders his plan to pursue his new business idea. In spite of his self-confidence and lucky feeling, his serious doubts about the government making an exception for his new idea overwhelmingly darkens his original optimism.

12.2.6 Augmenting Current Decision-Making Theories

Our model of the joint effects of efficacy and control can be used not only to predict risk perception but also to augment decision-making models and theories which are based on subjective probabilities. These models include but are not limited to expected utility theory (Bernoulli 1738; Schoemaker 1982), prospect theory (Kahneman and Tversky 1979), security-potential/aspiration theory (Lopes 1987; Lopes and Oden 1999), and cumulative prospect theory (Tversky and Kahneman 1992).

Expected utility theory, as proposed by Bernoulli (1738) and reviewed by Schoemaker (1982), states that people maximize the sum of the utilities (as opposed to absolute monetary gains) associated with outcomes weighed by the probabilities of the occurrence of these outcomes. Later empirical work has revealed that people do not weight utilities with the exact probabilities, but that they attach a decision weight that is a monotonic but nevertheless a nonlinear function of probabilities, e.g., overweighing of small and underweighting of large probabilities (e.g., prospect theory by Kahneman and Tversky 1979). While those early theories assumed that people hold precise beliefs about the probability of occurrence of an event, later theories relaxed this assumption and integrated uncertainty which implies that people do not need to have precise probability judgments, for example, cumulative prospect theory (Tversky and Kahneman 1992) and related non-expected utility theories (Machina 1989; Starmer 2000).

While recent empirical work suggests that the decision weights associated with various outcomes of a behavior may depend on whether or not one can influence the outcome (e.g., Heath and Tversky 1991; Kilka and Weber 2001), recent descriptive theories do not incorporate these findings. Building on the suggestion of Kilka and Weber (2001) that control beliefs and self-efficacy might influence the decision weighting in prospect theory, our production of perceived risk function based on the theory of mixed control provides a unified framework to explain how these beliefs interact. We thus provide a rationale for Goodie and Young's (2007) finding that sometimes self-efficacy and sometimes control beliefs are more relevant. Furthermore, by replacing the single variable for subjective probability (risk or expectancy) in the respective model with our multivariate function for the risk perception, the yet unresolved issue of source dependence raised by Tversky and Kahneman (1992) and discussed earlier in this chapter is resolved. Moreover, the issue of source dependence is resolved within the context of established decision-making theories and without having to design and validate a risky new decision-making theory.

The functional form of the subjectively perceived risk can, for instance, be embedded into cumulative prospect theory (CPT) (Tversky and Kahneman 1992) by replacing the argument of the probability weighing function with the risk production function suggested above. The source dependency is then combined with those characteristics captured by the CPT, e.g., the underweighting of small probabilities of extreme events. We believe that such models are a promising path for future research and will be better able to measure and predict entrepreneurs' risk-taking behavior in situations that are more complex and driven by multiple sources of risk (Mullins and Forlani 2005; Norton and Moore 2006; Simon et al. 2000; Wu and Knott 2006), instead of the simpler examples of single-risk-source situations, such as flipping coins or strategizing against opponents (Bernardo and Welch 2001; Camerer and Lovallo 1999; Forlani and Mullins 2000).

12.3 Dynamic Perspectives

In the previous section we developed the theory of mixed control. The theory is static, insofar as it postulates dependencies between expectancies without considering if and how these expectancies may evolve over time. As such, the theory has its limitations. The following section briefly discusses a more dynamic perspective on the various ways of how efficacy and control beliefs may change over time through reactive learning and proactive behaviors and how expectations of future events and decisions can affect current risk perceptions and decision making.

What do processes look like that change perceived odds, efficacy, or control beliefs? In general, these processes can be associated with one of two classes: learning about the world and changing the world. On the one hand, one can learn about how the world works through observation and thereby adjust one's behavior as a reaction to the environment; on the other hand, one can proactively engage in behaviors to change the world. These two classes parallel Sarasvathy's (2001) two logics of thought driving business people's behaviors. Learning about the world reflects the logic of "to the extent we can predict the future, we can control it" (2001: 252), while changing the world reflects the logic of "to the extent that we can control the future, we do not need to predict it" (2001: 252). Through both processes, learning about and changing the world, one updates one's beliefs about the impact and nature of the various sources of risk. One can, for instance, learn about the nature of a new business opportunity (see, for example, Bernardo and Welch 2001; Choi et al. 2008). One can also learn about other people and especially about potential competitors. As reported by Moore et al. (2007), this is, however, underutilized by business people. On the other hand, one could try to change the world and if one believes that these changes were successful, beliefs about the world will change too. If one actively engages in social networking and supports other people (i.e., creating and maintaining social capital), one might believe that these people are also willing to help once help becomes necessary for oneself (compare Adler and Kwon 2002; Fehr and Schmidt 1999).

Both types of processes that change efficacy and control beliefs, i.e., learning about and changing the world, refer to changes about how one perceives the world. It can nevertheless happen that one falsely believes that the world has changed or learns systematically or accidentally the wrong things about the world. While it is definitely worth investigating when such learning of false beliefs occurs (see, for example, Moore et al. 2007), for the theory of mixed control, only people's perceptions are relevant, whether or not their perceptions accurately reflect reality (for a more detailed discussion of perception, we refer the reader to Chapter 1 of this book). The distinction between learning about and changing the world will structure the following discussion. In particular, note that practicing and training has two effects: learning about one's capabilities and improving them. At the end of the discussion, we highlight that as a consequence of entrepreneurs being able to change the world, the perception of risk is moderated by entrepreneurs' future decision and actions and thus we suggest one mechanism of how future choice and preferences can affect one's risk perception, which then affects one's current choices.

12.3.1 Learning About the World

Beliefs about the world can change due to interactions with the world, observations of the world, or by communicating with others who know different things about the world. Beliefs change by perceiving new information, for instance, about whether other people are helpful or not and whether one's favored outcomes have high or low likelihood of occurring (Minniti and Bygrave 2001; Parker 2006). For instance, based on an experiment, Krueger and Dickson (1994) report that executives' positive and negative feedback about past risk taking affects their future risk taking. In contrast to negative feedback, positive feedback encourages people to see more opportunities instead of threats. Similar results were obtained by Gatewood et al. (2002) in a study with students. In the context of our theory, the new information can be related (1) to self, other, and chance efficacy beliefs, i.e., the perceived extent to which these internal and external factors help or hinder one's success; (2) to self, other, and chance control beliefs, i.e., the perceived degree to which different factors affect one's outcomes; or (3) to outcome expectancies, i.e., perceived risk.

In the first two cases, changes to efficacy and control beliefs through learning lead to corresponding changes in one's outcome expectancies and perceived risks as these are a function of the two sets of beliefs. In the third case, however, one only learns that the perceived risk needs to be adjusted, i.e., one was too optimistic or pessimistic, without knowing why. In contrast to mathematical models where the outcome expectancy is not explicitly considered to be composed of multiple sources of risk (Minniti and Bygrave 2001; Parker 2006), our model explicitly considers different sources of risk and types of beliefs and is closer to modeling reality. For example, when someone unexpectedly fails, there can be multiple reasons for that failure, and a person therefore needs to figure out which of the efficacy and control beliefs about the multiple sources of risk need to be adjusted. One might learn that one is not as good as expected, i.e., adjust self-efficacy beliefs downward. There are models of learning for efficacy beliefs, especially self-efficacy (Gist 1987, 1989; Gist and Mitchell 1992) in the management literature but are beyond the scope of this chapter. For more details on the antecedents of self-efficacy, we refer the reader to Chapter 11 in this book.

Just as one can learn about self-efficacy, one can also learn about the efficacy of external factors, such as others (e.g., markets, see Parker 2006) and chance (e.g., luck, see Minniti and Bygrave 2001). For adjustments of efficacy beliefs about internal or external factors, it is, however, necessary that the person believes that these factors have a controlling influence. Generalizing this, we claim that control beliefs affect the impact that experiences have on efficacy beliefs regarding the self and external factors. This is supported by Gist (1987; 1989), who argues that those with an internal locus of control adjust their self-efficacy beliefs faster.

Instead of learning that the efficacy of various factors is smaller than expected, one might also start believing that unfavorable external factors have more control than originally expected, i.e., adjust control beliefs more toward external control (i.e., other and chance). Such changes in control beliefs are at the heart of the theory of learned helplessness (Abramson et al. 1978; Peterson et al. 1993) and learned optimism (Seligman 1991). Seligman (1991) argues that optimists and pessimists differ with respect to their perception of the reasons for past successes and failures and how these beliefs apply to future events. This concept of learned helplessness has been applied by a number of management (Gist and Mitchell 1992; Sitkin and Pablo 1992; Sitkin and Weingart 1995) and entrepreneurship (Krueger et al. 2000; Markman et al. 2005) researchers who discuss reacting to and coping with failure. Seligman (1991) develops an idea of how control beliefs may change over time and what this change might depend on, thus establishing a learning perspective for control beliefs. There are also models of learning for control beliefs (Logan and Ganster 2005, 2007) in the management literature that are also beyond the scope of this chapter.

12.3.2 Changing the World: Beating the Odds

Changes in world beliefs can also be internally driven, for instance, when people change reality and the environment around them to change and beat the odds (Sarasvathy 2001). Instead of considering entrepreneurs as belief holders who only react to their environment, Sarasvathy (2001) puts forward the idea that entrepreneurs proactively create their environment and even believe that they are able to beat the odds. At the heart of this claim is the idea that entrepreneurship is a situation under partial control. Entrepreneurs change the odds and adjust the world to make success happen. A consequence of this logic is the exploitation of situations under one's control and the minimization of dependencies on external factors as much as possible. However, this leads to high outcome expectancies only if one perceives a high self-efficacy. Changing the world is thus related to internalization of control and to increasing self-efficacy.

The idea to take over control is consistent with Knight (1921), who argued that individuals, when faced with uncertainty, either try to reduce the uncertainty, e.g., take control of the situation, or choose to do something else. Along these lines, in his work on self-efficacy, Bandura (1997, 2001) proposes that one can internalize external control through social networking which provides proxy control. In contrast to direct control, proxy control is a socially mediated control, where a person convinces another person with influence to exert this influence to the benefit of the person out of direct control. In order to take control of the situation in an entrepreneurial context, Janney and Dess (2006) recommend the application of real options reasoning and leveraging social capital to gather specialized knowledge, to reduce information asymmetries, to convert chance and other control into internal/self control, and in turn to reduce perceptions of risk. Furthermore, learning by means of increasing one's competence and thus increasing one's efficacy complements Janney and Dess' strategies that target the social environment and the uncertainties about the outside world. All three strategies aim at changing the odds associated with the internal and external factors of one's success.

12.3.3 Anticipating Future Behavior: Endogeneity of Risk Perceptions

If potential and actual entrepreneurs can allocate their effort to change the odds, then compound-risk perception will also be a function of their allocation processes. Consider, for example, regulatory focus theory (Brockner et al. 2004; Higgins et al. 1997). Building on security-potential/aspiration theory (Lopes 1987; Lopes and Oden 1999), regulatory focus theory states that people choose their options according to the preferences for gains and losses. People with promotion focus try to maximize the gains while those with a prevention focus try to minimize the losses (Higgins et al. 1997). If we assume that entrepreneurship is a complex activity composed of a sequence of decisions, then a person may anticipate future decisions in making present decisions. Since these decisions can influence the risk structure, e.g., buying an insurance policy against losses or investing in a risky but highly innovative project, decision makers may anticipate such future decisions and perceive risk differently (Brockner et al. 2004). In such a situation, risk perception is thus moderated by future decisions and is therefore endogenous. For individuals with promotion focus, we expect that they would change the expectancies such that the expectancies for gains will increase, while those with prevention focus engage in activities that decrease expectancies for losses. Since future behavior is affected by one's preferences and evaluations of outcomes, these preferences and outcomes, therefore, indirectly affect one's perception of risk associated with a complex activity. Further models and mechanisms regarding how perceptions are affected by preferences are discussed by Krueger and Dickson (1994), Pablo et al. (1996) and Mullins and Forlani (2005). At the heart of these models is the central concept from prospect theory that risks regarding gains and losses are perceived differently (Kahneman and Tversky 1979; Tversky and Kahneman 1992).

12.4 Conclusions

As we have outlined in this chapter, existing decision theories cannot account for the typical characteristics of entrepreneurial decisions (multiple sources of risk, partial control, and endogenous risk). Our theory of mixed control and compound-risk perception framework make three key contributions. First, we explicitly combine efficacy and control beliefs into a formal model of risk perception and account for the moderating effect of control on the relationship between efficacy and expected outcomes. Second, we show that the three-dimensionality of self, others, and chance should be incorporated not only into control beliefs but also into efficacy beliefs. Control beliefs describe the extent to which different sources of risk affect outcomes and efficacy beliefs describe the expectations associated with these sources. Third, we augment our static view with a dynamic perspective and explain how risk perceptions can dynamically change over time and contexts, depending on the evolution of efficacy and control beliefs. In summary, our framework can explain more heterogeneity in entrepreneurial behavior than previous models and can therefore be applied in research and practice to better understand, improve, and increase the entrepreneurial performance of individuals and organizations.

Beyond these three explicit contributions, our chapter has the potential to provide theoretical and empirical support for other model and theories of entrepreneurship. For example, our model is complementary to the alertness model of opportunity recognition from Gaglio (1997) (see also Gaglio and Katz 2001), which proposes that entrepreneurs need to be alert to opportunities, have necessary skills (i.e., efficacy), and be able to extract a gain (i.e., control). In the mythical example related by Brännback and Carsrud (2008: 69), this system includes not only the Thor, the entrepreneur or self, but also Jormungander, the government official or powerful other. Our model, however, would suggest that Brännback and Carsrud should also consider adding Loki, a mischievous Norse deity, and the Norns, the Norse demigoddesses of destiny, to their Nordic tale of entrepreneurship.

There is, of course, room for future research. Our theory of mixed control is only one among other building blocks of a theory of entrepreneurial decision making. The question for antecedents of those control and efficacy beliefs that form the core of the theory of mixed control and the question how the perceived risk finally affects an entrepreneurial decision need to be addressed in much more detail. For instance, Harper (1998) argues that four factors within the institutional framework influence control beliefs: constitutional rules (political, legal, and economic system), operating rules (nature of economic policies), normative rules (cultural and social attitudes and norms), and characteristics of the family and educational environment during the development phase in an individual's life. For a more detailed discussion of antecedents of entrepreneurial self-efficacy, we refer the reader to Chapter 11.

To empirically test the theory, adequate measurement instruments have to be developed. It is a well-established belief that task-specific measures of self-efficacy (Bandura 1997) and locus of control (Furnham 1986; Spector 1988) are more reliable than general beliefs and measures in specific outcomes. Therefore, general measures of efficacy and control beliefs, for example, those used by Urbig (2008) and Urbig and Monsen (2009) in testing the theory of mixed control in a general context, need to be refined for more reliable use in the entrepreneurship context. In the entrepreneurship literature, for the measurement of entrepreneurial efficacy beliefs (see, for example, Baum et al. 2001; Chen et al. 1998; De Noble et al. 1999; Forbes 2005), there are relatively well-established instruments. However, a corresponding set of entrepreneurial control beliefs has not yet attained a correspondingly broad degree of acceptance (see, for example, Bonnett and Furnham 1991). Future research should, therefore, focus on the development and integrated testing of multidimensional efficacy and control belief measures that are more specific to the context and activities of entrepreneurship.

References

Abramson LY, Seligman ME, Teasdale JD (1978) Learned helplessness in humans: Critique and reformulation. Journal of Abnormal Psychology 87: 49–74

Adler PS, Kwon S-W (2002) Social capital: Prospects for a new concept. Academy of Management Review 27: 17–40

Ajzen I (2002) Perceived behavioral control, self-efficacy, locus of control, and the theory of planned behavior. Journal of Applied Social Psychology 32: 665–683

Astebro T, Thompson P (2007) Entrepreneurs: Jacks of All Trades or Hobos? (p. 33). Florida International University, Department of Economics, Working Papers: 0705

Bandura A (1982) The psychology of chance encounters and life paths. American Psychologist 37: 747–755

Bandura A (1997) Self-Efficacy: The Exercise of Control. W.H. Freeman, New York

Bandura A (1998) Exploration of fortuitous determinants of life paths. Psychological Inquiry 9: 95

Bandura A (2001) Social cognitive theory: An agentic perspective. Annual Review of Psychology 52: 1–26

Baron RA (1998) Cognitive mechanisms in entrepreneurship: Why and when entrepreneurs think differently than other people. Journal of Business Venturing 13: 275–294

Baron RA (2004) The cognitive perspective: A valuable tool for answering entrepreneurship's basic "Why" questions. Journal of Business Venturing 19: 221–239

Baum JR, Locke EA, Smith KG (2001) A multidimensional model of venture growth. Academy of Management Journal 44: 292–303

Bernardo AE, Welch I (2001) On the evolution of overconfidence and entrepreneurs. Journal of Economics & Management Strategy 10: 301–330

Bernoulli D (1738) Specimen theoriae novae de mensura sortis. In: Commentarri academiae sdentiarum imperialis petropolitanae, tomus v. Translated by Louise Sommer as "Expositions of a new theory on the measurement of risk," Econometrica (Jan. 1954) 22: 23–26.

Bonnett C, Furnham A (1991) Who wants to be an entrepreneur? A study of adolescents interested in a young enterprise scheme. Journal of Economic Psychology 12: 465

Brännback M, Carsrud A (2008) Do they see what we see? A critical nordic tale about perceptions of entrepreneurial opportunities, goals and growth. Journal of Enterprising Culture 16: 55–87

Brockner J, Higgins ET, Low MB (2004) Regulatory focus theory and the entrepreneurial process. Journal of Business Venturing 19: 203

Busenitz LW, Barney JB (1997) Differences between entrepreneurs and managers in large organizations: Biases and heuristics in strategic decision-making. Journal of Business Venturing 12: 9–30

Camerer C, Lovallo DAN (1999) Overconfidence and excess entry: An experimental approach. American Economic Review 89: 306–318

Chen CC, Greene P, Gene Crick A (1998) Does entrepreneurial self-efficacy distinguish entrepreneurs from managers. Journal of Business Venturing 13: 295–316

Choi YR, Lévesque M, Shepherd DA (2008) When should entrepreneurs expedite or delay opportunity exploitation? Journal of Business Venturing 23: 333–355

Cobb CW, Douglas PH (1928) A theory of production. American Economic Review 18(1, Supplement): 139–165

Cromie S (1987) Motivations of aspiring male and female entrepreneurs. Journal of Occupational Behavior 8: 251

Crossan M, Cunha MP, Vera D, Cunha J (2005) Time and organizational improvisation. Academy of Management Review 30: 129–145

Day L, Maltby J (2005) "With good luck": Belief in good luck and cognitive planning. Personality & Individual Differences 39: 1217–1226

De Noble AF, Jung D, Ehrlich SB (1999) Entrepreneurial self-efficacy: The development of a measure and its relationship to entrepreneurial action. In: Reynolds PD (ed) Frontiers of Entrepreneurship Research. Babson College, Babson Park, MA

DeTienne DR, Shepherd DA, De Castro JO (2008) The fallacy of "Only the strong survive": The effects of extrinsic motivation on the persistence decisions for under-performing firms. Journal of Business Venturing 23: 528–546

Fehr E, Schmidt K (1999) A theory of fairness, competition and cooperation. Quarterly Journal of Economics 114: 817–868

Felton J, Gibson B, Sanbonmatsu DM (2003) Preference for risk in investing as a function of trait optimism and gender. Journal of Behavioral Finance 4: 33

Fernández-Ballesteros R, Díez-Nicolás J, Caprara GV, Barbaranelli C, Bandura A (2002) Determinants and structural relation of personal efficacy to collective efficacy. Applied Psychology: An International Review 51: 107

Forbes DP (2005) The effects of strategic decision making on entrepreneurial self-efficacy. Entrepreneurship Theory & Practice 29: 599–626

Forlani D, Mullins JW (2000) Perceived risks and choices in entrepreneurs' new venture decisions. Journal of Business Venturing 15: 305

Furnham A (1986) Economic locus of control. Human Relations 39(1): 29

Gaglio CM (1997) The Entrepreneurial Opportunity Identification Process, Ph.D. Thesis, University of Chicago.

Gaglio CM, Katz JA (2001) The psychological basis of opportunity identification: Entrepreneurial alertness. Small Business Economics 16: 95

Gatewood EJ, Shaver KG, Gartner WB (1995) A longitudinal study of cognitive factors influencing start-up behaviors and success at venture. Journal of Business Venturing 10: 371

Gatewood EJ, Shaver KG, Powers JB, Gartner WB (2002) Entrepreneurial expectancy, task effort, and performance. Entrepreneurship Theory & Practice 27: 187–206

Gist ME (1987) Self-efficacy: Implications for organizational behavior and human resource management. Academy of Management Review 12: 472–485

Gist ME (1989) The influence of training method on self-efficacy and idea generation among managers. Personnel Psychology 42: 787–805

Gist ME, Mitchell TB (1992) Self-efficacy: A theoretical analysis of its determinants and malleability. Academy of Management Review 17: 183–211

Goodie AS, Young DL (2007) The skill element in decision making under uncertainty: Control or competence? Judgment and Decision Making 2: 189–203

Harper DA (1998) Institutional conditions for entrepreneurship. In: Koppl R (ed) Advances in Austrian Economics, vol. 5. Elsevier, Amsterdam

Hatch MJ (1998) Jazz as a metaphor for organizing in the 21st century. Organization Science 9: 556–557

Hatch MJ (1999) Exploring the empty spaces of organizing: How improvisational jazz helps redescribe organizational structure. Organization Studies 20: 75–100

Heath C, Tversky A (1991) Preference and belief: Ambiguity and competence in choice under uncertainty. Journal of Risk and Uncertainty 4: 5–28

Henahan D (1988, January 29, Friday) Music: The Cleveland. The New York Times, Section C, p. 36, Column 31, Weekend Desk

Higgins ET, Shah J, Friedman R (1997) Emotional responses to goal attainment: Strength of regulatory focus as moderator. Journal of Personality & Social Psychology 72: 515–525

Hmieleski KM, Corbett AC (2008) The contrasting interaction effects of improvisational behavior with entrepreneurial self-efficacy on new venture performance and entrepreneur work satisfaction. Journal of Business Venturing 23: 482–496

Janney JJ, Dess GG (2006) The risk concept for entrepreneurs reconsidered: New challenges to the conventional wisdom. Journal of Business Venturing 21: 385–400

Judge TA, Erez A, Bono JE, Thoresen CJ (2003) The core self-evaluations scale: Development of a measure. Personnel Psychology 56: 303–331

Judge TA, Locke EA, Durham CC (1997) The dispositional causes of job satisfaction: A core evaluations approach. Research in Organizational Behavior 19: 151

Judge TA, Locke EA, Durham CC, Kluger AN (1998) Dispositional effects on job and life satisfaction: The role of core evaluations. Journal of Applied Psychology 83: 17–34

Kahneman D, Tversky A (1979) Prospect theory: An analysis of decision under risk. Econometrica 47: 263–292

Keh HT, Foo MD, Lim BC (2002) Opportunity evaluation under risky conditions: The cognitive processes of entrepreneurs. Entrepreneurship Theory & Practice 27: 125–148

Kilka M, Weber M (2001) What determines the shape of the probability weighting function under uncertainty? Management Science 47: 1712–1726

Knight FH (1921) Risk, Uncertainty and Profit. Houghton Mifflin, New York

Krueger NF (2003) The cognitive psychology of entrepreneurship. In: Acs ZJ, Audretsch DB (eds) Handbook of Entrepreneurship Research: An Interdisciplinary Survey and Introduction, vol. 1. Springer, New York

Krueger NF, Dickson PR (1994) How believing in ourselves increases risk taking: Perceived self-efficacy and opportunity recognition. Decision Sciences 25: 385–400

Krueger NF, Reilly MD, Carsrud AL (2000) Competing models of entrepreneurial intentions. Journal of Business Venturing 15: 411–432

Kuratko DF, Hornsby JS, Naffziger DW (1997) An examination of owner's goals in sustaining entrepreneurship. Journal of Small Business Management 35: 24–33

Levenson H (1974) Activism and powerful others: Distinctions within the concept of internal-external control. Journal of Personality Assessment 38: 377–383

Levenson H (1981) Differentiating among internality, powerful others, and chance. In: Lefcourt HM (ed) Research with the Locus of Control Construct, vol. 1. Academic Press, New York

Levenson H, Miller J (1976) Multidimensional locus of control in sociopolitical activists of conservative and liberal ideologies. Journal of Personality & Social Psychology 33: 199–208

Lévesque M (2004) Mathematics, theory, and entrepreneurship. Journal of Business Venturing 19: 743–765

Logan MS, Ganster DC (2005) An experimental evaluation of a control intervention to alleviate job-related stress. Journal of Management 31: 90–107

Logan MS, Ganster DC (2007) The effects of empowerment on attitudes and performance: The role of social support and empowerment beliefs. Journal of Management Studies 44: 1523–1550

Lopes LL (1987) Between hope and fear: The psychology of risk. Advances in Experimental Social Psychology 20: 255–295

Lopes LL, Oden GC (1999) The role of aspiration level in risky choice: A comparison of cumulative prospect theory and sp/a theory. Journal of Mathematical Psychology 43: 286–313

Machina MJ (1989) Dynamic consistency and non-expected utility models of choice under uncertainty. Journal of Economic Literature 27: 1622–1668

Markman GD, Baron RA, Balkin DB (2005) Are perseverance and self-efficacy costless? Assessing entrepreneurs' regretful thinking. Journal of Organizational Behavior 26: 1–19

Miller KD (2007) Risk and rationality in entrepreneurial processes. Strategic Entrepreneurship Journal 1: 57–74

Miner JB, Raju NS (2004) Risk propensity differences between managers and entrepreneurs and between low- and high-growth entrepreneurs: A reply in a more conservative vein. Journal of Applied Psychology 89: 3–13

Minniti M, Bygrave W (2001) A dynamic model of entrepreneurial learning. Entrepreneurship Theory & Practice 25: 5

Monsen E, Boss RW (2009) The impact of strategic entrepreneurship inside the organization: Examining job stress and employee retention. Entrepreneurship: Theory & Practice 33: 71–104

Monsen E, Patzelt H, Saxton T (in press) Beyond simple utility: Incentive design and tradeoffs for corporate employee-entrepreneurs. Entrepreneurship Theory & Practice, DOI 10.1111/j.1540-6520.2009.00314.x

Monsen E, Saxton T, Patzelt H (2007) Motivation and participation in corporate entrepreneurship: The moderating effects of risk, effort, and reward. In: Zacharakis A (ed) Frontiers of Entrepreneurship Research. Babson College, Babson Park, MA

Moore DA, Oesch JM, Zietsma C (2007) What competition? Myopic self-focus in market-entry decisions. Organization Science 18: 440–454

Mullins JW, Forlani D (2005) Missing the boat or sinking the boat: A study of new venture decision making. Journal of Business Venturing 20: 47–69

Norton WI, Jr., Moore WT (2006) The influence of entrepreneurial risk assessment on venture launch or growth decisions. Small Business Economics 26: 215–226

Pablo AL, Sitkin SB, Jemison DB (1996) Acquisition decision-making processes: The central role of risk. Journal of Management 22: 723–746

Palich LE, Bagby DR (1995) Using cognitive theory to explain entrepreneurial risk-taking: Challenging conventional wisdom. Journal of Business Venturing 10: 425

Parker SC (2006) Learning about the unknown: How fast do entrepreneurs adjust their beliefs? Journal of Business Venturing 21: 1–26

Peterson C, Maier SF, Seligman MEP (1993) Learned Helplessness: A Theory for the Age of Personal Control. Oxford University Press, New York

Puri M, Robinson DT (2007) Optimism and economic choice. Journal of Financial Economics 86: 71–99

Rotter JB (1966) Generalized Expectancies for Internal Versus External Locus of Control of Reinforcement. Psychological Monographs 80(1, Whole No. 609)

Sarasvathy SD (2001) Causation and effectuation: Toward a theoretical shift from economic inevitability to entrepreneurial contingency. Academy of Management Review 26: 243–263

Schaubroeck J, Lam SSK, Jia Lin X (2000) Collective efficacy versus self-efficacy in coping responses to stressors and control: A cross-cultural study. Journal of Applied Psychology 85: 512–525

Schaubroeck J, Merritt DE (1997) Divergent effects of job control on coping with work stressors: The key role of self-efficacy. Academy of Management Journal 40: 738–754

Schindehutte M, Morris M, Allen J (2006) Beyond achievement: Entrepreneurship as extreme experience. Small Business Economics 27: 349–368

Schoemaker PJH (1982) The expected utility model: Its variants, purposes, evidence and limitations. Journal of Economic Literature 20: 529–563

Seligman MEP (1991) Learned Optimism. A. A. Knopf, New York

Shepherd DA, Krueger NF (2002) Cognition, entrepreneurship and teams: An intentions-based model of entrepreneurial teams' social cognition. Entrepreneurship Theory & Practice 27: 167–185

Simon M, Houghton SM, Aquino K (2000) Cognitive biases, risk perception, and venture formation: How individuals decide to start companies. Journal of Business Venturing 15: 113–134

Sitkin SB, Pablo AL (1992) Reconceptualizing the determinants of risk behavior. Academy of Management Review 17: 9–38

Sitkin SB, Weingart LR (1995) Determinants of risky decision-making behavior: A test of the mediating role of risk perceptions and propensity. Academy of Management Journal 38: 1573–1592

Spector PE (1988) Development of the work locus of control scale. Journal of Occupational Psychology 61: 335–340

Spreitzer GM (1995) Psychological empowerment in the workplace: Dimensions, measurement, and validation. Academy of Management Journal 38: 1442–1465

Starmer C (2000) Developments in non-expected utility theory: The hunt for a descriptive theory of choice under risk. Journal of Economic Literature 38: 332

Steel P, König CJ (2006) Integrating theories of motivation. Academy of Management Review 31: 889–913

Thomas KW, Velthouse BA (1990) Cognitive elements of empowerment: An "Interpretive" Model of intrinsic task motivation. Academy of Management Review 15: 666–681

Tversky A, Kahneman D (1992) Advances in prospect theory: Cumulative representation of uncertainty. Journal of Risk and Uncertainty 5: 297–323

Urbig D (2008) Beliefs of One's Own Performance, Social Support, and Luck: A Short Measure of Generalized Self-, Other-, and Chance-Efficacy. Jena Economic Research Papers Working Paper JERP #2008-020

Urbig D, Monsen E (2009) Optimistic, but not in Control: Life-Orientation and the Theory of Mixed Control. Jena Economic Research Papers Working Paper JERP #2009-013

Weber EU, Milliman RA (1997) Perceived risk attitudes: Relating risk perception to risky choice. Management Science 43: 123

Wilson F, Kickul J, Marlino D (2007) Gender, entrepreneurial self-efficacy, and entrepreneurial career intentions: Implications for entrepreneurship education. Entrepreneurship: Theory & Practice 31: 387–406

Wu B, Knott AM (2006) Entrepreneurial risk and market entry. Management Science 52: 1315–1330

Zhao H, Seibert SE, Hills GE (2005) The mediating role of self-efficacy in the development of entrepreneurial intentions. Journal of Applied Psychology 90: 1265–1272

Part V
Beyond Cognitions: From Thinking and Opportunity Alertness and Opportunity Identification to Behaving

Chapter 13
Entrepreneurial Decision-Making: Thinking Under Uncertainty

Veronica Gustafsson

13.1 Cognition in Psychology and Entrepreneurship

"Why, you never just stop like this. I mean, if the initial investment hasn't paid off and more money is required, you keep investing until you pull the project through; especially, if you feel confident about the whole thing."

The entrepreneur spoke with deep conviction. I ought to have been surprised by the reasoning, but I was not. I was collecting data on a project concerning escalation of commitment and virtually every entrepreneur I had met told me the same thing; money already invested was never regarded as sunk costs. Entrepreneurs were quite prepared to invest additional funds, even if the future of a project was uncertain.

According to the decision theories of rational choice, this was a demonstration of sunk cost fallacy; in other words, an irrational and erratic decision behavior, which subsequently leads to escalation of commitment. Instead of terminating a failing project, decision-makers continue investments, "throwing good money after the bad." This is a common decision bias, which has been studied extensively (Arkes and Blumer, 1985; Staw and Ross, 1978; Staw, 1981; Brockner, 1992).

Thus my lack of surprise was based on solid grounds of empirical observation and explained by theories of rational choice. The only thing that could be surprising was the persistence of the bias. As I have mentioned earlier, all the participants in the study regarded their decisions to continue investments as perfectly sound.

Since Socrates, Plato, and Descartes unaided decision-making was regarded as fault-prone and inconsistent (Cohen, 1993; Dreyfus and Dreyfus, 1989). Yet, if we look closer, this assumption may lead to a problem. Despite the existence of numerous, well-developed logical theories of decision-making, which ought to yield optimal results, decision-makers in real life almost never follow the prescribed procedures. Examples from all fields of human activity abound; people, even if they have received substantial training in applying statistical rules to decision-making,

V. Gustafsson (✉)
Jönköping International Business School, SE-551 11 Jönköping, Sweden
e-mail: veronica.gustavsson@ihh.hj.se

A.L. Carsrud, M. Brännback (eds.), *Understanding the Entrepreneurial Mind*,
International Studies in Entrepreneurship 24, DOI 10.1007/978-1-4419-0443-0_13,
© Springer Science+Business Media, LLC 2009

would fail to recognize a task as requiring statistical approach if this is not stated explicitly. This finding is confirmed by numerous studies of decision-makers being trained to use analytical models (cf. Payne et al., 1988; Zakay and Wooler, 1984), as well as studies on bias reduction training (cf. Bukszar and Connolly, 1988; Choo, 1976). Moreover, according to research in biases and heuristics rational decision-making is counterintuitive (Kahneman and Tversky, 1982).

Knowing all this, I could not help asking questions: what makes rational decision-making procedures counterintuitive and decision-makers reluctant to follow them? And if entrepreneurs are so reluctant to implement statistically grounded models, leading to optimal results, how can they ever make adequate decisions? Preparing for data collection, I have reviewed several broad theoretical perspectives concerning decision-making, such as theories of rational choice, the concept of bounded rationality, and naturalistic decision-making.

13.1.1 Theories of Rational Choice

One of the best known among the early normative models of choice is called maximization of subjective expected utility (SEU) created by De Finetti (1964) and Savage (1972). SEU does not imply procedures for decision-making; probabilities and utilities are defined by a decision-maker, according to a choice among gambles, and do not guide the choice (Cohen, 1993). In other words, the decision-maker is free to choose the desirable outcome of a gamble (utilities) and assign the probabilities of the desired outcome (weigh them) before making a decision.

The model was tested in laboratory experiments through the series of gambles in an artificial environment. It imposes mathematical consistency constraints on the participants' judgments but make no reference to actual mental procedures. So, some psychologists have questioned the cognitive plausibility of SEU even when the model fits behavior. According to Lopes (1983), for example, the real decision-makers are less concerned with an option's average outcome than with the outcomes that are most likely to occur.

Normative theories such as subjective expected utility was succeeded by another approach, most often called rational. It is critical of ordinary (intuitive, unaided) reasoning and promotes more valid methods of decision analysis, originating as a system of techniques for applying decision theory in management consulting (Ulvila and Brown, 1982). Unlike SEU that provides purely formal (mathematical) constraints for decision-making, decision analysis specifies procedures: Bayesian inference (for drawing conclusions or making forecasts based on incomplete or unreliable evidence), decision-tree analysis (for choices with uncertain outcomes), and multi-attribute utility analysis (for choices with multiple competing criteria of evaluation) (Brown, et al., 1974; Keeney and Raiffa, 1976). The problem-solving strategy is to deconstruct a problem into elements, to make the appropriate experts or decision-makers subjectively assess probabilities and/or utilities for the components, and then to recombine the components by the appropriate mathematical rule (Cohen, 1993).

The main attention within this approach is focused on classification of a constantly growing list of biases, defined as deviations from the normative theory (Anderson, 1990). Researchers hardly strive to provide alternative psychological explanations (Shanteau, 1989), to study systematically how and when the postulated biases occur (Fischoff, 1983), or to develop underlying theoretical principles and links with other areas of psychology, such as problem solving and learning (Wallsten, 1983). Few existing exceptions (cf. Klayman and Ha, 1987) do not affect the general trend.

As we can see, decision-making models of rational choice, being mathematically and statistically consistent, would indeed lead to optimal results. Also in this volume, Chapter 12 by Monsen and Urbig provides an interesting discussion related to rational choice theories and decision-making as seen from the economic perspective.

Yet real-life decision-makers, including entrepreneurs, do not implement these models. Quite often their thinking is based on heuristics, i.e., cognitive shortcuts or "rules of thumb." These are simple decision techniques, which make use of a limited number of cues and uncomplicated decision procedures.

13.1.2 Bounded Rationality

Decision-makers' propensity to ignore complex analytical procedures in favor of relatively simple rules has been long known to the theorists. As I have already mentioned, such behavior has been mostly considered erratic; normative models discussed above would prescribe following the rules of mathematics and statistics in order to reach adequate decisions.

A brilliant, Nobel Prize-winning attempt to explain such seemingly irrational behavior was made by Herbert Simon (Simon, 1955). Introducing the concept of bounded rationality he postulated the following:

- Human computational capacity or intellectual ability is not unlimited. This makes use of statistically based theories of choice, which require processing the large amount of data through complex calculations quite problematic.
- Rational theories of choice and decision-making imply that (a) an optimal decision exists and (b) it can be found or calculated, usually through complex procedures. However, real-life decision-makers seldom strive for the optimum; quite often they are contented with the satisficing decisions. These options, although suboptimal, the "next best," nevertheless satisfy the requirements of the decision-maker's or the decision task.

By introducing the concept of bounded rationality Simon has firmly stated that "natural," unaided decision-making was not inherently erratic, but quite capable to produce adequate, good enough if not optimal, results. In the subsequent research Simon developed the idea of decision-makers' expertise being intimately connected with their ability to make adequate decision, i.e., those meeting requirements of the decision situation (e.g., Chase and Simon, 1973).

13.1.3 Naturalistic Decision-Making

About 20 years ago study of decision-making had taken a new turn. Following Simon's lead, researchers in cognitive psychology moved from normative theorizing (how decision-makers ought to think, as in the theories of rational choice) and compiling ever-growing lists of decision biases to investigating the contingencies and antecedents of real-life decisions.

Proponents of this approach named it naturalistic decision-making (NDM) to highlight its attempt to, first, faithfully describe the empirical process of decision-making and then to evaluate it as being adequate or non-adequate, depending on, e.g., decision-maker's goals or requirements of the decision task.

NDM is versatile and incorporates numerous models. Lipshitz (1989) views decision as enactment of an action argument. Montgomery (1983) introduces a dominance search model, and Pennington and Hastie (1988) see decision-making as constructing a plausible explanatory model. Hammond (1988) is the author of cognitive continuum theory (CCT), and Noble (1989) discusses a situation assessment model. A decision-cycles model is introduced by Connolly (1988). All of these models were developed by different researchers using different methodologies to study quite different questions in a variety of realistic settings.

Despite the great diversity of models within the NDM paradigm, it is possible to distinguish a few themes that make a core of NDM approach, as described by Lipshitz (1993):

- Decisions in real world are made by many a way, which implies diversity of form within the approach. This diversity shows that the models agree on the futility of trying to understand and improve real-world decisions by means of a single concept, such as maximizing expected utility. On the other hand, diversity of forms is partly determined by the type of decisions studied.
- Situation assessment, or a "sizing up" and construction of a mental picture of a situation, is a critical element in decision-making. Unlike laboratory experiments, where problems are defined and presented by the researcher, the real-world problems have to be identified and defined by the decision-maker. Some researchers connect situation assessment directly to selections of actions; others suggest that it is a preliminary phase that initiates a process of alternatives' evaluation. In general, the majority of models suggest that making decisions in real-life settings is a process of constructing and revising situation representations as much as (not more than) a process of evaluating the merits of potential courses of action.
- Decision-makers often use mental imagery. The rational approach presents decision-making as a calculative cognitive process (that is, weighing the costs and benefits of alternative courses of action). NDM models emphasize different cognitive processes that are related to creating images of the situation, most notably categorization (for example, of the situation), the use of knowledge structures (for example, schema), and the construction of scenarios (for example, in the form of storytelling and mental modeling).

- As NDM is context-specific, understanding the context surrounding the decision process is essential.
- Normative models of decision-making must derive from an analysis of how successful decision-makers actually function, not how they "ought" to function. According to the naturalistic approach, prescriptions cannot be separated from descriptions because (a) some of the methods used actually make a good sense despite their imperfections and (b) people normally find it difficult to apply methods that are too different from the ones they would customarily use. The last statement is, however, questionable for two reasons. First, even if decision-making processes are natural, they are not always successful, for example, prescriptions should be derived from best practice. Second, although NDM is context-specific, theoretical generalizing might make the best practice even better (cf. Hammond et al., 1987; Hammond, 1988).

Once again I tried to make sense from the studies I had read. Rational theories of choice are mathematically and statistically sound, but counterintuitive. Real-life decisions are made differently, and that for good reason. Human cognitive abilities do not suffice in making optimal decisions (Simon, 1955) because, unlike theoretical models or laboratory experiments real-life problems and tasks would be unstructured, messy, and complex. Decision goals can be unclear or competing, which makes weighting options (in order to create preference) very difficult.

However, strategic management literature (especially its normative models) is often based on principles of rational decision-making and presupposes analytical, highly structured decision behavior through planning (Ansoff, 1987; Miles and Snow, 1978; Mintzberg, 1987). Even though several schools of thought within strategy focus on various aspects of decision-making (from power to emotions [Mintzberg et al., 1998]), departing from the strict, mathematically based models, rational approach is still highly influential.

Yet, as far as entrepreneurship context is concerned, I strongly believe that the applicability of the rational theories would be limited. This approach requires copious amounts of information to be collected. Further, the information obtained has to be processed in accordance with the established analysis techniques to eliminate potential flaws and biases and warrant optimal results. This can be a costly process, as Simon (1979) points out. Moreover, a decision-maker must possess substantial skills in order to perform the analysis correctly (cf. Abelson and Levi, 1985). These factors make it easy to understand the fact that managerial decision-making often falls short of the strict analytical approach (Simon, 1955).

Still, what of entrepreneurs? Moreover, what of cognitive studies within entrepreneurial context? I knew, from my previous research (Gustafsson, 2006), that entrepreneurs vary their cognitive models and far from always adhere to the statistically based models. I also knew that studies of entrepreneurial ways of thinking had already provided important insights, theoretical as well as empirical. Theoretical grounds for studying decision-making of entrepreneurs are now being amassed within the area of entrepreneurial cognition.

13.1.4 Entrepreneurial Cognition

This is a relatively new area within the field of entrepreneurship, based on cognitive psychology as well as on entrepreneurship theory and empirical research. The term "entrepreneurial cognition" was first used by Busenitz and Lau (1996). Some of the first works in entrepreneurial cognition were done in the areas of cognitive biases and heuristics in strategic decision-making (Busenitz, 1992), and in feasibility and desirability perception, planned behavior, and self-efficacy (Krueger, 1993). Almost at the same time entrepreneurial cognition-based concepts were first used to distinguish entrepreneurs from non-entrepreneurs (Mitchell, 1994). Then Palich and Bagby (1995) used cognitive theory to explain entrepreneurial risk-taking, and Mitchell and Chesteen (1995) demonstrated how a cognition-based entrepreneurial instruction pedagogy was superior to the traditional "business plan only" approach to teaching entrepreneurial expertise (Mitchell et al., 2002).

Since 2002 entrepreneurial cognition has become a more streamlined and structured approach within the field of entrepreneurship research. A milestone event was the first entrepreneurship cognition conference hosted by the University of Victoria, Canada. Since then the research agenda, methodology, challenges, and implications have been discussed at the 2005 Second Conference on Entrepreneurial Cognition hosted by the Ivey Business School, University of Ontario, Canada. Besides, *Entrepreneurship Theory and Practice* devoted three of its special issues to entrepreneurial cognition in 2002, 2004, and 2007.

From the very beginning, entrepreneurial cognition perspective was conceived of as providing a link between the entrepreneur and the new venture creation. Unlike earlier research streams, it focuses not on the personality traits, but on an individual's cognitive behavior. It introduces a theoretically rigorous and empirically testable approach that systematically explains the role of the individual as well as the context in the entrepreneurial process. This perspective provides an effective tool for probing and explaining the previously unexplained phenomena within the entrepreneurship research domain (Mitchell et al., 2002). Following discussions at the first cognition conference the authors defined entrepreneurial cognitions as "the knowledge structures that people use to make assessments, judgments or decisions involving opportunity evaluation and venture creation and growth" (Mitchell et al., 2002, p. 97).

As entrepreneurial cognition perspective took shape, researchers within the stream were able to formulate its key research question; again, summing up the discussions at the Second Entrepreneurial Cognition Conference, the main point of entrepreneurial cognition research was defined as "How do entrepreneurial context and individual cognitive mechanisms interact to create entrepreneurial attitudes, intentions and behaviours that drive new means-ends relationships?" (Mitchell et al., 2007, p. 17). Or, putting it in plain English, "How do entrepreneurs think?" (Mitchell et al., 2007, p. 2).

The 2007 Special Issue of Entrepreneurship Theory and Practice (Mitchell et al., 2007) also provides a comprehensive and up-to-date overview of the perspective. According to the authors, the research question becomes explored in the plethora of research streams within the frame of entrepreneurial cognition. What also unites these perspectives is the strong empirical evidence that, while making decisions, entrepreneurs tend to reject (whether consciously or not) the elaborate and complex procedures of collecting and analyzing data in order to archive the optimal result (as is required by the rational theories of choice, which I discussed earlier in this chapter). Quite to the contrary and not so surprisingly entrepreneurs seem to favor non-analytical cognitive activities. Mitchell et al. (2007) point out that this way of thinking has now become a research agenda for such streams within entrepreneurial cognition as entrepreneurs' use of heuristics (Busenitz and Barney, 1997; Simon et al., 2000); entrepreneurial alertness (Gaglio and Katz, 2001); the entrepreneurial expertise approach (Gustafsson, 2006; Mitchell, 1994; Mitchell et al., 2000, 2002); and the effectuation approach (Sarasvathy, 1999, 2001, 2008).

Driving inspiration and empirical foundation for research from the observations of entrepreneurs' decision behavior in real life entrepreneurial cognition perspective has, in fact, very much in common with other approaches within the naturalistic decision-making paradigm. As we know now, naturalistic decision-making is (as goes from the name) a preferred cognitive approach for people in many areas of life; would entrepreneurs subscribe to it as well?

13.2 Thinking "Naturally" – Thinking Entrepreneurially?

Entrepreneurship research, especially research within entrepreneurial cognition, provides quite a number of empirical evidence, which testifies that this might very well be the case. Already in 1993 McCarthy, Schoorman, and Cooper found out that in investment decisions, which would seemingly induce rational decision-making, entrepreneurs were quite prone to escalation of commitment, often based on over-confidence. In 1995, Cooper, Folta, and Woo confirmed that while seeking infor-mation, entrepreneurs would, again, often depart from rational decision-making and follow principles of bounded rationality instead. Again, overconfidence played sub-stantial role in this process.

Busenitz and Barney (1997) investigated potential differences between entrepreneurial and managerial way of thinking, concentrating on overconfidence and representativeness. Overconfidence is normally defined as decision-makers' propensity to overoptimistic initial assessment of the situation and their difficulty to incorporate additional information about the situation due to this initial optimism (Fischhoff et al., 1977). Representativeness, in its turn, is a propensity to generalize based on a small, non-random sample (Tversky and Kahneman, 1971, in Busenitz and Barney, 1997), with personal experience being the most common basis for gen-eralization (Kahneman and Tversky, 1982). Not surprisingly, the authors discover that entrepreneurs are much more prone to demonstrate decision biases than man-agers. In other words, entrepreneurs do think differently than managers and, subse-quently, their behaviors differ as well (Busenitz and Barney, 1997).

Risk management is an area thoroughly investigated by rational approaches to decision-making; normative theories of decision-making under risky conditions abound and are widely used. Or are they indeed? Research shows that entrepreneurs, also in managing risks, would rely on different strategies, compared, e.g., to bank managers, as Sarasvathy et al. (1998) pointed out. When bank managers make use of the rational theories in their risk management strategies, entrepreneurs are reluctant to use them.

These findings were subsequently supported in the study of Keh et al. (2002). Here, again, illusion of control and belief in the law of small numbers (representativeness) seemed highly prominent when entrepreneurs evaluated opportunities under risky conditions.

I should also point out that entrepreneurs' reluctance to use rational theories of choice seems to transcend national and cultural boundaries. Sarasvathy et al.'s (1998) study investigated American entrepreneurs, whereas Keh et al.'s (2002) research was conducted in Singapore. Despite cultural differences, both studies came to similar conclusions, namely that entrepreneurs, while managing risks, are much more prone to use "non-rational" decision-making.

Before proceeding to discuss further evidence of entrepreneurs departing from rational (or analytical) theories of choice in their decision-making, I would like to give a thought to the following issues: Does entrepreneurs' non-analytical way of thinking lead to adequate decisions? What factors would permit such "non-orthodox" decision-making to produce adequate results, nonetheless?

Baron (1998) confirms that, due to the peculiar characteristics of their environment (notably, high levels of uncertainty, novelty, emotions, and time pressure) entrepreneurs are apt to demonstrate decision-making biases. The list of these includes (a) counterfactual thinking – the effect of imagining what might have been; (b) affect infusion – the influence of current emotional state on decisions and judgments; (c) attributional style – a tendency to attribute various outcomes to either external or internal causes; (d) the planning fallacy – a strong tendency to underestimate the amount of time necessary to complete a given project, or the amount of work to be performed in a given time; and (e) self-justification – a tendency to justify previous decisions even if they produced undesirable outcomes.

In fact any (and all) of the cognitive processes investigated in Baron's (1998) paper may be regarded as a harmful decision bias, leading to potentially disastrous consequences. Yet it may not. For example, mental simulations and counterfactual thinking were studied by Gaglio (2004). Following, e.g., Sanna (2000) the author defines mental simulations as "imitative cognitive constructions of an event or series of events based on a causal sequence of successive interdependent actions" (Gaglio, 2004, p. 537). Counterfactual thinking, following, e.g., Roese (1997), is defined as "thinking in a way which is contrary to the existing facts" (Gaglio, 2004, p. 539).

Entrepreneurs are quite prone to use both cognitions. But are they harmful decision biases? According to Gaglio (2004) they are definitely not. On the contrary, she regards both mental simulation and counterfactual thinking as useful heuristics, which help entrepreneurs to control the unknown future and to start, at least mentally, shaping the desired outcome. According to Baron (2006) mental modeling plays a prominent role in entrepreneurial thinking; it also distinguishes cognitive processes of expert entrepreneurs from those of entrepreneurial novices. Models produced by expert entrepreneurs are deeper, much more varied, and incorporate cues relevant for the decision task.

The same theme, controlling of unknown and, according to Sarasvathy et al. (2003), even unknowable future, is germane for research on effectuation. Sarasvathy was first to recognize this specific cognition in entrepreneurial setting and is now extensively researching it (Sarasvathy, 1999, 2001, 2008). She posits that "effectuation processes take a set of means as given and focus on selecting between possible effects that can be created with that set of means" (Sarasvathy, 2001, p. 245).

Sarasvathy had first observed effectuation in 1999 while investigating entrepreneurial decision-making in non-existing markets. Being required to make marketing decisions in the non-existing markets, entrepreneurs would use effectuation, rather than the analytical model recommended by marketing literature (Sarasvathy, 1999, 2001, 2008). Through a given set of means entrepreneurs can pursue one (of several) possible scenario, without a necessity to predict often unpredictable future.

Once again, I have to conclude that entrepreneurs while making decisions are quite prone to depart from the norms of rational decision-making; or, at any rate, from the norms of rational decision-making theories. A cognitive psychologist, especially a proponent of the rational theories of choice, would call such behavior irrational and bias-prone. But is it inadequate? Indeed, although this question has been already asked, it is important and bears reiteration.

13.3 When Biases Become Heuristics

What are biases and what are heuristics? Proponents of rational decision-making, as discussed in the first part of this chapter, would define cognitive bias as unaided laymen's decision-making, which departs from the standard performance as prescribed by, e.g., subjective expected utility model, Bayesian inference, and least squares regression (Mellers et al., 1998). Researchers within this paradigm would use the terms "bias" and "heuristics" interchangeably, to denote discrepancies between the natural cognitive process and the normative rational strategies (cf. Goldstein and Gigerenzer, 2002; Gigerenzer and Murray, 1987). Yet this usage of the term "heuristics" is essentially deterioration of its initial meaning. "Heuristics" is a Greek word, meaning "serving to find out or discover"; this meaning was preserved by Dunker (1945). In later times, researchers, most notably Herbert Simon (1955), would use the term "heuristics" to denote specific strategies of information search and modification of the problems in order to find solutions. Yet, since the end of the 1960s and especially the beginning of the 1970s, following the rise of statistically based models of decision-making, e.g., ANOVA, heuristics became perceived as a poor substitute of sophisticated (and rational) normative strategies of decision-making; at times heuristics was associated with cognitive illusions and irrationality (Goldstein and Gigerenzer, 2002; Piatelli-Palmerini, 1994).

So, are "bias" and "heuristics" essentially the same? Yes, both terms denote cognitive processes that depart from the norms of statistically based theories of choice. Yet, there are connotations and habitual usage. "Bias" has a negative connotation (especially in cognitive psychology literature). The use of heuristics, however, becomes regarded by the growing number of cognitive psychologists as general, common decision behavior; this especially concerns the proponents of the naturalistic decision-making paradigm.

People do engage in the non-rational decision-making, and entrepreneurs, probably, even more so. To this there is ample empirical evidence, as we have seen from the discussion in the previous section of this chapter. Now it is time to find out whether such behavior is adequate; in other words whether it leads to the desired outcomes. Unfortunately, the answer to this question is not straightforward and would depend on a number of factors:

13.3.1 Theoretical Standing

As the previous discussion demonstrated, the researcher's theoretical standing plays an important role while determining whether the use of heuristics leads to adequate decisions. Proponents of statistically based theories of choice in psychology, economics, or strategy would regard any behavior, deviating from these norms, as suboptimal and inadequate.

13.3.2 Simple Heuristics that Make Us Smart

Ecological rationality is not an entirely new notion, but the ABC research group has infused it with a new meaning: ecological rationality now means that human decisions are usually fit to the cognitive requirements of a situation (Todd, 2007; Todd and Gigerenzer, 2003; Goldstein and Gigerenzer, 2002; Rieskamp and Hoffrage, 2008). According to the views of the ABC group, real-life, "natural" decision-making normally occurs in the environment, whose cognitive properties are specific. Information may be costly or difficult to obtain (Todd, 2007); benefits of a quick decision may outweigh the costs of making suboptimal decision; in other words, decisions are normally made under constraints of limited time, knowledge, and computational capacity (Rieskamp and Hoffrage, 2008).

Making decisions under such conditions people, as often as not, would perform quite well, without a necessity to resort to laborious and time-consuming data collection and complex statistically based analysis. Simple heuristics can perform quite well under such conditions, and they require less information and computation than more elaborate strategies (Gigerenzer et al., 1999). These heuristics are fast and frugal, because they are based on the limited search and non-optimized stopping rule (Goldstein and Gigerenzer, 2002). The ABC group has investigated a number of such fast and frugal heuristics, e.g., recognition heuristic and "take-the-best"; all these cognitive strategies would ignore most of the available information and rely on a few most important cues (at times on a single cue) (Todd, 2007; Todd and Gigerenzer, 2003; Goldstein and Gigerenzer, 2002; Rieskamp and Hoffrage, 2008). Yet despite being that "frugal" these heuristics can lead to surprisingly accurate judgments (Goldstein and Gigerenzer, 2002; Bröder and Eichler, 2006; Rieskamp and Hoffrage, 2008).

13.3.3 Level of Expertise

Although use of heuristics is a natural cognitive behavior, as we have seen from the discussion above, its results can (and do) vary. Heuristics made by novices in a field are hardly much better than a guess, whereas heuristically based decisions made by experts are most often adequate (Hammond et al., 1987). In general, experts' and novices' information perception and information processing differ immensely, with experts solving problems faster and with fewer errors (Read et al., 2003; Ericsson and Smith, 1991; Patel et al., 1996; Sweller and Cooper, 1985). Parallels in entrepreneurship research for this reasoning can be drawn using studies by Sarasvathy (2008) and Baron (2006). Baron demonstrated that heuristically based decisions in opportunity identification (creation of meaningful patterns or mental modeling), while performed by expert entrepreneurs, were much more refined and adequate than those of novices.

It is now possible to make a tentative conclusion that no decision is good or bad per se, but can be either adequate or non-adequate. This depends on the decision-maker's expertise in a field; an expert can depart from the strict norms of rational decision-making and nevertheless achieve adequate decisions.

But can we, in all honesty, claim that heuristically based decisions, especially if performed by experts, are superior to decisions based on any other cognition? Not entirely; well, in fact, not at all. First of all, heuristics are often frugal; even if the decision-makers use the most salient decision cues (as experts do), significant part of the available information is ignored. This leads, as we have pointed out, to decisions that are usually good (enough) but very seldom optimal. For majority of real-life decision tasks satisficing decisions are adequate; however, not always.

Heuristics are not general cognitive strategies; they are domain-specific, moreover, designed for a particular task (Todd and Gigerenzer, 2003). Apparently, some of the decision situations would prompt use of particular heuristics, but this is a skill which has to be learned.

It should be noted, though, that the champions of naturalistic decision-making paradigm (and research on heuristics by ABC group can be included in this approach) have never laid claims on heuristics-based decision-making being superior per se. Most comprehensive treatment of the potential fit between the properties of a decision task and required cognitions is presented in the cognitive continuum theory (CCT) (Hammond et al., 1987; Hammond, 1988). CCT introduces the concepts of task continuum, where tasks vary according to their uncertainty level (from very high to very low), and cognitive continuum, where cognitions range from intuition (one pole) to quasi-rationality/heuristics (middle) to analysis (the other pole).

According to the theory, every task within the task continuum would induce certain cognitive processes in order for the decision to be appropriate. Thus, highly uncertain tasks induce intuitive cognition, moderately uncertain tasks induce heuristics, and low uncertainty tasks induce analysis.

The correspondence-accuracy principle (CAP), which is a corollary to cognitive continuum theory, poses that no decision is good or bad per se; a decision can be solely regarded as adequate or inadequate depending on whether the cognitive processes employed correspond to the nature of the task for which a decision is made. According to CAP, the ability to make adequate decisions is a skill demonstrated by expert decision-makers.

The notion that different types of decision situations would induce different decision techniques starts taking hold also in entrepreneurship research. For example, Sarasvathy (2001, 2008) keeps pointing out that both effectual and rational ("causal," in her terms) thinking are an inherent part of human reasoning. Distinguishing the circumstances when either process (or combination of both) would provide particular advantages or disadvantages is, in her mind, an important task of future research.

Relying on Sarasvathy et al.'s (2003) research, in an earlier study I investigated the connection between a task's cognitive requirements and entrepreneurs' use of different cognitions (Gustafsson, 2006); then the following conclusions could emerge:

- Situations of low uncertainty, when the information is relevant, neither redundant, nor lacking and time to make decision is not constrained, would call for rational (analytical) decisions. In entrepreneurial settings low uncertainty is associated with opportunities when both supply and demand exist and are known, e.g., opening a franchise (Sarasvathy et al., 2003).
- In situations of high uncertainty, when information is scarce (or redundant), unreliable, or dynamic, and time for making a decision is restricted, adequate decisions are made by non-rational techniques: heuristics or intuitive judgments. In entrepreneurial settings such conditions are associated with opportunities when either supply or demand is unknown or when neither is known or existent. This last case represents ultimate, or Knightian, uncertainty (Knight, 1921).
- Expert entrepreneurs do recognize the nature of the decision task and are able, to a high extent, to match their decision-making techniques with the nature of the task. This means that the skill of entrepreneurial decision-making is expressed through the adaptable behavior of experts.
- Being a skill, the decision-making behavior in entrepreneurial tasks is different for expert and novice entrepreneurs. As has been mentioned above, the experts' behavior is adaptable and, in general, in compliance with CAP, i.e., expert entrepreneurs would make use of the ample array of decision-making techniques: analysis, heuristics, and intuition and match their cognitions with the requirements of the task. Novices, however, are to a high extent prone to analytical decision-making regardless of the nature of the decision task. This is especially true as far as students of business administration are concerned (they

participated in the study as novice or aspiring entrepreneurs); we can, then, make a tentative conclusion that modern business education seems to be highly conditioning toward analysis.

13.4 Methodology or Trekking Down the Entrepreneurial Mind

In 1988, MacMillan called on the entrepreneurship research community to move away from exploratory studies (in entrepreneurship context meaning mostly case studies) and start concentrating on establishing causality. This admonition was avidly supported by Chandler and Lyon (2001).

According to Chandler and Lyon, in the last few years entrepreneurship researchers indeed started demonstrating a shift in the research methodology from exploratory, non-theory-driven studies toward ones investigating causal relationships, including experimental research.

Not surprisingly, experimental studies (though still rather rare) are mostly conducted in entrepreneurial cognition research (Mitchell et al., 2002). One of the best-known studies in the area, although it cannot be called strictly experimental, is one by Baron and Brush (1999), devoted to investigation of social skills in entrepreneurial success. The authors had videotaped a number of entrepreneurs giving presentations of their venture concepts; the videotapes were subsequently evaluated by expert judges. Another interesting and very recent study was conducted by Gatewood et al. (2002) on entrepreneurial expectancy, task effort, and performance. Most notably, this experiment utilized an Internet-based computer simulation as well.

In recent years entrepreneurship studies have greatly benefited from an array of qualitative (or somewhat "mixed") research methods. For example, the present book provides an interesting and instructive discussion of cognitive mapping in Chapter 5 by Brännback and Carsrud. A broad array of qualitative methods, such as a lived experience using grounded theory, ethnographic, discourse, and narrative approaches, or, in other words, a toolbox of novel and established methods, is presented in the *Handbook of Qualitative Research Methods in Entrepreneurship* (Neergaard and Ulhøi, 2007).

13.5 Can We Teach Entrepreneurs Make Decisions? Conclusions and Implications

As I had to realize, decision-making is not a simple and straightforward matter as it might seem. First of all, decision tasks do differ in their cognitive nature. In some situations information is readily available (or can be collected at a low cost and during ample time, available for this collection) and salient cues are neither redundant nor missing; means and variables are independent (Todd and Gigerenzer, 2003). Under such conditions analytical (rational) decision-making is not only possible but indeed would provide the optimal results. According to CAP (Hammond, 1988) under such conditions as just described the cognitive properties of the task require analysis. An example in the entrepreneurial setting would mean that if both supply and demand are known (e.g., while introducing an incremental innovation to a mature market), entrepreneurs would do best, i.e., make an adequate decision by performing market, financial, etc., analysis.

Yet in the real world, such situations are far from forming a majority of decision environments. On the contrary, many a time decision-makers are faced with either lack or redundancy of cues; insufficient time to make decision (and especially to run an analysis); and correlations between means and variances, so that they can be seen as cues to infer each other (Einhorn and Hogarth, 1981). Under such conditions rational theories of choice cannot lead to optimal results; at times the costs of collecting data would make use of such theories prohibitive. The rational theories, as we have already discussed, are not commonly applied in the real-life decision-making. According to the notion of ecological rationality (Goldstein and Gigerenzer, 2002; Todd, 2007; Todd and Gigerenzer, 2003), there is a good reason for such behavior; when information is scarce and costly to come by, when time is a pressing issue, decision-makers would fall back to using "fast and frugal" heuristics – cognitive techniques that are based on simple procedures, few information cues, and avoid complex computations.

Experts in general and entrepreneurs in particular do possess a vast array of cognitive techniques (a "cognitive toolbox," in terms of Baron and Ward [2004]) and are quite capable to match cognitive requirements of the task and appropriate decision-making techniques, as I found out in an earlier study (Gustafsson, 2006).

However, there is still an under-researched issue which is worth attention; namely the correlation between performance and entrepreneurial cognition. Heuristically based decisions, made by experts, are supposed to be adequate, because they are matched to the cognitive requirements of the entrepreneurial task and are, therefore, ecologically rational. Yet this is a theoretical inference. To my best knowledge no research has been yet made, in real life, on connections between entrepreneurial cognitions and the entrepreneur's performance. Can we observe a single decision from the moment it is made, establish its cognitive nature (Is it heuristics? Is it analysis? Is it an intuitive flash of insight?), and trace it the whole way to the ultimate result? Would this result prove adequate? Would cognitive nature of the decision change, and how it would change? And, finally, could we by any chance watch another decision, in the same circumstances, to be made using different cognition and again trace it the whole way through and compare results?

Such a study would present substantial methodological difficulties; yet it seems to be desirable, especially if we think about providing normative advice to practitioners: students, aspiring and novice entrepreneurs. In general, development of normative advice for practitioners is an important and at times seemingly overlooked contribution. Entrepreneurship research is sometimes regarded as descriptive only; however, it should not be about mere investigation of the current practice. This is a very narrow and delimiting view that sentences entrepreneurship research to always lag behind entrepreneurship practice (Davidsson, 2002).

It is possible to argue that entrepreneurship research should take on a greater challenge than that; stop being entirely descriptive and start being (at least, to some extent) normative (Davidsson, 2002). Entrepreneurship research projects can ultimately provide important cues enabling researchers to predict what will happen in the market as a consequence of demographic, cultural, socioeconomic, and technological changes. Making a prediction of this kind is the same as pointing at entrepreneurial opportunities. To study what successful entrepreneurs have done is important, but an even more important and interesting question is what could be done right now, before somebody else pre-empts an opportunity that is open at this very moment. Entrepreneurship scholars should be able to answer this question and be able to translate the answer into normative recommendations for practitioners, and this is another implication of the present study. And, finally, but not the least important, entrepreneurship educators could emphasize developing such skills among their students. In the long run one more implication is to provide "hands-on" training that makes students not only smart critics but also competent actors (Davidsson, 2002).

With the above discussion in mind, I started considering the possible implications for education and practice. How, indeed, would I make use of my research results for students? For aspiring entrepreneurs without university education? For seasoned practitioners?

Theoretical side has now become more or less clear: Discussion on ecological rationality, taken together with the mindset of naturalistic decision-making paradigm, prompts theory-based inference that uncertainty is a powerful moderator, as far as real-life decision-making is concerned. Research on decision-making in entrepreneurship supports this view; studies by Baron (e.g., 1998, 2006), Gaglio (2004), Sarasvathy et al. (2003), Sarasvathy (2008), Gustafsson (2006) are but a few examples. Decision-making under uncertainty should be (and is) specific; decisions are made under more or less severe time and information constraints and are therefore based on heuristics or intuitive judgments.

Experts can produce adequate decisions under uncertainty; according to Hammond et al. (1987) and Hammond (1988) these decisions, though not entirely faultless, nevertheless produce more small mistakes with less severe consequences for each, compared with analytical decisions. On the other hand, novices do not yet possess this skill, and their decisions are hardly better than guesses. As such, both level of expertise and level of uncertainties pose as two powerful moderators.

Development of expertise requires a lot of time (no less than 7–10 years (Ericsson and Smith, 1991)), substantial efforts, and a lot of mistakes in order for cognitive schema to be developed. The chapter by Mitchell, Mitchell, and Mitchell in the present volume provides a comprehensive discussion on development of cognitive schemata and their importance for practitioner-entrepreneurs; so far, it is enough to mention that well-developed and numerous cognitive schemata (such as expert entrepreneurs possess) provide them with a possibility to make quick and adequate decisions across a variety of entrepreneurial settings cf. Mitchell and Morse, 2002.

One of the biggest problems is that the knowledge stored in cognitive schemata, or enabling use of appropriate heuristics, is tacit. How can it be taught to students and novice practitioners? In general, how can decision-making of practitioners be improved? Business plans are important and are taught extensively, but they provide adequate guidelines in situations of low to moderate uncertainty. High uncertainty settings are not dealt with in entrepreneurship education.

Is high uncertainty any common occurrence in entrepreneurship and business? According to Knight (1921) and Sarasvathy et al. (2003) – not altogether uncommon; entrepreneurs face this condition every time when "... neither supply nor demand exists in an obvious manner, one or both have to be 'created' and several economic inventions in marketing, financing etc. have to be made, for the opportunity to come into existence. This notion of opportunity has to do with the creation of new markets. Examples include Wedgwood Pottery, Edison's General Electric, U-Haul, AES Corporation, Netscape, Beanie Babies, and the MIR space resort" (Sarasvathy et al., 2003, p. 145). Hence, high uncertainty ought to be dealt with in entrepreneurship education.

People do make decisions under uncertainty in areas other than business. Examples would include testing airplanes and other machines; intelligence and warfare; and medicine.

Could decision procedures used in medicine (e.g., emergency room decision tree) be used in entrepreneurship and business education? In this case key cues ought to be identified.

How to avoid making fatal mistakes while studying? Tacit knowledge and cognitive schemata are not normally transferred via textbooks. Yet there exists solutions, such as providing to students training in a variety of entrepreneurial settings through simulations. Another successful approach is mentoring by expert entrepreneurs, which provides students with the access to entrepreneurial scripts, thus enabling development of their own schemata with fewer mistakes and under shorter time (Mitchell and Chesteen, 1995).

References

Abelson RP, Levi A (1985) Decision-making and decision theory. In Lindsey G and Aronson E (eds), The handbook of social psychology, vol. 1. New York, Random House

Anderson JH (1990) Cognitive psychology and its implications. New York, W.H. Freeman and Company

Ansoff HI (1987) The emerging paradigm of strategic behavior. Strategic Management Journal 8(6): 501–515

Arkes H, Blumer C (1985) The psychology of sunk cost. Organizational Behavior and Human Decision Process 35: 124–140

Baron RA (1998) Cognitive mechanisms in entrepreneurship: Why and when entrepreneurs think differently than other people. Journal of Business Venturing 13: 275–294

Baron RA (2006) Opportunity recognition as pattern recognition: How the entrepreneurs "connect the dots" to identify new business opportunities. The Academy of Management Perspectives 20(1): 104–119

Baron R, Brush C (1999) The role of social skills in entrepreneurs' success: Evidence from videotapes of entrepreneurs' presentations. In: Reynolds RP, Bygrave WD, Carter NM, Manigart S, Manson CM, Meyer GD, Shaver KG (eds), Frontiers of entrepreneurship research. Wellesley, MA, Babson College.

Baron RA, Ward TB (2004) Expanding entrepreneurial cognition's toolbox: Potential contributions from the field of cognitive science. Entrepreneurship Theory & Practice 28(6): 553–573

Brockner J (1992) The escalation of commitment to a failing course of action: Toward theoretical progress. Academy of Management Review 17(1): 39–61

Brown RV, Kahr AS, Peterson CR (1974) Decision analysis for the manager. New York, Holt, Rinehart, and Winston

Bröder A, Eichler A (2006) The use of recognition information and additional cues in inferences from memory. Acta Psychologica 121(3): 275–284

Bukszar E, Connolly T (1988) Hindsight bias and strategic choice. Some problems in learning from experience. Academy of Management Journal 31(3): 628

Busenitz LW (1992) Cognitive biases in strategic decision-making: Heuristics as a differentiator between managers in large organizations and entrepreneurs. Ph.D. Dissertation, Texas A&M University

Busenitz LW, Barney JB (1997) Differences between entrepreneurs and managers in large organisations: Biases and heuristics in strategic decision-making. Journal of Business Venturing 12: 9–30

Busenitz L, Lau C (1996) A cross-cultural cognitive model of new venture creation. Entrepreneurship Theory and Practice 20(4): 25–39

Chandler G, Lyon D (2001) Methodological issues in entrepreneurship research: The past decade. Entrepreneurship Theory & Practice 25(4): 101

Chase WG, Simon HA (1973) The mind's eye in chess. In: Chase WG (ed), Visual information processing. New York, Academic Press

Choo GTG (1976) Training and generalization in assessing probabilities for discrete events. Uxbridge, UK, Brunel Institute for Organisational and Social Studies

Cohen M (1993) Three paradigms for viewing decision biases. In: Klein GA, Orasanu J, Calderwood R, Zsambok C (eds), Decision-making in action: Models and methods. Norwood, NJ, Ablex Publishing Corporation

Connolly T (1988) Hedge-clipping, tree-felling and the management of ambiguity. In: McCaskey MB, Pondy LR, Thomas H (eds), Managing the challenge of ambiguity and change. New York, Wiley

Cooper AC, Folta TB, Woo C (1995) Entrepreneurial information search. Journal of Business Venturing 10(2): 107–120

Davidsson P (2002) A conceptual framework for the study of entrepreneurship and the competence to practice it. Jönköping, Jönköping International Business School

De Finetti B (1964) Foresight: Its logical laws, its subjective sources. English translation. In Kybert Jr RE, Smokler HE (eds), Studies in subjective probability. New York, Wiley

Dreyfus HL, Dreyfus SE (1989) Mind over machine: The power of human intuition and expertise in the era of computers. Oxford, UK, Basil Blackwell Ltd.

Dunker K (1945) On problem solving. Psychological Monographs 58, whole no. 270

Einhorn HJ, Hogarth RM (1981) Behavioral decision theory: Processes of judgment and choice. Journal of Accounting Research 19(1): 1–31

Ericsson KA, Smith J (1991) Prospects and limits of the empirical study of expertise: An introduction. In: Ericsson KA, Smith J (eds), Toward a general theory of expertise: Prospects and limits. Cambridge, Cambridge University Press

Fischoff B (1983) Predicting frames. Journal of Experimental Psychology: Learning, Memory, and Cognition 9: 103–116

Fischhoff B, Slovic P, Lichtenstein S (1977) Knowing with certainty: The appropriateness of extreme confidence. Journal of Experimental Psychology: Human Perception and Performance 3: 552–564

Gaglio CM (2004). The role of mental simulations and counterfactual thinking in the opportunity identification Process. Entrepreneurship Theory & Practice 28(6): 533–552

Gaglio CM, Katz JA (2001) The psychological basis of opportunity identification: Entrepreneurial alertness. Small Business Economics 16: 95

Gatewood E, Shaver K, Powers J, Gartner W (2002) Entrepreneurial expectancy, task effort, and performance. Entrepreneurship Theory & Practice 27(2): 187

Gigerenzer G, Murray DJ (1987) Cognition as intuitive statistics. Erlbaum, NJ, Hillsdale

Gigerenzer G, Todd PM, the ABC research group (1999) Simple heuristics that make us smart. New York, Oxford University Press

Goldstein DG, Gigerenzer G (2002) Models of ecological rationality: The recognition heuristics. Psychological Review 109(1): 75–90

Gustafsson V (2006) Entrepreneurial decision-making: Individuals, tasks and cognitions. Cheltenham, UK, Edward Elgar

Hammond KR (1988) Judgment and decision-making in dynamic tasks. Information and Decision Technologies 14: 3–14

Hammond KR, Hamm RM, Grassia J, Pearson T (1987) Direct comparison of the efficacy of intuitive and analytical cognition in expert judgment. IEEE Transactions on Systems, Man, and Cybernetics 17(5): 753–770

Kahneman D, Tversky A (1982) On the study of statistical intuitions. In: Kahneman D, Slovic P, Tversky A (eds) Judgment under uncertainty: Heuristics and biases, Cambridge University Press, Cambridge

Keeney RL, Raiffa H (1976) Decisions with multiple objectives: Preferences and value tradeoffs. New York, Wiley & Sons

Keh HT, Foo MD, Lim BC (2002) Opportunity evaluation under risky conditions: The cognitive process of entrepreneurs. Entrepreneurship Theory & Practice 27: 125–148

Klayman J, Ha YW (1987) Confirmation, disconfirmation and information in hypothesis testing. Psychological Review 94(2): 211–228

Knight FH (1921) Risk, uncertainty and profit. New York, Houghton Mifflin

Krueger N (1993) The impact of prior entrepreneurial exposure on perception of new business feasibility and desirability. Entrepreneurship Theory & Practice 18(1): 5–21

Lipshitz R (1989) Either a medal or a corporal: The effect of success and failure on the evaluation of decision making and decision makers. Organizational Behavior and Human Decision Process 44: 380–395

Lipshitz R (1993) Converging themes on the study of decision-making in realistic settings. In: Klein G, Orasanu J, Calderwood R, Zsambok C (eds), Decision-making in action: models and methods. Norwood, NJ, Ablex Publishing Corporation

Lopes LL (1983) Observations: Some thoughts on the psychological concept of risk. Journal of Experimental Psychology: Human Perception and Performance 9(1): 137–144

McCarthy AM, Schoorman FD, Cooper AC (1993) Reinvestment decisions by entrepreneurs: Rational decision-making or escalation of commitment? Journal of Business Venturing 8: 9–24.

Mellers BA, Schwartz A, Cooke ADJ (1998) Judgment and decision making. Annual Review of Psychology 49: 447

Miles R, Snow C (1978) Organization strategy, structure and process. New York, McGraw Hill

Mintzberg H (1987) Crafting strategy. Harvard Business Review 65(4): 66–75

Mintzberg H, Ahlstrand B, Lampel J (1998) Strategy safari: A guided tour through the wilds of strategic management. New York, Free Press

Mitchell RK (1994) The composition, classification and creation of new venture formation expertise. Ph.D. Dissertation, Management Department, University of Utah, Salt Lake City, UT

Mitchell RK, Busenitz LW, Bird B, Gaglio CM, Morse EA, Smith JB (2007) The central question in entrepreneurial cognition research. Entrepreneurship Theory & Practice 31(1): 1–27

Mitchell R, Busenitz L, Lant T, McDougall P, Morse E, Smith B, (2002) Toward a theory of entrepreneurial cognition: Rethinking the people side of entrepreneurship research. Entrepreneurship Theory & Practice 27(2): 93

Mitchell RK, Chesteen SA (1995) Enhancing entrepreneurial expertise: Experiential pedagogy and the new venture expert script. Simulation & Gaming 26(3): 288–306

Mitchell RK, Morse EA (2002) Developing market economies: The aboriginal case in north-west British Columbia. In: Chrisman JJ, Holbrook JAD, Chua JH (eds), Innovation and entrepreneurship in Western Canada: From family businesses to multinationals. Calgary, AB, University of Calgary Press

Mitchell RK, Smith JB, Seawright KW, Morse EA (2000) Cross-cultural cognitions and the venture creation decision. Academy of Management Journal 43(5): 974–993

Montgomery H (1983) Decision rules and search for dominance structure: Towards a process model of decision-making. In: Humpfreys P, Svenson O, Vari A (eds), Advances in psychology. Amsterdam, North-Holland

Neergaard H, Ulhøi JP (eds) (2007) Handbook of qualitative research methods in entrepreneurship. Cheltenham, UK, Edward Elgar

Noble D (1989) Application of a theory of cognition to situation assessment. Vienna, VA, Engineering Research Associates

Patel VL, Kaufman DR (1996) The acquisition of medical expertise in complex dynamic environments. In: Ericson KA (ed), The road to excellence: The acquisition of expert performance in the arts and sciences, sports and games. Mahwah, NJ, Erlbaum

Patel VL, Kaufman DR, Magder SA (1996) The acquisition of medical expertise in complex dynamic environments. In: Ericson KA (ed) The Road to Excellence: The Acquisition of Expert Performance in the Arts and Sciences, Sports and Games. Mahwah, NJ, Erlbaum

Payne JW, Bettman JR, Johnson EJ (1988) Adaptive strategy selection in decision-making. Journal of Experimental Psychology: Learning, Memory and Cognition 14(3): 534–552

Pennington N, Hastie R (1988) Explanation-based decision-making: Effects of memory structure on judgment. Journal of Experimental Psychology: Learning, Memory and Cognition 14(3): 521–533

Piatelli-Palmerini M (1994) Inevitable illusions: How mistakes of reason rule our minds. New York, Wiley

Read S, Wiltbank R, Sarasvathy S (2003) What do entrepreneurs really learn from experience? The difference between expert and novice entrepreneurs. Frontiers of entrepreneurship research

Rieskamp J, Hoffrage U (2008) Inferences under time pressure: How opportunity costs affect strategy selection. Acta Psychologica 127(2): 258–276

Roese NJ (1997) Counterfactual thinking. Psychological Bulletin 121(1): 133–148

Sanna LJ (2000) Mental simulations, affect and personality: A conceptual framework. Current Decisions in Psychological Science 9(5): 168–173

Sarasvathy S (1999) Decision-making in the absence of markets: An empirically grounded model of entrepreneurial expertise. Ph.D. Dissertation, School of Business, University of Washington

Sarasvathy S (2001) Causation and effectuation: Towards a theoretical shift from economic inevitability to entrepreneurial contingency. Academy of Management Review 26(2): 243–263

Sarasvathy S (2008) Effectuation: Elements of entrepreneurial expertise. Cheltenham, UK, Edward Elgar

Sarasvathy S, Dew N, Velamuri SR, Venkataraman S (2003) Three views of entrepreneurial opportunity. In: Acs ZJ, Audretsch DB (eds), Handbook of entrepreneurship research. The Netherlands, Kluwer Academic Publishers

Sarasvathy DK, Simon HA, Lave L (1998) Perceiving and managing business risks: Difference between entrepreneurs and bankers. Journal of Economic Behavior & Organization 33: 207–225

Savage LJ (1972) The foundations of statistics. New York, Dover

Shanteau J (1989) Cognitive heuristics and biases in behavioural audition: Review, comments and observations. Accounting Organizations and Society 14: 165–177

Simon HA (1955) A behavioral model of rational choice. Quarterly Journal of Economics 69: 99–118

Simon HA (1979) Information processing models of cognition. Annual Review of Psychology 30: 363

Simon M, Houghton SM, Aquino K (2000) Cognitive biases, risk perception and venture formation: How individuals decide to start companies. Journal of Business Venturing 15(2): 113–134

Staw BM (1981) The escalation of commitment to a course of action. Academy of Management Review 6(4): 577–587

Staw BM, Ross J (1978) Commitment to a policy decision: a multi-theoretical perspective. Administration Science Quarterly 23(1): 40–64.

Sweller J, Cooper GA (1985) The use of worked examples as a substitute for problem solving in learning algebra. Cognition and Instruction 2(1): 59–89

Todd PM (2007) How much information do we need? European Journal of Operational Research 177(3): 1317–1332

Todd PM, Gigerenzer G (2003) Bounding rationality to the world. Journal of Economic Psychology 24(2): 143–165

Tversky A, Kahneman D (1971) Belief in the law of small numbers. Psychological Bulletin 76: 105–110.

Ulvila JW, Brown RV (1982) Decision analysis comes of age. Harvard Business Review 60(5): 130–141

Palich LE and Bagby DR (1995) Using cognitive theory to explain entrepreneurial risk-taking: Challenging conventional wisdom. Journal of Business Venturing 10(6): 425–438

Wallsten, TS (1983) The theoretical status of judgmental heuristics. In RW Scholz (Ed) Decision making under uncertainty. Elsevier, Amsterdam, North-Holland

Zakay D, Wooler S (1984) Time pressure, training and decision effectiveness. Ergonomics 27(3): 273–284

Chapter 14
Entrepreneurial Alertness and Opportunity Identification: Where Are We Now?

Connie Marie Gaglio and Susan Winter

14.1 Introduction

Since its inception, entrepreneurship has struggled with the academic version of a new venture's liability of newness; the field was considered pre-paradigmatic (Ireland et al., 2005b), bereft of theory or conceptual frameworks (Phan, 2004; Zahra and Dess, 2001) and so lacking in understanding that investigators could not agree on what constituted the phenomenon of interest: any kind of self-employment? New venture creation? Corporate venturing? Something else? All of the above (Gartner, 1990; Ireland et al., 2005a; Low, 2001, Vesper, 1982)?

In 2000, Shane and Venkataraman wrote an article that they hoped would redress the discipline's liability of newness and legitimize the study of entrepreneurship as an area of scholarly interest rather than as "only a research setting or teaching application" (p. 218). Their declaration of independence asserts the discipline as one uniquely devoted to "the scholarly examination of how, by whom, and with what effects opportunities to create future goods and services are discovered, evaluated, and exploited ... the field involves the study of the sources of opportunity, the processes of discovery and evaluation, and the exploitation of opportunities and the sets of individuals who discover, evaluate and exploit them" (p. 218).

Eight years later, over 150 articles about the entrepreneurial opportunity process have been published in scholarly journals including several that summarize and review the output (e.g., Companys and McMullen, 2007; Hisrich et al., 2007; McMullen et al., 2007; Sarasvathy et al., 2003). This chapter examines whether and how the apparent trends emerging from this literature are useful in terms of improving our understanding of how entrepreneurs think and reason with regard to opportunity identification.

C.M. Gaglio (✉)
Ohrenschall Center for Entrepreneurship, San Francisco State University,
San Francisco, CA 94103, USA
e-mail: cmgaglio@sfsu.edu

Any opinions, findings, and conclusions or recommendations expressed in this material are those of the author(s) and do not necessarily reflect the views of the National Science Foundation.

A.L. Carsrud, M. Brännback (eds.), *Understanding the Entrepreneurial Mind*,
International Studies in Entrepreneurship 24, DOI 10.1007/978-1-4419-0443-0_14,
© Springer Science+Business Media, LLC 2009

The Trends. Examination of the 150 plus articles reveals three trends in current scholarship: (1) the application of the principles and dynamics of cognitive psychology; (2) the contemplation of the ontological nature of entrepreneurial opportunities; and (3) the re-emphasis of the social dimensions of the process. In addition, another trend is clearly evident although it appears to be unintended: (4) a widening schism between the theoretical and operational definitions of entrepreneurial opportunities.

The focus of this chapter is to explore whether and how useful these trends are in advancing our understanding of entrepreneurial cognitive processes. As such, the literature review is selective, not comprehensive. Many interesting articles fall outside the bounds of this focus; apologies to those colleagues in advance.

14.2 Trend #1: Cognitive Psychology

Undoubtedly, the biggest trend in the past eight years has been the application of the principles and dynamics of cognitive psychology to entrepreneurship (Hisrich et al.,2007; Mitchell et al., 2007; Mitchell et al., 2004). One might assume that this inherently precipitated a dramatic improvement in our understanding of the content and workings of the entrepreneurial mind. Not quite. As will be shown, progress has been hampered by what should be relatively tangential debates occupying center stage. However, on balance, consideration of cognitive dynamics is leading to higher quality questions about the entrepreneurial opportunity identification process. The net result is skewed toward questions because the number of theoretical articles outnumbers the empirical pieces.

The fundamental cognitive question regarding opportunity identification is how market environments are represented and interpreted in the minds of entrepreneurs such that they perceive and exploit opportunities (Shaver and Scott, 1991). More specifically, a cognitive explanation of the entrepreneurial opportunity process must answer (1) whether the content of an entrepreneur's mental model (schema) of a business situation or market environment differs significantly than that of non-entrepreneurs; (2) whether the entrepreneur uses this information differently than non-entrepreneurs; and (3) whether these unique properties of the mental models (content and uses) lead to the identification of more or qualitatively superior opportunities.

Based on Kirzner's theory of entrepreneurial alertness and opportunity identification, Gaglio and Katz (2001) developed a comprehensive profile regarding the likely contents of an entrepreneur's mental model of the business world and described the probable perceptual and information processing processes an entrepreneur would use to develop new innovative goods, services, and processes. Consistent with economic theory, they assume that the broad content of an entrepreneur's mental model of the marketplace does not differ significantly from that of other market actors because information about how markets work and what is "going on" must be rather widely available or the market process could not work at all. They argue that the significant differences between the entrepreneur and non-entrepreneur lay in what each chooses to notice, then in the importance or weight each gives to new information, and, finally, in the meaning each creates. The authors further argue that these differences are driven by the fact that the entrepreneur builds his or her mental model of the marketplace through the use of another mental model (alertness) which directs the entrepreneur's attention to any kind of stimuli or cue of change or anomaly and then directs interpretation of this information in atypical ways. Gaglio and Katz characterize alertness as a chronic schema meaning that the entrepreneur uses it habitually to the point where it is second nature, seemingly unconscious, unless someone else calls specific attention to it. The habitual or unconscious deployment creates the impression that alertness is effortless.

The attempt to translate entrepreneurial alertness into a cognitive process has not been successful to date as evidenced by the fact that far more scholarly attention has been given to a relatively tangential issue – the question of effort – than to more essential cognitive issues such as (1) whether entrepreneurs and non-entrepreneurs differ in the perception and interpretation of change and anomalies signals such as those Schumpeter (1950) and Drucker (1985) described; (2) whether entrepreneurs and non-entrepreneurs differ in the content of their schema about their industries, societies, what is going on, and so forth; (3) whether there are important behavioral differences in the cognitive operations performed on new and existing schema content; and (4) whether certain kinds of cognitive operations are more useful and reliable for transforming schema content into ideas for innovative products and services and ideas in action.

14.2.1 Search Effort

Unfortunately, Kirzner (1979) himself led the field to this detour with his definition of alertness as "the ability to notice without search opportunities that have hitherto been overlooked" (p. 48); the characterization conveys an image of pleasant strolls in a sunny meadow where one meets the opportunity leprechaun or as Demsetz (1983) phrased it, dumb luck. The face validity of such a conceptualization is preposterous and runs counter to the anecdotal evidence of people deliberately looking for business opportunities (Koller, 1988; Peterson, 1988).

Fiet (2007) takes the anecdotal evidence one step further by elaborating on the likely sequence of events and decision points involved in searches through his development of the theory of constrained systematic search. Attempting to be consistent with the cognitive principles of miserliness and bounded rationality, which state that people usually do the minimum cognitive work necessary to take action, he assumes that people who are searching for new venture ideas limit themselves to information sources with which they are familiar, usually because of prior experience and knowledge. There is empirical work demonstrating that constrained systematic search can be taught (DeTienne and Chandler, 2004; Fiet, 2002) and there is some evidence that some serial entrepreneurs do engage in systematic search (Fiet et al., 2004). These findings and the earlier anecdotal evidence led to the conclusion that deliberate searching is a valid route to opportunity identification.

However, evidence in support of systematic search does not by itself rule out the possibility of effortless search. Gaglio and Katz (2001) noted that the lack of effort could be attributed to the entrepreneur's use of a chronic schema. Shane (2000) proposes that effortless discovery can be explained as the result of the interaction between a person's idiosyncratic knowledge store and market events. Essentially, a person's background allows (or inhibits) him or her to apprehend the value of new information (the market event) and thus can notice without search. He offers evidence from a quasi-experiment demonstrating that idiosyncrasies in participants' prior knowledge led each to interpret information about a new invention differently; these differences led to different results. In some cases, participants did not discover any business concept based on the new invention but other participants did and in each of those cases, the concept was different from those identified by others. Unfortunately, his study does not really address the question of search versus discovery (his participants were given the information about the market event) so much as demonstrate that participants' prior knowledge (existing mental models) directs interpretation of information. This is important evidence, just not germane to the question of effort.

The debate between deliberate search and effortless discovery sparked a flurry of research activity; what does the evidence show? First, *we have evidence that people scan their environments* and that some entrepreneurs feel that actively searching for new ideas is essential to their success (Fiet et al., 2004; Ko and Butler, 2007). In at least some instances, the intensity of the search effort is positively associated with the number of potential business ideas articulated (Ucbasaran et al., 2008). It appears that the *motivation for the search – internal versus external – does not have an impact* on the success of the venture (Singh et al., 2008).

Second, amount of scanning and what one scans appear to depend in some measure upon the degree of change or turbulence (Stewart et al., 2008; Tang, 2008a) the entrepreneur perceives in his or her social, technological, economic, or personal environment. The area(s) perceived most volatile will be scanned more frequently than more stable areas. Most importantly, *search activity appears to be heavily influenced by the ease with which information is readily available* (Stewart et al., 2008). Regardless of environmental circumstances and degree of turbulence, if information is readily accessible, deliberate scanning is more likely. If the information is perceived to be inaccessible or difficult to obtain, active search is less likely to occur. This finding is an illustration of the principle of cognitive miserliness.

However, there is other evidence indicating that when an entrepreneur perceives his or her social and economic environment to be flush with resources to support new ventures, he or she is less likely to engage in deliberate search (Tang, 2008b) but rather allow discovery to occur in time. *The decreased likelihood of scanning when information is not easily accessible and the likelihood to use discovery in munificent environments suggest that entrepreneurs are probably using the availability heuristic (shortcut) to drive this stage of the opportunity identification process.*

Not surprisingly, at least one investigator (Berglund, 2007) found that, in response to the same market stimuli (rise of the mobile phone) some entrepreneurs used active search methods while others conformed to the discovery process. Indeed, a consensus appears to be forming within the discipline that both deliberate search and effortless discovery have a role in the opportunity identification process and if there is a salient question, it is which, when (Ardichvili et al., 2003; Casson and Wadeson, 2007; Fiet, 2007; Tang and Khan, 2007; Yu, 2001)? However, it would be more useful to the field if scholars can abandon this tangent altogether and concentrate on the more important questions such as how the availability heuristic affects the opportunity identification process (keeping in mind it could have a positive effect) or focus on the fundamental questions about the cognitive processes associated with opportunity identification that were enumerated earlier. For example, does the content of an entrepreneur's mental model (schema) of a business situation or market environment differ significantly from that of non-entrepreneurs?

14.2.2 Mental Models – Content

Shane's quasi-experiment demonstrated that differences in pre-existing mental models influence how new information is interpreted. This underscores the need to understand these mental models: their content, how they are formed, how they influence interpretation of new information, and whether and how they themselves are changed. Yet very little is known about an entrepreneur's mental model which, in the entrepreneurship literature, is also called schema (Gaglio and Katz, 2001), script (Chiasson and Saunders, 2005; Stewart et al., 2008), human capital (Fiet, 2007), or the mean-ends framework (Kirzner, 1979).

In one of the few empirical pieces directed at schema content, Baron and Ensley (2006) compared the differences between novice and serial entrepreneurs' schema regarding the opportunity to start a new venture. The differences in content clearly reflect experience as a venture founder. Serial entrepreneurs are more likely to mention and give weight to factors regarding the execution of a successful business: speed and ease of generating cash flow, ability to use networks, and so forth while novice entrepreneurs give more weight to the novelty and quality of the product or service idea. Bishop and Nixon (2006) compared the evaluation criteria of experienced venture capitalists and pre-nascent entrepreneurs and found that both groups essentially used the same criteria but the importance given to each item differed significantly by group.

Schema or mental models are representations of knowledge and so the recent empirical attention given to the influence of human capital on the opportunity identification process is relevant to this discussion. Researchers (Corbett, 2005; Fiet, 2007; Tang, 2008a; Shepherd and DeTienne, 2005; Ucbasaran et al., 2008) have typically distinguished between general human capital (generalizable knowledge acquired through education, life experience, social relations, and so forth) and specific human capital (technological experience, industry expertise, and so on). The findings indicate that the greater the amount of knowledge, whether general or specific, the higher the number of opportunities study participants report (Corbett, 2005; Ucbasaran et al., 2008). However, specific knowledge, particularly knowledge about customer problems, appears to influence the opportunities' degree of innovation (Shepherd and DeTienne, 2005). There is also some evidence that specific knowledge influences the decision to pursue opportunities (Ucbasaran et al.,2008) although this effect appears to be mediated by the interaction of an individual's learning style and the situational demands (Dimov, 2007).

The evidence raises more questions than it supports or disconfirms any theoretical position. The questions are especially useful for improving our understanding of the opportunity identification process and so deserve to be highlighted. First, the evidence indicates that, quite simply, *in order to discover or create opportunities, entrepreneurs have to know something; knowledge matters.* What do entrepreneurs need to know? *Efforts should be made to specify and elaborate on the contents of general knowledge and specific knowledge* much as Baron and Ensley did for the mental model of an opportunity so that we can understand what entrepreneurs need to know.

To begin this effort, it is possible to make logical inferences about what should be in an entrepreneur's mental model of the marketplace. For example, if alertness requires environmental munificence for deployment, then the entrepreneur must have a mental model of munificence to guide the decision regarding the activation of alertness. Tang (2008b) suggests this model probably includes concepts about a diversified economy; about other entrepreneurs as role models; about solid financial communities; about government incentives for businesses; about supporting infrastructure; and about the availability of skilled resources. Hsieh et al. (2007) note that the potential for gain triggers alertness; therefore, an entrepreneur must have a model that includes concepts about gain and about the characteristics of high gain potential markets. Gaglio and Katz (2001) describe a constellation of interacting mental models that depict the society's economic system (roles, rules, criteria); the society's sociopolitical culture (trends, tastes, technologies), as well as a fairly extensive model of how and why the industry of interest works the way it does. Finally, those who emphasize the role of prior knowledge mention that the entrepreneur has unique knowledge of markets; ways to serve markets; customer problems or needs; long-run trends; depletion of resources; and gaps (Ardichvili et al., 2003; Berglund, 2007; Casson and Wadeson, 2007; Ko and Butler, 2007; Shane, 2000).

It is inconceivable that all this information has equal weight although the cognitive psychology of expertise (Chase and Simon, 1973; Chi et al., 1982) indicates that it is the way in which information is organized in the mental model, particularly the number of connections made with other mental models, that matters most. Krueger (2007) recently challenged fellow scholars to move beyond our current stage of labeling and investigate the deep structures and the relationships among them. While Kruger is prescient in the general direction the discipline must take, it would be most useful to first test our implicit assumptions about schema content.

The association between the greater the amount of knowledge, the higher the number of opportunities reported also suggests that the issue of general intelligence, IQ, should be included in future studies rather than considered a third rail (Hisrich et al., 2007).

Third, *the fact that specific knowledge appears to have greater influence on the decision to pursue suggests that investigators should start to examine the mental models of different stages of the opportunity identification process* and not just the end point. Again, it becomes a question of what, when does one mental model facilitate or hinder the entire process from idea to venture or do different mental models come into play at different stages or perhaps have greater influence at difference stages, as the evidence suggests? Perhaps the discipline is doing itself a disservice by investigating the opportunity identification process in terms of its end point, the opportunity to start a business?

Finally, the evidence *that the kind of specific knowledge influences an opportunity's degree of innovation* suggests the need *to begin distinguishing among types of opportunities* (radical, innovative, imitative, and so forth) because it is highly likely that cognitive processes will vary by type of opportunity in important ways. Fiet's (2007) scale of innovation is a useful starting point as an operational measure.

14.2.3 Mental Models – Creation and Change

Kirzner (1979) claims that the quintessential moment of entrepreneurship and opportunity identification is the entrepreneur's decision to break the existing means – ends framework (mental model) and create another one that incorporates the new information, the new understanding, the new meaning and value, the new opportunity. Other entrepreneurship scholars have noted the importance of new interpretations or sense making in the opportunity identification process (Dutta and Crossan, 2005; Sarason et al., 2006a), and indeed Krueger's (2007) assessment of such deliberations led him to conclude that understanding how these models and other beliefs develop and change is the urgent scholarly question.

Based on the principles of cognitive dynamics, several skills and methods regarding schema alteration have been proposed: pattern recognition (Baron, 2006); framing and reframing (Lumpkin and Lichtenstein, 2005; Ward, 2004); bricolage (Baker and Nelson, 2005); and counterfactual thinking (Gaglio, 2004). We beg our fellow scholars not to consider whether these skills and techniques are used; at least check, entrepreneurs are human and rely on human cognitive processes. It would be more useful for the field to focus on whether entrepreneurs use these skills and techniques differently than non-entrepreneurs and if so, to what effect and under what circumstances. Let us start with an assumption that the useful questions about changing mental models are questions of which, when.

Pattern Recognition. The discussion regarding search versus discovery raises the question of what people do with the new information they seek out or encounter, particularly if the new information represents something unusual or atypical. The most obvious choices are to ignore it or incorporate it by revising their existing mental models or creating entirely new ones (Gaglio and Katz, 2001). Cognitive processes such as pattern recognition can help explain how people make sense of information when they choose not to ignore it. Pattern recognition (Baron, 2006) involves recognizing or creating relationships between currently unrelated pieces of information (e.g., the new information just acquired) in such a way that the relationship has meaning, can be connected to other mental models, and can guide action. For example, an alert entrepreneur comforting his or her small child who is crying after seeing desolate polar bears floating on shrinking icebergs might also create a pattern or connect the dots to the news heard on the Weather Channel a week earlier about the lack of rain in California resulting in government officials declaring a drought and start looking into desalinization processes and water right-of-ways.

There is evidence that *some entrepreneurs perceive themselves as looking to connect the dots among diverse pieces of information* (Baron, 2006: Ko and Butler, 2007), but this is not especially surprising because everyone engages in pattern recognition. It would be more useful to know whether entrepreneurs use the process differently such that it results in opportunity identification. Perhaps entrepreneurs are more likely to apply their pattern recognition skills to market environments while non-entrepreneurs apply their skills to other areas of life. If alertness is a chronic schema that directs attention to the unusual, then perhaps entrepreneurs simply look to connect the dots among these anomalies earlier and more often and perhaps even faster than non-entrepreneurs. It is also possible that connecting the dots among diverse pieces of information suggests that entrepreneurs are probably minimizing (perhaps even ignoring) the initial context in which the information was presented or uncovered, that is, the way in which the information was originally framed.

Framing. Cognitive psychologists (Fiske and Taylor, 1991) note that the way in which information is presented or framed influences which mental models an individual will recall from memory and use for sense making and decision-making. The persistence and power of the effects of information framing are well documented (Kuhberger, 1998). Evidence from three recent studies suggests some interesting and important directions for research about entrepreneurial cognition.

In an attempt to create the moment of Kirzner's pure entrepreneurial discovery several economists (Demmert and Klein, 2003; Kitzmann and Schiereck, 2005) devised a cute little experiment in problem-solving that allowed for obvious solutions and a clearly "out-of-the-box" solution that could be considered a Kirznerian alertness-type insight. Being economists, they focused on the influence of financial incentives in producing the alertness response; what they discovered was the power of framing. Their instructions presented participants with a problem to solve; the experimenters learned that even those participants who provided the out-of-the-box solution reported that they perceived the situation as simply a problem to be solved. None of the participants considered framing the situation as anything else even when prompted during debriefing. While the experimenters bemoan their failure to operationalize Kirznerian discovery, they successfully demonstrate the power of framing. Actually, it is rather reassuring to learn that alertness does not require events to be framed as extraordinary in order to be evoked and used to create an effective and innovative solution.

However, and more importantly for entrepreneurship scholars, these experiments also reveal that there are limits to framing effects. The participants who had the out-of-the-box insight had to apprehend that a small step stool, once inverted, could be used to carry water. To do so, they had to see beyond the initial label (frame) for the step stool. Cognitive psychologists explain that these participants did not suffer from functional fixedness, a cognitive bias to perceive objects and information in only one way or in only one relationship based on how first presented or encountered (Coleman, 2001). In this experiment, most people saw the step stool and once they mentally labeled it, they could not imagine any other use except to stand on it (which would not help solve the problem). On the other hand, the alert respondents did not allow the object's label to limit their imagined uses for the stool. In everyday life, functional fixedness has a purpose (effectiveness and efficiency in response) but it is considered a major barrier to creative thinking and solutions (Stein, 1989).

Ward (2004) examined the influence of initial framing on the solution's degree of innovation. He found that when problems are defined in abstract terms, solutions tend to be more innovative while problems that are defined in concrete terms tend to result in more familiar kinds of solutions. He theorizes that the presentation in concrete terms brings to mind very specific models (exemplars) that then limit thinking. Exemplars can be considered an example of functional fixedness for mental objects.

Thinking about framing as a kind of functional fixedness suggests that Yate's (2000) conceptualization of entrepreneurial alertness may be the most useful in guiding future investigations in alertness and opportunity identification.Yates believes that alert entrepreneurs simply understand and perhaps even assume that their beliefs about the way things work (the means – ends relationships or cause – effect connections in mental models) are probably incorrect and/or incomplete. Yate's entrepreneurs remain "alert" to the possibility that they may be surprised in any situation, that they may discover new relevant information that will require them to change their mental models – in cognitive terms, *entrepreneurs are especially sensitive to the problems engendered by framing effects and the functional fixedness bias and guard against them.*

Counterfactual Thinking and Bricolage. Guarding against framing effects and functional fixedness may be necessary steps for breaking the existing means – ends framework but they are by no means sufficient. Holcombe (2003) presses further and argues that all of the cognitive behaviors discussed so far are necessary but not sufficient. They lay the groundwork but are not themselves an entrepreneurial act. Whether one adopts the creativity or alertness or problem-solving or pattern recognition or any other explanation, at some point it becomes a question of what is the entrepreneur doing that breaks the existing means – ends framework and that changes his or her existing mental model of the world? We have little evidence but some suggestions about the probable cognitive dynamics.

Baker and Nelson (2005) provide the most direct evidence about the fact that at least some entrepreneurs are aware of their attempts to break existing mental models although their investigation focused on ventures that were already launched. The investigators observed that the founders whose firms that experienced growth showed a determined and conscious bias to test and push past the resources at hand (their existing means – ends framework). They describe several episodes in which *the entrepreneurs exhibit a "willful tendency to disregard limitations, commonly*

accepted definitions of material inputs, practices, and definitions and standards"
(p. 334) in order to experiment with re-combinations of inputs, reordering sequences
of events, and so forth which the authors label examples of bricolage.

The study provides evidence that entrepreneurs may intend to undo and redo what
exists but it does explain what or how entrepreneurs accomplished their intentions.
Gaglio (2004) suggests that the use of counterfactual reasoning and mental simulations is the driving force of these events. These cognitive processes work directly on
an individual's perceptions regarding a causal chain of events (e.g., means – ends).
Gaglio's theoretical development appears to run counter to Baron's (2000) assertion that entrepreneurs do not engage in counterfactual thinking but in fact, Baron
only examined the counterfactual processes associated with regret which is only
one of countless everyday situations in which people use counterfactual thinking.
It is used most often to solve problems. However, relative to opportunity identification, Gaglio proposes that entrepreneurs who, through active search or discovery,
identify anomalies or unexpected events (which are counter to the existing facts,
counterfactual) will place that information into their mental models and mentally
imagine what would happen. This kind of mental play leads to the identification of
market opportunities.

There is considerable room to expand this line of theory and research; its potential usefulness lay in shifting the focus of research to what entrepreneurs are doing
and on re-conceptualizing the entrepreneur as more than a response to stimuli. At
first glance, this sounds most useful but the discipline took another less than useful
detour into the consideration of the ontological nature of opportunities.

14.3 Trend #2: Ontological Nature of Entrepreneurial Opportunities

The question of whether an entrepreneurial opportunity can exist independently
of the entrepreneur appears to be a lightning rod for the discipline – nearly 10%
of the articles published in the last 8 years specifically address this issue (e.g.,
Baker and Nelson, 2005; Berglund, 2007; Buenstorf, 2007; Chiasson and Saunders,
2005; Companys and McMullen, 2007; Endres and Woods, 2007, Fletcher, 2006;
McMullen et al., 2007; Sanz-Velasco, 2006; Sarason et al., 2006a; Sarasvathy et al.,
2003; Shane, 2004).

From a cognitive perspective, the issue is a bit of a tangent because the act of
perception and interpretation inherently renders all human activity subjective. The
mystery lay in the fact that we manage to effectively interact with others and that
the world generally works despite the fact that each person introduces his or her
subjectivity at every turn. However, an individual's "subjectivity" is guided by his
or her mental models which are the results of worldly interactions, so what is presumed subjective actually has a strong social, if not objective, flavor. Cognition then
is both social and individual (Fiske and Taylor, 1991). The discipline appears to
be resolving the ontological debate in this direction by importing the theories of

social construction (Fletcher, 2006; Gartner et al., 2003; Gaglio and Katz, 2001) and structuration (Chiasson and Saunders, 2005; Sarason et al., 2006a) or concluding that the opposing sides in the debate are actually complementary (Companys and McMullen, 2007). Yet the debate proved useful in that it highlighted the need for the discipline to address two issues if we want to improve our understanding of opportunity identification. As scholars pulled in examples of subjective, objective, and enacted opportunities in support of their respective positions, it became clear that they were more often than not considering opportunities of a different scale. This implies that there may be more than one kind of entrepreneurial opportunity. Second, by proposing social construction or structuration theory as a resolution to the controversy, scholars will need to direct more attention to the social dimension of the opportunity identification process.

14.3.1 More than One Kind of Entrepreneurial Opportunity

The most interesting pattern to emerge from this literature review is that at some point, at least one scholar from each ontological camp came to the conclusion that the field needs to make distinctions among types of opportunities in order for further discussions to be productive. Readers interested in each position's line of argument leading to this conclusion are referred to the literature cited above. What is more fascinating and far more useful is the fact that a similar conclusion was reached.

One approach distinguishes between opportunities based on scale. Yu (2001) recommends differentiating between what he calls ordinary opportunities and extraordinary opportunities. Ordinary opportunities reflect restructuring the existing way of doing things (cf. causal chain or existing means – ends framework) so that the process is cheaper, better, and/or faster; the determining feature is that the entrepreneur works within the existing situation (p. 56). Extraordinary opportunities, on the other hand, are on the order of Schumpeter's creative destruction. Their identifying feature is that the entrepreneur is trying to make sense out of the uncertainties associated with anomalies and such; nothing like the new product or service idea has ever been seen before and the entrepreneur will probably have a hard time convincing others of its possibilities. Shane (2004) echoes the need to distinguish between the small-scale opportunities (which he calls Kirznerian) and the larger ones (which he also calls Schumpeterian). From a cognitive perspective, the recommendation has face validity because it would seem logical that the cognitive processes associated with each would differ somewhat and that these differences would be important differences.

Other scholars (Endres and Woods, 2007) urge that a distinction be made between existing opportunities and newly created opportunities precisely because the cognitive processes associated with accomplishing each is assumed to differ. Recall that there is evidence to support this assumption; the previous section reviewed studies which indicate that the way in which a problem was framed and an individual's store-specific human capital had an influence on an opportunity's degree of innovation.

Plummer et al. (2007) offer several examples distinguishing between ideas for products and services that almost everyone would agree are new to the world versus those ideas that really are instances of an underexploited or incompletely exploited opportunities (p. 374). However, the authors offer an even more interesting idea that an *opportunity be thought of in terms of its life cycle* where it moves over time from pure novelty to underexploited to exploited to saturated. Thinking in terms of a life cycle is consistent with the theory of evolutionary economics (Buenstorf, 2007; Companys and McMullen, 2007) which reminds us that the actions of entrepreneurs spawn additional opportunities both mundane and grand. Buenstorf observes that a complete explanation of entrepreneurial opportunities would have to account for those cases in which the entrepreneur only knows that he or she has found the opportunity to create an opportunity which is probably about as abstract a problem frame as one can have (Ward, 2004).

It would appear that between consideration of the ontological nature of entrepreneurial opportunities and consideration of the influence of human capital, the *pressure is mounting to include measures that distinguish among types of opportunities.* While the concept of an opportunity's life cycle is probably more useful to theoretical development, measures for it need to be developed and validated. Meanwhile, measures regarding level of innovation already exist and increased deployment of these measures may provide data for a speedier and better measure of opportunity life cycle.

The second direction emerging from the debate regarding the ontological nature of entrepreneurial opportunities is pressure to re-introduce social variables into the discussion of the opportunity identification process. But interest in the social dimension is not limited to this debate, it represents the third major trend of the past eight years.

14.4 Trend #3: Re-emphasis of Social Dimensions

As noted earlier the mental models that represent market environments are developed over time through a variety of interactions with other market actors – through learning, buying, selling, working, scanning, and so forth. Therefore, while the concept of mental models is primarily an individual level phenomenon, it is also a social phenomenon because its creation requires social interaction.

14.4.1 Structuration Theory

Giddens (1984) theory of structuration provides a comprehensive description at a meta-level of how the world comes to be represented in an individual's mind and how the individual can take action and even change the world. Central to this description is the concept of scripts (mental models) which summarize and represent an individual's understanding of what works and what does not work based on the feedback an individual receives from social interactions.

Chiasson and Saunders (2005) and Sarason et al. (2006a) provide detailed examples demonstrating that the entrepreneurial opportunity process can be recast in structuration terms but the contribution of these efforts is uncertain and yet to be realized. Both articles point to the need to understand the contents of an entrepreneur's script because the contents codify what the entrepreneur believes to be effective, legitimate, and powerful. Sarason et al. (2006a) also state that the entrepreneur's idiosyncratic selection of the facts is the driving force of the process; this is analogous to cognitive psychology's presupposition that what one chooses to attend to or ignore drives all cognitive processes. The authors also contend that structuration underscores the importance of signification structures which facilitate the construction of meaning but this line of reasoning needs more development before it can be a useful guide to research efforts. Currently, scholars who are interested in the social dimensions of the opportunity identification process continue to demonstrate the influence of the environment of a geographic location and the influence of social networks.

14.4.2 Environmental Munificence

Kirzner (1979) claimed that the very exercise of entrepreneurial alertness depends on the type of society within which the entrepreneur lives and acts. If the entrepreneur does not perceive incentives, he or she will not engage his or her alertness skills. Tang (2008b) provides some empirical support for this claim; she found that individuals are more likely to engage their alertness abilities as well as commit to starting a business if they perceive their social environment to be munificent, that is, abundant with the necessary resources and social support.

From the cognitive perspective, information is a resource, so one would expect that entrepreneurs would prefer environments rich in information. The uneven clustering of entrepreneurial activity geographically in places like Silicon Valley, Route 123, and so on suggests this to be the case. Cooper and Park (2008) document the fact that entrepreneurs move to these clusters in order to take advantage of the tacit knowledge and informal information flows as well as to add to the knowledge flow themselves. Audrestsch and Keilbach (2007) suggest that the knowledge spillover caused by unexploited or underexploited opportunities is also part of the attraction. This explanation is consistent with the evolutionary economics perspective (Buenstorf, 2007; Casson and Wadeson, 2007).

The most striking fact about the existence of these clusters is that they are concrete examples of information asymmetries, which according to both the search and discovery approaches conveys considerable advantage for opportunity identification. Recent research (Minniti, 2004) shows that alert entrepreneurs are less interested in starting businesses when information is evenly distributed than when there is an unbalance in information distribution (in their favor of course). The other advantage regional clusters have is the existence of and access to entrepreneurial role models, which research demonstrates is most predictive of perceptions regarding environmental munificence (Arenius and Minniti, 2005; Tang, 2008b) even today after decades of media blitzes.

The power of role models as a predictor of perceptions emphasizes *the need to move beyond assertions regarding the importance of social environments to investigation of what really matters.* The increasing role of the Internet and other forms of telecommunication and video communication points to the probable diminishing importance of geography per se (connect the dots: the rise in concerns about global warming; the cost of travel; the expanding bandwidth; cell phone cameras). It would be useful to know more what factors lay behind the proxy variable called geographic clusters had.

14.4.3 Social Networks

Entrepreneurship scholars have long maintained that an entrepreneur's social network is an important source of information as well as an important influence on the way an entrepreneur thinks. It is commonly believed that for entrepreneurs, a network of weak ties is more useful for the identification/creation and pursuit of opportunities (Granovetter, 1982). Social construction and structuration theories emphasize the give and take interaction between entrepreneurs and stakeholders in ways that would both facilitate and constrain the opportunity identification process.

The empirical record of the past eight years is disappointing in that it offers little to deepen or expand our understanding of the role of social networks in the opportunity identification process; however, the role of networks in opportunity exploitation is better understood. We have evidence that entrepreneurs believe that their social networks are very important to the development of their opportunities (Ko and Butler, 2007; Thorpe et al., 2006) but we do not have any insights into what these networks actually do for the entrepreneur, whether all networks and network members contribute equally, and whether or when entrepreneurs' interactions with networks create problems. Arenius and DeClercq (2005) claim to offer evidence in support of the power of weak ties but the measure was so indirect (rural versus city living) that it would be misleading to draw conclusions from this study about an individual's network, which has a stronger focal point.

It is time to begin asking more sophisticated questions such as whether and how social networks influence the content of entrepreneurial mental models and whether and how they influence the kinds of connections made within those mental models. The role of mentors in shaping the content of an entrepreneur's mental model would be an excellent place to start. The rise of the cleantech industry also affords the opportunity to examine how mental models are formed by all stakeholders and how they influence each other – this situation is most exciting as it is virtually a clean slate.

14.5   Trend #4: Widening Schism in Definitions of Entrepreneurial Opportunities

The single most striking impression one gains from a review of the opportunity identification literature of the past eight years is that there is an elephant in the room and no one wants to talk about it. Perhaps no one recognizes it? The elephant is the widening gap between the theoretical and empirical definitions of entrepreneurial opportunities. An examination of the literature published since Shane and Venkataraman's declaration reveals three basic conceptualizations of entrepreneurial opportunities:

(1) introducing new to the world raw materials, goods, services, or processes (Ardichvili et al., 2003; Baron, 2006; Companys and McMullen, 2007; Eckhardt and Shane, 2003; Gaglio and Katz, 2001; Sarasvathy et al., 2003; Yu, 2001)
(2) starting a business (Arenius and Minniti, 2005; Arenius and DeClercq, 2005; Baker and Nelson, 2005; Baron and Ensley, 2006; Berglund, 2007; Fletcher, 2006; Sanz-Velasco, 2006; Sarason et al., 2006b; Tang et al., 2008)
(3) introducing new to the world goods, services, or processes by starting a business (Ardichvili et al., 2003; Lee and Venkataraman, 2006).

Two dimensions are implicit in these definitions: (1) the scale of the product, service, or process (i.e., new to the world or not) and (2) organizational form (new business or not). Theoretical work tends to favor a strict constructionist view of Shane and Venkataraman's declaration and discusses opportunity in terms of new to the world goods and services. Empirical work tends to favor new venture creation, partly because new venture founders can be considered an "ideal type" of entrepreneur who just happens to be easier to locate when constructing a sample and partly because of the wider use of data sets such as the PSED and Global Entrepreneurship Monitor.

The implications regarding the scale of the product or service have been discussed earlier and will not be repeated here. The question is whether the de facto use of new ventures in empirical work presents serious repercussions, particularly for the discipline's desire to move away from being an applied research setting. If the current pattern is maintained going forward, the discipline will define itself as the study of an organizational form, new ventures, and the task will be to demonstrate that the issues confronting new ventures are unique and their solutions are equally unique.

If the discipline would prefer to avoid this outcome, then journal editors need to encourage more studies about opportunities for new goods and services in the corporate and non-profit settings. Brown et al. (2001) reported some curious findings in their attempt to operationalize Stevenson's (Stevenson and Jarillo, 1990) theory of entrepreneurial firms. Their sample consisted of established firms and while their factor analysis confirmed many of the expected dimensions such as resource orientation, reward structure, and growth orientation, it is somewhat puzzling that the factor analysis was unable to support both the strategic orientation and an opportunity orientation; they found the opportunity orientation was subsumed in the strategic orientation scale. This study needs to be replicated before one can draw definite inferences but it would be an extremely important theoretical development if opportunity identification or the kind of opportunity identified were bounded by the organizational form. Articles comparing and contrasting the same opportunity across settings can help sort this out. It is food for thought.

14.6 People – The Game's Afoot!

Table 14.1 summarizes the key findings and insights culled from this review of the work of the past eight years. As we sit here discussing the implications of these findings and develop our recommendations for building upon these insights while trying to find ways to make the same old platitudes about research designs and methods sound more compelling (or at least fresh), we keep coming back to fact that right now, a rare and unusual set of circumstances exist and we have the feeling that perhaps complying with the traditional format of summary and next steps creates a discussion analogous to a debate about the number of angels that can dance on the head of a pin rather than pointing to the opportunity afforded by the rare events – the game's afoot!

We are going to take the chance and assume that our colleagues in entrepreneurship would prefer not to miss out. We are, of course, referring to the complete meltdown of the global financial markets, which theoretically can be seen as a moment of creative destruction – no one ever said it would look pretty. In addition, a new industry, cleantech, is emerging in response to the global warming crises. In each case, the existing means – ends frameworks are broken; new ones must be created which will give rise to new products and services that will compete in the marketplace. Opportunity identification and creation must occur; a significant amount of opportunity identification must occur.

These circumstances provide at least two avenues of investigation that can dramatically advance our understanding of the opportunity identification process. The first route is to take each of the perspectives outlined in this chapter (search versus discovery; general versus specific knowledge; objective versus subjective versus enacted; weak versus strong ties; and so on) and pit each explanation against the data emerging in either (or both) industry. This is the moment for adherents of structuration theory to make *predictions* about how industry structures, rules, and norms will unfold. The nature of events in these industries allows us to test competing explanations and determine which provides a more useful, more internally consistent, more elegant explanation of the data.

The second avenue is to conduct *good* longitudinal grounded theory studies regarding the development of the mental models, especially their content and change over time. Cognitive maps from each stakeholder group, perhaps even key members of an entrepreneur's network, would prove especially useful as a tracking tool. Content analysis of think-aloud protocols in which entrepreneurs and other stake-

Table 14.1 Summary of key findings and insights

- **We have evidence that people scan their environments**
    - ○ Both deliberate search and effortless discovery are viable explanations. Which, when?
    - ○ Amount of scanning depends first upon ease of access to information and then upon degree of perceived turbulence in relevant environment
    - ○ Motivation for search does not seem to have an impact on long-term success

- **Knowledge matters, in order to discover or create opportunities, entrepreneurs have to know something**
    - ○ The greater the amount of knowledge, the more higher the number of opportunities reported
    - ○ Degree of specific knowledge, particularly knowledge about customer problems, influences the degree of innovation in reported opportunities
        - ▪ Need to distinguish among different types of opportunities
    - ○ Decisions to exploit opportunities are mediated by the kind of specific knowledge an individual has and the interaction of an individual's learning style and the situational demands
    - ○ Serial and novice entrepreneurs appear to have different mental models about what constitutes an opportunity
    - ○ Novice entrepreneurs and venture capitalists appear to have similar models about what constitutes an opportunity but give different weights to the factors
    - ○ If knowledge matters, IQ must play a role

- **Entrepreneurs have some awareness of how they use their mental models**
    - ○ Reported awareness of attempts to connect the dots among information acquired
    - ○ Awareness that their mental models may be incorrect or incomplete, open to the possibility of surprise and change
        - ▪ Steps to guarding against framing effects
        - ▪ Steps to guarding against functional fixedness
    - ○ Conscious and intentional recombination of inputs, reordering of sequences (counterfactual thinking)

- **Social environment matters**
    - ○ Environments with asymmetric information advantage foster entrepreneurial activity
    - ○ Geographic clusters experience knowledge spillovers which result in unexploited or underexploited opportunities which attract entrepreneurial activity
    - ○ The presence of and access to entrepreneurial role models is the most powerful predictor of perceptions of environmental support

- **Emerging consensus that discipline needs to distinguish among types of opportunities**
    - ○ Scale of innovation
    - ○ Stage in opportunity's life cycle

- **Schism in the definition of entrepreneurial opportunities**
    - ○ Theoretical work tends to define entrepreneurial opportunities in terms of future goods and services
    - ○ Empirical work tends to define entrepreneurial opportunities in terms of new ventures
    - ○ Is entrepreneurship becoming the study of an organizational form?

---

holders explain their understanding of events as well as their opinions about where the industry is heading should facilitate identification of pattern recognition and/or counterfactual thinking, bricolage, and so forth. One of the most exciting aspects of current circumstances is that some of these ideas and opportunities are bound to fail so that we can finally start to examine the effectiveness of the various cognitive strategies used. Obviously, the work on mental models can be ramped up to the development of shared understanding, and then to the development of industry standards and norms.

This is the most exciting time for any scholar interested in the opportunity identification process. We have good tools and theories to use but we also need to be entrepreneurial enough to rigorously test these in the marketplace. Why should our respondents have all the fun? This is the time, seize the opportunity.

References

Ardichvili A, Cardozo R, Ray S (2003) A theory of entrepreneurial opportunity identification and development. Journal of Business Venturing 18(1): 105–123.

Arenius P, DeClercq D (2005) A network-based approach to opportunity recognition. Small Business Economics 24(3): 249–265.

Arenius P, Minniti M (2005) Perceptual variables and nascent entrepreneurship. Small Business Economics 24(3): 233–247.

Audrestsch DB, Keilbach M (2007) Journal of Management Studies 44(7): 1242–1254.

Baker T, Nelson RE (2005) Creating something from nothing: Resource construction through entrepreneurial bricolage. Administrative Science Quarterly 50(3): 329–366.

Baron R (2006) Opportunity recognition as pattern recognition: How entrepreneurs 'connect the dots' to identify new business opportunities. The Academy of Management Perspectives 20(1): 104–119.

Baron R, Ensley MD (2006) Opportunity recognition as the detection of meaningful patterns: Evidence from comparisons of novice and experienced entrepreneurs. Management Science 52(9): 1331–1344.

Baron R (2000) Counterfactual thinking and venture formation: The potential effects of thinking about "what might have been". Journal of Business Venturing 15(1): 79–91.

Berglund H (2007) Opportunities as existing and created: A study of entrepreneurs in the Swedish mobile internet industry. Journal of Enterprising Culture 15(3): 243–273.

Bishop K, Nixon RD (2006) Venture opportunity evaluations: Comparisons between venture capitalists and inexperienced pre-nascent entrepreneurs. Journal of Developmental Entrepreneurship 11(1): 19–33.

Brown TE, Davidsson P, Wiklund J (2001) An operationalization of Stevenson's conceptualization of entrepreneurship as opportunity-based firm behavior. Strategic Management Journal 22: 953–968.

Buenstorf G (2007) Creation and the pursuit of entrepreneurial opportunities: An evolutionary economics perspective. Small Business Economics 28: 323–327.

Casson M, Wadeson N (2007) The discovery of opportunities: Extending the economic theory of the entrepreneur. Small Business Economics 24(4): 285–300.

Chase WG, Simon HA (1973) The mind's eye in chess. In: Chase RD (ed.) Visual Information Processing. New York, NY: Academic Press, pp. 215–281.

Chi MTH, Glaser R, Rees E (1982) Expertise in problem-solving. In: Sternberg RS (ed.) Advances in the Psychology of Human Intelligence, volume 1. Hillsdale, NJ: Erlbaum, pp.1–75.

Chiasson M, Saunders C (2005) Reconciling diverse approaches to opportunity research using the structuration theory. Journal of Business Venturing 20(6): 747–767.

Coleman AM (2001). "functional fixedness." A Dictionary of Psychology. 2001. Retrieved February 07, 2009 from Encyclopedia.com: http://www.encyclopedia.com/doc/1O87-functionalfixedness.html

Companys YE, McMullen JE (2007) Strategic entrepreneurs at work: the nature, discovery and exploitation of entrepreneurial opportunities. Small Business Economics 28(4):301–322.

Cooper SY, Park JS (2008) The impact of 'incubator' organizations on opportunity recognition and technology innovation in new entrepreneurial high tech ventures. International Small Business Journal 26(1): 27–56.

Corbett A (2005) Experiential learning within the process of opportunity identification and exploitation. Entrepreneurship Theory & Practice 29(4): 473–491.

Demmert H, Klein DB (2003) Experiment on entrepreneurial discovery: an attempt to demonstrate the conjecture of Hayek and Kirzner. Journal of Economic Behavior and Organization 50: 295–310.

Demsetz H (1983) The neglect of the entrepreneur. In: Ronen J (ed.) Entrepreneurship. Lexington, MA: Lexington Books.

DeTienne DR, Chandler GN (2004) Opportunity identification and its role in the entrepreneurial classroom: a pedagogical approach and empirical test. Academy of Management Learning and Education 3: 242–57.

Dimov D (2007) From opportunity insight to opportunity intention: The importance of person-situation learning match. Entrepreneurship Theory & Practice 37(4): 561–583.

Dutta DK, Crossan M (2005) The nature of entrepreneurial opportunities: understanding the process using the 4I organizational learning framework. Entrepreneurship Theory & Practice 29(4): 425–445.

Drucker PF (1985) Innovation and Entrepreneurship: Practice and Principles. New York: Harper & Row.

Eckhardt J, Shane S (2003) Opportunities and entrepreneurship. Journal of Management 29(3): 333–349.

Endres AM, Woods CR (2007). The case for more 'subjectivist' research on how entrepreneurs create opportunities. International Journal of Entrepreneurial Behaviour and Research 13(4): 222–234.

Fiet J (2007) A prescriptive analysis of search and discovery. Journal of Management Studies 44(4): 592–611.

Fiet J (2002) The Systematic Search for Entrepreneurial Discoveries. Westport, CT: Quorum Books.

Fiet JO, Clouse VGH, Norton Jr WI (2004) Systematic search by repeat entrepreneurs. In: Butler J (ed.), Research in Entrepreneurship and Management, volume 4. Greenwich, CT: Information Age Publishing, pp. 1–27.

Fiske ST, Taylor SE (1991) Social Cognition, 2nd ed. New York, NY: McGraw Hill.

Fletcher DF (2006) Entrepreneurial processes and the social construction of opportunities. Entrepreneurship and Regional Development 18(5): 421–440.

Gaglio CM (2004) The role of mental simulations and counterfactual thinking in the opportunity identification process. Entrepreneurship Theory & Practice 28(6): 533–552.

Gaglio CM, Katz J (2001) The psychological basis of opportunity identification: Entrepreneurial alertness. Small Business Economics 16(2): 95–111.

Gartner WB (1990) What are we talking about when we talk about entrepreneurship? Journal of Business Venturing 5: 15–28.

Gartner WB, Carter NM, Hills GE (2003) The language of opportunity. In: Steyaert C, Kjorth D (eds.), New Movements in Entrepreneurship. Cheltenham, UK: Edward Elgar, pp. 103–104.

Giddens A (1984) The Constitution of Society. Berkeley, CA: University of California Press.

Granovetter M (1982) The strength of weak ties. In: Marsden PV, Lin N (eds.), Social Structure and Network Analysis. Beverly Hills, CA: Sage Publications.

Hisrich R, Langan-Fox J, Grant S (2007). Entrepreneurship research and practice: A call to action for psychology. American Psychologist 62(6): 575–589.

Holcombe RG (2003) The origins of entrepreneurial opportunities. Review of Austrian Economics 16(1): 25–43.

Hsieh C, Nickerson JA, Zenger TR (2007) Opportunity discovery, problem solving and a theory of the entrepreneurial firm. Journal of Management Studies 44(4): 1255–1277.

Ireland RD, Reutzel CR, Webb JW (2005a) Entrepreneurship research in AMJ: What has been published and what might the future hold? Academy of Management Journal 48(4):556–564

Ireland RD, Webb JW, Coombs JE (2005b) Theory and methodology in entrepreneurship research. In: Ketchen D, Berg KD (eds.), Research Methodology in Strategy and Management, 2nd edn. New York: Elsevier JAI, pp. 1–32.

Kirzner I (1979) Perception, Opportunity and Profit. Chicago: University of Chicago Press.

Kitzmann J, Schiereck D (2005) Entrepreneurial discovery and the Demmert/Klein experiment: Another attempt at creating the proper context. The Review of Austrian Economics 18(2): 169–178.

Ko S, Butler J (2007) Creativity: A key link to entrepreneurial behavior. Business Horizons 50: 365–372.

Koller RH (1988) On the source of entrepreneurial ideas. In: Kirchoff BA, Long W,McMullan W, Vesper KH, Wetzel WE (eds.), Frontiers of Entrepreneurship Research, Wellesley, MA: Babson College, pp. 194–207.

Krueger NF (2007) What lies beneath? The experiential essence of entrepreneurial thinking. Entrepreneurship Theory & Practice 31(1): 123–138.

Kuhberger A (1998) The influence of framing on risky decisions: A meta-analysis. Organizational Behavior and Human Decision Processes 75(1): 23–55.

Lee JH, Venkataraman S (2006) Aspirations, market offerings and the pursuit of entrepreneurial opportunities. Journal of Business Venturing 21(1): 107–123.

Low MB (2001) The adolescence of entrepreneurship research: Specification of purpose. Entrepreneurship Theory and Practice 26(4): 17–25

Lumpkin GT, Lichtenstein B (2005). The role of organizational learning in the opportunity recognition process. Entrepreneurship Theory & Practice 29(4): 451–472.

Minniti M (2004) Entrepreneurial alertness and asymmetric information in a spin-glass model. Journal of Business Venturing 19(5): 637–658.

Mitchell RK, Busenitz LW, Bird B, Gaglio CM, McMullen JS, Morse EA, Smith JB (2007) The central question in entrepreneurial cognition research 2007. Entrepreneurship Theory & Practice 31(1): 1–27.

Mitchell RK, Busenitz L, Lant T, McDougall P, Morse EA, Smith JB (2004). The distinctive and inclusive domain of entrepreneurial cognition research. Entrepreneurship Theory & Practice 28(5): 506–518.

McMullen JS, Plummer LA, Acs ZJ (2007) So what is an entrepreneurial opportunity? Journal of Small Business Economics 28: 273–283.

Peterson RT (1988) An analysis of new product ideas in small business. Journal of Small Business Management 26: 25–31.

Phan PH (2004) Entrepreneurship theory: Possibilities and future directions. Journal of Business Venturing 19: 617–620.

Plummer LA, Haynie JM, Godesiabois J (2007) An essay on the origins of entrepreneurial opportunity. Small Business Economics 28(4): 363–379.

Sanz-Velasco SA (2006) Opportunity development as a learning process for entrepreneurs. International Journal of Entrepreneurial Behaviour and Research 12(5): 251–271.

Sarason Y, Dean T, Dillard JF (2006a) Entrepreneurship as the nexus of individual and opportunity: A structural view. Journal of Business Venturing 21(3): 286–305.

Sarason Y, Shepherd D, Dillard JF (2006b) Entrepreneurship as the nexus of individual and opportunity: A structural view. Journal of Business Venturing 21(3): 286–305.

Sarasvathy S, Dew N, Velamuri R, Venkataraman S (2003) Three views of entrepreneurial opportunity. In: Acs ZJ, Audretsch DB (eds.), Handbook of Entrepreneurship Research. New York, NY: Springer, pp. 141–160.

Schumpeter JA (1950) Capitalism, Socialism, and Democracy, 3rd ed. New York: Harper.

Shane S (2004) A General Theory of Entrepreneurship: The Individual-Opportunity Nexus. Cheltenham, UK: Edward Elgar.

Shane S (2000) Prior knowledge and the discovery of entrepreneurial opportunities. Organizational Science 11(4): 448–469.

Shane S, Venkataraman S (2000) The promise of entrepreneurship as a field of research. Academy of Management Review 25: 217–226.

Shaver KG, Scott LR (1991) Person, process, choice: The psychology of new venture creation. Entrepreneurship Theory & Practice 16(2): 23–45.

Shepherd DA, DeTienne DR (2005) Prior knowledge, potential financial reward and opportunity identification. Entrepreneurship Theory and Practice 29(1): 91–112.

Singh RP, Knox EL, Crump MES (2008) Opportunity recognition differences between black and white nascent entrepreneurs: A test of Bhave's model. Journal of Developmental Entrepreneurship 13(1): 59–75.

Stein BS (1989) Memory and creativity. In: Torrance EP, Glover JA, Ronnin R, Reynolds CR (eds.) Handbook of Creativity. New York, NY: Springer.

Stevenson HH, Jarillo JC (1990) A paradigm of entrepreneurship: Entrepreneurial management. Strategic Management Journal 11: 17–27.

Stewart W, May R, Kalia A (2008) Environmental perceptions and scanning in the US and India: Convergence in entrepreneurial information seeking. Entrepreneurship Theory & Practice 32(1): 83–105.

Tang J (2008a) Entrepreneurial Alertness: A Review, Reconceptualization and Extension: A Three-Essay Approach. PhD thesis, University of Alabama.

Tang J (2008b) Environmental munificence for entrepreneurs: entrepreneurial alertness and commitment. International Journal of Entrepreneurial Behaviour and Research 14(3): 128–151.

Tang J, Khan S (2007) Dynamic interactions between alertness and systematic search: a yin and yang perspective on opportunity recognition and innovation. International Journal of Entrepreneurship and Innovation 8(3): 175–187.

Tang J, Tang Z, Lohrke F (2008) Developing an entrepreneurial typology: The roles of entrepreneurial alertness and attributional style. International Entrepreneurship and Management Journal 4(3): 273–294.

Thorpe R, Gold J, Holt R, Clarke J (2006) Immaturity: The constraining of entrepreneurship. International Small Business Journal 24(3): 232–250.

Ucbasaran D, Westhead P, Wright M (2008) Opportunity identification and pursuit: Does an entrepreneur's human capital matter? Small Business Economics 30(2): 153–173.

Vesper KH (1982) Introduction and summary of entrepreneurship research. In: Kent CA, Sexton DH, Vesper KH (eds.), Encyclopedia of Entrepreneurship. Englewood Cliffs, NJ: Prentice-Hall.

Ward TB (2004) Cognition, creativity and entrepreneurship. Journal of Business Venturing 19(2): 173–188.

Yates AJ (2000) The knowledge problem, entrepreneurial discovery and the Austrian market process. Journal of Economic Theory 91(1): 59–85.

Yu TF-L (2001) Entrepreneurial alertness and discovery. Review of Austrian Economics 14(1): 47–63.

Zahra S, Dess GD (2001) Entrepreneurship as a field of research: Encouraging dialogue and debate. Academy of Management Review 26(1): 8–11.

Chapter 15
Entrepreneurial Behavior: Its Nature, Scope, Recent Research, and Agenda for Future Research

Barbara Bird and Leon Schjoedt

An action is the perfection and publication of thought.

Ralph Waldo Emerson

The end of all the cognition and motivation of entrepreneurs is to take some action in the world, and by doing so, give rise to a venture, an organization. Thoughts, intentions, motivations, learning, intelligence without action does not create economic value. The very nature of organizing is anchored in actions of individuals as they buy, sell, gather and deploy resources, work, etc. The values created by exploiting of opportunity undoubtedly include some that are intrapsychic and personal, but those we study, those of value to the readers of this book, are inherently interpersonal and social and thus observable and learnable. This chapter provides a brief overview of entrepreneurial behavior using a limited but hopefully representative lens on recent research. We call for more research on what entrepreneurs do and that this research be both more rigorous than what we currently have and also more creatively sourced.

15.1 The Nature and Scope of Entrepreneurial Behavior

Entrepreneurial behavior as an academic interest is the study of human behavior involved in finding and exploiting entrepreneurial behavior opportunity through creating and developing new venture organizations. Entrepreneurial behavior is the proximal outcome of the cognitions and emotions of entrepreneurial actors; it is also the proximal individual-centric cause of venture outcomes. The major goals of research are to explain, predict and control (change and change) behavior of individuals and teams. Knowledge of entrepreneurial behavior has value to actors – entrepreneurs as it allows them to shape and change their behaviors for better outcomes and to venture stakeholders, such as investors, local governments, and employees, insofar as entrepreneurial outcomes meet their respective goals.

B. Bird (✉)
Kogod School of Business, American University, Washington, DC 20016, USA
e-mail: bbird@american.edu

A.L. Carsrud, M. Brännback (eds.), *Understanding the Entrepreneurial Mind,*
International Studies in Entrepreneurship 24, DOI 10.1007/978-1-4419-0443-0_15,

Knowledge of entrepreneurial behavior is important to educators, students, news media, and creative writers. Entrepreneurial behavior eventually results in the creation of innovations, new competition, new jobs, and new revenue streams, and scholars from several disciplines such as economics, sociology, psychology, social psychology, and organizational design may find interest as well.

Entrepreneurial behavior as a research construct is the concrete enactment of individual or team tasks or activities required to start and grow a new organization. As we will argue, behaviors are best understood as discrete units of action that can be observed by others and which are "sized" to be meaningful. These activities are consciously chosen by individuals with the intention of finding and exploiting an opportunity and forming an organization of human, financial, physical, social, and intellectual resources. Examples of such activities are illustrated in a study by Carter et al. (1996). The resulting organization may be for profit or not, may vary on a continuum of virtuality and size, but it contributes economic and social value to its surroundings (Davidsson et al. 2006; Mitchell et al. 2007). This behavior (these actions) draws upon the experience, knowledge, skills, abilities, cognitions, intelligence, learning, intentions, and motivations of entrepreneurial individuals and teams. Behavior is visible, auditory, and/or kinesthetic and if others are present, social or potentially interpersonal in nature. Thus deciding is a cognitive process invisible to others and is different from the action of writing down the decision, orally communicating the decision, or taking other action to implement the decision. In the same way, learning is a cognitive process and objective assessment of learning results from behaviors.

15.1.1 Differentiating Concepts

First, entrepreneurial behavior is individual behavior, not firm behavior. Thus work on entrepreneurial orientation (Lumpkin et al. 2009; Wiklund and Shepherd 2003) and the operationalization of Stevenson's dimensions (which items are also attitudinal and ipastive) do not fall into our purview (Brown et al. 2001).

At the individual level of analysis, often researchers and certainly students and laypeople fail to differentiate behavioral terms. Behaviors are actions and therefore also *activities* of individuals (entrepreneurs). *Responses* are behaviors that follow from and presumably caused or evoked by some preceding stimulus. *Performance* is usually understood as results achieved by an action and when measured is often a complex aggregation of many behaviors (e.g., a high-performing student combines reading, writing, exam-taking, critical thinking, life-management behaviors, and many other behaviors).

Ability is a relatively stable broad characteristic of individuals that underlies their maximum performance and would include various forms of intelligence and physical attributes, such as strength or height. In general, abilities are difficult to change; however, they can be enhanced over time with education and experience. For example, intellectual ability refers to individuals' all-around effectiveness in activities directed by thought, such as thinking, reasoning, and problem solving, and in one approach (Sternberg 1988) has three facets: (1) analytic intelligence (*g*), (2) practical intelligence ("street smarts") which is domain specific, and (3) creative intelligence which is the ability to produce something that is, both, novel and useful. *Skills* are abilities to perform specific tasks and can be either broadly or narrowly construed (e.g., general skill at negotiation or more specific skill at bluffing). *Knowledge* is information the individual has in specific areas (e.g., knowledge about a market or how to make an oral presentation) acquired through education and experience. Knowledge can be either explicit or tacit and general or specific. *Competence* may be defined as abilities, knowledge, skills, traits, and concepts of self such as self-efficacy beliefs that are "causally related to criterion-referenced effective and/or superior performance in a job or situation" (Spencer and Spencer 1993). These capacities (abilities, skills, knowledge, and competencies) enable behaviors but are not behaviors themselves.

Processes may involve behavior but not necessarily. Decision making is a process that is largely cognitive and which leads to a choice among alternatives and may result in some action. Creativity is also a process often largely cognitive, of producing something new or partially new (Amabile 1996). Searching for opportunity is a process that may share elements of cognition, creativity, learning, and behavior (Corbett 2007; Sternberg 2004).

Whereas behavior is observable, performance, capacities, and processes are derived by inference from behaviors. For capacities to result in action, motivation and opportunity must also be present for behavior. For processes to have an impact in adding economic and social value, action or behavior must follow.

15.2 Recent Research on Entrepreneurial Behavior

15.2.1 Conceptual Efforts

In assessing the recent research on entrepreneurial behavior, we reviewed conceptual and theoretical articles that aim squarely at our topic. Action theory advanced by Frese (2007) builds on the cybernetic control model of Miller et al. (1969) and links the chapters which define this book to "action." This model, as well as that discussed by McMullen and Shepherd (2006), describes the judgmental processes which precede action or behavior and the cognitions which either enable or impede individuals from acting entrepreneurially when faced with an opportunity. Both models define action as consciously chosen (intentional) responses of individuals. While Frese (2007) focuses on behavioral control through planning, feedback, cognitive regulation, and traits of individuals such as initiative, McMullen and Shepherd (2006) focus on how decision uncertainty is perceived and impacts entrepreneurial action (which they leave undefined). Thus both of these efforts discuss action, address precursors to action but offer little insight into the action or behavior itself.

An initial effort to bring the field of organizational behavior to entrepreneurship came in 1989 when the first author (Bird 1989) summarized the then extant research pertaining to entrepreneurial behavior, defining it as "opportunistic, value-driven, value-adding risk-accepting, creative activity where ideas take the form of organizational birth, growth or transformation" (p. 5). The book included chapters on the person-centered variables (i.e., experience, education, motivation, values, and emotions), social and political contexts of entrepreneurial behavior, careers, teams, staffing, governance, leadership, competencies, and learning. Following that, Gartner et al. (1992) had one of the earliest journal articles that attempted to map organizational behavior onto emerging (compared to existing) organizations. They reviewed managerial work as a field of research, hoping for guidance in framing entrepreneurial behavior but found managerial work literature to be as atheoretical as entrepreneurship at the time. They recommended richer description of entrepreneurial behavior. It is interesting to note that this article has been cited only 43 times in the past 10 years and of these only 16 reference the behavior of entrepreneurs. A more recent effort to extend this bridge from organizational behavior to entrepreneurship was forged by Baron (2002). His review addressed the basic OB model (found as a framework in most textbooks) of individual, interpersonal, and organizational/social factors at three phases of the entrepreneurship process (pre-launch, launch, and operations). Much of his contribution here and elsewhere (Baron 2008) anchors on individual cognition and decision making but he has also introduced OB links for some specific person-centric predictors of outcomes that include learning from a mentor, social competence, successful and emotional intelligence, charismatic, visionary, and situational leadership, influence processes, and group dynamics of teams. In same vein, Shook et al. (2003) review behavioral research in entrepreneurship with a focus on judgment (cognition) but pointing to emerging interest in individuals who engage in active search for opportunities (see discussion on active search below) briefly mentioning opportunity exploitation activities. Shook and colleagues observe: "Perhaps the most under-researched aspect of individual and venture creation is exploitation activities. We know very little about the role of the individual in acquiring resources and organizing the company" (p. 390). We concur.

Several scholars have postulated behaviors that are important to opportunity exploitation without testing or measuring these. For example, Shepherd et al. (2000) suggest venture survival depends on organizing activities such as specifying tasks, allocating people to tasks, defining authority structures, and building communication channels. The next section of this chapter offers a brief review of recent empirical research that includes entrepreneurial behavior. Following that, we attempt to frame entrepreneurial behavior concretely and call for better measurement. Finally, we offer five research areas wherein entrepreneurship scholars can build upon the foundation of organizational behavior.

15.2.2 Empirical Efforts

To examine contemporary entrepreneurial behavior research, we reviewed empirical papers published over the last 3 years (2005–2007) in two top entrepreneurship journals – *Entrepreneurship Theory and Practice* and *Journal of Business Venturing*.

While we recognize that research on entrepreneurial behavior is published in other journals, like *Journal of Applied Psychology* (Baum and Locke 2004), and *Management Science* (Baron and Ensley 2006), we chose to focus our attention on *Entrepreneurship Theory and Practice* and *Journal of Business Venturing* as they, in our view, represent the two most recognized entrepreneurship journals and should provide a reasonable approximation of the approaches and findings of scholars. We identified articles pertaining to behavioral constructs at the individual and group levels. To focus on research addressing the entrepreneur, we excluded research addressing strategic firm decisions such as competitive stance or internal policies, corporate entrepreneurship including that of small organizations, older firms, and venture capital, and other stakeholders. We included only empirical papers as these efforts show operationalizations of behavioral constructs, which we consider important in assessing the state of entrepreneurial behavioral research. A total of 28 empirical articles that address behavior are shown in Table 15.1. The total number of articles published in these two journals was 223+, so empirical studies of behavior constituted about 12% of published efforts in this time period.

This limited review of the literature is insufficient for a theory-based approach to entrepreneurial behavior but it does serve to highlight the relative lack of attention to behavior in recent entrepreneurship literature. This is surprising insofar as individual and group levels of analysis remain a strong focus in entrepreneurship. While there has been some fertilization from organizational behavior, with its extensive research (Gatewood et al. 2002; Vecchio 2003b), much more could be done. To illustrate the fragmented nature research on entrepreneurial behavior, we have divided the articles into four groups – entrepreneurial behavior as a criterion for sampling, as an independent variable, as a dependent variable, and description of behaviors based on social theories.

Behavioral precision began with the initiation of a national panel study of startups in the United States where the first data collection and test of the sampling procedure was done in 1992 with the adult population in Wisconsin (Reynolds 2000; Reynolds and White 1997). Eventually, this led into the Panel Study of Entrepreneurial Dynamics (PSED) conducted by telephone and mail from 1998 to 2000. See Garnter et al. (2004) and Reynolds (2000) for details on methods and sampling. This was followed by similar studies internationally as part of the Global Entrepreneurship Monitor (Arenius and DeClercq 2005; Langowitz and Minniti 2007). Embedded within the survey two questions were designed to identify nascent entrepreneurs: (1) Are you, alone or with others, now trying to start a business? (2) Are you, alone or with others, now starting a new business or new venture for your employer?

Together the telephone interview and mail questionnaire provided information on a broad range of topics including activities of individuals that might be related to success in organizing an entrepreneurial business. There are two primary advantages to the PSED data set. First, the data were collected contemporaneously with the new venture creation process, unlike samples based on retrospective accounts. Second, the PSED data set allows for generalizations to the United

Table 15.1 Summary of literature

Year/journal	Citation	I, D, C variable	Exemplar behaviors
2005/ETP	Corbett (2005)	?	Market testing, selecting options, finalizing choices
	Forbes (2005)	I	Implied delegation, consulting with outsiders, scanning, analysis, planning
	Fiegener (2005)	D	Involvement of board
	Rauch et al. (2005)	I	Training/development of employees, encourage others to participate initiate, communicate goals
	(Singh and Lucas 2005)	D	Prepare business plan
	Hite (2005)	?	Working for partner, problem solving, communicating
2006/ETP	Orser et al. (2006)	D	Apply for external capital
	Alsos et al. (2006)	I	Adding, hiring a new team member
	Forbes et al. (2006)	D	Adding, hiring a new team member
	Vanaelst et al. (2006)	?	Joining or leave team, roles
2007/ETP	Schjoedt and Shaver (2007)	C	Trying to start a business
	Hanlon and Saunders (2007)	I	Receiving support
	DeTienne and Chandler (2007)	D	Self-reports on behavior sequences
	Langowitz and Minniti (2007)	C	Trying to start
	Cloninger and Oviatt (2007)	D/C	Internationalize
JBV/2005	Talaulicar et al. (2005)	I	Decision-making processes
	Grandi and Grimaldi (2005)	?	Articulation of roles, interaction with external agents
	Chrisman and Hall (2005)	I	Guided preparation in the research, planning and "activities" by advisors
JBV/2006	Kolvereid and Isaksen (2006)	D	Starting up a self-employment entity
	Ebben and Johnson (2006)	D	Bootstrapping such as delaying payments, joint utilization
	Ensley et al. (2006b)	I	Transformational and transactional behaviors
	Lichtenstein et al. (2006)	I/D	Strategic organizing – many behaviors talking with friends, formatting book
JBV/2007	(Watson 2007)	I	"Networking"
	Gruber (2007)	I	Market mix planning
	Tornikoski and Newbert (2007)	I/D	Categories of activities
	Lichtenstein et al. (2007)	I	Activities
	Haber and Reicheil (2007)	I	Writing business plan

States as a whole when post-sampling stratification weights are employed as these make the aggregate sample match the population in sex, race, age, and education level.

Subsequent research with this data set has developed a behavioral criterion for when an individual is a "nascent" entrepreneur by whether or not they have engaged in a number of behaviors, such as having developed a product/service, established credit with suppliers, filed a tax return for a new business, hired employees for pay, or invested own money (Garnter et al. 2004). Other studies categorize a respondent as having an operating business based on some of these behaviors (e.g., Edelman et al. 2008). In this way, *behaviors are a sampling criterion*.

Entrepreneurship research uses *behavior as an independent variable*. Here specific behaviors such as locating the business in a specific area, writing a business plan, opening a business bank account, seeking outside advice (Haber and Reicheil 2007; Lichtenstein et al. 2007; Tornikoski and Newbert 2007), or the degree of improvisation or number or pacing of activities (Hmieleski and Corbett 2008; Lichtenstein et al. 2007) might predict something, usually venture outcomes. In other studies, behavior is less specific and more cognitive to include self-reports of planning and time spent on planning (Alsos et al. 2006; Chrisman and Hall 2005; Gruber 2007) or initiating investor relationships measured in part by a self-report of confidence in "identifying sources of finance" (Alsos et al. 2006). Often behavior is global in nature (e.g., as an indicator of transformational leadership, "provides vision," Ensley et al. 2006b). Just as often, it is global in nature and poorly measured. For example, employees reported "support for personal initiative" and "communicating business goals" using single items (Rauch et al. 2005). In most cases, the entrepreneur's behavior is self-reported, but in other cases (as with Rauch et al. 2005) it is captured through the perception of a stakeholder such as a member of the venture team. Usually the focus is individual behavior of the self-reporting entrepreneur, but occasionally the focus is team behaviors such as decision-making processes (Forbes 2005; Talaulicar et al. 2005).

Other research seeks to predict behavior, treating *behavior as a dependent variable*. In some cases demographic variables that reflect human capital and individual differences such homemaker status, sex of entrepreneur, and prior experience are used to predict self-reported behaviors (e.g., preparing business plans, choosing a location, or seeking funding, Orser et al. 2006; Singh and Lucas 2005; Wright et al. 2008). For example, DeTienne and Chandler (2007) using sex and human capital as predictors, asked CEOs of young firms to choose among four sequences of actions those they themselves or their organization took in finding and acting on their start-up opportunity. In other cases, categories of context such as organizational size, board composition, need for strategic decision making, or operations predict CEO (entrepreneur) behavior such as bringing issues to the board of directors (Fiegener 2005) or deciding to open foreign operations (Cloninger and Oviatt 2007). Organizational age was used to predict bootstrapping behaviors (Ebben and Johnson 2006). In less frequent cases, cognitions such as beliefs and intentions as well other individual differences predict nascent behaviors such as those developed by PSED or the GEM (Langowitz and Minniti 2007) or a self-reported measure of "working" in a start up (Kolvereid and Isaksen 2006). In some cases, the actual entrepreneur is not wholly visible as decision maker or implementer (Cloninger and Oviatt 2007).

While prediction is the focus of most studies, some only *seek to describe or explain behavior in the context of extant social theories.* For example, Forbes and his colleagues (2006) sought to explain new venture hiring of new team members based on theories of attraction and resource dependence. In another example, using a single in-depth case study, Lichtenstein and his colleagues (Lichtenstein et al. 2006) observed three modes of organizing some of which are clearly behaviorally anchored: organizing the vision (expressing a strong vision) but also less behaviorally (changing thoughts and vocabulary about the opportunity); strategic organizing (tangible events such as formatting a book, deciding to publish as book or web page; committing personal funds, and coping with non-venture responsibilities); and tactical organizing (developing a product/service, establishing credit with suppliers, filing a tax return for a new business, hiring employees for pay, or investing own money).

In most cases, the behaviors are self-reports and are broad and unspecific in nature (e.g., initiating investor relationships, preparing a business plan, articulating a business idea). These behavioral constructs are not necessarily linked to observable objective behaviors and could be interpreted in very different ways by different audiences, but these kinds of constructs are often used in entrepreneurship research. For example, in the DeTienne and Chandler (2007) study, behaviors were self-reports of action sequences, which included "I/we found or developed a product or technology then looked for a market". A would-be or even successful entrepreneur might have some understanding of concrete referents for "product or technology" but may not differ widely on what is done to "look for a market." Another example is the use of self-reports by entrepreneurs of their strategic actions of exploration and exploitation (e.g., "We are usually one of the first companies in our industry to use new, breakthrough technologies"; "We frequently adjust our procedures, rules, and policies to make things work better" [Bierly and Daly 2007). We suspect that different audiences will concretely interpret "use of new, breakthrough technology" and "adjusting rules" in behaviorally very different ways.

In only one case in our review did an empirical article include behavior as both an independent and a dependent variable. Tornikoski and Newbert (2007) used PSED data for both independent and dependent variables. They looked at venture improvising (prepare business plan, start marketing, apply for patent, project financial statement, open bank account, list in phone book), resource combination (develop prototype, purchase raw materials, purchase facilities), and networking (ask for funds, establish credit, received outside assistance) as predictors of organizational emergence (make a sale, hire employees, received external funding).

Finding a paucity of empirical research and a lack of conceptual clarity on entrepreneurial behavior, we propose further refinement of our behavioral research methods. Following that we propose four broad organizational behavior areas from which entrepreneurship scholars can borrow, as long as we borrow wisely.

15.3 Behavioral Research Methods for Entrepreneurship

Entrepreneurial behaviors are discrete units of individual activity that can be observed by an "audience" and that have a meaning that is likely to be shared between actor and audience. By this definition, teams and organizations do not behave but individuals comprising them do. By this definition making a decision is not a behavior, announcing a decision is a behavior.

Many of the "behaviors" of entrepreneurship research are not discrete but complex and often ill defined. Planning a business is not a discrete unit of activity but a complex set of activities, some done sequentially, most done iteratively, almost always with interruptions for other activities, some done alone and others done by outsiders, such as consultants or teams of local college students. The behaviors embedded in "planning" might include consulting a text or template for business plan components (market size, competition, costs, legal protection, potential financing sources, board of advisors, etc.) and gathering information on various plan components through the discrete acts of web search, telephone calls, business meetings, etc. Planning also includes codifying and prioritizing the information and sense making through writing and speaking of the plan.

Bhide (2000) in his review of the process new ventures take to become large and enduring organizations draws on data from these large firms (no longer start up, nascent, or entrepreneurial by most definitions). He sees "critical tasks" for new ventures to include articulating audacious goals, formulating strategy, and implementing strategy which are likely comprised of many different behaviors of individuals (or teams). Only in his discussion of implementation of strategy does Bhide give hints at what behaviors one might want to engage to grow a venture (e.g., finding specific store locations, negotiating leases). Unfortunately other implementation behaviors are quite broad (e.g., upgrade resources, build infrastructure).

Behaviors need to be distinguished from their results. Asking for funds is a behavior (from whom, how, and when might usefully be specified), whereas receiving funds is a result. Writing a business plan is a behavior, having a written business plan is a result. In this particular case, entrepreneurs who hire others to write their plan are behaviorally distinct from those who write their own plan. When we use results as a surrogate for behavior, we infer behavior. Sometimes this is sensible, but it leaves the audience to our research to imagine what the entrepreneur actually did to achieve the result.

15.3.1 Molarity Issues

Just how specific should our behavioral variables be? Early behavioral psychologists applied the term "molarity" to behavior to focus attention on meaningful perceptual behavioral units or activities. Just as in chemistry a "mole" is a unit of matter that is often more useful and an atom or molecule, the meaningful unit of behavior is more useful than its component behaviors. For example, using the Internet for 4 hours to research markets or competition is more useful than the specific flexing muscles, moving joints or in our example, keystrokes. These "molecular" behaviors are less visible and combine together to make the observable behavior qualitatively different from underlying physiological processes (W. Baum 2002; Hauser 2006). We apply the concept here to focus attention on the wildly divergent sizes of behavioral units that are reported in the entrepreneurship literature. Whereas behavioral psychologists (e.g., Edward Toleman and others) differentiated holistic units of behavior from reflexive, simple stimulus–response connections, entrepreneurship scholarship errs in making our behavioral units far too galactic in size.

Behavior is concrete, not abstract. To pass the test of being behavior, it must be theoretically, if not practically observed by someone (or something in the case of a recording) other than the actor. It refers to an action or set of actions that can be seen, heard, or measured. Many of the behaviors of entrepreneurship research are under-specified and operationalizations unique to the particular manuscript and purpose (and far too often based on self-reports and single-items). A respondent, another researcher or a student wishing to learn to act as an entrepreneur, may not know what specific action is called for.

The behaviors listed in the PSED/GEM studies come close to the specificity we may need; some moreso than others. For example, one PSED behavior is "applied for patent." We may not need to know that the entrepreneur read the requirements and completed and submitted the paper work and paid the fees for patent or that they hired a patent attorney to do this for them. However, other PSED behaviors remain less specified. What specifically does one do to "define market opportunities/customers, competitors"?

We do not expect or suggest that entrepreneurship scholars drill down to keystrokes or "molecular" behaviors. We do think that just as scholars recognized the need to collect and report demographic data on respondent individuals and firms (so that context and comparisons could be made), we need to present greater unity on how we measure behavior. One step is finer granularity and another to begin to use similar if not identical operationalizations of key behaviors.

15.3.2 Need to Move Beyond Self-Report Methods

Since the behaviors of interest to entrepreneurship scholars are consciously undertaken, individual actors can reasonably report on their behaviors. But as is true in other research critiques (e.g., Chandler and Lyon, 2001), self-reports are limited by recall and social desirability bias. Self-reports of behavior can be more reliably and accurately obtained with any variant of an experience sampling diary (beeper) method (Spain et al. 2001) to capture frequency, sequence, duration of behaviors within and across entrepreneurs. These methods suffer from being intrusive but could provide us with a finer grain on what entrepreneurs actually do. Behavior can be assessed with other methods including observation both in the field and in the laboratory. Field observations are done and done well (Lichtenstein et al. 2007; Lichtenstein et al. 2006) but suffer from the inability to gather sufficient sample sizes to generalize. Laboratory studies (using experimental designs) in entrepreneurship are few and none, to our knowledge, observe behavior. Often these types of studies use students (not entrepreneurs) as subjects (Grichnik 2008), are often time consuming, and require the subject to be in a laboratory environment. It might also be possible to obtain unobtrusive measures of behaviors (Webb et al. 2000) if entrepreneurs could reasonably be expected to show up at a conference, meeting, or web site. This type of measure could count clicks, visits, or even employ photography or video methods. Finally, of course, is ask others who observe entrepreneurs to report on their observations, a method best used if triangulation (multiple observers) is employed.

As a field of research, let us move beyond self-reports as our primary way to measure behavior. If we must use self-reports, control for social desirability, which is the tendency to report socially desirable but possibly untrue results (Arnold and Feldman 1981). Let us employ the rigorous methods of other social scientists.

15.3.3 Need to Move Beyond Single Items

One of the most serious threats to research on entrepreneurial behavior, which was evident in the early research on entrepreneurial traits, is poor construct measurement. Considering the relatively complex nature of new venture creation and of entrepreneurial behavior, quality measurement is crucial (Boyd et al. 2005; Godfrey and Hill 1995). While advanced statistical methods allow single items to serve in statistical models, a real question must be raised about not only reliability but also validity since a single-tem measure can be ambiguous with respect to the intended meaning and can be changed by the context of previous items. Reliance on single-item measures at the exclusion of multi-item measures weakens results. More than two decades ago, marketing researchers (Churchill 1979; Jacoby 1978) critiqued the use of single-item measures to assess constructs. As Jacoby puts it:

> Given the complexity of our subject matter, what makes us think we can use responses to single items (or even to two or three items) as measures of these concepts, then relate these scores to a host of other variables, arrive at conclusions based on such an investigation, and get away calling what we have done Quality research? (1978, p. 93).

Considering the majority of research in entrepreneurship, even recent research, in the context of Jacoby's comment, how can we, as entrepreneurship scholars, claim that we have advanced the literature instead of adding clutter to our collective understanding of entrepreneurship.

Reliability of measurement is better assured and often obtained through psychometric development of scales comprised of multiple items. Reliability is a requirement for self-reports and other reports of behavior but also a requirement for measures of cognitive, motivational, attitudinal, and perceptual constructs. Reliability refers to the extent to which a measure is repeatable (Nunnally and Bernstein 1994) and consistent (Torabi 1994). Since reliability is a necessary condition for validity, unreliable measures lessen the observed correlation between measures. Consequently, if the correlation between two construct measures is low, it is not possible to determine whether there is no relationship between the two constructs or whether the measures are unreliable (Peter 1979). A single item to assess behavior not only is psychometrically unreliable, but often grossly over-simplifies behavior.

A good example of a study that used multiple items for all independent and dependent variables is offered by Baum and Bird (forthcoming). Of particular interest here is the behavior scale of "multiple improvement actions" which used eight items such as "We frequently experiment with product and process improvements" and "Continuous improvement of our products and processes is a priority".

15.3.4 Need to Include Time

There are critical time lag issues in translating cognitions into behavior and behavior into results. There are issues of how long a behavior takes to complete (when it begins and when it is finished and a new behavior begins). In the experimental design framework, the time between an independent variable change and a dependent variable measurement for the effects of that change is subject to "errors" that include history. Things happen between the formation of an intention and action based on that intention, especially when dealing with complex and relatively "galactic" behaviors such as defining markets and competition. These historical effects are likely to be more confounding the longer the behavior takes to complete. When does the entrepreneur begin planning and when is she finished? When does she begin to ask for funds and when does she get an answer (or the funds)? When does she approach her first customer and when does she make the first sale? These are identifiable behaviors and results, which are considered clear indicators of venture start-up according to Carter et al. (1996).

Undoubtedly, the entrepreneur is juggling these "behaviors" with other behaviors such as filing for patents, purchasing equipment, leasing space, etc. An illustrative example of juggling "behaviors" (activities) is *Heather Evans* (Roberts 1998). In this case, Heather incorporates the business, designs a clothing line, hires and pays an employee, arranges for factoring and production, locates a location for her store, and more while still attending classes at Harvard Business School and conducting a field study as well as moving from Boston to New York to further facilitate her venture creation process.

15.4 Behaviorally Anchored Research Agenda

As we addressed the very large issue of entrepreneurial behavior, we considered finding links between the issues and problems of entrepreneurs and the theories and research in the more mature field of organizational behavior. Clearly, entrepreneurship scholars are importing many ideas from OB, such as leadership (Ensley and Pearce 2001); job characteristics and satisfaction (Schjoedt forthcoming; Schjoedt and Shaver 2007); and team formation, composition, and processes (Forbes et al. 2006). We also recognize that this book is individual centric and cognition/motivation focused, and while personality, diversity, human capital, and attitudes such as satisfaction are important and they have a longer history of inclusion and extension into entrepreneurship, they are not behavioral but rather precursors to or moderators of behavior. For example, the growing body of research on women and minority entrepreneurship (Alsos et al. 2006; DeTienne and Chandler 2007; DeTienne et al. 2008; Essers and Benschop 2007) and the extensive research on personality characteristics of entrepreneurs (e.g., Stewart and Roth 2007) has applied OB insights but are not behavioral. Much of the rest of the OB domain is less directly relevant (e.g., political behavior, organization culture and design). Rather than repeat the overview of possibilities of OB-inspired research covered by Baron (2002), we choose to point to five areas of potential use to entrepreneurship scholars and practitioners. Three are strongly anchored in behavior (1) leadership (including shared leadership), (2) communication, (3) behavioral roles and two are less behavioral but critically important areas of (4) creativity and (5) opportunity discovery.

15.4.1 Leadership

We believe that the vast body of leadership research does pertain to entrepreneurship and excellent reviews of intersections for entrepreneurship scholars are offered by Cogliser and Brigham (2004) and Vecchio (2003a). Leadership is simultaneously about individual leader/entrepreneur behavior and the relationship of the leader/entrepreneur to the "followers" or "constituents" and external environment of the organization being formed and grown. It bridges the individual to the team and to the eventuality of dissent, political behavior, and organizational culture. We will provide a short review of the OB approach to leadership behavior framed as that stream of research shifted from traits to behaviors. Then we add the more recent work on shared leadership that may of particular interest to new ventures.

Leadership research began with attention to traits of executives. When those traits (e.g., intelligence, achievement motivation, power motivation) did not sufficiently discriminate between leaders and those in other roles such as managers and did not predict who would become a leader, attention shifted to leader behaviors. However, important trait-related leadership research continues (Kouzes and Posner 2002) as it does in entrepreneurship research (Ciavarella et al. 2004; Zhao and Seibert 2006). The behavioral study of leaders (Fleishman 1998) which is discussed below found two sets of behaviors that describe leaders – initiating structure/task focused and consideration/people focused. Again, the power of these tools to predict and shape leaders proved to be less than ideal and researchers proceeded to develop the currently most advanced theories, which address contingencies for when specific leadership behaviors or styles are more effective in achieving organizational results (House 1996).

The behavioral study of leaders, which was undertaken by a large interdisciplinary team including personnel officers of the military services, foundations, and firms and led by researchers at the Ohio State University, began with a definition of leadership: "behavior of an individual when he is directing the activities of a group toward a shared goal" (Hemphill and Coons 1957). The team held long discussions during which apparent conflicts arose over issues of independence of dimensions of leader behavior, linkages to existing theory, the molar–molecular level of analysis, and whether objective measurement was possible from asking about frequency of behavior (in a Likert-type scale). With some reservations, the team settled on nine leadership dimensions (integration, communication, production emphasis, representation, fraternization, organization, evaluation, initiation, domination). The team and two advanced classes at Ohio State University, based on their experience and knowledge, used these dimensions and their descriptions to create 1,790 potential items for an instrument. The team used their own expertise to determine items that belonged to only one of the nine dimensions and eliminated items that overlapped content and reduced the number to 150 behavioral descriptions, a number which would fit on an IBM test answer sheet (remember this study was published in 1957 and conducted before the development personal computers in the 1960s or SPSS and SAS in 1968). In creating Likert-like scales for each item, the team debated and eventually structured an approach selecting the frequency and extent adverbs to use (e.g., Always-Never, Often-Very seldom, A great deal-Not at all, each with five anchors). They empirically tested the Leader Behavior Description Questionnaire (LBDQ) on 357 individuals (205 were describing a leader of their group and 152 describing themselves as a leader). Groups included educational, social, military settings, and a diversity of respondents. From this and subsequent studies, two factors (initiating structure and consideration) and shorter scales with strong psychometric properties were developed (Stogdill and Coons 1957).

We believe that entrepreneurship scholars could apply the methods used in the behavioral approach to leadership to achieve more highly consistent measures of entrepreneurial behavior. Once those dimensions and measures have been psychometrically tested, entrepreneurship scholars can advance to our own contingency approach to entrepreneurship behavior. We believe this is the optimal way to "borrow" from OB research and that merely applying extant leadership measures and models to entrepreneurs will not suffice if indeed entrepreneurs are different from executives, team leaders, or supervisors who are the focus and respondents in mainstream OB leadership research. As "sexy" as it may be to apply new models, such as transformational–transactional leadership (Avolio and Yammarino 2002) to entrepreneurs, these efforts move away from entrepreneurship as a distinct phenomenon.

15.4.2 Shared Leadership

Although leadership is a social process involving both leaders and followers (Lord et al. 1999), leadership scholars have largely focused on the leader as an individual in a hierarchical system which makes sense given the history of OB leadership emerging from studies of the military and large organizations (Campbell et al. 1970). Hierarchical or vertical leadership is based on unity of command that stems from an appointed or formal leader of a team (e.g., the CEO) (Daft 2004). In contrast, shared leadership is a form of distributed leadership that occurs when all team members are engaged in the leadership of the team. Shared leadership is "a dynamic, interactive influential process among individuals in groups for which the objective is to lead one another to the achievement of group or organizational goals or both" (Pearce and Conger 2003). Thus when leadership is shared within the team, the member with the most relevant experience, knowledge, skills, or abilities pertaining to the situation facing, the team communicates and influences others on the team. Through debate (i.e., the statements, action, and reactions of the debating team members) the team develops commitment to a decision to take action. For shared leadership to emerge, members of the team must have a shared purpose (i.e., venture success), provide support to one another by communicating their agreement or support, and opportunity to voice their views via debate (Carson et al. 2007).

At least five factors influence the appropriateness of shared leadership (Pearce and Manz 2005) – situational urgency, need for creativity and innovation, team member commitment, task interdependence, and degree of complexity. In situations with a high level of urgency, hierarchical leadership may be more appropriate than shared leadership. Even though there are few truly urgent situations facing most organizations, urgent situations may be more prevalent in new ventures. For example, bootstrapping to meeting payroll on a week-to-week basis may present an urgent situation where delegation to one team member is appropriate. Even though shared leadership is not necessarily appropriate in urgent situations, shared leadership may provide a basis for avoiding urgent situations in the first place by providing creative solutions to reoccurring problems.

In contrast, creativity and innovation are important factors for the development for the new venture and its product/service offerings. When members of the entrepreneurial team share their various points of view and influence each other in problem solving and decision making, they build a collective creative capacity. The commitment of team members to go beyond what is minimally required might be expected in new venture teams when each member has a stake in its success and this commitment contributes to the potential for shared leadership. When task interdependence is high and the tasks are complex, as when team members take on different specific roles such as technical development, market creation, and financing, shared leadership becomes more important and possibly more likely. In addition, shared leadership lowers monitoring costs and provides a system of checks and balances of team members' actions and performance (Barker 1993; Pearce et al. 2008).

There is some emerging evidence of the effectiveness of shared leadership in new venture teams. Ensley et al. (2006a) studied 66 top management teams drawn from Inc. Magazine's annual list of the 500 fastest growing US firms and 154 randomly sampled top management teams of start ups from Dun and Bradstreet. They found that both shared and hierarchical leaderships predicted new venture performance, with shared leadership having a stronger effect in both samples. We believe that these findings and the novelty of shared leadership as a research topic point to shared leadership as a fruitful avenue for entrepreneurial behavior research. To get objective team behaviors of the appropriate "molarity" will be an important research problem to solve. Clearly teams provide a minimum of triangulation on the emergent behaviors of shared leadership.

This setting may also be one where participant observation is appropriate and useful. It may also be worthwhile to return to systematic observation of behavior in new venture teams rather than relying on self-reports. Bales and others (Bales 1951; Hare et al. 1955) developed a system of observing, counting, and categorizing group interaction which may be useful to those truly interested in new venture groups and the emergence and evolution of shared leadership as well as group-level communication, role development, creativity, and systematic search (below).

15.4.3 Communication

Communication is critical to entrepreneurial organizations – from writing a business plan through incorporation and team building to selling a product or service, some form of communication occurs. Communication is critical to overcoming the liabilities of newness since actions taken to legitimize, create a positive perception or reputation, and establish reliable production, delivery, and accountability systems all involve communication or display. Given its critical role and potential for easy observability (Ziegler et al. 1992), it is surprising that little research directly addresses communication behaviors of entrepreneurs.

Communication briefly defined is information exchange, which can be one way or two way in dyad linkages. That is, the communication process has sender, receiver, and mediating variability. Communication can be seen as precursor to and outcome of intentions. As a precursor/mediator, we ask what role communication plays in forming the intention. Receiving information through listening (reading) or watching may be more critical for shaping an intention than is sending information through speaking or writing. As an outcome of intention, one of the earliest acts entrepreneurs take to manifest their intentions is to speak/write about it. Speaking and writing are entrepreneurial behaviors that warrant additional academic research. If a product is developed, prototyping and displaying become critical. For both directions (the sending and receiving of information), cognitive errors can become communication errors but at the same time communication can reduce those perceptual or cognitive errors through feedback and iteration.

There is a scattering of conceptual and theoretical work that addresses or touches upon communication in the entrepreneurship process or setting. One example is debate about the impact of written business plans on venture outcomes (Honig 2004). Others have theorized about the translation of entrepreneur's mental models (sense making) into communication (sense giving), entrepreneurial vision communication (written and spoken), and the importance of linguistic metaphors (Hill and Levenhagen 1995). More recently, empirical studies found vision communication to have significant impact on venture growth (Baum et al. 1998). Communication is sometimes assumed and sometimes measured as "frequency of contact" in the growing literature on entrepreneur's social network and social capital (West 2007; West and Wilson 1995) and entrepreneurial teams (Forbes et al. 2006; Schjoedt forthcoming). Extending beyond the start-up processes and early opportunity identification communication is critical to venture financing, alliances, and technology choices (Redoli et al. 2008; Roodt 2005). Included here is the choice of what information to share, with whom and when and includes the issues of non-disclosure and protection of intellectual property. In addition, communication is critical and problematic for entrepreneurs who internationalize or establish virtual workplaces (Matlay and Westhead 2007; Todd and Javalgi 2007). Finally communication takes on greater complexity and perhaps more importance in teams. Sharing leadership and working as a team requires individuals to listen more and talk less, ask more questions and offer fewer answers, and openly share information.

Entrepreneurship scholars could more precisely link the cognitions, which are the foci of this book, to venture outcomes (start ups, organizations, growth of organizations) through careful attention to communication as a mediator of those intentions, with stories and narrative methods as important considerations (see discussion below). One highly cognitive turn on communication is the potential of entrepreneurs "inner conversation" or self-talk (an element of thought self-leadership) (Neck et al. 1999). Thinking out loud protocols are a way to operationalize this (Sonnentag 1996).

To develop our research on communication as entrepreneurial behavior, we might usefully form research relationships with communications scholars (from a range of specialties including rhetoric, social construction, and public relations) and scholars in information technology who are grounded in communications theories. Among the many questions we might ask are: How does a web-centric start up communicate effectively to gain legitimacy and reputation? What forms of communication best lead to commitments of others to the intention? What channels of communication are most useful and for what purposes? What types of communication errors are most likely among entrepreneurs of different types (novices, experts, gender, ethnic, and age differences) and at different stages in the venture creation process?

15.4.4 Behavioral Roles

Roles are abstractions and aggregations of behaviors, tasks, activities that comprise sensible, meaningful clusters (Mintzberg 1973) and differ from what Vesper (1980) and others refer to as "types of entrepreneurs." So while we have argued for precision and finer-grained accounting of behavior, we also believe that aggregation of individual behavior into roles is of potential value. Mintzberg found ten *managerial* roles in three clusters – interpersonal, informational, and decisional (one of which was "entrepreneurial" and referred to planned change inside organizations). If entrepreneurial behavior is to be distinct from managerial, entrepreneurship scholars need to follow Mintzberg's model, observe entrepreneurs, and "chunk" behavior into roles that they perform. These might be opportunist (finding, shaping opportunity), resource acquirers, salesman, etc. To do this, we must be clear on what constitutes role and the dynamics of role processes.

The concept of role derives, in part, from the dramaturgical approach to behavior (Goffman 1959), which uses theater as a metaphor for social interaction of many kinds. Many conceptual and some empirical efforts have hinted at the dramaturgical approach to entrepreneurship. The seminal paper by Gartner et al. (1992) tiled itself "Acting as if." One of the original outlines for that paper included a section on roles and scripts, entrepreneur as actor. Gartner (personal communication, 1990) commented "I want to get as much in about Stanisklavski's book CREATING A ROLE as possible, but there is a lot of material on roles that would be valuable to have." The dramaturgical approach would consider (among other elements) the relationship between actor, audience, backstage and outsiders (Goffman 1959), props, timing, costumes, impression management, rehearsals, and, importantly, the story being told. That section never got written into the text of the 1992 article. Nor did that manuscript make good use of the "if" of its title. In theater, the "if" is a method acting instruction that allows the actors to bring authenticity to the stage or screen (e.g., acting as if there were a man with a gun in corner). "*If* acts as a lever to lift us out of the world of actuality into the realm of imagination" (Stanislavski 1948). Insofar as ventures operate to create novelty, "something out of nothing" (Baker and Nelson 2005) or fulfill a vision (Baum et al. 1998), this *if* is important. Finally, the manuscript left out the mystification of the audience (its willingness to believe in the story of possibilities). For mystification to occur one of the five elements of social interaction is absent or obscure: the act (what is done), the scene (when and where), the agent (actor, here the entrepreneur), the agency (how the actors do it), or purpose (Manghan and Overington 1983).

Since then there has been some attention to role-related improvisation in the entrepreneurship literature (Baker et al. 2003; Hmieleski and Corbett 2008) which has both musical and theatrical roots. However, entrepreneurial behavior as drama and storytelling has not been developed other than the efforts by Martens et al. (2007) and Gartner (2007) who develop a narrative method issue of the *Journal of Business Venturing*, methods which are discursive, reflexive, and sense making and deal with story meaning and context.

There has been virtually no research on role taking and role making or role theory as it applies to entrepreneurs.[1] Scholars who do use the term "role" use it in different ways, lending to imprecision. When the role concept has been applied to entrepreneurship it often refers to how entrepreneurs are different in economic and organizational functions compared to other individuals. Thus some research and commentary refer to the role of entrepreneur as venture creator, change agent, risk bearer, or champion for innovation (Gartner 1988; Hayek 1985). Some use the term or imply the term when comparing nascent entrepreneurs to others (Carter et al. 2003) and when looking at categories of experience prior to becoming an entrepreneur (Dorbrev and Barnett 2005; e.g., previous work roles). Markman and

---

[1] ABIinform found only two articles with the joint search fields of entrepreneur and role behavior. The same two articles surfaced with search terms of entrepreneurship and role behavior. One article, Ortqvist et al. (2007), is in an obscure journal and described below. The other article dealt with corporate entrepreneurship.

Baron (2003) conceptualize person-role fit for entrepreneurs but do not cite role theory or operationalize that fit.

Katz and Kahn (1978) have defined role as a set of expectations about the behaviors of the role holder (here, the entrepreneur). Expectations about conduct are sent by individuals or groups that have formal, organizational relationship to the entrepreneur (e.g., investors, customers, and employees) and by those in informal relationships (e.g., family and friends). These expectations can be explicit (telling) or implicit (nonverbal signals or observed in a role model) and inform a "role schema" or prototype about what an entrepreneur is supposed to do (generally or in a specific situation). These expectations can conflict among senders resulting in role conflict for the entrepreneur; they can vary in clarity or change over time, resulting in role ambiguity for the entrepreneur; they can exceed the skills, resources, and time of the entrepreneur, resulting in role overload for the entrepreneur. Role conflict, ambiguity, and overload are sources of stress for entrepreneurs (Ortqvist et al. 2007; Schindehutte et al. 2006).

Role theory as described above was developed for organizational behavior settings (existing, often large, and formalized organizations) where roles and jobs are more clearly defined, not for organization creation. As we have discussed, the work, job, tasks, and expected behaviors of entrepreneurs are conceptually underdeveloped. However, social psychological constructs related to role such as identity and self-efficacy have found a place in the entrepreneurship literature (Down 2006; Elfring and Hulsink 2007; Martens et al. 2007). Of potential value is the literature on role taking or shaping and role transitions which entrepreneurial literature treats in the context of careers (Burke et al. 2008; Schjoedt and Shaver 2007) and learning (DeTienne and Chandler 2004). However, the role behaviors of the entrepreneur are not developed.

The novice entrepreneur, before becoming an entrepreneur, has had other roles and must transition from employee, student, etc., to entrepreneur. The early work of Nicholson (1984) provocatively suggested that entrepreneurs might take on that role with less change to themselves and more proactive determination of the content and structure of their role or work than organizational employment transitions (e.g., from individual contributor to supervisor). To date, only one study has attempted to empirically test this assertion. Ortqvist and associates (2007) measured entrepreneurs' perception of their role redefinition (self-reports of negotiating different expectations or changing personal priorities or expectations of self) and role behavior (increasing performance or passively withdrawing or engaging in diversions). They found that negotiating expectations and increasing performance to meet role expectations associated with higher venture performance.

More research on role taking and shaping of entrepreneurs could follow and use a finer grained approach to self- and other expectations about behavior as entrepreneurs develop. While there are many provocative research questions, we propose these: To what extent and how accurately and effectively do role schemas develop out of active experience (class room activities, role modeling) compared conceptualizing (reading/watching about entrepreneurs in the media)? To what extent do entrepreneurs experiment with imitation and find "true-to-self" behavioral strategies or roles and evaluate those strategies (Ibarra 1999) and are these more effective than other processes that result in behavioral strategies? How much novelty, autonomy, and discretion (Nicholson 1984; Parasurman et al. 1996) do entrepreneurs have in creating their role at the various transitions from nascent, start up, small business, family business, growth business, publicly traded/acquired business? To what extent do factors such as cognitive complexity, role breadth, self-efficacy, and situational attributes such as feedback and time spent "acting as if" mediate transitions in entrepreneur's roles (Neale and Griffin 2006)?

15.4.5 Creativity

This section takes a turn from our previous considerations above insofar as entrepreneurial creativity is an enormous construct worthy of a book on its own merits. Creativity research is also far from being "behavioral" in the way we call for. Creativity in entrepreneurs encompasses traits, intelligence, processes, abilities, competencies, and behaviors that produce effective novelty, generating variations that have relevance to the situation or task at hand (Amabile 1996). This creativity applies importantly to opportunity identification (Corbett 2005; Ward 2004). In addition to playing an important role in shared leadership (Pearce and Manz 2005), creativity competence plays a role in the growth stages of a venture (Baum and Bird forthcoming).

Generally most scholars accept that creativity is a cognitive and behavioral process (Csikszentmihalyi 1996), similar to problem solving, that begins with some sort of tension, followed by preparation (information collection and immersion), incubation, insight (articulation or expression), evaluation, followed by elaboration and iteration where the "devil is in the details." The process is rarely linear but iterative and recursive and includes both conscious search and expression but also often deeply subconscious incubation. Most creative insight comes as a result of immersion in an intellectual, economic, or social domain and/or immersion in a problem or object of curiosity. In many organizational and educational settings, the problems are presented and the individual asked to apply themselves to develop a solution. Presented problems often have a "rightness" or rationality criteria applied (or implied) to solutions, from cost-effectiveness, political correctness, timeliness to fit with prototype (as in educational settings where we grade exams, case solutions, and research assignments).

Finding problems (opportunities) worthy of solution (or new venture creation) may emerge from the three sources provided by Csikszentmihalyi (1996). One source is personal life experience, including overcoming deprivations and setbacks, a life-long habit of curiosity, or frustration with a product or process in the marketplace. The second source is knowledge of the domain and recognition of anomalies or gaps in knowledge and/or the ability to bridge to other domains. The third source is the larger social environment that might include having trusted "think tank" friends or advisors and the emotional intelligence or "presence of mind" while experiencing social or economic chaos. Whatever the source, creativity takes incubation time, time for reflection, and puttering – sometimes only moments and at other times, years.

Most of the approaches to creativity in entrepreneurship and the larger domains of organizational behavior and psychology have not addressed creative behavior in the way we call for in this chapter (molecular enough to specify the observable actions taken). It turns out that measures of individual creativity in these larger domains vary widely in what they measure, what audience is appropriate for the measure, and usefulness in surveys, field studies, and experimental design. Most psychology and organizational behavior approaches look for personality precursors (openness to experience, tolerance for ambiguity), while others more in line with this book focus on cognition to assess individual creative capacity (Simonton 2003).

Psychologists partition the measurement of creative capacity into *creative products* such as drawings, lists, stories, etc., and *creative cognitions* which individuals use to generate these products (Cropley 1999, 2000). Organizational behavior researchers have looked at patents or idea disclosures and superior/peer ratings of individual innovativeness (which are correlated) (Keller and Holland 1982; Tierney et al. 1999). Creative products (perhaps including patents and idea disclosures) require an expert panel of judges whose expertise is in itself a source of variance although rigorous methods for this type of qualitative measurement have been developed (Boyatzis 1998).

Although there are measures of creative cognition (Guilford 1962; Torrance 1965; Treffinger 2003; Treffinger et al. 1971), these measures and others less well known are inappropriate for surveys and for field studies of entrepreneurs as they are timed and generally oriented to a school environment. In addition, these measures which focus on divergent thinking have been criticized as not tapping the whole of creative capacity (Torrance 1965). In addition, debate lingers over whether divergent thinking (or creative intelligence for that matter) is a generalized capacity or domain specific.

More recent efforts show a broad range of creative processes (problem construction or problem finding, information encoding, category selection, and category reorganization and combination) can be assessed and significantly contribute to problem solution quality and originality (Mumford et al. 1997). Of these, problem construction is the earliest to operationalize and closest to opportunity identification and thus to entrepreneurship. These scholars (Mumford et al. 1994; Mumford et al. 1993) used four complex and ill-defined problems and respondents chose four alternative definitions of the problem from a previously developed list of 16, which varied in use of original goals, approaches, information, and restriction of problem construction. Both of these studies used unidentified expert judges to rate quality and originality of solutions. The four problems include (1) diplomat with State Department sees colleague who has had too much to drink at a social event, (2) athlete representing your country told by a doctor he/she is going to need surgery, (3) principal at an elementary school with a snake that got loose, and (4) student on a team project with a member not showing for meetings. An additional two problems perhaps more relevant to entrepreneurship are not published.

Thus when Baum and Bird (forthcoming) wanted to assess creative intelligence of entrepreneurs using survey methods, they chose Mednick's (1968) Remote Word Association Test (RAT) as extended by Bowden and Jung-Beeman (2003). RAT measures divergent and creative thinking by testing individuals' ability to see associative concepts among 30 sets of three words (e.g., Water:Tobacco:Stove = Pipe). RAT is a commonly used measure of creativity and has been shown to correlate with supervisor ratings of creativity (Fong 2006), which is the most common operationalization of individual creativity in OB. This worked well in their study of successful intelligence, which helped to predict new venture growth.

What of the behaviors that lead to outputs judged creative? Getzels and Csikszentmihalyi (1976) looking at problem finding and construction found that art students faced with the task of drawing still life images who did more manipulation of more of the objects (of a fixed set provided), who chose unusual combinations of objects, and who erased and changed their drawing more often produced drawings that were judged (by lay people, artists, and expert judges) as being more creative. This study found that time spent finding the problem and working out the "devilish details" of solutions is important for esthetic value and originality.

Creative problem finding and problem solving seems to engage the whole person. Gelb (1998) who consults on creativity in organizations thinks that curiosity (perhaps behaviorally assessed by asking good questions), actively engaging all senses, and developing kinesthetic or physical grace, poise, and fitness are important (and behavioral) contributors to creativity. He also proposes "mind mapping" as a way to actively and concretely explore the relationships among facets or ideas (that may be part of an opportunity or problem). Likewise Twyla Tharp, a noted dancer and choreographer speaks of developing rituals of preparation, organizing in boxes (literally), and "scratching" for a good idea which for a fashion designer maybe visiting vintage stores, for an actor it may be doing theater games or improvisation, for others it is reading, talking with others, etc. (Tharp 2003). These writers suggest that creativity is indeed behavioral and not "merely" a function of predispositions or cognitions.

15.4.6 Opportunity Discovery

Like creativity, opportunity recognition and discovery is a largely cognitive process (and thus not behavioral). However, there is an emerging behavioral approach to this important competency of entrepreneurship. This approach begins with identifying the differences in cognition and behavior between novice and repeat entrepreneurs who become "experts" in opportunity recognition. Thus while some scholars claim that entrepreneurs discover opportunities by accident or luck by being alert (Kirzner 1997), other research shows that repeat entrepreneurs actually engage in an active search for opportunities based on their existing knowledge. One scholar in particular, James Fiet, has made substantial contributions to this area (Fiet 2002, 2007). Based on information economics (e.g., Hayek 1945), Fiet argues that repeat entrepreneurs engage in a constrained, systematic search when they discover opportunities. In an experiment, Fiet and Patel (2008) found individuals in the alertness group found 35 ideas of which one was high potential, whereas the group using constricted, systematic search identified 24 ideas of which nine were high in wealth-generating potential.

Fiet (2002, 2007) argues that specific knowledge (knowledge about people, places, technology, timing, and special conditions), which is a subset of prior experience and which is also seen as practical intelligence (Baum et al. 2009), is the basis for active opportunity discovery. In effect, opportunity discovering behaviors of repeat entrepreneurs are focused intentional acquisition and use of specific knowledge. These "behaviors" would include selection, identification, choice, specification, interpretation, revision, and interaction with other people.[2] These behaviors are evident in the opportunity discovery process as follows: First, based on the entrepreneur's prior specific knowledge, the entrepreneur selects information channels. An information channel is a relatively low-cost source of new specific information capable of directing the entrepreneur's attention toward opportunity discovery based on what and whom they know already. The search is thus actively constrained by the entrepreneur's prior knowledge and choice of information channels. Second, after choosing the information channels, the entrepreneur clusters the information channels into consideration sets to maximize results. A consideration set is a group of information channels that hold promise to be helpful for the entrepreneur to locate opportunity. Third, from the consideration sets the entrepreneur searches for signals (new information that provides view of the future, especially as it relates to new venture creation and wealth generation) that the entrepreneur interprets as the existence of an opportunity.

While constrained, systematic search for opportunity discovery is illustrated above for the individual; it is also applicable to teams. Actually, it may justify why entrepreneurial teams outperform ventures created by an individual (Baum and Silverman 2004; Chandler and Hanks 1998; Schjoedt 2009; Schjoedt and Kraus forthcoming). The benefits of team search for opportunity are based on team diversity expanding the number of information channels that comprise the consideration sets. This may also explain why shared leadership and intra-team communication (e.g., debate) enhance venture performance (Ensley et al. 2006a).

Clearly more refinement on opportunity search behaviors could help expand the knowledge and usefulness of entrepreneurial behavior. Search behaviors must necessarily include some communication behaviors (e.g., listening and reading). How is search behavior different from communication behavior? What methods and sources of search are used, how frequently, and in what order? While constrained by existing knowledge, do differences exist in systematic search behavior across industries? Are search behaviors different at different times in industry development? These and other research questions warrant our further attention.

---

[2] Other than interaction with others, these behaviors may or may not be observable. As stated, they are lacking specificity we recommend.

15.5 Concluding Remarks

One cannot think one's way to creating a new venture. Actions in the form of concrete behaviors are necessary for new venture creation and organizational birth. Thus for the field of entrepreneurship research to provide valuable contributions to entrepreneurs, educators, and society, advances in the area of entrepreneurial behavior are critical. While 12% of the articles published in two top entrepreneurship journals – *Entrepreneurship Theory and Practice* and *Journal of Business Venturing* – over a 3-year period (2005–2007) addressed entrepreneurial behavior, more can be done to clarify what entrepreneurs do to enact their intentions. Greater specificity of behaviors will benefit our research and teaching.

With this chapter, we offered five behaviorally anchored research areas – leadership, communication, behavioral roles, and two less behavioral but critically important areas – creativity and opportunity discovery. These areas have scholars, research, and methods (organizational behavior, sociology, and behavioral psychology), which may be adapted and joined to our specific domain. In doing this, we emphasize three critical issues. First, entrepreneurial behavior consists of *discrete units of action that can be observed by others* – they are visible, auditory, and/or kinesthetic and if others are present, social or potentially interpersonal in nature – *they are "sized" to be meaningful.* However, today many of the "behaviors" considered in entrepreneurship research are not discrete but complex and often ill defined as they are broad and unspecific in nature (e.g., initiating investor relationships, preparing a business plan, articulating a business idea).

Second, we need to develop our own agreed-upon set of core behaviors and from this develop psychometrically sound empirical tools (similar to the work on leadership). Entrepreneurial behavior may be inherently more complex or multidimensional than the leadership in extant organizations that has been well measured and which spawned the situational and contingency approaches. Entrepreneurs face a process and stage of organization phenomena that may require different behaviors. However, if we begin with a manageable context such as start-up and nascent ventures, we stand a chance to accomplish our equivalent Entrepreneurial Behavior Description Questionnaire. A common core of behavioral constructs, if not measures, would allow theories of and empirical research on entrepreneurial behavior to accumulate. From this, we could also advance observational studies of entrepreneurial teams, role taking, communication, and creativity of individuals and teams as well as opening other fertile areas for research.

Third, however we measure behavior we need to do so more rigorously than the current state of the field. Single-item measures and self-reports need to be supplemented with methods drawn from the other disciplines of organizational behavior, sociology, and behavioral psychology. Minimally we need to control for social desirability bias. More innovatively, we could do behavioral sampling (beeper or diary studies), laboratory and field experiments (or quasi experiments) where behavior is a specified variable.

In sum, we call for more studies and better operationalizations of entrepreneurial behavior. We also caution against blindly adopting models, theory, and even measures from organizational behavior, which have evolved in studies of larger, mature organizations. We have no reason a priori to expect entrepreneurs to behave as the leaders studied by the Ohio State researchers (Hemphill and Coons 1957) nor do we have any reason to suppose that there is a path-goal model to entrepreneurship such as that developed by House (1996). Likewise, the received knowledge of organizational behavior, sociology, and behavioral psychology needs to be well understood and critically applied to our domain.

Finally, if the postulates of this book are even in part true or verified, then entrepreneurial behavior broadly defined, would likely be seen in contexts that extend beyond the start-up new venture. With careful theorizing and better (general) measures of the entrepreneurial mind and entrepreneurial behavior, we might find people forming intentions, making choices and behaving entrepreneurially in a myriad of contexts including governmental agencies, non-governmental organizations, communities, families, and temporary settings such as rush hour subways, twitter collectives, singles bars, and natural disaster management.

> We have to understand the world can only be grasped by action, not by contemplation. The hand is more important than the eye .... The hand is the cutting edge of the mind. – Jacob Bronowski

References

Alsos G, Isaksen E, Ljunggren E (2006) New venture financing and subsequent business growth in men- and women-led businesses. Entrepreneurship Theory and Practice 30(5): 667–686

Amabile TM (1996) Creativity in Context. Westview Press, Boulder, CO

Arenius P, DeClercq D (2005) A network-based Approach on opportunity recognition. Small Business Economics 24(3): 249–265

Arnold HJ, Feldman DC (1981) Social desirability response bias in self-report choice situations. Academy of Management Journal 24(2): 377–385

Avolio B, Yammarino F (2002) Transformational and Charismatic Leadership: The Road Ahead. JAI Press, New York

Baker T, Miner AS, Eesley DT (2003) Improvising firms: Bricolage, account giving and improvisational competencies in the founding process. Research Policy 32(2): 255–276

Baker T, Nelson RE (2005) Creating something from nothing: Resource construction through entrepreneurial bricolage. Administrative Science Quarterly 50: 329–366

Bales RF (1951) Interaction Process Analysis: A Method for the Study of Small Groups. Addison-Wesley, Cambridge, MA

Barker JR (1993) Tightening the iron cage: Concertive control in self-managing teams. Administrative Science Quarterly 38(3): 408–437

Baron RA (2002) OB and entrepreneurship: The reciprocal benefits of closer conceptual links. Research in Organizational Behavior 24: 225–269

Baron RA (2008) The role of affect in the entrepreneurial process. The Academy of Management Review 33(2): 328–340

Baron RA, Ensley MD (2006) Opportunity recognition as the detection of meaningful patterns: Evidence from comparisons of novice and experienced entrepreneurs. Management Science 52(9): 1331–1344

Baum W (2002) From molecular to moral: A paradigm shift in behavior analysis. Journal of Experimental Analysis of Behavior 78(1): 95–116

Baum JR, Bird BJ, Singh S (2009) The practical intelligence of growth oriented entrepreneurs: Antecedents and a link with new venture growth, Working Paper: University of Maryland

Baum JR, Bird B (forthcoming) The successful intelligence of high growth entrepreneurs: Links to new venture growth. Organization Science

Baum JR, Locke EA (2004) The relationship of entrepreneurial traits, skill, and motivation to subsequent venture growth. Journal of Applied Psychology 89: 587–598

Baum JR, Locke EA, Kirkpartrick SA (1998) A longitudinal study of the relation of vision and vision communication to venture growth in entrepreneurial firms. Journal of Applied Psychology 83(1): 43–54

Baum JA, Silverman BS (2004) Picking winners or building them? Alliance, intellectual, and human capital as selection criteria in venture financing and performance of biotechnology startups. Journal of Business Venturing 19(3): 411–436

Bhide AV (2000) The Origin and Evolution of New Businesses. Oxford University Press, New York

Bierly P, Daly P (2007) Alternative knowledge strategies, competitive environment, and organizational performance in small manufacturing firms. Entrepreneurship Theory and Practice 31(4): 493–516

Bird B (1989) Entrepreneurial behavior. Scott Foresman, Glenview, IL

Bowden EM, Jung-Beeman M (2003) One hundred forty-four remote associate problems: short insight-like problems with one-word solutions. Behavioral Research Methods, Instruments, and Computers 35: 634–639

Boyatzis R (1998) Transforming qualitative information. Sage, Thousand Oaks, CA

Boyd BK, Gove S, Hitt MA (2005) Construct measurement in strategic management research: illusion or reality? Strategic Management Journal 26(3): 239–257

Brown TE, Davidsson P, Wiklund J (2001) An operationalization of Stevenson's conceptualization of entrepreneurship as opportunity-based firm behavior. Strategic Management Journal 22: 953–968

Burke AE, R. FF, Nolan MA (2008) What makes a die-hard entrepreneur? Beyond the 'employee or entrepreneur' dichotomy. Small Business Economics 31(2): 93–115

Campbell JP, Dunnette MD, Lawler EE, Weick KE (1970) Managerial Behavior, Performance, and Effectiveness. McGraw-Hill, New York

Carson JB, Tesluk PE, Marrone JA (2007) Shared leadership in terms: An investigation of antecedent conditions and performance. Academy of Management Journal 50(5): 1217–1234

Carter NM, Gartner WB, Reynolds PD (1996) Exploring start-up event sequences. Journal of Business Venturing 11(3): 151–166

Carter N, Gartner W, Shaver K, Gatewood E (2003) The career reasons of nascent entrepreneurs. Journal of Business Venturing 18: 13–39

Chandler GN, Hanks SH (1998) An examination of the substitutability of founders human and financial capital in emerging business ventures. Journal of Business Venturing 13(5): 353–369

Chandler GN, Lyon DW (2001) Issues of research design and construct measurement in entrepreneurship research: The past decade. Entrepreneurship Theory and Practice 25: 101–113.

Chrisman JEM, Hall J (2005) The influence of guided preparation on the long-term performance of new ventures. Journal of Business Venturing 20(6): 769–791

Churchill GA (1979) A paradigm for developing better measures of marketing constructs. JMR, Journal of Marketing Research (pre-1986) 16(000001): 64–73

Ciavarella MA, Buchholtz AK, Riordan CM, Gatewood RD, Stokes GA (2004) The big five and venture survival: Is there a linkage? Journal of Business Venturing 19: 465–483

Cloninger P, Oviatt B (2007) Service content and the internationalization of young ventures: An empirical test. Entrepreneurship Theory and Practice 31(2): 233–256

Cogliser CC, Brigham KH (2004) The intersection of leadership and entrepreneurship: Mutual lessons to be learned. Leadership Quarterly 15: 771–799

Corbett AC (2005) Experiential learning within the process of opportunity identification. Entrepreneurship Theory and Practice 29(4): 473–491

Corbett AC (2007) Learning asymmetries and the discovery of entrepreneurial opportunities. Journal of Business Venturing 22(1): 97–118

Cropley AJ (1999) Creativity and cognition: Producing effective novelty. Roeper Review 21(4): 253–261

Cropley AJ (2000) Defining and measuring creativity: Are creativity tests worth using? Roeper Review 23(2): 72–79

Csikszentmihalyi M (1996) Creativity. HarperCollins, New York

Daft RL (2004) Organization Theory and Design. South-Western, Mason, OH

Davidsson P, Delmar F, Wiklund J (2006) Entrepreneurship and the Growth of Firms. Edward Elgar, Northampton, MA

DeTienne DR, Chandler GN (2004) Opportunity identification and its role in the entrepreneurial classroom: A pedagogical approach and empirical test. Academy of Management Learning & Education 3(3): 242–257

DeTienne DR, Chandler G (2007) The role of gender in opportunity identification. Entrepreneurship Theory and Practice 31(3): 365–386

DeTienne DR, Shepherd DA, De Castro JO (2008) The fallacy of "only the strong survive": The effects of extrinsic motivation on the persistence decisions for under-performing firms. Journal of Business Venturing 23(5): 528–546

Dorbrev S, Barnett W (2005) Organizational roles and transition to entrepreneurship. Academy of Management Journal 48(3): 433–449

Down S (2006) Narratives of Enterprise: Crafting Entrepreneurial Self-identity in a Small Firm. Elgar, Northhampton, MA

Ebben J, Johnson A (2006) Bootstrapping in small firms: An empirical analysis of change over time. Journal of Business Venturing 21(6): 851–865

Edelman LF, Manolova TS, Brush CG (2008) Entrepreneurship education: Correspondence between practices of nascent entrepreneurs and textbook prescriptions for success. Academy of Management Learning & Education 7(1): 56–70

Elfring T, Hulsink W (2007) Networking by entrepreneurs: Patterns of tie-formation in emerging organizations. Organization Studies 28(12): 1849–1872

Ensley MD, Hmieleski KM, Pearce CL (2006a) The importance of vertical and shared leadership within new venture top management teams: Implications for the performance of startups. Leadership Quarterly 17(3): 217–231

Ensley MD, Pearce CL (2001) Shared cognition in top management teams: Implications for new venture performance. Journal of Organizational Behavior 22(2): 145–160

Ensley MD, Pearce C, Hmieleski K (2006b) The moderating effect of environmental dynamism on the relationship between entrepreneur leadership behavior and new venture performance. Journal of Business Venturing 21(2): 243–263

Essers C, Benschop Y (2007) Enterprising identities: Female entrepreneurs of Moroccan or Turkish origin in the Netherlands. Organization Studies 28(1): 49–69

Fiegener M (2005) Determinants of board participation in the strategic decisions of small corporations. Entrepreneurship Theory and Practice 29(5): 627–650

Fiet JO (2002) The Systematic Search for Entrepreneurial Discoveries. Quorum Books, Westport, CN

Fiet JO (2007) A prescriptive analysis of search and discovery. The Journal of Management Studies 44(4): 592–611

Fiet JO, Patel PC (2008) Entrepreneurial discovery as constrained, systematic search. Small Business Economics 30(3): 215–229

Fleishman E (1998) Consideration and structure" another look at their role in leadership research. In: Dansereau F, Yammarino F (eds) Leadership: The Multiple-Level Approaches. JAI Press, Stamford, CT

Fong CT (2006) The effects of emotional ambivalence on creativity. Academy of Management Journal 49(5): 1016–1030

Forbes D (2005) The effects of strategic decision making on entrepreneurial self-efficacy. Entrepreneurship Theory and Practice 29(5): 599–626

Forbes D, Borchert P, Zellmer-Bruhn M, Sapienza H (2006) Entrepreneurial team formation: An exploration of new member addition. Entrepreneurship Theory and Practice 30(2): 225–248

Frese M (2007) The psychological actions and entrepreneurial success: An action theory approach. In: Baum JR, Frese M, Baron RA (eds) The Psychology of Entrepreneurship. Lawrence Erlbaum, Mahwah, NJ

Garnter W, Shaver KG, Carter NM, Reynolds PD (2004) Handbook of Entrepreneurial Dynamics. Sage, Thousand Oaks, CA

Gartner WB (1988) "Who is an entrepreneur?" Is the wrong question. American Journal of Small Business 12(4): 11–32

Gartner WB (2007) Entrepreneurial narrative and a science of the imagination. Journal of Business Venturing 22(5): 613–627

Gartner WB, Bird BJ, Starr JA (1992) Acting as if: Differentiating entrepreneurial from organizational behavior. Entrepreneurship Theory and Practice 16(3): 13–31

Gatewood EJ, Shaver KG, Powers JB, Gartner WB (2002) Entrepreneurial expectancy, task effort, and performance. Entrepreneurship Theory and Practice 27(2): 187–206

Gelb MJ (1998) How to Think like Leonardo da Vinci. Delacorte, New York

Getzels JW, Csikszentmihalyi M (1976) The Creative Vision. Wiley, New York

Godfrey PC, Hill CWL (1995) The problem of unobservables in strategic management research. Strategic Management Journal 16(7): 519–533

Goffman E (1959) Presentation of Self in Everyday Life. Anchor, New York

Grandi A, Grimaldi R (2005) Academics' organizational characteristics and the generation of successful business ideas. Journal of Business Venturing 20(6): 821–845

Grichnik D (2008) Risky choices in new venture decisions – experimental evidence from Germany and the United States. Journal of International Entrepreneurship 6(1): 22–47

Gruber M (2007) Uncovering the value of planning in new venture creation: A process and contingency perspective. Journal of Business Venturing 22(6): 782–807

Guilford JP (1962) Potentiality for creativity. Gifted Child Quarterly 6: 87–90

Haber S, Reicheil A (2007) The cumulative nature of the entrepreneurial process: The contribution of human capital, planning and environment resources to small venture performance. Journal of Business Venturing 22(1): 119–145

Hanlon D, Saunders C (2007) Marshaling resources to form small new ventures: Toward a more holistic understanding of entrepreneurial support. Entrepreneurship Theory and Practice 31(4): 619–641

Hare AP, Borgatta EF, Bales RF (eds) (1955) Small Groups: Studies in Social Interaction. Alfred Knopf, New York

Hauser L (2006) The internet encyclopedia of philosophy

Hayek FA (1945) The use of knowledge in society. American Economic Review 35: 519–530

Hayek FA (1985) Richard Cantillon. The Journal of Libertarian Studies 7(2): 217–247

Hemphill J, Coons A (1957) Development of the leader behavior description questionnaire. In: Stogdill R, Coons A (eds) Leader Behavior: Its Description and Measurement. Ohio State University, Columbus, OH

Hill R, Levenhagen M (1995) Metaphors and mental models: Sensemaking and sensegiving in innovative and entrepreneurial activities. Journal of Management 21(6): 1057–1074

Hite J (2005) Evolutionary processes and paths of relationally embedded network ties in emerging entrepreneurial firms. Entrepreneurship Theory and Practice 29(1): 113–144

Hmieleski KM, Corbett AC (2008) The contrasting interaction effects of improvisational behavior with entrepreneurial self-efficacy on new venture performance and entrepreneur work satisfaction. Journal of Business Venturing 23: 482–496

Honig B (2004) Entrepreneurship education: Toward a model of contingency-based business planning. Academy of Management Learning and Education 3(3): 258–273

House R (1996) Path-goal theory of leadership: Lessons, legacy, and a reformulated theory. Leadership Quarterly Autumn: 323–352

Ibarra H (1999) Provisional selves: Experimenting with image and identity in professional adaptation. Administrative Science Quarterly 44(4): 764–791

Jacoby J (1978) Consumer research: A state of the arts review. Journal of Marketing 42(2): 87–96

Katz D, Kahn RL (1978) The Social Psychology of Organizations. John Wiley, New York

Keller RT, Holland WE (1982) The measurement of performance among research and development professional employees: A longitudinal analysis. IEEE Transactions on Engineering Management EM 29(2): 54–58

Kirzner IM (1997) Entrepreneurial discovery and the competitive market process: An Austrian approach. Journal of Economic Literature 35(1): 60–85

Kolvereid L, Isaksen E (2006) New business start-up and subsequent entry into self-employment. Journal of Business Venturing 21(6): 866–885

Kouzes J, Posner B (2002) Leadership Challenge, 3rd edn. Jossey-Bass, San Francisco

Langowitz N, Minniti M (2007) The entrepreneurial propensity of women. Entrepreneurship Theory and Practice 31(3): 341–364

Lichtenstein B, Carter N, Dooley K, Gartner WB (2007) Complexity dynamics of nascent entrepreneurship. Journal of Business Venturing 22(2): 236–261

Lichtenstein B, Dooley K, Lumpkin G (2006) Measuring emergence in the dynamics of new venture creation. Journal of Business Venturing 21(2): 153–175

Lord RG, Brown DJ, Freiberg SJ (1999) Understanding the dynamics of leadership: The role of follower self-concepts in the leader/follower relationship. Organizational Behavior and Human Decision Processes 78(3): 167–203

Lumpkin GT, Cogliser CC, Schneider DR (2009) Understanding and measuring autonomy: An entrepreneurial orientation perspective. Entrepreneurship Theory and Practice 33(1): 47–69

Manghan IL, Overington MA (1983) Dramatism and the theatrical metaphor. In: Morgan G (ed) Beyond Method: Strategies for Social Research. Sage, Beverly Hills, CA

Markman GD, Baron RA (2003) Person – entrepreneurship fit: Why some people are more successful as entrepreneurs than others. Human Resource Management Review 13: 281–301

Martens ML, Jennings JE, Jennings D (2007) Do the stories they tell get them the money they need? The role of entrepreneurial narratives in resource acquisition. Academy of Management Journal 50(5): 1107–1132

Matlay H, Westhead P (2007) Innovation and collaboration in virtual teams of e-entrepreneurs: Case evidence from the European tourism industry. International Journal of Entrepreneurship and Innovation 8(1): 29–36

McMullen J, Shepherd D (2006) Entrepreneurial action and the role of uncertainty in the theory of the entrepreneur. The Academy of Management Review 31(1): 132–152

Mednick SA (1968) Remote associates test. Journal of Creative Behavior 2: 213–214

Miller A, Galanter E, Pribram K (1969) Plans and the Structure of Behavior. Holt, London

Mintzberg H (1973) The Nature of Managerial Work. Prentice-Hall, Englewood Cliffs, NJ

Mitchell R, Busenitz L, Bird B, Gaglio C, McMullen J, Morse E, et al. (2007) The central question in entrepreneurial cognition research 2007. Entrepreneurship Theory and Practice 31(1): 1–27

Mumford M, Baughman WA, Supinski EP, Costanza DP, Threlfall KV (1994) Cognitive and metacognitive skill development: Alternative measures for predicting leadership potential (No. Tech. Rep. No. MRI 93-2). Bethesda, MD: Management Research Institute

Mumford M, Baughman WA, Supinski EP, Threlfall KV (1993) Cognitive and metacognitive skill development: Alternative measures for predicting leadership potential (No. rep. No. SBIR A92-154, US Army research Institute for Behavioral and Social Sciences). Bethesda, MD: Management Research Institute

Mumford M, Supinski EP, Baughman WA, Costanza DP, Threlfall KV (1997) Process-based measures of creative problem-solving skills: V. overall prediction. Creativity Research Journal 10(6): 73–85

Neale M, Griffin MA (2006) A model of self-held work roles and role transitions. Human Performance 19(1): 23–41

Neck CP, Neck HM, Manz CC, Godwin J (1999) "I think I can: I think I can": A self-leadership perspective toward enhancing entrepreneur thought patterns, self-efficacy, and performance. Journal of Managerial Psychology 14(6): 477–501

Nicholson N (1984) A theory of work role transitions. Administrative Science Quarterly 29: 172–191

Nunnally J, Bernstein I (1994) Psychometric Theory. McGraw Hill, New York

Orser B, Riding A, Manley K (2006) Women entrepreneurs and financial capital. Entrepreneurship Theory and Practice 30(5): 643–665

Ortqvist D, Drnovsek M, Wincent J (2007) Entrepreneurs' coping with challenging role expectations. Baltic Journal of Management 2(3): 288–304

Parasurman S, Purohit YS, Godshalk VM (1996) Work and family variables, entrepreneurial career success, and psychological well-being. Journal of Vocational Behavior 48: 275–300

Pearce CL, Conger JA (2003) Shared Leadership: Reframing the Hows and Whys of Leadership. Sage, Thousand Oaks, CA

Pearce CL, Manz CC (2005) The new silver bullets of leadership: The importance of self- and shared leadership in knowledge work. Organizational Dynamics 34(2): 130–140

Pearce CL, Manz CC, Sims HP (2008) The roles of vertical and shared leadership in the enactment of executive corruption: Implications for research and practice. Leadership Quarterly 19(3): 353–359

Peter PJ (1979) Reliability: A review of psychometric basics and recent marketing practices. Journal of Marketing Research 16(000001): 6–7

Rauch A, Frese M, Utsch A (2005) Effects of human capital and long-term human resources development and utilization on employment growth of small-scale businesses: A causal analysis1. Entrepreneurship Theory and Practice 29(6): 681–698

Redoli J, Mompo R, Garcia-Diez J, Lopez-Coronado M (2008) A model for the assessment and development of Internet-based information and communication services in small and medium enterprises. Technovation 28(7): 424–435

Reynolds PD (2000) National panel study of US business start ups: Background and methodology. Databases for the Study of Entrepreneurship 4: 153–227

Reynolds PD, White SB (1997) The Entrepreneurial Process: Economic Growth, Men, Women, and Minorities. Quorum Books, Westport, CT

Roberts MJ (1998) Heather Evans. Cambridge, MA: Harvard Business School Publishing

Roodt J (2005) Self-employment and the required skills. Management Dynamics 14(4): 18–33

Schindehutte M, Morris M, Allen J (2006) Beyond achievement: Entrepreneurship as extreme experience. Small Business Economics 27(4–5): 349–368

Schjoedt L (2009) Defining entrepreneurial teams and modeling team performance. In: Fink M, Kraus S (eds) The Management of Small and Medium Enterprises. London, Routledge

Schjoedt L (forthcoming) Entrepreneurial job characteristics: An examination of their effects on entrepreneurial satisfaction. Entrepreneurship Theory and Practice

Schjoedt L, Kraus S (forthcoming) Entrepreneurial teams: Definition and performance factors. Management Research News

Schjoedt L, Shaver KG (2007) Deciding on an entrepreneurial career: A test of the pull and push hypotheses using the panel study of entrepreneurial dynamics data 1. Entrepreneurship Theory and Practice 31(5): 733–752

Shepherd D, Douglas E, Shanley M (2000) New venture survival: Ignorance, external shocks, and risk reduction strategies. Journal of Business Venturing 15: 393–410

Shook C, Priem R, McGee J (2003) Venture creation and the enterprising individual: A review and synthesis. Journal of Management 29(3): 379–399

Simonton DK (2003) Scientific creativity as constrained stochastic behavior: The integration of product, person, and process perspectives. Psychological Bulletin 129(4): 475–494

Singh R, Lucas L (2005) Not just domestic engineers: An exploratory study of homemaker entrepreneurs. Entrepreneurship Theory and Practice 29(1): 79–90

Sonnentag S (1996) Planning and knowledge about strategies: their relationship to work characteristics is software design. Behaviour & Information Technology 15(4): 213–225

Spain JS, Eaton LG, Funder DC (2001) Perspective on personality: The relative accuracy of self versus others for the prediction of emotion and behavior. Journal of Personality 68(5): 837–867

Spencer LM, Spencer SM (1993) Competence at Work: Models for Superior Performance. John Wiley & Sons, New York

Stanislavski K (1948) An Actor Prepares. Theatre Arts, New York

Sternberg R (1988) The Triarchic Mind. Viking, New York

Sternberg R (2004) Successful intelligence as a basis for entrepreneurship. Journal of Business Venturing 19: 189–202

Stewart WH, Roth PL (2007) A meta-analysis of achievement motivation differences between entrepreneurs and managers. Journal of Small Business Management 45(4): 401–421

Stogdill R, Coons A (1957) Leader Behavior: Its Description and Measurement. Ohio State University, Columbus, OH

Talaulicar T, Grundei J, Werder A (2005) Strategic decision making in start-ups: the effect of top management team organization and processes on speed and comprehensiveness. Journal of Business Venturing 20(4): 519–541

Tharp T (2003) The Creative Habit. Simon & Schuster, New York

Tierney P, Farmer SM, Graen GB (1999) An examination of leadership and employee creativity: The relevance of traits and relationships. Personnel Psychology 52(3): 591–620

Todd PR, Javalgi RG (2007) Internationalization of SMEs in India. International Journal of Emerging Markets 2(2): 166–180

Torabi MR (1994) Reliability methods and number of items in development of health instruments. Health values: the Journal of Health Behavior, Education and Promotion 18(6): 56–59

Tornikoski E, Newbert S (2007) Exploring the determinants of organizational emergence: A legitimacy perspective. Journal of Business Venturing 22(2): 311–335

Torrance EP (1965) Rewarding Creative Behavior: Experiments in Classroom Activity. Prentice-hall, Englewood Cliffs, NH

Treffinger DJ (2003) Assessment and measurement in creativity and creative problem solving. In: Houtz JC (ed) The Educational Psychology of Creativity. Hampton Press, Cresskill, NJ

Treffinger DJ, Renzulli JS, Feldhusen JF (1971) Problems in the assessment of creative thinking. Journal of Creative Behavior 5: 104–111

Vanaelst I, Clarysse B, Wright M, Lockett A, Moray N, S'Jegers R (2006) Entrepreneurial team development in academic spinouts: An examination of team heterogeneity. Entrepreneurship Theory and Practice 30(2): 249–271

Vecchio RP (2003a) Entrepreneurship and leadership: Common trends and common threads. Human Resource Management 13: 303–327

Vecchio RP (2003b) Entrepreneurship and leadership: common trends and common threads. Human Resource Management Review 13: 303–327

Vesper KH (1980) New Venture Strategies. Prentice-Hall, Englewood Cliffs, NJ

Ward TB (2004) Cognition, creativity, and entrepreneurship. Journal of Business Venturing 19(2): 173–188

Watson J (2007) Modeling the relationship between networking and firm performance. Journal of Business Venturing 22(6): 852–874

Webb EJ, Campbell DT, Sechrest L, Schwartz R (2000) Unobtrusive Measures. Sage, Thousand Oaks

West GP (2007) Collective cognition: When entrepreneurial teams, not individuals, make decisions. Entrepreneurship Theory and Practice 31(1): 77–102

West GP, Wilson E (1995) A simulation of strategic decision making in situational stereotype conditions for entrepreneurial companies. Simulation & Gaming 26(3): 307–327

Wiklund J, Shepherd D (2003) Knowledge-based resources, entrepreneurial orientation, and the performance of small and medium-sized businesses. Strategic Management Journal 24(13): 1307

Wright M, Liu X, Buck T, Filatotchev I (2008) Returnee entrepreneurs, science park location choice and performance: An analysis of high-technology SMEs in China. Entrepreneurship Theory and Practice 32(1): 131–155

Zhao H, Seibert SE (2006) The big five personality dimensions and entrepreneurial status: A meta-analytical review. Journal of Applied Psychology 9(2): 259–271

Ziegler M, Rosenzweig B, Ziegler P (1992) The Republic of Tea: Letters to a Young Zentrepeneur. Currency Doubleday, New York

About the Editors and Authors

Barbara Bird, Ph.D., is currently associate professor of management in the Kogod School of Business at American University in Washington, DC. At Kogod she teaches organizational behavior and leadership courses. She holds a B.A. in psychology from California State University, Fresno, a M.A. in social psychology from the University of Western Ontario, and a Ph.D. in business administration from the University of Southern California. Her research interests include entrepreneurial cognition and entrepreneurial behavior. She has research projects examining technology of new venture liabilities of newness and strategic alliances. She has authored *Entrepreneurial Behavior*, several scholarly journal articles in *Academy of Management Review*, *Organization Science*, and *Journal of Applied Psychology*. She is past chair of the Entrepreneurship Division of the Academy of Management and currently serves as a historian. Her travels have taken her to EU, Brazil, Peru, China, Turkey, and Syria and across the United States by car (alone) five times. She is currently taking a course on comedy improvisation and enjoys swing dancing, jazz, and wine tasting.

Kristie Brandt, M.A., received her M.A. degree in May 2009 and B.A. in 2006 from Florida International University (FIU) with a major in psychology and a minor in marine biology where she was in the Honors College. She received the award for Outstanding Academic Achievement in Psychology from the FIU. She will receive her M.S. degree in industrial/organizational psychology from FIU in the spring of 2009, she then will pursue a doctoral degree in applied psychology. Ms. Brandt has been actively involved with research in a variety of fields including marine biology, several areas within psychology as well as entrepreneurship. Her current research interests include leadership, motivation within organizational settings, and occupational health. She is a member of the National Golden Key Honor Society.

Malin Brännback, D.Sc., is chair of international business at Åbo Akademi University where she received her doctoral degree in management science in 1996. She also holds a B.Sc. in pharmacy. Prior to her return to Åbo Akademi University in 2003, she served as associate professor in information systems at University of Turku and professor of marketing at Turku School of Economics. She is docent at the Turku School of Economics where she taught prior to returning to Åbo and is also docent at the Swedish School of Economics and Business Administration in

Stockholm. She has held a variety of teaching and research positions in such fields as information systems, international marketing, strategic management, and pharmacy. She has published widely on entrepreneurship, biotechnology business, and knowledge management. Her current research interests are in entrepreneurial intentionality, entrepreneurial cognition and entrepreneurial growth, and performance in technology entrepreneurship, especially within the field of life sciences.

Melissa S. Cardon, Ph.D., received her doctorate in organizational behavior from Columbia University. She is currently assistant professor of management at Pace University's Lubin School of Business. Her research focuses on unleashing human potential within entrepreneurial firms, including a dual interest in human resource practices that maximize employee potential, and the emotional, relational, and cognitive aspects of entrepreneurs that contribute to optimizing their behavior and performance. Recent work of hers includes a focus on entrepreneurial passion, entrepreneurial failure, and the organizational attractiveness of small firms to applicants. Her work has been published in journals such as *Academy of Management Review, Human Resources Management Review, Human Resources Management, Journal of Business Venturing, Journal of Management Studies*, and *Journal of Developmental Entrepreneurship*. She has received several awards for both conceptual and empirical research studies.

Alan L. Carsrud, Ph.D., is professor of entrepreneurship and strategy and holds the Loretta Rogers Chair in Entrepreneurship in the Ted Rogers School of Management at Ryerson University in Toronto, Canada. His B.A. degree from Texas Christian University was in psychology, sociology, history, and anthropology. He received his doctoral degree in social psychology from the University of New Hampshire in 1974 and did postdoctoral work in applied psychology at the University of Texas at Austin. He is docent in entrepreneurship at Åbo Akademi University in Finland. Prior to his appointment at Ryerson he was professor of industrial and systems engineering, clinical professor of management, and executive director of the Eugenio Pino and Family Global Entrepreneurship Center at Florida International University. He previously has served on the graduate entrepreneurship faculties of the Anderson Graduate School of Management of the University of California, Los Angeles, The Australian Graduate School of Management, Bond University – Australia, The University of Southern California, Pepperdine University, and the University of Texas at Austin. He has published over 160 articles, chapters, and books in entrepreneurship, family business, biotechnology, industrial and applied psychology, social psychology, and clinical psychology.

Evan Douglas, PhD., is currently professor of entrepreneurship and dean of the Faculty of Business at The University of the Sunshine Coast, Queensland, Australia. His first two degrees were from the University of Newcastle in Australia and his doctorate is from Simon Fraser University in Canada. He initially taught and researched in economics but converted to entrepreneurship about 20 years ago, and has now taught entrepreneurship, new venture strategy, new venture funding and business planning to MBA students in more than a dozen business schools in

North America, England, Australia, China, India, and Thailand. His current research interests include entrepreneurial attitudes and abilities, the self-employment decision, new venture risk analysis, new venture funding, new venture strategy, and workaholism and work enthusiasm in entrepreneurs.

Mateja Drnovsek, Ph.D., is assistant professor of entrepreneurship at the Faculty of Economics at the University of Ljubljana, Slovenia, where she also got her doctorate. Her research is immersed in cognitive aspects of entrepreneurship and their influence on formation of entrepreneurial intentions, new venture creation, and overall entrepreneurial effectiveness. She has also done several studies of gender entrepreneurship, entrepreneurship, and job creation contribution of small businesses to a national economy. Her work has been published in journals such as *Academy of Management Review, Baltic Management Journal, Economic and Business Review, Scandinavian Management Journal, Journal of Enterprising Culture, Small Business Economics*, and others.

Jennie Elfving, D.Sc., received her D.Sc. in 2009. She now works as development manager at Kosek, the regional development company in Kokkola, Finland. She is responsible for the strategic development of the boatbuilding industry as well as the welfare industry in the region. She has previously held a research position at Åbo Akademi University, Department of Business Studies, and has published articles and conference papers on entrepreneurship and regional development. Her current research interest lies in entrepreneurial cognition, small business marketing, and regional development.

Connie Marie Gaglio, Ph.D., director of the Ohrenschall Center for Entrepreneurship and associate professor of management at San Francisco State University became interested in the parallels between the theory of entrepreneurial alertness and the fundamental cognitive dynamics of schema theory, framing effects, and counterfactual thinking while earning her doctorate in social psychology at the University of Chicago. She continues to pursue a research, publishing, and teaching agenda on these topics in the context of emerging industries.

Veronica Gustavsson, Ph.D., is assistant professor in entrepreneurship and a research fellow at CISEG at Jönköping International Business School, Jönköping, Sweden. She has been working at her home university upon receiving her doctoral degree from Jönköping. Her dissertation titled *Entrepreneurial Decision-Making: Individuals, Tasks and Cognitions* has been acclaimed for the relevance of the topic, solid as well as innovative theoretical framework and an innovative and courageous approach to the methodology. Her subsequent research has been focused on entrepreneurial decision-making under uncertainty. She has undertaken a number of research projects in the area and has published monographs and book chapters as well as numerous conference papers. Her research often reflects her varied cultural, educational and working background. She was born and obtained the university degree in the Soviet Union (later Russia). Her university studies have included Germanic languages and literature (major), economics and psychology (minor).

Kevin Hindle, Ph.D., is professor emeritus of Swinburne University, Australia, professor of entrepreneurship at the University of Southern Denmark, and international director of the Venture Intelligence Institute. He has over 80 peer-reviewed publications and global experience in teaching, research, management consulting, and private equity investment. All his work focuses on building entrepreneurial capacity – the ability to turn new knowledge into new value for defined stakeholders. This includes new venture evaluation; entrepreneurial business planning; market and financial modeling; change management; organizational design; corporate strategy; and management training. His research agenda centers on the nature of entrepreneurial process and the role that contextual and community factors play in entrepreneurial process. He is a pioneer in the field of indigenous entrepreneurship. On an international scale, he has initiated and developed a wide range of new ventures, innovative teaching programs, and insightful, applied research.

Daniel F. Jennings, Ph.D., PE, is the Andrew Rader Professor of Industrial Distribution and Program Director for the Master of Industrial Distribution degree within the Dwight Look College of Engineering at Texas A&M University in College Station, Texas. Professor Jennings has published over 300 articles in academic and practitioner journals and has authored or coauthored 21 textbooks in addition to writing 18 chapters in textbooks authored by others. His research has been described in the *Wall Street Journal* and the *New York Times*. Dr. Jennings has been either the principal investigator or co-principal investigator for applied research projects totaling $1.85 million dollars. His research focuses on strategy–structure–performance relationships in entrepreneurial and non-entrepreneurial organizations.

Kim Klyver, Ph.D., received his Ph.D. in 2005. Since then, he has worked as a post-doctoral fellow at Australian Graduate School of Entrepreneurship at Swinburne University of Technology (Australia) and as an assistant professor at the University of Southern Denmark (Denmark). Currently, he is working as a postdoctoral fellow at Stanford University after been awarding the "Scancor Postdoctoral Fellowship Award 2009." Kim has been a member of the Global Entrepreneurship Monitor (GEM) project since 2000 and has been part of both the Australian national team and the Danish national team. He has more than 80 publications and has published several peer-reviewed journal articles in journals such as *International Entrepreneurship and Management Journal, International Journal of Entrepreneurial Behaviour and Research, International Journal of Entrepreneurship and Small Business*, and *Journal of Small Business and Enterprise Development*. He has won several awards for his research. Kim's main research interests are entrepreneurial networks, nascent entrepreneurship, women entrepreneurship, entrepreneurship policy, and advisory of entrepreneurs.

Norris Krueger, Ph.D., received his doctorate from Ohio State University in 1989. A mentee of the late Al Shapiro, he often describes himself as a recovering entrepreneur-turned entrepreneurship scholar and educator. Today his interests have turned to social entrepreneurship. He continues to balance his entrepreneurial bent with highly cited cutting edge academic work in entrepreneurial cognition, with cognitive science and social entrepreneurship. His work on intentions is at the heart of his interests. Throughout, he has been passionate in his curiosity about how entrepreneurs think, especially how they see opportunities and act on them. He is concerned with how we use that knowledge to design programs to encourage more – and better informed – entrepreneurial activity. He sees this as critical in advancing our understanding of entrepreneurial thinking in areas like entrepreneurial learning, social ventures, technology commercialization, and entrepreneurial economic development. Currently, he works in entrepreneurial economic development through his consulting firm, Entrepreneurship Northwest, located in Boise, Idaho. He formerly served on the faculty of Boise State University, but now maintains his academic research in entrepreneurship through his fellowship with the Max Planck Institute of Economics in Jena, Germany.

Anne Kirketerp Linstad, Ph.D., is a recent graduate teaching entrepreneurship in an enterprise perspective from the University of Southern Denmark. She is currently engaged in a number of large-scale quantitative and qualitative research projects, involving different teaching strategies due to enhanced innovation and creativity. Her research involves looking at teaching methods and pedagogy in the field of creativity and enterprising behavior from primary school to university level. She is currently working in a private research center, the Danfoss Universe Research Lab, whose aim is to explore novel teaching methods to enhance enterprise, innovation, and creativity at all levels of the school system. She teaches in various Master Programs at the Aarhus Business School, in Denmark, including an E-M.B.A. program, all in the area of conditioning of the mind and specifically how to stimulate enterprising behavior among university students.

René Mauer, M. Sc., is an entrepreneurship researcher and student in the Ph.D. program at RWTH Aachen University in Germany. He received a M.Sc. in economics and business administration at WHU Otto Beisheim School of Management in 2004, with concentrations in entrepreneurship, marketing, and management accounting. René has studied at the Amos Tuck School of Business in Boston and at the LUISS in Rome. He has worked for 3 M, startups, a consulting firm, and been in investment banking. He is co-proprietor of a family business in landscaping services. After joining RWTH Aachen University in 2005, he acquired substantial funding and built up the Center for Entrepreneurship. In 2008, he was awarded a DAAD research grant that allowed him to join research projects with colleagues both in the US and Europe. René does research in technology entrepreneurship and entrepreneurial cognition. He is specifically interested in effectuation, bricolage, and improvisation, the latter of which he is applying to the business and theater stage.

Theresa Michl, M.Sc., is a Ph.D. student in economics at the Munich School of Management of the Ludwig-Maximilians-University (LMU), Munich, Germany. At present she is also working as an assistant professor for telecommunications and innovation management at the Department for Information, Organization, and Management of the Ludwig-Maximilians-University (LMU), Munich, Germany, and for statistics, methodology, and organization theory at the University of Applied Management (FHAM), Erding, Germany. Theresa Michl is working in many theoretical and empirical research projects of economics and psychology such as *entrepreneurship, innovation management, cognitive emotion theories, management trainings, and coaching.*

Benjamin T. Mitchell, M.Sc., is currently a Ph.D. student in the Carlson School of Management at the University of Minnesota. He holds Bachelor's and Master's degrees in management information systems from the Marriott School of Management at Brigham Young University. He has worked as a network operations analyst at a global network operations center and as a researcher examining the vendor side of outsourcing relationships. His current research interests include cognition, human information processing, expertise, and how information technologies can enable greater human performance.

J. Robert Mitchell, Ph.D., is an assistant professor of entrepreneurship and management at the University of Oklahoma. He received his doctorate in entrepreneurship from the Kelley School of Business at Indiana University. Prior to pursuing a Ph.D. at the Kelley School, he worked in a technology startup in Salt Lake City, Utah, and was involved in emerging enterprise consulting in Victoria, British Columbia. At OU, he teaches opportunity and venture creation and is actively involved in research in entrepreneurship and strategy. His research has appeared in *Entrepreneurship Theory and Practice, Journal of Business Venturing,* and *Strategic Entrepreneurship Journal.* In his research, he bridges entrepreneurship and strategic management by studying how cognitive, environmental, and behavioral factors lead to the creation of new value at multiple levels of analysis.

Ronald K. Mitchell, Ph.D., is a professor of entrepreneurship and holds the Bagley Regents Chair in Management at Texas Tech University. Previously he was Winspear Chair in Public Policy and Business at the University of Victoria, and jointly appointed professor of public policy and strategy at the Guanghua School of Management at Peking University. He is a CPA, former CEO, consultant, and entrepreneur; he received his doctorate from the University of Utah; and he won the 1995 Heizer Award for his dissertation *The composition, classification, and creation of new venture formation expertise.* Ron publishes and serves in editorial review capacities in the top entrepreneurship and management journals and is also 2008–2009 chair of the entrepreneurship division of the Academy of Management. He is coauthor of the Ivey Casebook, *Cases in Entrepreneurship,* one of the first texts to apply entrepreneurial cognition research focused specifically on the development of students' "entrepreneurial minds." He researches, consults, and lectures worldwide.

Erik Monsen, Ph.D., is a senior research fellow in the entrepreneurship, growth, and public policy group of the Max Planck Institute of Economics in Jena, Germany. He earned his doctorate in organization management at the University of Colorado at Boulder (2005), where he earned an M.B.A. in entrepreneurship and technology management (2001). Before entrepreneurship, he was an aerospace engineering researcher (B.S., Rensselaer Polytechnic Institute, 1991; M.S., Stanford University,

1992) at the German Aerospace Center (DLR) in Braunschweig, Germany, from 1994 to 1999. Instead of designing better aircraft, he now researches how to design better entrepreneurship systems from the employee perspective and has published in *Entrepreneurship Theory and Practice* and the *Zeitschrift für betriebswirtschaftliche Forschung*. Further, he teaches at the University of Jena, the Leipzig Graduate School of Management (HHL), and the International Graduate Business School Zagreb.

Charles Y. Murnieks, Ph.D., is an assistant professor of management at the United States Air Force Academy. He received his doctorate in business administration, with a concentration in entrepreneurship from the Leeds School of Business at the University of Colorado, Boulder (2007), where he studied under Dean Shepherd and Elaine Mosakowski. He also received an M.B.A. from the Anderson School of Management at the University of California, Los Angeles (2001). For the past 15 years, he has served as an officer in the US Air Force, first as an engineer and now as a faculty member of the Air Force Academy. Where his passion once revolved around building bridges and buildings, now it involves researching the drives and emotions that fuel individuals, like entrepreneurs, to persist in their endeavors. He is convinced that passion is a critical ingredient both to the study of entrepreneurship and to the practice of scholarship.

Helle Neergaard, Ph.D., received her doctorate in international business in 1999 for her dissertation titled "Networks as Vehicles of Internationalization" from the Aarhus School of Business in Denmark. As assistant and then associate professor at the Department of Organization and Management she quickly became involved in a comprehensive research project aimed at studying technology-based entrepreneurs. She is a very active researcher and has produced more than 40 conference papers, journal articles, and book chapters over the last 4 years as well as giving numerous presentations and interviews. One pillar of her research is a strong interest in qualitative methods. She is lead editor of *Handbook of Qualitative Research Methods in Entrepreneurship* published by Edward Elgar (2007). Her other research passion is female entrepreneurs and in particular the influence of self-efficacy on women's propensity to become entrepreneurs and grow their businesses, and in her teaching she applies a pedagogy based on effectuation thinking.

Arnold Picot, Ph.D., holds the chair of the Institute for Information, Organization and Management at the Munich School of Management at Ludwig-Maximilians-Universität (LMU), Munich, Germany. Arnold Picot's research and teaching activities focus on core fields of management, namely organization theory, theory of the firm, strategy and entrepreneurship, innovation, management implications of new technologies, telecommunications, media, and regulation. Beside LMU he has taught at Stanford University, Technical University of Munich, University of Hannover, Georgetown University, and University of Strasbourg, among others. His research has been supported by the German National Science Foundation (DFG), the Volkswagen Foundation, the German Federal Ministry of Research and Education, and other funding agencies. He is an editorial board and review member of various academic and professional journals, book series, and yearbooks. Arnold Picot is the (co)author of around 30 books and over 400 journal articles and book chapters.

Leon Schjoedt, Ph.D., received his doctoral degree from the University of Colorado at Boulder. He currently is assistant professor of entrepreneurship at the College of Business, Illinois State University. His research focuses on entrepreneurial behavior. His work has appeared in *Entrepreneurship Theory and Practice, Journal of High Technology Management Research, Management Research News, The Journal of International Management Studies*, and *International HR Journal*, as well as in a number of book chapters, and has been presented at numerous academic meetings, including the annual meeting for the Academy of Management and Babson College Entrepreneurship Research Conference. Leon serves on the editorial review board for *Entrepreneurship Theory and Practice* and *Academy of Management Learning and Education*. In 2008, he won the *Entrepreneurship Theory and Practice* Best Reviewer Award. Leon has taught at Copenhagen Business School (Denmark), Wake Forest University (USA), University of Colorado at Boulder (USA), and Thammasat University (Thailand).

Kelley Shaver, Ph.D., is professor of entrepreneurial studies and chair of the Department of Management and Entrepreneurship in the School of Business and Economics at the College of Charleston. His prior affiliations include the National Science Foundation, the College of William & Mary, and the Entrepreneurship and Small Business Research Institute (ESBRI) in Stockholm. For 5 years Dr. Shaver was editor of *Entrepreneurship Theory and Practice*. He is the author or coauthor of 10 books and 69 articles emphasizing social psychology. He began studying entrepreneurship in the late 1980s, participating in the creation of 5 books, 7 chapters, and 39 articles related to entrepreneurship. Professor Shaver is a fellow of the American Psychological Society, a member of the Society of Experimental Social Psychology, an elected member of the PSED1 executive committee, and is past chair of the Entrepreneurship Division of the Academy of Management. His web pages are located at www.cofc.edu/~shaverk.

Matthias Spörrle, Ph.D., studied psychology at the Ludwig-Maximilians-University (LMU), Munich, Germany (Diploma in 2001, Ph.D. in 2006). He has worked in many empirical research projects of applied psychological science such as *usability engineering, organizational evaluation, customer profile analysis, and customer satisfaction.* At present he is professor for statistics and methodology at the University of Applied Management (FHAM), Erding, Germany, as researcher at the Department of Psychology at the Ludwig-Maximilians-University (Institute of General Psychology and Institute of Methodology), as lecturer for the Technology Transfer Office of the University of Munich, and as organizational consultant. His current academic research topics are questionnaire design, sociometry, cognitive emotion theories, emotional intelligence, and entrepreneurship research

Diemo Urbig is a research fellow in the Entrepreneurship, Growth, and Public Policy Group of the Max Planck Institute of Economics in Jena, Germany. After studying in Berlin and Copenhagen, supported by the German National Academic Foundation, Diemo Urbig received diploma degrees in management with major in organization theory (2001) and computer science (2003) from Humboldt University of Berlin (HUB). His work on the simulation of social processes was published in the *Journal of Artificial Societies and Social Simulation* and *Advances of Complex Systems*. As a research associate at the School of Business and Economics of HUB he investigated aspects of behavioral economics focusing on social learning, overconfidence, and their welfare implications. He is completing his doctorate at Utrecht University using a model-based and theory-driven approach to understand optimism, overconfidence, and risk perception.

Isabell Welpe, Ph.D., holds the chair for strategy and organization at the Technical University of Munich, Germany. She researches and consults in strategy, entrepreneurship, organization theories, and organizational behavior. Her research interests lie at the intersection of economic and psychological concepts, the role of communication (technologies) for cooperative behavior, and their impact on organizational collaboration. She teaches strategy, organization theories, human resource management, empirical research methods, and entrepreneurship. She has taught on the faculty of Claremont University, EM Lyon, France, Ludwig-Maximilians-University in Munich, Germany, and the University of Berne, Switzerland. She is an editorial board and review member of several academic and professional journals and the author of several books and edited volumes as well as over 40 articles and book chapters. Her research has appeared in journals such as *Journal of Business Venturing, International Journal of Technology Management, Financial Markets and Portfolio Management*, and others.

Susan J. Winter, Ph.D., received her PhD from the University of Arizona, her MA from the Claremont Graduate University, and her BA from the University of California, Berkeley. She is currently an associate professor of MIS at Portland State University with over 20 years of international managerial and consulting experience. Her interests include the impact of ICT on the organization of work and its symbolic aspects. Her research has resulted in 18 publications, 7 grants, and over 25 refereed conference presentations (including 3 Best Paper awards). Her work has appeared in such journals as *Information Systems Research, Information & Management, Frontiers of Entrepreneurship Research* and the *Journal of Vocational Behavior*, been presented at the *International Conference on Information Systems* and at the *Academy of Management*, and been included as chapters in scholarly books. She currently serves on the editorial boards of the *Journal of Information Technology, Information and Organization,* and *Group* and *Organization Management*.

Index

Note, The locators in bold with 't' and 'f' refers to 'tables' and 'figures'.

Lightning Source UK Ltd.
Milton Keynes UK
UKOW020709030212

186579UK00001B/28/P